CHARTING
THE
FUTURE

Contributions in Legal Studies
Series Editor: *Paul L. Murphy*

Stability, Security, and Continuity: Mr. Justice Burton and Decision-Making in the Supreme Court 1945-1958
Mary Frances Berry

Philosophical Law: Authority, Equality, Adjudication, Privacy
Richard Bronaugh, editor

Law, Soldiers, and Combat
Peter Karsten

Appellate Courts and Lawyers: Information Gathering in the Adversary System
Thomas B. Marvell

CHARTING THE FUTURE

THE SUPREME COURT RESPONDS TO A CHANGING SOCIETY, 1890-1920

John E. Semonche

CONTRIBUTIONS IN LEGAL STUDIES, NUMBER 5

GREENWOOD PRESS
WESTPORT, CONNECTICUT • LONDON, ENGLAND

Library of Congress Cataloging in Publication Data

Semonche, John E., 1933-
Charting the future.

(Contributions in legal studies ; no. 5 ISSN
0147-1074)
Bibliography: p.
Includes index.
1. United States. Supreme Court—History.
I. Title. II. Series.
KF8742.S44   347′.73′2609   77-94745
ISBN 0-313-20314-8

Library of Congress Catalog Card Number: 77-94745
ISBN: 0-313-20314-8
ISSN: 0147-1074

First published in 1978

Greenwood Press, Inc.
51 Riverside Avenue, Westport, Connecticut 06880

Printed in the United States of America

10 9 8 7 6 5 4 3 2 1

For Two Very Special
and Lovely Young Women, **Barbara and Laura**

CONTENTS

PREFACE

In the period from 1890 to 1920, Americans sought to cope with the substantial political, economic, social, and even psychological changes generated by an emerging industrial society by demanding that government, both local and national, expand its functions to redress imbalances and re-establish some order.[1] The Supreme Court's special task was to determine whether a fundamental law, fashioned in a much simpler time, could accommodate these new exertions of governmental power.

Aside from the general importance of this watershed period in American history, changes in the Court's personnel both at the beginning and end of these thirty years clearly demarcate an era in Supreme Court history. Beginning late in 1890 and extending over the next four years, five new appointees came to the High Bench; their arrival strengthened a dissident faction on the Court and paved the way for a wave of judicial activism. The battle to save the federal structure had absorbed their immediate predecessors, and although the new men were not insensitive to the demands of federalism, they assumed its continued existence and faced the problems of the present freed from the lurking shadows of the past. Seemingly ready to interpose its will in reviewing exertions of federal, state, and local power, the reconstituted Court actually exercised its new authority with caution. Substantial personnel changes again came with the administration of William Howard Taft, but the Court's basic approach to its task remained intact. The decisive change came with the four men that Warren G. Harding put on the High Bench during his short tenure. Again, the result was to strengthen a dissident faction, which this time became a majority that readily found constitutional obstacles to the exercise of governmental power.

The generation from 1890 to 1920 surveyed here encompasses a most significant, but too little appreciated, seminal period in the history of the Supreme Court. Searching for a usable past saves the historian from antiquarianism, but it also strews his path with obstacles. We are attracted by the dramatic event, and it invites us to view what came before and what came after in its reflection. Such a dramatic event in the Court's history was the crisis of 1937 precipitated by Franklin D. Roosevelt's postelection resolve to do something about the Court's invalidation of New Deal legislation. In interpreting this crisis of the mid-1930s, writers reached back in time to another depression decade, the 1890s, and connected the two periods to provide a seemingly consistent picture of a conservative, if not reactionary, Court.[2] Though there has been some recognition that such a characterization is an oversimplification, enough evidence in the form of some notable cases exists to lend plausibility to such a thesis. Further confirmation can be found in the opinions of contemporaries who made the Supreme Court a special target. Charles Warren, a friendly interpreter and later historian of the Court, asked his fellow Americans in the 1910s to take a more balanced view of the work of the High Bench and, in the process, to realize how quantitatively insignificant were the cases that excited popular disapproval.[3] His words generally fell upon deaf ears, and even later historians have preferred to concentrate on the judicial opinions that seemed to thwart the reform impulses of the generation. Even when writers did recognize that the Court's work could not be adequately characterized as conservative or laissez-faire, they sought new overarching explanations that postulated an economic and social theory behind the diverse and wide-ranging work of the Justices.[4]

The significance of the period 1890 to 1920 has not only been obscured because of the tendency to view it within the long shadow cast by the crisis of 1937 but also because of a decided preference to treat the Court's work thematically rather than chronologically. The attractiveness of the thematic approach is obvious: models are provided; the material is easily retrieved; and the task of analysis is considerably simplified. Despite such advantages, a chronological approach captures with less abstraction the actual processes of decision making, for it encourages a focus on results, rather than on the rhetoric of opinions. For the lawyer's purposes, the segregation of cases in doctrinal areas serves a useful function, but unless the historian transgresses these boundaries, he cannot provide the synthesis necessary to an understanding of how the Court functioned during a discrete period.

This study proceeded from certain largely negative assumptions: first, that the Court's work during the era from 1890 to 1920 could not be adequately captured by the two dozen or so cases that had etched themselves into the historical literature; second, that it was time to get out from under the shadow of the 1937 crisis and look at the earlier period afresh without an implicit condemnation of judicial activism; and finally, that prevailing characterizations of Justices and interpretations of their work in terms of personal economic and social views would have to be tested by a consideration of their total work product.

From these starting points, all the cases decided by the Supreme Court from the 1889 term through the 1920 session were collected and analyzed.

Legal indices are abundant, but they have limited use for the historian. A historical index was constructed that brought within its ken a host of cases with minimal legal significance but with some historical value, either in terms of illuminating the operation of the Court and its group attitudes or in terms of providing insight into the work of individual Justices. The result is not only a more complete story of the Court during these years but a more human one as well.

From 1890 to 1920 the Court issued some unfortunate opinions, but it handed down many others based upon an implicit recognition of new societal needs. As relatively old men from confined socioeconomic strata grappling with the problems of a changing America, the Justices took their responsibilities seriously and tried to contend fairly with circumstances often far beyond the boundaries of their common cultural heritage. Valuing flexibility more than consistency, they willingly subjected their prior views to the test of new fact situations. True to the common law heritage, law and its institutions were found resilient enough to cope with society's new problems. A Court changing its mind dramatically in 1937 found support for such a shift because the recent precedents could be rejected in favor of those that were set during the 1890 to 1920 period—an era in which the Justices were doing no less than modernizing the fundamental law.

As the writer puts the finishing touches to his work, he realizes how, in reality, he is putting his name to a collaborative effort. Mention should first be made of the Justices of the Supreme Court, whose work has been too little appreciated and upon which so much of this volume rests. Second, any study of the Supreme Court owes much to the prior labors of historians, political scientists, and legal scholars, who have made the Court the focus of their study. Such indebtedness is only partially recognized in my notes. Finally, appreciation is due my students who, with their "unsophisticated" questions, have led me to reinspect and reevaluate the fundamental assumptions and interpretations upon which so much of the literature on the Court rests.

The University of North Carolina at Chapel Hill provided me with crucial support at various stages. I was able to begin my study with the aid of a research leave, and the University Research Council provided funds for two expeditions that enabled me to comb through the records of the Supreme Court in the National Archives. In addition, the interest of my colleagues in both the history department and the law school and their continued encouragement have aided the final product.

Of the numerous people who provided input into the work, there are three whose contributions deserve special mention. Margaret A. Blanchard, a journalist and now a historian as well, never once suggested that the Eighth Amendment might constitute a bar to her many readings of the manuscript. Her help was invaluable, especially in terms of tightening the organization and in eliminating jargon that could only interfere with the reader's understanding. Jordan M. Smith, also a lawyer and a historian, took time from his own work and gave each chapter a thorough reading. His demand for clarity and his keen stylistic sense are, I hope, reflected in the writing. Finally, Lawrence D. McMahon, Jr., my research assistant in the law school, so dedicated himself to the task of checking my sources that he contributed a research dimension of his own.

Many typists in the history department and the law school worked on various parts of the manuscript, and for their patience and good humor I give thanks. Special appreciation, however, is due Daria Primerano, Rosalie I. Radcliffe, Brenda Hunt, and Secily Jones. The pride they took in their work cannot be purchased.

Finally, my wife and daughter made contributions to this work that they would not consider large, but their support, encouragement, and patience cannot be measured. Without their faith in me and their belief in the value of what I was doing, there would be no book at all.

NOTES

1. For some useful general interpretations of the period, see Samuel P. Hays, *The Response to Industrialism, 1885-1914* (Chicago: University of Chicago Press, 1957); Ray Ginger, *Age of Excess: The United States from 1877 to 1914* (New York: Macmillan Co., 1965); and Robert H. Wiebe, *The Search for Order, 1877-1920* (New York: Hill and Wang, 1967).

Historians of the first two decades of the twentieth century, most commonly labeled the Progressive Era, agree that governmental activity increased substantially in efforts to cope with the problems of an industrialized society, but they differ in their explanations of who initiated, supported, guided, and profited from the reforms effected in the period. As historians broke through the boundaries of reformer rhetoric, they found that businessmen and lawyers, who had been primary targets of such rhetoric, were, in fact, supporters of much reform legislation. On the matter of the role of business interests in the period, see Robert H. Wiebe, *Businessmen and Reform: A Study of the Progressive Movement* (Cambridge: Harvard University Press, 1962); Gabriel Kolko, *The Triumph of Conservatism: A Reinterpretation of American History, 1900-1916* (Glencoe, Ill.: Free Press, 1963); and James Weinstein, *The Corporate Ideal in the Liberal State: 1900-1918* (Boston: Beacon Press, 1968). And for a study of how leaders of the bar were drawn to support certain reform legislation and recommend approval of it by the courts in an effort to halt an emerging class consciousness and the more radical proposals that they feared would follow in its wake, see Barbara C. Steidle, "Conservative Progressives: A Study of the Attitudes and Role of Bar and Bench, 1905-1912" (Ph.D. dissertation, Rutgers University, 1969). At the very least, such studies of the period suggest that the term "progressive" has become fuzzy and of questionable analytical value.

2. For instance, in Arnold M. Paul, *Conservative Crisis and the Rule of Law: Attitudes of Bar and Bench, 1887-1895*, Torchbook ed. (New York: Harper & Row, 1969), p. 237, the author states that "the neo-Feudalism of the 1890's opened the door to what was to prove in succeeding decades a full proliferation of judicial obstructionism. The Supreme Court of

the United States became, instead of an instrument of constitutional democracy, an impediment to constitutional democracy. Exaggerating its powers beyond proportion in the period 1890-1937, confusing its proper role in the American scheme of government, the Court for a long while seriously weakened its real value."

3. Charles Warren, "The Progressiveness of the United States Supreme Court," and "A Bulwark to the State Police Power—the United States Supreme Court," *Columbia Law Review* 13 (April, December 1913): 294-313, 667-95.

4. See John P. Roche, "Civil Liberty in the Age of Enterprise," *University of Chicago Law Review* 31 (Autumn 1963):103; "Entrepreneurial Liberty and the Fourteenth Amendment," *Labor History* 4 (Winter 1963):3-31; and "Entrepreneurial Liberty and the Commerce Power: Expansion, Contraction and Causistry in the Age of Enterprise," *University of Chicago Law Review* 30 (Summer 1963): 680-703. The articles have been collected and published in *Sentenced to Life* (New York: Macmillan Co., 1974), pp. 205-308.

Roche argues, quite correctly, that the Supreme Court in the period roughly from 1870 to 1920 cannot legitimately be characterized in terms of a conservative or laissez-faire attitude. He then substitutes a description of the Supreme Court built around a concept of entrepreneurial liberty, which he defines as opportunistic in its dedication to freeing business enterprise from shackles of any kind. The result of this shift is to give the traditional interpretation of the Court's work during the era a more current and precise formulation. Roche, however, does provide hints of an explanation that would be broader, more comprehensive, and more liberating than the one he chose to develop.

CHARTING
THE
FUTURE

chapter 1

SETTING THE SCENE: THE MEN AND THE COURT

To climax a decade and a half of national centennial celebrations, President Benjamin Harrison, in his inaugural address of March 4, 1889, suggested commemorating the establishment of the United States Supreme Court. Appropriately, since a number of its members were prominent advocates before the High Bench and since the Court first sat in New York City, the New York State Bar Association eagerly grasped the idea and began devising plans for a celebration worthy of the opulent era.[1]

With some effort the Metropolitan Opera House was procured for the morning and afternoon of February 4, 1890; the magnificent and impressive structure seemed especially fit for honoring the Justices and the institution they served. Red, white, and blue streamers covered the dome, and the galleries were draped with large silk flags. Between the first and second tier of boxes were replicas of the seals of the states and the territories. Although some of the scenery from the Metropolitan's production of "Tristan and Isolde" could be seen in the background, a straddling arch draped with flags was placed across the stage. On both sides of the arch portraits of the Chief Justices were placed upon easels. The solemn procession headed by the members of the Supreme Court began at 10:30 A.M. and included as many members of the federal and state judiciaries as could be assembled, along with Senators, members of the House Judiciary Committee, and the most prominent members of the New York Bar.[2]

Never before and never since has the Supreme Court been paid the public homage it was paid on that dark and rainy day in February. Neither the uncooperative weather nor the absence of the President and his cabinet, due to the accidental death of the wife and daughter of the Secretary of the Treasury, dulled the luster of the occasion. The hall was packed, and spontaneous applause greeted the arrival of the nine Justices who led the procession down the center aisle. Those persons fortunate enough to be fairly close to the aisle got a good look at the members of the Court.[3]

At the head of the Court was the Chief Justice of the United States, Melville Weston Fuller, then in the middle of his second term. Selected by President

Grover Cleveland in 1888, Fuller was little known beyond the confines of Chicago in his adopted state of Illinois. Except for a short term in the Illinois legislature during the Civil War, Fuller had held no public office. But he was no stranger to the Justices, for he had appeared regularly as an advocate before the Court from 1872 to the time of his nomination. In Chicago Fuller had been known as a lawyer's lawyer, a man to summon after an adverse trial decision because he had mastered the special skills of appellate litigation. Although his relative public obscurity inspired some negative reactions to his appointment, he did bring to his new post a wealth of experience garnered on the other side of the bench.[4]

The dignity that Fuller manifested in his appearance and manner was heightened by his conception of his role. To one of the many reporters present for the occasion, Fuller had a poetic face, a characterization that might have pleased the Chief Justice who earlier had dabbled in poetry.[5] What observers could not help noticing was that Fuller, at fifty-six, was a lean man, less than five and one-half feet tall, and weighing about one hundred and thirty pounds. Most striking was his long silver white hair and his glossy, slightly bushy mustache. He wore his hair long and combed back; it partially covered his ears and fell upon the collar of his gown. His forehead was high and full, his nose large and straight with flared nostrils, and his eyes a clear blue. When he smiled, which was not infrequent, his mouth reached to the ends of his mustache, and good-natured wrinkles framed his eyes.

Fuller had not coveted a position on the Court, but once there, he seemed to enjoy his role. The new Chief fully recognized the task that confronted him in heading a Court already composed of "giants," some of whom were less than pleased with his selection. In a note to the Court reporter, Fuller remarked: "No rising sun for me with these old luminaries blazing away with all their ancient fires." He deliberately and successfully courted the friendship of his new colleagues, working from a basic warmth and graciousness that proved irresistible. The two leading "luminaries" to whom the Chief referred were Samuel F. Miller and Stephen J. Field; both were appointed by Abraham Lincoln, both were mentioned as candidates for the post Fuller filled, and both had served under three previous Chief Justices. But even they eventually succumbed to the Chief's overtures.[6]

Perhaps when Fuller referred to "giants" on the Court, he was unconsciously revealing something more than that these men were intellectual leaders, for both Miller and Field were big men, well built and six feet tall. Size, of course, does not make the man, but in a traditionally oriented masculine society, these men had a commanding presence that the new Chief could not share. When Fuller found himself on the bench sandwiched between Miller and Field, he decided to have his seat raised. Now he could see over the bench and was on the same level with his two senior associates; the gap left between his feet and the floor he filled with a hassock.[7]

Right behind Fuller in the procession was Samuel F. Miller. Except for those who were acquainted with the man's forceful personality and his keenly analytical mind, few could have predicted that this former physician with his pragmatic, pleasant manner would distinguish himself on the United States Supreme Court. But Miller, a plain-speaking man who had moved to Iowa from Kentucky in his early thirties, had done just that. He had been appointed in 1862, and at seventy-four he was the senior associate. Miller had a large head, a wholesome rosy face, and a Roman countenance. He weighed about two hundred and twenty pounds, and his easygoing corpulence was probably the image reporters conjured up when they characterized the Court as comfortable looking. Miller's hair was white, worn full on both sides of a bald streak starting from his forehead and moving back. Unlike Fuller and Field, Miller tended to be tough with the attorneys who appeared before the Court, peppering them with questions and taking some delight in their discomfiture.[8]

Next in line was the Court's most well-known member, Stephen J. Field, whose colorful California apprenticeship, rugged individualism, and political ambitions attracted public interest. Appointed to the Court in 1863, the California Democrat was serving long enough to see his earlier dissents capture the majority. Of all the men on the Court, Field seemed to project an image that fully conformed to juristic eminence. Newspaper reporters used the term "awe-inspiring" and saw in him the visage of an Old Testament prophet.[9] His deep voice with its theatrical tone only served to further the image. He had a classic face with a high forehead, a prominent but thin nose, and cheekbones that seemed to strengthen his piercing eyes. Curly, sable grey hair left the top of his head and tumbled down the sides of his face over his ears into sideburns that split into a mustache and a long grey beard. For a man of his size, his hands were delicate and sensitive and yet somehow strangely in keeping with his image. Well might the Chief Justice fear that if his pace did not quicken, the two aging "giants" would overwhelm him.

After Field came Joseph P. Bradley, the oldest member of the Court, who was nearing his seventy-seventh birthday. Bradley, appointed with William Strong in 1870 by Ulysses S. Grant, was well skilled in the mechanics of the law, and his craftsmanship has been the subject of admiration. A little shorter than Fuller, Bradley had a tight-lipped face and a nasty temper.[10] His normal expression came perilously close to a frown, and his pale face was dominated by a large nose and bright eyes. He still had some iron grey hair on top of his head, which he wore shorter and more closely trimmed than the other members of the Court. His face was quite wrinkled, and he clearly looked like the oldest member of the bench.

Bradley was followed by John Marshall Harlan, who, as he strode down the aisle, caused one reporter to remark that he walked with the dignity of a king. A Southern Republican from Kentucky, he was forty-four years old when Rutherford B. Hayes appointed him to the Court in 1877. At fifty-seven he was still one of the Court's youngest members. Standing six-feet, two inches tall, he had a large frame, topped by a large dome of a head with puffy white fringes of hair above the ears. His face was equally strong, and his prominent nose inspired comparisons to Daniel Webster and Louis XIV.[11] His mouth was wide with thin lips, and his eyes were clear and sparkling. When excited, his cheeks flushed, and the redness overtook his entire face. Harlan was much in demand as an after-dinner speaker, and he was assigned the task of making the Court's response at the evening banquet that would conclude the day's festivities.

After Harlan came Horace Gray, who had been plucked from his position as chief justice of the Massachusetts high court by Chester Arthur in 1881. Gray at sixty-two was about six feet, four inches tall, and he weighed close to three hundred pounds. His broad shoulders and big bones supported his weight well, and his pink-cheeked, smooth complexion was highlighted by a bald head. His brown hair had begun to turn grey as the remaining fringe circled his long head and drooped into modest side whiskers. Long a bachelor, a rare breed on the Court, Gray the previous year had married the daughter of his former colleague, Stanley Matthews. The Massachusetts Justice was the Court's acknowledged scholar and legal historian, and his opinions often revealed this bent. Gray had a tendency to doze during counsel's arguments before the Court.[12]

Samuel Blatchford was next in line behind Gray, whose bulk effectively screened off the other appointee of Chester Arthur. Blatchford, a New Yorker, came on the Court in 1882, but neither his personality nor his opinions, often in the technical areas of patent and admiralty law, earned much public attention. He was a man of regular habits with an emphasis on punctuality, and at sixty-nine he was about the same height and build as Bradley. He had a flat face without much color, outlined with frosted silver hair from ear to ear. The public had heard little of Blatchford, but what they now saw was a pleasant-looking man.

Following Blatchford was Lucius Quintus Cincinnatus Lamar, the first Cleveland appointee and the first secessionist to sit on the Court following the Civil War. Although Lamar's famous eulogy delivered as a Congressman from Mississippi in the House of Representatives on the death of Charles Sumner revealed a politically wise man intent upon binding up the wounds of the past, his appointment in 1888 provoked controversy. To his past was added the burden of his age, sixty-two, and a record of poor health, but these difficulties were surmounted and the Senate approved his appointment by a vote of thirty-two to twenty-eight. He became the second oldest man ever appointed to the Court, but the worry about his health seemed misplaced, for as he moved down the aisle he carried his sixty-four years comfortably. About the same general physical size as Bradley and Blatchford, Lamar had a long head that was distinguished by a full-flowing mustache and long, greying beard. His hair, receding from his forehead, was darker than his beard, and he wore it long, over his ears. His features were well proportioned.

The last member of the Court was David Joseph Brewer, who had been sworn into service less than a month earlier. He replaced Stanley Matthews, whose last illness preceding his death greatly limited his participation in the Court's work. At fifty-two Brewer was the Court's youngest member and nephew of one of the Court's oldest members, Stephen J. Field. This man from Kansas must have been impressed by the glamour of the occasion, an affair certainly worth celebrating in the doggerel verse he regularly turned out for his colleagues' amusement. But if he did so celebrate the occasion, no such evidence has been found. Brewer was a little less than six feet tall, but a slight stoop in his broad shoulders made him look shorter. He had a broad, full forehead, a Roman nose, and black hair growing a little thin at the top. What was most striking and what excited the most comment, since his arrival on the Court, were his glossy black mustache and shaggy chin whiskers. His facial adornment minimized a dour, piercing look, which became more apparent in the next year when he shaved his face clean. Then, observers remarked, he looked like a Jesuit priest.[13] But this solemn face well masked a playful personality that livened the Justices' conferences.

When the long procession had reached the stage, the proceedings began with a short introductory address by ex-President Grover Cleveland, who had played a significant part in shaping this celebration. Before the Court was given the opportunity to respond, five speeches were made, consuming over four hours. Newspaper reports echoed the unspoken comments of the weary audience in the assessment that lawyers were unnecessarily long-winded and not very perceptive critics of their own efforts. The Court's logical spokesman was the Chief, but he deferred to Stephen J. Field. Fuller had made a widely acclaimed speech to both houses of Congress the previous December commemorating the inauguration of George Washington. That effort, combined with a desire to win the support of Field, led Fuller to appoint the Californian to respond to the public accolade. The long-windedness of the other speakers may have annoyed Field, but it did not deter him from delivering his full speech. In fact, the applause generated by his introduction confirmed that the audience was still responsive. Field acknowledged the uniqueness of this special celebration dedicated to a body that through its unobtrusive labors, simplicity, and small clientele tended "to escape rather than attract popular attention and applause." His speech covered considerable ground, including both his own interpretation of the Constitution and his support for some relief for the terrible work burden of the Court.[14]

The audience was spared the final address that the absent President was to give but not the full efforts of the Liederkranz Society. Twenty-five hundred voices strong, the chorus first sang "Ave Marie." The leader of the assembled orchestra, aware that the program was running painfully long, thought one chorus of "America, the Beautiful" sufficient and swung into the Doxology, but the trumpets were overwhelmed by the chorus that refused to yield. Defeated, the orchestra fell into line.[15] The program was over but with little time to spare before the gala banquet celebration planned at the Lennox Lyceum that evening.

In terms of menu, size, and decorations the banquet was indeed a lavish affair. James C. Carter, an eminent constitutional lawyer well known to the Court, was the toastmaster. Speeches in the evening were appropriately shorter, and at least the audience could listen with a full stomach. John Marshall Harlan responded to the toasts offered, but the Justice appeared subdued by the occasion, and none of the color and witticism that generally graced his speeches came through.[16]

The Court had done its duty; it had left Washington, traveled to New York, and listened to the encomiums. Perhaps all agreed that one such celebration in a hundred years was just about right. Leaving this alien experience behind, the Justices returned to the comfortable and certainly far less hectic environment that enveloped the Court and its work.

Although it was no longer a hub around which society swarmed, the Supreme Court did figure in Washington social life in the early 1890s. While Fuller was Chief, the Court met socially on a regular basis, but gradually the larger social orbit of the Court was contracted. This Fuller did for a combination of personal and professional reasons. He had heard the rumor that his predecessor, Morrison Waite, had been sped to his grave by a burdensome social schedule. The new Chief preferred the quiet of his home and relatively small and congenial social groupings. Also, Fuller's conception of his role as Chief Justice made him more rigid and uncomfortable in large social gatherings. His insistence upon proper official respect for the office he occupied led to further difficulties; at one presidential reception when foreign ambassadors were placed before the Court the Chief fumed and withdrew.[17]

In 1890 the Justices were paid $10,000 a year with the Chief receiving $500 more.[18] Although some considered the salary princely, many Justices, if not most, took a considerable cut in income when they came to the High Bench. Gray, after the death of his father, was independently wealthy; Fuller had amassed enough of a personal fortune through his earlier investments to augment his income; but Miller, so long in judicial service, would leave his widow a subject for charity.

Housed in the Capitol, the Supreme Court had moved up from the ill-ventilated, cramped basement quarters to the original Senate Chamber shortly after the upper house found a new home in one of the wings added to the building in 1859. Comfortably ensconced in the Old Senate Chamber at the beginning of the 1860 term, the Court now had a courtroom that advocates and the public alike deemed suitably impressive. Little change could be discerned in the thirty years court had been held there.[19]

The half-domed ceiling gave a spaciousness to the room. Nine upholstered leather chairs stood behind the long, imposing raised bench, separated from the attorneys by a decorative iron railing. The Chief Justice sat in the center, and the remaining members were distributed to his right and left, alternately in terms of their seniority, with the most recent arrival to the far left of the Chief. Directly behind the center chair was a crimson-draped arch, above which a sculptured eagle with outstretched wings stood guard. Above the eagle, as a constant reminder to the advocates, was a clock by which oral arguments could be precisely measured. Deep green marble pillars stood as a backdrop to the Justices, and the side walls were decorated with marble busts of the Chief Justices. Tables, with freshly cut quill pens laid out, and arm-chairs were available to counsel directly in front of the bench. Reporters and guests were accommodated to the left of the Court in the gallery.[20]

Twelve other rooms were set aside for the Court, including the old courtroom that had become a library for the Justices. Across from the courtroom was a small anteroom in which the Justices donned their robes. Robes were not the common apparel for the judiciary that they have since become, but they were for the Supreme Court. They were made of black Chinese silk and cost each Justice between $60 and $90. A conference room was outfitted in the basement of the Capitol, but during Fuller's years he often made his home available for conferences as well.[21]

Despite the space the Supreme Court commanded, there were no private offices. Since each Justice had responsibility for every case, much work had to be done outside the confines of the Capitol. Such work was generally done in the Justice's private study at home, furnished out of the Court's current expense budget. Limited to a total of $2,000, the amount covered everything from lighting fixtures to decorative accessories. The new appointee fell heir to the library of his predecessor, which was augmented by a $50 yearly allotment. Upon the death or resignation of a Justice, the marshal of the Court was an early visitor checking the inventory of the study. Often this government property was auctioned off, but the marshal had no objection to family purchases as long as they were made at the appraised value.[22]

The single term of court began in mid-October and ended in May or June, depending upon the pressure of the docket. Most of the Justices, as long as their physical vigor lasted, walked from their homes to the Capitol. There they congregated in the robing room, where an attendant exchanged their outerwear for the black gowns in strict order of seniority. The robes flowed in loose folds from shoulders to the floor, completely covering their street clothes. Duly outfitted, the procession, headed by the marshal and the clerk, precisely at noon made its way across the hall, through the courtroom, to the seats at the bench. As each Justice stood behind his chair and as the attorneys and spectators remained standing, the official crier intoned the traditional words: "Oyez! Oyez! Oyez! All persons having business before the honorable, the Supreme Court of the United States, are admonished to draw near and give their attention, for the Court is now sitting. God save the United States and this honorable Court." The Court sat for four hours, usually the time required to hear oral arguments on both sides of a single case, although at times oral arguments were cut to a single hour each. When the Court was convinced that the first advocate had not made a case, it did not hear the opposing lawyer, and in certain instances cases were submitted without oral argument. During the two-hour presentation, attorneys were frequently interrupted by questions from the bench.

Advocates before the Court were also interrupted by Justices slipping behind a partition where tables were set up to serve lunch. The sounds of dining echoed in the courtroom, but Chief Justice Fuller hesitated to break with tradition. Supposedly, the stimulus for change came near the turn of the century when an advocate noted that the bench had been reduced to five, one less than the quorum required. Fuller assured counsel that the missing Justices could still hear the argument, but soon afterward the Chief established a half-hour recess so lunch would not be such a disturbing event in the Court's workday. With this change, the Court sat until precisely 4:30 P.M. when it adjourned for the day.[23]

After a week of hearing oral argument, the Court met on Saturday morning in conference to decide pending cases. Here the Justices were sealed off from the Court's auxiliary personnel and the rest of the world, and here the Justices, freed from the solemnity required by the courtroom, could enter into the give and take that characterize healthy, collective decision making. The atmosphere of the conference room depended upon the personalities of the men and the control exercised by the Chief. Fuller, with his intrinsic respect for his colleagues and his pacifying spirit, tried to keep the discussions from becoming too personal. To prevent disagreements from festering, Fuller introduced the practice of the Justices exchanging handshakes each morning.[24]

After votes were counted in conference, the Chief Justice, if he had voted with the majority, assigned the writing of the opinion to a member of the majority. If the Chief disagreed with the Court's resolution of a case, the senior associate Justice had the task of either writing the opinion or assigning it to one of the other majority Justices. Only with the assignment of an opinion does the collective work of the Court fall more heavily upon a single Justice. The task of the writer of the Court's opinion is to explain the decision to the satisfaction of the previously determined majority. Often this submission of a draft opinion elicits requests for changes, resulting in the fact that an opinion of the Court, though announced by its writer, is often a group, rather than an individual, product. Only in a lone dissent is a Justice unchecked in the airing of his personal views.

On Monday morning the opinions were read in open court. The Court's decision binds the parties to the litigation, but more significantly the rule announced in the case becomes binding in the federal trial courts and in federal constitutional matters on the state courts as well. The idea that prior cases, or precedent, should be paid great respect is based upon the assumption that conduct has been geared to the rules announced in prior cases. No appellate court could completely ignore precedent and settle each matter anew; neither justice nor the work load of the courts would support such an undertaking.

In addition to the structured decision-making process and the inhibitions of precedent, the Justices during this era worked within an environment heavily laden with formality and regularity. Individual members of the Court differed in their respect for Court ritual, but there have always been some like Horace Gray who made decorum and formality a personal crusade. As the self-appointed sartorial leader of the Court, Gray took a personal interest in ensuring that all men connected with or appearing before the bench were properly attired. Harlan's casual and sloppy dress bothered Gray, who saw the robe that enveloped his colleague as a godsend. Advocates appeared in either frock coats or cutaways, and the marshal kept a supply of the proper dress on hand to clothe untutored counsel. In fact, the clerk and the marshal carried on a continual school for the indoctrination of counsel into the manners and procedures of the Supreme Court. Nor were new Justices without a ready supply of tutors both within and without the membership. For instance, Brewer's unruly beard would soon be a casualty of bench disapproval.[25] But such collegial influence was only one of the various pressures that weighed heavily upon new arrivals.

The new Justice could hardly escape the tradition-bound environment that enveloped him. Tenure for life was constitutionally prescribed for the federal judiciary, but the supporting personnel of the Court acquired it by custom.[26] The clerk of the Court in 1890 was James R. McKenney, whose $6,000 salary gave little indication of the power he wielded or of the way in which he was courted by the more highly paid lawyers that appeared before the High Bench. Before becoming clerk in 1880, McKenney had been employed by the Court for twenty-two years. When he died in 1913, he was succeeded by his deputy, James D. Maher, who had served the Court for the preceding forty-eight years. The marshal in 1890 was Major John M. Wright, who would serve in that capacity for twenty-seven years prior to his death in 1915.

If this longevity and devotion to the Court seem astonishing, look at the record of those who served the Justices as body servants, or messengers, as they were officially labeled. These men, all blacks, were employed by the marshal's office and assigned to individual Court members. As the books of a deceased Justice passed to his successor, so did his body servant. Although the marshal tried to consider the preferences of the Justice, in a showdown the body servant won. Some evidence exists that the sinecure the body servant had was passed on to his son when the father died or became incapacitated. The one common duty of the body servants was to serve lunch, but their prime unofficial duty seemed to be the careful, deliberate, and stubborn indoctrination of the Justice into the ways of the Court. One observer of the practice concluded that these men in the guise of servants rule "the private life of the justices with iron authority and discipline that persons in the South have long been familiar with in old family servitors."[27] Some body servants, as they aged, found new jobs with the Court. Archie Lewis, who began his service as a body servant in 1849, later became the robing-room attendant. He died in 1913 after sixty-four years of total service. His close friend William H. Bruce began as a servant in 1867 and finished his life as the doorkeeper. Such records of service were not exceptional.

The Justices, however, did have control over one employee, a secretary they could hire on a salary allotted by the Department of Justice. Horace Gray had broken with the prevailing tradition by hiring a new secretary each year, a graduating Harvard Law School student recommended by Professor John Chipman Gray, Horace's brother. This practice of hiring recent law school graduates as secretaries or clerks for a single year was not easily established on the Court, for the other members preferred continuity throughout their years of service.[28]

Many observers were led to conclude that the Court abhorred novelty and change in its immediate world. Such a characterization was not inappropriate. When furniture began to look shabby, it was never replaced: instead it was carefully refinished. When chairs had to be reupholstered, if at all possible the fabric used was of the same material, texture, and pattern as the old. When the rug in the courtroom had been practically reduced to threads, a new one was furnished that was an exact duplicate of the old one in its better days.[29]

Within this environment, one can understand the subtle and the not-so-subtle pressures to reinforce a respect for the past and a suspicion of change.

NOTES

1. Hampton L. Carson, *The Supreme Court of the United States: Its History*, 2d ed., 2 vols. (Philadelphia: A.R. Keller Co., 1892), 2:587-88. This publication was sponsored by the centennial committee and contains a full account of the celebration including all the speeches.

2. Ibid., pp. 593-94; and *New York World*, February 5, 1890.

3. *New York World*, February 5, 1890.

4. Short biographies of varying quality of all the men who have served as Supreme Court Justices through 1969 are found in Leon Friedman and Fred L. Israel, eds., *The Justices of the United States Supreme Court 1789-1969: Their Lives and Major Opinions*, 4 vols. (New York: R. R. Bowker Co. and Chelsea House Publishers, 1969).

5. *New York World*, February 5, 1890. The author has drawn his descriptions by synthesizing contemporary portrayals with a study of photographs. Many newspaper and

magazine articles dealing with the Court and its members are collected in fourteen scrapbooks kept by the Clerk of Court. They are generally arranged chronologically and maintained with some thoroughness from the late 1880s to 1913. See Scrapbooks on Court's History, 1880-1935, Records of the Supreme Court of the United States (Office of the Clerk), Record Group 267, National Archives, Washington, D.C., hereafter referred to as Clerk's Scrapbooks.

6. Willard L. King, *Melville Weston Fuller: Chief Justice of the United States*, Phoenix ed. (Chicago: University of Chicago Press, 1967), pp. 125-27.

7. Ibid., p. 137.

8. Charles O. Fairman, *Mr. Justice Miller and the Supreme Court* (Cambridge: Harvard University Press, 1939); and *New York Sun*, September 26, 1892.

9. *New York World*, May 7, 1895.

10. Charles O. Fairman, "What Makes a Great Justice? Mr. Justice Bradley and the Supreme Court," *Boston University Law Review* 30 (January 1950):49-102, and "Mr. Justice Bradley," in *Mr. Justice*, ed. Allison Dunham and Philip B. Kurland, rev. & enl. ed. (Chicago: University of Chicago, Phoenix Books, 1964), p. 81.

11. *New York World*, February 5, 1890, May 7, 1895.

12. Robert M. Spector, "Legal Historian on the United States Supreme Court: Justice Horace Gray, Jr., and the Historical Method," *American Journal of Legal History* 12 (1968):181-210; and unsigned limericks on Gray's tendency to doze on the bench can be found as early as 1886 in Clerk's Scrapbook No. 1, National Archives.

13. *New York Recorder*, February 18, 1891.

14. *New York Times*, February 5, 1890; and Field's address in Carson, *The Supreme Court*, 2:705.

15. *New York Times*, February 5, 1890.

16. Charles H. Butler, *A Century at the Bar of the Supreme Court of the United States* (New York: G. P. Putnam's Sons, 1942), pp. 141-42; *New York Times*, February 5, 1890; and for Harlan's speech, see Carson, *The Supreme Court*, 2:725-32.

17. King, *Fuller*, pp. 152-54, 317-18.

18. In 1903 the salaries were raised to $12,500 and $13,000 respectively, in 1911 to $14,500 and $15,000, and in 1926 to $20,000 and $20,500.

19. Charles Warren, *The Supreme Court in United States History*, rev. ed., 2 vols. (Boston: Little, Brown & Co., 1926), 2:361-62; and for a picture of the courtroom, circa 1900, see Glenn Brown, *History of the United States Capitol*, 56th Cong., 1st sess., 1900, *Senate Document No. 60*, 2 vols. (Washington: Government Printing Office, 1900-1903), 2:plate 103.

Today visitors to the Capitol can see the old basement courtroom as it was when the Supreme Court held its formal sessions there before 1860 and the old Senate Chamber as it was furnished before its occupancy by the Court. In 1935 the Supreme Court moved to its present building.

20. Edward G. Lowry, "Justice at Zero: The Frigid Austerities Which Enrobe the Members of the United States Supreme Court," *Harpers Weekly*, May 21, 1910, p. 8. This article also includes a picture of the courtroom from which some of the textual description has been drawn.

21. Warren, *Supreme Court*, 2:362; Brown, *History of the Capitol*, 2:148, which also includes a picture of the new library at 1:plate 94; J.M. Wright to F. E. Hinckley, May 13, 1908, in "Court, Robes for" file, Records of the Supreme Court (Office of the Marshal), National Archives; and King, *Fuller*, p. 152.

22. This material has been collected from folders under the general subject heading, "Court Room and Chambers—Furniture and Furnishings, 1867-1910," Records of the Supreme Court (Office of the Marshal), National Archives.

23. George Shiras, III, *Justice George Shiras, Jr. of Pittsburgh*, ed. and compl. Winfield Shiras (Pittsburgh: University of Pittsburgh Press, 1953), pp. 99, 135-36; and Butler, *A Century at the Bar*, pp. 87-88, 121-22.

24. King, *Fuller*, p. 134.

25. Butler, *A Century at the Bar*, pp. 85-86; and *New York Recorder*, February 18, 1891.

26. *New York Times*, June 12, 1910.

27. Undated memorandum, "Court Room and Chambers—Furniture and Furnishings, 1867-1910," Records of the Supreme Court (Office of the Marshal), National Archives.

28. Ibid.; and King, *Fuller*, p. 133. King states that Gray was the first Justice to employ secretaries with legal training. Apparently the practice of hiring recent law school graduates as temporary clerks was fairly well established by 1920.

29. Lowry, "Justice at Zero," p. 34.

chapter 2

SHIFTING MEMBERSHIP AND SHIFTING DOCTRINE, 1890-93

Following the midwinter sojourn in New York City, the Justices returned to a crowded docket that included the major cases of the 1889 term. The sustenance, if that is what it was, that they had received from the public tribute would soon be consumed. Hopes for the creation of intermediate federal appeal courts were brightening, but the docket was still crowded with a host of relatively unimportant cases hardly worth the time of the nation's highest court. Such work had the potentiality of diverting the Justices from a close and careful consideration of the more significant cases.

After the return to Washington, the first important case to be decided was one involving a Mississippi statute directing railroads in the state to provide separate accommodations, either cars or compartments divided by partitions, for "white and colored races." Attorneys for the railroad argued that the Mississippi law commanding segregation was an impermissible burden on interstate commerce. The Court had pronounced a Louisiana law commanding integration just such a burden in 1878. The seven-man majority, in an opinion written by Brewer, distinguished the earlier case on grounds that Mississippi's highest court had confined the reach of the statute to intrastate commerce, something Louisiana had not done. With the act so restricted, the majority concluded, congressional power was not infringed.[1]

In many ways this Mississippi case was more pivotal than the more widely known *Plessy* v. *Ferguson*, in which the Court confronted a challenge to segregated public transportation under the terms of the Fourteenth Amendment. In 1890 the challenge was mounted on the more limited grounds of the commerce clause, where a decision against the state would not forbid the enactment of other state segregation statutes. Although continually sensitive to the distribution of power within the federal system, the Court had not hesitated to find state acts in violation of the interstate commerce clause. Its decision here favoring Mississippi's law seemed a silent acquiescence in the South's solution to the problem of race relations. Harlan, joined by Bradley, dissented on the basis of the 1878 decision and the law's inhibitive effect on interstate commerce.[2]

In March 1890 the Court announced its decision in *Chicago, Milwaukee and St. Paul Railway Co.* v. *Minnesota,* a case that has etched its way into legal and historical literature as the culmination of a determined and concerted drive to find a lodging for vested rights in the Constitution. The story is a dramatic one of issues, interests, and attorneys, played against the backdrop of great industrial growth and the creation of a national economy. It involves the attempt to wring new meaning from the worn phrase "due process of law."[3]

Due process of law has a long and honored tradition in Anglo-American law, often traced back to the words "law of the land" in the Magna Carta. It entered our Constitution as part of the Bill of Rights in the Fifth Amendment, which provides that "No person shall . . . be deprived of life, liberty, or property, without due process of law." Its understood meaning was properly constituted procedures prescribed by valid law. The first hint that the phrase could be interpreted as a broader check on the lawmaking power came in Chief Justice Roger Taney's much discredited opinion in the *Dred Scott* case of 1857. In a long and rambling opinion the Chief Justice had suggested that property in slaves might be invulnerable to legislative proscription. Due process again appeared as a substantive limitation in 1870 when the Supreme Court declared federal legal tender legislation unconstitutional. But that decision did not survive the following year when the Court reversed itself.[4] So the only two decisions in which the Supreme Court lent some credence to a new interpretation of the due process clause were rather short-lived.

In 1868 the Fourteenth Amendment was added to the Constitution as an essential step in the reconstruction of the Union following the Civil War. Its very significant first section was little debated, and subsequent attempts to decipher its meaning fill shelves in any law library. In part, the first section reads "nor shall any State deprive any person of life, liberty, or property, without due process of law." The Fifth Amendment had imposed such a restriction upon the federal government in 1791; now it became a restriction upon the states as well. Obviously the sponsors of the first section of the amendment sought to overturn the *Dred Scott* decision by conferring national citizenship on blacks and to restructure the federal union by empowering the federal government to supervise certain state action. Despite primary concern for the newly freed slave, the language was broadly drawn in keeping with the American constitutional tradition. It was a tantalizing invitation to those with property interests to protect, especially since the states were now regulating business enterprises more aggressively.

It is ironical that an amendment that had to be imposed upon the former Confederate states would become a vehicle not for emancipation but rather for a type of legislative enslavement. Blacks received a few favorable decisions under the terms of the Fourteenth Amendment, but the Court seemed content in the latter quarter of the nineteenth century to join the other branches of the federal government in entrusting the future of blacks to the states.

Although its original purpose was sidetracked, the Fourteenth Amendment quickly became a target for litigation. This initial interest in, and then constant attention paid to, the amendment seems a necessary prelude to its later use. Wording in the Constitution can atrophy through disuse. Ongoing concern about specific constitutional language keeps it alive; it may come to mean different things or may be applied in novel ways, but it remains in the mainstream of constitutional law.

The *Slaughter-House Cases* in 1873 gave the Court an initial opportunity to contend with the meaning of the Fourteenth Amendment's first section. A broad challenge was hurled at an act of the Louisiana legislature granting a monopoly of the slaughtering business in New Orleans to a newly formed corporation. The butchers put out of business by the law carried their cause to the Supreme Court. The chief attorney, ex-Justice John A. Campbell, who had resigned from the Court in 1861 when his home state of Alabama left the Union, appeared before the bench seeking to convince the Justices that the Fourteenth Amendment had effected sweeping changes in the nature of the federal union. Summoning history and philosophy to his side in his effort to aid the Court in interpreting the amendment, he essentially argued that the monopolistic grant was unconstitutional because it deprived men of the right to work at their chosen trade. The amendment, he said, "was designed to secure individual liberty, individual property, and individual security and honor from arbitrary, partial, proscriptive and unjust legislation of governments."[5] The argument was novel and its presentation impressive, but a bare majority of the Justices refused to accept the broad supervisory function that Campbell urged upon them.

Samuel J. Miller, for the Court, read the Fourteenth Amendment narrowly and confined its language to the emancipated slave. What is surprising is not that Campbell lost but that he convinced four members of the Court, including Field and Bradley. Field in dissent emphasized the right a man had to his own labor free from state interference, a proposition he touched upon again in his centennial speech. The dissents do not focus on the due process clause; the clauses of the amendment are bunched together very much in the way that Campbell had presented his case. For one reason or another, four members of the Court believed the Fourteenth Amendment did preclude the state from passing certain legislation because its effect would deprive certain individuals of their property rights. Although five to four decisions are as final as unanimous decisions, they do seem to offer, as the decision did here, greater hope to litigants seeking to change the Court's mind. Over the next decade and a half the due process clause became more and more the focus of arguments made to the Court.

The majority of such cases concerned railroads. Certainly railroad corporations were large national enterprises with sufficient financial resources to hire legal talent, but this does not explain why railroads were most often the special targets of state regulatory measures. The railroad was a powerful vehicle for welding together a truly national economy, and the railroad was a major factor in the shaping of American law. After the War of 1812 Americans realized the key to economic growth and prosperity lay in improved methods of transportation. Turnpikes, canals, and the development of the steamboat caught the fancy of Americans, but the excitement caused by the railroad was unparalleled. The iron horse was the answer to all men's prayers; it would bring the hitherto illusive prosperity men sought; and towns engaged in skirmishes to attract the railroad. Opening up a new world of market opportunities, railroads were courted and they came, but with them came an increasing dependence. Hailed as unmitigated blessings, railroads, with their control of the highways of commerce, soon became targets of attack. In this power struggle, the farmers and their supporters gained ascendancy in certain state legislatures; they had no wish to cripple the iron horse, just limit the rates it extracted. Arising from this battle in the Midwest came the Granger cases in which the Supreme Court was called upon to referee the contest.

In *Munn* v. *Illinois* and the related Granger cases the Court held firm against the due process argument as it was leveled against state attempts to regulate the business of corporations. *Munn* involved the regulation of grain elevators, rather than railroads, but the principle was the same. A seven-man majority upheld the regulatory measures challenged, but in so doing the Court confined the ambit of state regulatory power to property in which the public has an interest. This was an opening wedge that the proponents of substantive due process could exploit. Field dissented from the majority's determination in the grain elevator case and focused his argument more clearly on the due process clause. He alleged that no line could be drawn on the basis of public interest; either the states had such regulatory power across the board or they did not. Field denied they did.[6] He lost Bradley's support, for the New Jersey Justice could not accept his colleague's broad-ranging ban on state regulation.

Those seeking to expand the ambit of due process seemed to be losing ground for only one Justice agreed with Field in *Munn*, but the stakes were high and eminent lawyers were available. In 1878 Justice Miller sought valiantly but unsuccessfully to stem the tide by describing the attempt to extract new meaning from the due process clause as "a strange misconception" without support in the law. Working for the advocates of this new meaning was attrition; four new Justices joined the Court in the period from January 5, 1881 through April 3, 1882. New Justices were less nurtured in the pre-Civil War tradition with its respect for the old federal-state balance.

Also, the Court never imposed a ban on the argument, and the simple task of having to respond to it repeatedly forced the Justices, whether consciously or not, to give ground. Although the majority continued to rebuff in strong language wholesale challenges to the power of the states to establish rates, by 1886 it had given a blueprint to advocates seeking more limited success. In *Stone* v. *Farmers' Loan and Trust Co.*, Chief Justice Morrison Waite described the target:

This power to regulate is not a power to destroy, and limitation is not the equivalent of confiscation. Under pretense of regulating fares and freights, the State cannot require a railroad corporation to carry persons or property without reward; neither can it do that which in law amounts to a taking of private property for public use without just compensation, or without due process of law.[7]

The two dissenters in *Stone*, Harlan and Field, had already accepted a fuller blown definition of due process.

With the stage now set, the Court awaited a case that would directly pose the problem the majority in *Stone* considered hypothetically. That case was *Chicago, Milwaukee and St. Paul Railway Co.* v. *Minnesota* before the High Bench in 1890. The Court's decision, subscribed to by five Justices, was written by Samuel Blatchford. Blatchford may have been chosen by the Chief because his workmanlike approach would produce the most acceptable opinion; certainly both Brewer and Field in their belief in the constitutional invalidity of much state regulation of property would have been poor choices to hold the majority together. Even Blatchford could not hold Miller, who concurred in a special opinion.

Minnesota, through its legislature, had delegated power to a commission to set railroad rates in the state, and the state's highest court had ruled that the rates set were not subject to judicial examination. Although Blatchford at times wrote as if a matter of procedure were involved, his decision clearly asserted that the fairness and reasonableness of the commission's work is a proper matter for the courts: "If the company is deprived of the power of charging reasonable rates for the use of its property, and such deprivation takes place in the absence of an investigation by judicial machinery, it is deprived of the lawful use of its property, and thus in substance and effect, of the property itself, without due process of law and in violation of the Constitution of the United States."[8] Citing the significant wording of Waite in the *Stone* case as authority, though those words in that case were *obiter dicta*, that is, not necessary to the Court's decision and therefore not binding as precedent, Blatchford's opinion concealed the novelty of the Court's decision. Prior to 1890 what a state legislature or commission did, assuming no violation of its established procedures, was presumed reasonable. Now the Court carves out a role for the judiciary, and since that role is predicated on federal constitutional grounds, appeal is possible all the way to the Supreme Court. Since 1873 the Court has consistently rejected sweeping due process attacks on state legislation, but in 1890 it accepted a limited application of that argument and clothed it in the sacred garb of the Constitution.

Hesitatingly Miller concurred in the result reached by the Court. He was primarily concerned that piecemeal challenges to rates would overburden the courts, and he suggested what he considered the proper procedure for bringing a rate determination before the judiciary. Still this Justice, who twelve years earlier characterized the substantive due process argument as "some strange misconception," now accepted its limited application.

Miller, in trying to cope with counsel's arguments, had backed into acceptance, but Joseph P. Bradley did not. Asserting that a determination that the state possessed regulatory power carried with it the full authority to set rates, he contended that the instant decision had the effect of overruling the *Granger* cases. "The governing principle of those cases was that the regulation and settlement of the fares of railroads and other public accommodations is a legislative prerogative and not a judicial one."[9] If, he continued, the legislature simply provides that reasonable rates be imposed, the courts can properly act to determine what is reasonable, but when the legislature or its surrogate sets rates, it, in effect, is declaring what is reasonable. The Justice condemned his colleagues for assuming an authority that resides in the people and their chosen representatives. A fear of popular majorities would mount in the years ahead, but Bradley did not share that phobia. Bradley's dissent captured Gray and Lamar, but in less than three years Bradley and Lamar would both be dead, and Gray had neither the conviction nor the inclination to carry on the fight.

With its insistence that any imposed rate provide a fair, just, and reasonable return on capital, the Court had accepted the due process clause as a substantive limitation on state legislative power, a course legal writers like Thomas Cooley had been urging since 1868.[10] With the great outpouring of state regulatory measures in the last quarter of the nineteenth century, certain business interests were alarmed. Legislatures are not immune to such interests, but politicians are an unpredictable breed, and, if defeats in the halls of state legislatures could be reversed by this new access to the judiciary, the future would look considerably brighter. Although all judges are far from alike, judges, advocates, and successful businessmen shared similar cultural backgrounds and often indulged in the same suspicion of the ascendant mob. The argument that property interests were being threatened struck a responsive chord. Just how far could this opening wedge be pushed, and just how far would a changing Supreme Court extend its reach?

Although Blatchford's majority opinion in the Minnesota case clearly upheld the state's power to regulate, Bradley suggested in his dissent that the

Court's decision in *Munn* v. *Illinois* had been placed in jeopardy. Railroads with their state and federal charters and their public character were clearly subjects of state regulation, but what about other property, especially the grain elevators dealt with in *Munn*? Was Bradley right? Would the Court reverse the 1877 decision? The prospect was intriguing and would not go untested. In November 1891 the Court heard arguments in *Budd* v. *New York*, another case involving state regulation of grain elevators. An eight-man court split five to three in favor of the law's constitutionality. The question was posed in the framework of a criminal prosecution of Budd for exceeding the legislatively prescribed rates. No argument was made that the rates imposed were unreasonable; instead the Court was summoned to invalidate the state's power to regulate such a business. Blatchford was again selected to write the Court's opinion. He gave counsel's argument a full hearing but refused to undermine the rationale of *Munn*. Field, who dissented in 1877, dissented again, as did the new arrival on the Court, Henry B. Brown, both men joining in the opinion by David J. Brewer.[11]

Brewer's dissent forcefully delineated his ideas on governmental regulation of property and included that oft-quoted phrase, "The paternal theory of government is to me odious." The Justice took to task the public interest qualification for legitimating state regulation, first enunciated in *Munn*. Arguing that practically all business can be housed under that standard, he suggested that regulation be confined to instances where a special privilege is conferred by government, where the service performed is a public service, or where property is devoted to a public use. Railroads clearly fell into the latter two categories, Brewer ruled in a Court opinion issued on the same day as his dissent in *Budd*. In such cases, he said, the Court's only function is to assess the reasonableness of the rates when they are challenged. But Budd's grain elevator, he continued, was beyond the legitimate scope of the state's power over private business. "The utmost possible liberty to the individual and the fullest protection to him and his property," Brewer concluded, "is both the limitation and duty of government."[12]

Often mistakenly chosen to typify the Court of the 1890s, Brewer lost many battles on the High Bench. Some of his views struck his more pragmatic brethren as too dogmatic, but his tenacity in urging them, both in strong dissenting opinions and in frequent public speeches, gave them wide circulation.

Reaffirming *Munn* v. *Illinois* in 1892 seemingly settled the issue, but in 1894 the Court faced the question once again. In the interim three new Justices had taken their seats, all replacements for Justices who had been wedded to *Munn*. If Brewer could gain two of the three new votes, assuming the dissenters in *Budd* stood firm, he would obtain the reversal he sought. In fact, in *Brass* v. *North Dakota* Brewer did receive the votes of both Edward Douglas White and Howell Edmunds Jackson, but a reversal of *Munn* was not to be. Justice Henry B. Brown had switched sides, which made the vote five to four in favor of reaffirming the *Munn* decision. Brown had been attracted to Brewer's logic in their early mutual service on the Court, but by 1894 the junior Justice was becoming more independent. Also, Brown had an aversion to five to four decisions, a fact that may explain the inconsistency some observers have found in the Justice's decision making. A five to four decision could not be avoided in *Brass*, but Brown may well have felt the authority of *Munn* should not now be undermined by the narrowest of margins. At any rate, Brown's vote decided the case. A disappointed Brewer concluded "that the country is rapidly traveling the road which leads to that point where all freedom on contract and conduct will be lost."[13]

So the Court stood firm on the constitutionality of state regulation of private property affected with a public interest, but the accommodation the Court reached with the due process argument in 1890 also had a lasting effect. Advocates zeroed in on the target the Court displayed. In 1894 a unanimous Court enjoined enforcement of the rates set by a Texas commission on grounds they were "unjust and unreasonable." In 1898 in the case of *Smyth* v. *Ames*, a unanimous Court invalidated a Nebraska attempt to set rates by statute, finding the prescribed rates a deprivation of property without due process of law.[14]

In viewing the Court's work in the area, the due process argument levied against the power of the states to regulate was continually repulsed. Beginning in 1890, however, the Justices asserted that rates set either by commission or by the legislature were vulnerable to a judicial veto if the attack was centered on the failure of the rate to provide a fair return on capital. The Court, then, took upon itself the extensive responsibility of determining what was the actual capital base and what was a fair rate of return. The railroad managers could now count upon their day in court. On the one hand, the attempt of the judiciary to protect property rights, when an imbalance in state governmental power threatened them, seemed only to be serving the ends of justice in a growing capitalistic system. On the other hand, the chain of decisions did represent a departure from the past as both an inroad upon the power of the state legislatures and an expansion of judicial power. Advocates and the interests they represented worked diligently to bring the judiciary into the picture because of its cultural sympathy with a traditional American concern for the protection of property. An argument could be mounted that this accretion to judicial power was in keeping with the basic constitutional principles that sought to limit the power of the majority. Doctrine had to be developed, but the end sought was the same.

Substantive due process had arrived, and even its quite limited acceptance gave the doctrine a new respectability. With renewed vigor counsel introduced the argument in a great variety of cases, but with little success. For instance, no headway was made when it was urged against taxes levied by the states, for the Court in the 1890s read the state's taxing power broadly.

The primary grounds for overruling state acts, a power granted to the Court by the Judiciary Act of 1789, continued to be the no impairment of contracts and the interstate commerce clauses. Decisions in the 1890s reflect the weakening of the contract clause as a bar to state regulation. The states had been told how the obstacle posed by the contract clause in the Constitution could be surmounted. In any grant, corporate charter, or other contract, the state could write into the agreement the right to modify its terms. Furthermore, the Court increasingly construed these contracts in favor of the public interest, and claimed exceptions from taxation or regulation had to be explicitly stated. The protection afforded by the contract clause was severely limited, thereby making the due process argument far more attractive.

Although the Court in the 1889 term was finding new meaning in the due process clause as it related to property rights, it could find no merit in the novel argument presented on behalf of William Kemmler. As a device for carrying out the sentence of death, the electric chair was replacing the hangman's noose throughout the country. Kemmler's attorney argued that electrocution constituted a cruel and inhumane punishment that violated his client's right not to be deprived of life without due process of law. A unanimous Court concluded that the Fourteenth Amendment had not changed the nature of the federal union and that the protection of life, liberty, and property rested with the states.[15]

Such a conclusion is really quite misleading in its assertion of business as usual under the terms of the pre-Civil War union, as the fascinating case of *Cunningham* v. *Neagle* well illustrates. The case was the culmination of one of the most bizarre episodes in the history of the High Bench and its members.[16] Colorful California was the setting of the story, and the cast of characters included Justice Stephen J. Field; David S. Terry, a former chief justice of the highest state court; Sarah Althea Hill, an attractive, adventurous, and hot-tempered woman; William Sharon, an aging former United States Senator and millionaire with banking and mining interests; and David Neagle, a deputy sworn into special federal service. Sarah Hill, in her early twenties, formed a liaison with Senator Sharon, who provided her a room at a hotel he owned. After a year or so his ardor cooled, and Sarah could neither reclaim his affections nor continue to live in her room after the door had been removed. Eventually she countered by producing a "marriage contract" and a batch of otherwise nonincriminating letters purportedly from Sharon, addressed "Dear Wife." The race to court was won by Sharon, who filed a suit in federal court to have the so-called contract voided on grounds of fraud. Claiming to be Mrs. Sharon, Sarah Hill filed a suit for divorce in the state court. Sarah's divorce case caught the public fancy, and a sympathetic judge, encouraged by a favorable press that condemned the philandering millionaire, granted the divorce and a handsome settlement. Sharon took separate appeals on the decision and the settlement to the California Supreme Court.

While these appeals were pending, Sarah and her attorney sought to delay action in the federal court. All the attacks to the jurisdiction of the federal court were rejected by Judge Lorenzo Sawyer. Sharon and, after his death late in the autumn of 1885, his heirs concentrated their efforts on the federal action. Extensive testimony was taken in the summer of 1885 designed to discredit Sarah and her alleged "marriage contract." Because of the hysterical conduct of Sarah and her threats of harm to the lying witnesses, the hearing examiner had to adjourn the proceedings. The federal circuit court was asked to restore order. This time Judge Sawyer asked for the assistance of Field, then on circuit duty in California, and both men joined in a vigorous condemnation of Sarah and her attorneys for their conduct. In December 1885 the decision in the federal case was announced by the circuit judge, who had jurisdiction of the original suit. Declaring the "marriage contract" void as a forgery, the judge spread a long, detailed, and highly unflattering portrayal of Sarah Hill on the public record. A federal court decided that no marriage had ever existed, while a state court had granted a divorce, a paradoxical result quite compatible with our federal system. Sharon's death preceded the verdict, and his heirs deliberately took no action to enforce the federal court's judgment.

In early 1886 David S. Terry entered the picture, drawn to the defense of this lovely woman who had been so thoroughly condemned and tainted in the federal court's proceedings. His sense of chivalry was matched by a personal attraction, and the two were married in early January 1887. Now Terry's legal talents and prestige were committed to his new wife's cause. First, he took what he thought was the proper action to appeal the decision of the federal circuit court; then, he concentrated on the appeals to the state supreme court. In a four to three decision in January 1888 the California supreme court upheld the divorce decree but reduced the amount of the settlement. The Sharon heirs took another appeal from the California trial court when it refused to grant a motion for a new trial. Perhaps because of his personal involvement in the case, Terry had committed a fatal error in his efforts to appeal the federal court's decision on the fraud issue. Before an appeal could be taken to the decision, the action, which had abated with Sharon's death, had to be revived. This Terry had not done, and after the passage of the two-year period in which appeals were permitted, the Sharon heirs revived the action and sought enforcement of the original judgment. The case was scheduled for the coming term of circuit court, which had shown no sympathy to the claims of the new Mrs. Terry. Outduelled on the legal battleground, Terry was frustrated and little inclined to act as a restraining influence on his wife. For instance, in August 1888 Sarah Terry encountered Judge Sawyer on a train; she seized his long hair, gave his head a vigorous shake, and then laughed as she continued down the aisle.

Justice Field became a special target for the enmity of the Terrys when he announced the decision of the three-man federal circuit court on September 3, 1888. As he began to read the opinion and its drift became clear, Mrs. Terry interrupted Field's reading with cries that the Justice had been bought. Field ordered her ejection from the courtroom, and when the marshal sought to comply, her husband replied with a blow that flattened the law officer. Chaos reigned until the Terrys were removed from the courtroom; then Field continued with his reading, which ended by ordering the surrender of the "marriage contract." After a further skirmish in the hall, the Terrys were jailed, although the sheriff, so impressed with having a former chief justice of the California high court in his custody, persuaded his wife to relinquish their bed to the couple.

Terry had second thoughts after the affair and prepared a petition for his release from a six-month contempt of court sentence. He put a benign interpretation upon his conduct, but Field, horrified as judges have always been by disruptions in the courtroom, handled the petition in a prejudicial manner. After obtaining evidence contradicting Terry's rendition and without prior notice, he introduced the petition and denied it. Later, when he returned to Washington, Field used his influence to keep Terry imprisoned for the full six months. His colleagues on the Court sustained Field's denial of Terry's petition, and President Cleveland refused to act in Terry's behalf.

Field was urged to let the whole affair cool and not perform circuit court duties in 1889. The Justice, however, refused to be intimidated by threats to his personal safety. Responding to the situation, the United States Attorney General approved the hiring of special deputies to ensure order in what was expected to be a tumultuous term of circuit court. All hope for a piece of the Sharon estate had vanished, but the Terrys still faced criminal charges for their conduct of the preceding summer. David Neagle, one of the specially appointed deputies, met Justice and Mrs. Field in Reno, Nevada, and escorted them to San Francisco. Field expressed his objection to Neagle's presence, but the deputy stuck close. Without incident Field traveled from San Francisco to Los Angeles for the session of circuit court. He left Los Angeles by train on August 13. Occupying the sleeping berth opposite Field's, Neagle asked the porter to awaken him when the train reached Fresno, where the Terrys lived. There the Terrys did embark on their way to San Francisco to answer the charges pressed against them. (In the preceding month the California supreme court, whose membership had changed, overturned the earlier decision in the divorce case by granting a new trial. State and federal court decisions thus were fully harmonized to the detriment of Mrs. Terry and her claims against the Sharon estate.)

That morning Field chose to have his breakfast at the Lathrop station, where the train had stopped. Field and Neagle found a table near the center of the dining room; a little later the Terrys entered. David Terry proceeded to take a table off to one side, but his wife, on spotting Field, went back to the train. When she returned with the bag that was rumored to contain the pistol she often carried, her entrance was barred by the restaurant manager. Terry eventually got up from his table and walked down the aisle toward the entrance. As he reached the spot behind Field, he whirled around and struck the Justice on the head. Apparently Neagle thought that Terry was reaching for a gun or a knife; at any rate he fired two quick shots that killed Terry instantly. No weapon was found, although some would later contend that the bereaved widow, as she bent over the body, covertly removed a knife. Mrs. Terry's desire for immediate revenge was stymied when the growing crowd failed to respond to her suggestion of a lynching. Because the actual details of the shooting were muddied and because Terry, despite his recent fall from social favor, had considerable support within the state, Field and Neagle were arrested, Neagle in Tracy, a stop along the way, and Field in San Francisco. With able support from the local bar, Field met the arrest warrant with a petition for habeas corpus. Neagle was less fortunate and prospects for a trial in Stockton, where considerable pro-Terry sentiment existed, were not encouraging. To free Neagle from the hazards of California justice, a petition was filed in the federal circuit court seeking his release. On September 16, 1889, Judge Sawyer found that Neagle had acted lawfully and ordered his release from custody.

Judge Sawyer's action was the occasion for the appeal that the Court faced in the case of *Cunningham* v. *Neagle*. Field disqualified himself, but his strong feelings did not go unnoticed by his brethren. He had warmly commended Neagle's action, and he secured the talents of two eminent constitutional lawyers, Joseph H. Choate and James C. Carter, to aid the Attorney General in Neagle's behalf. The question the case posed was whether the federal court was legally empowered to intervene in the state's criminal process. Miller, for the majority, did not find the case difficult. He relied, as had the circuit court, on a federal statute that provided for the writ of habeas corpus when an individual was held in custody for an act done pursuant to federal law. Assuming that the authority to protect the life of a Justice of the Supreme Court must exist under the Constitution, Miller viewed the term "law" broadly as embracing any action of a federal deputy derived from the general scope of his duties under the laws of the United States. A habeas corpus petition, Miller concluded, is the proper way to assert the claim, and its granting does not unduly interfere with California's criminal processes. Since the practicalities of the situation seemed to call for an assertion of federal power, the majority tried to soft pedal the decision's effect on federal-state relationships. All the Justices concurred in Neagle's innocence and in the fairness of the California courts, and the majority saw no reason to drag out an issue that could be promptly resolved, thus eliminating *any* possibility of error.[17]

That the Court's opinion provoked dissent is quite interesting, for both dissenters, Lamar and Fuller, must have realized that Field considered a decision in favor of Neagle a matter of personal loyalty. Furthermore, the Chief must have sensed the potential damage that could be done to the relationship he was cultivating with the Californian. Because the dissenters believed the case raised an issue of far more importance than the facts at first indicated, they resisted the pressure for unanimity. Lamar's dissenting opinion, in which the Chief concurred, stressed the dangers lurking in the Court's decision.

Not only does it invade state power, the Justice began, but also it aggrandizes federal power. Lamar's concern extended beyond the federal-state balance to the balance among the branches of the national government. *Law*, as used in the habeas corpus act, he defined as a statute passed by Congress; without such legislative authorization the executive department could not proclaim that the actions of a deputy assigned to protect the life of a Supreme Court Justice are pursuant to law. Lamar's view of law was purposefully narrow, for he feared the majority's willingness to acknowledge a large domain of undefined national authority. Willing to trust California justice, the dissenters considered it presumptuous for the Court to grant immunity to an individual accused of murder under state law.

Lamar was less concerned with supporting state's rights than he was with condemning the Court's approval of an increase in executive power. What seemed to bother the ex-Confederate was the spectre of Abraham Lincoln, the prime expander of the executive office. Lamar had risen in politics and tried to gain a hearing for the new South by attempting to heal old wounds, but one lesson the past had taught was that the executive department must be watched and its power closely confined. In the long run the Mississippi Justice was fighting a losing battle in what now appears an inexorable trend toward expanding presidential power. Fuller was probably more sensitive to the state-federal balance, but during their common years on the bench, Lamar and the Chief would ponder issues presented to the Court from approximately the same perspective and join each other's dissents.

Two weeks after the *Neagle* decision, Lamar, speaking for a unanimous Court, reversed an obscenity conviction secured by the government under the terms of the Comstock Act of 1876. Although the national government had no delegated power to supervise the morals of its citizens, Congress had used its power over the mails to proscribe the mailing of obscene material.

Penalties were stiff and prosecution was zealous. Lamar was able to nip some of this zeal by rejecting the broad and sweeping interpretation of the law that the government urged; he said that since the sender's plain envelope gave no hint of its contents, due regard for the security of private correspondence necessitated the reversal.[18]

Another target of moral reformers was liquor, and prohibitionists had waged successful crusades in a number of states, including Iowa and Michigan. The Court in 1887 had upheld the constitutionality of prohibition against charges that such statutes deprived persons of their property without due process of law. Such state prohibition laws clearly resulted in a taking of private property, but the legislature's judgment of what was necessary for the protection of the public health, safety, morality, and welfare was deemed conclusive. States found that prohibiting the manufacture and sale of liquor within their borders did not ensure dryness. Undaunted citizens simply procured their supplies from other states. When Michigan and Iowa tried to invoke the terms of their laws to penalize such access, the "criminals" appealed to the Supreme Court on grounds that the application of the prohibition law to shipments from out of state was an impermissible restraint on interstate commerce. The six-man majority in the major case of *Leisy* v. *Hardin* agreed. As long as the shipment was retailed in its original package, the Court decided, it was immune from state regulation. Essentially the Court-developed doctrine was designed to foster interstate commerce by immunizing the product in the original package or container in which it was shipped from state interference. Justice Gray dissented, along with Brewer and Harlan, drawing attention to the fact that the Court's opinion, in effect, undermined state prohibition laws. Minimizing the restraint on interstate commerce, the dissenters emphasized the state's police power. Gray was unwilling to read the silence of Congress to mean that interstate commerce was to be free from all restraint, or to mean that the states were precluded from acting on matters to which Congress had not specifically addressed itself.[19] Although the wets in the dry states had won, their victory would be short-lived.

In *Leisy* v. *Hardin* the Court had to give meaning to a century of congressional silence. Whether interpreting such silence or a statute, the Court's decision is final in the case before it, but the prospective application of the rule announced can be overturned by legislative action that breaks the silence or amends the statute. Congress cannot so overrule a decision the Court bases upon the Constitution, but a simple majority with the President's concurrence is enough in many other matters. Confronted with such Court decisions, states, with their regulatory effects thwarted, can petition Congress for relief. That is precisely what happened here, and Congress responded with the Wilson Act, which sought to give the states effective control over liquor found within their borders.[20]

Just as Iowa and Michigan ran afoul of the commerce clause, if only temporarily, so did Minnesota with its meat inspection law. That statute provided that all meat on the hoof had to be inspected within twenty-four hours before its slaughter. Already dressed meat could be imported freely by the buyer. Suspicion of the genuineness of the inspection act as a protection of the public health, especially with no concern being paid to dressed meat, led the Court to invalidate the act as a burden on interstate commerce. In the next term the Justices struck down two Virginia inspection statutes, one relating to meat and another, tracing its ancestry to 1867, relating to flour.[21] This brief flurry of activity in striking down state inspection statutes came to an abrupt end. Either states drafted better statutes more clearly protective of health and not plagued by suspicious loopholes, or inspection acts were not challenged. In the following generation no such laws were again voided by the Court.

In the last major case of the term the Court joined in the national crusade against the Mormons and their practice of polygamy. In 1887 Congress, drawing upon its power over the territories, annulled the charter of the Mormon Church and directed proceedings to forfeit its property. Not called upon to determine the fate of the property but rather to pass upon the constitutionality of the statute, the Court responded with the most forceful assertion of congressional sovereignty over the territories in its annals.[22] Throughout the whole opinion and, in fact, throughout the whole crusade, one gains the impression that the condemnation of polygamy was uppermost and all devices for its eradication were presumed legal.

Chief Justice Fuller wrote a brief dissent, joined by Field and Lamar, in which he expressed his alarm at the majority's eager support of such total congressional power. Always one to peer through the smoke screen arising from the emotionalism of the moment, Fuller agreed that polygamy could be made illegal and its practice punished. But, he added, Congress does not possess the naked power to seize and confiscate property. In a dissent made more eloquent by its terseness, Fuller concluded that the property's diversion "under this Act of Congress is in contravention of specific limitations in the Constitution; unauthorized, expressly or by implication, by any of its provisions; and in disregard of the fundamental principle that the legislative power of the United States as exercised by the agents of the people of this Republic is delegated and not inherent." Earlier in the term the Court had decided that, though polygamy was an article of the Mormon faith, the free exercise of religion clause in the First Amendment did not protect this abhorrent social practice. Gradually polygamy withered, more the result of the wise invocations of the President's amnesty power than of criminal prosecutions.[23]

The 1889 term ended, but, with the substantial and still growing backlog of cases, one could hardly say the Court had completed its work. May was almost gone, and the Chief was exhausted. The one bright spot on the horizon came from the serious activity in Congress directed toward the creation of intermediate federal courts of appeal. In assessing the term, followers of the Court's work must have noted that the commerce clause argument had been the most successful in challenging state action. On the other hand, the Court continued to speak in broad terms of the state's taxing power where the commerce clause had no relevance or where the challenge was made in terms of the Fourteenth Amendment.[24]

Only eight of the seats were occupied when the Court reassembled in October 1890. Earlier in the month Samuel F. Miller died after over twenty-eight years of service, the last nine as senior associate. Highly regarded for the thoroughness and distinction he brought to his work, Miller came to the law late and to the Supreme Court without either the training or the cultivation of some of his colleagues, but he etched his influence into constitutional law. Miller's estate was so meager and his widow so ill-provided for that the New York Bar sent her $2,500, part of the surplus remaining from the centennial celebration.[25]

To fill the vacancy, President Benjamin Harrison recalled the consideration that had produced the nomination of Brewer a year earlier. Apparently Henry Billings Brown was Harrison's first choice, but Brewer's unselfish recommendation of his Yale classmate so impressed the President that Harrison chose Brewer rather than Brown. Now with the added urging of Harrison's old friend, Circuit Judge Howell E. Jackson, Brown received the appointment. Brown came from a prominent family, and his marriage in 1864 eased all financial worries. A district judge in eastern Michigan since 1875, Brown now found his hopes for promotion fully realized.[26] At fifty-four the new Justice was among the Court's shorter members. He had a smooth-shaven face without much color, a receding forehead, and greyish hair that he brushed over his ears. Bushy eyebrows emphasized his clear eyes. He had a wide mouth with thin lips, but his most prominent feature was a large, bulb-like nose. Despite the stern visage portrayed in photographs, he was amiable and cheerful. Since the new Justice was not sworn in until early January 1891, the Court was one man short in the early months of the 1890 term.

Without too much competition from a docket of largely routine cases, the highlight of the session was the long-awaited Circuit Court of Appeals Act of March 3, 1891. Before this date the Supreme Court was the only full-fledged federal appellate court; previous changes in the judicial system had coped with the territorial growth of the United States but had left undisturbed the basic judicial organization established in 1789. The great industrial growth following the Civil War pressed insistently upon the Supreme Court's docket, and friends of the Court regularly proposed bills that would relieve the total appellate burden from the Justices.[27]

Before his appointment to the Court, Melville Fuller had joined a growing chorus of bar support beseeching Congress to provide badly needed relief. Now personally confronted with the unwieldy case load, the Chief used his influence to procure reform. In the 1889 term 1,648 cases were on the Court's docket. Fuller's gentle manner of cultivating his adversaries paid off. The crucial body in Congress was the Senate Judiciary Committee, headed by George F. Edmunds, who had opposed the Chief's appointment. Edmunds could hardly refuse the olive branch that Fuller so graciously tendered. In a dinner given in honor of David J. Brewer in January 1890, the rest of the bench was joined by all the members of the Senate Judiciary Committee. Less than a month later Field needed no special urging to mention the need for reform in his centennial speech. Soon thereafter, the Chief received copies of all pending bills for judicial relief from the committee, along with a request for the Justices' comments. Justice Gray was assigned the task of preparing the official response, which, of course, strongly urged the creation of intermediate federal appellate courts.[28]

Less than a year later, Congress created nine Circuit Courts of Appeal. Without much reason the old circuit courts were retained, but a new tier had been added to the federal judicial system. To the disappointment of Fuller and the other members of the Court, the act did not provide for the transfer of cases already docketed on the Supreme Court calendar. But additions to that docket decreased from a high of 623 in the 1890 term to 290 in the session of 1892. Although still a long way from the practically total control of its docket that was to come in the 1920s, the Court was now freed from a host of unimportant cases, including the many that found their way to the federal courts simply because the opposing parties were citizens of different states. Under the act of 1891 the rulings of the Courts of Appeal were final in these diversity cases and in cases arising under patent, revenue, admiralty, and most criminal laws of the federal government. In cases with substantial policy implications, the Court had the discretion to review the work of the lower appellate courts. Also, where the Courts of Appeals needed guidance in view of a division of opinion among the judges, the Court could settle the matter of law.[29]

Buoyed by the prospect of some relief from its crowded docket, the Court undertook the work of the 1890 term. Justice Harlan dealt with two claims from New York defendants seeking writs of habeas corpus because neither the juries, nor the pools from which they were drawn, included members of the defendants' minority race. Harlan's opinion for the Court recognized that a constitutional claim might be validly presented, even in the absence of a discriminatory statute, but he said the defendant first must work through the hierarchy of New York courts. Concurring, Field categorically denied that the Reconstruction amendments gave any defendant the right to a nondiscriminatory jury-selection process. [30]

In a test of the Wilson Act passed in response to *Leisy* v. *Hardin* the previous term, the liquor interests argued that the statute unlawfully delegated national power to the states. Theoretically the problem the argument posed was a substantial one, for if a state does close its borders to a product of commerce, interstate traffic is burdened. With ingenuity, Fuller, for the Court, explained that the congressional act simply removed an impediment to the enforcement of state law and did not confer any new power upon the state. "No reason is perceived why," the Chief wrote, "if Congress chooses to provide that certain designated subjects of interstate commerce shall be governed by a rule which divests them of that character at an earlier period of time than would otherwise be the case, it is not without its competency to do so."[31] Certainly a Court that for so long had to struggle to find meaning in congressional silence was not about to censure Congress for breaking that silence. Harlan, Gray, and Brewer concurred without opinion. In *Leisy* they had urged unsuccessfully that the state already possessed the requisite power. Now Congress so provided.

In interpreting the interstate commerce clause, the Court's decision making provided precedent no matter which way the Justices chose to resolve a particular case. Theory was less important than the subject matter of the case. Where the product regulated was considered dangerous, unhealthy, or morally corrupting, the Court was usually sympathetic to the exercise of the state's police power. Perhaps the Court had erred in the *Leisy* case; at least Congress thought so. Should the original package doctrine have held firm, demand for national prohibition might have peaked much earlier than it did. Essentially, shared assumptions were responsible for relegating certain property to a less-favored status. When the Court heard a claim that a San Francisco liquor licensing ordinance was discriminatorily applied, it responded that such business "may be entirely prohibited or subjected to such restrictions as the governing authority of the city may prescribe."[32]

The Court also refused to interpose a commerce clause bar against state attempts to tax large interstate corporations, such as Pullman's Palace Car Company and Western Union. Pennsylvania sought to tax the Pullman Company on a proportion of its capital stock, determined by taking the ratio of the miles operated in the state to the national total. With the cars moving in and out of the state, Pennsylvania's formula was aimed at providing a rough estimate of the property that could be subjected to its tax. The company argued that this tax was levied on its interstate traffic and could not be sustained under the interstate commerce clause. Gray, for the majority, relied upon a string of precedents to support the state's taxing power, concluding that Pennsylvania's scheme was not inequitable. Bradley, in a dissent joined by Harlan and Field, said that the tax was impermissible because, in reality, it was a tax on the company's capital stock, property the state could not legitimately reach. What bothered the dissenters was the real possibility that an interstate operation like the Pullman Company, under the terms of the Court's opinion, could be crippled by a vast array of state tax exactions. On that same day in May when Pennsylvania won its victory over the Pullman Company, the Court pronounced Massachusetts the victor over Western Union in a similar case.[33]

That the Justices struggled with the problem presented in the two cases is obvious, and Bradley's contention that the states involved could not directly levy a tax on capital stock is sound. But the majority preferred to accept the states' rationale that their levies were not imposed on capital stock. Although the Court did not hesitate to void state taxes imposed on ticket agents or on interstate telegrams, the Justices refused to use interstate commerce doctrine to immunize large corporations from the states' power to tax. No federal corporate or income taxes existed, and a contrary decision in these cases would have conferred a substantial privilege on corporations already large enough to excite American fears about bigness. Examining the cases in a broad social setting, the majority was willing to gloss over the problem that plagued the dissenters to reach a roughly equitable result.

As the 1890 term was drawing to a close, a case that shed some light on the relationship of three members of the Court with an ex-President was decided. The ex-President was Grover Cleveland, who had appointed both Lamar and Fuller to the Court. Early in the session Cleveland had appeared before the High Bench as an advocate in a complicated case involving the liability of the city of New Orleans on some drainage warrants. Cleveland lost the case against the city, but that loss was dwarfed by the embarrassment suffered by the ex-President during oral argument. Late on an October afternoon Cleveland asked the Court's indulgence so he could finish his presentation; perhaps, as he addressed the Chief, he felt that was little enough to ask. He did not know that few things were more sacred than the Court's adjournment time. Quickly he learned, for Fuller responded by adjourning Court and telling Cleveland he could continue on the morrow.[34]

Probably no member of the Court enjoyed Cleveland's discomfiture more than Stephen J. Field. Field had long coveted the presidency, but odds had been stacked against the Democrats, and the Justice, despite his availability, never received the party's nod. If this plum was to be denied him, then perhaps the chief justiceship would satisfy his ambition. Cleveland's election in 1884 promised some hope, but the new President and the Justice did not get along. The President rebuffed Field on a number of patronage matters, and when Cleveland named Fuller Chief Justice, the animosity grew. When Benjamin Harrison defeated Cleveland's bid for a second term, Field shed no tears, and when Cleveland won the rematch in 1892, Field personally resolved not to retire and give his adversary the opportunity to nominate a successor.[35]

McAllister v. *United States* involved Cleveland's removal, without warning or announced cause, of a district judge in Alaska. A territorial judgeship was not covered by the life tenure provisions of the Constitution. Contending that the specified term of years did not limit the Chief Executive's inherent removal power, the majority upheld Cleveland's suspension of the judge. This finding of a new inherent source of executive power should have disturbed Fuller and Lamar, but both Cleveland appointees silently accepted the majority's determination. Both had agreed that Cleveland, the advocate, could not prolong the Justices' day, but both also agreed to a recognition of presidential power that usually excited their firm disapproval. Predictably Field dissented. Since he carried Gray and Brown with him, the votes of Fuller and Lamar were crucial. With special enthusiasm Field condemned the presidential action as arbitrary, insisting that the term of years was conditional only on good behavior. The President's removal power was not unlimited, said the Californian, and even less-favored federal judges, like McAllister, should receive the protection of the law.[36]

Vacation time, or more accurately recuperation time, was again upon the Court. The pace the Court's work exacted from aging men was, and still is, exhausting. Late in the term Bradley celebrated his seventy-eighth birthday, and early on that morning he confided to his diary that he was finding it increasingly difficult to keep up with the "awful hard work of the court."[37] Too few Justices find retirement palatable, and the Court's history is packed with aging men struggling to meet the demands placed upon them. Retirement was made attractive by providing full pay for any federal judge who had served ten years, but the absence of any external standard and the tenacious human desire to hold on to power was too strong for most Justices to resist. This was especially true for Bradley, who, although he complained about the work burden, found it life-sustaining.

Bradley did not live to enjoy his seventy-ninth birthday, dying in mid-term on January 22, 1892. For almost twenty-two years he had served on the Court. Despite President Grant's failings, he had put a number of good men on the Court, and Bradley was considered one of the best of them.[38] Bradley's rigid personality was not appealing, and his immersion in the details of the law often precluded his taking the larger perspective that some of his colleagues did. But Bradley was steadfast in his convictions. Although his brethren slowly backed into an acceptance of substantive due process, he held firm. If his vision of the future was sometimes limited, he at least made sure his colleagues did not forget the wisdom of the past. Increasingly in his later years Bradley indicated his opposition to the trends he saw emerging. The more comfortable world he knew was passing.

As the Court convened for the 1891 term, the recently passed judiciary act had little immediate effect. Corporations seemed to have an inexhaustible supply of funds for legal expenses, for the challenge to state regulatory and taxing acts continued unabated. The only such case that troubled the Justices involved a Maine excise tax on railroads; decided early in the term by a vote of five to four, it provided Bradley with his final opportunity to write a dissent. Here the state took a percentage of the railroad's transportation receipts as the taxing base. Rejecting the familiar commerce clause argument, the majority said the mode of determining the tax did not undermine the state's long-acknowledged power. Field, often criticized as a pawn of railroad interests, wrote a majority opinion that drew a distinction between a tax on receipts and the use of the receipts as a taxing base. This distinction Bradley would not accept, and his dissent won the votes of Harlan, Lamar, and Brown. This last Bradley dissent was characteristic; precise and factual, it took the majority to task. Such a tax, the dissenters argued, substantially burdened interstate commerce, and the majority's willingness to approve almost any mode of state taxation reflected society's "jealousy of corporate institutions."[39]

Such cases involving railroads continued to press upon the Court; the technological drama was well matched by a continuing legal drama. The subject matter of the suit might be relatively unimportant, but railroads chose to fight rather than concede because of the basic principles involved. City authorities in Yakima, Washington, the county seat, sought to compel the Northern Pacific Railroad to establish a depot and stop in their town. On technical grounds the majority decided against the city, but in a blistering dissent, joined by Field and Harlan, Brewer condemned the majority for its rationale and lack of perception. Brewer speculated that the railroad promoters decided to bypass Yakima in favor of some other less densely populated area because the city had refused to pay tribute. At any rate, the dissenters, seeing a conflict between public service and private interest, broadly asserted that the Court has the power to force the railroad to give priority to the public interest.[40]

In a number of cases during the 1891 term the Court refused to act on the federal issue presented because of its determination that the lower court's judgment was supported by independent state grounds. This is a doctrine the Court had developed in part as a concession to the federal system.

Whether state grounds were truly independent sometimes posed a difficult problem, and a consistent pattern is difficult to find, even by focusing upon a single Justice. For instance, Field unsuccessfully sought to invoke the doctrine in *Boyd* v. *Nebraska*. James Boyd had won the gubernatorial race in Nebraska, but upon taking office he was subjected to a suit for his ouster on grounds that he was not a citizen. In two opinions seven members of the Court acknowledged jurisdiction and upheld Boyd's claim of citizenship, contending that a decision concerning citizenship necessarily involves a federal question. The undescribed story behind the scenes is intriguing, but apparently the majority felt that Boyd, who had been active in the politics of the state for forty years, was the victim of political action that sought to wrest from him the office that he had rightfully won. Field denied that the Court had jurisdiction and argued the practical difficulty of enforcing a decision against the opposition of the state. In a federal system already subject to strain, Field urged restraint upon his brothers.[41]

The California Justice found himself on the other side of the independent state grounds argument in *O'Neil* v. *Vermont*. John O'Neil, a New York liquor vendor, took orders from Vermont citizens and shipped the goods via an express carrier to the state, where upon payment the carrier turned over the liquor. Vermont authorities closed in on the traffic and prosecuted O'Neil. He was found guilty of 307 offenses against the state prohibition law. His penalty was fixed at $6,638.32, or, if payment was not made by a certain date, imprisonment on the basis of three days for each dollar of fine, or a total of over 54 years. *Leisy* had not been decided by the Supreme Court when O'Neil appeared before the county court, and on appeal the Vermont Supreme Court refused to consider its applicability. Blatchford, for the Supreme Court in a five to three decision, dismissed the appeal on the ground that Vermont law was broad enough to support the conviction. He said that how the liquor got to Vermont was immaterial, thereby sidestepping the commerce clause argument. Next, the statutory requirement that a sale be made in the state, Blatchford said, was met by the money passing hands from customers to the express company, O'Neil's agent, in Vermont. Nowhere in the opinion is there an acknowledgment that the state had dealt harshly with the defendant; he was trafficking in a commodity considered dangerous to health and morality.[42] At any rate, the majority avoided any responsibility for determining whether the sentence levied on a guilty party was reasonable or just, though the Court did not so defer when a property right was threatened.

Field had no sympathy for the Vermont action, saying the majority had evaded its responsibility in the case. "It will, I think," he wrote, "strike many men with surprise to learn that filling an order for the purchase of goods and their transmission from one State by an express carrier, to be paid on delivery to the buyer in another State can be turned into a criminal offense of the person filling the order in the State where he was not present." The Californian's argument is telling, and one cannot escape the belief that the majority's conclusion was muddied by the character of the commodity. Field, however, was not finished. He saw the indictment charging a single offense, not hundreds. With dismay, Field grappled with the sentence, saying its severity was unmatched in nineteenth-century American law. Since the jail term exceeded by sixfold the state's maximum punishment for manslaughter, Field had no trouble characterizing it as "unusual and cruel."[43] Although recognizing that the Eighth Amendment binds only the federal government, he found in the Fourteenth Amendment the authority to force the states to respect certain basic rights, including, here, the right to be free from cruel and unusual punishment.

In a separate dissent, Harlan argued that under the *Leisy* ruling, which was controlling, the Vermont law offended the commerce clause. He also agreed with Field that the Court possessed the power to consider whether the sentence imposed violated the defendant's rights. Since the Kentuckian in 1884 had stated his opinion that the Fourteenth Amendment made the Bill of Rights binding upon state action, he had no difficulty in finding a violation of O'Neil's rights. Now hesitatingly Field seemed to be moving in the same direction, stirred in part by his outrage at the Court's disposition of O'Neil's appeal. Also Brewer authorized Harlan to note an "in the main" concurrence in the dissent.[44]

Much of the Court's important work in the present term and throughout its history consisted of responding to claims that certain federal legislation violated the Constitution. The authority to rule on the constitutionality of federal legislation was not specified either in the Constitution or in any congressional act, but the Court had assumed that power early in John Marshall's tenure. A few of the term's cases illustrate the nature of this power. *Counselman* v. *Hitchcock* arose from the refusal of a witness to answer questions put to him by a grand jury investigating violations of the Interstate Commerce Act. His Fifth Amendment privilege against self-incrimination was met by a governmental promise of immunity from prosecution. Still Counselman refused. In a unanimous decision Blatchford upheld the contention that the promised immunity did not cover the full range of protection offered by the Fifth Amendment. It failed because it did not preclude the possibility of using the witness' admissions as a base for unearthing sufficient independent evidence to support a conviction. In view of the constitutional guarantee, Blatchford wrote, ". . . a statutory enactment, to be valid, must afford absolute immunity against future prosecution for the offense to which the question relates." Congress responded with a legislative act attempting to meet the Court's requirements.[45]

While *Counselman* forced the Justices to explore the dimensions of the Fifth Amendment's protection, Brewer took the opportunity in another case of the session to expound upon a portion of the First Amendment. As part of a growing pattern of immigration restriction, Congress passed a statute in 1885 that prohibited assistance in or encouragement of the importation or migration of an alien under a contract to perform labor or services. Unwittingly, the Church of the Holy Trinity ran afoul of the act when it contracted for the services of an English pastor. An eager federal prosecutor won his case, as the trial judge dutifully imposed the $1,000 fine. In the act Congress had exempted certain occupational categories, but not ministers. At times statutes are unclear in their wording or in their intended application, and the Court is forced to decipher their meaning by considering congressional intent. Here, however, the words were clear and the application logically unassailable.

Unanimously the Court decided to rescue the church from the long-armed statute by reversing the conviction. The decision commended itself to common sense, but it was not easy to rationalize. Brewer's active view of the

Court's role made him a logical choice to develop a rationale. Acknowledging that the church was trapped within the literal words of the statute, he refocused attention on the act's purpose. What he found was a policy designed to restrict the inflow of cheap, unskilled labor, a policy the church's action did not violate. So an application of the act completely consistent with its wording was voided because it offended the spirit and underlying purpose of the act. Because this rationale was unsettling to the canons of statutory construction, the Kansan sought additional support for the Court's determination. Because we are a religious people, he continued, no action against religion can be imputed to any legislative body. With a slight nod to history, he tried to demonstrate this conclusion and wound up with a recitation of the free exercise of religion clause in the First Amendment. If, contrary to the Court's interpretation, Congress did intend to make the employment of ministers subject to the act, then its application would violate First Amendment rights. Not imputing such an intention to the legislative branch, he drew attention to the issue of religion to support further his conclusion that the statute was written too broadly. Although the weakness of the opinion invited dissent, all Brewer's colleagues agreed.[46] This case remains an oddity, but it does illustrate the wide discretion available to the Court, even in those areas where Congress has spoken with as much clarity as language permits.

Congress actually had little interest in barring alien pastors from American pulpits, and on those matters of greater importance to the legislative branch, the Court was quite deferential. When counsel James C. Carter challenged legislation banning matter concerning lotteries from the mails on the grounds that Congress was delegated no power to legislate on matters concerning the health, safety, morality, and general welfare of the people, the Court paid him little heed. Fuller simply said that the authority to establish the postal service carries with it the right to determine what it will distribute. On the basis of the obscenity precedent, the federal government could forbid the dissemination of materials tending to promote crime or immorality. To the claim that the citizen's freedom to communicate was abridged, the Chief simply denied that the regulation had that effect.[47] In the years ahead Congress would use its specifically delegated powers, especially those relating to the postal service and interstate commerce, to reach indirectly, but often quite effectively, subjects over which it had no direct control.

The last congressional act to weather the term was the tariff of 1890. Many objections were mounted, but a unanimous court affirmed the tariffs imposed. First, the Justices were invited by counsel to overturn the legislation on grounds that the bill the President signed varied from the terms of the bill passed by Congress. This invitation to enter into the procedural aspects of the legislative process had been accepted by a number of state supreme courts, but the Court refused to enter the arena. On a second issue, involving the empowering of the President with authority to adjust the tariff schedules,

Lamar and Fuller dissented from the broad approval given by the majority. Although little concerned about the Court's approval of an implied congressional power to reach lotteries, they expressed again their worry about a too powerful President. Congress had given the President the right to determine when the introduction of tariff-free goods should be stopped; the dissenters insisted that Congress had impermissibly delegated an exclusive legislative function.[48]

On May 26, 1892, the term ended, with the Court having reduced its appellate docket by almost a third. The Circuit Court of Appeals Act of 1891 was finally having some effect on the work of the Court.

During the summer recess Bradley's vacated seat received the attention of President Harrison, now faced with the task of making his third appointment to the High Bench. This time he had no candidate waiting in the wings, and a sensitive political situation demanded caution. Bradley had come from New Jersey, in the Third Judicial District, and apparently the President decided that the replacement should come from the largest state in that district, Pennsylvania. What gave Harrison pause was the fact that an entrenched Republican machine was controlled by the state's two Senators, James Donald Cameron and Matthew Quay, with whom the President was at odds. Bypassing the traditional practice of senatorial courtesy, which called for the President to clear his appointee with the state's Senators, would be both difficult and politically hazardous. What Harrison sought in an appointee was a lawyer of substantial standing, obviously not aligned with Cameron and Quay and not sufficiently involved in state politics to have incurred the personal enmity of the two Senators. This tended to push the search westward, and with the advice of a personal friend, Congressman John Dalzell of Pennsylvania, Harrison found George Shiras, Jr. Shiras's handsome income, estimated at about $75,000 a year, had come in part from his service to corporate clients. But he was generally well regarded and was considered to be a man of broad sensibilities.[49]

Certainly President Harrison's failure to consult Cameron and Quay meant that opposition would be forthcoming in the Senate. But the choice had been well made and a six-month delay in making the appointment gave the President time to maneuver skillfully. When in desperation the Pennsylvania Senators sought to gain Democratic support for their personal opposition, they were fairly well isolated. The best they could do was prevent the Senate Judiciary Committee from making any recommendation on the nomination. Politically astute enough to recognize defeat, Quay moved for Shiras's unanimous confirmation on July 26, 1892.[50]

At sixty, George Shiras, a practicing lawyer for thirty-seven years, was one of the older appointees to the Court. About six feet in height, he did not approach Gray's girth, but he was heavily built. He had bushy side whiskers that met together in a mustache and enough gray hair to be the envy of his younger colleagues. The side whiskers occasioned adverse newspaper comment and probably some internal criticism; at any rate they would go the way of Brewer's beard and mustache within a short time. Shiras's eyes were bright and alert, and careful observers noted a slight twinkle that sharply contrasted with the traditional solemn look. Actually this easygoing but frank man was quite a wit. He shared with Brewer not only unfashionable facial adornment but also a fine sense of humor that livened the conference room.[51]

Shiras was not sworn in until the Court was ready to convene for the 1892 term. When he took his seat, he could not help but recognize that his colleague, Justice Lamar, looked weak and drained. The Mississippian heard only a few cases before he was forced to return home, where he died on January 23, 1893. Despite his earlier reputation as a temporizer, Lamar in his five years of service demonstrated he was a man of vigorous and strongly held views. He tried to draw attention to the danger of expanding the President's power, and he believed fervently in the value of the prevailing federal system and its separation of powers.

Often at less than full strength during the early 1890s, the Court hoped for a quick replacement, but Harrison had been defeated in the November election. With Grover Cleveland resuming office in March, the lame-duck Republican President seemed to offer little hope. Harrison, a more skillful politician than is often recognized, was determined to fill the vacancy and prevent Cleveland from placing another former secessionist on the Court. The Senate was controlled by Democrats, so the appointee had to be a Democrat and by tradition had to come from the South. Justice Brown, Harrison's second appointee, suggested, in part as a return favor for earlier support of his candidacy, Howell E. Jackson of Tennessee. Jackson had been appointed a federal judge in the Sixth Judicial Circuit by Cleveland in 1887. Harrison had been friendly with Jackson during a concurrent term in the Senate and had been in contact with him during the last four years. These fortuitous circumstances made Jackson an ideal choice, for the Democrats in the Senate could hardly protest this elevation of a former Cleveland appointee.[52] Jackson was sworn into service on March 4, 1893, only forty days after Lamar's death.

Jackson was sixty-one when he took his seat on the Court, a seat recently plagued by limited service, but none as short as Jackson's would be. Vigorous and healthy at the time of his appointment, he soon entered a physical decline that took his life. During his two official years on the High Bench, Jackson was the smallest member in physical stature. He had a small face with a white tuft of beard and deeply set eyes. A deep wrinkle across his forehead coupled with the required stern pose etched a permanent frown in his face.

Again railroad matters pressed upon the Justices in the 1892 term, but despite able and at times ingenious arguments by counsel, the great majority of these cases were handled without division. Contractual tax exemptions were not transferable when the railroad so favored was absorbed into a larger unit, and immunity from taxation did not exempt railroads from special levies for local improvements. When Minnesota imposed treble damages on railroads in suits by citizens injured by the failure to fence tracts, advocates argued that this was a taking of property without due process of law. The Court responded in strong words, saying that states had the power to inflict substantial economic injury to "ensure prompt obedience to their requirements." When John Dillon tried to combat Colorado's antidiscrimination freight rate statute by arguing that some discriminations are just, the Court disparaged the argument.[53]

Before Lamar fell ill, his vote became crucial in a case determining the title to property bordering Lake Michigan, contested by the city of Chicago and the Illinois Central Railroad. The suit went all the way back to 1883 and turned on the legitimacy of a state act passed in 1873. Fuller had argued the case for the railroad in the lower court before he came to the High Bench, so he disqualified himself, as did Blatchford, who acknowledged that he held stock in the Illinois Central. The seven remaining members of the Court split four to three in favor of the city. Field wrote the majority opinion, which rejected, among other contentions, the argument that the railroad's reclamation of the land gave it a vested interest. Shiras, joined by Gray and Brown, disagreed. They pronounced the statute of 1873 "an arbitrary act of revocation, not passed in the exercise of any reserved power."[54]

Field and Brewer had helped compose the narrow majority in the Chicago lakefront case, but they divided in a contest between the United States and the Southern Pacific Railroad. When the majority decided that the land had reverted to the government under the terms of its grant, Field fumed and carried Gray along with him. The dissenters sympathized with the Southern Pacific, for the company had made improvements under the assumption that it owned the lands. Field said that the majority's decision encouraged the government to operate on ethical standards different from those that bound private individuals.[55]

In both cases only Horace Gray sided consistently with the railroad, while Brewer and Harlan consistently favored the government. Field, who divided his votes, was far from being an uncritical supporter of the railroads. At times he pondered their impact on society with a special understanding.

One area in which Field was more sensitive than most of his colleagues concerned the many injuries and deaths occasioned by the iron horse. In a society enamoured of technological change, rarely was the cost of that change evaluated. In the nineteenth century contract law assumed center stage with its recognition of the power of individuals to bind themselves to agreements that courts would enforce. Tort law, that is the law of personal injury, little developed at the start of the century, increasingly was shaped by the needs of the railroad.[56] To allow the railroad to fulfill its potential, state after state accepted, as part of the common law, certain defenses that the railroads could use in personal-injury suits. If an employee brought suit, the railroad defended successfully if it could convince the court that the employee had assumed the risk as part of his employment, or that the injury was caused by the actions of a fellow servant, or that the employee had in some manner contributed to his accident.

Some states had recognized the plight of the employee and passed statutes modifying or voiding these common law defenses. When Kansas and Minnesota acts were challenged in the Supreme Court in the 1880s, the Justices saw no objection to such legislative modification of the common law. Railroads, however, were interstate enterprises with access to the federal courts on diversity of citizenship grounds, and since 1842 the federal courts had developed their own common law doctrine. The Supreme Court, then, was free to develop its own policy in the area, and in the case of *Baltimore and Ohio Railroad Co.* v. *Baugh*, it was invited to adopt the policy of the more enlightened states. Baugh, employed as a fireman, was seriously injured when the engineer ran into an oncoming train. In the federal trial court the judge instructed the jury that under Ohio law the fellow servant defense was not a bar to recovery if the injury was caused by an employee who had supervisory responsibilities over the injured party. The jury returned a verdict in favor of Baugh. Brewer, for the majority, reversed the decision, saying the trial court had erred in instructing the jury in terms of Ohio law. Federal courts, Brewer asserted, have a responsibility to define common law independent of the states. The Justice concluded that the engineer and fireman were fellow servants, and, if that was not enough, that Baugh had accepted such a risk with his employment. Fuller dissented on the grounds that when one employee had supervisory authority over the injured worker, the fellow servant doctrine did not apply.[57]

Earlier Field had expressed his feeling that the fellow servant rule was a relic that should be discarded, and in such cases he often dissented without opinion, but in the *Baugh* case he released his pent-up feelings. Although agreeing with Fuller, Field in his extensive opinion covered much more ground. Sensing that a federal common law in conflict with the state's common law could lead to different decisions depending upon the chosen courtroom, the Justice totally rejected the idea of a federal common law. Acknowledging that he might have erred earlier, he now stoutly maintained that the Ohio rule of decision should control. Stirred by his dislike of the fellow servant doctrine, he hit upon a basic problem that would continue to plague and strain the judicial system for the next forty-five years. To make sure that both the majority and the general public did not interpret his condemnation of a federal common law as an avoidance of the fellow servant issue, he continued: if we must live with a federal common law, let it be "most in accordance with justice and humanity to the servants of a corporation."[58] At the least he would read federal common law liberally enough to sustain the verdict in Baugh's favor. Finally, in part moved by the plight of Baugh, he castigated the majority for its uncritical support of exempting corporations from this potentially large area of liability.

Despite his personal idiosyncracies and his strong emphasis upon individual effort, Stephen J. Field was acutely sensitive to the changes taking place in society and to the oppression that could come in their wake. Doctrinaire in his assertation that certain individual rights must be zealously guarded, never did he limit the boundaries of his concern and never was his keen sense of fairness myopic. Running through Field's opinions was a strong current of morality.[59] Often his associates did not approach questions in moral terms, but we can imagine Field asking, how else can important questions be decided?

The last case heard by the Court in the 1892 term involved a challenge to an act designed to prohibit the entry of Chinese migrants into the United States. Argued on May 10, the Court announced its conclusion in five days, though the written opinions were filed later. The legislation of May 5, 1892, was the most recent installment in the continuing congressional campaign against the Oriental. Section six required a Chinese resident in the United States to apply to the district collector of internal revenue for a certificate of residence within one year from the passage of the act. Refusal to comply or being found without such a certificate was grounds for arrest. The arrested individual was then taken before a federal judge, who was required to order deportation unless the procurement of a certificate had been impossible and the individual's residence at the time of the act was verified by at least "one credible white witness." Essentially, Congress had provided an administrative procedure in which the courts had a closely confined role, the burden being placed on the petitioner to show clear administrative error. What made this burden especially difficult was the fact that wide administrative discretion existed in granting such certificates.[60]

Chinese had been prohibited from becoming citizens; they were refused entry into the United States; and now long-term residents were placed in jeopardy. Obviously framed as a test of section six, the case of Fong Yue Ting was argued by the renowned constitutional lawyer Joseph H. Choate. Choate brought his full talents to bear, as he sought to convince the Justices that Congress had in section six subverted clear constitutional guarantees.[61]

With the Court at full strength, Justice Gray, indulging his tendency to engage in historical surveys of both international and domestic law, wrote the majority opinion. Working from earlier Court decisions that had acknowledged the government's right to prohibit Chinese entry, Gray simply pronounced the act a legitimate exercise of national sovereignty. Such power is not limited by the Constitution, he contended, because aliens are beyond the reach of its protection. Skirting the constitutional issues, in part by denying that deportation is a criminal penalty, Gray was sensitive to the political dimensions of the question and considered acquiescence to the legislative branch desirable. To the argument that the act contravened certain provisions in treaties with China, Gray responded that the will of Congress could not be thwarted. The rather arbitrary administrative procedure Gray considered an act of grace, for, from his perspective, the nation has the naked power to remove aliens.[62] The six-man majority was obviously deferring to the racial phobia of Congress, certainly not the last time the Court would avoid disturbing sensitive political determinations.

Brewer, Field, and Fuller protested vigorously. Although each wrote a dissenting opinion, they were collectively appalled by the Court's approval of "tyranny." Brewer led the attack, contending that section six of the 1892 act violated many of the provisions of the Bill of Rights. These rights, he said, protect all, including aliens. The expulsion of a race, he acceded, may be within the power of a despot, but certainly not within that of a government of limited powers checked by a written constitution. Brewer, the son of a missionary, asked why we continued to send missionaries to China to preach a Christian ethic that is denied by such legislation. To make sure the potential result of the majority's approval of the passions of the moment did not escape attention, Brewer concluded:

It is true this statute is directed only against the obnoxious Chinese; but if the power exists, who shall say it will not be exercised tomorrow against other classes and other people? If the guarantees of these amendments can be thus ignored, in order to get rid of this distasteful class, what security have others that a like disregard of its provisions may not be resorted to?[63]

Brewer's uncle, Stephen J. Field, was no less harsh in his condemnation of the majority. The Californian denied that his earlier opinion upholding the government's right to exclude aliens in any way implied the right to banish residents from this country in time of peace. Field vehemently condemned the despotic spectre that emerged from Gray's opinion, saying that under the Constitution "brutality, inhumanity, and cruelty cannot be made elements in any procedure for the enforcement of the laws of the United States."[64]

Chief Justice Fuller was slightly more restrained in his dissent. He centered on the majority's rationale that the matter presented is best solved by the legislative branch of government. Fuller was not insensitive to the claim of judicial restraint, but he argued that the question presented to the Court was not political but judicial, precisely the type of conflict that the courts should be best equipped to settle. The deportation that now awaited Fong Yue Ting and his two countrymen Fuller considered a punishment, as did the other two dissenters. In a stirring paragraph, he concluded:

No euphemism can disguise the character of the act in this regard. It directs the performance of a judicial function in a particular way, and inflicts punishment without a judicial trial. It is, in effect, a legislative sentence of banishment, and, as such, absolutely void. Moreover, it contains within it the germs of the assertation of an unlimited and arbitrary power, in general, incompatible with the immutable principles of justice, inconsistent with the nature of our government, and in conflict with the written Constitution by which that government was created and those principles secured.[65]

During Fuller's five terms other cases had stirred dissent, some of it heated, but no single case better captures the drama of the Court's role better than that of *Fong Yue Ting.* The majority was not in error when it recognized that the matter was highly charged and that strong congressional feelings were involved, but the dissenters argued that these facts should not paralyze the Court in performing its intended function. The activism of Brewer and Field was not confined by the perimeter of property protection, and when the issue was basic, Fuller subordinated his position as Chief and harmonizer and spoke out forcefully. Despite their age, the dissents in *Fong Yue Ting* have a modern ring, mainly because of the work of the Court in recent times. More than any other litigation in the 1890s, the cases dealing with the actions of the federal government against the Chinese gave some members of the Court the opportunity to appraise the Bill of Rights and seek, if not always successfully, to expound its meaning.

With President Harrison's success in easing Jackson on the Court in the waning days of his administration, the Court finished the term in May 1893 at full strength. But the recess brought another casualty, when, on July 7, 1893, Samuel Blatchford died at seventy-three after eleven years of service. Even though the Justice was assigned some major opinions during his later years, he remained out of the limelight.[66] Blatchford rarely dissented; to one who took the institutional perspective of his role as his own, the collective work of the Court was the important thing. Fuller tended to rely upon Blatchford's compromising tendency in the early 1890s to write opinions that could hold less than firm majorities together. Since Justices like Blatchford tend to submerge their personalities in the group product of the Court, they do not attract study and their importance in the ongoing work of the Court is not fully appreciated.

President Grover Cleveland, now in the second of his interrupted terms, sought to fill the vacancy with another New Yorker. In his home state he confronted a problem similar to the one Harrison faced in the process that led to the appointment of George Shiras. David B. Hill was the Senator from New York that Cleveland sought to bypass; relations between the two men were already strained and a stubborn President determined that he would not bend to Hill's wishes. Instead of trying to outmanuever Hill, as Harrison had done with Cameron and Quay, Cleveland sprung the nomination of the young and talented William B. Hornblower upon the Senate. Apparently Cleveland felt that a frontal assault would bring the desired results, for no advance notice was given to the Senate Judiciary Committee. Hill was vehemently opposed to Hornblower and was able to invoke the rule of senatorial courtesy to defeat the appointment by a vote of thirty to twenty-four. An angered Cleveland responded with the name of Wheeler H. Peckham, who, to Hill, carried the same disability as Hornblower. That disability was participation, even more direct in Peckham's case, in a New York bar investigation that involved Hill and destroyed the political career of a friend. Forcing the matter to a showdown, Cleveland lost again, forty-one to thirty-two. An exuberant Hill let it be known that the vacancy would go unfilled until Cleveland observed the proper procedure and consulted with the New York Senator.[67]

Although twice defeated, Cleveland refused to capitulate. In a surprise, flanking move the President turned from the battleground of New York and appointed the junior Senator from Louisiana, Edward D. White. The appointment seemed strange to many observers, for White was valiantly striving against the administration in its efforts to lower the tariff schedules. Cleveland, however, respected the Louisianian's integrity and welcomed his support. What better way could be found to silence Hill's boasts? Just as senatorial courtesy had blocked the President's first two appointments, it now demanded rapid approval of the appointment of one of the Senate's own members to the Court. Despite considerable criticism of his conduct, White remained in the Senate after his confirmation to continue his fight against tariff reform; only when, almost a month later, he had met the responsibilities he felt he owed his constituents did he retire.[68] He was sworn into service on the Court on March 12, 1894.

In contrast to the two preceding appointments, White, at age forty-nine, was the youngest man to be appointed since Harlan. White was one of the secessionists Harrison had hoped to keep off the High Bench and a Roman Catholic as well. White had served in the forces of the Confederacy, but he was identified with the new image of the Democratic party embodied in the leadership of Cleveland. In his short two and one-half years in the Senate he had made himself heard. He stood about five feet, ten inches tall, weighed well over two hundred and fifty pounds, and had plump cheeks and a double chin. White had a rich, full voice, and, what was a rarity on the Court, a full head of thick and curly brown hair. He had a well shaped large nose, clear eyes, and a prominent cleft in his chin. His immaculate dress might well have caused Gray to wonder if his position as the Court's sartorial leader was in jeopardy.

NOTES

1. Hall v. De Cuir, 95 U.S. 485 (1878); and Louisville, New Orleans & Texas Ry. v. Mississippi, 133 U.S. 587 (1890).

2. Plessy v. Ferguson, 163 U.S. 537 (1896); and Louisville, New Orleans & Texas Ry. v. Mississippi, 133 U.S. 587 (1890).

3. Chicago, Milwaukee & St. Paul Ry. v. Minnesota, 134 U.S. 418 (1890). For detailed studies of how the Supreme Court came to find new meanings in the due process clause, see Benjamin R. Twiss, *Lawyers and the Constitution: How Laissez Faire Came to the Supreme Court* (Princeton: Princeton University Press, 1942), and Walton H. Hamilton, "The Path of Due Process of Law," *Ethics* 48 (April 1938): 269-96.

4. U.S. Const. Amend. V; Dred Scott v. Sandford, 60 U.S. (19 How.) 393 (1857); and Hepburn v. Griswold, 75 U.S. (8 Wall.) 603 (1870), *reversed by* Knox v. Lee (Legal Tender Cases), 79 U.S. (12 Wall.) 457 (1871).

5. Slaughter-House Cases, 83 U.S. (16 Wall.) 36 (1873); and Campbell's argument is quoted in Twiss, *Lawyers and the Constitution*, p. 49.

6. Munn v. Illinois, 94 U.S. 113 (1877).

7. Davidson v. New Orleans, 96 U.S. 97, 104 (1878); and Stone v. Farmers' Loan & Trust Co., 116 U.S. 307, 331 (1886).

8. Chicago, Milwaukee & St. Paul Ry. v. Minnesota, 134 U.S. 418, 458 (1890).

9. Id. at 461.

10. For an attempt to assess the influence of certain legal writers upon the judiciary, see Clyde D. Jacobs, *Law Writers and the Courts: The Influence of Thomas M. Cooley, Christopher G. Tiedeman, and John F. Dillon upon American Constitutional Law* (Berkeley: University of California Press, 1954).

11. Budd v. New York, 143 U.S. 517 (1892).

12. Id. at 551; and the railroad case is Chicago & Grand Trunk Ry. v. Wellman, 143 U.S. 339 (1892).

13. Brass v. North Dakota, 153 U.S. 391, 410 (1894).

14. Reagan v. Farmers' Loan & Trust Co., 154 U.S. 362 (1892); and Smyth v. Ames, 169 U.S. 466 (1898).

15. *In re* Kemmler, 136 U.S. 436 (1890).

16. The story summarized here is drawn from Carl B. Swisher, *Stephen J. Field: Craftsman of the Law* (Washington: Brookings Institution, 1930), pp. 321-61.

17. Cunningham v. Neagle, 135 U.S. 1 (1890).

18. United States v. Chase, 135 U.S. 255 (1890).

19. Mugler v. Kansas, 123 U.S. 623 (1887); and Leisy v. Hardin, 135 U.S. 100 (1890). The same result was reached in *Lyng* v. *Michigan* (135 U.S. 161 [1890]).

20. Wilson Act, ch. 728, 26 Stat. 313 (1890).

21. Minnesota v. Barber, 136 U.S. 313 (1890); Brimmer v. Rebman, 138 U.S. 78 (1891); and Voight v. Wright, 141 U.S. 62 (1891).

22. The Late Corporation of the Church of Jesus Christ of the Latter-Day Saints v. United States, 136 U.S. 1 (1890).

23. Id. at 68; and Davis v. Beason, 133 U.S. 333 (1890). The amnesty proclamations of Presidents Benjamin Harrison and Grover Cleveland are in James D. Richardson, ed., *Compilation of the Messages and Papers of the Presidents, 1789-1897*, 53rd Cong., 2d sess., 1894, *House Miscellaneous Document No. 210*, 10 vols. (Washington: Government Printing Office, 1896-99), 9:368-69, 510-11.

24. McCall v. California, 136 U.S. 104 (1890); Norfolk & Western R.R. v. Pennsylvania, 136 U.S. 114 (1890); Western Union Telegraph Co. v. Alabama State Board of Assessments, 132 U.S. 472 (1889); and for instance, see Home Insurance Co. v. New York, 134 U.S. 594 (1890).

25. For a favorable appraisal, see Charles O. Fairman, *Mr. Justice Miller and the Supreme Court* (Cambridge: Harvard University Press, 1939); and Charles H. Butler, *A Century at the Bar of the Supreme Court of the United States* (New York: G.P. Putnam's Sons, 1942), pp. 146-47.

26. Joel Goldfarb, "Henry Billings Brown," in *The Justices of the United State Supreme Court 1789-1969: Their Lives and Major Opinions*, ed. Leon Friedman and Fred L. Israel, 4 vols. (New York: R.R. Bowker Co. and Chelsea House Publishers, 1969), 2:1554-55.

27. The legislative history through the 1891 act is summarized in Felix Frankfurter and James M. Landis, *The Business of the Supreme Court: A Study in the Federal Judicial System* (New York: Macmillan Co., 1927), pp. 56-102.

28. Willard L. King, *Melville Weston Fuller: Chief Justice of the United States 1888-1910*, Phoenix ed. (Chicago: University of Chicago Press, 1967), pp. 148-50.

29. Circuit Court Appeals Act, ch. 517, 26 Stat. 826 (1891).

30. *In re* Wood, 140 U.S. 278 (1891); and *In re* Jugiro, 140 U.S. 291 (1891).

31. *In re* Rahrer, 140 U.S. 545, 562 (1891).

32. Crowley v. Christensen, 137 U.S. 86, 94 (1890).

33. Pullman's Palace Car Co. v. Pennsylvania, 141 U.S. 18 (1891); and Attorney General of Massachusetts v. Western Union Telegraph Co., 141 U.S. 40 (1891).

34. Peake v. New Orleans, 139 U.S. 342 (1891); and King, *Fuller*, pp. 161-62.

35. Swisher, *Field*, pp. 310-19, 414.

36. McAllister v. United States, 141 U.S. 174 (1891).

37. Quoted in Leon Friedman, "Joseph P. Bradley," in *Justices of the Supreme Court*, 2:1199.

38. See Charles O. Fairman, "What Makes a Great Justice? Mr. Justice Bradley and the Supreme Court," *Boston University Law Review* 30 (January 1950):49-102, and "Mr. Justice Bradley," in *Mr. Justice*, ed. Allison Dunham and Philip B. Kurland, rev. & enl. ed. (Chicago: University of Chicago Press, Phoenix Books, 1964), pp. 65-89.

39. Maine v. Grand Trunk Ry., 142 U.S. 217, 235 (1891).

40. Northern Pacific R.R. v. Washington, 142 U.S. 492 (1892).

41. Boyd v. Nebraska, 143 U.S. 135 (1892).

42. O'Neil v. Vermont, 144 U.S. 323 (1892).

43. Id. at 337, 339. An illuminating view of the aging Field battling over the headnotes to this case is found in Alan F. Westin, "Stephen J. Field and the Headnote to O'Neil v. Vermont: A Snapshot of the Fuller Court at Work," *Yale Law Journal* 67 (January 1958):363-83.

44. O'Neil v. Vermont, 144 U.S. 323, 371 (1892).

45. Counselman v. Hitchcock, 142 U.S. 547, 586 (1892); and Act of February 11, 1893, ch. 83, 27 Stat. 443.

46. Church of the Holy Trinity v. United States, 143 U.S. 457 (1892).

47. *In re* Rapier, 143 U.S. 110 (1892).

48. Field v. Clark, 143 U.S. 649 (1892).

49. George Shiras, III, *Justice George Shiras, Jr. of Pittsburgh*, ed. and comp. Winfield Shiras (Pittsburgh: University of Pittsburgh Press, 1953), pp. 87-92, 77.

50. Ibid., pp. 92-97.

51. Ibid., p. 125; and *Washington Evening Star*, February 17, 1894.

52. Irving Schiffman, "Howell E. Jackson," in *Justices of the Supreme Court*, 2:1610-11.

53. Wilmington & Weldon R.R. v. Alsbrook, 146 U.S. 279 (1892); Illinois Central R.R. v. Decatur, 147 U.S. 190 (1893); Minneapolis & St. Louis Ry. v. Emmons, 149 U.S. 364, 367 (1893); and Union Pacific Ry. v. Goodridge, 149 U.S. 680 (1893).

54. Illinois Central R.R. v. Illinois, 146 U.S. 387, 475 (1892).

55. United States v. Southern Pacific R.R., 146 U.S. 570 (1892).

56. J. Willard Hurst, *Law and the Conditions of Freedom in the Nineteenth-Century United States* (Madison: University of Wisconsin Press, 1956), pp. 2-32; and Lawrence M. Friedman and Jack Ladinsky, "Social Change and the Law of Industrial Accidents," *Columbia Law Review* 67 (January 1967):51-52.

57. Missouri Pacific Ry. v. Mackey, 127 U.S. 205 (1888); and Minneapolis & St. Louis Ry. v. Herrick, 127 U.S. 210 (1888); and Baltimore & Ohio R.R. v. Baugh, 149 U.S. 368 (1893).

58. Baltimore & Ohio R.R. v. Baugh, 149 U.S. 368, 411. Only in 1938 with the decision in *Erie R.R. v. Tompkins* (304 U.S. 64) did the Court eradicate the injustice caused by conflicting federal and state common law rules, deciding that the federal courts were bound by the state's common law.

59. See Robert G. McCloskey, *American Conservatism in the Age of Enterprise 1865-1910* (New York: Harper & Row, Torchbooks, 1964), pp. 104-5, 125-26. For an interesting suggestion about the influence of antislavery thought on Field's views, see William E. Nelson, "The Impact of the Antislavery Movement Upon Styles of Judicial Reasoning in Nineteenth Century America," *Harvard Law Review* 87 (January 1974):551-54.

60. Act of May 5, 1892, ch. 60, 27 Stat. 25.

61. Brief for Appellant, Fong Yue Ting v. United States, 149 U.S. 698 (1893).

62. Fong Yue Ting v. United States, 149 U.S. 698 (1893).

63. Id. at 743.

64. Id. at 756.

65. Id. at 763.

66. For an assessment of Blatchford, see Arnold M. Paul, "Samuel Blatchford," in *Justices of the Supreme Court*, 2:1401-14.

67. Allan Nevins, *Grover Cleveland: A Study in Courage* (New York: Dodd, Mead & Co., 1933), pp. 569-71.

68. Ibid., pp. 571-72; and James F. Watt, Jr., "Edward Douglas White," in *Justices of the Supreme Court*, 3:1640-41.

chapter 3

INTO THE POLITICAL
MAELSTROM, 1893-96

When the eight members of the Supreme Court convened in October for the 1893 term, they could have anticipated the task of reviewing some murder convictions, but they could hardly have foreseen the role they would play in a drama of the wild west. Generally, the crimes of murder and rape were punishable only under state law, but in the territories the federal circuit courts had jurisdiction. Until 1889 the verdict of these trial courts was final, but in that year the Supreme Court was given obligatory jurisdiction to hear appeals in capital cases coming from federal courts.[1] During the first three terms the Court considered such appeals, ten cases were reviewed, but in the 1893 session it faced sixteen such cases, thirteen coming from the Western District of Arkansas alone.

On the federal bench at Fort Smith sat Judge Isaac C. Parker. Quickly after his arrival in 1875 Parker established the integrity of his court through his hard work and determination that justice be done. With criminal jurisdiction over that vast area of land known as Indian Territory, the Fort Smith judge dispensed an Old Testament law that wrathfully descended upon the guilty. What brought notoriety to his court was the volume of serious criminal cases and Parker's predeliction for group hangings. Six men fell through the gallows trap on September 3, 1875, and five more followed in April. Parker's reputation as "the hanging judge" was assured; the terror of the outlaw was now met by the terror of the law. Whether in acting as an assistant prosecutor, instructing the jury, or in passing sentence, Parker was the voice of an outraged society, a voice that indiscriminately blended the will of God with the will of the people.[2]

From his first term of court through 1890, Parker sentenced 113 persons to death, although only 63, in fact, died on the Fort Smith gallows. A number of presidents had been moved not only by pleas for mercy but by the fact that no other avenue of review existed. Executive clemency was granted to 40 percent of the defendants that Parker had sentenced to die in his first fifteen years on the bench. The Fort Smith judge resented the highly paid lawyers, who, in their often successful appeals for clemency, were thwarting the exactions demanded by law. The Criminal Appeals Act of 1889 was very definitely aimed at Parker and his court, and the judge lamented that the certainty of punishment would be further eroded.[3]

Before the 1893 term the Supreme Court had heard four capital cases from Fort Smith, and in only one case did the Justices uphold the conviction. The Court said it would not inspect a voluminous record without specific objections to certain rulings having been made at the time of the trial, a wise admonition that the Justices would not always follow in later cases coming from Fort Smith. Two of the reversals were based upon the Court's decision that Parker had admitted evidence that had prejudiced the accused. In the third case the Court avoided deciding whether "the language of the learned judge went beyond the verge of propriety," and based the reversal upon the assumption that the defendant had not been brought face to face with the potential jurors in the case.[4]

This early success in the Supreme Court heartened Fort Smith attorneys who pressed thirteen appeals during the 1893 term. When the dust had settled, Parker had been overturned nine times. Two reversals were based upon Parker's failure to honor objections to portions of the prosecution's closing argument, another because the trial judge had improperly admitted evidence, and yet another because he entrusted to the jury an issue that he should have decided himself. The other five reversals were grounded in the High Bench's objections to Parker's instructions to the jury. That the Fort Smith judge believed he had to help the jurors make up their minds and discharge responsibly the burden placed upon them is quite clear. Repeatedly the Court censured the judge for abusing his discretion and attempting to lead the jury. Three of the convictions were reversed because the majority determined that Parker had misled the jury with his instructions on self-defense.[5]

Parker's worst fears about the effect of appeals to the Supreme Court had been confirmed, and the Justices, as they searched the trial court records, could not resist directing some barbed comments to the "learned judge." The cases coming from Fort Smith totaled about 4 percent of the Court's work load in the 1893 term, certainly a record in terms of appeals from the rulings of a lone federal judge. If the Justices had hoped that their admonitions to Parker would make him a more circumspect and impartial judge, they were disappointed, as his cases continued to dot the agenda for the next four terms.

In the subsequent session, the Justices rendered four decisions, two of which concerned second installments of cases the Court had heard previously. The defendants had been retried, and in both instances Parker again had levied the death sentence. In one case the Court said the trial judge erred in not instructing the jury on self-defense, and in the other it objected to Parker's conclusions that manslaughter would become murder if the killing revealed "brutality, barbarity, and a wicked and malignant purpose." In the remaining two cases, the Court affirmed one conviction and reversed the other on the now familiar grounds of Parker's instructions on self-defense.[6]

The relative quiet of the 1894 term was the lull before the storm that broke in the following session. Sixteen capital punishment cases from the Fort Smith bench reached Washington, including another retrial. Five cases were handled summarily by the Court. In two of these cases the Justice Department acknowledged that Parker had erred; so the Justices reversed the convictions. Without opinion, the Justices upheld the conviction of six men in two cases. The fifth case was dismissed because the defendant had been hanged for another offense. In the eleven opinions of the term, the Court affirmed four convictions and reversed seven. One conviction was overturned because the Justices determined that Parker's court did not have jurisdiction, one because of the judge's rulings on the admissibility of evidence, and another because of Parker's view that the burden of proof shifted with an insanity plea. In the four other cases, Parker was censured for leading the jury with inferences of the defendant's guilt, once for his "injurious epithets" and once for his "animated argument."[7]

Seven more Parker-imposed death sentences came to the Court in the 1896 term; four were the result of retrials in which the same sentence had been levied. In only one of the seven cases was the judge's work affirmed. The Justices ruled that the courts of the Cherokee Nation were the proper seat of jurisdiction in one case and in another that the trial judge had erred on an evidentiary ruling. In three other reversals the Court found error in Parker's instructions to the jury: the theme remained the same, for the Fort Smith judge, the High Bench concluded, had led the jury or prejudiced the accused in his instructions. On the basis of the Court's prior work in the Parker cases, the Justice Department confessed error in the sixth case.[8]

The Supreme Court's last response to a death sentence levied by Parker came in the 1897 term, when once again the Justice Department refused to defend the trial court decision.[9]

Just in terms of statistics, Judge Isaac C. Parker and the Justices of the Supreme Court had a most significant relationship. During slightly over seven terms of Court, beginning with the 1890 session, the Justices reviewed forty-four death sentences imposed by Parker, counting each installment of a case separately. In written opinions the Court reversed twenty-seven convictions and affirmed only ten. Summarily the Court reversed four, affirmed two, and dismissed one, making a total of thirty-one reversals in forty-four cases. In over two out of every three cases, the criminal lawyers of Fort Smith, often with the aid of appellate counsel in Washington, were successful in staving off the hangman's noose. A further tribute to the bar can be seen in the fact that only fifteen men swung from the rope in the six and a half years since February 1890, although sixteen had met a similar fate in the two preceding years.[10] In the same six-and-a-half-year period the Court affirmed ten capital crime convictions and reversed nine in cases coming from all other federal jurisdictions. That the Justices more closely inspected the Parker decisions is clear from the record; apparently, they felt more comfortable erring, if they had to, in favor of the defendant.

Justice Brewer was Parker's most insistent defender during this series of cases. Eight times he dissented from the majority decisions to reverse, and five times Justice Brown agreed. The Kansan criticized his colleagues for straying from proper appellate review procedures and for unduly interfering with the discretion of the trial judge. The result, Brewer said, was to frustrate the ends of justice.[11]

Although the Supreme Court had the last word on his cases, Parker could keep his silence just so long. He was increasingly disturbed by seeing his hard work overturned, by what he perceived to be a related increase in the incidence of serious crime, and, finally, by congressional action that chopped away at the jurisdiction of his court. In 1892 a federal court had been established with full criminal jurisdiction over a portion of the Indian Territory, but the final blow came when Congress provided that the Fort Smith court be stripped of its remaining criminal jurisdiction over the Territory on September 1, 1896. The once mighty court at Fort Smith, whose jurisdiction at one time extended over 74,000 square miles, was on its way to becoming an ordinary federal district court with jurisdiction limited to the western counties of Arkansas.[12]

With his court's authority being phased out and with a growing feeling that the federal government, which he had served so devotedly, had turned upon him, Parker took to the public press. His initial foray came after he had received news that Cherokee Bill, a convicted murderer awaiting the result of his appeal to the High Court, had killed a respected deputy in an escape attempt. To a reporter who caught up with Parker on a trip to St. Louis in July 1895, he spilled out his feelings. Accusing the Supreme Court of ignoring its responsibility to society by freeing guilty men on mere technicalities, he concluded that the only explanation possible was that the Justices were personally opposed to capital punishment.[13]

Having transgressed judicial etiquette by frontally attacking the Court, Parker defended his words, saying that he meant no disrespect, just honest criticism. More such honest criticism followed. Becoming more pointed in his indictment of the High Bench, he said the Justices were "knifing the trial judge in the back and allowing the criminal to go free." He questioned the Court's competence to deal with criminal appeals, saying that the Justices with their exclusive training in the civil law looked "to the *shadow* in the shape of technicalities instead of the *substance* in the form of crime." A tribunal schooled in the criminal law, he continued, would not be obsessed with minor procedural points and would better serve its obligations to society.[14]

Parker had carefully avoided any personal attack on the Justices, but when his aim shifted to Assistant Attorney General Edward B. Whitney and his superior, Judson Harmon, all restraint was lost. When the Justice Department early in 1896 confessed error in three Parker cases, the Fort Smith judge was incensed. He responded publicly in a letter published in a St. Louis newspaper. The government's legal officers, he said, "are supposed to speak for this court when cases go up on appeal, but they have blundered badly and let the opposition run off with the show." Parker continued: "I think my duty to the public, my duty to the law, my duty to peace and order, my duty to the innocent and unoffending people, and my duty to the murdered dead, all demand that I should, in the name of right and justice, protest against this extraordinary and unusual method of getting rid of important criminal cases."[15]

Edward Whitney, who had carried the brunt of the government's work in the Parker cases, was provoked into verbal combat. Responding in an open letter, he called the judge's interpretation of the law of self-defense "obsolete" and "ridiculous." Whitney advised "the learned judge" to confine himself to statement of law and not to undertake the task assigned to the jury. Now enraged, Parker called Whitney a "legal imbecile," whose words had been "croaked by every foul bird of evil, hissed from every wicked serpent of crime...for all these twenty years." Parker's aligning Whitney with the criminal elements caused the Assistant Attorney General to come up with some invective of his own. It was the "ignorant and careless" judge, Whitney said, who through his gross errors aided criminals more effectively than could the best trained lawyers. Parker had been stirred to frenzy by what he viewed as the capitulation of the Justice Department, and he insisted that liberty and "life are precarious unless those in authority have sense and spirit enough to defend them under the law." An unbowed Whitney responded that the Justice Department had little difficulty in convincing the Supreme Court to uphold murder convictions in other jurisdictions. If blame must be laid, Whitney suggested, it would be placed upon an overeager judge whose conduct in the courtroom resulted in upsetting the convictions of "probably guilty" men.[16]

Parker never repented, but he was thoroughly whipped by his adversaries; his spirit was broken and he fell ill in the summer of 1896. As most of the remaining jurisdiction of his beloved court was withdrawn, so, too, was his hold on life beginning to weaken. Within three months he was dead.

The Supreme Court would continue to review capital cases until 1911, but the cases were relatively few and devoid of the special circumstances of the Parker work that had forced the Justices into an insistent confrontation with the criminal law and its ultimate sanction.[17] The Court had refused all invitations to find federal rights violated in state murder prosecutions and even determined that the absence of an appeal in state capital crime convictions did not violate any federal right, but the Criminal Appeals Act of 1889 brought the Court into the area of the criminal law. In this unfamiliar arena, the Justices responded conscientiously, seeing its role in terms of rebalancing the scales of justice that had been tipped unfairly by an overzealous trial judge. Certainly the majority of Justices felt that Parker was not the impartial judge posited by the legal system. The trial judge had made himself a combatant in the war against crime; the Supreme Court's view of his role, however, was superior in both institutional and qualitative terms.[18]

Although the drama of Judge Parker's court and of the reverberations felt in Washington during the 1893 term occupied center stage, the work of any court, including the nation's highest, encompasses a host of minor human dramas. For instance, the Justices held an insurance company liable when an insured man committed suicide, despite a clause in the policy excluding payment in cases of suicide. Accepting the trial judge's interpretation that the exception could only be honored if the insured had been sane when he took his own life, the Court further ruled that the beneficiary was entitled to the presumption that a sane man would not commit suicide. (Insurance companies responded to the decision by redrafting contracts to exempt suicide "whether sane or insane.") The Court, however, had less sympathy for Belva A. Lockwood, that colorful, pioneering woman lawyer who had been the first of her sex to be admitted to practice before the Supreme Court, when it ruled that no federal right had been violated by Virginia's refusal to admit her to the state bar, even if the reason had been her sex.[19]

Due process of law was invoked to strike down the railroad rates established by a Texas commission, but the Court, despite its changing membership, continued to give broad support to the local police power. Claims of exemption from taxation often made by railroads were now and then successful, but states had generally preempted the claim by writing into charters the proviso that the legislature could alter the initial arrangements. Any doubt the Justices usually construed in favor of the legislature, and if the railroad corporation underwent reorganization or consolidation, any preexisting tax exemption was lost. Connecticut could order a railroad to remove a grade crossing at its own expense, and Ohio was virtually unchecked in subjecting to taxation a foreign corporation absorbed by a domestic company. When the state of New York seized some fishing nets used in violation of its fish and game law, the Court agreed that plaintiffs could not recover the cost of the nets. New York, the majority said, could declare such nets a nuisance and summarily destroy them. Again concerned about the broader policy implications of such unchecked power, Chief Justice Fuller dissented, along with Field and Brewer. To the argument that the nets were not worth much, the Chief responded that this fact did not justify any weakening of the clear protections of the Constitution.[20]

Brewer, who closely contended with Harlan as the leading dissenter in the mid-1890s, disagreed with the majority in two other cases of the 1893 term. Both cases involved the United States government; the majority decided against the government in the first case but upheld it in the second, and only

Justices Gray and Shiras would have decided against the government in both cases. In the first instance the government contended that it could control the use of certain land it had granted to the Illinois Central Railroad. The majority said that the grant passed control to the grantee, but Brewer, with Brown, saw no reason why the United States should not be able to insist on restricting use to the purposes specified. The second case was far more important to the government, for at stake was the ownership of valuable lands with important reserves of minerals. Field, for the majority, sided with the government in its contest with the Northern Pacific Railroad, upholding the argument that such lands were excluded from the grant. In his annual report Attorney General Richard Olney specifically mentioned the decision as a tribute to the Justice Department and the wisdom of the Court.[21] No such crowing would have been possible if Brewer, Gray, and Shiras had been able to win two more votes for their view that the Court had ignored precedent and had imposed an unreasonable burden on the railroad. The dissenters may have had weightier precedent on their side, but the majority relied upon the basic proposition that doubt in a case was to be resolved in favor of the public interest.

The final case argued in the term involved the Interstate Commerce Commission (ICC) in an attempt to break through a judicial wall of resistance to its effective operation. As amended in 1889 and 1891, the basic act required the federal circuit courts to use their authority in aid of inquiries conducted by the ICC. Although the future would be strewn with similar federal administrative agencies, the ICC was the first such agency, and, as such, continually had to meet attacks on its jurisdiction and power. Here the ICC had requested W. C. Brimson to testify and bring certain documents with him to the hearing. His refusal led the ICC to summon the circuit court's aid, but the court refused to do the commission's bidding. Justice Harlan, for the majority, reversed and upheld congressional authority to use the federal judiciary in the manner it chose. In a long opinion Harlan denied that this newly conferred jurisdiction conflicted in any way with constitutional provisions. Field did not participate in the decision, although earlier he announced that Congress could not force the federal courts to become assisting agencies to such a commission. Brewer carried the burden in dissent, gaining the votes of both the Chief and Jackson. What bothered the dissenters was that the courts were being asked to punish individuals like Brimson for contempt of court when their only contempt was that of an administrative agency.[22]

When the session ended in May 1894 the Justices had little hint of what lay in store for them. Whether the bench would be at full strength when it convened in the fall was in doubt, for Justice Howell Jackson, who had begun his tenure with a vigor that belied his age, missed a month of work because of illness.

As the Justices scattered, they must have been aware of a deepening of the economic depression that had descended the previous year. For instance, on May 1, 1894, the month-and-a-half march of Coxey's Army, which had begun its trek in Massillion, Ohio, culminated on the steps of the Capitol. Police easily subdued the demonstrators, but these unemployed men, augmented by infusion from similar groups, brought to national attention some of the trouble of the times. Jacob S. Coxey's program with its proposal of a massive highway-building program to improve transportation and provide employment sponsored by the federal government, was simply an offshoot of the new fervor found in the midsection of the country. On the heels of this Washington demonstration came the strike of the Pullman Palace Car workers, which brought a notoriety to the hitherto comfortable company town of Pullman, Illinois. In late June 1894 the newly organized American Railway Union, under the leadership of Eugene V. Debs, lent its support to the strike effort by boycotting trains hauling Pullman cars. The intervention of federal troops, summoned over the protests of the Illinois governor, John P. Altgeld, quickly broke the strike. Using the federal court the United States moved against Debs and his cohorts for their refusal to obey an injunction against the boycott.[23]

Some members of the Supreme Court may not have spent much time contemplating the headlines, but Justice Brewer was deeply concerned about these events. The Kansan seemed to conceive of his judicial role as embracing a broader responsibility to educate people from the lecture platform. The preceeding year he had railed against the "black flag of anarchism flaunting destruction to property and therefore the relapse of civilization to barbarism." Socialists inviting a redistribution of property, he said, were "assassins of liberty" and their supporters were fiends, fools, or fanatics.[24]

As if to give further credence to such views, Congress, during the fateful summer of 1894, passed an income tax as part of a tariff act. It levied a flat rate of 2 percent on individual incomes over $4,000 and on all corporate income. The Wilson-Gorman tariff started out as a substantial downward revision, and to fill the expected gap in federal revenue, supporters of an income tax eagerly pressed their solution to the projected deficit. From 1874 to 1894 no less than sixty-eight income tax bills were introduced in Congress; the last of these proposals survived the attack that had doomed its predecessors, despite the fact that the final tariff bill provided little reduction in federal revenue. Even the major party leaders could not completely ignore the Midwest discontent that had produced the Populist movement and its plea for an income tax.[25]

Whether the political matters of the past summer would intrude upon the serene world of the Supreme Court was not clear as the Justices convened in October. The bench was full during the early weeks, but before much could be done Jackson was forced to leave. His illness was diagnosed as some form of lung disease, and before he made his dramatic return late in the term, dropsy had been added to his ailments.[26] Looking at the docket from the perspective of October 1894, the Justices saw only one major case, the federal government's prosecution of E.C. Knight and Company for allegedly violating the restraint of trade provisions in the Sherman Antitrust Act of 1890. This first test of the power of the act embodied the hope of many who feared increased business consolidation. The decision in this case, coupled with two others arising from the preceding summer, would be of major importance, but the Court also contended with other matters.

For instance, when a touchy Congress sought to prevent the federal courts from interfering with administrative determinations concerning the exclusion of aliens, the Court capitulated. Earlier the Justices had read the Chinese Exclusion Act to permit a previously resident Chinese merchant to reenter the country after a vacation in his homeland. Congress greeted this decision with an act in August 1894 commanding judicial noninterference with the exclusion process. This new legislation was considered when Lem Moon Sing, after having been denied reentry, petitioned for a writ of habeas corpus. Harlan, for the majority, never reached the merits of the case; he simply accepted the authority of the legislative branch to delegate decision-making authority to immigration and customs officials, whose decisions were subject only to an appeal to the Secretary of the Treasury. A somewhat chastened Court simply found ample precedent for this new exercise of legislative power. Without opinion Brewer dissented.[27]

Certainly the acknowledgment of congressional power to exclude the courts from even this limited area was a potentially harmful precedent. But the legislative sensitivity on this issue was unusual, and this inroad on judicial power might easily be confined. As a whole, the Court probably did not resent the fact that its case load would be lightened in an area of little flexibility. The episode, however, does reveal some dimensions of Court-Congress interaction. Justices are appointed for life and freed from many political pressures, but they are by no means isolated from all such pressures.

In a bevy of cases challenging state action, the Justices continued to allow the states considerable latitude. When Kansas abolished the fellow servant defense in employee suits against railroads, the Court unanimously rejected a broad Fourteenth Amendment attack on the statute. Railroads could be singled out for special legislative treatment, the Justices said, because of the recognized hazards of rail employment. When defective equipment was the cause of accident, the Court continued to hold the railroads responsible for employee injuries. A Missouri peddler's tax weathered a commerce clause challenge, as did a Louisiana inspection statute that imposed a penalty in favor of charity on uninspected coal. Arkansas could impose a penalty on a railroad for charging more than the prescribed rate, and Pennsylvania could levy taxes on rentals paid for the use of a railroad within the state.[28]

Jackson participated in the business of the Court in its first week, but he left for home before the *E. C. Knight* case was argued on October 24, 1894. That this would be the first of a trio of cases that would make the 1894 term one of the Court's most significant was little anticipated in the rather routine oral argument. The E.C. Knight Company was indicted under the Sherman Antitrust Act, which prohibited every "contract, combination in the form of trust or otherwise, or conspiracy, in restraint of trade of commerce among the several states." Agreements among various sugar refiners had resulted in the creation of an entity known as the American Sugar Refining Company, which controlled 95 percent of the sugar refining business in the country. The government asked the federal circuit court for an injunction commanding the cancellation of certain agreements and the surrender of stock the company had received. Deciding that no violation of the law had been established, the circuit court refused to grant the injunction. In the Supreme Court Attorney General Richard Olney made a laconic argument, in part the result of his personal belief that the Sherman Act was neither wise nor useful.[29] The Chief Justice chose to write the Court's opinion.

Fuller said the ligitation hinged on the question of whether the manufacture of sugar was in itself a subject of interstate commerce. Drawing upon a strong belief in the viability of federalism and in the duty of the Court to draw the line between competing sovereignties, the Chief decided against the government. After quoting from recent precedent on the distinction between commerce and manufacture, the Chief determined that commerce "succeeds to manufacture, and is not a part of it." Then he detailed some of the reasoning behind the conclusion:

It is vital that the independence of the commercial power and of the police power, and the delimitation between them, however sometimes perplexing, should always be recognized and observed, for while the one furnishes the strongest bond of union, the other is essential to the preservation of the autonomy of the States as required by our dual form of government; and acknowledged evils, however grave and urgent they may appear to be, had better be borne, than the risk be run, in the effort to suppress them, of more serious consequences by resort to expedients of even doubtful constitutionality.[30]

To hold that the intent to use the channels of interstate commerce subjects a monopoly to federal control, Fuller continued, would result in depriving the states of their primary control over business operations. Although the Chief had supported the use of congressional power over commerce to reach subjects over which the federal legislative branch could not exert direct control, such as obscene materials, he refused to extend the reach of the power where no transportation was directly involved. The government's suit, he concluded, offered no proof of the company's intent to monopolize commerce.

The Chief's relatively short opinion drew the votes of all sitting members except Harlan, who expressed his outrage at the majority's conclusion that the Constitution did not provide sufficient power "to deal with gigantic monopolies holding in their grasp, and injuriously controlling in their own interest, the entire trade *among the States* in food products that are essential to the comfort of every household in the land." No undue reverence for the federal system, he continued, should blind us to the need to preserve the "just authority of the General Government." Quite legitimately the Justice read the Court's precedents to embrace more than transportation. Agreeing that congressional power cannot reach state monopolies, Harlan reminded the majority that the Sherman Act "does not strike at the manufacture of articles that are legitimate or recognized subjects of commerce, but at *combinations* that unduly restrain, because they monopolize, *the buying and selling of articles* which are to go into interstate commerce."[31]

Rhetorically Harlan asked, is not trade restrained when a monopolistic supplier can extract whatever price he desires for his goods? If a legislature attempted to levy a tax on refined sugar coming into the state, he continued, the Court would surely invalidate the enactment as a burden on interstate commerce. Harlan pointed to a paradoxical result that flowed from the majority's opinion: a state could not take such tribute, but a monopolistic corporation could. Citing state court decisions that uniformly held such a monopoly to be contrary to public policy because of its inevitable tendency to restrain trade, the Justice said: "Whatever a State may do to protect its completely interior traffic or trade against unlawful restraints, the general government is empowered to do for the protection of the people of all the states—for this purpose one people—against unlawful restraints imposed upon interstate traffic or trade in articles that are to enter into commerce among the several States." Reading the Court's opinion as undermining the Sherman Act, Harlan contended that a doctrine of state sovereignty "cannot properly be invoked to justify a denial of power in the national government to meet such an emergency, involving as it does that freedom of commercial intercourse among the States which the Constitution sought to attain."[32]

Justice Harlan was unable to sway any of his colleagues, but through his dissenting opinion ran the winds of the future. The creation of a national economy necessitates national controls; they might be delayed, as they were here, but they could not ultimately be denied. In periods of transition, especially with a Congress far from convinced about the need for greater governmental intervention, the Court could question the methods of regulation. Harlan, however, was quite right in his assertion that the Constitution could not long be interpreted contrary to the felt needs of the people. Joining the Kentuckian in his condemnation of the majority's opinion were many other critics, who interpreted the Court's action as a death blow to the Sherman Antitrust Act.[33]

As the term progressed, critics of the Court's work would soon find an even more vulnerable target. Arrangements were under way to bring the income tax of 1894 before the High Court. William D. Guthrie, at thirty-five a partner in a well-established New York law firm and already a weathered advocate before the Supreme Court, came to an understanding with Solicitor General Lawrence Maxwell on two suits filed in the federal circuit court in mid-January 1895. Guthrie had devised a means for a quick judicial determination by circumventing the statutory requirement that no suit to restrain the collection of a tax could be heard in any court. The income tax law, Guthrie figured, could be challenged indirectly in a suit brought by a stockholder against his company seeking to enjoin it from paying the allegedly illegal tax. Such suits were instituted against two trust companies, and, without consulting either President Cleveland or Attorney General Olney, Maxwell agreed to expedite proceedings in the lower court. Demurrers—formal replies to claims denying that the facts as alleged are sufficient to establish a case under the law—were filed by the Solicitor General. The circuit court sustained the government's position without opinion, thereby clearing the way for an appeal to the Supreme Court. When Maxwell's superiors learned of his agreement, they forced his resignation.[34] Maxwell, however, was only the first to be manipulated.

One week after its decision in E.C. Knight, the Court agreed to hear the two cases and to advance the argument so a decision could be reached in the present term. What caused the Justices to be so accommodating and apparently willing to overlook the obvious circumvention of the revenue statutes and the friendly nature of the suit is unclear. Perhaps the Court's members were swayed by the appeal to their responsibility to contend as quickly as possible with this most important economic matter. Also one of the companies involved, the Continental Trust Company, hired James C. Carter, an eminent constitutional lawyer, to argue in favor of the constitutionality of the tax.[35] Possibly this good faith attempt to have adverse interests represented blunted the charge of a friendly suit.

Because of the absence of a lower-court hearing and opinion, five full days were set aside for the presentations of counsel. In opposition to the tax were the eminent constitutional lawyers William D. Guthrie, Clarence A. Seward, Joseph H. Choate, and George F. Edmunds, while the case for the tax was presented by the Attorney General, Richard C. Olney, Assistant Attorney General Edward B. Whitney, and James C. Carter.[36] If the opponents of the tax had a greater mass of legal talent on their side, the supporters had clear precedents supporting the taxing power of government generally and an income tax in particular. But this was an unusual case, heard in unusual haste in an unusual national environment. Initially stymied by the precedents against them, antitax forces began to see some hope. If the full horror of the effect this little wedge, the 1894 tax, might have on the grand tenets of the

American tradition could be made clear, the Justices might be persuaded to use their power to save a temporarily distressed society from grave error. The legislative campaign in opposition to the tax had failed, but perhaps the Court would proclaim a new winner.

Although certain Justices could be counted upon to be sympathetic to repulsing an attack of the majority upon wealth, the argument had to encounter a strong judicial traditionalism, reinforced by the atmosphere in which the Court worked. Traditionalism implies a respect for the precedents of the Court, wherever those precedents might lead, even if, as in this matter, they lent substantial constitutional support to the validity of an income tax. Conservatism, on the other hand, is a term long buffeted by the forces of history, that can be confined here to an economic and social view that emphasizes the need for a vigorous protection of property interests. Judicial traditionalism and conservatism can be mutually supportive, but in the income tax case they came into conflict. The Justices were now summoned to reverse a century of error and come to the defense of imperiled property interests.[37]

Oral argument in the cases, generally known by the title *Pollock* v. *Farmers' Loan and Trust Co.*, began on March 7 and continued through the 13th. Swelling crowds of spectators watched the display of forensic ability. Guthrie began the argument in a low and formalistic key with little hint of the fireworks to come. He argued against the tax on grounds that its many exceptions precluded its meeting the constitutional requirement that a tax be uniform. The senior partner of the New York firm, Clarence A. Seward, followed by dealing with the issue that was to become the central one in the Court's ultimate resolution. That was the claim that an income tax was a direct tax, and, as such, it had to be apportioned among the states. Here precedent was strongly against the antitax advocates, but Seward urged the Justices to make up their minds in a fresh consideration of the issue. Whitney countered the Guthrie and Seward arguments well, citing ample precedent on the direct tax issue and insisting that the uniformity requirement was met by the universal applicability of the tax throughout the United States. Acknowledging that a $4,000 exemption did result in a tax levied primarily upon the wealthy, he argued that Congress was simply redressing an imbalance in which the federal tax burden had been placed primarily upon the consumer.[38]

On March 11, the tempo of the arguments picked up when former Senator George Edmunds warned the Court that such a tax imposed on the relatively few, so "intentionally and tyrannically and monstrously unequal," was the initial invasion upon property that would inevitably lead to "communism, anarchy, and then the ever following despotism."[39] As the oratory picked up so did the hyperbole. The Justices would not be allowed to escape full knowledge of the social and economic implications of the hated tax. Next came Richard Olney, now a far different advocate than he was in *E.C.*

Knight. Forceful and effective, he cautioned the Court, reminding the Justices that this is a government in which powers are separated and that they should not tred upon the legislative domain. Addressing himself to the attempt to reopen the direct tax question, Olney said that a contrary decision now would "set a hurtful precedent and would go far to prove that government by written constitution is not a thing of stable principles, but of the fluctuating views and wishes of the particular period and the particular judge when and from whom its interpretation happens to be called for."[40]

James C. Carter's defense of the act was so strong and powerful that his clients, the officers of the Continental Trust Company, were dismayed. This past president of the American Bar Association was too much a man of integrity to do any less than prepare the most able defense of the act possible. His argument was broadly addressed to the social and economic questions raised, as he claimed that justice demanded that the wealthier classes shoulder a larger tax burden than they had in the past. On all issues, he was responsive and thorough. He closed, as did Olney, with words of caution to the Court:

Nothing could be more unwise and dangerous—nothing more foreign to the spirit of the Constitution—than an attempt to baffle and defeat a popular determination by a judgment in a lawsuit. When the opposing forces of sixty millions of people have become arrayed in hostile political ranks upon a question which all men feel is not a question of law, but of legislation, the only path of safety is to accept the voice of the majority as final.[41]

Carter had done his job so well and with such apparent relish that he was widely condemned by fellow lawyers and others who saw him as a traitor to his own class. Especially alarmed was the conservative press, and Joseph Choate, who followed Carter, repeatedly took the opportunity to swipe at Carter in his argument. Having acquired a considerable reputation as a most effective trial lawyer, Choate was a perfect match for Carter. Calling the income tax "communistic in its purposes and tendencies," Choate asserted that "one of the fundamental objects of all civilized government was the preservation of the rights of private property." Should this "very keystone of the arch upon which all civilized government rests" be eroded, all that Americans held dear would be threatened. Then Choate settled down to furnish the Court with a rationale for a favorable decision. Carefully he tried to distinguish the cases of the past, drawing the close and fine distinctions that have always attracted lawyers. With this debris shunted to one side, Choate argued that a tax on income from property, whether real or personal, was in fact a tax on the property itself and therefore a direct tax that must be apportioned. While the opposition lawyers urged the Court to be cautious, Choate said the Justices must be brave and courageous in exercising their duty:

I do not believe that any member of this court has ever sat or ever will sit to hear and decide a case the consequences of which will be so far-reaching as this. . . . If it be true as my friend said in closing, that the passions of the people are aroused on this subject, if it be true that a mighty army of sixty million citizens is likely to be incensed by this decision, it is the more vital to the future welfare of this country that this court again resolutely and courageously declare, as Marshall did, that it *has* the power to set aside an act of Congress violative of the Constitution, and that it will not hesitate in executing that power, no matter what the threatened consequences of popular or populistic wrath may be.[42]

Choate was right in suggesting that few cases in the history of the Supreme Court seemed, at the time, as momentous as this one. Ably argued, the issue was now placed in the laps of the Justices. No charge of decision making in a vacuum could be levied, because the extensive arguments repeatedly drew attention to political, social, and economic consequences. In spite of the extremes of Choate's and Edmunds's arguments, they did highlight the fact that an income tax as part of the revenue-raising apparatus of the federal government would work a substantial change in American society.

Diligently the Justices worked toward a solution of the issues raised, and on April 8 a hushed audience awaited the judgment. When Chief Justice Fuller reached the end of his reading, no one was satisfied. The majority had only reached a decision on two matters: first, that a tax on the income from municipal bonds was invalid because it was a restriction on the power of the state to borrow money; and second, that a tax on income from real property was in effect a tax on that property and therefore a direct tax that could not be levied in the manner the federal government chose. The government had conceded the first point, but it had strongly contested the second.

Fuller's opinion, which has been acclaimed his best and derided as his worst, depending upon the perspective of the critic,[43] seemed more extensive than a resolution of the two matters necessitated, but even in deciding the question of the constitutionality of a tax on rentals the majority had to contend with the hitherto settled state of precedent. Prior to the Court's partial resolution of the income tax problem, a string of precedents had coalesced with a popular understanding that direct taxes were taxes on land itself or taxes on persons, such as a poll tax. What made the labeling of the income tax a direct tax so crucial was the Constitution's provision that such taxes had to be apportioned among the states. In practical terms such apportionment would make an income tax an absurdity because property or income and population had little correlation.

If Congress is thereby precluded for levying an income tax, Fuller argued, it is because the framers of the Constitution intended to prevent "an attack upon accumulated property by mere force of numbers." Warming to his new interpretation, he called the direct tax limitation "one of the bulwarks of private rights and private property."[44] In fact one of the creative dimensions of Fuller's opinion was the transferral of this alleged fear into a modern setting; so although precedent would have to be evaded, Fuller justified this by a reading of the basic intent of the framers of the Constitution. If Fuller was right, history until 1895 served the framers poorly.

After asserting the Court's right to read the Constitution anew and reconsider the framers' intent, Fuller contended with the Civil War income tax. An earlier Court had determined its validity, so Fuller had to cast aspersions on that result. He suggested, although the earlier decision affords no such indication, that the Justices were affected by wartime emergency conditions; now in a time of peace, he wrote, more thought and care were necessary in reaching a just result. In handling precedent Fuller did not directly overrule the earlier decisions; instead he interpreted them narrowly and skirted their implications. Then returning to one of his favorite themes, he said that "by calling a tax indirect when it is essentially direct, the rule of protection could be frittered away" thus trespassing "the boundary between the Nation and the States."[45]

The Chief's opinion seemed to be building toward an invalidation of the income tax, so careful listeners were quite surprised to find that the eight-man Court had split equally on three major questions. That six members of the Court could have fully subscribed to Fuller's reasoning and its implications and then divided equally on the remaining questions seems inconsistent. The three unresolved issues were: first, whether the invalidity of the tax on income from real property voided the entire act; second, whether the taxing of income from personal property was a direct tax; and third, whether any part of the tax was invalid for lack of uniformity.

Justice Field indicated his concurrence with the majority's determination, but he then added a rather long opinion arguing that the act's arbitrary and capricious provisions clearly indicated a failure to meet the test of uniformity. Forcefully asserting his personal sympathy with the antitax advocates, he asked, "if the provision of the Constitution can be set aside by an act of Congress, where is the course of usurpation to end? The present assault upon capital is but the beginning. It will be the stepping stone to others, larger and more sweeping, till our political contests will become a war of the poor against the rich; a war constantly growing in intensity and bitterness."[46]

In dissent the newest member of the Court, Edward White, delivered a thoughtful and careful opinion well anchored in precedent. That an income tax is not a direct tax, he argued, is no longer an open question prey to the whims and caprice of those who just happened to constitute the Court. He warned of dangers lurking in the majority's view:

Teach the lesson that settled principles may be overthrown at any time, and confusion and turmoil must ultimately result. . . . If the permanency of its conclusions is to depend upon the personal opinions of those who, from time to time, may make up its membership, it will inevitably become a theatre of political strife, and its action will be without coherence or consistency. . . . Break down this belief in judicial continuity, . . . and our Constitution will, in my judgment, be bereft of value and become a most dangerous instrument to the rights and liberties of the people.[47]

To the argument that the Court must also act to save the capitalistic system from erosion, White responded that the Court must not act if it is to preserve our governmental system. Harlan concurred in White's dissent and then added a few words indicating his belief that the circumvention of the revenue statutes should have caused the Court to refuse jurisdiction.

The three major opinions in *Pollock* are more philosophical in their essence than they are legal. An intensive legal analysis of their wording is really beside the point. To Fuller the balance between state and federal power should be maintained and the Court is doing the job it was designed to do when it staves off the attacks of a democratic majority on property. To Field arbitrary legislative action must be condemned and the Court must accept the responsibility to nip an incipient class war in the bud. To White settled precedent must be the guide and the Court must not forget its prescribed role in the governmental system.

Antitax advocates had won a clear victory in the decision of April 8. Fuller's opinion not only disposed of the initial question of whether the Court would consider the direct tax matter anew but also indicated considerable sympathy with the antitax advocates. Still, although shorn of two sources of revenue, the tax stood. One week later Guthrie filed a petition for a rehearing. Attorney General Olney responded with a counterpetition requesting that, if a rehearing was granted, it extend to the Court's determination that a tax on rentals was a direct tax. Apparently, after consulting the absent Jackson, who assured the Chief that he was well enough to join the Court for a rehearing, the petitions were granted and argument set for May 6. The ailing Jackson became the center of attention, and newspapers were rife with speculation about his views. All commentators concluded that Jackson's vote would determine the fate of the income tax.[48] Such an intense focus on Jackson was highly dramatic, and only by fully appreciating the effect of this press campaign can we understand the dramatic events to follow.

Since each side was limited to two lawyers on the reargument, the ranks were chopped to Richard Olney and his assistant, Edward Whitney, on the protax side and William Guthrie and Joseph Choate on the antitax side of the case. The oral arguments were now pitched to the Court's first opinion. Olney spent much more of his time contending with the direct tax issue. Choate sought to use the leverage of Fuller's opinion to equate personal property and real property, since the Court had previously decided a tax on income from real property was direct. Again the courtroom was packed, but counsel were generally more restrained.[49] Also these opponents of the tax had a new confidence that made the appeal to emotionalism less necessary.

On May 20, with no hint of either the drama behind the scenes or the one to follow in the courtroom, Fuller read the majority's decision. The income tax of 1894 was declared invalid. Perfunctorily indicating that the Court fully appreciated the gravity of voiding an act of Congress, Fuller reiterated the majority's earlier decision on rental income and then came to the same conclusion about a tax on investment income. The Court had hesitated in its first opinion to declare the entire act void as a result of its determination that a tax on real property was unconstitutional, but that determination now inevitably followed.[50] Remaining taxes on occupations and wages would have gravely distorted the act's purpose.

Fuller's opinion, clearly intended to supplement and not displace his first one, was terse and dignified, but the dissenters were anything but terse and dignified. As the readings progressed, four dissenters, each filing an opinion, were counted. When Fuller finished with the opinion of the five-man majority, the focus shifted to Justice Harlan. The assembled spectators were about to witness one of the most spectacular displays ever staged by a member of the Court. Harlan, who had written a short, nonrhetorical dissent in the first case, now released his pent-up fury. At the outset the Kentuckian was agitated, more the result of what he knew was ahead rather than anything discernible in the early paragraphs in which he criticized the majority's shameful reading of precedent. His flushed face grew redder as he continued, and if his stinging words alone were insufficient castigation, he reinforced them with pointed looks and gestures.[51]

"I have a deep, abiding conviction," Harlan began, "which my sense of duty compels me to express, that it is not possible for this court to have rendered any judgment more to be regretted than the one just rendered." It excites the "gravest apprehensions" and "strikes at the very foundation of national authority" and reestablishes that helplessness that characterized the central government under the Articles of Confederation. The picture counsel drew of the threatened and beseiged rich elicited no sympathy from the Justice. He expressed dismay that his brothers could decide that income derived from the sweat of the brow, or the skill or intelligence of the individual, could be taxed but not income from invested capital. His colleagues, he advised, should not be intimidated by the cries of socialism; such arguments belong in a legislative chamber and not in a court of law. Shaking his finger at the Chief, he said that the hands of Congress have been bound, leaving that body no recourse except to propose an amendment to the Constitution. With a cracking voice, he concluded:

I cannot assent to an interpretation of the Constitution that impairs and cripples the just power of the National Government in the essential matter of taxation, and at the same time discriminates against the greater part of the people of our country.

The practical effect of the decision to-day is to give to certain kinds of property a position of favoritism and advantage inconsistent with the fundamental principles of our social organization, and to invest them with power and influence that may be perilous to that portion of the American people upon whom rests the larger part of the burdens of the government, and who ought not be subjected to the dominion of aggregated wealth any more than the property of the country should be at the mercy of the lawless.[52]

The work of the Court as exhibited on that day in May would long invite comment, and Harlan's impassioned performance was vigorously assailed. He was disrespectful to his colleagues; he had forgotten about judicial proprieties; he was acting like an advocate, not a judge; and so on.[53] But the whole matter of the income tax had stirred deep emotions, and despite the bad press Harlan received, it remains heartening that the seemingly impenetrable veneer of solemnity and decorum can fall before the strength of one man's conviction.

Brown followed Harlan. In the first opinion Brown had agreed in labeling the tax on rentals a direct tax, but now he repented and changed his mind. In an opinion much shorter than Harlan's he indicated his full conversion to a protax view. Insisting that the Court is not empowered to reverse the long-established meaning of direct tax, he refused his assent to this enfeebling of Congress. The suggestion of apportioning an income tax was foolish, Brown argued, for it would lead to gross and insupportable inequities. Cries of socialism he exposed as a smoke screen, for how is socialism established by a tax levied "upon the people in proportion to their ability to pay." Expressing his faith in the ingenuity of Congress to escape the Court's confinement, Brown still worried that the majority's decision might paralyze the legislative branch in a time of national emergency. "I hope," he added, "it may not prove the first step toward the submergence of the liberties of the people in a sordid despotism of wealth. As I cannot escape the conclusion that the decision of the court in this great case is fraught with immeasurable danger to the future of the country, and that it approaches the proportion of a national calamity, I feel it my duty to enter my protest against it."[54]

Howell Jackson called the decision "the most disastrous blow ever struck at the constitutional power of Congress," and Justice White, preferring, as did Fuller, to stand on his earlier opinion, dissected the majority's opinion point by point. He concluded by deploring the resurrection of "a long repudiated and rejected theory of the Constitution, by which the government is deprived of an inherent attribute of its being, a necessary power of taxation."[55]

Shock, dismay, jubilation, and relief were a varied set of reactions to the decision, but when the smoke cleared the more sober-minded critics began to ask what had happened. Howell Jackson was supposed to be the swing vote, the lone justification for imposing the trip to Washington upon the man. Jackson voted in favor of the tax, but the majority decided against it. From the perspective in which the rehearing was viewed, some Justice who previously favored the tax must now have voted against it. Thus began "the mystery of the vascillating jurist." Justices do change positions in response to an argumentative process that assumes minds are not closed, but the Court's work in *Pollock* was subjected to an uncommon public scrutiny. Despite the fact that five votes were required to invalidate the income tax, the one errant judge was the special target of the press. A Chicago newspaper, which had leaked some correct details concerning the Court's resolution of the case, claimed it had solved the mystery when it named George Shiras of Pennsylvania. Although some praise for Shiras's resolute final judgment was heard, it was drowned out by the opprobrium that descended upon the often light-hearted but now troubled judge. Upholding the tradition of not revealing the alignment of particular members on unresolved questions, the Justices met the charge with silence. Shiras suffered quietly, though somewhat resentfully, for the rest of his life. Denying privately that he had changed his mind, he futilely hoped that either Fuller or his successor would set the record straight.[56]

Early observers accepted without question that Shiras was the Justice who changed his mind, but his insistent denial and some support for it led historians to reopen the matter. As the focus shifted from Shiras, all members of the final majority became suspects except the steadfast Chief. In all the different solutions no one suggested that Fuller could possibly have vascillated, for the obvious reason that his first opinion reveals a strong feeling against the tax. But, in turn, Gray and even those strong protectors of property, Field and Brewer, became suspects.[57]

The trouble with the "vascillating jurist" theory is not that it is illogical but rather that it neglects other possibilities. The most attractive rival explanation has been that the Justices did not vote consistently on all three reserved issues, and, though five had decided the tax was unconstitutional, they could not agree upon a rationale. That the unresolved questions did not invite a consistent response is easy to appreciate, as is Fuller's hesitancy to release a decision striking down a major piece of congressional legislation with no consensus on precisely why it violated the Constitution.

With the Chief's reporting an even division on the three unresolved questions, the assumption has been that all routes to invalidating the income tax were equally open after the first decision. The narrowest grounds—that without the tax on rentals the whole tax must fall—could have held no appeal for the Chief, Field, and quite probably Brewer. Although the argument based upon the requirement that federal taxes be uniform in more than a geographical sense had support, Field's opinion detailing the implications of such a position might well have eroded that support. The third alternative, deciding that a tax on the income from personal property was a direct tax, flowed most consistently from Fuller's first opinion in which "direct tax" had been redefined. This seemed to be the area in which consensus was sought, but not achieved, in the first hearing.

Scholars who have speculated on how the Justices might have voted on the three issues have generally centered their inquiry on Shiras and Gray, the prime suspects under the "vascillating jurist" theory. These men retain their appeal as the key to the mystery primarily because their presence on the antitax side is difficult to explain. Both were moderates and both showed considerable respect for precedent. But the unasked question is how either of these men could have held out against substantial internal pressure to agree upon a rationale. Gray hardly revealed himself as a recalcitrant holdout in a letter to the Chief complimenting Fuller on the first opinion.[58] There is no evidence in Shiras's career on the High Bench to indicate he could or would have resisted the demand for consensus.

Only one Justice in favor of invalidating the tax was stubborn and irascible enough to have withstood the demand for agreement at the first hearing. That was Stephen J. Field. In his later years on the Court, the Californian had a substantially reduced work load, and periods of vagueness increasingly outnumbered periods of clarity. His weakening mental and physical condition, however, seemed only to strengthen his beliefs; he became more tenacious, righteous, and unyielding. In the Court's internal discussions, Justice Harlan said, Field acted "like a mad man during the whole of this contest about the income tax."[59] Actually, the Californian was running no risk by refusing to agree that the tax on personal property was a direct tax, for a rehearing was inevitable, and Jackson's vote, even if cast the other way, would not save the hated tax. What Field had to gain was the acceptance of his argument on uniformity, a position he desired to etch into constitutional law.

When at the second hearing Jackson sided with the protax Justices, Field had no choice but to capitulate and subscribe to Fuller's opinion for the five-man majority. That the Californian eventually subscribed to a different rationale to reach the desired result is clear, but hardly could he be called the vascillating Justice that the mystery initially posited. Because of the need to substitute assumptions and speculation for hard evidence, no claim of a definitive solution can be made. But if five members of the Court did come to the conclusion that the income tax was unconstitutional at the first hearing, as seems likely, Stephen J. Field was the one man in the majority who could have resisted the demand for consensus.

At any rate, the income tax decision called attention both to the power of the Court and to the fact that constitutional decisions could not be divorced from the personal predilections and political and economic views of the men who made them. *Pollock* injected the Court into the political mainstream and subjected it to vilification as a body working against the interests of the people.[60] Attempts were made to get Congress to enact another income tax law in the hope that a changed membership might sustain it, but the Court's decision would rule the area for eighteen years. The majority had flexed its muscles and halted the taxing of the rich, but whether this exertion of power was indicative of a future in which a philosophical type of adjudication would come to characterize the Justices' work was unclear.

Rehearing the income tax case put the Court behind schedule, and the Justices delayed their vacation to consider the last of the famous trio of cases of the 1894 term. They were asked to issue a writ of habeas corpus to free Eugene V. Debs, the leader of the American Railway Union (ARU), from jail. Debs was ably represented by former Senator Lyman Trumbull and Clarence Darrow, whose fame as a criminal lawyer was just beginning to spread. Although the legal profession as a whole was divided over matters like the income tax and trust regulation, little, if any, support could be found for the boycott of Pullman cars. American society was just beginning its rather long and painful adjustment to the activity of labor unions. Consolidation was an ongoing reality in many other areas of economic life, but when workers sought to organize and increase their bargaining strength their activity was viewed by many as un-American. The notes of class warfare in the refrain of advocates' arguments in the income tax case were occasioned perhaps more by a fear of massive, organized labor than by a single act of a misguided Congress.

Late in June 1894 the refusal of the members of the American Railway Union to handle Pullman cars paralyzed rail transportation at its heart, Chicago. The paralysis spread west and south. On July 2 Attorney General Olney directed the United States attorney in Chicago to seek an injunction against the leaders of the ARU, ostensibly for obstructing the passage of the mails. A broad injunction was granted against Debs and all others "to desist and refrain from in any way or manner interfering with, hindering, obstructing, or stopping any of the business of any of the following named roads." This expansive, omnibus injunction was widely criticized, but apparently Debs and the three other leaders involved received copies and deliberately refused to honor its provisions. Finally federal troops, although initially escalating the difficulties through violence, broke the strike. Proceedings for contempt were brought against the leaders of the ARU. To the argument that such an injunction went beyond judicial authority, the trial court responded that the defendants had engaged in a combination in restraint of trade and thereby had violated the terms of the Sherman Antitrust Act. The circuit court judge imposed a six-month contempt sentence upon Debs and three-month sentences upon three other defendants.[61]

On May 27, 1895, one week after the final income tax decision, the Supreme Court considered for the first time the question of the validity of the use of an injunction in a labor dispute. Two years earlier the Court had unanimously refused to uphold a federal conviction for conspiracy to obstruct justice in a labor dispute on grounds that the jurisdiction of the federal courts did not directly or indirectly embrace the state's criminal law process. Since Debs was imprisoned for actions done in Illinois and imprisoned under the federal court's contempt power, the earlier case seemed in point. Brewer blithely ignored the precedent and discussed the injunction as a special form of relief for abating a nuisance or preventing irreparable damage to property that could not adequately be compensated in an action at law. What was novel here was the resort of the government to the injunction process and the absence of an irreparably threatened property interest. At a time when labor unions seemed to pose new threats to the American way of life, the Court was being asked to approve a new and mighty weapon for use by the government against labor. The trial court seemed less sensitive to the novelty of the whole question, but Brewer recognized that a denial of the writ of habeas corpus would confirm a substantial extension of federal equity jurisdiction.[62] Instead of protecting the rights of private parties, as had been its traditional area of application, the injunction was now being called into service to preserve public rights and punish public wrongs.

In broad language, Brewer upheld the authority of the circuit court to issue the injunction. Although the lower court had rested its decision on the Sherman Act, the Justice found broader grounds, perhaps preferring not to find too much vitality in an act that the Court had just severely limited in *E.C. Knight.* Asserting that both Congress and the Court have long recognized the federal government's power over interstate commerce and the mails, Brewer concluded "that the national government may prevent any unlawful and forcible interference therewith." To the argument that the federal system precludes the national government from interfering with crimes within the jurisdiction of the state, Brewer simply responded that he saw "no such impotency in the national government." The Justice had just joined in the opinion of the Court in the second *Pollock* case, which found a substantial impotency within the federal government, but even in the absence of any legislation he found no such incapacity here. "The strong arm of the national government may ... brush away all obstructions," and, Brewer continued, summon military force to ensure obedience to the law. Since such recourse to military might was legitimate, the resort to the legal process was not only permissible but commendable. The Kansan asserted that the government did have a sufficient property interest in the mails to support injunctive relief, but then he added:

Every government, entrusted, by the very terms of its being, with powers and duties to be exercised and discharged for the general welfare, has a right to apply to its own courts for any proper assistance in the exercise of one and the discharge of the other, and it is no sufficient answer to its appeal to one of those courts that it has no pecuniary interest in the matter. Preventing wrongdoing is sufficient reason for standing. The obligations which it is under to promote the interest of all, and to prevent the wrongdoing of one resulting in injury to the general welfare, is often of itself sufficient to give it standing in court.[63]

Fitting injunctive relief into its traditional model, the Justice pronounced the action of the strikers a public nuisance, saying that the government could seek a court's help in enjoining a public nuisance as an individual could a private nuisance. If the remedy seemed strange, he argued that a strange and compelling case for its use was demonstrated. As with all novelty, the Court sought to clothe this newly discovered governmental power in the garments of an honored past.

Brewer's opinion found a new reservoir of power in the federal government, and in the executive branch at that, but Chief Justice Fuller did not dissent. Perhaps he shared the prevailing horror of mass union action, or perhaps after his grueling experience with the income tax issue he sacrificed his principles to tactical necessity. Although the decision was unanimous and although there was little general public support either for Debs or for the cause of unionized labor, it did provoke concern. "Government by injunction" became a rallying cry, and legal scholars worried about the implications of this new injunctive power in the hands of the government.[64]

From one perspective this trio of major decisions of the 1894 term revealed that what the Court took away with one hand it gave back with the other. Congress could not reach manufacturing, no matter how completely the business monopolized its field, and it could not pass an income tax under the terms of the present Constitution, but this was balanced against the potentially great power the Court discerned in the federal government when the public highways of interstate commerce were threatened. From another perspective the three decisions were part of a single whole; they all protected property at the expense of the working class. This latter interpretation quickly preempted the field. Without any protection existing within the framework of government, members of the laboring class were to be forced to pay for refined sugar, and by implication other products, at prices set by monopolistic corporations; they were to be denied a more equitable taxing system; and they were to be subjected to injunctions and contempt charges should they seek to organize and use their combined strength to redress imbalance in the industrial society. Despite the legal jargon and technical discussions, the philosophical implications of these decisions were both clearly intended and clearly perceived.

So a Supreme Court that had begun the decade with the fanfare of a centennial celebration and the public respect it implied was now viewed as a staunch protector of special business interests. What the critics saw was not a tribunal of justice, whose members sought their guidance from the Constitution, the wisdom of the past, and the public conscience, but instead a body of appointed men seeking to protect propertied interests by rejecting the past and rigging the future. These decisions helped widen the split in the ranks of the Democratic party, a split that resulted in the insertion of planks in the party's 1896 platform attacking the judiciary and in the nomination of

William Jennings Bryan for president.[65] That the Court had dealt itself a blow and brought on a new wave of condemnation is undisputed, but it had weathered such blows before. Despite the analogy often drawn to the *Dred Scott* decision and despite contemporary fears, society was not rent asunder. The Court had not in any way alienated the most powerful political and economic forces; in fact, it had strengthened their allegiance. William McKinley, the Republican candidate, would defeat Bryan in 1896, and the gloom of depression would be rapidly displaced by the euphoria of a new prosperity.

This change in national mood also affected the Court's critics in the legislative branch. Although the decisions of the 1894 term generated considerable activity in the 53rd and 54th Congresses seeking to curb the power of the High Bench, the proposals for such bills dwindled thereafter.[66]

While the Justices were on vacation after the hectic session, they received news of another casualty of the *Pollock* case. Justice Howell Jackson died on August 8, 1895. Lured from his home in Tennessee by a sense of responsibility, Jackson found that his vote had made no difference. His recovery, however, had received a fatal setback. During one of the shortest tenures in the Court's history, he had been deprived of his one opportunity to play the major role that had been promised him.

President Cleveland once again had to confront the hurdles of appointing a man to the Supreme Court. David Hill was still in the Senate, and Cleveland, who in desperation last time had chosen the Senator from Louisiana, Edward White, now acknowledged that the appointee must come from New York. When reports circulated that the President would send William B. Hornblower's name to the Senate, the New York lawyer quickly wrote to Cleveland and politely but firmly requested that his name be withdrawn from consideration. So, too, did Frederick R. Coudert, another prominent New York lawyer, who had been considered for the chief justiceship in 1888. Coudert also had been involved in the bar association's investigation that was the source of Senator Hill's ill will. With neither of these men willing to play the pawns in Cleveland's struggle with Hill, the President quit the field. An easy way out of the dilemma had always been present, for Senator Hill in 1894 had indicated he would have no objection to Rufus Peckham, Wheeler's younger brother. The President thought highly of Rufus Peckham and earlier said he would bring him to Washington, but he stubbornly refused Hill's accommodation in 1894. Now, with Hornblower and Coudert out of the picture, Cleveland sent Hill a respectful letter soliciting the Senator's reaction to Rufus Peckham. A victorious Hill warmly endorsed Peckham, who took his seat on the Court on January 6, 1896.[67]

Rufus Peckham had served on New York's highest court, and his judicial philosophy showed an inclination to favor the property interest. In outlook he seemed close to David Brewer, but unlike Brewer, who was the Court's most visible member, Peckham tended to be quiet and withdrawn from the public. About five feet, seven inches tall, he was of slight build. At fifty-eight he had an attractive white mustache, a receding forehead, and shocks of white wavy hair over both ears. His features were well-proportioned and sharply defined, and keen eyes contributed to his distinguished appearance.

When the Supreme Court convened in October for the 1895 term, it may have been viewed with greater suspicion, but the disposition of cases in the session revealed no basic change in approach. For instance, the invalidation of the federal income tax did not invite any change in the Court's approval of the exercise of state taxing power.[68] As before, when questions of interstate commerce were involved, the Court pragmatically responded to the differing fact situations. With little apparent consistency, the Court unanimously decided that Illinois could not force a fast mail train to detour to the county seat, but Georgia could prohibit the running of freight trains, fast or slow, intrastate or interstate, on Sundays in the absence of any congressional legislation. Such inconsistency bothered Chief Justice Fuller and White, who saw in the latter decision an interference with congressional power; the silence of Congress, the dissenters argued, should be interpreted as a commitment to free and unrestricted intercourse.[69]

Field and Harlan had failed to discern any conflict in the previous two cases, but they vigorously disagreed with the majority in a Connecticut case. The state sought to punish any individual who transported or intended to transport beyond Connecticut's boundaries game birds killed within the state. With Brewer and Peckham not participating, White wrote for the five-man majority and upheld the Connecticut law. White sidestepped the argument that interstate commerce was impeded by ruling that "the commerce in game, which the state law permitted, was necessarily only internal commerce since the restriction that it should not become a subject of external commerce went along with the grant and was part of it." Since the law was designed to conserve a valuable food supply, White added, it clearly fell into the domain of the state's police power. Such an opinion had broad implications, for it seemed to say that if a state could bring a regulation within its traditional authority to legislate in the interest of its citizens' health, morality, safety, and welfare, it could conclusively determine what was or was not a subject of interstate commerce. Field denied such a proposition and filed his dissent. Harlan also dissented, saying that Connecticut's law was "not consistent with the liberty of the citizen, or with the freedom of interstate commerce."[70]

Despite continued suspicion and close analysis of the work of the Interstate Commerce Commission,[71] the Court did, by a narrow margin, uphold an immunity act passed by Congress, in the wake of *Counselman* v. *Hitchcock*, designed to facilitate investigations by the commission. In *Brown* v. *Walker*, Justice Brown, the Court's spokesman, expressed satisfaction that the earlier objections of the Justices had been met. To the claim that the grant of immunity did not extend to state prosecutions, he simply asserted that the immunity granted would extend "whenever and in whatever court such prosecution may be had."[72] To the rather novel argument that the President's constitutionally conferred pardoning power exhausted federal governmental authority in the area, Brown answered that it in no way precluded congressional acts of general amnesty.

Justice George Shiras filed a dissent in which Gray and White concurred. Considering the broad protection offered by the Fifth Amendment, Shiras questioned whether any statute seeking to exchange immunity for compulsory testimony could truly pass constitutional scrutiny. Assaulting the logic of the majority, he questioned how a federal statute, provided in lieu of a right that protected the individual from the federal government only, could possibly bind state governments. Admittedly the majority had been caught in a dilemma. The individual has a constitutional right to remain silent, and if he chooses to exercise that right there could be no possibility of his conviction in a state court on the basis of his own admissions. If, then, the Fifth Amendment right was to be protected fully, the majority was forced to conclude that the federal act had, in some manner, immunized the individual from state prosecution as well. Since the Fifth Amendment was not viewed as restricting state action, both logic and state power were affronted by the Court's rationale. The majority had succumbed to the government's argument that the ICC could not hope to enforce its delegated power without this type of access to witnesses. The dissenters saw only danger in this erosion of constitutional rights, suggesting that if such a problem really existed "the remedy must be found in the right of the nation to amend the fundamental law, and not in appeals to the courts to substitute for a constitutional guaranty the doubtful and uncertain provisions of an experimental statute."[73]

Also dissenting, Field preferred to go his own way, which included an acceptance of counsel James C. Carter's contention that the pardoning power of the president precluded congressional acts of immunity. More importantly, what Field's dissent contributed to the discussion was the recognition that the self-incrimination provision is designed to do more than shelter its invocator from prosecution. Forcing the individual to speak, Field said, can undermine the dignity and self-respect that the amendment protects. With considerable sensitivity the Justice noted that a trial in a courtroom is only one of the trials that a self-confessed criminal must endure in his society. Few would deny the usefulness of immunity as an option available to the government, but whether the compulsory extraction of testimony is necessary is an entirely different question.

Despite changing membership and occasional dissent, the Court continued to read the police power broadly, apparently willing to afford state governments considerable room for experimentation within the federal system. Speaking for the Court in another case of the term, Brown summed up the prevailing attitude: ". . . whatever is contrary to public policy or inimical to the public interests is subject to the police power of the State, and within legislative control, and in the exertion of such power the legislature is vested with a large discretion, which if exercised *bona fide* for the protection of the public, is beyond the reach of judicial inquiry."[74] Such a policy gave the Justices discretion to decide if the state action was truly in the public interest or if it was designed to undermine some vested interest, but the cases of the 1890s revealed little use of this discretion to limit state power.

In January 1896, during his first week as a member of the Court, Rufus Peckham heard arguments in a case entitled *United States* v. *Gettysburg Electric Railway Company*. Fuller assigned Peckham the task of writing the opinion; in more ways than one Peckham's maiden effort was highly significant. A congressional act in 1888 authorized the Chief Executive to condemn land for public use. Specific legislation in 1893 and 1894 authorized the preservation of the Gettysburg battlefield. Condemnation proceedings failed in the federal circuit court on the grounds that the contemplated public use was not incident to some power delegated to that government. Unanimously the Supreme Court reversed the decision.[75] Much of the federal government's power to develop national parks and to conserve land for public accessibility lay in the balance, and the Justices' instincts in the case were sound. When Peckham was handed the task of writing the opinion, he might not have anticipated the difficulties of translating an instinctual resolution into the form of a judicial opinion. He soon found out.

Starting out, Peckham drew upon principle from John F. Dillon's *Municipal Corporations* to the effect that the legislature properly determines what is a public use and that the courts accept that determination unless it is "palpably without reasonable foundation."[76] But whether the state authority that Dillon used to support his proposition was sufficient to sustain such power in the federal legislature is doubtful. Next, the New York Justice asserted that the presumption of constitutionality that the Supreme Court regularly extends to acts of Congress can only be overcome by clear and unmistakable contrary evidence. Because neither of these conclusions reached the basic argument that Congress had exceeded its delegated authority, Peckham tried to find a source in the Constitution for the action of the government. Since no express delegation of power could be found, the federal government's authority to condemn land must be implied.

Attacking the problem, Peckham argued: "Any act of Congress which plainly and directly tends to enhance the respect and love of the citizen for the institutions of his country and to quicken and strengthen his motives to defend them, and which is germane to and intimately connected with and appropriate to the exercise of some one or all of the powers granted by [*sic*]

Congress must be valid." Then he asserted that the matter here fell well within the area described. Still unconvinced and unconvincing, Peckham tried to make something of the fact that the area involved was a battlefield. Talking of the glorious heritage of the war and the heroism of the men who fought, he suggested that the public taking might be justified under the war power with its emphasis upon protecting and preserving the whole country. He asked, could anyone object to the taking of property to bury deceased soldiers? Realizing that his search for some specific source of implied power had been fruitless, Peckham concluded with an assertion of faith:

No narrow view of the character of this proposed use should be taken. Its national character and importance, we think, are plain. The power to condemn for this purpose need not be plainly and unmistakably deduced from any one of the particularly specified powers. Any number of those powers may be grouped together, and an inference from them all may be drawn that the power claimed has been conferred.[77]

With a smile we may seek to dismiss Peckham's public groping as the work of an inexperienced Justice, but the New Yorker had considerable state appellate court experience. Another Justice, more sensitive to the pitfalls that lay ahead, might have avoided contending with counsel's basic argument by simply developing further the idea that the question should be resolved by the legislative branch, but Peckham's opinion is more generally illuminating. The New Yorker was convinced that Congress had the power claimed, but he was frustrated in his inability to find it. His sense of responsibility spurred him on to make the search, but the more he wrote the more involved he got and the less convincing was his rationale. He was searching for something that did not exist; certainly the power should have been delegated, but it was not. Such constitutional gaps can obviously be filled by amendment, but they are often filled in less cumbersome ways. Confronted with the offer of the Louisiana Territory by Napoleon, President Jefferson found no authority in the Constitution to enable the government to make the purchase. Expediency and national necessity overcame the President's scruples. That initial act of purchase solved the constitutional problem ever after. So, too, did this strange Supreme Court decision settle conclusively Congress's right to condemn land for what it deemed to be a public purpose.

During the term in *Wong Wing* v. *United States* the Court again contended with the congressional campaign against the Chinese, but this time the Justices concluded that the legislation had transgressed constitutional boundaries. The case turned on the constitutionality of a provision in the infamous Immigration Act of 1892 that provided that Chinese aliens found to be in the United States illegally would be imprisoned at hard labor for up to one year. The government's vigorous denial that the Constitution protected aliens enraged Justice Field. He wrote a separate opinion that differed from the majority only in its castigation of the Assistant Attorney General for insulting the Court with such an argument. In a more moderate tone Shiras, for the rest of the Court, granted Wong Wing's petition for habeas corpus. Acknowledging that earlier decisions had upheld administrative regulations commanding deportation, Shiras said that such previous action hardly entailed approval of what the government sought to do here. Although the majority of the Court had concluded that deportation was not a punishment, there was no other way to characterize imprisonment at hard labor. With some exasperation at the intensity of the government's campaign, Shiras said it "is not consistent with the theory of our government that the legislature should, after having defined an offense as an infamous crime, find the fact of guilt and adjudge the punishment by one of its own agents."[78] Saying that the courts could not be bypassed, the Justice ruled that the provision violated both the due process clause of the Fifth Amendment and the Sixth Amendment's requirement of indictment by a grand jury. Willing to go a long way with the federal government, the Court could not square the new crime of unlawful residency punished summarily by administrative officials with the Constitution.

When the focus shifted from the Oriental to the American Indian, the majority seemed less worried about the federal government's obligation. In 1868 Congress had established a territorial government in Wyoming with the proviso that Indian rights protected by treaty not be extinguished. Less than a year later the United States signed a treaty with the Shoshonee and the Bannock Nations providing for the establishment of reservations and "the right to hunt upon the unoccupied land of the United States so long as game may be found thereon, and so long as peace subsists among the whites and Indians on the borders of the hunting districts." When Wyoming was admitted as a state in 1890 no mention was made in the enabling act about Indian rights; it simply admitted the state into the Union "on an equal footing with the original states in all respects whatever."[79] Under its police power Wyoming passed a game law and sought its enforcement against a Bannock. Wandering far from the reservation, a brave named Race Horse had killed seven elk in a large, uninhabited tract of land owned by the federal government. Obviously designed to evaluate the conflicting claims of Wyoming and the Bannocks, *Ward* v. *Race Horse* sought to determine whether the hunting rights accorded by treaty survived on federal government lands now within the boundaries of a state.

Examining the treaty as a whole, Justice White, for the Court, argued that the government, in anticipating the "necessities of civilization," made the hunting "privilege" absolutely dependent "upon the will of Congress." White was correct in asserting that the treaty provision left the hunting right subject to cancellation, but only when the peace was broken, or the government parted with title to the lands, or the land was occupied. The Justice supported his peculiar reading of the treaty by contending that otherwise Congress's creation of Yellowstone Park out of what had been previously designated hunting districts would "necessarily imply that Congress had violated the faith of the government and defrauded the Indians." Since this conclusion was unthinkable to White, he concluded that the government could not be bound to the literal terms of the treaty. Although the Justice's objective slowly began to surface, his involuted reasoning still left him considerably short of his goal. Step number two involved showing how power in the federal government became power in the state government. Relying upon precedent, White stated that Congress through legislation could supercede the provisions of a treaty. As well established as the general rule White cited was its corollary, that the terms of a treaty are not to be nullified by implication. Ignoring the corollary, he sought to show how congressional action indirectly extinguished the hunting rights. When Congress admitted Wyoming as a state on an equal footing with the others and did not reserve Indian rights as it did in the 1868 territorial act, Wyoming, White contended, gained full control over the territory within its borders. The so-called rights of the Indians, which were "essentially perishable and intended to be of a limited duration," he ruled, were subordinated to the state's police power. The alleged sanctity of treaty rights, White added, "should not be made an instrument for violating the public faith by distorting the words of a treaty, in order to imply that it conveyed rights wholly inconsistent with its language and in conflict with an act of Congress and also destructive of the rights of one of the States."[80]

As in a number of other areas, the Court here was an abetter of dominant social views. White's opinion made it clear that the Indian had little protection within the turn-of-the-century society; a scrupulous regard for rights incompatible with the tide of civilization had few supporters. Indians might well understand that the Chief Executive, with his access to military force, could renege on prior pledges and make his will dominant, but the white man talked much of his courts and the justice that was found there. Here in the highest court in the land the Indian found no justice and little sympathy, for the High Bench seemed only to encourage further incursions on the rights of the Indians. What Race Horse received was a judicial song and dance that could only be interpreted by a high priest of constitutional law. No less an apostle could fathom how the federal system could be manipulated to reach the result desired. That clear, unequivocal treaty rights could be overridden by a maneuvering of legal assumptions was probably beyond the Indian's ken, as well as that of Justice Henry Brown.

Brown's eloquent dissent illustrates well that the fallacies of the Court's opinion did not have to await the exposure of a future generation. He attacked the view that the congressional act admitting Wyoming to statehood implicitly abrogated the treaty rights of the Bannock Indians. A public treaty, Brown continued, should not be set aside on the basis of "doubtful language." Displaying a sympathy for Indian culture totally lacking in the majority's opinion, the Justice said that hunting for the Indian was a matter of survival, not of sport. Despite Wyoming's law, he continued, the public faith must be kept even as it relates to the "helpless Indian." Brown implied that a reading of state power that enables it to "deprive the Indians of their principal means of subsistence" is no less than shameful.[81] Then recognizing how the majority's opinion piles assumption upon assumption to reach a result that clearly violates the language of the treaty, he concluded that the requirement that a new state be admitted on an equal footing with the rest cannot justify an abrogation of preexisting rights.

The Justices' lack of sensitivity to minorities in American society, except in cases of the most flagrant violations of constitutional rights, was also apparent in their resolution of cases dealing with blacks. Two state murder convictions, one in Mississippi and the other in Louisiana, came before the Court. In the Mississippi case the defendant, John Gibson, was represented by two able black lawyers, but they had no success in convincing the Justices of the deficiencies of Southern justice. Their hope that the Court might change its mind and favor removal of state criminal prosecutions to the federal court upon a showing that blacks were not included on state jury lists was without foundation. Even if error had been committed in the trial, the unanimous bench ruled, its correction was beyond the revisory power of the Supreme Court. The Justices simply trusted the state courts "to see to it that the accused had a fair and impartial trial, and to set aside any verdict of guilty based on prejudice of race." Similar contentions were presented in the Louisiana case with the same result.[82]

Of far greater social significance was the Court's decision in *Plessy* v. *Ferguson*, which posed a challenge to a Louisiana act of 1890 imposing penalties upon train passengers who refused to honor the prescribed segregation pattern.[83] John Adolph Plessy refused to sit in the compartment reserved for blacks and was ejected and arrested. The Supreme Court received the case when the highest court in Louisiana denied Plessy's petition for a writ of prohibition directing the lower court judge not to proceed with a trial. In 1890 the Justices had decided that a state could command segregation on railways within the state without violating the interstate commerce clause. Now the litigation was framed in terms of whether the Louisiana statute ran afoul of either the Thirteenth or Fourteenth Amendment, or both, a claim that had been consistently rejected in the lower federal courts.[84]

Justice Brown gave the Thirteenth Amendment claim little credence, as he simply asserted that a distinction based on color "has no tendency to . . . re-establish a state of involuntary servitude." In the Fourteenth Amendment, with its due process and equal protection clauses obviously designed to protect the black man, Plessy's attorneys found greater reason to contend that the Louisiana segregation act was unconstitutional. In his majority opinion Brown did not distinguish between the due process and equal protection clauses of the amendment, often addressing both at the same time. Acknowledging that the purpose of the amendment "was to enforce the absolute equality of the two races before the law," Brown then added a caveat: ". . . in the nature of things it could not have been intended to abolish distinctions based upon color, or to enforce social, as distinguished from political, equality, or a commingling of the two races unsatisfactory to either." He assumed that both races wanted separation with its minimization of contact, and to this end he saw the police power of the state legitimately directed. Attempting to prove this legitimacy by saying that such power has long been recognized, he drew special attention to the common practice of establishing "separate schools for white and colored children."[85] Viewing segregation as the common system of race regulation, he found nothing unreasonable in the Louisiana law. Brown seemed to be saying, if segregation is so generally accepted, it cannot be unconstitutional.

To the claim that Plessy was denied the equal protection of the law Brown responded:

We consider the underlying fallacy of the plaintiff's argument to consist in the assumption that the enforced separation of the two races stamps the colored race with a badge of inferiority. If this be so, it is not by reason of anything found in the act, but solely because the colored race chooses to put that construction upon it. . . . The argument also assumes that social prejudices may be overcome by legislation, and that equal rights cannot be secured to the negro except by an enforced commingling of the two races. We cannot accept this proposition. . . . Legislation is powerless to eradicate racial instincts or to abolish distinctions based upon physical differences, and the attempt to do so can only result in accentuating the difficulties of the present situation. If the civil and political rights of both races be equal, one cannot be inferior to the other civilly or politically. If one race be inferior to the other socially, the Constitution of the United States cannot put them upon the same plane.[86]

Much of this discussion about the ineffectiveness of legislation as a tool for overcoming racial prejudice is quite beside the point, for what was involved in Plessy's case was legislation grounded in such prejudice. Plessy was not arguing that the state should command integration, just that it not forbid it.

Nowhere in the Court's fuzzy opinion is the phrase "separate but equal" actually used, but that phrase is not an inaccurate summary of the fundamental idea upon which the opinion rests. If Brown's reasoning lacked clarity, certainly the result the Court reached did not. As read by the majority, the Constitution did not interpose any obstacle to segregating the races. The Justices shared the common assumption that such separation would minimize racial conflict. In the Old South slavery had been not only a system of forced labor but also a regulator of the relationship between the races. Its abolition required a new adjustment, which was complicated by the strange mixture of fear, distrust, and envy with which whites confronted blacks. The fateful but inevitable decision of the national government at the conclusion of Reconstruction to entrust blacks to dominant white governments in the South let loose the forces of segregation. By its decision in *Plessy* v. *Ferguson* the Court did not create segregation or perhaps even spur its use, but it did for almost two generations place blacks beyond the pale of certain constitutional guarantees. The majority could do little else, for no more than the other branches of the federal government was it prepared to move beyond the social consensus.

A decision in 1896 that the Constitution precluded segregation is impossible to conceive. The Supreme Court could invalidate the income tax and count on the support of the wealthy and powerful to stay its critics, but from where would support come for forcing the states to renounce their power in regulating race relations in the only way then deemed feasible? Certainly Cleveland's administration gave no indication that the executive arm of the government would be willing to participate in this campaign. The constitutional argument in *Plessy* invited a decision that would have dealt a death blow to official segregation everywhere and would have required an active, ongoing executive supervision, wholly incompatible with the nature of the federal union in 1896.

Throughout the 1890s Harlan was the leading and often the most perceptive dissenter on the Court. After his earlier objection to the majority's resolution of the *Civil Rights Cases*, his response in *Plessy* was predictable. What was involved in the case, Harlan began, were state criminal penalties for "the use of a public highway by citizens of the United States solely upon the basis of race." The Justice promptly condemned such legislation as "inconsistent, not only with the equality of rights which pertains to citizenship, National and State, but with the personal liberty enjoyed by every one within the United States." He exposed the majority's reliance on state decisions, noting that most of them antedated the Reconstruction amendments and that none of them was relevant to the constitutional issue before the Court. Reading the Thirteenth Amendment, the Kentuckian determined that the state act should fall, for that amendment forbad "any burdens or disabilities that constitute badges of slavery or servitude." Together the three Reconstruction amendments, he continued, "removed the race line from our governmental systems." To the majority's contention that segregation was not in itself discriminatory, Harlan responded by lifting the veil and revealing that the clear purpose of the statute was to exclude blacks from the company of whites. "If a white man and a black man choose to occupy the same public conveyance on a public highway," he said, "it is their right to do so, and no government, proceeding alone on grounds of race, can prevent it without infringing the personal liberty of each."[87] If race is a legitimate base for separation, Harlan asked, what about religion or citizenship? The majority is wrong, he contended, for the issue is not the reasonableness of the regulation but the authority of the state to act at all.

Condemning the Court for a decision fully as "pernicious" as the one in *Dred Scott*, the Kentuckian asserted that the "Constitution is color-blind." Interpreting the Civil War and the Reconstruction amendments as commanding that our institutions be purged of notions of racial superiority, he said that state enactments "conceived in hostility to, and enacted for the purpose of humiliating citizens of the United States of a particular race" are designed to "defeat the legitimate results of the war" and render true peace impossible. With uncanny insight, the Justice continued: "The destinies of the two races, in this country, are indissolubly linked together, and the interests of both require that the common government of all shall not permit the seeds of race hate to be planted under the sanction of law." Nothing less, he said, than a new form of slavery is rearing its head in such "sinister legislation." Condemning the majority for the "legal inferiority" it had imposed on blacks, the irate Justice concluded: "The thin disguise of 'equal' accommodations for passengers in railroad coaches will not mislead anyone, or atone for the wrong this day done."[88] So thoroughly anticipatory of a later generation's views was Harlan that the reader of his opinion cannot help but marvel.

Although the Justice, like his colleagues, did not wish to examine the realities faced by black criminal defendants in the state courts, his opinion here realistically grapples with the meaning of segregation. Perhaps Harlan's personal understanding of the Southern life, enabled him to expose the distortive abstractions of the Court's opinion. As is quite evident, Harlan was a peculiar white Southerner.[89] There were other men from that region on the High Bench, but none felt any inclination to support this renegade.

With the *Plessy* decision in late May 1896 the term came to an end. A Court that had so consistently suffered membership losses over the past six years was still at less than full strength. David Brewer missed a few months of the term and did not participate in a number of important cases, including *Wong Wing*, *Race Horse*, and *Plessy*. His absence was caused by service as chairman on a commission established by President Cleveland to determine for purposes of American foreign policy the boundary line between British Guiana and Venezuela.[90] The Kansan's absence was temporary, but age was catching up with his uncle, Stephen J. Field.

For the last few years Field had alternated between periods of lucidity and fuzziness. In recognizing these growing physical and mental problems, Fuller assigned the Californian only three opinions during the term.[91] With Brewer writing only sixteen opinions, a substantial maldistribution of the work load resulted. Fuller shouldered more than his share with sixty opinions; Brown wrote forty-three; and Harlan, Shiras, and White each contributed over thirty. Death had a way of claiming those Justices who could no longer meet their obligations, but the record is not barren of men who lapsed into senility and posed special problems for the Court. Officially a senile Justice could cling to his seat until death; he could not be removed against his will, though this fact did not preclude the exertion of both internal and external pressure for his resignation. As the Justices left for vacation, they hoped that a looming battle with Stephen Field could be avoided.

NOTES

1. Act of February 6, 1889, ch. 113, 25 Stat. 655, 656.
2. Glenn Shirley, *Law West of Fort Smith: A History of Frontier Justice in the Indian Territory, 1834-1896* (New York: Henry Holt & Co., 1957), pp. 35-39; and Fred H. Harrington, *Hanging Judge* (Caldwell, Idaho: Caxton Printers, 1951), pp. 58-59, 122-23, 129.
3. Shirley, *Law West of Fort Smith*, pp. 209-37 (appendices from which statistics are collated), 144-46.
4. Crumpton v. United States, 138 U.S. 361 (1891); Alexander v. United States, 138 U.S. 353 (1891); Boyd v. United States, 142 U.S. 450 (1892); and Lewis v. United States, 146 U.S. 370, 379 (1892).
5. Hall v. United States, 150 U.S. 76 (1893); Graves v. United States, 150 U.S. 118 (1893); Brown v. United States, 150 U.S. 93 (1893); Smith v. United States, 151 U.S. 50 (1894); Hicks v. United States, 150 U.S. 442 (1893); Gourko [sic] v. United States, 153 U.S. 183 (1894); Allen v. United States, 150 U.S. 551 (1893); Hickory v. United States, 151 U.S. 303 (1894); and Starr v. United States, 153 U.S. 614 (1894).
6. Allen v. United States, 157 U.S. 675 (1895); Brown v. United States, 159 U.S. 100, 102 (1895); Johnson *alias* Overton v. United States, 157 U.S. 320 (1895); and Thompson v. United States, 155 U.S. 271 (1894).
7. Luckey v. United States, 163 U.S. 692 (1896); Thornton v. United States, 163 U.S. 707 (1896); Buck v. United States 163 U.S. 678 (1896); Wilkey *alias* Davis v. United States, 163 U.S. 712 (1896); Goldsby *alias* Cherokee Bill v. United States, 163 U.S. 688 (1896); Isaacs v. United States, 159 U.S. 487 (1895); Goldsby *alias* Cherokee Bill v. United States, 160 U.S. 70 (1895); Pierce v. United States, 160 U.S. 355 (1896); Wilson v. United States, 162 U.S. 613 (1896); Lucas v. United States, 163 U.S. 612 (1896); Carver v. United States, 160 U.S. 553 (1896); Davis v. United States, 160 U.S. 469 (1895); Hickory v. United States, 160 U.S. 408 (1896); Alberty v. United States, 162 U.S. 499 (1896); Smith v. United States, 161 U.S. 85, 89 (1896); and Allison v. United States, 160 U.S. 203, 217 (1895).
8. Davis v. United States, 165 U.S. 373 (1897); Nofire v. United States, 164 U.S. 657 (1897); Carver v. United States, 164 U.S. 694 (1897); Brown v. United States, 164 U.S. 221 (1896); Starr v. United States, 165 U.S. 627 (1897); Mills v. United States, 164 U.S. 644 (1897); and King v. United States, 164 U.S. 701 (1897).
9. Kettenring v. United States, 168 U.S. 703 (1897).
10. Statistics compiled from Shirley, *Law West of Fort Smith*, pp. 222-31.
11. Brewer's position is revealed in his dissents in the following cases: Hicks v. United States, 150 U.S. 442 (1893); Allen v. United States, 150 U.S. 551 (1893); and Brown v. United States, 164 U.S. 221 (1896).
12. Shirley, *Law West of Fort Smith*, pp. 156-57, 192-94.
13. Ibid., pp. 156-57.
14. Harrington, *Hanging Judge*, pp. 185-86; and Shirley, *Law West of Fort Smith*, pp. 186-87.
15. Shirley, *Law West of Fort Smith*, pp. 187-89.
16. Ibid., pp. 187-90.

17. Not again until the 1960s, and then by means of interpreting the constitutional reach of the Bill of Rights, would the Court become so involved in an active role in the administration of criminal justice.

18. For a more comprehensive treatment of the Supreme Court's consideration of the Parker cases, of the judge himself, and of the environment in which he worked, see John E. Semonche, "Conflicting Views on Crime and Punishment in the 1890s: 'Hanging Judge' Parker Confronts the United States Supreme Court," publication forthcoming.

19. Connecticut Mutual Life Insurance Co. v. Akens, 150 U.S. 468 (1893); and *In re Lockwood*, 154 U.S. 116 (1894).

20. Reagan v. Farmers' Loan & Trust Co., 154 U.S. 362 (1894); Mobile & Ohio R.R. v. Tennessee, 153 U.S. 486 (1894); Keokuk & Western R.R. v. Missouri, 152 U.S. 301 (1894); New York & New England R.R. v. Bristol, 151 U.S. 556 (1894); Ashley v. Ryan, 153 U.S. 436 (1894); and Lawton v. Steele, 152 U.S. 133, 144 (1894).

21. United States v. Illinois Central R.R., 154 U.S. 225 (1894); Barden v. Northern Pacific R.R., 154 U.S. 288 (1894); and U.S., Department of Justice, *Annual Report of the Attorney-General*, 1894, p. v.

22. ICC v. Brimson, 154 U.S. 447, 155 U.S. 3 (1894).

23. For Coxey's Army, see Donald L. McMurry, *Coxey's Army: A Study of the Industrial Army Movement of 1894* (Boston: Little, Brown & Co., 1929); and Arnold M. Paul, *Conservative Crisis and the Rule of Law: Attitudes of the Bar and Bench, 1887-1895*, Torchbook ed. (New York: Harper and Row, 1969), pp. 132-42.

24. Quoted in Edward S. Corwin, *Court over Constitution: A Study of Judicial Review as an Instrument of Popular Government* (Princeton: Princeton University Press, 1938), pp. 197-98.

25. Wilson-Gorman Tariff Act, ch. 349, 28 Stat. 509, 553, 556 (1894); and Paul, *Conservative Crisis*, pp. 160-62.

26. Irving Schiffman, "Howell E. Jackson," in *The Justices of the United States Supreme Court 1789-1969: Their Lives and Major Opinions*, ed. Leon Friedman and Fred L. Israel, 4 vols. (New York: R. R. Bowker Co. and Chelsea House Publishers, 1969), 2:1605.

27. Lau Ow Bew v. United States, 144 U.S. 47 (1892); and Lem Moon Sing v. United States, 158 U.S. 538 (1895).

28. Chicago, Kansas & Western R.R. v. Pontius, 157 U.S. 209 (1895); Baltimore & Potomac R.R. v. Mackey, 157 U.S. 72 (1895); Emery v. Missouri, 156 U.S. 296 (1895); Pittsburgh & Southern Coal Co. v. Louisiana, 156 U.S. 590 (1895); St. Louis & San Francisco Ry. v. Gill, 156 U.S. 649 (1895); and New York, Lake Erie & Western R.R. v. Pennsylvania, 158 U.S. 431 (1895).

29. Sherman Antitrust Act, ch. 647, 26 Stat. 209 (1890); William F. Swindler, *Court and Constitution in the Twentieth Century: The Old Legality 1889-1932* (Indianapolis: Bobbs-Merrill Co., 1969), pp. 27-28; and Allan Nevins, *Grover Cleveland: A Study in Courage* (New York: Dodd, Mead & Co., 1933), p. 671.

30. United States v. E. C. Knight Co., 156 U.S. 1, 13 (1895).

31. Id. at 19, 35.

32. Id. at 42, 43.

33. Paul, *Conservative Crisis*, pp. 182-84.

34. Robert T. Swaine, *The Cravath Firm and Its Predecessors, 1819-1947*, 3 vols. (New York: privately printed by Ad Press for Cravath, Swaine & Moore, 1946-48), 1:518-22.

35. Paul, *Conservative Crisis*, p. 190, n. 13.

36. Because the constitutionality of a federal act was the issue, the Court permitted the government to argue, though, of course, the United States was not a party to the suit. The legal system does result in private parties litigating matters of supreme governmental interest, and, as a matter of practice, the Court regularly grants the request of the federal government to file briefs and participate in the argument of the case.

37. Advocates play an important role in the Court's decision-making process, though rarely is credit given even when the writer of opinion in the case borrows significantly from the lawyers' briefs and oral arguments. The lawyers are part of the ensemble, quite pleased with their contribution to the production's success and usually equally pleased with their low public visibility. For a focus on the role lawyers played in some work of the Court in the latter nineteenth and early twentieth centuries, see Benjamin R. Twiss, *Lawyers and the Constitution: How Laissez Faire Came to the Supreme Court* (Princeton: Princeton University Press, 1942).

38. Pollock v. Farmers' Loan & Trust Co., 157 U.S. 429 (1895). The oral arguments are included in the official report of the case.

39. This oral argument is more fully reported in the Lawyers' Edition of Supreme Court Reports, published by Lawyers Co-operative Publishing Co., Rochester, New York, and cited L. Ed. For the quoted extracts, see Pollock v. Farmers' Loan & Trust Co., 39 L. Ed. 759, 788, 786 (1895).

40. Pollock v. Farmers' Loan & Trust Co., 157 U.S. 429, 502 (1895).

41. Id. at 531-32.

42. Id. at 532, 534, 553.

43. See Willard L. King, *Melville Weston Fuller: Chief Justice of the United States, 1888-1910*, Phoenix ed. (Chicago: University of Chicago Press, 1967), p. 204; and Louis B. Boudin, *Government by Judiciary*, 2 vols. (New York: William Godwin, 1932), 2:224-26. For a scholarly critique of Fuller's opinion, see Corwin, *Court over Constitution*, pp. 177-209.

44. Pollock v. Farmers' Loan & Trust Co., 157 U.S. 429, 583 (1895).

45. Springer v. United States, 102 U.S. 586 (1881); and Pollock v. Farmers' Loan & Trust Co., 157 U.S. 429, 583 (1895).

46. Pollock v. Farmers' Loan & Trust Co., 157 U.S. 429, 607 (1895).

47. Id. at 650-52.

48. See, for instance, *New York World*, May 7, 1895.

49. For brief summaries of the arguments, which this time were not printed in the official report, see Sidney Ratner, *American Taxation: Its History as a Social Force in Democracy* (New York: W.W. Norton & Co., 1942), pp. 206-8.

50. Pollock v. Farmers' Loan & Trust Co., 158 U.S. 601 (1895).

51. *New York Sun*, May 22, 1895; David G. Farrelly, "Harlan's Dissent in the Pollock Case," *Southern California Law Review* 24 (February 1951): 175-82; and Elmer Ellis, "Public Opinion and the Income Tax," *Mississippi Valley Historical Review* 27 (September 1940):177. The courtroom scene on the day the opinion was rendered is described by Henry H. Ingersoll, "The Revolution of 20th May, 1895," *Proceedings of the Fourteenth Annual Meeting of the Bar Association of Tennessee* (1895):161-80.

52. Pollock v. Farmers' Loan & Trust Co., 158 U.S. 601, 664-65, 671, 685 (1895).

53. Harlan considered much of the criticism unfair, suggesting it came from "large newspapers with vast incomes." Farrelly, "Harlan's Dissent," pp. 178-81.

54. Pollock v. Farmers' Loan & Trust Co., 158 U.S. 601, 689, 695 (1895).

55. Id. at 706, 715.

56. The phrase *vascillating jurist* was coined by Corwin in *Court over Constitution*, p. 194; and George Shiras, III, *Justice George Shiras, Jr. of Pittsburgh*, ed. and compl. Winfield Shiras (Pittsburgh: University of Pittsburgh Press, 1953), pp. 168-73.

57. Charles Warren, *The Supreme Court in United States History*, rev. ed., 2 vols. (Boston: Little, Brown & Co., 1926), 2:700; Charles Evans Hughes, *The Supreme Court of the United States* (New York: Columbia University Press, 1928), p. 54; and the historical search is ably summarized and documented in Paul, *Conservative Crisis*, pp. 214-18. Other attempts at solving the mystery can be found in Corwin, *Court over Constitution*, pp. 194-201; Shiras, *Justice George Shiras, Jr.*, pp. 168-83, and King, *Fuller*, pp. 214-21.

58. Gray to Fuller, April 5, 1895, in King, *Fuller*, p. 204.

59. Harlan's letter to his sons dated May 24, 1895, in Farrelly, "Harlan's Dissent," pp. 178-81.

60. Warren, *Supreme Court*, 2:703, n. 1.

61. Paul, *Conservative Crisis*, pp. 134-42, 153.

62. Pettibone v. United States, 148 U.S. 197 (1893); and *In re* Debs, 158 U.S. 564 (1895).

63. *In re* Debs, 158 U.S. 564, 581, 582, 584 (1895).

64. See William D. Lewis, "Protest Against Administering Criminal Law by Injunction—the Debs Case," *American Law Register & Review* 42 (December 1894):879-83, Charles N. Gregory, "Government by Injunction," *Harvard Law Review* 11 (March 25, 1898):487-511, and W.G. Peterkin, "Government by Injunction," *Virginia Law Register*, 3 (December 1898):549-63. "Government by Injunction" received further currency when it was included in the Democratic party platform in 1896, found in Kirk H. Porter and Donald B. Johnson, comps., *National Party Platforms 1840-1960*, 2d ed. (Urbana: University of Illinois Press, 1961), p. 99.

65. See Alan F. Westin, "The Supreme Court, the Populist Movement and the Campaign of 1896," *Journal of Politics* 15 (February 1953):3-41.

With obvious references to the *Pollock* and *Debs* decisions, the Democratic platform read:

We declare that it is the duty of Congress to use all the Constitutional power which remains after that decision, or which may come from its reversal by the court as it may hereafter be constituted, so that the burdens of taxation may be equally and impartially laid, to the end that wealth may bear its due proportion of the expense of the Government. . . .

We denounce arbitrary interference by Federal authorities in local affairs as a violation of the Constitution of the United States, and a crime against free institutions, and we especially object to government by injunction as a new and highly dangerous form of oppression by which Federal Judges, in contempt of the laws of the States and rights of citizens, become at once legislators, judges and executioners; and we approve the bill passed at the House of Representatives, relative to contempts in Federal courts and providing for trials by jury in certain cases of contempt. (Porter and Johnson, *National Party Platforms*, pp. 98-99).

66. Stuart S. Nagel, "Court-Curbing Periods in American History," *Vanderbilt Law Review* 18 (June 1965):926.

67. Richard Skolnik, "Rufus Peckham," in *Justices of the Supreme Court*, 3:1693-94.

68. For instance, see Phoenix Fire & Marine Insurance Co. v. Tennessee, 161 U.S. 174 (1896); Central Pacific R.R. v. California, 162 U.S. 91 (1896); Bank of Commerce v. Tennessee, 163 U.S. 416 (1896); and United States v. Perkins, 163 U.S. 625 (1896).

69. Illinois Central R.R. v. Illinois, 163 U.S. 142 (1896); and Hennington v. Georgia, 163 U.S. 299 (1896).

70. Geer v. Connecticut, 161 U.S. 519, 532, 544 (1896).

71. See Texas & Pacific Ry. v. ICC, 162 U.S. 197 (1896).

72. Counselman v. Hitchcock, 142 U.S. 547 (1892); and Brown v. Walker, 161 U.S. 591, 608 (1896).

73. Brown v. Walker, 161 U.S. 591, 627 (1896).

74. Louisville & Nashville R.R. v. Kentucky, 161 U.S. 677, 701 (1896).

75. United States v. Gettysburg Electric Ry., 160 U.S. 668 (1896).

76. Id. at 680.

77. Id. at 681, 683.

78. Wong Wing v. United States, 163 U.S. 228, 237 (1896).

79. Ward v. Race Horse, 163 U.S. 504, 505, 506 (1896).

80. Id. at 507, 509, 510, 515, 516.

81. Id. at 517, 518.

82. Gibson v. Mississippi, 162 U.S. 565, 585 (1896); and Murray v. Louisiana, 163 U.S. 101 (1896).

83. The background of the *Plessy* case is well developed in C. Vann Woodward, "The Case of the Louisiana Traveler," in *Quarrels That Have Shaped the Constitution*, ed. John A. Garraty (New York: Harper & Row, 1964), pp. 145-58.

84. For instance, see United States v. Dodge, 25 F. Cas. 882 (No. 14, 976) (W. D. Texas 1877); Bertonneau v. Board of Directors of City Schools, 3 F. Cas. 294 (No. 1, 361) (C. C. La. 1878); and Green v. Bridgeton, 10 F. Cas. 1090 (No. 5, 754) (S. D. Ga. 1879).

85. Plessy v. Ferguson, 163 U.S. 537, 543, 544 (1896).

86. Id. at 551-52.

87. Id. at 553, 555, 557.

88. Id. at 559, 560, 563, 562.

89. See Alan F. Westin, "John Marshall Harlan and the Constitutional Rights of Negroes: The Transformation of a Southerner," *Yale Law Journal* 66 (April 1957):637-710.

90. King, *Fuller*, pp. 250-51.

91. One of his opinions was so confusing that he had to clarify it when the Court denied a petition for a rehearing in the case. See Telfener v. Russ, 162 U.S. 170, 163 U.S. 100 (1896).

chapter 4

A "GIANT" FALLS, BUT HIS SHADOW LINGERS, 1896-1900

Stephen J. Field was in his seat to the right of the Chief when the Court convened for the 1896 term. Even though Grover Cleveland would be leaving the presidency soon, Field seemed little inclined to step down. Both the presidency and the chief justiceship had eluded him, but he might well establish a new record for longevity in office. The existing record was held by John Marshall, but breaking that record required service beyond the present term. Field's health was failing and his periods of lucidity were of shorter duration, but his will remained strong.[1]

Fuller and his colleagues pondered the question of how best to convince the Justice that the time for retirement had come. The case of Justice Robert C. Grier suggested a solution. In 1869 Grier was growing increasingly senile and his inconsistent votes in conference revealed a befuddled mind. Ultimately a committee of Grier's colleagues prevailed upon the Justice to retire. That delegation included Stephen J. Field. Late in 1896 Harlan was deputized to stir the Californian's memory of this episode. The long-time colleague found Field half asleep on the settee in the robing room. After arousing him Harlan reminded the Justice of the Grier matter. Gradually absorbing the subject, Field's eyes sparkled and he vigorously responded: "Yes! And a dirtier day's work I never did in my life!" Somewhat taken aback by the force of Field's response, the Kentuckian reported his failure to the Chief. For the time being the conspirators were stymied.[2]

Although the Justices rejected repeated attempts to immunize property from state regulation, they did in two notable cases of the 1896 term find in the due process clause of the Fourteenth Amendment new and sweeping meanings. In the first of the two decisions announced on that same winter day, *Allgeyer* v. *Louisiana*, the Court announced a general principle of due process that would haunt the Justices and American society for the next four decades. Louisiana had passed a law seeking to tighten regulation of the marine insurance business by assessing a $1,000 fine on any person or organization obtaining insurance on property within the state from a firm not licensed to do such business. Allgeyer had an open marine policy with a New

York firm; his obligation was to notify that firm when he was ready to ship cotton covered under the policy out of state. This he did by letter. He was prosecuted in Louisiana and convicted of violating the state law. His argument in the Supreme Court was that the statute was a violation of due process of law and that it could not be applied to a contract made in New York. Both sides conceded that the contract had been made in New York and that certain actions had been taken by Allgeyer in Louisiana that would bring him within the terms of the state act. The highest court in Louisiana had concluded that any restraint on liberty found in such a situation "must give way to the greater right of the collective people in the assertion of well-defined policy, designed and intended for the general welfare."[3]

For a unanimous Court, Justice Peckham responded. Acknowledging that the police power was broad, he said it still could not justify the state's treading upon constitutionally protected rights. If insurance had then been recognized as a subject of commerce, the state's restriction would obviously have infringed the commerce clause.[4] But since this route was closed, Peckham had to deal with the protection of the citizen under the Fourteenth Amendment. Emphasizing that the contract was made out of state, even though it concerned goods within the state, the Justice concluded that a right to contract was embraced by the due process clause. Focusing on the subject of notification to the New York insurance company, he said that Allgeyer was free to so perform, and the state, being bound by the federal constitution, could not restrict such freedom. The presence of the citizen, Peckham continued, did not alone vest the state with the type of control it sought to exercise here. In the freedom to pursue a calling, the citizen could make the necessary contracts to conduct his business. Since Louisiana sought to forbid the making and performance of such contracts by imposing a penalty on a resident contractor, the Justice concluded, its action violated the due process clause. The Court had arrived at a novel conclusion, and Peckham sought to buttress it by broad language about the meaning of the Fourteenth Amendment:

The liberty mentioned in that amendment means not only the right of the citizen to be free from the mere physical restraint of his person, as by incarceration, but the term is deemed to embrace the right of the citizen to be free in the enjoyment of all his faculties; to be free to use them in all lawful ways; to live and work where he will; to earn his livelihood by any lawful calling; to pursue any livelihood or avocation, and for that purpose to enter into all contracts which may be proper, necessary and essential to his carrying out to a successful conclusion the purposes above mentioned.[5]

This exposition is somewhat question begging in its use of the term *lawful*, but it provides the base Peckham sought.

Peckham's language, which alternately was narrow and broad, read into the due process clause of the Fourteenth Amendment a protection of the liberty to contract. The nineteenth century was the age of contract law in

American legal history, but only here late in the century, when the social and economic conditions of society were in a rapid state of transition leading to gross inequality in the bargaining process, was some federal constitutional guarantee found to protect this essentially private lawmaking process.[6]

Before *Allgeyer* read new protection into the Constitution, a state could place what restrictions it desired upon future contracts. *Allgeyer* still left the state free to prescribe requirements for out-of-state insurance companies seeking to do business within the state and to punish agents of such companies for violations, but it also provided an exception that could undermine state regulatory policy. Apparently the state's policy could be circumvented by the elimination of an agent; the citizen was free to enter into a contract of insurance with a foreign company and insure goods in the state free from any local interference. This abrupt break with the past did not escape contemporary notice and criticism.[7]

The second case in which the Court found a sweeping prohibition housed within the simple language of the due process clause was *Chicago, Burlington, & Quincy Railroad Company* v. *Chicago. Allgeyer* stole the public spotlight in part because the majority upheld the governmental interest in the *Chicago* case. But those who looked behind the result found in the case as revolutionary a reading of the due process clause as that announced in *Allgeyer* and one that could be made only by implicitly overruling a precedent less than two decades old. Chief Justice Fuller did not participate in the case, apparently because of his earlier service as counsel for the railroad, but the remaining eight Justices, including the dissenter Brewer, agreed on the general principles announced in the Court's opinion. Chicago had decided to build a street, a portion of which would cross the railroad's tracks; acting under the power of eminent domain the city condemned the railroad's property. In the judicial proceedings the railroad was awarded $1 as compensation by a jury, even though it had lost property approximately the size of other landholders who had been awarded compensation of $5,000 and even though it would now be forced to spend money to make the new crossing safe.[8]

In appealing from the state supreme court, which upheld the decision, counsel for the railroad insisted that the company had been deprived of its property without due process of law. Counsel for the city said that the matter was solely a matter of local law and that no federal question had been presented; the city's case was buttressed by the Court decision in *Davidson* v. *New Orleans* holding that the due process clause of the Fourteenth Amendment gave the federal courts no authority to supervise the eminent domain power of local government. In 1878 the Court had reached this conclusion on the basis that the Fifth Amendment, which includes the identical due process clause found in the Fourteenth, contains additional language saying "nor shall private property be taken for public use, without just compensation."[9]

In the intervening years new personnel made the Court more receptive to the due process claim. Harlan, for the majority, did not directly overrule the *Davidson* case; in fact, he quoted approvingly from it and disguised the fact that the Court had come to a very different result. The Justice denied that a trial in conformance with duly respected procedures in which the party has a right to be heard exhausts the meaning of the due process clause in the Fourteenth Amendment. "In determining what is due process of law," Harlan ruled, "regard must be had to substance, not to form." Just as government arbitrarily taking the property of one and giving it to another would violate the prohibition of the Fourteenth Amendment, he continued, so, too, would a public taking without just compensation. This is so, he said, in any country where a judiciary has the responsibility to interpret a written constitution. Just compensation for a public taking of property is, he continued, "a vital principle of republican institutions."[10]

Having boldly asserted the general principle, avoiding entirely the fact that while such wording is included in the Fifth Amendment it is absent from the Fourteenth Amendment, Harlan went on to determine whether in this case the principle had been violated. His surprising answer was no, a result he reached by concluding that the federal courts are precluded by the Seventh Amendment from reinspecting a fact determination made by a jury. Since the Justice concluded that no errors of law are found in the judge's charge to the jury, the jury's verdict must stand. The fact that the railroad must incur expense to make the new crossing safe, Harlan said, is simply a burden it must bear since it took its charter subject to the power of government to provide for the safety of its citizens. Such a damage to property, the Kentuckian added, is not within the scope of the due process and eminent domain clauses of the Constitution. Finally, to the claim that the equal protection of the laws had been denied by the vast differences in compensation to other landholders in comparison to the railroad, the Justice said this inequality is justified on the basis that the other owners were deprived of the entire use of their property while the railroad still retained the use for which the property was held, namely, the authority to run its tracks over it.

Although indicating his support for the Court's broad delineation of the meaning of due process in eminent domain proceedings, Brewer in dissent expressed dismay at the majority's avoidance of the principle's application in the case. Since the Court had clearly stated that no governmental department, including the judicial, could take property without just compensation, how, he asked, could the Court carve out an exception for a jury verdict. The Kansan lamented that the "abundant promises of the fore part of the opinion vanish into nothing when the conclusion is reached."[11]

Brewer's lament provides a most illuminating insight into the activist Court of this era. A majority of, and often all, the Justices seemed quite willing to read sweeping principles into the law of due process, which, if applied in conformance with the breadth of their statement, would have had a devastating effect on the ability of state and local governments to respond to the needs of society. But the way the majority habitually coped with such principles was to temper logical deduction in favor of a determination of whether within the total facts of a case their application seemed advisable. Other judicial decision makers before and since have preferred to be more cautious in making sweeping constitutional pronouncements, inclined more to pick their way through the cases toward a qualified general statement, but the activist Court of the 1890s was attracted to the formulation of a general rule, the application of which it would judge anew with practically each relevant case.

More than any other tendency in this Court's approach, this one has led observers astray. A concentration on the Justices' general pronouncements of constitutional law distorts the picture of what the Court was actually doing. The reach for broad principles gave the Court a formalistic look, but repeatedly and consistently it responded pragmatically to the facts, seemingly little troubled by the disparity between the broad statement and the result reached. Brewer was not immune to this pragmatic approach, but here his assessment of the facts led him to the conclusion that the case in which the new principle was announced was one in which it should be applied. The strange feature of the *Chicago* case is that despite the unqualified language of Harlan's view of the relation between due process and the power of eminent domain, the principle was modified in the very case in which it was so boldly proclaimed. In *Allgeyer* the new principle of a freedom to contract was both proclaimed and applied, but concern about the Court's unthinking application of the new doctrine in the future was premature. One thing was certain—the general freedom to contract would extend only so far as the Justices felt comfortable in extending it. As a group, they showed an amazing lack of reverence for general rules of decision making.

The other facet of *Chicago, Burlington, & Quincy Railroad Company* v. *Chicago* concerns the Court's willingness to read the due process clause of the Fourteenth Amendment to encompass specific wording found in the Bill of Rights. In their concern for the property interest the Justices were willing to supervise the exercise of the eminent domain power by states and municipalities. This first step, however, brought them no closer to accepting Harlan's view that the due process clause incorporated the entire Bill of Rights and made it applicable to state and local government. But what has not been adequately recognized is that Harlan in his opinion formulated an alternative approach to the goal he sought. This approach focused on the due process clause, which, having been accepted as a substantive check upon the states, can now be read as a general requirement that the states act fairly and justly in dealings with their citizens. Fairness and justice are determined by the Justices within the particular context of both the case and the times. In the *Chicago* case the idea that government could take property without being burdened with the payment of just compensation struck the Justices as beyond the pale of responsible government. So the constitutional requirement that state and local government pay a fair price for a public taking was made binding not because of its concrete formulation in the Fifth Amendment but rather because it was no less than a matter of essential fairness protected by the due process clause of the Fourteenth Amendment.[12]

Almost a generation would pass before the Court would be willing to embrace this approach to find in the due process clause other provisions spelled out in the Bill of Rights, but the path was charted clearly in 1897. Harlan had failed to win his colleagues or the vast majority of future Justices to his view that the due process clause in the Fourteenth Amendment was designed to be a shorthand method of making the Bill of Rights applicable to the states, but the *ad hoc* approach he used in the *Chicago* case would eventually be used to accomplish approximately the same result.[13] Despite the public wrath often triggered by a particular decision that would periodically descend upon the activist Court of this era, the men on the High Court, were, in fact, forging a new body of constitutional law.

Although Louisiana could not restrain its citizens from making out-of-state insurance contracts, and all governmental units were bound to pay just compensation for the taking of property, the Court continued to speak approvingly about the reach of the police power.[14] For instance, the Justices had no difficulty in upholding a conviction of a man for making a speech on the Boston Common without obtaining a license from the mayor. Talking in terms of the right of the state government to regulate the use of public land, Justice White rejected the claim that any individual right was violated. The Louisianian approved the words of Oliver Wendell Holmes, Jr., who, in the state court opinion, had equated the power of the legislature over public areas with that of an individual over his own home.[15]

Cases in earlier terms had demonstrated that the Justices were willing to give states considerable latitude in taxing interstate corporations by placing a stamp of approval on many differing schemes for determining the portion of the company's property that could legitimately be subject to the state's taxing power. A series of cases during the present term, many concerning the Adams Express Company, the largest such company in the nation, asked the Court again to rule that the states had transgressed constitutional boundaries. Presenting the argument for Adams Express, James C. Carter said that the inequities imposed, if carried out by all the states, would destroy the company. In all the cases the Court divided five to four in favor of upholding state action. Fuller, supported by Gray, Brewer, Shiras, and Peckham, wrote the majority opinions.[16] Lurking behind the Court's resolution in favor of the state's taxing authority was a recognition of the difficulty of evaluating the company's property within the state and an acceptance of the premise that in the absence of any federal taxes these large corporations would escape all taxation if such state schemes were deemed unconstitutional.

White, the dissenters' consistent spokesman, continued to emphasize Carter's arguments that approval of one state's taxing system was simply an invitation for other states to join in and wreck the finances of a company. To the repeated argument that a contrary decision would enable such companies to escape taxation, White said, this was no reason to violate the Constitution. He saw sufficient congressional power to remedy the situation and was not moved by the argument that we have "entered a new era requiring new and progressive adjudications" by the Court.[17] White said that our institutions were sufficient to cope with the problem without the distortion of misguided constitutional interpretation.

Brewer, for the majority, however, had the last word on the matter in his denial of a petition for a rehearing of one of the cases:

> In conclusion, let us say that this is eminently a practical age; that courts must recognize things as they are and as possessing a value which is accorded to them in the markets of the world, and that no finespun theories about situs should interfere to enable these large corporations, whose business is carried on through many States, to escape from bearing in each State such burden of taxation as a fair distribution of the actual value of their property among those States requires.[18]

Often Brewer vigorously protected property interests, but here he was sensitive to the real issue. Just as his uncle Stephen Field often looked beyond the facts of the case to the real world, so, too, did Brewer. White's dissents in the cases were well done and logically appealing, but the bare majority favored the state's interest, thereby avoiding the possibility of immunizing the most affluent corporations from taxation. Two years earlier the Court was condemned for its activism in the income tax decisions, but that same activism, sensitive to the broader issues behind the cases, resulted here in accretions to public treasuries. A more passive Court certainly would have upheld the 1894 income tax, but it might also have been persuaded by White's reasoning in these tax cases.

As previously noted, Congress had passed legislation that dealt with traditional subjects of the state's police power by drawing upon its taxing and postal authority. A federal tax on margarine had been imposed by Congress in 1886, and the statute provided that dealers making sales of the product not packaged and branded as directed by administrative officials "shall be fined for each offense not more than $1,000 and be imprisoned not more than two years." Israel C. Kollock was convicted of selling a half pound of margarine without the requisite packaging and stamps. He petitioned for habeas corpus on grounds that Congress had no authority to protect the consumer and that a crime could not be defined by administrative officers. Fuller, for a unanimous Court, rejected these contentions. The crime, he said, was defined by statute, though determinations as to packaging and the particular brands required as evidence of complying with the revenue act were left to administrative officials. Fuller labeled the measure a revenue act and said that protection of the consumer was not its primary object. Disingenuous though this may seem, the Court consistently accepted the characterization that Congress used in passing such legislation. The requirements of packaging, stamps, and brands were incidental to the revenue purpose, the Chief continued, and the congressional directive was sufficiently clear so no legitimate claim could be made that elements of the crime were left to administrative definition.[19] With the Court's sanction, the federal taxing act was a much more effective measure in halting the growth of the margarine industry than a host of state regulations.

During the term the Court was faced with two habeas corpus petitions in which the petitioners claimed their personal service had been forced. Damages caused by the breaking of a contract can be assessed, but a court cannot command personal service. In the first case a railroad engineer claimed he had resigned from his employment and could not be jailed for contempt for refusing to obey a court order that his train carry a particular railroad car. The Court found his resignation spurious, since his subsequent actions bespoke a continued service with the railroad. In *Robertson* v. *Baldwin* the Justices could not escape the claim that personal service was being compelled, for the seaman who jumped ship spoke eloquently with his feet. Congress had conferred upon certain local officials the power to arrest deserting seamen without a warrant and deliver them on board the vessel. Robertson and his fellow deserters claimed this process violated their Fifth Amendment rights and that the Thirteenth Amendment's provision banning involuntary servitude precluded this compulsion of forced personal service.[20]

Brown, for the Court, disposed of the claim that Congress had unlawfully delegated judicial power to state officials by citing some old cases and arbitrarily classifying such a summary procedure as not within the constitutional definition of the judicial power. So went the petitioners' Fifth Amendment arguments. But was not Congress ordaining involuntary servitude in violation of the Thirteenth Amendment? Brown contended that if the seamen agreed to the terms of an employment contract, their service under it could not be termed involuntary. Next, he said that if such a transaction was within the letter of the amendment, it was not within its spirit. From a historical base he argued that the often unequivocal language of the Constitution must be read with the exceptions implicit at the time the language was constructed. He contended that seamen and military men have always been regarded as exceptions. Then in a comparative law survey he tried to demonstrate how seamen, because of their indispensable service in completing the voyage of the ship, have been consistently treated differently in the law. Such legislation existed sixty years before the Thirteenth Amendment, the Justice continued, and similar foreign legislation stretched much further back in time. He saw the protection of seamen in federal legislation against fraud and cruelty of masters, boardinghouse keepers, and so on as the *quid pro quo* for the disabilities imposed. Harlan, again a lone dissenter, took issue with the majority.

Refusing to be limited by the historical context and seeing the Court's duty to interpret the plain language of the Constitution, Harlan said seamen *are* protected by the reach of the Thirteenth Amendment: ". . . a condition of enforced service, even for a limited period, in the private business of another, is a condition of involuntary servitude."[21] The Justice ridiculed the majority's reliance upon history, which he suggested would support imprisonment at hard labor and rations of bread and water. Then taking up Brown's arguments that seamen are protected from cruelty and fraud, Harlan shook his head over the majority's deduction that such protection explained how seamen could be compelled to render personal service. Such burdens, he continued, placed upon a special class of employees for private business are different from the situation of military service and are clearly unconstitutional. The Kentuckian accused the majority of legislating by creating a new class of second-class citizens in substituting for the category of runaway slaves that of runaway seamen.

What makes *Robertson* v. *Baldwin* instructive is its illustration of two approaches to constitutional interpretation. Brown and the majority acknowledged that the Thirteenth Amendment's ban on involuntary servitude reached the facts of this case, but they denied its applicability on historical grounds. The right conferred must not be interpreted literally because of the supposed exemptions that an earlier society implied. Clear language of the Constitution is muddied by a historical fixing of its language. What lies behind the seeming abstract discussion of how the Constitution is to be interpreted is a more complex problem presented by the facts of the case. Unlike the situation in other litigation where the broader social and economic matters affected the Court's resolution, here the discussion seems curiously abstract and little related to reality. The majority relied upon past practice to justify the discriminatory treatment of seamen and accepted no obligation to determine whether those special conditions still existed. Brown simply implied that such discrimination was essential to the success of this private sector of the economy. Without a realistic assessment of contemporary conditions, Harlan's opinion is more convincing. There is a certain simplicity in Harlan's constitutional literalism, but its logic is unassailable.

During the session the Justices were generally sympathetic to the federal government's claims, even to the surprising extent of finding new life in the Sherman Antitrust Act. The decision in *E.C. Knight* seemed to sound the death knell of that piece of congressional legislation, but a bare majority of the Court now found new life in its provisions. Acting under the terms of the

Sherman Act, the government sought an order seeking the dissolution of an association of railroads, the Trans-Missouri Freight Association, formed to establish and maintain reasonable rates and regulations on freight traffic. The significance of the suit could be seen in the presence of John F. Dillon, James C. Carter, and William Guthrie as attorneys for the railroads involved.

Justice Peckham, for the majority, rejected the contention that since railroads were governed by the Interstate Commerce Act, the antitrust legislation did not pertain to their business. Such an exemption, he said, would leave little "for the act to take effect upon." Meeting the argument that the statute should be read to prohibit only unreasonable restraints, Peckham said that the difficulty of making such a distinction might well have caused Congress, as it did, to prohibit all restraints whether reasonable or not. He added that the government was not obligated to prove the intent to restrain trade, for the "necessary effect of the agreement is to restrain trade or commerce, no matter what the intent was on the part of those who signed it."[22] Competing railroads that sought to work together to determine rates, he concluded, violated the Sherman Act's provision against restraints of trade.

The dissenters were led by Edward White, who here began a continuing campaign to read the adjective *unreasonable* into the Sherman Act. According to the Justice, not all restraints were proscribed, only those found to be unreasonable. White, for Field, Gray, and Shiras, referred to the common law and its definition of restraint of trade to show how needful was the addition of the word *unreasonable.* Reading the Sherman Act as a protection of the liberty of contract and the freedom of trade, he saw such an intention frustrated, if not destroyed, by the construction of the majority. Worried about the possibility that many business contracts to some extent tend to restrain trade, White concluded that the Interstate Commerce Commission provided the needed supervision over the matter of rates. White made a plausible case for limiting the range of the Sherman Act, but he failed to garner the other vote he needed, and his opinion stirred no congressional activity to so amend the Sherman Act. From this initial expression of opinion, the Justice continued the fight to make what he felt was necessary sense out of the Sherman Act.

Although railroad managers protested the Court's interpretation of the range of the Sherman Antitrust Act, they appreciated the Court's literalism when it was applied to the Interstate Commerce Act. In the previous session a unanimous High Bench, after upholding an ICC order directing a railroad to eliminate a discriminatory rate, offered its opinion that the ICC's power to condemn unreasonable rates conferred no authority to set rates. In the 1896 term with that issue squarely presented to the Court, Brewer, for the majority, issued the definitive ruling. He concluded that Congress had conferred no direct or implied power upon the commission to fix minimum, maximum, or absolute rates. Dissenting, Harlan accused the majority of undermining the essential purposes of the Interstate Commerce Act.[23]

That the Court would insist upon measuring the ICC's power by a close inspection of the enabling legislation was now crystal clear, but in the ensuing term the High Bench went one step further and, in effect, read out of the basic legislation an important regulatory provision. A section of the act prohibited a carrier from charging more for a short haul than a long one. The ICC could provide an exception if the carrier could establish the fairness of the apparently discriminatory rate by showing a dissimilarity of circumstances. When a railroad simply proceeded to charge more for a short haul, the commission sought an injunction against the practice. Following the lead of the lower federal courts, the High Bench refused to do the commission's bidding. Shiras, for the majority, rejected the ICC's claim that a railroad seeking to charge more for a short than a long haul had to proceed first through the commission to gain approval for the deviation from the basic rule. Maintaining that the courts were well equipped to determine whether the railroad's rates met the legislative test for an exemption, the Pennsylvania Justice denied the commission's request and, in effect, voided the clear regulatory intent of the long-and short-haul provision in the Interstate Commerce Act. Harlan again protested, claiming the majority's decision went far toward making the ICC "a useless body for all practical purposes."[24]

Such decisions have been explained in terms of a prorailroad bias on the part of the Justices, but this interpretation cannot survive an examination of the totality of railroad cases decided by the Court in this period. Others have argued that the prorailroad characterization is also deficient for it neglects the detrimental effect Supreme Court decision making had on the order and stability the railroads sought.[25] Rather, the explanation of the Court's attitude in these ICC cases lies in its belief that the Interstate Commerce Commission posed a substantial institutional threat to the authority of the judiciary. Under the sway of a long-honored belief in the desirability of a separation of powers, the Justices viewed an agency that blended legislative, executive, and judicial powers with considerable suspicion. Feeding this institutional suspicion was the Justices' belief that the ICC continually tried to exaggerate the scope of its delegated power. From this perspective judicial supervision of the commission's claimed authority and its work was both salutary and necessary.

With the end of the 1896 session came a resolution of the matter of Stephen J. Field. Harlan's lack of success in hinting to the senior associate that he should resign proved only a temporary setback. Chief Justice Fuller enlisted the aid of Brewer, Field's nephew, to procure the resignation. During the past term Field had been assigned no opinions and in the preceding three terms he had been assigned a total of only nineteen, far below his average yearly output of about thirty. Apparently he was lucid enough in the ensuing negotiations to make clear his desire both to establish a record for longevity on the High Bench and to have some assurances about his successor. If he served beyond August 16, 1897, Field would better John Marshall's record, and the

Chief promised that this could be done. Then, with Brewer acting as agent, President-elect McKinley was approached concerning Field's successor. Field's desire to be replaced by a Californian and McKinley's warm regard for Joseph McKenna, then sitting on the federal circuit court in California and soon to be appointed Attorney General, enabled the incoming President to meet the retiring Justice's wishes.[26]

With these details worked out and with the urging of Fuller and Brewer, Field's brother, the prominent clergyman Henry Field, procured a resignation in the spring of 1897. Upon receiving it the Chief fixed the termination date of service as December 1, 1897, and hurried to present it to the President. No publicity was given to the resignation, and during the summer and early fall Fuller and Brewer were troubled when Field gave indications that he might not stay resigned. But such ramblings were only the final protests of a fallen giant. Brewer's suggestion that President McKinley formally accept the resignation to head off any change of mind was followed, and Field formally notified his colleagues of his imminent departure on October 12, 1897.[27]

Coming to the Court in March 1863 and leaving it near the turn of the century, Field served during a period of rapid change. Apparently he sought to make his official letter to the Court a narrative of his judicial life, but the pruned result was more of a summary and a reassertion of the Justice's view of the significance of the Court and its work. He pointed to the total of six hundred and twenty opinions he had written for the Court and indicated his pride in being, in part, responsible for its success.[28] He had longed for a more active political role, but now he was willing to emphasize the importance of the role he played. After his formal separation from the Court, Field survived until April 9, 1899, when he died at the age of eighty-two.

Characterizing the Justice's work on the Court is not an easy task, both because of its scope and because of its many-sided nature. He was an active jurist, who brought to his work personal conviction and a sense of moral righteousness. He could be both dogmatic and doctrinaire in his preference for the individual or the minority against the weighty force of society and the power of organized government.[29] But Field was too politically sensitive to arrive at his decisions solely on the basis of theory; he was often acutely aware of the social, economic, and political realities that encircled cases, and his choices were often consciously made in recognition of such realities. Viewing the judiciary as a defender of individual rights from abridgment at the hands of a grasping majority, he saw a need to establish a strong constitutional underpinning for the right most precious and most valued by society— that of property.

Today we distinguish between the property right and other individual rights, and, when the two are in conflict, we tend to make the choice against the property right. But in the nineteenth century there was no such conflict. The threat posed by society then was not to the individual's right to speak freely or to his life-style but rather to his property. Adjusting to the growing demands of an industrialized society was a difficult process that would eventually necessitate further restrictions on the property interest, but in nineteenth-century terms to protect a person's property was tantamount to protecting him as an individual. "It should never be forgotten," Field said in his centennial speech in 1890, "that protection to property and to persons cannot be separated. Where property is insecure, the rights of persons are unsafe. Protection to the one goes with the other; and there can be neither prosperity nor progress where either is uncertain."[30] The Justice's words echoed those of John Locke over two centuries earlier, but the proposition that the individual should be accorded security in his enjoyment of property is still very much within our social consensus today.

The problem that Field did not face, and that Americans only slowly recognized in the twentieth century, was that this Lockean philosophy, impregnable in a capitalistic society on the individual level, produced new problems when applied to those entities called corporations. From the mid-1880s when corporations were labeled "persons" for purposes of the Fourteenth Amendment, the individualistic philosophy became warped by the presence of large business organizations seeking refuge behind it. Law's tendency to categorize made corporations artificial citizens with essentially the same rights as natural citizens. With this equation, the philosophy became a bulwark against a government acting in the public interest, not to deprive an individual of his property, but to regulate and restrict the tremendous economic and political power of large business organizations. The failure to realize that an age of organization necessitated less simple legal adaptations was not only Field's but the society's as well. Protections that made sense in relation to the lone businessman made no sense when applied to Standard Oil. Field was not blind to the fact that often the "individual" protected was a large railroad corporation, but, he believed, if the basic proposition was sound its implications could not be thwarted. In this sense, then, Field's approach was simplistic.

Worried about the potential abuse of power that could issue from majorities heedless of their encroachment upon the rights of the individual, Field saw the Supreme Court's role as a nay-sayer. A constitution confers legitimacy and empowers a government to act, but it also places limitations on the range of that action. As the Californian said, the Court's role is one of resistance based upon the guarantees spelled out in the Constitution. Any weakening of this restraining power, he said, "is a blow to the peace of society and to its progress and improvement."[31] The power to say no highlights the importance of the High Bench and continually subjects it to attack as a frustrator of the majority will. Against the backdrop of nineteenth-century individualism and the peculiar institutional role of the Supreme Court, Field must be measured and evaluated.

Stephen J. Field was one of the most creative men ever to have served on the Supreme Court. We might not like the edifice he constructed; time may change our tastes; and we may even finally conclude that the construction did not advance but rather retarded growth. But the creator is always a target. The fact remains that Field seized upon the due process clause of the Fourteenth Amendment, breathed life into it, and eventually gained the concurrence of his brethren. This early development of the Fourteenth Amendment appears to be a necessary prelude to its later service in behalf of other individual rights, and Field, along with Harlan, was responsible for weaving its clauses into the fabric of a working constitutional law. The protection the due process clause afforded property interests, even after its acceptance in the 1890s, was never as complete as Field wished, but few Justices have been able to bequeath a similar heritage to posterity.

To Field's mind the Fourteenth Amendment imposed a new and substantial restraint upon the states, and the Court was charged with the duty to invoke this restraint whenever individual rights were jeopardized. In the very first case in which the Justices considered that amendment, the Californian in dissent asserted that it protected the individual's right to pursue his chosen occupation. That a "right to labor" was not simply a passing fancy extracted from the facts of the *Slaughter-House Cases* is established by its forceful restatement in Field's centennial speech. The Californian did battle mightily against the income tax of 1894; he did seek to limit governmental power to regulate business; and he was a forceful protector of the property interest. But he was far from an uncritical supporter of such claims, being, at times, keenly aware of the social disadvantages such protection could have. His attack on the fellow servant rule, so often invoked by railroad companies in defense against suits by injured employees, revealed a sensitivity to the human condition and a recognition of the need to redress an imbalance created by the industrial society. His concern for due process did not stop at the perimeter of property protection, for he attacked the federal government for its excesses in the campaign against the Chinese. Although he did not accept Harlan's view that the Fourteenth Amendment made the Bill of Rights binding upon the states, he had some empathy for the position, as his dissent in *O'Neil* v. *Vermont* demonstrated. Also, late in his career Field recognized that the Supreme Court had erred in encouraging the development of a federal common law that created substantial and unnecessary problems for the federal system. At the time his plea for its abrogation fell upon deaf ears, but eventually his perception would win the Court.

One of the most colorful Justices ever to sit on the Court, Field served that institution well. With strong ideas and a forceful personality, he often reacted personally to disagreement, but he took his role seriously and brought to it the stamp of an individual. Field had left, but his ideas lingered.

When news of the Californian's resignation became public in mid-October 1897, newspapers reported the seat would be filled by McKinley's Attorney

General, Joseph P. McKenna. Born in Philadelphia in 1843 of recent Irish Catholic immigrants, McKenna moved with his family to the more tolerant environment of California in 1855. Leaving his family's traditional Democratic allegiance behind, he joined the Republican party. After brief study he was admitted to the bar, and hitching his professional and political interests to those of the Republican machine, controlled by the railroad magnate Leland Stanford, he attained the success he sought. He served four terms in the House of Representatives and came to the favorable attention of William McKinley, then chairman of the powerful Ways and Means Committee. With the sponsorship of McKinley and Stanford, with whose interests McKenna was closely identified, President Benjamin Harrison in 1892 selected the California Congressman to fill a vacancy on the Ninth Circuit Court of Appeals. When McKinley became President he offered McKenna the post of Attorney General. Hesitating to give up the security the federal bench provided, McKenna was assured that he would be appointed to the Supreme Court on Field's retirement. With such assurances the Californian accepted the post of Attorney General. As negotiations with Field reached their final stages and as the press talked of the imminent retirement, mention of McKenna's succession to the seat gave opponents of the nomination opportunity to mount an attack.[32]

McKenna's candidacy for the Supreme Court was hotly contested. Even though McKinley was victorious in his battle for the presidency over William Jennings Bryan, the 1896 campaign had projected nationally the fear of large corporate enterprise with tentacles reaching into all corners of government. Many of the Justices had earlier served corporations as attorneys, but none had such a thorough identification with a single interest as McKenna did with Leland Stanford's Southern Pacific Railway. Added to this disability were numerous derogatory evaluations from fellow judges and lawyers: his legal education was superficial; his legal experience was minimal; his work habits were sloppy; his opinions were often confusing and poorly written; and his impartiality was questionable. Even Chief Justice Fuller, when informed of the pending nomination, sought to intercede and prevent the appointment. But the bargain had been struck, and McKinley did not falter. Most of this material came out in the lively Senate hearing, but the Republican Senate hewed to the party line and put its stamp of approval upon the President's choice.[33]

On January 26, 1898, Joseph P. McKenna was sworn into service on the Court. Admittedly, few men have possessed as many apparent disabilities as McKenna faced upon becoming a member of the Supreme Court. Recognizing his limitations, he spent some time at Columbia Law School attempting to prepare for his new work. His early years on the Court would be difficult. Often his opinions were bounced back and sometimes had to be rewritten more than once. Fuller, always so intent on winning the favor of the Court's membership, seemed to spend little time courting McKenna. The new

Justice was aware that he had been thrust in a position that seemed too large for him, and his unhappiness reflected itself in a nervous and irritable manner.[34] If ever the proposition that the job can make the man was to be tested, McKenna was the ideal subject. Few would have expected the new Californian to survive the ordeal.

Fifty-four years of age, McKenna stood five feet, seven inches tall with a well-proportioned frame. The new Justice had regular features and bright clear eyes, and the solemnity that traditionally greeted the photographer, in McKenna's case, did not emerge as a frown. He had a full set of chin whiskers and was either unaware or uncaring that this was a departure from Court tradition. Perhaps the retention of the whiskers was McKenna's way of demonstrating that, despite common gossip, he was his own man.

With the 1897 term came some cases inviting the Court to expand further on the tantalizing idea of freedom of contract developed in *Allgeyer*. A challenge was mounted to Iowa's attempt to prohibit common carriers from exempting themselves from liability for negligence. Gray, writing for the majority, said nothing about a freedom to contract, as he rejected the contention that such a law was a restraint upon interstate commerce. He then added that "any contract by which a common carrier of goods or passengers undertakes to exempt himself from all responsibility for loss or damage arising from the negligence of himself or his servants is void as against public policy."[35] Here at least, the Court was not willing to broaden freedom of contract to protect contracts deemed to be at variance with public policy. Implicitly, Gray recognized the inequality of the parties and the need for imposing such liability upon the public carrier.

Actually one of the early cases argued in the term, *Holden* v. *Hardy*, did squarely put the freedom of contract claim before the Court. Albert F. Holden was prosecuted under an 1896 Utah statute that forbade the employment of workers in mines for more than eight hours a day. The Utah court had imposed a fine of $50 and imprisonment for fifty-seven days; the Supreme Court was asked to review the denial of the writ of habeas corpus by the state court. Although Holden's counsel did not cite the recently decided *Allgeyer* case, he did focus on the Fourteenth Amendment with its latent supervisory power over state action. Utah's exercise of power was without precedent, he said, in its violation of the liberty of the parties, for the business was not a public one, nor was it one affected with a public interest. Attorneys for Utah simply argued that the statute was well within the state's power to protect the health and safety of its citizens.

Brown, for the Court, reviewed litigation under the Fourteenth Amendment for the purpose of illustrating the Court's need to be sensitive to changes in the economic and social order. Because of the difficulty of amendment, the Constitution, he said, "should not be so construed as to deprive the States of the power to amend their laws as to make them conform to the wishes of the citizens as they may deem best for the public welfare without bringing them into conflict with the supreme law of the land." The "law is to a certain extent, a progressive science," the Justice continued, and it must "adapt itself to new conditions of society, and, particularly, to the new relations between employers and employees, as they arise." Without denying that due process ensures certain fundamental rights, he refused to accept this invitation to censure state action. Contending with *Allgeyer* and the freedom of contract idea, Brown stated that such freedom "is itself subject to certain limitations which the State may lawfully impose in the exercise of its police powers."[36]

Characterizing these powers as inherent, the Justice noted their great expansion in the past century due to the increase in dangerous and unhealthy occupations and conditions. A conflict does exist between employers and workers, Brown added, when the self-interest of one group does not accord with the self-interest of the other. The parties are far from equal bargaining partners, he continued, and the contention that such a statute impairs the freedom of the worker seems disingenuous coming from the lips of the employer. The state, the Justice ruled, can protect the worker where his health is in issue and where obvious inequality is present. Taking judicial notice of conditions in the mining industry, he was satisfied with the rationale of state's interference. Then seeking to generalize, Brown concluded that the "question in each case is whether the legislature has adopted the statute in exercise of a reasonable discretion, or whether its action be a mere excuse for an unjust discrimination, or the oppression, or spoilation of a particular class."[37]

Although the majority ignored counsel's argument that state police-power legislation should be presumed constitutional, certain language in the opinion, along with its immediate result, gave heart to those who believed that further governmental interference would be necessary before certain economic imbalances could be redressed. Peckham, the author of *Allgeyer*, and Brewer dissented without opinion, but even the majority did not deny to the Court an active role in assessing such state action. Freedom of contract advocates might have hoped for a bold pronouncement staying the hand of state legislatures in regulating the employment contract, but Brown did not foreclose the possibility of successful challenge when regulations did not strike the majority as reasonable exercises of the police power.

The term also produced a decision in the case of *Smyth* v. *Ames*, in which a Nebraska rate-fixing statute was declared unconstitutional as depriving a railroad corporation of due process of law. Clearly, legislatures or commissions could set rates, but those rates had to assure the railroads a fair return upon property. If the Court's role in this process had not been established earlier in the decade, *Smyth* v. *Ames* forcefully asserted that the judiciary had the final say on whether the return was just. Harlan, speaking for the Court, said that in determining the property base for purposes of calculating a fair rate of return, the cost of construction and improvements, the value of bonds and stock, and the railroad's earning capacity and operating expenses were all to be considered.[38] This listing was far from a useful formula, and its very vagueness was an invitation to corporations to seek reversals of legislative and administrative determinations. If the most optimistic hopes of the advocates of due process had not been realized, this judicial check upon legislatures and commissions did represent a clear victory.

In contrast, *Williams* v. *Mississippi* again demonstrated the Court's unwillingness to interfere with the state criminal process, but in affirming the conviction of a black defendant for murder, the Justices really did much more. They gave tacit approval to state use of a literacy test as a means of restricting, if not eliminating, black suffrage. Williams challenged his indictment by an all-white grand jury on grounds that Mississippi's constitution and the laws passed thereunder restricting jury service to qualified voters, coupled with the requirement that an applicant for the franchise pass a literacy test to the satisfaction of local election officials, effectively barred blacks from qualifying for jury service. This system, the defendant contended, denied him the equal protection of the law guaranteed by the Fourteenth Amendment. In upholding the constitutionality of a poll tax provision in the Mississippi constitution, the highest state court had explained the work of the drafters of the suffrage provisions of the new constitution as follows: "Within the field of permissible action imposed by the Federal Constitution, the convention swept the field of expedients, to obstruct the exercise of suffrage by the negro race."[39] With the administration and evaluation of the literacy test placed in the hands of local officials, the practical result, clearly argued in the defendant's brief, was the exclusion of blacks from the ballot box. With a cultivated myopia, the unanimous Supreme Court confined its scrutiny to the text of the Mississippi law.

None of the provisions of state constitutional or statutory law are constitutionally defective, said McKenna, for they apply equally to both races. The recent arrival went on to distinguish an 1888 case in which the Court invalidated a San Francisco ordinance because it found a clear pattern of discriminatory enforcement by saying that here no such discriminatory enforcement has been proved. The bare possibility that local election officials will act in a discriminatory fashion, he continued, is to substitute allegation and speculation for proof. Concluding that Williams's appeal was without merit, McKenna affirmed the murder conviction. The majority also indicated approval of the use of the poll tax, saying in response to the state court's opinion on the subject that whatever is sinister in the constitutional and statutory provisions, if anything, "can be prevented by both races by the exertion of that duty which voluntarily pays taxes."[40]

The California Justice's opinion is weak; it is neither well written nor well organized, and it relies heavily upon quotations. Fuller's assignment of the opinion to McKenna is illustrative of the slight importance the Chief attached to the case. Yet in this single inartful opinion the Supreme Court placed its approval upon laws designed to cut down the rights of blacks, saying it would not presume the discriminatory enforcement of such laws. Such enforcement reflected well the realities of Southern political life, but the Court of the 1890s, though active and sensitive to certain constitutional claims, was ill-equipped to grapple with the underlying issues the case presented. The Justices were still respectful of the contours of the federal system and quite hesitant to interfere, even on the basis of federal constitutional guarantees, with policy determinations in which state authority had been consistently respected.

Harlan offered no dissent in *Williams*. To reach the issues raised in the case required a different context and a different time, and even Harlan, who championed loudly and clearly the rights of blacks within the constitutional system, was unwilling to dig beneath the surface here. Although his dissents in racial cases have a modern ring to them, his approach to them was still bound within a late nineteenth- and not a midtwentieth-century context.

The 1897 term did produce a notable victory for the Indians and for Justice Henry B. Brown. *New York Indians* v. *United States* posed substantial difficulty for the Justices. It was argued in December 1896 and again in March 1898. Congress in 1883 had provided for the adjudication of certain Indian claims against the federal government. Members of various New York tribes claimed certain rights under the Treaty of Buffalo Creek of 1838 in which the government sought to effect the removal of the Indian nations to the area now known as Kansas. In the treaty the Indians had ceded their rights to 500,000 acres in Wisconsin in return for the new grant. Just before the Civil War the government put that land in Kansas on the market, and eventually it was sold. With the Indians now claiming the proceeds from the sale, government counsel argued that removal was an essential condition of the grant and that the failure of, and in certain instances resistance to, removal defeated the Kansas grant. As the case was discussed in conference, both the Chief and Harlan, the Court's most senior members, were in the minority, leaving Gray as the senior Justice responsible for assigning the opinion. With satisfaction Justice Brown accepted the assignment.

Brown stuck to the legal issues in determining whether the Indians had rights under the 1838 treaty. Acknowledging that Congress can override the provisions of a treaty through inconsistent action, the basis the Court used to decide against Race Horse and the Bannocks, Brown found no clear congressional action that divested the Indians of their right to the Kansas land. The crucial question was whether the treaty vested the Indians with a legal title in the lands. One of the problems Brown faced was an amendment to the treaty that made the land grant dependent upon removal, but he concluded that this amendment, not in the published treaty nor in the proclamation by the President, could not now be invoked to defeat the rights of the Indians. "There is something, too, which shocks the conscience," the Justice continued, "in the idea that a treaty can be put forth embodying the terms of an arrangement with a foreign power or an Indian tribe, a material provision of which is unknown to one of the contracting parties, and is kept in the background to be used by the other only when the exigencies of a particular case may demand it." There was provision for forfeiture in the treaty, but Brown argued that more than inconsistent executive action was required to accomplish the forfeiture. The last point relied upon by the government was that, in effect, the Indians had abandoned their claim, but the Justice said the government had not proceeded upon this assumption and was now barred from using it. Brown consistently resolved the doubt that lay within the government's actions in favor of the Indians, and the final result, determined by the Court of Claims and upheld by the Supreme Court, was an award of $1,967,056.[41]

During the term the Justices gave notice that they would not follow uncritically the antiliquor and antimargarine advocates. For instance, in interpreting the Wilson Act, which gave to the states control over liquor found in the state, the Court refused to sanction Iowa's conviction of a stationmaster for moving liquor from the station platform to a warehouse. Gray, who was least sensitive to the commerce clause claim and most inclined to support such state regulation, dissented, along with Harlan and Brown. When the Court allowed South Carolina to monopolize the sale of liquor and prevent private competition under the terms of the Wilson Act, Shiras, Fuller, and McKenna dissented. The dissenters argued that the essential purpose of the commerce clause was to protect lawful subjects of commerce from hostile state action. When the focus shifted to state regulations imposed on margarine, the absence of federal legislation like the Wilson Act made no difference to Gray and Harlan, who, in dissent, argued that "questions of danger to health, and of likelihood of fraud or deception, and of the preventive measures required for the protection of the people, are questions of fact and of public policy, the determination of which belongs to the legislative department, and not to the judiciary." The majority, however, concluded that Pennsylvania's ban on the sale of margarine and New Hampshire's mandate that margarine be colored pink were impermissible restraints on interstate commerce.[42]

Apparently in this area of conflict between the commerce clause and the police power of the states, Fuller and Gray were the prime antagonists.[43] Gray was willing to defer to the state police power, while Fuller was more concerned about safeguarding the channels of commerce. In interpreting the Wilson Act the two approaches resulted in broad and narrow readings respectively. The majority of the Court, however, proceeded to pick its way through the cases and react to their factual dimensions. The result of this practice tended to favor Fuller's view, for although the police power was accorded considerable respect, the majority was sensitive to the possibility of state intrusions upon the federal domain.[44]

Fuller had some success in gaining support for his stand on protecting interstate commerce from exertions of the police power, but he lost the biggest battle of the 1897 term. In fact, the Chief's biographer has called Fuller's failure in the case of Wong Kim Ark "perhaps his worst defeat on the Court." Gray and Fuller were the rival spokesmen and contenders for their colleagues' votes, and this case, more than any other, revealed sharp differences between the two men. The question the case posed was deceptively simple: was a child born in the United States to alien Chinese parents a citizen of the United States? Some indication of the internal wrangling over the case can be seen in its timetable: it was submitted in May 1896, ordered for oral argument in November 1896, argued on March 5, 1897, and not decided until March 28, 1898. When the opinions were announced, even a defeated Fuller was relieved, and the Court's unofficial poet, David Brewer, echoed a similar sentiment in doggerel verse.[45]

From the battles of the conference room, Gray emerged the victor and brought the sanctity of the Constitution to bear upon Wong Kim Ark's claim of American citizenship. Justice Gray in his stolid, unswerving, and determined way carried the Court to a momentous decision. The logic of the Massachusetts Justice won five of his colleagues and bucked a political current that seemed to demand a contrary decision. Since McKenna did not hear the oral arguments, he did not participate in the decision. The Chief's dissent won only the next most senior Justice, Harlan. Gray, next in seniority, received all the votes of the appointees of the 1890s and made the most of this invitation to explore the domain of Anglo-American law and practice.

Wong Kim Ark was born in 1873 in San Francisco of Chinese parents, and the family continued to reside there until 1890, when he and his parents left for China. Wong Kim Ark returned in the same year and was admitted on the claim that he was a natural-born citizen of the United States. After another visit to China in 1894, he returned the following year to find his claim of citizenship denied and his entry barred. The government appealed the habeas corpus writ granted by the district court.

Gray began by saying the claim of citizenship must be measured against the wording of the first section of the Fourteenth Amendment: "All persons born or naturalized in the United States, and subject to the jurisdiction thereof, are citizens of the United States and of the State wherein they reside." Such constitutional language on its face appears to cover the situation of Wong Kim Ark, but both internal division and the external political environment demanded a more extensive rationale. Gray stated that a constitutional provision must be measured by the law as it stood before its adoption. Finding the words *natural-born citizens* in various places in the Constitution without any clarification of their meaning, the Justice sought a definition in the common law. Drawing upon the English experience, Gray found a settled principle that birth within the jurisdiction of the king conferred nationality, with only children born to foreign diplomats and to enemy aliens excepted. Saying that this rule was in force in all the British colonies, he saw its continuance after Independence and under the Constitution as originally drafted. What the Fourteenth Amendment does, the Justice continued, is reaffirm "in the most explicit and comprehensive terms" the prevailing rule, its primary purpose being to ensure the former slave of citizenship.[46] Although the original purpose of the amendment might be limited, its language is not, and Gray noted that all members of the Court in 1873, when the language was first considered, clearly recognized that it related to place and jurisdiction and not to race or color.

Gray then sidestepped language in earlier opinions of the Court that said children born of alien parents are not citizens by saying, in effect, that such conclusions were gratuitous statements not necessary to the decisions in those cases and therefore entitled to no weight as precedent. Accepting the earlier direct ruling that Indians are not citizens because they are not "subject to the jurisdiction" of the United States, he refused to widen the exception, contending that it would be incompatible with the need of the country to govern those within its domain. The Justice read the legislative record as supporting this conclusion, noting that Congress had consistently treated aliens residing in this country as subject to its jurisdiction. Then Gray cited the opinions of Attorneys General since the time of the Fourteenth Amendment, which, he said, consistently imply that birth within the country confers citizenship. A contrary rule, Gray concluded, would "deny citizenship to thousands of persons of English, Scotch, Irish, German, or other European parentage, who have always been considered and treated as citizens of the United States."[47] Measured against this background, the amendment, he continued, is affirmative and declaratory and intended to allay doubts, not impose any new restrictions upon citizenship. He suggested that the language of the 1866 act requiring that the individual not be subject to any foreign jurisdiction was confusing and that its deletion in the Fourteenth Amendment places emphasis entirely upon the affirmative grant.

Gray hinted that the challenge to Wong Kim Ark's citizenship may have been racially inspired. Whatever motivated Congress in its firm determination to prevent the naturalization of Chinese, he said, cannot constrain a court whose duty is to give full effect to the meaning of the Constitution. Although the common law can be changed by statute, a constitutional provision interpreted in light of the common law is beyond the reach of the legislature. Since the dissent charged inconsistency between the majority's determination here and its earlier rulings on Chinese exclusion cases, Gray responded by drawing a key distinction:

The acts of Congress, known as the Chinese Exclusion Acts, the earliest of which was passed some fourteen years after the adoption of the Constitutional Amendment, cannot control its meaning, or impair its effect, but must be construed and executed in subordination to its provisions. And the right of the United States, as exercised by and under those acts, to exclude or to expel from the country persons of the Chinese race, born in China and continuing to be subjects of the Emperor of China, though having acquired a commercial domicile in the United States, has been upheld by this court for reasons applicable to all aliens alike, and inapplicable to citizens, of whatever race or color.[48]

Recognizing that Congress with its exclusive power over naturalization can, as it had with the Court's approval, declare Chinese to be ineligible for naturalization, he ruled that such authority can be used to confer citizenship but not to take it away. If the naturalization power was interpreted to allow the legislative branch to exclude certain classes from becoming citizens by birth, "it would be in the power of Congress, at any time, by striking negroes out of the naturalization laws, and limiting those laws, as they were formerly limited, to white persons only, to defeat the main purpose of the Constitutional Amendment." Such an anomaly could only be resolved, Gray concluded, by giving full effect to the provision in the Fourteenth Amendment. Wong Kim Ark and other Chinese born in the United States are now declared to be citizens. That the same decision had been made by Stephen J. Field, while on circuit court, did not go unnoticed.[49]

Chief Justice Fuller began his dissent by accusing Gray and the majority of undercutting the congressional policy of Chinese exclusion. With a comparative-law approach, he stated that the modern rule is that citizenship descends from the parents. Fuller argued that the old English rule no more survived the American Revolution than it did the French, for the recognition by the government of the right of expatriation is inconsistent with the common law rule. The Chief was horrified by the idea that by accepting the geographical determination of natural citizenship, as the majority did, a Wong Kim Ark could become president while a child born to American parents overseas could not. To reach the result that Wong Kim Ark was not a citizen and yet preserve the right to citizenship of children born to other aliens in the United States, he drew a distinction. Reading the constitutional phrase, "subject to the jurisdiction thereof," to mean completely subject, he said that American-born Chinese are disabled from becoming citizens because their parents are prevented by Chinese law from renouncing their allegiance to the Emperor and are barred from the naturalization process by American law. Paternalistically, he added that the Chinese have not wanted to become American citizens and accused the majority of tearing up "parental relations by the roots."[50]

Fuller had fought long and hard for his resolution of this case. Personally, he had no objection to the congressional policy toward the Chinese, and professionally, he was fearful of frustrating a clearly expressed congressional attitude and precluding the ability of the President and the Senate to settle such matters in treaties with the foreign power. Wisdom, he seemed to feel, dictated deference on this touchy issue. His fears, however, did not materialize. Late in March 1898 Congress was almost completely absorbed by the situation in Cuba and in efforts to convince the administration that war with Spain was necessary. The decision tumbled into this environment without much notice.[51]

In an age of illiberality toward Orientals, the Supreme Court wrapped a cloak of protection around a portion of these people, giving to the children of often despised parents a new status within the society. While Fuller and Harlan would have held such children in bondage to a distant emperor, Gray and his colleagues voted for their emancipation. The Justice from Massachusetts had consistently supported the exercise of federal power over aliens and was assertive in his belief that the government had power to deal with Orientals as it saw fit. In this instance, however, he saw a conflict between this inherent governmental power and what he interpreted to be a clear constitutional mandate. His opinion illustrates well the creative amalgam that can be wrought by mixing the archaic past with the present.

The term ended on the last day of May with the country involved in that "splendid little war" with Spain. Despite the government's renunciation of any territorial desire in Cuba, a perceptive Justice might well have realized that even a short war could leave a troublesome legacy for the Court. The session had been difficult for the Chief; although he would have denied a quest for ideological leadership, he did lose a number of battles upon whose outcome he had staked some prestige. But, being the man he was, his contests with Gray seemed to end at the conference room door, for their personal friendship was little affected.[52]

As if to aid Fuller in his search for harmony, the docket the Court returned to in October 1898 was mainly composed of cases with little potential for exacerbating recent disagreement. In fact over the next eight months the ratio of agreement among the Justices would be higher than in any of the four preceeding terms.

Three antitrust cases were decided early in the session. Rufus Peckham had become Fuller's preferred writer in Sherman Act cases, and all three decisions, announced on October 24, 1898, carried Peckham's name. The most devisive case was a reincarnation of the *Trans-Missouri Freight Association* case dealing with an agreement among railroads on the matter of rates. In the earlier litigation Peckham and the bare majority had fought off the challenge that the antitrust act did not apply where the Interstate Commerce Commission had jurisdiction. The dissenters were White, Gray, Shiras, and Field. Field had left the Court, and his replacement, McKenna, did not hear the arguments and did not participate in the decision. The three remaining members again dissented, this time without opinion. Peckham, in his majority opinion, scolded eminent counsel James C. Carter, Edward J. Phelps, and George F. Edmunds for raising the same arguments that had failed to convince the Court earlier. Obviously counsel hoped the decision in *Trans-Missouri* could be reversed, but Peckham and the majority held firm, disabusing counsel of the notion that a five to four decision indicated vulnerability in the majority's resolution. Counsel for the railroads had tried to play upon the freedom of contract doctrine, and Peckham, while acknowledging its value, added the substantial caveat that government has the power to pronounce contracts "which shall restrain trade and commerce by shutting out the operation of the general law of competition" illegal.[53]

Although an area of applicability for the Sherman Act had been found, the Court was reluctant to broaden that area. In the two other cases the Court decided the act did not reach the activities of the Traders' Livestock Exchange operating in Kansas City. The exchange was a monopolistic organization in part dedicated to freezing out nonmembers. The Sherman Act, Peckham said, could only be applied to restraints of trade in interstate commerce, and the bolstered majority concluded that these traders were not engaged in interstate commerce.[54] Whether the activity had a direct or indirect effect on interstate commerce, the touchstone of *E. C. Knight*, remained for the Court a crucial question.

The Justices continued to afford the states considerable latitude in their police-power legislation. For instance, when an insurance company claimed it was being singled out by Missouri for discriminatory treatment, the Justices said that legislative classification does not have to be based upon a scientific or common-sense demarcation: "It suffices if it is practical, and is not reviewable unless palpably arbitrary."[55] Such a statement is really far-ranging, but it is quite consistent with the way the Court continued to view state power.

As usual, many of the cases involved railroads, whose attorneys claimed either that Fourteenth Amendment rights were violated or that the state regulation was an unconstitutional burden upon commerce. A unanimous Court held an Arkansas statute providing for the payment of earned wages upon discharge well within the police power. Some such litigation, however, did give the Justices trouble. A case from Ohio posed the recurring problem of a state's authority to command interstate trains to stop at certain towns. Harlan, for a bare majority, sustained the regulation and tried to draw a line between the police power of the state and the preemptive power of the federal government under the commerce clause. Recognizing that much state regulation touched interstate commerce, Harlan used a test of reasonableness, saying that the federal commerce power did not preclude states from passing laws to secure the convenience of the public that had only incidental or remote effects on interstate commerce. The argument of the railroad was typical: when a state regulation was challenged, counsel drew grandoise pictures of the reach of congressional power; when, on the other hand, the regulation was federal, counsel claimed it encroached upon state power. In dissent, Shiras, joined by Brewer, White, and Peckham, accused the majority of ignoring both precedent and the purpose of the commerce clause.[56] Opinions like Harlan's that pragmatically sought to balance federal and state action were always subject to such criticism.

With a similar lack of agreement the Court also decided in favor of a Kansas regulation of railroads. State legislatures were not only interested in regulating rate structures, they were also desirous of imposing liability upon such powerful corporations for both direct and indirect damage done to the public. A Kansas act passed in 1885 made railroads responsible for damages from fire caused by the operation of trains. The legislation required no proof of negligence on the part of the railroad; the property holder simply had to establish that his loss was caused by a fire started by a train. Attorneys for the railroad claimed the law singled out railroads for special liability that deprived them of the equal protection of the laws as specified in the Fourteenth Amendment. This time Justice Brewer wrote the opinion for the five-man majority, ruling that the inequality of the burden imposed had "no significance upon the question of constitutionality."[57] Harlan, for the dissenters, contended that this type of class legislation was condemned by the Fourteenth Amendment.

In these two five to four decisions Fuller and Gray consistently upheld the state regulation, while only Peckham dissented in both cases in favor of the railroad's claim. One of the long-standing myths about the Court during this era is that it was unduly hospitable to railroad claims, but only Peckham in this pair of cases favored the railroad's interest, while the majority of his colleagues cast their votes with no such consistency. The record simply does not bear out the prorailroad charge, and although many votes were close, the decisions of the Court in the area were generally sensitive to the public interest.

With the Court winding up its business late in May, two Justices had a special commitment for the summer. Both the Chief and Brewer had accepted appointments in early 1897 to a five-man arbitration panel empowered to settle a long-standing controversy between Venezuela and British Guinea. Because of Fuller's insistence that the work of the Supreme Court be as little disturbed as possible, an initial session held in January 1899, which Brewer attended in Paris, quickly adjourned until after the Court's term ended. So Fuller, his family, and Brewer spent over two hot months in Paris during the summer of 1899. Arguments on both sides lasted for fifty-five days, a wearying experience for both of the Justices.[58]

Presidents throughout American history have looked to the Court as a source of manpower for special governmental assignments.[59] The men on the High Bench are afforded a preeminent legal position, and with that position are associated a host of desirable characteristics—impartiality, reasoned judgment, political invulnerability, and so on. President Cleveland sought to exploit this tradition, when in 1893, upon returning to office, he offered Fuller the position as Secretary of State. The Chief, always acutely sensitive to the dignity of his office, mulled over the offer for a few days and then responded: "The surrender of the highest judicial office in the world for a political position, even though so eminent, would tend to detract from the dignity and weight of the tribunal. We cannot afford this." Cleveland was disappointed, but he felt called upon to apologize for the impropriety of his invitation.[60]

President McKinley also sought to tap the services of the Chief by urging him to accept a position with the American delegation seeking to conclude a peace treaty with Spain. After some equivocation, Fuller refused. Explaining his decision, he said that conditions had changed greatly since Chief Justices John Jay and Oliver Ellsworth in the 1790s had performed diplomatic services for the administration. His considered opinion was that Justices should confine their public service to the Court. Undaunted, the President then sought the services of Justice White, who also refused.[61]

After the long summer ordeal in Paris, Fuller probably hoped the coming term of Court would be as quiet and uneventful as the preceeding one had been. He was to be disappointed, as the number of divided cases would reach a new high during his tenure. Fuller continued to carry a disproportionate share of the opinion-writing load, in part because he was assuming part of Gray's burden. The Massachusetts Justice, who wrote unneccessarily lengthy opinions, avoided new assignments. As a result, his opinion output was the lowest on the Court since the departure of Field.

In one of the first decisions announced in the 1899 term, *Jones* v. *Meehan*, the Court administered a rebuke to the other branches of the federal government. Individual land allotments were authorized by a 1863 treaty with the Chippewa Nation. An Indian, who was heir to an individual land grant under the treaty, had leased his land to Meehan in 1891. Over a three-year period the railroad had come and the land had increased greatly in value. In 1894 the same land was leased to Jones for a twenty-year period. Then in August of the same year Congress passed a joint resolution authorizing the Secretary of the Interior to approve the second lease with or without modifying its terms. The Secretary approved the lease after doubling the rental and making the proceeds payable to the agent in charge of the Chippewas, who in turn was to determine to whom the money would be paid. Gray concluded that the original treaty had vested absolute title. The first lessee, Meehan, had a valid lease and his suit to quiet title was upheld. Although the suit was between private parties and the federal government was not directly involved, Gray lectured the other branches of the government, saying that neither the practice of the Secretary of the Interior nor the authority of Congress, expressed in the 1894 resolution, could divest the title and the valid lease. Except "in cases purely political," Gray said, "Congress has no constitutional power to settle the rights under a treaty, or to affect titles already granted by the treaty itself."[62] The 1894 resolution was pronounced null and void. Normally receptive to claims of federal authority, the Justices here, however, saw their role in terms of protecting the judicial function from usurpation by the other branches.

Just as Justice Peckham began the previous term with an imprimatur of approval for the government's prosecution of railroads under the Sherman Antitrust Act, he, this time for a unanimous Court, sustained the government in the *Addyston Pipe and Steel Company* case. What was novel here was that the corporation, a manufacturing enterprise not directly engaged in transportation, was held liable under the Sherman Act. Recognizing that manufacturing and commerce were not mutually exclusive categories, Peckham distinguished *E.C. Knight* by saying that in the earlier case no agreement looking toward the future disposition of the product in interstate commerce had been shown. Here he found the pipe company had combined with others to divide the national market into regional areas and rig the bidding to prevent effective competition. As Peckham concluded:

The direct and immediate result of the combination was therefore necessarily a restraint upon interstate commerce in respect of articles manufactured by any of the parties to it to be transported beyond the State in which they were made. The defendants by reason of this combination and agreement could only send their goods out of the State in which they were manufactured for sale and delivery in another State, upon the terms and pursuant to the provisions of such combination.[63]

Although the Court still required the government to prove an agreement restrained interstate commerce, the federal officials had made just such a showing. This intent to restrain interstate commerce was not absent from the sugar refining prosecution in 1895, but there the government developed the case in such a way as to obscure rather than focus on the interstate dimension. Three Justices had dissented in the railroad case of the preceeding term, but here there were no dissents. This episode demonstrates that when the government carefully prepares its case and brings it within the confines of the antitrust act's provisions, even the most dubious of Justices found little room to disagree.

So entrenched was the Court's respect for the state police power that at times the Justices were willing to take judicial notice of factors justifying its exercise. When the United States sought to prosecute a state agent for damming a navigable stream in Louisiana without obtaining approval from the Secretary of War, a unanimous Court overturned the conviction. Although the record was largely barren of traditional police-power justification, the Court filled the gap:

We think that the trial court might well take judicial notice that the public health is deeply concerned in the reclamation of swamp and overflowed lands. If there is any fact which may be supposed to be known by everybody, and therefore, by courts, it is that swamps and stagnant waters are the cause of malarial and malignant fevers, and that the police power is never more legitimately exercised than in removing such nuisances. The defendant was not deprived of the defense that the act which he was charged with was performed in order to promote the health of the community, by the fact, if fact it was, that the order under which he acted did not say anything about the subject of health, but, simply authorized the erection of the dam, so as to exclude the overflow from the river.[64]

Despite the Court's respect for state power, some cases presented complex fact situations that made for hard decisions. Lindsay & Phelps Company found $15,000 worth of its logs seized on a lien given to the surveyor general of Minnesota to pay him for his task of surveying and scaling logs run through chartered booms. The company felt especially aggrieved because its logs were seized to pay the charges due on all the logs in the boom, including those of other owners. Counsel contended that such a procedure violated due process of law, and that the lien being imposed upon its logs, cut in another state, was an unconstitutional burden on interstate commerce. In a majority opinion written by Justice Brewer, the company's arguments were rejected. Justice Peckham dissented, along with Harlan, Brown, and White. The New Yorker said that this case is a clear example of "the illustration that is generally made for the purpose of showing that there are some things so contrary to justice as to admit no doubt of their utter illegality; such as the arbitrary taking, under the form of legislative enactment, of the property of one man and bestowing it upon another."[65]

This particular decision typifies the scrutiny to which due process claims were put. One would think that with any respect for substantive due process as a legitimate doctrine of constitutional law, Peckham's opinion should have carried the Court. But a searching and sympathetic inquiry into the facts of the case tended to be typical of the Court's pragmatic approach to its task. The writer of the Court's opinion was Brewer, who in his public speeches seemed most philosophically committed to a laissez-faire position. As a Justice, however, he regularly scrutinized the facts and issues before the Court and came to a decision with no apparent regard for its general philosophical implications. Based upon such opinions Brewer must be seen as a Justice who was quite sensitive to the need to grant considerable latitude to the states.

During the term a majority of Justices avoided involvement in politically charged matters. Louisiana sought to sue Texas to enjoin an alleged maladministration of the latter state's quarantine laws. Louisiana claimed the enforcement of such laws effectively impeded trade between New Orleans and the Lone Star State. Chief Justice Fuller, for the majority, concluded that Louisiana had no standing to bring a suit concerning interstate commerce, a subject over which the state itself had no control. The Chief acknowledged the political overtones of the action, stating that the Court's jurisdiction "does not embrace the determination of political questions."[66] Written concurrences of Harlan and Brown accepted the result but indicated objection to the idea of noninvolvement in all such matters.

A second politically charged plea called upon the Court to reverse a determination that Kentucky's governor be ousted from office. When the Republican candidate for governor had outpolled his rival by less than 2,500 votes, the Democrats refused to accept the electoral defeat. Using the state constitutional procedures for resolving a disputed election, the Democratically controlled legislature declared the defeated candidate the victor. State courts upheld the decision. Again Chief Justice Fuller, for the majority, took the easy way out. He denied both that the Court had any power to act under the constitutional provision guaranteeing each state a republican form of government and that the election to the office conferred any property right upon the claimant that was protected under the Fourteenth Amendment. Knocking out the two pins upon which the Republican's appeal rested, the majority simply dismissed the writ of error. Brown concurred with no opinion, but the Court's two activists, Brewer and Harlan, wrote at length.

Brewer took issue with Fuller's passive approach and reminded the Court that over a period of twenty-five years the Court had reached a decision in three similar cases and had only dismissed a fourth because the claim raised was frivolous. Quite willing to decide the merits of the case; he was ready to approve the Kentucky court's decision to oust the Republican. Justice Harlan, a Kentucky Republican not untutored in the nature of his home state's politics, agreed with Brewer only in that the Court should take jurisdiction of the case.

In his dissent, Harlan called the Kentucky legislature's procedure a farce, "discreditable in the last degree and unworthy of the free people whom it professed to represent." In light of such an appraisal the Justice could not "believe that the judiciary is helpless in the presence of such a crime." Harlan argued that the people should be protected in their right to select their rulers free from "action taken outside the law" and that the property right of the Republican in office should be recognized. Liberty is insecure, he said, "if the judiciary must be silent when rights existing independently of human sanction, or acquired under the law, are at the mercy of legislative action taken in violation of due process of law."[67] Obviously Harlan was right in his appraisal of the Kentucky situation, but the type of interference in state affairs he urged was far too drastic for his brethren.

The 1899 term also produced two cases involving claims of racial discrimination. Texas authorities were told by the Court that systematic exclusion of blacks from a grand jury that brings in an indictment against a black violates the equal protection clause of the Fourteenth Amendment whether the exclusion results from legislative, judicial, or administrative action. In such cases the Justices consistently required the complaining party to carry the burden of proof, but here the defendant had been precluded by the Texas court from doing so; therefore a new trial was ordered.[68] The second case was peculiar in the way in which the issues were framed.

Cumming v. *County Board of Education* did not raise the matter of racial segregation in schools; the record shows an acceptance of the practice by all parties. With the turn of the century public school education in the South still lagged considerably behind the national standard. In Georgia a county was under no obligation to establish high schools, but the county here had partially provided for this level of education by subsidizing private white high schools and by providing a high school for blacks, charging tuition for those attending. A decision to divert the black high school facility to primary education was the cause of the controversy: the high school serving some sixty students was to become a primary school serving about three hundred blacks hitherto unprovided for within the system. Instead of trying to force the board to maintain a black high school, the plaintiffs sought to enjoin the board from financially supporting private white high schools and the tax collector from collecting that portion of the taxes channeled into this venture. The county court refused an injunction against the tax collector but did order the board not to use any of its funds to aid private schools until some provision was made for black high school students. Georgia's supreme court reversed this decision, and the plaintiffs appealed to the High Bench.

Justice Harlan wrote the unanimous opinion. The Kentuckian earlier had shown his sensitivity to charges of racial discrimination by exposing the underlying prejudice of certain state action, but here he demonstrated little inclination to probe behind the issues framed. Harlan acknowledged that any taxing structure is inequitable in terms of the disbursements made, but he discredited the plaintiffs' claim by saying that under such a theory parents of boys could argue they should not support a girls' high school. Then the Justice queried how the cutting off of support to the white high schools would in any way aid the cause of black education. Of course, Harlan was sharing the myopia that afflicted his brothers in *Plessy* v. *Ferguson*, for behind the plaintiff's action was the hope that a successful suit would force the board to reestablish the black high school rather than deny a high school education to whites. Finally, Harlan unquestioningly accepted the board's contention that its controversial decision was made solely for sound economic and educational reasons. Since segregation went unquestioned and since the plaintiffs were unable to offer any proof of discrimination in the board's decision, the board appeared justified.[69]

The almost cavalier way the Court assumed in *Cumming* that segregated education was a "given" in American society could only buttress the system that would take substantial time, effort, and dedication to uproot. Perhaps only a later generation could fully empathize with George F. Edmunds, who, upon hearing of the Court's decision, expressed sympathy for his "poor colored clients ... in their aspirations for equal rights in public education."[70]

To view Harlan's opinion in *Cumming* as a retreat from the Justice's expansive reading of the protection he found within the Fourteenth Amendment would be erroneous, for the Kentuckian, during the term, forcefully reiterated his earlier views. In two cases before the Court in which defendants claimed that states had violated their constitutional rights because they had not been indicted by a grand jury, the Court responded that the requirement of the Fifth Amendment of indictment by a grand jury was not made binding upon the states by means of the due process clause in the Fourteenth Amendment.[71] Harlan dissented without opinion in one case but detailed his position in the other, *Maxwell* v. *Dow*, which also presented the question of whether a jury composed of eight people was barred by the Sixth Amendment. Peckham in his majority opinion quoted extensively from earlier cases and denied that the rights the defendant asserted were any more protected by the due process clause than they were by the privileges and immunities clause of the Fourteenth Amendment.

Harlan began by reasserting his opinion, first expressed in 1884, that the Fourteenth Amendment made all provisions of the Bill of Rights binding upon the states. This time, however, after simply restating that an infamous crime can only be prosecuted by an indictment handed down by a grand jury, he moved on to the issue of the eight-man jury. All on the Court agreed that the word *jury* in the Sixth Amendment must be translated as meaning twelve men. Harlan argued that even before the Fourteenth Amendment the right of an individual to a jury trial was well established as a privilege or immunity. How, after the amendment, which includes that specific phraseology as a limitation on state action, he asked, can the majority take a position that the right to a jury trial, as that term is commonly understood, is not fundamentally protected? He suggested that the Court's reasoning leads to the conclusion that a state could abolish a jury trial completely without violating any constitutional right. "I cannot assent to this interpretation," he continued, "because it is opposed to the plain words of the Constitution and defeats the manifest object of the Fourteenth Amendment."[72]

Noting that the Justices had agreed that the amendment precludes the taking of private property without compensation, although that requirement is not expressly stipulated, he censured his colleagues for their apparent views "that the protection of private property is of more consequence than the protection of the life and liberty of the citizen." The full panoply of rights in the first ten amendments, the Kentuckian maintained, must be enforced against the states, for no judicial tribunal "has authority to say that some of them may be abridged by the states while others may not be abridged." To the Justice the Court's duty was clear; it should recognize that the Fourteenth Amendment imposes barriers to state oppression that "should not be destroyed or impaired by judicial decisions."[73]

Harlan was a consistent believer in the Court's responsibility to supervise the actions of state and local government under the broad guidelines of the Fourteenth Amendment. The profound implications of such a view for the old system of federalism were well recognized by his reluctant colleagues. As his dissent in *Maxwell* so aptly demonstrated, Harlan refused to draw the line at property protection; for, after all, life and liberty were also protected by the due process clause. This logic the Kentuckian saw clearly, but he was frustrated by an inability to reach his colleagues. In a very real sense Harlan was both a man of his times and a man ahead of his times. Through Harlan we can perceive how the early interpretations of the Fourteenth Amendment were a stepping stone to later readings. The willingness of the Court to interpret and then reinterpret the commands of the amendment in a changing society paved the way for the future.

Officially the Court's first contact with the ramifications of the Spanish-American War came in the preceding term when the Justices unanimously rebuffed a limited challenge to the War Revenue Act of 1898. The Court said it would not impede the federal taxing power by heeding abstract distinctions that rested "more upon the differing theories of political economists than upon the practical nature of the tax itself." Now the Justices confronted a more wide-ranging challenge to the revenue measure in the major case of *Knowlton* v. *Moore*. The result was the same, as White, for the majority, responded to the challenge in an extensive opinion. The federal tax, the Louisianian said, did not have to be apportioned among the states because it was not a direct tax on property but rather an excise, a type of tax long and consistently characterized as indirect. On the question of uniformity, the issue that so bothered Justice Field in *Pollock*, White could now say for the Court that this constitutional test was met because the tax was geographically uniform throughout the United States. Finally, on the point that most disturbed property-conscious conservatives, the progressive feature of the tax, the Justice said it offended no fundamental principles of fairness and justice. The question of whether such a tax was more just than a proportional one, White continued, was exclusively a matter for legislative determination. Counsel's arguments had painted a doleful picture of the future should this innovation be deemed constitutional, but the Court was unmoved.[74]

Brewer could gain no support for his view that the tax's progressive feature was unconstitutional, but in the following term he did garner a narrow majority to rule that a levy placed by the War Revenue Act on foreign bills of lading was a tax on exports forbidden by Article I, section 9, of the Constitution. The Kansan dismissed the argument that such levies had not been contested earlier because of their presumed constitutionality with the following words: "Indeed, it is only of late years, when the burdens of taxation are increasing by reason of the great expenses of government, that the objects and modes of taxation have become a matter of special scrutiny."[75] Harlan, in dissent with Gray, White, and McKenna, scolded the majority for bringing a discredited idea back into constitutional law—the idea that a tax on a paper document was viewed as a tax on the items listed therein. Consistent congressional action imposing like duties for the past century, he concluded, should have adequately disposed of the constitutional claim.

In other litigation arising from the recent war, the Court decided nine prize cases, but only one unanimously. In that case, in an opinion written by McKenna, the Court concluded that, although the authorities had probable cause to seize a British steamship for attempting to run the blockade in Cuba, the proof offered by the government was insufficient to sustain forfeiture. Fuller and McKenna in the eight divided cases consistently voted to uphold the action of the government in seizing prizes during the war. The Court decided six cases in favor of the condemnation by the United States and two against.[76] Brown consistently sided with the majority, and Gray also favored the United States in six cases, although he resolved two actions differently. Harlan favored the United States in all but one of the cases, while Brewer split the eight evenly. Peckham and White, although not agreeing on particular cases, voted six to two against the government. Finally, Shiras found the United States' claim meritorious in only one action. Certainly it is not surprising that national judges would tend to decide cases involving their government with less than an impartial eye, and the statistics bear out this obvious surmise, for the same five Justices favored the government in six of the eight cases. What is surprising is the voting record of the remaining four Justices to whom is attached the same suspicion of bias.

Despite the elaborate arguments in the cases, votes were lined up in terms of how willing the individual Justice was to hold his government to perceived rules of international law. For instance, in *The Paquete Habana*, when Gray, for the majority, traced the byways of international law to find an exemption from seizures for fishing vessels, Fuller in dissent clearly indicated how he viewed such cases: "I am unable to conclude that there is any such established international rule, or that this court can properly revise action which must be treated as having been taken in the ordinary exercise of discretion in the conduct of war."[77] Baldly, then, the Chief stated that the Court's role in such cases was one of deference to the executive branch. Often the Court has assumed just this role, but rarely has this attitude of deference been so blatantly voiced.

In some of the cases British interests were involved, and in *The Adula* a British steamship was seized for attempting to run a blockade established at Guantanamo Bay, Cuba. Placing the mantle of legitimacy on the American action, Brown wrote the opinion for the Court. Shiras, writing for Gray, White, and Peckham as well, wrote a heated dissent, which concluded as follows:

This is no time, in the history of international law, for the courts of the United States, in laying down rules to affect the rights of neutrals engaged in lawful commerce, to extend and apply harsh decisions made a hundred years ago, in the stress of the bitter wars then prevailing, when the rights of the comparatively feeble neutral states were wholly disregarded. Still less should our courts, as it seems to me was done in this case by the District Court, adopt strained and unnatural constructions of facts and circumstances, in order to subject vessels of nations with whom we are at peace to seizure and condemnation.[78]

Obviously Shiras was troubled. The United States through need and philosophy had championed neutral rights in the past, and Shiras was ashamed that the nation, now holding the upper hand, should treat its principles so casually. Of all the Justices this man from Pittsburgh, who achieved notoriety in the *Pollock* case, was most willing to subject the actions of his government to careful judicial scrutiny and to accept the responsibility for casting his vote in a way that would further proper rules of international law.

Only four men who completed the term in early June 1900, the Chief, Harlan, Gray, and Brewer, were on the High Bench in 1890. The Court was often divided and not immune from flares of temper, but the Chief had established a good working relationship and a fairly efficient operation. Even McKenna was pulling his own weight, although in these early years of his tenure the Chief was careful to assign him relatively simple opinions.

The 1890s had been a difficult period for both the nation and the Supreme Court. Starting the decade with fanfares, the High Bench found its image transformed by the political battles of the mid-1890s. Bryan's campaign in 1896 had made the Court a political issue, emphasizing how its decisions could be conditioned by the "right" appointments to its ranks. With this clear recognition of the Court as a policy-making factor in the life of the nation, the modern era of its history was introduced. With the new century the Justices would be drawn more and more into resolving difficult questions where the past offered infirm guidance and the future demanded charting.

NOTES

1. Carl B. Swisher, *Stephen J. Field: Craftsman of the Law* (Washington: Brookings Institution, 1930), pp. 441-43.

2. Frank O. Gatell, "Robert C. Grier," in *The Justices of the United States Supreme Court 1789-1969*, ed. Leon Friedman and Fred L. Israel, 4 vols. (New York: R. R. Bowker Co. and Chelsea House Publishers, 1969), 2:883; and Charles Evans Hughes, *The Supreme Court of the United States* (New York: Columbia University Press, 1928), pp. 75-76.

3. State court opinion quoted in Allgeyer v. Louisiana, 165 U.S. 578, 585 (1897).

4. In 1869 the Court had ruled that the business of writing insurance contracts was not a subject of commerce, thereby leaving to the states full power to regulate the insurance industry. Early in the present term the Justices had upheld Alabama's right to impose personal liability upon an insurance agent acting in behalf of a company not licensed to do business within the state (Paul v. Virginia, 75 U.S. [8 Wall.] 168 [1869]; and Noble v. Mitchell, 164 U.S. 367 [1896]).

5. Allgeyer v. Louisiana, 165 U.S. 578, 589 (1897).

6. Essentially, contract law gave to private parties the opportunity to make their own rules in the agreement they reached; courts would generally enforce the "law" agreed upon by the parties. This freedom existed at the sufferance of the society and was heralded as a positive contribution to economic growth. Private parties could make their own "law" not because the government was disabled from making it but rather because of a fundamental decision that entrusted this responsibility to the parties themselves.

7. See J. Willard Hurst, *Law and the Conditions of Freedom in the Nineteenth-Century United States* (Madison: University of Wisconsin Press, 1956); and Roscoe Pound, "Liberty of Contract," *Yale Law Journal* 18 (May 1909):454-87.

8. Willard L. King, *Melville Weston Fuller: Chief Justice of the United States 1888-1910*, Phoenix ed. (Chicago: University of Chicago Press, 1967), p. 94; and Chicago, Burlington & Quincy R.R. v. Chicago, 166 U.S. 226 (1897).

9. Davidson v. New Orleans, 96 U.S. 97 (1878); U.S. Const. Amend. V.

10. Chicago, Burlington & Quincy R.R. v. Chicago, 166 U.S. 226, 235-36 (1897).

11. Id. at 259.

12. In the preceding term Harlan had carried most of his colleagues with him in another path-breaking due process ruling. In *Crain* v. *United States* (162 U.S. 625 [1896]), a noncapital criminal case coming from Judge Isaac C. Parker's court, the Court ruled that the failure of the official record to show that the defendant had pleaded to the charge was a denial of due process. Eighteen years later, however, in *Garland* v. *Washington* (232 U.S. 642 [1914]), the Court overturned the *Crain* precedent, saying that such technicalities could no longer be viewed as a denial of due process. For a fuller discussion of the episode, see John E. Semonche, "Conflicting Views on Crime and Punishment in the 1890s: 'Hanging Judge' Parker Confronts the United States Supreme Court," publication forthcoming.

13. For a brief summary of this later development, see Henry J. Abraham, *Freedom and the Court: Civil Rights and Liberties in the United States*, 3rd ed. (New York: Oxford University Press, 1977), pp. 33-105.

14. See St. Louis & San Francisco Ry. v. Mathews, 165 U.S. 1 (1897); Gladson v. Minnesota, 166 U.S. 427 (1897); New York, New Haven & Hartford R.R. v. New York, 165 U.S. 628 (1897); Lake Shore & Michigan Southern Ry. v. Ohio, 165 U.S. 365 (1897); and Long Island Water Supply Co. v. Brooklyn, 166 U.S. 685 (1897).

15. Davis v. Massachusetts, 167 U.S. 43 (1897).

16. The major case is Adams Express Co. v. Ohio State Auditor, 165 U.S. 194 (1897), *rehearing denied*, 166 U.S. 185 (1897).

17. Adams Express Co. v. Ohio State Auditor, 165 U.S. 194, 254 (1897).

18. Adams Express Co. v. Ohio State Auditor, 166 U.S. 185, 225 (1897).

19. Act of August 2, 1886, ch. 840, 24 Stat. 209, 210; and *In re* Kollock, 165 U.S. 526 (1897).

20. *In re* Lennon, 166 U.S. 548 (1897); and Robertson v. Baldwin, 165 U.S. 275 (1897).

21. Robertson v. Baldwin, 165 U.S. 275, 292 (1897).

22. United States v. Trans-Missouri Freight Assn., 166 U.S. 290, 313, 342 (1897).

23. Cincinnati, New Orleans & Texas Pacific Ry. v. ICC, 162 U.S. 184 (1896); and ICC v. Cincinnati, New Orleans & Texas Pacific Ry., 167 U.S. 479 (1897).

24. ICC v. Alabama Midland Ry., 168 U.S. 144, 176 (1897).

25. See Gabriel Kolko, *Railroads and Regulation, 1877-1916* (Princeton: Princeton University Press, 1965), pp. 80-83.

26. King, *Fuller*, pp. 224-26; and Swisher, *Field*, pp. 444-45.

27. King, *Fuller*, pp. 226-27. Field's official letter of resignation is at 168 U.S. 713. His record of over thirty-four years and seven months of service on the high court was finally bettered by William O. Douglas before his retirement in 1975.

28. Field's letter of resignation at 168 U.S. 713.

29. Field's "philosophical" bent has invited just such interpretations. See Robert G. McCloskey, *American Conservatism in the Age of Enterprise 1865-1910* (New York: Harper & Row, Torchbooks, 1964), pp. 72-126; and Charles W. McCurdy, "Justice Field and the Jurisprudence of Government-Business Relations: Some Parameters of Laissez-Faire Constitutionalism, 1863-1897," *Journal of American History* 61 (March 1975):970-1005.

30. Speech printed in Hampton L. Carson, *The Supreme Court of the United States: Its History*, 2d ed., 2 vols. (Philadelphia: A.R. Keller Co., 1892), 2:723.

31. Ibid.

32. James F. Watts, "Joseph McKenna," in *Justices of the Supreme Court*, 3:1719-26.

33. See *New York World*, December 17, 18, 1897, and *New York Times*, January 22, 1898; and King, *Fuller*, pp. 228-29.

34. Brother Matthew McDevitt, *Joseph McKenna: Associate Justice of the United States* (Washington: Catholic University Press, 1946; reprint ed., New York: Da Capo Press, 1974), pp. 105, 202.

35. Chicago, Milwaukee & St. Paul Ry. v. Sloan, 169 U.S. 133, 135 (1898).

36. Holden v. Hardy, 169 U.S. 366, 387, 385, 387, 391 (1898). Brown here stresses the Court's need to be sensitive to changing realities in performing its task of constitutional interpretation, an admonition Brown and the majority apparently neglected in the Court's consideration of *Robertson* v. *Baldwin* (165 U.S. 578 [1897]) in the previous term.

37. Holden v. Hardy, 169 U.S. 366, 398 (1898).

38. Smyth v. Ames, 169 U.S. 466 (1898).

39. Williams v. Mississippi, 170 U.S. 213, 222 (1898).

40. Yick Wo. v. Hopkins, 118 U.S. 356 (1888); and Williams v. Mississippi, 170 U.S. 213, 222 (1898).

41. New York Indians v. United States, 170 U.S. 1, 23 (1898); and United States v. New York Indians, 173 U.S. 464 (1899).

42. Rhodes v. Iowa, 170 U.S. 412 (1898); Vance v. W.A. Vandercook Co., 170 U.S. 438 (1898); Schollenberger v. Pennsylvania, 171 U.S. 1, 30 (1898); and Collins v. New Hampshire, 171 U.S. 30 (1898).

43. King, *Fuller*, pp. 238-41.

44. A later Justice concluded that, although little would have changed in the basic system of government if the Court did not have the power to declare federal legislation in conflict with the Constitution, much would have been different had the Court not had this

review power over state legislation (Oliver Wendell Holmes, "Law and the Court: Speech at a Dinner of the Harvard Law School Association of New York on February 15, 1913," in *Collected Legal Papers* [New York: Harcourt, Brace & Co., 1921], pp. 295-96).

45. King, *Fuller*, p. 235; and attached in Clerk's Scrapbook No. 1, Records of the Supreme Court of the United States (Office of the Clerk), Record Group 267, National Archives, Washington D.C., is the following poem:

> At last the end of Wong
> We've studied, written long,
> And may be wholly wrong;
> Yet join the happy song
> Goodby, goodby to Wong
> No more, no more of Kim!
> We've had enough of him,
> And close this case with vim
> So raise the gladsome hymn
> Goodby, goodby to Kim.
> The last, the last of Ark!
> His prospects have been dark
> If Gray had missed his mark;
> But now he's on a lark
> Goodby, goodby to Ark!
>   Brewer

46. United States v. Wong Kim Ark, 169 U.S. 649, 675 (1898).

47. Slaughter-House Cases, 83 U.S. (16 Wall.) 36, 73 (1873); Elk v. Wilkins, 112 U.S. 94, 102 (1884); and United States v. Wong Kim Ark, 169 U.S. 649, 694 (1898).

48. United States v. Wong Kim Ark, 169 U.S. 649, 699 (1898).

49. Id. at 704; and see *In re* Look Tin Sing, 21 Fed. 905 (1884), cited in United States v. Wong Kim Ark, 169 U.S. 649, 694, 697 (1898).

50. United States v. Wong Kim Ark, 169 U.S. 649, 726 (1898).

51. Not until late in the second decade of the twentieth century, and then in response to what was seen as the Japanese problem, was a constitutional amendment proposed in Congress seeking to overturn the Court's broad ruling in *Wong Kim Ark* (U.S., Congress, House, *Proposed Amendments to the Constitution*, House Doc. No. 551, 70th Cong., 2d sess., 1928 [Washington: Government Printing Office, 1929], pp. 180-81).

52. King, *Fuller*, p. 235.

53. United States v. Joint-Traffic Assn., 171 U.S. 505, 569 (1898).

54. Hopkins v. United States, 171 U.S. 578 (1898); and Anderson v. United States, 171 U.S. 604 (1898).

55. Orient Insurance Co. v. Daggs, 172 U.S. 557, 562 (1899).

56. St. Louis, Iron Mountain & Southern Ry. v. Paul, 173 U.S. 404 (1899); and Lake Shore & Michigan Southern Ry. v. Ohio, 173 U.S. 285 (1899).

57. Atchison, Topeka & Santa Fe R.R. v. Matthews, 174 U.S. 96, 106 (1899).

58. The final resolution largely fulfilled British expectations, though the desire of the commission to achieve unanimity did allow Fuller to gain some concessions for Venezuela (King, *Fuller*, pp. 249-60).

59. For a partial listing of both governmental and nongovernmental activities of the Justices, see U.S., Congress, House, Committee on the Judiciary. *Associate Justice William O. Douglas: Final Report by the Special Subcommittee on H. Res. 920*, 91st Cong., 2d sess., 1970, pp. 431-32, 437-50.

60. King, *Fuller*, pp. 165-66.

61. Ibid., pp. 246-47.

62. Jones v. Meehan, 175 U.S. 1, 32 (1899).

63. Addyston Pipe & Steel Co. v. United States, 175 U.S. 211, 240-41 (1899).

64. Leovy v. United States, 177 U.S. 621, 636 (1900).

65. Lindsay & Phelps Co. v. Mullen, 176 U.S. 126, 155 (1900).

66. Louisiana v. Texas, 176 U.S. 1, 23 (1900). The political question doctrine, created by the Court and first clearly expounded in *Luther* v. *Borden* (48 U.S. [7 How.] 1 [1849]), is a device of judicial restraint, used when the Justices determine that the dispute should be resolved through the processes of political decision making and not in a legal forum.

67. Taylor v. Beckham, 178 U.S. 548, 605, 608, 609 (1900).

68. Carter v. Texas, 177 U.S. 442 (1900).

69. Cumming v. County Board of Education, 175 U.S. 528 (1899), overruled by Brown v. Board of Education, 347 U.S. 483 (1954).

70. G. F. Edmunds to James H. McKenny, December 30, 1899, in Apellate Case Files, Docket No. 17206, Records of the Supreme Court of the United States, Record Group 267, National Archives, Washington, D.C.

71. Bollin v. Nebraska, 176 U.S. 83 (1900); and Maxwell v. Dow, 176 U.S. 581 (1900).

72. Hurtado v. California, 110 U.S. 516 (1884); and Maxwell v. Dow, 176 U.S. 581, 612 (1900).

73. Maxwell v. Dow, 176 U.S. 581, 614, 616, 617 (1900). Harlan was vindicated when the *Maxwell* decision was overruled in *Duncan* v. *Louisiana* (391 U.S. 145 [1968]).

74. Nicol v. Ames, 173 U.S. 509, 515 (1899); and Knowlton v. Moore, 178 U.S. 41 (1900).

75. Fairbank v. United States, 181 U.S. 283, 312 (1901).

76. The Newfoundland, 176 U.S. 97 (1900); cases decided in favor of the government: The Pedro, 175 U.S. 354 (1899); The Guido, 175 U.S. 382 (1899); The Adula, 176 U.S. 361 (1900); The Panama, 176 U.S. 535 (1900); The Benito Estenger, 176 U.S. 568 (1900); and The Carlos F. Roses, 177 U.S. 655 (1900); and cases decided against the government: The Buena Ventura v. United States, 175 U.S. 384 (1899); and The Paquete Habana, 175 U.S. 677 (1900).

77. The Paquete Habana, 175 U.S. 677, 715 (1900).

78. The Adula, 176 U.S. 361, 398 (1900).

chapter 5

DEFERENCE, NOT
ABDICATION, 1900-1903

In October 1900 the capital was buzzing with the upcoming presidential election. The candidates were the same as they had been in 1896, the now incumbent President William McKinley and the Democratic challenger William Jennings Bryan, but there was none of the panic that characterized the election of 1896, when apocalyptic visions were conjured up in the event of a Bryan success. Perhaps most observers recognized that McKinley was in a secure position, not only with a growing national prosperity but also as the beneficiary of a most successful war against Spain. Less hospitable to the alleged radicalism of Bryan, the voters were no more sympathetic to his anti-imperialistic stance. When the votes were counted McKinley had outdrawn Bryan by about 240,000 more votes than in 1896. Of some interest was the election with McKinley of the former governor of New York and hero of San Juan Hill, Theodore Roosevelt. Roosevelt had accepted the vice-presidential bid reluctantly, viewing it as the end of his political career. Prophetically, it was McKinley's friend and advisor Mark Hanna who said that now only one man stood between that "mad man" and the presidency of the United States.[1]

Encountering the work of the 1900 term, the Justices contended with a raft of cases claiming that governmental action had impaired the obligation of contract. Although the area had been a busy subject of litigation for generations, and although the claim was usually met by rejection, often because modification by the government had been accepted as part of the agreement, there were a few cases during the term that fell into the diminishing grey area. The Justices divided five to four in three cases involving water companies. In *Freeport Water Company* the majority held that the municipality could only contract with the company within the limitations set down by a state statute. The town's contract fixed rates for the life of the charter, while the state statute provided for changes by municipal ordinance. McKenna, for the majority, concluded there was no impairment of the contract when the municipality sought to change the rates. White, Brewer, Brown, and Peckham dissented. In two other water company cases where similar contentions were raised, the lineup of Justices remained unchanged.[2] The majority was obviously willing again to draw every inference that would protect the public interest in regulating the rates of these enterprises.

Another pair of cases illustrates well the nature of the Court's decision making. All nine Justices agreed in two cases from Minnesota that local governmental units had acted unconstitutionally. What posed the difficulty was the rationalization of the result, important not only as a defense of the decision but also as precedent. In *Stearns* v. *Minnesota* there was no opinion of the Court, just three different rationales. The public little understood how the Justices could unanimously decide a case in favor of one party, yet fail to agree on the reasons. Such public debates among the Justices only provided fuel to the growing criticism that these men in black robes were virtually unrestrained as they approached their solemn duty. Succinctly, the issue involved in *Stearns* was whether Minnesota could tax certain land owned by a railroad after providing in a contract that the property would be exempt in return for a tax of 3 percent upon the gross receipts of the railroad. Minnesota still claimed the 3 percent while it sought to impose the regular rate of taxation on certain railroad property. Brewer, with Fuller, Shiras, and Peckham agreeing, concluded that such action constituted an impairment of the contract and was therefore void. Brown found his own path, saying that, since the Minnesota legislature and courts had for thirty years recognized the agreement with the railroad, state authorities were now prevented from changing it.[3]

White, for the others, acknowledged the power of the state to change the terms of the contract. But such power, he said, "cannot be so exercised as to violate fundamental principles of justice by depriving of the equal protection of the laws or of the constitutional guarantee against the taking of property without due process of law."[4] The Louisianian found that the statutory attempt to tax the property under the regular system of taxation, while insisting upon the gross-receipt exaction, was unconstitutional. Despite his failure to command a majority, White had introduced an intriguing idea into this area of the law: even if the state did have the power to amend a contract, it could not amend it in a way that violated the equal protection and due process clauses. Certainly this could herald a new approach for advocates seeking to contest state action. If the state had the power to amend a contract, the inquiry would not stop there, but the effect of that amendment would, if White could command a majority, now be subject to a new scrutiny. For the present only Harlan, Gray, and McKenna were prepared to tread this new path with the man from Louisiana.

The divisions in *Stearns* became public on December 3, 1900, but one week later White had won over Brown and was able to deliver a majority opinion in the *Duluth & Iron Range Railroad Company* case, the other

Minnesota case, argued seven months after *Stearns* and dealing essentially with the same issue. White, for the majority, wrote into constitutional law this new addition to substantive due process. For the first time the majority looked at an alleged impairment of contract, found state authority to change its terms, but then concluded that the action had violated another constitutional guarantee. White's opinion was short, just long enough to state the pertinent facts and reiterate the conclusion the quartet had earlier reached in *Stearns*. On the basis of this pair of cases, White and his cohorts were willing to go further in using the Court's power to define due process than were Brewer, Fuller, Shiras, and Peckham, who simply concurred in the result.[5]

The conclusion that this majority of five was more inclined to use the due process clause to check state action than was the minority of four should be approached with caution. Although the Justices were fully aware of the central issue involved in their disagreement, this lineup, even in other due process cases, had little solidity. Each case would have to be inspected on its own terms and if this process led to philosophical inconsistency, that was simply the price paid by the Justices for their desire to approach each case independently rather than be bound by deductions from precedent.

For example, Harlan, a member of this new majority, thought that the Court two terms ago had established a rule that an assessment for paving levied on abutting property owners had to be justified by proving that a benefit had been conferred. The absence of such a consideration would be a violation of due process. But there were other factors present in that case, including the fact that the assessment was greater than the condemnation award. Now Harlan saw his earlier six-man majority dissipate in two cases during the term. Shiras wrote majority opinions legitimating such an assessment without consideration of benefit. Harlan's extensive dissent carried along only White and McKenna. At least a trio of the five-man majority in the second Minnesota case was still intact. But, to show the hurdles the due process argument had to face on the Court, a property owner's claim that the United States had deprived him of access to the water by erecting a pier won only three votes, those of Shiras, Gray, and Peckham, an entirely new trio. No member of the Court found merit in the due process claim of a resident of the city of Brockton, Massachusetts, that an assessment for the construction of a sewer constitutionally precluded an annual charge for its use.[6]

During the session the Court turned away all challenges to state action based upon the argument that such action violated the commerce clause. The type of multipronged argument that was used by counsel before the Court was well demonstrated in a challenge to a Georgia statute, which imposed a license tax on agents hiring laborers for work outside the state; agents employing laborers for work within the state were free from any such obligation. The Court disposed of privileges and immunities and equal protection arguments and then saw no unconstitutional burden upon interstate commerce. Minnesota could require railroads to provide rail connections for the exchange of cars and require a license for elevators and warehouses on the right of way of railroads; Nebraska could enforce a judgment for illegal charges on the Western Union Telegraph Company; and Kentucky could impose racial segregation on railroad companies operating within the state.[7]

A commerce clause case that provoked division was *Austin* v. *Tennessee*, which concerned a determination that cigarettes were detrimental to one's health. Tennessee sought to prevent the selling or other disposition of cigarettes within the state, and Austin was fined $50 for violating the ban. Although refusing to take judicial notice that cigarettes were harmful, a narrow majority in two opinions did agree that Tennessee had the authority to enact such a measure to protect the public health. The problem the case posed was the recurrent one of what was the original package. The American Tobacco Company packaged its products in paper containers containing ten cigarettes each, which were carried in baskets to their interstate destinations by an express company. Seemingly forced to find an original package, Brown for the four-man plurality casually said it was the basket. White, who with his concurring opinion made up a majority to uphold the Tennessee action, was at pains to make clear that he was still wedded to the original-package doctrine. To the question, was the ten-cigarette package an original one, White answered: "I am constrained to conclude that this question is correctly answered in the negative, not only from the size of each particular parcel, but from all the other surrounding facts and circumstances."[8] For White, especially, an original package was not something that could be defined; rather it was a conclusion that attached when various facts coalesced to make it desirable. In a case in the previous term, involving the original-package concept,[9] White had been a silent member of the majority, but here he spoke out, worried that Brown's opinion might be taken as indicating that the Court was abandoning the doctrine.

Brewer, in dissent with Fuller, Shiras, and Peckham, wrote an extensive opinion explaining the rationale of the original-package doctrine and its importance to interstate commerce. After this exploration, he added: "I regret that the decision of a great constitutional question like that here presented turns on the shifting opinions of individual judges as to the peculiar facts of a particular case. . . . No case, involving a constitutional question should be turned off on the simple declaration that upon its peculiar facts it falls on one side or the other of some undisclosed line of demarcation." The Justice well recognized the purpose of the Tennessee regulation, which was effectively to preclude the shipment of cigarettes into Tennessee. Brewer argued that the majority's contention "that an imported package must be of a large size in order to secure the right of sale is simply a convenient way of declaring that the right of importation for purposes of sale may be denied." Although believing that many things may be restrained, the Kansan argued that the proper body to make such a determination is Congress, not the individual states. It "is better," Brewer concluded, "that in certain instances one State should be subjected to temporary annoyance rather than that the whole framework of commercial unity created by the Constitution should be destroyed."[10]

The Court had taken a year to decide *Austin* v. *Tennessee*. Gray, Harlan, and Brown were not in sympathy with the original-package doctrine, and they had captured the votes of both McKenna and White in the previous term. Brewer had worked hard to win the Louisianian to his side, and possibly his failure led to pointed words in his dissent that came close to ridiculing White's concurring opinion.

Strangely, despite the strong words in support of congressional control over interstate commerce, none of the dissenters in *Austin* saw any such inroad in a Texas law prohibiting the importation of cattle from Louisiana. At the same time the Texas case was decided, a unanimous Court upheld an Idaho sheep quarantine act giving the governor authority to prohibit the importation of sheep when he believed that such animals might be carriers of an infectious disease. Brewer, for the Court, found nothing that would cast suspicion on the state's contention that this was a legitimate quarantine measure well within the state's police power. The Texas case posed a more difficult question, not only because of continual commercial squabbling between the two states, but because of the presence of other factors. McKenna, for a majority of six, ruled that an embargo by Texas on all livestock shipped from Louisiana, because of a perceived threat of anthrax, was a legitimate exercise of the state's police power. Two dissenting opinions were written. Harlan, for himself and White, questioned the absence of evidence to sustain such a drastic measure and pronounced the action "an unauthorized obstruction to the freedom of interstate commerce."[11] Brown also dissented, contending that the facts developed in the record failed to justify this substantial interdiction of trade.

Overshadowing all other business of the 1900 term were the cases that forced the Court to square American imperialism with the Constitution. The ease with which the Justices agreed that Cuba was a foreign country, despite continued American occupation,[12] gave little hint of the battles that lay in store over the more difficult questions yet to be reached. Because of a self-denying congressional resolution passed at the outset of the Spanish-American War, Cuba could not be annexed to the United States, but the Treaty of Paris at the war's conclusion did place in American control both Puerto Rico and the Philippines. How these possessions were to be treated within the

American constitutional system was the knotty problem presented in the *Insular Cases*. Not surprising was the Court's failure to find an easy solution to a politically charged issue deceptively presented in abstract terms.

All three *Insular Cases—De Lima* v. *Bidwell, Dooley* v. *United States*, and *Downes* v. *Bidwell*—involved commercial matters. Arguments in the three cases took almost a full week in early January, and the decisions were not announced until May 27, 1901. In the first two decisions Brown wrote for the Court with the support of Fuller, Harlan, Brewer, and Peckham. In the *De Lima* case Gray dissented alone, while McKenna's dissent attracted both Shiras and White. In *Dooley* White emerged as the leader of a faction on the Court. In the final case of the trio, *Downes*, Brown defected, leaving the former members of the majority to join together in a dissenting opinion by Fuller. The difficulty with the new majority was that it could not coalesce. Brown wrote for himself; White concurred and carried Shiras and McKenna along; and Gray added additional words of his own. Rarely had the Court faced a more difficult problem, for just as novel as the nation acquiring colonies was the reconciliation of this new development with the nation's constitutional structure.

In *De Lima* the Court had to decide whether, after the cessation of Puerto Rico to the United States by the Treaty of Paris but before any congressional action, customs duties could be legally collected on goods imported into the United States from that island. Brown and the majority concluded that the resolution of this question turned on whether Puerto Rico was still a "foreign country" under the terms of the tariff laws. After an extensive review of executive, legislative, and judicial action respecting territories of the United States, he ruled that, whether technically organized or not, Puerto Rico was a territory of the United States. As such, the Constitution barred the collection of such duties. Although the federal government argued that some action by Congress was necessary to convert a foreign country into a domestic territory, the majority recognized no such need. Brown also rejected the contention that a territory might be domestic for some purposes and foreign for others. This initial majority seemed unwilling to allow the other branches of government to draw lines at will, preferring instead to see a definite and important role for the judiciary in checking arbitrary and inconsistent action by the other branches.

In dissent Gray said that the decision was inconsistent with an early precedent of the Court and with the decision reached in the *Downes* case. Except for the wayward Brown, all the others agreed that the two cases were inconsistent. McKenna wrote the major dissent, in large part based upon a middle ground that the majority said could not exist—"that Porto Rico occupied a relation to the United States between that of being a foreign country absolutely and of being domestic territory absolutely, and because of that relation its products were subject to the duties imposed by the Dingley act."[13] Although the fundamental issue of the extent of judicial power lurked beneath the surface, the dispute involved whether the term *foreign country* could have different meanings for different purposes. The majority sought an all-purpose definition; the more vocal minority stressed the malleability of words and the relativity of definition.

Possibly receiving some aid from White, who was busy preparing his opinions in the remaining two cases, McKenna's opinion was well done. The Constitution, practice under it, judicial authority, and the treaty with Spain all support, he said, placing Puerto Rico in a status that is both foreign and domestic at the same time. McKenna seemed especially concerned about not trapping the administration within a constitutional bind. Concluding his opinion, he revealed some of the strong feeling behind the dissenters' position:

It vindicates the government from national and international weakness. It exhibits the Constitution as a charter of great and vital authorities, with limitations indeed, but with such limitations as serve and assist government, not destroy it; which, though fully enforced, yet enable the United States to have—what it was intended to have— an equal station among the Powers of the earth, and to do all Acts and Things which Independent States may of right do—and confidently do, able to secure the fullest fruits of their performance. All powers of government, placed in harmony under the Constitution; the rights and liberties of every citizen secured put to no hazard of loss or impairment; the power of the nation also secured in its great station, enabled to move with strength and dignity and effect among the other nations of the earth to such purposes as it may undertake or to such destiny as it may be called.[14]

The rhetoric was in part the result of the high emotionalism the issue provoked and the conviction of the dissenters that the Constitution should not be an obstacle to the nation in its search for great power status.

Second among the trio of cases was *Dooley* v. *United States*. Here the lineup remained the same, but White consolidated the dissenters in a single opinion. The new wrinkle in *Dooley* was that the duties were imposed on goods coming into Puerto Rico from the United States after the island had been acquired. Brown, for the majority, conceded that duties exacted before the cession of the island to the United States were permissible, but he ruled that after cession Puerto Rico no longer was a foreign country and "until Congress otherwise constitutionally directed, such merchandise was entitled to free entry." Brown said that to hold otherwise would place the island in a disastrous position of "practical isolation."[15]

White began his dissent by summarizing the dissenting position in *De Lima*, concluding with the earlier trio's attitude toward the effect of the Treaty of Paris: "The rule of the immediate bringing, by the self-operating force of a treaty, ceded territory inside of the line of the tariff laws of the United States denies the existence of powers which the Constitution expressly bestows, overthrows the authority conferred on Congress by the Constitution, and is impossible of execution." Even if the Treaty of Paris had incorporated Puerto Rico into the United States, he said, this fact, in itself, would not exempt the island from the tariff act. Only Congress, by specifically addressing the matter, could provide the needed exemption. To the majority's charge that the dissenting position was one of expediency, not of law, White countered:

But this is fallacious. For, if it be demonstrated that a particular result cannot be accomplished without destroying the revenue power conferred upon Congress by the Constitution, and without annihilating the conceded authority of the government in other respects, such demonstration shows the unsoundness of the argument which magnifies the results flowing from the exercise by the treaty-making power of its authority to acquire, to the detriment and destruction of that balanced and limited government which the Constitution called into being.[16]

The dissenters here were arguing not only that it was wise to entrust this difficult question to the other branches of government but also that this deference was essential to protect the powers that had been constitutionally delegated to those branches.

Brown had written the first two Court opinions, because he, among the majority Justices, was least committed to the need for judicial supervision. In both of his opinions there is a recognition that, should Congress act, Puerto Rico could indeed be placed in that middle ground between foreign and domestic status. When that question was presented in *Downes* v. *Bidwell*, Brown upheld congressional authority and joined with the quartet of earlier dissenters to create a new majority. *Downes* dealt with duties paid under the authority of the Foraker Act, by which Congress provided for a temporary civil government for Puerto Rico. Section three of that act provided for a duty of 15 percent on merchandise imported into the United States from the island. Obviously, if Puerto Rico was part of the United States, such exaction would be unconstitutional, and this was what counsel for Downes contended. Brown wrote an extensive opinion announcing the judgment of the Court, which sustained the tariff.

He contended that a decision in favor of the exaction of tariff duties does not lead inevitably to the result that no provisions of the Constitution extend to Puerto Rico. There "is a clear distinction," Brown said, "between such prohibitions as go to the very root of the power of Congress to act at all, irrespective of time or place, and such as are operative only 'throughout the United States' or among the several states." The Justice stated that the relative silence of the Constitution on the subject of territories afforded Congress considerable latitude. "The executive and legislative departments of the government," he continued, "have for more than a century interpreted this silence as precluding the idea that the Constitution attached to these territories as soon as acquired, and unless such interpretation be manifestly contrary to the letter or spirit of the Constitution, it should be followed by the judicial department."[17]

Implicitly recognizing an anti-imperialistic movement growing in the United States, Brown labeled such territorial acquisition strictly a political question. In the absence of language in the Constitution demanding a different result, he believed, Congress should be allowed to consider each case upon its merits. "A false step at this time," the Justice continued, "might be fatal to the development of what Chief Justice Marshall called the 'American Empire.' " Content with having Congress determine how quickly "Anglo-Saxon principles" should be extended to "alien races," he concluded that Puerto Rico "is a territory appurtenant and belonging to the United States" but not one embraced by the revenue clauses of the Constitution. The Justice gained no adherents because of his strong assertion, contrary to an earlier opinion of John Marshall, that the constitutional requirement mandating uniform taxation applied only to the states and not to the territories.[18] From a position that originally put him in union with Fuller, Harlan, Brewer, and Shiras, Brown had emerged taking a stronger and more unqualified position on congressional authority than the original dissenters. To unequivocal congressional leadership, he would defer.

White responded for himself, Shiras, and McKenna, asserting that in "the case of the territories, as in every other instance, when a provision of the Constitution is invoked, the question which arises is not whether the Constitution is operative, for that is self-evident, but whether the provision relied upon is applicable."[19] The Louisianian contended that a decision in favor of the constitutionality of the duties does not imply that Congress could destroy the liberties of the people of Puerto Rico. The only issue, he said, is whether this tax on imports from that island offends the Constitution.

The key to White's opinion, and to what would in the years ahead become the Court's clear position, was that a treaty in itself could not incorporate territory into the United States without the express assent of Congress. Incorporation "does not arise," he said, "until in the wisdom of Congress it is deemed that the acquired territory had reached that state where it is proper that it should enter into and form a part of the American family." White was unclear how, in the absence of the use of the word *incorporate*, such action was to be signaled, but he *was* clear in his insistence that Congress, not the Court, must determine when a territory should receive the full benefits of the Constitution. Viewing the Treaty of Paris as not providing specifically for incorporation of the territory into the United States, he agreed with Brown in characterizing Puerto Rico as an "appurtenant" possession.[20]

Gray in a short, laconic opinion said that, in substance, he agreed with White. The Justice drew a distinction between territories previously acquired by the United States and those it now had obtained as spoils of war. He accepted the concept of incorporation and the authority of Congress to establish temporary governments in such territories "not subject to all the restrictions of the Constitution."[21]

Some arguments by counsel in the cases were wide-ranging, and the Court was asked to protect these new territories from potential oppression at the hands of the other branches of the government. In emotional overtones the arguments were similar to those in *Pollock*, that is, the Court must act to save the country. White had no sympathy for this approach. Should the United States never incorporate such territories and continually hold them in subjection, he said, judicial interference with legislative discretion would be far more disastrous. Unwilling to impune the integrity of the legislative and executive branches, White found a solution that was to his mind both constitutionally sound and expedient, but he would have to work to gain a majority.[22]

The dissenters in *Downes* were led by the Chief, who earlier had delegated the writing of opinions to Brown. Fuller, who was, along with McKenna, most inclined to support the actions of the wartime government in seizing ships, was now more critical. Calling attention to his colleagues' inability to agree in a single opinion, he said that the splintered majority had misread precedent, which clearly dictates that the tariff on Puerto Rican goods violates the constitutional requirement of geographical uniformity. Fuller agreed that the nation has the power to acquire territory, but he argued that, once the territory is obtained, the government is restricted in its exercise of sovereignty by the terms of the Constitution. Contending with White, the Chief continued:

Great stress is thrown upon the word "incorporation," as if possessed of some occult meaning, but I take it that the act under consideration made Porto Rico, whatever its situation before, an organized territory of the United States. Being such, and the act undertaking to impose duties by virtue of clause one of section eight, how is it that the rule which qualifies the power does not apply to its exercise in respect of commerce with that territory? . . .

That theory assumes that the Constitution created a government empowered to acquire countries throughout the world, to be governed by different rules than those obtaining in the original States and territories, and substitutes for the present system of republican government, a system of domination over distant provinces in the exercise of unrestricted power.[23]

This argument of saving the Constitution from the actions of the other branches won Fuller, Brewer, and Shiras, three of the four remaining Justices who composed the majority in *Pollock*.

Harlan, in addition to concurring in Fuller's opinion, wrote a dissent of his own. Agreeing that the tariff imposed by the Foraker Act is unconstitutional, he felt compelled to deal with some of the more general propositions involved in the other opinions. From a low-key start Harlan warmed up, disturbed by the majority's apparent willingness to sacrifice the protection of constitutional liberty upon the altar of "legislative absolutism." To the conclusion that Congress was relatively unchecked in its dealings with the territories, Harlan responded:

In my opinion, Congress has no existence and can exercise no authority outside of the Constitution. . . . The idea that this country may acquire territories anywhere upon the earth, by conquest or treaty, and hold them as mere colonies or provinces—the people inhabiting them to enjoy only such rights as Congress chooses to accord to them—is wholly inconsistent with the spirit and genius as well as with the words of the Constitution.[24]

These words express well the crisis of conscience that the American people were experiencing in the aftermath of the Spanish-American War. On one hand, the acquisition of colonies meant new status for the nation; on the other, our heritage as colonies of Great Britain, engaging in the first great war for colonial liberation, made our new position somewhat uncomfortable. Harlan said that rather than distort the Constitution the administration should determine before acquisition whether a territory and its people could be assimilated successfully.

Although the *Insular Cases* concerned tariff problems, they did excite considerable popular and legal interest. An eager public was somewhat frustrated by such divided and equivocal judicial responses to the issues. What was clear, however, was the emergence of a majority that would not hinder the establishment of an American empire. Bryan in 1900, seeking to inspire a lethargic electorate, had sought to make imperialism a campaign issue, saying that the Constitution must follow the flag. Commenting on the implications of Bryan's defeat, Finley Peter Dunne's Mr. Dooley said: "no matter whether the Constitution follows th' flag or not, th' Supreme Coort follows th' ilicition returns."[25]

During the summer recess Harlan and Fuller worried that Brown, in one of the two similar cases yet to be publicly decided, would defect from the five-man grouping he had initially joined. To save the majority Harlan suggested that Fuller write an opinion and send it to Brown. The Chief's diplomatic approach to Brown might have strengthened the Justice's resolve, for he responded that he had asked that the opinion be postponed simply to reply more effectively to some of the points raised by the dissenters. When he saw the draft opinion Brown indicated that he would concur in it and add a few additional remarks. Despite their summertime effort, Harlan and Fuller failed to capture their colleague's vote in the other remaining case.[26]

Before the Justices returned to the capital, the public was shocked by the shooting of President William McKinley on September 6, 1901, just six months after his second inauguration. Eight days later McKinley died, and a somber Theodore Roosevelt, resolving to carry on the policies of the dead President, took the oath of office. Roosevelt had been catapulted from the limbo of the vice-presidency into the nation's top office. If for no other reason than his power to select future colleagues, the Justices, along with the people of the nation, were interested in the type of leadership this exuberant hero of the last war and former governor of New York would bring to the presidency.

When the Court convened for the October 1901 term, Horace Gray was not present. Illness prevented his return until three weeks after the beginning of the session, and then he stayed only until mid-February, when he returned home.[27]

Early in the session the Justices issued their opinions in the two insular cases remaining from the previous term. Fuller's success with Brown over the past summer was reflected in *Fourteen Diamond Rings* v. *United States*. The draft Fuller had sent to Brown became the majority opinion. Brown wrote a concurrence, but he indicated that he fully subscribed to the Chief's opinion. The case introduced the Philippines into the record of the Court. Harlan and Fuller had considered Brown a shaky adherent to this majority because the tariff duties were imposed after a Senate resolution had been passed. That resolution specifically denied incorporation and any intention to annex the islands permanently.

The question posed was whether confiscation by customs officials of diamond rings brought back by a soldier who had served with his regiment in the Philippines, after the cession of that territory by Spain to the United States, was lawful. An answer turned on whether the soldier had any obligations to declare and pay duties upon the rings. Relying heavily upon the *De Lima* opinion by Brown, Fuller said the same result should be reached here. He pronounced the Senate resolution, passed only by a simple majority, "absolutely without legal significance on the question before us."[28] Finally, Fuller had to face the fact that, unlike Puerto Ricans, Filipinos were rebelling against American control. Since the United States had legal title to the Philippines, the Chief said, insurrection against that authority did not result in impairing the islands nonforeign status. Gray, Shiras, White, and McKenna dissented, citing references to their opinions in the three preceding cases. Brown, in his special concurring opinion, addressed himself to the Senate resolution. He considered it neither a part of the treaty, nor, since it did not have the concurrence of the House, a legislative act.

Brown's adherence to *Downes* was demonstrated in the second case, in which he spoke also for Brewer, Gray, and McKenna; White added a concurring opinion. *Downes* had determined that a tariff could be imposed on goods imported from Puerto Rico; the present decision applied the correlative, that under the authority of the congressional act a duty could be imposed on goods imported into Puerto Rico from the United States. Acknowledging that the earlier case was decided by a fractured majority, Brown noted that all five Justices agreed that certain provisions of the Constitution applied to Puerto Rico, but other provisions, including the constitutional restriction on the taxing power, did not. Here the Justice reached his conclusion by relying upon "a wide difference between the full and paramount power of Congress in legislating for a territory in the condition of Porto Rico and its power with respect to the States, which is merely incidental to its right to regulate interstate commerce."[29] Fuller answered for the dissenters, again refusing to accept the categorization of the territory of Puerto Rico as in a different class from the continental territories of the United States. Congress under the terms of the Constitution, he asserted, cannot lay any tax on exports, and, irrespective of its place of collection, this tax had to be so categorized.

With the opinions announced in these two divisive cases, the Justices put this matter behind them for the time being and concentrated upon cases that reflected a mounting activity in state government. If critics bemoaned the lack of leadership and activity in the national sphere at this time,[30] they could little complain about state government. Such activity sought to cope not only with corrupt government but also with government that was apathetic to the need to redress the economic and social dislocations caused by the rapid industrial growth following the Civil War. Part of this campaign would involve the reshaping of law into a social tool, and already that task had the support of both laymen and legal scholars. If this reform thrust, in part characterized by legislative and constitutional experimentation, was to achieve success, sooner or later this action would have to pass the scrutiny of the Supreme Court. In a psychological sense the Supreme Court had the opportunity to legitimate change; obstruction on its part could delay change though not prevent it, while approval meant something more than mere acquiescence. It was a way of saying that the new could be embraced without cutting the moorings of the past. To get the Supreme Court to fulfill this role, there had to be a successful attack on certain doctrines that could substantially hinder reform efforts. One such doctrine was liberty of contract. If the Court was determined to read liberty to contract firmly into the due process clause, many efforts of government to redress bargaining imbalances would be constitutionally barred.[31]

During the 1901 term the Court showed little inclination to widen the scope of the liberty of contract doctrine. For instance, to protect employees Tennessee passed a law in 1899 providing that employers, on demand, had to redeem store orders and scrip for money. A practice had grown up in company towns to pay in scrip and thereby limit the range of spending options open to the employee. Shiras, for the majority, upheld the law saying that "the right to contract is not absolute in respect to every matter, but may be subjected to the restraints demanded by the safety and welfare of the state and its inhabitants." With approval the Justice quoted the Tennessee court's conclusion that the state could attempt to prevent "strife, violence and bloodshed" by reducing the inequality between employer and employee. The two holdouts in *Holden* v. *Hardy*, Brewer and Peckham, again dissented. This same duo, again without opinion but presumably upon liberty of contract grounds, dissented when the Court ruled that an Illinois law prohibiting options to buy and sell commodities at a future time did not violate the due process clause. Harlan, for the majority, insisted that the Court's task was not to pass on the wisdom of such legislation.[32]

Continually, commerce clause claims called for judicial line drawing. If state courts interpreted broadly worded statutes as applicable only to commerce within their borders, the Justices accepted this interpretation and saw no impermissible restraint on interstate commerce. On the other hand, when Tennessee sought to extract a privilege tax on agents soliciting business with local dealers for shipments from out of state, a unanimous Court ruled this action unconstitutional. The tenuous nature of the Court's categorizing of cases is well illustrated in two cases involving the Louisville & Nashville Railroad and the state of Kentucky. Both involved rate discriminations. In the first case Shiras, for a unanimous bench, wrote a forceful opinion upholding the state's right to regulate the roads. Kentucky could penalize the railroad for charging more for the carriage of goods over a shorter distance than it did for a longer distance. Both routes were traversed within the state's borders, and Shiras pronounced any effect on interstate commerce remote and indirect. But seven Justices saw a difference in the second case where the long haul, to which the short haul was being compared, terminated outside the boundaries of Kentucky. This standard of measurement was held to be a direct restraint on interstate commerce. Amazed that his colleagues could distinguish the cases, Brewer dissented with Gray. Kentucky, the Justice said, had full authority to regulate its internal commerce and to establish standards. The fact that here it chose as its standard the interstate rate, Brewer concluded, did not vitiate its power.[33] Although the Kansan was opposed to expanding the range of state regulatory power, he had long ago accepted that the railroad and other such public service corporations were exceptions.

The term's most unusual commerce clause claim was urged by the Kansas & Texas Coal Company against action by the state of Arkansas. Seeking to prevent nuisances and danger to the public safety, the state sought an injunction in its courts against the company to prevent it from importing strikebreakers in a labor dispute. The company argued that the granted injunction was a restraint on interstate commerce, but a unanimous Court rebuffed the claim.[34] Largely because of its decision in *Debs*, the High Bench was accused of hostility to organized labor, but here it showed no willingness to interfere on behalf of the company.

During the term the Court also found some new vitality within the equal protection clause of the Fourteenth Amendment. In numerous cases counsel raised the equal protection argument, but the Justices usually were willing to accord state legislatures considerable leeway in classifying businesses. *Connolly* v. *Union Sewer Pipe Company* was an exception. Connolly sought to defend himself in a suit for payment by relying upon a section of the state antitrust law that provided that any purchaser of goods from a company in violation of the act was not liable for payment. Harlan, for the majority, did not directly confront this section of the law. Instead he singled out the act's exemption of "agricultural products and livestock in the hands of producers and raisers" as a classification that undermined the law on equal protection grounds.[35] Since Harlan, for the majority, concluded that the state legislature would not have drawn the act as it did if this exemption were missing, he invalidated the entire law and held Connolly liable under the purchase agreement.

McKenna dissented; the persuasiveness of his opinion suggests that the majority, disfavoring the provision invoked and yet not able to invalidate it directly, sought other grounds for favoring the company. Far more descriptive of the work of the Court in this area is McKenna's general statement that the "equality prescribed by the Constitution is fulfilled if equality be observed between the members of the class." McKenna refused to recognize the distinction the majority sought to make on the classification issue between tax and other cases, concluding:

The equality of operation which the Constitution requires in state legislation cannot be construed, as we have seen, as demanding an absolute universality of operation, having no regard to the different capabilities, conditions and relations of men. Classification, therefore, is necessary, but what are its limits? They are not easily defined, but the purview of the legislation should be regarded. A line must not be drawn which includes arbitrarily some persons who do and some persons who do not stand in the same relation to the purpose of the legislation. But a wide latitude of selection must be left to the legislature. It is only a palpable abuse of the power of selection which can be judicially reviewed, and the right of review is so delicate that even in its best exercises it may lead to challenge. At times, indeed, it must be exercised, but should always be exercised in view of the function and necessarily large powers of a legislature.[36]

Obviously McKenna did not believe Illinois had overstepped the bounds, but those bounds could be transgressed, as the full bench agreed in a Kansas case. In *Cotting* v. *Kansas City Stock Yards Company* the issue was the legality of a general statute ostensibly pertaining to all public stockyards but, in fact, because of the volume of business required, applicable only to the stockyards in Kansas City. Because the statute discriminated in terms of the quantity of business, all Justices agreed that this was one of those special instances, to which McKenna referred, where equal protection had been violated. After the agreement in conference, Fuller assigned the opinion to Brewer. The Kansan grasped the opportunity to go beyond the range of

agreement. Although he rested the determination of invalidity on equal protection grounds, he also sought to invoke the due process clause. Failing in
the 1890s to restrict the category of property affected with a public interest,
Brewer seemed ready to try again. Recognizing his lack of success in urging
immunity from state regulation, he now suggested that a property holder
might rightfully object when he was deprived "of the ordinary privileges of
others engaged in mercantile business."[37] The Justice was urging upon his
colleagues a standard that would compel states regulating such business to be
more "reasonable" than they would be with regard to railroads or utilities.

Brewer's colleagues rebelled. The Kansan announced the judgment of the
Court in an opinion that only Fuller and Peckham accepted. The other Justices joined a one-paragraph statement by Harlan, which said that no decision on due process was called for in the case. Trying an end run, Brewer had
failed. He knew he could count upon Peckham, and he did win Fuller, but the
others were unmoved and possibly disturbed. In the time-honored tradition
of the Court, the majority saw no reason to make new law in a case that could
be resolved without any such tinkering.

Justice Horace Gray had been absent for most of the term, which had
extended into June 1902. His absence from the bench revived rumors of his
retirement. Facing the inevitable in July, the Massachusetts Justice sent a
letter of resignation to President Theodore Roosevelt, to take effect upon the
appointment of a successor. Before that process was completed, Gray died on
September 15, 1902.

Fuller personally mourned the loss of Gray, for though the two men argued
about the resolution of certain cases, their personal relationship remained
close. In fact, all told, Gray and Fuller agreed in approximately 75 percent of
the divided cases. In responding to the resolutions offered by the Supreme
Court bar after Gray's death, the Chief paid tribute to the man's cautiousness
in arriving at his conclusions and to his tenacity in defending them. Fuller,
who had personally borne the brunt of both characteristics, graciously said
that the Justice's aim was to settle not only the case but the law as well.[38]

Horace Gray had served for almost twenty-one years on the Court, well
above the average tenure; yet he excited little contemporary interest. His
ponderous size, insistence upon propriety, and rigid manner gave him a
pompous air. He had a reputation for being lazy, but such a characterization
misrepresents his deliberateness. With a keen interest in legal history, he
appointed himself teacher of his colleagues, the bar, and the public. This
practice, along with his tendency to write little essays on law, made his
opinions long and somewhat heavy. Rarely pithy and quotable, the opinions, however, were scholarly and thorough. Gray's work was respected,
and he approached his obligations seriously, even to the extent of writing the
headnotes to his opinions, a task normally left to the reporter. His acknowledged competence in matters of international and admiralty law tended to

take him away from more lively domestic issues. He was a legal technician on the Court, a service more generally appreciated by other judges and lawyers than interpreters of the Supreme Court's history. Gray generally supported the federal government, as he did in the *Insular Cases*, but, compared to most of his colleagues, he was willing to afford more latitude to state power, as in the matter of the original package doctrine. His tendency to look toward the past often precluded his furthering the forward thrust of the Constitution. The most important exception, and perhaps his most important legacy, was his opinion in the case of Wong Kim Ark. There the backward look dove-tailed into a reading of the citizenship clause to protect the birthright of Chinese-Americans.

In the spring of 1902, as Gray's health was declining and as he was wres-tling with the decision to retire, moves were afoot to find a replacement. Since Gray was from Massachusetts in the First Judicial Circuit, geographical con-siderations dictated a choice from that circuit. Senator Henry Cabot Lodge approached President Roosevelt in May 1902 with the suggestion that Oliver Wendell Holmes, Jr., be appointed as Gray's replacement.[39] For twenty years, the last three as Chief Justice, Holmes had served on the Supreme Judicial Court of Massachusetts. When Roosevelt received Gray's resigna-tion in July, he wrote to Lodge seeking more information about Holmes.

This vacancy was the Court's first in five years, and Roosevelt was espe-cially interested in making sure his appointee would reflect the administra-tion's interests. Instinctively recognizing the significance of his task, the Pres-ident sought a Justice in tune with his political philosophy. Specifically, he wanted an appointee who would be sympathetic to the government's recently instituted prosecution of the Northern Securities Company under the anti-trust law and who could be counted upon to take the "right" view regarding America's new island possessions. Writing to Lodge, the President outlined his views:

The majority of the present Court who have, although without satisfactory unanim-ity, upheld the policies of President McKinley and the Republican party in Congress, have rendered great service to mankind and to this nation. The minority—a minority so large as to lack but one vote of being a majority—have stood for such reactionary folly as would have hampered well-nigh hopelessly this people in doing efficient and honorable work for the national welfare, and for the welfare of the islands them-selves, in Porto Rico and the Philippines.

In this correspondence with the Massachusetts Senator, Roosevelt acknowl-edged Holmes's attributes but sought assurances that the judge shared the President's perceptions. Roosevelt suggested showing the letter containing this appraisal to Holmes, adding that in a recent speech the judge seemed to miss the essence of John Marshall's contribution to his party and his country. The President asked Lodge, was the judge a party man?[40] To such queries the

Senator responded that the candidate had the highest character and professional standing and was free from class bias.

It seems strange that in our system of government the President should be required to make a nomination without obtaining all facts he deems relevant, but even Roosevelt implicitly recognized the impropriety of seeking prior commitment from a nominee on matters likely to come before the Supreme Court. As Presidents before and after Roosevelt would discover, the appointment of a Justice is a hazardous task.

With Lodge's assurance that Holmes was the man for the job, President Roosevelt, in early September 1902, called the Massachusetts judge in for a personal interview and offered him the position. Since Holmes spoke of the "joy of the way" the appointment was offered,[41] Roosevelt, who was not always respectful of propriety or protocol, obviously had decided not to seek further assurances. Holmes's nomination received easy confirmation in the Senate, and he was sworn in as the junior Justice on December 8, 1902. Oliver Wendell Holmes would become one of the great names in Supreme Court history, but in 1902 he was less well known than his father, the physician-poet. The younger Holmes was recognized in legal circles as a prominent state judge and an able and innovative legal scholar and speaker, but his arena of activity had been circumscribed. Now at sixty-one, when retirement beckoned others, the Massachusetts judge was assuming his seat, center stage.

Widely described as handsome and attractive, the new arrival stood over six feet with his weight well distributed over an erect frame. His features were perfectly proportioned, and although his full angular mustache was white, his full head of brown hair was greying only at the temples. Holmes dressed impeccably and his four-in-hand tie set a new standard for the Court. Both physically and mentally vigorous, he looked considerably younger than his colleagues.

Roosevelt had filled his first vacancy, but before any Senate action on Holmes, which would have to await the midterm elections, a second vacancy developed. Justices rarely retire unless prompted by ill health or senility, but George Shiras resolved, when he accepted the post at age sixty, that he would retire after the ten years of service that entitled him to full pay. In October 1902 Shiras sent the President his notice of resignation,[42] to take effect when his successor was commissioned.

After leaving the Court Shiras lived for over twenty-one more years. To many observers his retirement provided a sterling example for others on the federal bench. During his active career he eagerly planned fishing expeditions, but apparently he found fishing a better avocation than a full-time pursuit. His periodic returns to Washington were times of uneasy nostalgia. When a younger Justice lamented that Shiras could fish in Michigan in the summer and in Florida in the winter and still draw full pay, an older colleague responded that Shiras had often regretted his decision to retire.[43]

In almost eleven years of service on the Court the man from Pittsburgh had written 259 opinions and 14 dissents. Rarely did he dissent alone, and often he indicated his opposition without opinion. In addition to his forceful defense of the principles of international law based on his conviction that the nation must maintain faith with its principles, he demonstrated a concern for people and the human consequences involved in the operation of law. His thoroughness and general high level of competence has led to his being ranked as one of the Court's ablest lawyers during his years of service. Shiras was a strong supporter of state police power and was generally more sympathetic to individual rights than was the majority. Although unwilling to follow Harlan's dogmatism in the area and trusting more in a judicious pragmatism, he was sensitive to claims asserting the abridgment of such rights. His concern for individual rights embraced the property interest, and the frightening spectre conjured up by the antitax advocates in *Pollock* had an effect upon him. The public picture of Shiras as the Justice who changed his mind to invalidate the income tax was the one episode that plagued the man. Pathetically he hoped that some pronouncement would be made by the Court exonerating him of this charge, and to his dying day he waited.

This episode did truly bother the Pennsylvanian, but it did not dampen his good humor. Shiras was the Court's humorist, and his wit enlivened the conference room and, at times, even the courtroom. For instance, in a case where a claimant was attempting to obtain a patent for a new type of collar button, Shiras said that he would favor the patent if an affirmative answer could legitimately be given to the question he would pose. Ever eager to capture a vote, counsel listened intently as Shiras asked: "Will this hump prevent the collar button from rolling under the bureau when you drop it?" His fellow Justices, especially Harlan and Brown, traded their solemnity for snickers and then laughs, and some time elapsed before serious argument could begin again. Despite his success here, Shiras found his brethren were not always receptive to levity on the bench. When he once made a humorous reference to Mr. Dooley, his colleagues greeted the remark with a stony silence.[44]

When the President received Shiras's letter of resignation, he probably wished that the letter had come from one of the Justices whom he had accused of "reactionary folly." According to Roosevelt's calculations, Shiras had been on the right side in the crucial cases. Now, not inclined to gamble, he turned to a man whose party regularity was not in doubt. That man was William Howard Taft, now serving as Governor-General of the Philippines. Taft had been a young federal judge and Solicitor General before his assignment in the new American possession. From his early days on the bench Taft had been interested in a seat on the Supreme Court. Now Roosevelt had the opportunity to make this dream a reality, while at the same time eliminating a potential rival for the 1904 presidential nomination.

Although Taft personally had no desire to be President, this attitude was not shared by his wife, who felt that she and her husband deserved more than the limbo of the judiciary, no matter how high the place. Her long-range goal and Taft's short-range goal coalesced at this time, leading Taft to respond to Roosevelt's invitation by declining the office. The Governor-General enjoyed his post as "boss" of the Philippines, and, as an administrator who did not have to cope with strong rival governmental interests, he was most successful. What he had started in the islands, Taft said, he wanted to finish. Roosevelt, however, was not easily convinced. He cabled Taft, saying that only the President could see the total picture and that the Governor-General would have to defer to the wishes of his leader. Taft could hardly refuse, and he did not, though he did offer a final plea, writing, "I presume on our personal friendship even in the face of your letter to make one more appeal, in which I lay aside wholly my strong personal disinclination to leave work of intense interest half done." In addition to supporting letters from other members of the governing commission came an outcry from prominent Filipinos and demonstrators chanting, "We want Taft." Defeated, Roosevelt cabled the Governor-General to stay where he was.[45]

As an alternate choice the President, probably still thinking of strengthening his position in 1904, turned to William R. Day, a fellow townsman, confidant and able lieutenant of the deceased McKinley. When the former President placed Day on the bench of the United States Court of Appeals for the Sixth Circuit just three years earlier, McKinley was in all likelihood grooming his friend for a position on the Supreme Court. Roosevelt's elevation of the federal judge certainly would not hurt his standing with those party members more closely allied with McKinley than with the new incumbent. Also, on the crucial antitrust issue, Day, as a judge, seemed in tune with the new President's views.[46]

Day had been an able and successful Ohio lawyer, in whom McKinley had perceived significant qualification for higher office. Day's first position in the administration was as First Assistant Secretary of State. McKinley had needed a person he could trust in the State Department. The Secretary's position was occupied by former Senator John Sherman, who had been persuaded to accept the position and vacate his seat in the Senate so it could be filled by Mark Hanna, McKinley's close personal advisor. Sherman, however, gave little leadership to the department. After a fact-finding tour of Cuba, Day was offered the First Assistant's position. The Canton lawyer had none of that enthusiasm for war with Spain that gripped some Republicans, but, like McKinley, he found himself drawn toward war. When it came, the President secured Sherman's resignation and temporarily put Day in the top slot. After four months Day resigned to head the American delegation to the Peace Conference in Paris. Then in February 1899 McKinley appointed his friend to the Sixth Circuit bench, a congenial appointment not only because of the court's prominence but also because of its location in Cincinnati. On the bench he found William Howard Taft, the chief judge, and Horace H. Lurton, who with Day made up a trio who would all, in time, become Justices of the Supreme Court.[47]

In January 1903 Roosevelt journeyed to Canton in celebration of McKinley's birth and was introduced by Judge Day. Roosevelt made the nomination both public and official, when he responded thanking his friend, "Mr. Justice Day."[48] The nominee was confirmed quickly and sworn in on March 2, 1903.

Day was physically different from the other recent arrival, Holmes. About five feet, six inches tall, he weighed less than one hundred fifty pounds. Almost fifty-four, the appointee was of frail build and often worried about his health and energy. His head was nearly bald with a neatly trimmed white fringe above the ears. He had an intense look with small features, sunken eyes, and a modest, partially greyed mustache that drooped ever so slightly. Day played some billiards and golf, but his main passion was baseball; he found this latter interest shared by Justices White and McKenna. The trio went to as many home games of the Washington Nationals as time permitted. Like so many of his physical type and constitution, Day took pains to conserve his energy and strength. Perhaps it should come as no surprise that he would outlast many of his more vigorous contemporaries both on and off the bench.

Roosevelt's subtle announcement in Canton had been preceded by a news leak that Taft had refused the post and that it would be offered to Day. The "trial balloon" or "government by news leak" probably originated with Theodore Roosevelt, for the President took this nonquoted opportunity to see if he could oil the wheels of the governmental machinery. Quoting only a White House source, the story continued that Taft would be appointed to the High Bench when he had finished his work in the Philippines. "The suggestion is made," the report ran, "that Chief Justice Fuller may soon wish to retire and that Governor Taft would be a suitable man for the vacancy." Obviously Taft, who so desperately wanted any appointment to the High Bench in the 1890s, was now coveting only the top spot. Perhaps Roosevelt hoped that Fuller, who was also seventy years of age, would follow Shiras's example and step down gracefully. Fuller had voted on the wrong side in the *Insular Cases*, and the President would personally welcome the Chief's departure. The trial balloon set off a raft of printed and nonprinted speculation. Fuller responded to the rumors by assuring an emissary of the President that he had not given any thought to the subject. But Taft's ambition and Roosevelt's determination gave the Chief little rest over the next several years. To these constant anonymous suggestions of retirement, Fuller once responded to Holmes, "I am not to be 'paragraphed' out of my place."[49]

When Justice Day was given the traditional welcoming dinner at the Fullers, Mrs. Fuller engaged in an interesting exchange with a young military officer who had just been ordered to the Philippines. Mrs. Fuller said her good-bye over the upstairs banister, but as the officer was leaving, she called, "And when you get to the Philippines you tell Willie Taft not to be in too much of a hurry to get into my husband's shoes."[50] Taft had not been responsible for the rumors and was sincerely desirous of remaining where he was, but Mrs. Fuller's comment was uncannily predictive of Taft's future actions.

Skirmishes were to be fought over the next four years, and in Fuller's wry way he acknowledged Taft's ambition in an introduction prepared as president of the Harvard Law School Association upon Taft's return to Washington in 1904. Fuller said:

When the late Governor of the Philippines arrived at Washington, as soon as I penetrated the dense thicket of laurels that embowered him, he posed this question: "How's the Docket?" I recognized at once the demonstration of his fitness for the highest judicial station. It is very true that I knew my friend had been a professor and Dean of a law school, and had been a judge of the state court, had been Solicitor General of the United States and Judge of the Circuit Court of the United States, and Governor as aforesaid and had discharged the duties of all these positions to great acceptance, but I had not realized before that he felt that interest in the docket which is considered a principal qualification of Chief Justices.[51]

Fuller aptly demonstrated that, although over seventy, he was far from senility.

When the Court convened in October 1902, Gray had died, Holmes had not yet been confirmed, and Shiras had just submitted his resignation. Not too long after Holmes arrived in early December, he became a full-fledged working member of the Court, but Day, who took his seat in early March, did not write a single opinion and sided with the majority in every case.

In part to handle business that was on the rise again after the respite afforded by the establishment of intermediate federal courts of appeal in 1891, the Court seemed more inclined than usual to dispose of cases on technical grounds. Often the appellant was told that the federal question had not been raised early enough in the trial process to merit review.[52] The Justices really had substantial discretion to overlook certain irregularities and proceed to adjudicate the case on the merits. Beginning with the 1902 term, however, the Chief seemed eager to save the Court from having to render a decision if escape was at all possible.

Yet many issues remained that could not be evaded, including the immunity of government from suit and from taxation by other governmental units, issues upon which the Chief, joining a dissenting opinion by White, could not agree with the majority. White stated one of the general rules of intergovernmental tax immunity: "Nothing is better settled than that the United States has no power to tax the governmental attributes of the States, and that municipal corporations are agencies of the States and not subject, as to their

public rights and duties, to direct or indirect taxation by the United States."
The entire Court was satisfied with the application of this rule in one case
early in the session, but later a majority found an exception in permitting the
federal government to tax a bequest to a city on grounds that the tax was
levied on the executor of the will before the money passed to the municipality. Peckham joined with White and Fuller in protesting this inroad on the
doctrine of sovereign immunity.[53]

Even in the absence of any governmental consent to be sued, there was
another possible avenue open to a claimant when his property was damaged
by federal governmental action. Clearly the Fifth Amendment requires the
government to pay for property taken for public use, and it was this argument that Lynah urged upon the Court as a justification for compensation.
He had seen his rice plantation "permanently flooded, wholly destroyed in
value, and turned into an irreclaimable bog" by the action of the federal
government in building a dam to improve navigation on the Savannah River.
Brewer, for the majority, did not dispute the government's power to improve
navigation but insisted that it had taken Lynah's property without compensation. Five Justices agreed with Brewer, including Holmes, for whom a reargument had been ordered, and Shiras, who was serving his last day as a Justice.
White, with the Chief and Harlan in tow, dissented, deeply worried about
the precedential implications of the majority's decision, especially in its
discovery of an implied contract. White contended that this was not a case of
public taking, for Lynah had no right to insist "that the mean low tide of the
river should be forever unchanged." According to the Louisianian, the "loss
of drainage does not constitute an appropriation of the property by the
United States, and is but the result of the natural situation of the land."[54]

Although inclined to uphold various state taxes and exercises of police
power, the Court did recognize its role as an umpire of the federal system.
Wyoming could not tax sheep in transit through the state; North Carolina
could not levy a tax on an agent for out-of-state concerns; Kentucky exceeded
its authority in taxing a ferry company on a basis that included the value of a
franchise awarded by a neighboring state; and Washington could not enforce
a lien on ocean-going vessels. When Nebraska sought to protect itself from
suit in the matter of establishing maximum railroad rates, the Court informed
the state that it could not invoke the Eleventh Amendment to shield itself
from violations of the Fourteenth.[55]

If blacks in the United States were encouraged by the presence of Booker T.
Washington at the White House for lunch early in Theodore Roosevelt's
administration, the Justices offered no evidence of greater sympathy to this
particular minority. From the blacks' perspective the Court seemed to be
drifting backward. A black man convicted of murder in South Carolina
appealed on grounds that members of his race, although constituting four-
fifths of the county's population and registered voters, were excluded from

service on the grand jury. Holmes, in one of his first opinions for the Court, acknowledged that the case raised grave questions, but, he continued, the record in the case was so deficient of supporting facts that no other course was open but to affirm the state court. From the bare opinion there seems to be little more in the record than the allegation and the judge's comment that he would presume in the absence of other evidence that the jury commissioners had "done their duty."[56]

A second Court opinion delivered by Holmes in the next month involved more substance and provoked division among his colleagues. Jackson W. Giles sought to compel the Montgomery County, Alabama, Board of Registry, to enroll him as a qualified voter. Giles sought to be put on the rolls before a new state constitutional amendment went into effect providing that all persons on the voting rolls before the effective date of the change would be permanently registered, while those enrolled later would have to pass a literacy test or own substantial property. Giles said that the refusal to register him and other members of his race was part of a general conspiracy to disenfranchise blacks.

Holmes denied that the Court had jurisdiction but then proceeded to a consideration of the merits. What is disturbing about Holmes's opinion is not only its lack of sensitivity but its lack of responsibility. After dealing with the matter of jurisdiction, Holmes added that, although that difficulty could be overcome, two others could not. The first was that a decision in favor of Giles would make the Court a party to what the petitioner claims is an unlawful and fraudulent scheme to prevent blacks from voting. Second, Holmes said that equity cannot be used to enforce political rights, for the Court has no power to control the state. He concluded that "relief from a great political wrong, if done, as alleged, by the people of a State and the State itself, must be given by them or by the legislative and political department of the government of the United States."[57] In separate dissents Brewer and Harlan contended that the relief Giles sought should be granted.

Giles was not easily discouraged, for in the next term the Court considered two other cases brought by the aggrieved black, one for damages for the refusal of the local board to register him, and the second for a writ of mandamus to compel the board to register him. The Montgomery city court sustained a demurrer to both suits, and the Alabama Supreme Court affirmed. To sustain a demurrer the court must accept the plaintiff's allegations as true, and this was what once again trapped Giles. The Alabama court concluded that, if the board was indeed discriminating against blacks, it was constituted in violation of the Fourteenth and Fifteenth Amendments and its action was therefore illegal and could not result in the disqualification of a legal voter. In the second suit, again accepting the allegations as true, the state court said it could not issue a mandamus because, if the board was indeed practicing the type of discrimination that the plaintiff alleged, it would have no legal existence and therefore could not be legally compelled to register Giles. The Supreme Court accepted the lower court's reasoning, saying that suits had failed upon an independent state ground: accepting all the plaintiff's allegations as true, relief could not be granted. Day, for the Court, concluded, as had Holmes in the first case, that the remedies judicially available are ill-adapted to political matters. Even though the claims were grave and substantial, Day said, the Court's right of review "is circumscribed by the rules established by law."[58] McKenna concurred, while Harlan, still the most sensitive Justice to such claims, dissented without elaboration.

Even more disturbing than its response in the *Giles* cases was the Court's invalidation of a section of the Civil Rights Act of 1870. Henry Bowman had been indicted for bribing certain blacks not to vote in an election. The question the case presented was whether Congress possessed the power to pass a statute punishing the crime of bribery in elections. Brewer, for the Court's majority, concluded that the Fifteenth Amendment's protection of the right to vote, restricted only governments and not private individuals. Since the 1870 provision was broad and covered the franchise in both state and federal elections, the Kansan said the Court could not narrow the scope of the statute to save its constitutionality.[59] Brewer disguised the fact that precedent existed whereby the statute could have been confined to the federal sphere and then upheld. Justice McKenna did not sit in the case, and Harlan and Brown dissented without opinion.

Court invalidation of a federal act usually sets off some blustering in Congress, but in that body there was little proprietary interest in this old civil rights act. As the Alabama case graphically demonstrated, states were proceeding in their own ways to obstruct the exercise of the franchise by blacks. All in all, these decisions of the Court demonstrate the apathy of the nation to the black-suffrage issue. Rarely did the inconsistency of the democratic ideal with the position of blacks in American society provoke much thought, let alone a program for action.[60]

From the contemporary congressional perspective, *Champion* v. *Ames* was a far more significant case. At issue was nothing less than federal legislative authority to prohibit interstate commerce in certain goods. First argued in February 1901, and then again in October of the same year, no decision had been reached when the present term began. An even division results in the affirmance of the lower court's decision, but here Chief Justice Fuller apparently thought the case was of such importance that it necessitated an opinion by the Court. In November the Court ordered a second reargument after Holmes had taken his seat. *Champion* v. *Ames* was handed down on Shiras's last day of service, and Harlan took upon himself the task of writing the opinion for the narrow majority. To the uninitiated the case looked innocuous enough; it was simply another denial of habeas corpus by the Court. The defendant had been charged with conspiring to cause lottery tickets to be carried from one state to another. The importance of the case was revealed by the battery of lawyers arraigned on the side of the appellant, a battery that included William D. Guthrie. What really was involved was a reading of congressional power under the commerce clause, for in 1895 Congress sought by statute to suppress interstate traffic in lottery tickets.[61]

Charles F. Champion and Charles B. Park engaged the Wells Fargo Express Company to transport Paraguayian lottery tickets from Texas to California. The appellants argued that the carrying of lottery tickets by an express company does not constitute the commerce among states that Congress was empowered to regulate. Responding, the government contended that express companies are instruments of commerce, that the carrying of lottery tickets is commerce that Congress can lawfully regulate, and that such regulation can make criminal the act of arranging for the transportation of such tickets.

Harlan began by searching precedent for a definition of commerce, after which he concluded that the cases establish that

. . . commerce among the States embraces navigation, intercourse, communication, traffic, the transit of persons, and the transmission of messages by telegraph. They also show that the power to regulate commerce among the several States is vested in Congress as absolutely as it would be in a single government, having in its constitution the same restrictions on the exercise of the power as are found in the Constitution of the United States; that such power is plenary, complete in itself, and may be exerted by Congress to its utmost extent, subject *only* to such limitations as the Constitution imposes upon the exercise of the powers granted by it; and that in determining the character of the regulations to be adopted Congress has a large discretion which is not to be controlled by the courts, simply because, in their opinion, such regulations may not be the best or most effective that could be employed.[62]

After stating this general conclusion, the Justice questioned the existence of any solid foundation upon which to rest the exclusion of lottery tickets from the range of this power. To the argument that they in themselves had no value, Harlan had little sympathy: they were sold in the expectation that they might have considerable value and, as such, Congress was justified in designating them as subjects of traffic. The regulation of their carriage, he continued, is a regulation of commerce.

Next Harlan addressed himself to the contention that Congress within the sphere of its delegated power can regulate but not prohibit. In inspecting the evil to be suppressed, he saw no objection to regulation in this form. Just as a state can prohibit lotteries, he said, Congress can use its plenary power over interstate commerce in a like way. Harlan ridiculed the assertion of a right "to introduce into commerce among the States an element that will be confessedly injurious to the public morals." To the contention that the Tenth Amendment reserved this power over lotteries to the states, the Kentuckian responded that Congress was supplementing such action. "We should hesitate long," he continued, "before adjudging that an evil of such appalling character, carried on through interstate commerce, cannot be met by the only power competent to that end."[63] To further support this prohibition the Justice cited a federal act prohibiting transportation of diseased livestock and then went on to deal with the subject of liquor regulation.

To head off the claim that the upholding of this lottery act would give Congress the authority to exclude from the channels of interstate commerce whatever it chose, Harlan asserted that such power cannot be exercised arbitrarily. The "possible abuse of a power," he maintained, "is not an argument against its existence." No general rule can now be promulgated, he said, because the "whole subject is too important, and the questions suggested by its consideration are too difficult of solution, to justify any attempt to lay down a rule for determining in advance the validity of every statute that may be enacted under the commerce clause."[64]

Harlan may not have had time to draft the opinion with great care. Certainly the opinion stresses heavily the odious nature of the traffic in lottery tickets and relies upon a universal suspicion of them. But what the Justice in his majority opinion did that the Court had not done before was equate the state's police power with a new found matching power within the commerce clause of the Constitution. Constitutional gospel had long recognized the plenary police power of the states in contrast to the delegated power of the federal government. Now the majority, made so by the agreement of Holmes, found within the commerce clause a source of authority for federal governmental action in the general area of commerce that would permit legislation for the welfare of the people. Earlier, in upholding the federal margarine act, the Court had impliedly recognized the legitimacy of using the federal tax power to achieve police-power purposes,[65] but *Champion* opened an even wider door. Although Harlan tried to soften the blow of this new doctrine by saying he would venture no applications beyond the instant case, the majority had extended to the federal government a broad new regulatory power, nothing less than the police power in the guise of the commerce clause. The federal government had long used its control over the mails to enact laws prohibiting the dissemination of obscene materials, but that power to legislate morality was based firmly on the federal government's complete control of the mail service.

Fuller, joined by Brewer, Shiras, and Peckham, began his dissent by distinguishing between congressional control over the mails and the power exercised here. Citing the title of the act as evidence, the Chief said the intent of Congress was to suppress lotteries. States are competent to do just this, but the dissenters claimed the Tenth Amendment precludes Congress from pursuing a similar policy. "To hold that Congress," Fuller continued, "has general police power would be to hold that it may accomplish objects not entrusted to the General Government, and to defeat the operation of the

Tenth Amendment." Scorning the implications of the majority's decision, he suggested that calling a lottery ticket an article of commerce invites a similar label for an insurance policy, and "an invitation to dine or take a drive." Such reasoning, the Chief contended, led to including within the commerce clause "the absolute and exclusive power to prohibit the transportation of anything or anybody from one State to another." Citing Harlan's contention that, since state suppression of lotteries had not proved fully effective, the public interest sustained this new reading of the commerce clause, he responded: "In countries whose fundamental law is flexible it may be that the homely maxim, 'to ease the shoe where it pinches,' may be applied, but under the Constitution of the United States it cannot be availed of to justify action by Congress or by the courts."[66]

No one could accuse the Justices in *Champion* of missing the fundamental issues involved, and the jurisprudential flourishes in the opinions testify to the significance they attached to the case. It was a tough fight, but as in many five to four decisions the majority perceived the future far better than the minority. This ability to provide for the future by adjusting the law without wrenching it from its moorings is the genius of the American system of constitutional adjudication. The majority Justices in *Champion*, perhaps for differing reasons, saw the need to afford the federal government room to cope with the problems of a nation. Fuller, with his reverence for the federal system, sought to put his finger in the dike and argue that the present Constitution did not sanction such federal regulation. To overemphasize the importance of this case would be difficult, especially with the advantage of hindsight. Somewhat hesitatingly and only by a bare majority, the Court had entered the twentieth century and was willing to rationalize the actions of a revived Congress. It seemed to say that greater activity by the legislative branch at the national level would not be thwarted by an archaic and unyielding interpretation of the fundamental law. If the problems of an industrial society were going to be effectively handled, action would eventually have to come from the federal government.

Fuller's alarm at the recognition of a federal police power was shared by some legal commentators, who viewed the decision with disquietude. Although a portion of the legal community remained disaffected, Congress welcomed this judicial approval of its reading of the range of the commerce power. Congressional response came in terms of a spate of new legislation over the next thirteen years, much of it based upon this new quasi-police power.[67]

Still on the docket for decision on the last day of the term was *Hawaii* v. *Mankichi*, a case that President Roosevelt watched with great interest. One of the first cases heard by the newly installed Justice Day, it raised again the principles of the *Insular Cases* before the Court. Hawaii had been annexed to the United States by the Newlands Resolution of July 7, 1898, which made the

islands "a part of the territory of the United States and subject to the sovereign dominion thereof." Local legislation of the islands not inconsistent with
the resolution "nor contrary to the Constitution of the United States" was
continued in effect.[68] In the *Mankichi* case the Hawaiian territorial court had
granted a writ of habeas corpus to Mankichi, who had been convicted of
manslaughter. Since the defendant was not indicted by a grand jury and since
the verdict was rendered upon the concurrence of nine out of twelve jurors,
the lower court ruled that the proceedings had violated the standards specified in the Bill of Rights.

Justice Brown, for the majority, began by saying the question the case
posed was simple; the "difficulty" he continued, "is in fixing upon the principles applicable to its solution." He conceived the question in terms of whether
Congress intended to substitute the guarantees relating to criminal procedure
in the Fifth and Sixth Amendments for those preexisting in Hawaii. Citing
cases that called for a sensible reading of statutes to effect legislative intent,
the Justice concluded that there "are many reasons which induce us to hold
that the act was not intended to interfere with the existing practice when such
interference would result in imperiling the peace and good order of the
islands." Brown said the annexing resolution did not intend any change in the
government in the islands, for when Congress so acted to establish a government in 1900 it provided that "the laws of the United States, which are not
locally inapplicable, shall have the same force and effect within the said
Territory as elsewhere in the United States." (Included in that act of 1900
"was a provision requiring grand juries and unanimous verdicts," but
Mankichi had been convicted before the passage of the 1900 act.) Brown then
added that to read the Newlands Resolution of 1898 as displacing pre-existing
law "might be so disastrous that we might well say that it could not have been
within the contemplation of Congress." What worried Brown was the effect
a contrary interpretation would have on criminal convictions in the islands in
the two-year period. Then to counter the argument that he had made the key
phrase in the resolution meaningless, Brown responded

. . . that most, if not all, the privileges and immunities contained in the bill of rights of
the Constitution were intended to apply from the moment of annexation; but we place
our decision of this case upon the ground that the two rights alleged to be violated in
this case are not fundamental in their nature, but concern merely a method of procedure which sixty years of practice had shown to be suited to the conditions of the
islands, and well calculated to conserve the rights of their citizens to their lives, their
property, and their well being.[69]

In a concurring opinion, White, joined by McKenna, grasped the opportunity to expound upon his idea of incorporation, starting off with the
proposition that the Newlands Resolution had not incorporated the islands
into the United States. The resolution, he said, left to Congress the subse-

quent determination of the relationship. Only when Congress acted in the legislation of April 30, 1900, did incorporation take place and fully make the islands part of the United States. He begged the question on the key phrase in the resolution of 1898 that subjected local legislation to the constitutional test by saying it referred only to applicable sections of the Constitution.

In dissent with Harlan, Brewer, and Peckham once again, Chief Justice Fuller argued that the Newlands Resolution "is plain and unambiguous, and resort to construction or interpretation is absolutely uncalled for. To tamper with the words is to eliminate them."[70] Whether Congress intended to make the Bill of Rights immediately applicable or not, the Chief said, the mandate of the resolution could not be avoided. Harlan, who concurred with Fuller, added his own dissent striking to the heart of congressional authority. Convinced that the trial of Mankichi tested by the resolution of 1898 was constitutionally improper, he justified his long dissent by citing the exceptional importance of the majority's principles. Not only did he take issue with the Court's reading of congressional intent, but the Justice detailed action of the Secretary of State and his subordinates that buttressed the conclusion that the full range of the Constitution's guarantees came to the islands with annexation.

Of far more importance to Harlan was the majority's implicit view that Congress, through nonaction, could have indefinitely denied the protection of the Bill of Rights to the islands' inhabitants. Passionately, the Justice rejected a doctrine that would leave the liberties of a people under the sovereignty of the United States to the despotic will of an uncaring Congress. "It is," he continued, "impossible for me to grasp the thought that that which is admittedly contrary to the supreme law can be sustained as valid."[71] Disturbing Harlan further was the fact that three members of the present majority had agreed in *Downes* v. *Bidwell* that the Constitution was applicable to annexed territories; in that case they differed from Harlan in their denial that the provision relied upon was applicable. Any analogy between customs duties and individual rights he rejected, saying that Congress had been delegated authority to levy duties but not to limit the protections of the Constitution. Scorning Brown's view that the rights Mankichi claimed were not fundamental, Harlan said there was no other possible way to classify them. Even if Congress specifically denied such personal liberties, he would hold the legislative branch powerless to do so. The Kentuckian's resolution was broader than that of the other dissenters. Harlan would hold that the acquisition of complete sovereignty by the United States over any territory, foreign or domestic, brought with it the full protection of the Constitution.

On tariff questions Harlan was content to let others speak for him, but this case involved more than simple commercial matters. What was at stake was a constitutional system, designed to protect individuals from arbitrary acts of government. The majority's tendency to defer to Congress on this question incensed Harlan, who considered the matter inherently judicial in its nature. The attitude of his colleagues he labeled an abdication of the Court's duty to defend the Constitution.

After *Mankichi* the Justices were probably quite ready to leave the turmoils of the session behind them and scatter for vacation. Personnel changes had caused some disruption, even though the late-arriving Holmes was able to carry his full share of opinion writing. In fact, after Fuller, Holmes tied with two of his colleagues for the largest number of opinions written during the term. Holmes's high output, unusual for a new Justice and unique for a partial termer, was the result of the man's indefatigable energy and initiative. Although his brethren at times moaned under their opinion load, Holmes wrote to the Chief asking for more opinions to write.[72] In part, this strange plea was the result of an efficient personal organization, but it also reflected a determination of what kind of opinion was necessary to justify a decision. It is rare to find a Holmes opinion occupying more than twelve pages in the official reports. Believing in brevity and reacting against his colleagues who often rambled and extended their prose repetitively and unmercifully, Holmes saw no reason for doing more than was strictly necessary to explain the decision. Although at times this stylistic preference led to a lack of clarity, Holmes sought to get to the point quickly and not clog up his prose with heavy and extensive citations of precedent. A man of lesser ability could easily have become careless, and even Holmes wrote some sloppy and hasty opinions, but generally he did the job with some grace.

As President Theodore Roosevelt appraised the work of his two appointees, he hardly had any reason to be disappointed. Both Holmes and Day had come out right on the matter of the overseas possessions, as was illustrated in *Mankichi*, and Holmes had cast the decisive vote in *Champion* v. *Ames*. Perhaps it was too early for the President to form any conclusions. Certainly he was pleased with both Holmes and his wife as ingredients in the buzzing social life of Washington.[73] As Lodge had promised, the President found the Holmeses urbane, sophisticated, and pleasurable social associates. Neither the President nor the Justice could have known that this honeymoon would not last another term of Court.

NOTES

1. Margaret Leech, *In the Days of McKinley* (New York: Harper & Bros., 1959), p. 537.
2. Freeport Water Co. v. Freeport, 180 U.S. 587 (1901); Danville Water Co. v. Danville, 180 U.S. 619 (1901); and Rogers Park Water Co. v. Fergus, 180 U.S. 624 (1901).
3. Stearns v. Minnesota, 179 U.S. 223 (1900).
4. Id. at 259.
5. Duluth & Iron Range R.R. v. St. Louis, 179 U.S. 302 (1900).
6. Norwood v. Baker, 172 U.S. 269 (1898); French v. Barber Asphalt Paving Co., 181 U.S. 324 (1901); Cass Farm Co. v. Detroit, 181 U.S. 396 (1901); Scranton v. Wheeler, 179 U.S. 141 (1900); and Carson v. Brockton Sewerage Commission, 182 U.S. 398 (1901).

7. Williams v. Fears, 179 U.S. 270 (1900); Wisconsin, Minnesota & Pacific R.R. v. Jacobson, 179 U.S. 287 (1900); Western Union Telegraph Co. v. Call Publishing Co., 181 U.S. 92 (1901); and Chesapeake & Ohio Ry. v. Kentucky, 179 U.S. 388 (1900).

8. Austin v. Tennessee, 179 U.S. 343, 364 (1900).

9. F. May & Co. v. New Orleans, 178 U.S. 496 (1900).

10. Austin v. Tennessee, 179 U.S. 343, 383, 386, 387 (1900).

11. Rasmussen v. Idaho, 181 U.S. 198 (1901); and Smith v. St. Louis & Southwestern Ry., 181 U.S. 248, 260 (1901).

12. Neely v. Henkel, 180 U.S. 109 (1901).

13. De Lima v. Bidwell, 182 U.S. 1, 220 (1901). The Court's opinions consistently referred to Puerto Rico as Porto Rico.

14. Id.

15. Dooley v. United States, 182 U.S. 222, 235, 236 (1901).

16. Id. at 238, 243.

17. Downes v. Bidwell, 182 U.S. 244, 277, 286 (1901).

18. Id. at 286, 287; and Loughborough v. Blake, 18 U.S. (5 Wheat.) 317 (1820).

19. Downes v. Bidwell, 182 U.S. 244, 292 (1901).

20. Id. at 339, 342. For the apparent source of White's incorporation theory, see Abbott L. Lowell, "The Status of Our New Possessions—A Third View," *Harvard Law Review* 13 (November 1899):155-76.

Although White in his opinion did not credit the young Boston lawyer, who would later become president of Harvard University, the article did seem to aid White in constructing the basis for his deference to Congress. While other legal scholars were trying to undermine Chief Justice Marshall's conclusion that the term *United States* included the territories, Lowell sought the same end by seeking to distinguish earlier acquisitions of territory. The young scholar concluded that the earlier treaties and resolutions acquiring territory had brought the inhabitants of the area into the Union as citizens, and the treaty with Spain had left Congress free to determine the civil and political rights of the residents.

21. Downes v. Bidwell, 182 U.S. 244, 346 (1901).

22. Fuller's biographer has suggested that White may have been attracted to this position because of his views as a Senator supporting a protective tariff, especially on sugar (Willard L. King, *Melville Weston Fuller: Chief Justice of the United States 1888-1910*, Phoenix ed. [Chicago, University of Chicago Press, 1967], p. 270). Fuller was a Cleveland Democrat and was opposed to a protective tariff. Certainly, American interests seeking protection had been responsible for the drive to maintain the duties on products coming from the new territories, and votes in favor of validating such duties could be interpreted as favorable to those interests. But White had traveled a long way from his days as a freshman Senator pledged to fight for the protection of the Louisiana sugar industry, and his opinions in this series of cases demonstrate a sincere breadth of concern.

23. Downes v. Bidwell, 182 U.S. 244, 373 (1901).

24. Id. at 379, 380.

25. King, *Fuller*, pp. 267-69.

26. Ibid., pp. 271-73.

27. Ibid., p. 278.

28. Fourteen Diamond Rings v. United States, 183 U.S. 176, 180 (1901).

29. Dooley v. United States, 183 U.S. 151, 157 (1901).

30. Loren P. Beth, *The Development of the American Constitution 1877-1917*, New American Nation Series (New York: Harper & Row, Torchbooks, 1971), pp. 29-30.

31. For a scholarly critique, see Roscoe Pound, "Liberty of Contract," *Yale Law Journal* 18 (May 1909):454-87.

32. Knoxville Iron Co. v. Harbison, 183 U.S. 13, 22, 21 (1901); and Booth v. Illinois, 184 U.S. 425 (1902).

33. Erie R.R. v. Purdy, 185 U.S. 148 (1902); Stockard v. Morgan, 185 U.S. 27 (1902); Louisville & Nashville R.R. v. Kentucky, 183 U.S. 503 (1902); and Louisville & Nashville R.R. v. Eubank, 184 U.S. 27 (1902).

34. Arkansas v. Kansas & Texas Coal Co., 183 U.S. 185 (1901).

35. Connolly v. Union Sewer Pipe Co., 184 U.S. 540, 557 (1902).

36. Id. at 570. McKenna's view became the Court's in *Tigner* v. *Texas* (310 U.S. 141 [1940]), when the High Bench concluded that the earlier decision could no longer stand.

37. Cotting v. Kansas City Stock Yards Co., 183 U.S. 79, 95 (1901).

38. King, *Fuller*, p. 342; and Fuller's comments in the memorial proceeding, 187 U.S. xxxvii-xxxix.

39. Roosevelt to George F. Hoar, July 30, 1902, in Elting Morison, ed., *The Letters of Theodore Roosevelt*, 8 vols. (Cambridge: Harvard University Press, 1951-54), 3:302; and King, *Fuller*, p. 278.

40. Roosevelt to Henry Cabot Lodge, July 10, 1902, in Morison, *Letters of Roosevelt*, 3:288-89; and Henry J. Abraham, *Justices and Presidents: A Political History of Appointments to the Supreme Court* (New York: Oxford University Press, 1974), pp. 147-48.

41. Holmes to Lady Pollock, September 6, 1902, in Mark D. Howe, ed., *Holmes-Pollock Letters*, 2d ed., 2 vols. (Cambridge: Harvard University Press, Belknap Press, 1961), 1:105.

42. George Shiras, III, *Justice George Shiras, Jr. of Pittsburgh*, ed. and compl. Winfield Shiras (Pittsburgh: University of Pittsburgh Press, 1953), p. 197.

43. Charles H. Butler, *A Century at the Bar of the Supreme Court of the United States* (New York: G. P. Putnam's Sons, 1942), pp. 198-99.

44. Ibid., p. 89; and Shiras, *Justice George Shiras, Jr.*, pp. 126-27.

45. Alpheus T. Mason, *William Howard Taft: Chief Justice* (New York: Simon & Schuster, 1965), pp. 20-23. Roosevelt's letter to Taft summoning him to the Supreme Court dated November 26, 1902 is in Morison, *Letters of Roosevelt*, 3:382-83.

46. Vernon W. Roelofs, "Justice William Day and Federal Regulation," *Mississippi Valley Historical Review* 37 (June 1950):42-43. On such matters Roelofs concluded that Day's decision making on the High Court did not disappoint Roosevelt.

47. James F. Watts, "William R. Day," in *The Justices of the United States Supreme Court 1789-1969*, ed. Leon Friedman and Fred L. Israel, 4 vols. (New York: R.R. Bowker Co. and Chelsea House Publishers, 1969), 3:1775-82.

48. Ibid., pp. 1782-83.

49. King, *Fuller*, pp. 302-3.

50. Ibid., p. 304. The source of the story is Butler, *A Century at the Bar*, pp. 164-66.

51. Quoted in King, *Fuller*, pp. 305-6.

52. See, for instance, Layton v. Missouri, 187 U.S. 356 (1902).

53. Snyder v. Bettman, 190 U.S. 249, 255 (1903). The case in which all the Justices agreed was *Ambrosini* v. *United States* (187 U.S. 1 [1902]).

54. United States v. Lynah, 188 U.S. 445, 469, 485 (1903). White's concern was shared by a later Court in *United States* v. *Chicago, Milwaukee, St. Paul & Pacific R.R.* (312 U.S. 592 [1941]), which repudiated the idea that damage to property in the bed of a navigable stream caused by governmental attempts to improve navigation would entitle the owner to compensation from the government.

55. Kelley v. Rhoads, 188 U.S. 1 (1903); Caldwell v. North Carolina 187 U.S. 622 (1903); Louisville & Jefferson Ferry Co. v. Kentucky, 188 U.S. 385 (1903); The Roanoke, 189 U.S. 185 (1903); and Prout v. Starr, 188 U.S. 537 (1903).

56. George E. Mowry, *The Era of Theodore Roosevelt and the Birth of Modern America 1900-1912*, New American Nation Series (New York: Harper & Row, Torchbooks, 1962), pp. 165-66; and Brownfield v. South Carolina, 189 U.S. 426, 428 (1903).

57. Giles v. Harris, 189 U.S. 475, 488 (1903).

164 CHARTING THE FUTURE

58. Giles v. Teasley, 193 U.S. 146, 167 (1904).

59. James v. Bowman, 190 U.S. 127 (1903).

60. See Dewey W. Grantham, "The Progressive Movement and the Negro," *South Atlantic Quarterly* 54 (October 1955):461-77.

61. Act of March 2, 1895, ch. 191, 28 Stat. 963.

62. Champion v. Ames, 188 U.S. 321, 352-53 (1903).

63. Id. at 357-58.

64. Id. at 363.

65. *In re* Kollock, 165 U.S. 526 (1897).

66. Champion v. Ames, 188 U.S. 321, 365, 371, 366, 372 (1903).

67. For instance, see William A. Sutherland, "Is Congress a Conservator of the Public Morals?" *American Law Review* 38 (January-February 1904):194-208, and Paul Fuller, "Is There a Federal Police Power?" *Columbia Law Review* 4 (December 1904):563-88. For a list of such federal acts, see Charles Warren, *The Supreme Court in United States History*, rev. ed., 2 vols. (Boston: Little, Brown & Co., 1926), 2:736-37.

68. Newlands Resolution of July 7, 1898, Res. 55, 30 Stat. 750, 751.

69. Hawaii v. Mankichi, 190 U.S. 197, 209, 214, 215, 217-18 (1903).

70. Id. at 223.

71. Id. at 241.

72. King, *Fuller*, pp. 290-91.

73. Catherine Drinker Bowen, *Yankee from Olympus: Justice Holmes and His Family* (Boston: Little, Brown & Co., 1944), pp. 361-65.

chapter 6

ROOSEVELT PROPOSES, THE COURT DISPOSES, 1903-6

As the Justices assembled for the 1903 term, the man in the White House was especially interested in the antitrust prosecution of the Northern Securities Company. The government had won in the lower court, but President Roosevelt was still worried about the reaction of the Justices.[1] Such anxiety was not misplaced, for although the Rough Rider had made two appointments to the High Bench he had not strengthened what he considered his party's faction. Gray and Shiras had been moderates and were not part of the "reactionary" group that Roosevelt condemned.

That a President cannot accurately predict how an appointee to the Supreme Court will vote in diverse matters that arise should occasion no surprise. To assume that a more thorough knowledge of the appointee would enable him to predict with accuracy votes in particular cases makes the whole decision-making process too simplistic. Cases very often present hard choices between values of roughly equivalent worth. In such instances the choice is difficult and often unsystematic. Second, the collegial atmosphere of the Court has a restraining effect. Both Court traditions and precedent can constrain the individual's voting. Each Justice must establish a working relationship with his colleagues if he expects to have some influence on the Court's decisions. As a member of a collective body, he must be prepared to compromise personal views. Unanimous opinions, by which most cases are decided, do not result from the complete meeting of nine minds but rather from a willingness to accept the resolution of the majority. Dissent arises when a Justice's assessment cannot be compromised, and though Fuller was personally disturbed by the division that characterized the Court, he, unlike others who have held the top spot, did not hesitate to dissent.

That the two Roosevelt appointees could hold the balance of power in closely contested cases became clear early in the session. Their uncritical willingness to apply the fellow servant bar to an injured employee's claim left the Chief, Harlan, and McKenna still in the minority in this type of litigation, but the votes of Holmes and Day were crucial in *Atkin* v. *Kansas*, the term's first major case. The Kansas legislature had made an employer engaged in public work criminally liable if he required or permitted an employee to work more than an eight-hour day. The opponents of the law contended that it was an obvious infringement of the liberty to contract.

Framing the issue in terms of power, Harlan, for the majority, saw "no possible ground" to dispute the state's ability to prescribe conditions under which work for the government will be performed. To the alleged right of all to dispose of their own labor on their own terms, the Justice responded "that no employee is entitled, of absolute right and as a part of his liberty, to perform labor for the State; and no contractor for public work can excuse a violation of his agreement with the State by doing that which the statute under which he proceeds distinctly and lawfully forbids him to do." To the claim that such legislation "is mischievous in its tendencies," Harlan answered:

No evils arising from such legislation could be more far-reaching than those that might come to our system of government if the judiciary, abandoning the sphere assigned to it by the fundamental law, should enter the domain of legislation, and, upon grounds merely of justice or reason or wisdom annul statutes that had received the sanction of the people's representatives.

Counsel had urged the Court to protect individual rights from arbitrary power; Harlan agreed, but he added that legislative enactments embodying the will of the people should be upheld unless "plainly and palpably" in violation of the Constitution. As far as the Kansas law was concerned, "its constitutionality is beyond all question."[2] Brewer and Peckham could be expected to dissent, and they did without opinion, this time joined by Fuller.

Harlan's majority opinion with its strong and forceful language did not bury the relatively new doctrine of freedom of contract, but it did considerably limit its reach. Early in the nineteenth century the Justices found state contracts embraced within the constitutional provision against the impairment of contracts, but now their successors did not find similar breadth in the freedom of contract concept. In fact, the rule announced in *Atkin* substantially increased governmental power at a time when other state action was being subjected to close Court scrutiny. With governmental activity in the economy and society on the rise, the Court told private parties contracting with government that the High Bench would not interfere with the provisions of the bargain struck. Although the Court might well continue to be suspicious of legislation seeking to regulate wholly private contracts, it had served notice that in the economic marketplace the government could use its bargaining advantage in behalf of what it determined to be the public interest.

Freedom of contract came up in another case in the 1903 term. At issue was an Ohio mechanics law that gave those who furnished material to a contractor a lien on the property where the material was used. A hotel company claimed the statute interfered with its liberty to contract with the general contractor. A unanimous Court said this statutory addition to the terms of the contract was neither arbitrary nor oppressive and that such legislation "was sanctioned by the dictates of natural justice, and, as must be conclusively presumed, was known to the owner." What made the case especially interesting was that, after it was instituted in the federal courts, the Ohio supreme court had invalidated the statute in another action as a violation of the state constitutional provision that read as follows: ". . . one of the most valuable and sacred rights is the right to make and enforce contracts. The obligation of a contract, when made and entered into, cannot be impaired by act of the General Assembly." The Justices agreed with the federal court of appeals "that the meaning and scope of constitutional provisions substantially like those to be found in the Constitution of Ohio is, in our opinion, against the conclusion reached by the learned state court."[3] Of course, had the state decision preceded the filing of this suit, the federal court would have had to follow the state court's ruling. Since the suit was filed earlier, the result saw the Supreme Court upholding the enforcement of a judgment based on a state statute that had been declared invalid by the highest state court.

Despite claims that the Supreme Court was less than a liberal body, state courts, such as the one in Ohio, seemed much more restrictive of the permissible range of legislation.[4] The greater visibility of the United States Supreme Court and the fact that in a few notorious decisions it did strike down reform legislation skews the general picture. What is surprising is not that the Supreme Court tends to be conservative, for that is its appointed constitutional role, but that it has been so receptive to change. The general impression that state courts were more wary of state legislative experimentation than the Supreme Court remains.

High Bench support for state and municipal action was demonstrated in a batch of cases. Unanimously, the Justices upheld pure food and drug acts in New York and Ohio. Denver could forbid women in places where liquor was sold, whether they were imbibers or waitresses, and local option liquor laws were upheld in Ohio and Texas. In Texas, where preferential treatment was afforded prohibitionists, Justice Holmes said that a state had no obligation to treat both sides equally. St. Louis could banish dairies and cattle barns from the city limits, and Illinois could cancel the right of an insurance company to do business in the state should it seek to remove a suit to federal court. Texas could impose liability upon railroad corporations in favor of contiguous landholders for allowing Johnson grass and Russian thistle to go to seed. Brown, White, and McKenna felt that singling out railroads from others plagued by the same problem was an impermissible classification under the equal protection clause. But Holmes, for the majority, was willing to assume that the state had acted in good faith and had perceived special conditions that justified such legislation. Then he added: "Great constitutional provisions must be administered with caution. Some play must be allowed for the joints of the machine, and it must be remembered that legislatures are the ultimate guardians of the liberties and welfare of the people in quite as great a degree as the courts."[5]

Although the Justices were generally sensitive to a perceived need to minimize conflict between federal and state judiciaries, the term produced three decisions that cut the other way. Despite the Court's prior reluctance to interfere with actions in state courts, the Justices did enjoin North Carolina from proceeding with a sale of railroad property that had been included in a federal judicial decree of foreclosure. Indiana relied on the Court's rule that a federal court would not issue an injunction to stop the exaction of a tax, but the Justices said the rule did not apply when the tax was based upon unconstitutional principles.[6] These checks to state power, however, were minor compared with the ruling in *South Dakota* v. *North Carolina*. North Carolina had issued bonds secured by a mortgage of railroad stock. When the state refused to honor the obligation, the individual holders, barred from suing the state under the Eleventh Amendment, gave the bonds to the state of South Dakota.[7] Would this attempt to evade the state's immunity be successful?

Brewer, for the majority, answered in the affirmative, characterizing the action as the type of controversy between states that gave the Supreme Court original jurisdiction under the Constitution. Although acknowledging the difficulties generally involved in enforcing such judgments, the Kansan saw no problem here. Should the state refuse to honor the verdict of the Court, the marshal of the Supreme Court would be directed to order the sale of the railroad stock. Brewer deemed irrelevant the argument that the original holders had made the gift to South Dakota with the expectation that the successful state would be generous. In a much longer opinion, White, joined by Fuller, McKenna, and Day, disputed the majority's contentions. Not only did the dissenters question the effectiveness and desirability of a decree in the case, but they saw the majority opinion eroding the protection the Eleventh Amendment provided. White said that this attempt to use the vehicle of the state to enforce the claim was sheer subterfuge.[8]

Justice Brewer was the Court's most consistent dissenter in cases where the majority invalidated state or local action on impairment of contract or due process grounds. Again contrary to the image often projected, the Kansan seemed willing to afford local government considerable discretion in business regulation. In one case where the majority accepted a bank's argument that prior practice had established the bank's immunity from taxation, Brewer, joined by Fuller, lectured his colleagues: ". . . it must be remembered that objects and means of taxation were not in years past sought for with the same avidity as at present. The demand for revenue was not so great. . . . So the mere fact that a particular kind of tax was not sought to be enforced upon any institution is not conclusive of the fact that it was necessarily exempt therefrom." Brewer was also with the dissenters when a bare majority of the Court, holding a bank exempt from a state exaction, said that, though the technical application of legal rules might give rise to hardship, the Constitution, at times, necessitated such results.[9]

When the matter before the Court did not concern state and municipal commercial regulation, the Justices were content to validate local discretion. Maryland could require potential voters to appear before a county clerk and make a declaration of their intent to become state citizens. When some blacks in Virginia, claiming disenfranchisement, sought to enjoin the canvass of votes in a congressional election, the Court sidestepped the issue by dismissing the case because the votes had already been canvassed. Repeated attempts to subject state criminal procedure to high court review failed. For instance, only Harlan dissented when the Court decided that depositions could be used in Louisiana in lieu of the presence of out-of-state witnesses.[10]

However, the Justices unanimously reversed a murder conviction in Alabama, where a black defendant had moved to quash his indictment on the ground that all black men had been excluded from jury service. What made this case different from others raising similar claims was that, instead of denying the allegation, the prosecutor moved to strike the claim on the basis that it was wordy and rambling, a sufficient objection under the state's procedural code. The trial judge agreed with the prosecutor and the defendant was convicted. Holmes, for a unanimous Court, said that a substantial constitutional claim could not be submerged in a matter of state practice. The state would have to retry the defendant and at least consider his claim.[11]

Except for the *Atkin* case, the real excitement of the term was produced by cases involving federal governmental interests. Dissenters in *Lynah* in the previous term had worried that the federal government would be held liable for indirect public takings. Now compensation was refused to a landholder who claimed that public work on the Mississippi River had injured his land. And when the government condemned property for military purposes, the Court upheld the limited award, ruling that evidence of other offers for the land and of injury to the remaining land were matters properly excluded in determining compensation.[12]

In *Buttfield* v. *Stranahan* a federal tea inspection act was upheld by a unanimous Court, which repulsed the argument that Congress had unlawfully delegated power to federal officials. White said the legislative branch had ordained the basic policy while leaving its implementation to executive officers. "To deny the power of Congress to delegate such a duty," he concluded, "would, in effect, amount but to declaring that the plenary power vested in Congress to regulate foreign commerce could not be efficaciously exerted."[13] Realizing the practical necessities of entrusting a limited policy-making function to the executive department, the Court was, in effect, refusing to use the separation of powers doctrine to impede effective interbranch cooperation. The long-term result of the Court's acquiescence would be an enlargement of the Chief Executive's power.

Despite the long-term significance of the *Buttfield* decision, the Court's resolution of *Northern Securities Company* v. *United States* occasioned far more contemporary interest. President Roosevelt's capacity for self-dramatization was revealed both in the prosecution of this holding company and in the intense personal interest he had in the case's outcome. After getting some feel for the office following McKinley's death, Roosevelt and Attorney General Philander C. Knox announced the prosecution on February 19, 1902. Conservative leaders in Congress and the financial community were stunned. The stock market dropped sharply. Roosevelt's action was characterized as a "thunderbolt out of a clear sky." A public, surfeited with stories of the power of a financial oligarchy and large trusts and the dangers they posed to the people, responded joyously to the President's initiative. For Roosevelt and the nation at large, the suit was a symbolic act of the first magnitude. The President, who was miffed by the attitude of J. P. Morgan during an early call by the financial baron at the White House, saw an opportunity to put Morgan in his place, while asserting the power of the federal government.[14] The modern presidency began with Roosevelt, and his dramatic use of the antitrust law illustrates the type of leadership, with its investment of personal ego, that has characterized successful presidents in the twentieth century.

Under the leadership of J. P. Morgan and James J. Hill, representing the interests of John D. Rockefeller, the Northern Securities Company was chartered in New Jersey, that hospitable mother of corporations, on November 31, 1901. Capitalized at $400 million, the company's assets consisted of a controlling stock interest in three major railroads, the Northern Pacific, the Great Northern, and the Chicago, Burlington & Quincy. The question posed by the suit was whether this incorporation of a holding company, which in itself operated no railroads, was a combination or conspiracy in restraint of trade in violation of the Sherman Antitrust Act. Attorney General Knox made a dramatic plea to the High Court, contending that an adverse decision might well pave the way for the absorption of the entire system of railroads into a single national unit.[15]

Splitting four-one-four, the Supreme Court affirmed the circuit court's decision to order the dissolution of the holding company. Harlan announced the judgment of the Court in an opinion in which Brown, Day, and McKenna concurred. Many issues were raised in the briefs including arguments of federalism and of liberty of contract, but the heart of the matter was whether the Sherman Act embraced the activity of the Northern Securities Company, and, if it did, was the statute beyond the authority of Congress.

Harlan approached the language of the Sherman Act literally and determined that no qualification of reasonableness could be read into its prohibi-

tion of every contract, combination, or conspiracy in restraint of trade.
Citing precedent to sustain general propositions upholding the suit of the
government, he evaluated the particular contentions of the company. No
state, the Justice added, can imbue a corporation with the authority to escape
congressional control over commerce. He then continued:

So long as Congress keeps within the limits of its authority as defined in the Constitution, infringing no rights recognized or secured by that instrument, its regulations of
interstate and international commerce, whether founded on wisdom or not, must be
submitted to by all. Harm and only harm can come from the failure of the courts to
recognize this fundamental principle of constitutional construction. To depart from it
because of the circumstances of special cases, or because the rule, in its operation, may
possibly affect the interests of business, is to endanger the safety and integrity of our
institutions and make the Constitution mean not what it says but what interested
parties wish it to mean at a particular time and under particular circumstances.[16]

Claims that such enforcement of the antitrust law would be disastrous and
lead to financial ruin have been made in all cases, Harlan said, adding that
such fears have not been realized in the past. After finding nothing wrong
with the relief granted by the lower court, he concluded that the congressional act clearly sought to embrace just such a combination as was now
before the Court.

Brewer was the swing man in the case. "I have felt constrained," he wrote,
"to make these observations for fear that the broad and sweeping language of
the opinion in the court might tend to unsettle legitimate business enterprises,
stifle or retard wholesome business activities, encourage improper disregard
of reasonable contracts, and invite unnecessary litigation."[17] The Kansan
accepted the dissenters' view that only unreasonable restraints of trade are
proscribed, but unlike them, he had no trouble characterizing the restraint
here as unreasonable. The abstract analogy the minority drew equating the
rights of an individual with those of a corporation, he contended, should not
take precedence over the factual situation presented. Brewer said the prosecution had clearly demonstrated the existence of a combination of persons
seeking to suppress competition. Agreeing with the government that approval here would logically lead to a total monopoly of the rail system, he
pronounced this restraint of trade unlawful and agreed with the dissolution
order.

Perhaps no opinion Brewer wrote during his long tenure on the Court
better illustrates his integrity, competence, and sophistication than this short
concurring opinion. Because he believed fervently in protecting the property
of the individual from increasing governmental interference, he objected to
the Harlan generalities that seemed to intrude upon this sacred domain. But
the Kansan possessed a sophisticated, if not fully developed, understanding
of the limitations of the artificial person-natural person analogy that often

enamoured his colleagues. Determining that the corporation was a person in terms of the protections of the Constitution may have solved certain conceptual problems for his brethren, but for Brewer the analogy had to be reinspected in terms of the case before the bench. He recognized substantial governmental power over the economy, and despite sweeping antiregulatory comments in some off-the-bench speeches, he approached cases pragmatically. Here his vote afforded the administration the power it sought under the antitrust act.

In an extensive dissent, which Fuller, Peckham, and Holmes joined, White took Harlan to task. In the 1890s White had arrived at the conclusion that the Sherman Act only outlawed unreasonable restraints of trade; such unreasonableness he did not find here. He agreed with counsel that a decision against the company would be an intrusion upon power reserved to the states by the Tenth Amendment. This new authority that the majority had found in Congress to deem a particular ownership of property unlawful, he said, conflicts "with the most elementary conception of the rights of property." Extensively reviewing commerce clause decisions, he concluded that the national legislature cannot regulate "that which is not interstate commerce," in which category he placed the ownership of stock.[18] To White full power to regulate corporations rested with the state, and this situation could only be changed by amending the Constitution, not by the Court's filling in a perceived gap in federal authority. White then deferred to Holmes on the question of the proper construction of the statute. Throughout his opinion the Louisianian contended that the majority's construction of the statute was inconsistent with the federal system, but he also agreed with Holmes, who denied that the majority understood the Sherman Act.

In this strange two-stage dissent Holmes's opinion was also joined by all the dissenters. In his first written dissent on the Court the Justice expressed the feeling that dissent was generally "useless and undesirable," indeed a strange statement as measured against Holmes's future career on the Court. After expressing this caveat, he continued in one of his most quoted passages:

Great cases, like hard cases, make bad law. For great cases are called great, not by reason of their real importance in shaping the law of the future, but because of some accident of immediate overwhelming interest which appeals to the feelings and distorts the judgment. These immediate interests exercise a kind of hydraulic pressure which makes what previously was clear seem doubtful, and before which even well settled principles of law will bend.

Although acknowledging that, at times, "judges need for their work the training of economists or statesmen," here, he argued, all that was needed was an intelligent reading of the English language. Holmes said the act must be interpreted fairly to leave no doubt as to its legitimacy. The government's interpretation of it, he argued, left "hardly any transaction concerning commerce between the states that may not be made crime by a finding of a jury or a court."[19]

For Holmes this problem did not arise, because he determined that the statute did not encompass the transactions involved in the case. He sought his definitions in the common law. Contracts in restraint of trade "were contracts with strangers to the contractor's business, and the trade restrained was the contractor's own," and combinations or conspiracies in restraint of trade, on the other hand, "were combinations to keep strangers to the agreement out of business." Seeking to undermine the Harlan position, he interpreted the antitrust act to say that "whatever is criminal when done by way of combination is equally criminal if done by a single man." Asking under which of the two common law definitions the transactions in the case fell, he answered, neither. Noting the popular view that the act was directed against bigness, he saw no such definite focus in its language. Holmes was willing to presume that the company's desire was to suppress competition, but he would await the commission of some illegal act. Concluding, the Justice said he was

... happy to know that only a minority of my brethren adopt an interpretation of the law which in my opinion would make eternal the *bellum onmium contra omnes* and disintegrate society so far as it could into individual atoms. If that were its intent I should regard calling such a law a regulation of commerce as a mere pretense. It would be an attempt to reconstruct society. I am not concerned with the wisdom of such an attempt, but I believe that Congress was not intrusted by the Constitution with the power to make it and I am deeply persuaded that it has not tried.[20]

What the opinions in the case reveal so well are the personal predilections of the writers. Harlan was in tune with the government's campaign against mammoth business enterprise; Brewer thought railroads with their monopolistic tendencies should be regulated even where that regulation was once removed; White was worried about the tendency to restrict economic growth and development and the intrusion of the power of the federal government into the realm of the states; and Holmes indicated that, despite his disclaimer, the government campaign against bigness was unwise and that the general theory behind it threatened the liberty of the people. Holmes enjoyed his posture of Olympian detachment, but he did not maintain it here. His feeling of enmity toward the act was evident. Privately he conveyed his feeling "that the Sherman Act is a humbug based on economic ignorance and incompetence."[21]

When the smoke had cleared, the President had won a narrow victory. Marring the victory, however, was Holmes's dissent, which Roosevelt interpreted as a lack of courage. Whether or not the President ever said "I could carve out of a banana a judge with more backbone than that," the quotation accurately reflected his reaction. A few years later he confessed to Senator

Lodge that from all indications Holmes should have been a great judge rather than the "bitter disappointment" he was. The President was so personally disturbed by this "treason" that he wanted to banish the Justice forever from the White House, but his advisors prevailed upon him to check the impulse. The relationship between the two men disintegrated, and Holmes privately found little generous to say even after the Rough Rider died.[22]

President Roosevelt had to accept his victory in the antitrust litigation knowing that the votes of Harlan and Brewer, two Justices that Roosevelt accused of "reactionary folly," were crucial. In his votes in the *Insular Cases* Justice Harlan was the most consistent opponent of the administration's view, and Brewer often agreed with his senior colleague. The Kansan, however, went further as he delivered off-the-bench speeches castigating the President's cult of masculinity and the concept of America's destiny and questioning the compatibility of the excursion into the Philippines and the resulting war against the Filipinos with basic democratic principles.[23] But these very men were the key to the President's victory.

Although the government had narrowly won a victory in *Northern Securities*, more of the Justices were quite willing to give administrative officers considerable discretion. For instance, Postmasters General had repeatedly asked Congress to modify legislation that apparently classified books in paper covers published regularly as entitled to the preferential mailing rate for periodicals. Displaying more initiative than his five predecessors, Henry C. Payne issued an order denying the more favorable rates to such publishers. The Court majority concluded that this order of the Postmaster General was authorized. Harlan dissented vigorously, and Fuller agreed that Payne had usurped a legislative function. The Court did rule that a Puerto Rican immigrant could not be classified as an alien after the cession of the island to the United States and that certain Chinese persons were entitled to classification as merchants, but the majority generally deferred to the administrative decisions of the immigration service. From this attitude of deference Brewer usually silently dissented, content to let his earlier words in the area stand. But the denial of the habeas corpus petition of Sing Tuck by his colleagues enraged Brewer. The Court of Appeals reviewing the lower federal court's decision had ordered the petition granted. The majority Justices, however, took the position that the judiciary could not interfere with an administrative decision on the matter of the petitioner's citizenship until that determination had been reviewed by the Secretary of Commerce and Labor.[24]

To the majority's deference, Brewer responded: "I cannot believe that the courts of this republic are so burdened with controversies about property that they cannot take time to determine the right of personal liberty by one claiming to be a citizen." To accept the decision of an administrative official over the calm reflection of a court seemed to the Kansan the height of absurdity. The Justice contended that legislation in 1902 mandated a new scrutiny of the treatment of the Chinese, one which would better comport with the provision in the treaty between the two nations promising treatment in accordance with the status of citizens of the most favored nation. "I am not astonished," he said, "at the report current in the papers that China has declined to continue this treaty for another term of ten years." As if his previous words were not enough to condemn those both on and off the Court who blithely accepted such prejudicial treatment, Brewer prophetically concluded:

Finally, let me say that the time has been when many young men from China came to our educational institutions to pursue their studies, when her commerce sought our shores, and her people came to build our railroads, and when China looked upon this country as her best friend. If all this be reversed and the most populous nation on earth becomes the great antagonist of this republic, the careful student of history will recall the words of Scripture, "they have sown the wind, and they shall reap the whirlwind," and for cause of such antagonism [we] need look no further than the treatment accorded during the last twenty years by this country to the people of that nation.[25]

In the next term Brewer, this time joined by Peckham, again castigated his colleagues for preferring the decision of an administrator to that of a court in a similar claim of citizenship. "I cannot believe," he said, "that Congress intended to provide that a citizen, simply because he belongs to an obnoxious race, can be deprived of all the liberty and protection which the Constitution guarantees, and if it did so intend, I do not believe it has the power to do so."[26] Giving voice to his noble aspirations, the Kansan confronted a nation either apathetic or hostile to the Asiatic. Realizing that the principles he espoused might fall upon deaf ears, he tied them to the very real self-interest of the country. The Kansan did not hesitate to express himself on policy issues, and though historians have rescued Harlan from the limbo of obscurity for his views on the Bill of Rights and on the need to treat blacks equally, they have not acknowledged Brewer's assault on a different type of racial injustice— discrimination toward the Oriental.

As the long term was finally drawing to an end, the Court, as it often does, was saving some of its major decisions for the last opinion day. One such case was *McCray* v. *United States*. Just as *Champion* in the previous term found a quasi-police power inherent in the commerce clause, *McCray* reaffirmed a similar power within the taxing authority of Congress. This story takes us back to 1886 when Congress responded to the fear of dairy interests that margarine was a formidable competitor. The 1886 act imposed a license tax on manufacturers and dealers in margarine and contained numerous regulations relating to packaging, marketing, and manufacture. The manufacturer was forced to pay a tax of two cents a pound, payment of which was confirmed by the appearance of revenue stamps. Demand for more protection bore fruit in an amendment to the original act passed in 1902. The tax was now raised to a prohibitive level of ten cents a pound, but, if the margarine was free of any artificial coloration and did not resemble butter, the tax would be one-quarter cent per pound.[27] McCray, a licensed dealer in margarine, was convicted of having purchased for resale yellow margarine bearing only stamps showing a tax paid at the lower rate. He claimed the act violated due process, that it interfered with the police power of the states, and that it so arbitrarily discriminated against margarine in favor of butter that it offended fundamental principles of the Constitution.

White wrote the Court's opinion. He cited the first consideration by the Court of the margarine tax, where Fuller had disposed of the question of the motive of Congress, as follows: "The act before us is on its face an act for levying taxes, and although it may operate in so doing to prevent deception in the sale of oleomargarine as and for butter, its primary object must be assumed to be the raising of revenue." Rather than simply rest on precedent, White responded to the full-dress argument of counsel. He accused the defendant of seeking a ruling from the Court on the wisdom of the congressional action. According to the Justice, correction of alleged errors would be judicial usurpation that would eradicate the "entire distinction" among the departments upon which our government is founded. To the allegation that a lawful power is here exercised for an unlawful purpose, White responded that such an argument "reduces itself to the contention that under our constitutional system, the abuse by one department of the government of its lawful powers is to be corrected by the abuse of its powers by another department." The remedy for any abuse lies with the people, not with the judiciary, said the man from Louisiana. He concluded that "the taxing power conferred by the Constitution knows no limits except those expressly stated in that instrument" and that the Court cannot determine that a tax is excessive without fastening limitations on the legislature that do not exist.[28]

To the more general contention that fundamental principles of justice were not in tune with the act, White answered that the Court had already determined that states can regulate or prohibit the article without violating due process. So it could hardly be held, even if the defendant's contention of prohibition of the product were true, that the activity of the federal government had violated a right that "no free government could destroy."[29] White conceded that a case might be hypothesized where the taxing power was being used as a sham to destroy rights that freedom and justice could not tolerate. Then he would describe such a situation not as an abuse of power but rather as the attempted exercise of a nondelegated power, but this case, he concluded, bore little resemblance to that hypothetical one.

Fuller, who had written the Court opinion upholding the original federal taxing act, dissented silently with Brown and Peckham. Both Fuller and Peckham were dissenters in *Champion*, but in *McCray* Brewer and Brown changed places. The fourth dissenter in *Champion* was Day, who now subscribed to White's opinion. Under both the commerce and the taxing power, Congress had a reservoir of authority earlier associated only with the states. The Justices here did not really disagree with the defendant that Congress was using its power to drive margarine colored like butter out of the market, but at least six members of the Court pronounced that consideration constitutionally irrelevant.

On that last opinion day the overseas possessions again figured in the Court's work. A federal district court in Puerto Rico had convicted an individual in the postal service of embezzlement. The defendant sought to prohibit the court from proceeding by attacking the competency of the grand jury that brought in the indictment. He had no success in the lower court, but a unanimous Supreme Court, speaking through Harlan, held that the local court, established in 1900, was bound by the rules of the domestic federal district courts. Alleging that the failure of certain jurors to meet the requisite property qualification was a defect of form only, counsel cited a curative statute designed to make minor defects insufficient to challenge an indictment. Harlan labeled the claim "a matter of substance, which cannot be disregarded without prejudice to an accused."[30]

This unanimity was short-lived, as the Justices faced other criminal questions in the new Imperial America. In the case of Thomas E. Kepner the issue was whether the government could appeal an acquittal. Kepner was found not guilty of embezzlement, apparently a common crime in the overseas possessions, but the Philippine Supreme Court reversed the decision and found him guilty. This was permissible under an early military order maintaining prior judicial practice, but Kepner contended that this procedure did not survive a congressional act of 1902 providing for the establishment of a civil government in the islands. In that act Congress followed the President's earlier orders and restated that the Bill of Rights applied to the islands. The government's contention was based on section nine of the same act, which recognized the preestablished jurisdiction of the local courts. Day, for the majority, found that the more specific protections overrode any implication drawn from section nine. Reviewing cases on the double jeopardy provision, he concluded that an initial verdict of acquittal was final and definitive.[31]

This case revealed some interesting new lineups on the Court. Day's opinion garnered Fuller, Harlan, Brewer, and Peckham, all of whom had consistently taken a position more in favor of extending constitutional guarantees to the overseas possessions. For the moment Day was a new adherent, giving those with whom the President disagreed a majority. Shiras and Gray, consistent advocates of the government's position, were gone, but Holmes joined White and McKenna, two of the remaining three consistent supporters of the government. Brown, also in dissent, again charted his own way.

Holmes's dissent shows both his willingness to support the government in its action in the recently pacified Philippines and his lack of sensitivity to the protection afforded by the double jeopardy provision of the Constitution. The Massachusetts Justice worried about the domestic implications of the majority's interpretation of the Fifth Amendment. He expressed concern about fastening "upon the country, a doctrine covering the whole criminal law, which . . . will have serious and evil consequences. At the present time in this country there is more danger that criminals will escape justice than that they will be subjected to tyranny." After this tirade, Holmes asserted that such sentiments had nothing at all to do with the decision he reached. Acknowledging that double jeopardy meant being tried twice for the same offense, he still maintained that "there is no rule that a man may not be tried twice in the same case." Noting that a defendant can appeal a conviction, Holmes implied that the government should have an equivalent right to contest the verdict in the first instance. The constitutional protection, he contended, is not vitiated by the Philippine procedure that allows either party to appeal the verdict, for a "second trial in the same case must be regarded as only a continuation of the jeopardy which began with the trial below."[32] Holmes seemed to equate the situation here to a game in which the players are held to the same set of rules.

Brown dissented, not from the majority's reading of the double jeopardy provision but rather from the determination that it was applicable in the instant case. The Justice said the use of the term *double jeopardy* in the 1902 act should be read in light of prior criminal procedure beginning with the military order. Congress, he continued, sought in section nine to preserve this practice. Brown found it "impossible to suppose that Congress intended to place in the hands of a single judge the great and dangerous power of finally acquitting the most notorious criminals."[33] What Congress really intended to do is a mystery, but, if the administration was in harmony with Congress, Brown's reading may not be in error. The majority, however, felt that the Court's task was to interpret the words Congress used and not explore the murky realm of intent.

The final case of the term was *Dorr* v. *United States*, which again involved a conviction in the Philippines. Once more Day, although for a far different majority, was assigned the task of writing the opinion. Fred L. Dorr was convicted for libel under an act passed by the Philippine Commission; he was tried before a court without a jury in the city of Manila. Essentially the question was, did the act of 1902 prescribe trial by jury for criminal offenses? Day concluded that the right was not extended by the Constitution itself and that the act of 1902 neither extended the right nor sought to incorporate the Philippines into the United States. Seeing no obligation on the part of Congress to afford the right of trial by jury, Day added a passage that reflected the patronizing attitude of the administration:

If the right to trial by jury were a fundamental right which goes wherever the jurisdiction of the United States extends, or if Congress, in framing laws for outlying territory belonging to the United States, was obliged to establish that system by affirmative legislation, it would follow that, no matter what the needs or capacities of the people, trial by jury, and in no other way, must be forthwith established, although the result may be to work injustice and provoke disturbance rather than to aid the orderly administration of justice. If the United States, impelled by its duty or advantage, shall acquire territory peopled by savages, and of which it may dispose or not hold for ultimate admission to Statehood, if this doctrine is sound, it must establish there the trial by jury. To state such a proposition demonstrates the impossibility of carrying it into practice.[34]

Peckham, in a concurring opinion, joined by Fuller and Brewer, simply conceded defeat on the basis of the majority's decision in the *Mankichi* case. The trio was, however, disturbed by Day's capitulation to White's incorporation theory. Reliance on *Downes* v. *Bidwell*, they maintained, was misplaced in the case at hand. Harlan added a short dissent reiterating his belief that the right to a trial by jury is fundamental and cannot be denied. Harkening back to his words in *Mankichi*, he said that wherever the United States is sovereign, action against life, liberty, or property cannot take the form of any procedure inconsistent with the Constitution.

This spate of decisions brought the term to an end. The work load had been fairly well spread out, but Brown and Harlan wrote only about half as many opinions as the other Justices. Harlan's frequent and lengthy dissents, however, gave him ample representation in the official reports. Day put in a productive year, though it can hardly be said that all his opinions made the President happy. In fact, before long Roosevelt would adjudge both of his appointees failures. Of all the Justices the term really belongs to Brewer, not only because of his highlighting of the patently discriminatory policies of the government toward the Chinese, but also because of his concurrence in the *Northern Securities Company* case.

During the Court's recess the national parties went through their quadrennial ordeal of nominating presidential candidates. With careful preparation, including safely ensconcing his potential rival, Taft, in the War Department, and despite his anxiety, Theodore Roosevelt had no difficulty capturing the Republican nomination. Like all vice-presidents who have attained the high office on an incumbent's death, Roosevelt had a desperate need to have his claim to the office ratified by the people. The Democrats, disaffected by the so-called radicalism of Bryan, swung back to the Cleveland wing, and Bryan's western support was insufficient to block the nomination of an orthodox New York Democrat, Judge Alton B. Parker. Winning respect for his noninvolvement in the bitter internal party controversies of the last eight years, Parker won an easy victory over Bryan on the first ballot. There was some talk of the possibility that large financial interests might prefer the conservative Parker over the less reliable Roosevelt, but money flowed generously into the Republican till.[35] Shortly after the Court convened for the 1904 term Roosevelt won a smashing victory. He garnered over 56 percent of the vote, winning by a margin of almost 19 percentage points, the greatest electoral victory since such votes were first recorded in 1824.

When the Court met in October 1904 all the Justices were present. Fuller's wife had died during the recess, but the Chief responded to reactivated rumors of his resignation, spurred on by both Roosevelt and Taft, with a determined resolve to stay on. After all, at age seventy-one he was still carrying the heaviest opinion load on the Court.

Despite the Court's continued willingness to defer to the lower courts' handling of matters of criminal justice, the majority, early in the term did deliver a setback to the administration's attempt to enforce the federal criminal statute against peonage. A defendant had been indicted and convicted for returning individuals to a state of peonage. Brewer, for the majority, insisted upon the letter of the statute, so unlike his decision in the *Holy Trinity Church* case, and said that the evidence did not show that the two blacks involved had ever been in a prior state of peonage; therefore, they could not be returned to that condition. On this technical basis, the majority overturned the jury verdict and ordered a new trial. In dissent, Harlan described how the blacks were found in Florida and forcibly returned to Georgia to work off an alleged debt. Lecturing his colleagues for their insensitivity to the plight of these men, he said: "The accused made no objection to the submission of the case to the jury, and it is going very far to hold in a case like this, disclosing barbarities of the worst kind against these negroes, that the trial court erred in sending the case to the jury."[36]

With state legislative activity continually increasing, the Justices were faced with more cases in which state action was claimed to have violated the commerce clause. The Court again responded pragmatically to the cases, avoiding the argument if it was raised too late in the proceedings and accepting a construction of state taxing laws that would save them from invalidation under the commerce clause. Also, the majority ruled that the Wilson Act had conferred sufficient authority upon the states so an inspection tax could be levied on imported beer equal to the tax on the product imposed on domestic producers. Brown dissented in an opinion joined by Fuller, Brewer, and Day, claiming that the decision opened the door generally to obstructions of interstate commerce.[37]

Just as challenges to state and local taxes were generally repulsed by the Court during the term, so were attacks levied against other police power regulations. Massachusetts' compulsory vaccination law was sustained by the Court over the silent dissent of Brewer and Peckham, who apparently were more sensitive to the defendant's claim that his liberty had been abridged. Holmes, for the majority, took judicial notice of the belief that vaccination prevented the spread of smallpox and said that this was a proper exercise of the state's police power to protect the public health. The Justices unanimously upheld Texas and Kansas antitrust laws and accepted Wisconsin's determination that the attempt of a group of newspapers to injure a rival by engaging in preferential advertising contracts was actionable. Utah, because of local conditions, could allow a private landowner to exercise the power of public condemnation to enlarge an irrigation ditch across a neighbor's property. Peckham was careful in his majority opinion to limit the reach of the decision, saying the Court's decision did not imply approval of the broad concept "that private property may be taken in all cases where the taking may promote the public interest and tend to develop the natural resources of the State."[38]

Until *Lochner* v. *New York* was decided in mid-April, there was little evidence that the concept of liberty of contract was making any headway on the Court. In earlier sessions, when the issue was squarely presented in a labor situation, both Brewer and Peckham believed this freedom was abridged by state regulation. In *Atkin* Fuller joined the duo, but if Joseph Lochner was to win his case, two more votes were needed.

On its face the case appeared unassuming, even though its importance was recognized by allowing counsel two days for argument in late February. Lochner had been convicted of violating a state law making the employment of a worker in a bakery for more than ten hours a day or sixty hours a week a misdemeanor. One of the interesting features of the case was that Lochner was represented in the lower court by Henry Weismann, a former baker turned lawyer. The story was that Weismann, at the time the law was passed by the New York legislature, was so convinced of its unconstitutionality that he was inspired to study law and prove it so. By special leave, because his brief practice had not made him eligible for membership in the Supreme Court bar, he was allowed to argue the case before the High Bench.[39] In such labor cases the allegation of the employer that his employees' rights were being violated by a regulation of work conditions always had a hollow ring; now here was Henry Weismann to afford some substance to that contention.

Weismann and co-counsel Frank Harvey Field attacked the law on due process and equal protection grounds. Their main point was that, since the trade of a baker was not dangerous to one's safety or health, it was not a legitimate subject of the state's police power. This statute, they urged, was arbitrary and a clear violation of the parties' freedom to contract. To lend weight to their contention they cited numerous state decisions overturning similar legislation, again a reminder that the doctrine of liberty of contract had much more appeal and success at the state rather than at the federal level. Opposing counsel stressed not only the approval of the New York courts but also the large measure of legislative discretion that properly belongs to the state legislature.[40]

Apparently the Justices in conference decided to agree with the lower court and uphold the legislation; with Fuller in dissent, Harlan accepted the task of writing the Court's opinion. Peckham agreed to write for the dissenters.

When the opinions were read on April 17, 1905, however, the New York Justice began with the majority opinion. Harlan dissented for White and Day, and Holmes filed a separate opinion. From their internal construction, especially taking into account Harlan's usual style, the opinions were apparently reversed. Someone had switched sides in an episode reminiscent of the earlier *Pollock* case. Since Peckham and Brewer were the strongest advocates of freedom of contract, their positions seem fixed, and the Chief had shown himself a recent convert. Excluding the final four dissenters leaves Brown and McKenna. Since in the past both Justices had expressed their belief that the police power afforded the states wide latitude, their presence in the *Lochner* majority is surprising. Without further evidence, either internally or externally, the selection of the "vascillating jurist" defies resolution. Fortunately, as Shiras well knew, the fact that a member of the Court had apparently changed his vote did not become public knowledge. Still, upon this single vote rested not only much similar state legislation but also the prestige of the Court in a reform-minded society. Few of those who attacked the *Lochner* result put it into the context of the Court's total work product.[41]

Especially disturbing in Peckham's opinion is the broad language limiting the range the Court repeatedly had given to the police power. After stating the facts, the Justice immediately condemned the statute as an abridgment of the individual's freedom to contract protected by the due process clause of the Fourteenth Amendment. Relying upon his opinion in *Allgeyer*, the decision creating the doctrine and the only instance of its prior application, Peckham then reviewed some police power cases including *Holden* v. *Hardy*. He limited this precedent to demonstrably unhealthy labor, adding that in the Utah statute, unlike that of New York, there was an exception for emergencies. As for *Atkin* v. *Kansas*, he confined its reach to the right of a governmental unit to prescribe how public work is to be done.

Asserting that the police power must be limited by the Fourteenth Amendment, Peckham said that determining whether a statute is "unreasonable, unnecessary and arbitrary" is not a matter of substituting a judicial for a legislative judgment, but rather one of demarcating the line that the Fourteenth Amendment draws. He rejected the argument that the law could be sustained as a labor law without reference to the police power, saying there was no reason to make bakers "wards of the State." Contending that there can be no public interest in the terms of a labor contract, he argued that the only possible justification the state may use is health. Concluding that neither the health of bakers nor of the general public was involved in the New York legislation, Peckham pronounced it beyond the range of the state's power. Were the Court to uphold such an act, he said, "there would seem to be no length to which legislation of this nature might not go." Painting with a broad brush, the New York Justice made clear his desire to protect the freedom of individuals from the "restrictive sway of the legislature." Noting that state enactments with only "the most remote relation" to the public health or welfare were on the rise, Peckham implied that the Court has a duty to stamp out or retard this unfortunate development.[42] Henry Weismann, the former baker had won his case, and a dozen years would pass before the back of the *Lochner* precedent would be broken.

Harlan's dissent was heavily laced with precedent and carried less of the sting characteristic of his dissenting opinions. The Justice acknowledged that the legislature may have been motivated to equalize the bargaining power of employer and employee, but whatever the underlying motive, Harlan accepted what the majority rejected—that the New York legislature could pass such acts when in its judgment they protected the health of workers. Reminding the majority that the Court's duty is not to second guess the legislature, he said, "I find it impossible, in view of common experience, to say that there is here no real or substantial relation between the means employed by the State and the end sought by its legislation." The invasion of fundamental rights that Peckham perceived was lost on Harlan, who reminded his colleagues that by annulling such legislation they were transcending the judicial function. He then cited studies, drawn from the state's brief, that sustained what the majority said could not be sustained—that there was evidence that prolonged work in a bakery can be detrimental to an employee's health. Recognizing that the question of how long a man should work was much disputed by political economists, Harlan argued that this controversy itself precludes labeling New York's action arbitrary. "We are not," he continued, "to presume that the State of New York has acted in bad faith. Nor can we assume that its legislature acted without due deliberation, or that it did not determine this question upon the fullest attainable information, and for the common good."[43] Then the Kentuckian rested his case by citing the Court's opinion in *Atkin*, an opinion he wrote and from which only Fuller, Brewer, and Peckham had dissented, saying it sustains in the broadest terms legislative discretion in such matters.

Holmes dissented alone in one of those short, quotable dissents that multiply as the years go by. "This case," he wrote, "is decided upon an economic theory which a large part of the country does not entertain." Whether a Justice agrees with such a theory or not, he said, "has nothing to do with the right of a majority to embody their opinions in law." Our Constitution, he concluded,

... is made for people of fundamentally differing views, and the accident of our finding certain opinions natural and familiar or novel and even shocking ought not to conclude our judgment upon the question whether statutes embodying them conflict with the Constitution of the United States.

General propositions do not decide concrete cases. The decision will depend on a judgment or intuition more subtle than any articulate major premise. But I think that the proposition just stated, if it is accepted, will carry us far toward that end. Every opinion tends to become a law. I think that the word liberty in the Fourteenth Amendment is perverted when it is held to prevent the natural outcome of a dominant opinion, unless it can be said that a rational and fair man necessarily would admit that the statute proposed would infringe fundamental principles as they have been understood by the traditions of our people and our law. It does not need research to show that no such sweeping condemnation can be passed upon the statute before us.[44]

With this dissent Holmes came of age on the Court. It attracted much attention and was widely approved. Harlan's opinion was more solidly anchored and more fully developed, but Holmes's rhetoric, expressing a deference to the democratic majority, struck a most responsive chord in the generation. There is evidence that the Justice personally had little sympathy for such laws;[45] yet here he was practicing what he preached—judicial restraint. Holmes, at times, could be infuriating in his posture of detachment, but in an era of legislative activity and experimentation he provided support from the High Bench. By taking the high ground he made the majority look self-interested and made Peckham and his colleagues, despite their disclaimer, look like they were not judging at all but simply writing their personal preferences into law.

Not since the debacle of 1895 had a case stirred as much protest in the popular press and professional journals.[46] What was at issue was not simply the law in the case but a nationwide movement to use government to redress imbalances in the industrial society. The theory of contract with its parties of equal bargaining power was out of touch with the realities of early twentieth-century America. Industrialization had taken place under the guidance of entrepreneurs who relied upon their relative freedom from regulation and their ability to dictate the terms of an employment contract. As Holmes indicated, what was at stake was not simply the reach of the state's police power but whether or not the economic theories and practices of the past could be adjusted to the realities of the present.

Theodore Roosevelt found the decision in *Lochner* a confirmation of his fears about the Court, but the Justices struck closer to home when they dealt a blow to the President's conservation policy. A mining company was prosecuted for cutting timber on leased land in violation of an order promulgated by the Secretary of the Interior. The Court decided that the conviction could not stand because the Secretary's order conflicted with an 1878 congressional act permitting such cutting. Justice Brown, joined by Harlan and Peckham, saw no such fatal conflict. In tune with the conservationist policy of Secretary Ethan A. Hitchcock and the administration, Brown said that bearing "in mind that the policy of the government has been to preserve its rapidly diminishing area of forest lands for the benefit of the whole people, any statute which permits timber to be cut by individuals should be narrowly construed."[47] Just as Brown had demonstrated an unusual sensitivity to the plight of the American Indian, he indicated here that the Court should not be blithely insensitive to the need for a policy of conservation.

One bright spot in the session for President Roosevelt was the Court's unanimous resolution of a major antitrust case, *Swift & Company* v. *United States*. Despite Holmes's personal antipathy to the Sherman Act his opinion for the Court furthered the legislation's reach. The circuit court had granted an injunction against the company for violations of the statute. Swift was engaged in buying livestock, slaughtering it, and selling it to dealers and customers throughout the United States, transactions involving substantial interstate commerce. The government accused the company of entering into a combination for the purpose of purchasing the livestock without substantial competition. In an attempt to fix favorable prices, the dominant dealers in the country joined together; blacklists were maintained; improper charges for cartage were established; and railroads were forced to lower their rates. Swift conceded the allegations of the government and appealed the adverse lower court decision.

First, Holmes passed on the sufficiency of the indictment, holding that the scheme outlined "as a whole seems to us to be within the reach of the law." Responding to the argument that the transactions took place within a single state, the Justice said their "effect upon commerce among the States is not accidental, secondary, remote or merely probable." The purpose of the agreements "is to restrain and monopolize commerce among the States in respect to such sales." He ruled that

... commerce among the States is not a technical legal conception, but a practical one, drawn from the course of business. When cattle are sent for sale from a place in one State, with the expectation that they will end their transit, after purchase, in another, and when in effect they do so, with only the interruption necessary to find a purchaser at the stock yards, and when this is a typical, constantly recurring course, the current thus existing is a current of commerce among the States, and the purchase of the cattle is a part and incident of such commerce.[48]

With these latter words the Court introduced the stream of commerce concept into antitrust law. In ten years the Court had come a long way from *E. C. Knight*, where it had failed to look at the practical effects of the sugar monopoly. The Sherman Act had been given a new dimension, continuing the tradition of *Northern Securities*, but there railroads were indirectly involved; here a major business corporation, using the transportation facilities after the fact, was deemed to be within the prohibitions of the antitrust act.

Near the end of the session the Justices decided an important case in favor of Indian treaty rights. McKenna wrote the opinion, from which only Harlan dissented. Under a treaty in 1859 the Yahima Indians were afforded fishing rights in the Columbia River. Such rights were granted in return for relinquishing land, and McKenna said that they survived the actions of both the Land Department and the state of Washington. Even private purchases from the federal and state governments, the Justice continued, were burdened by the treaty rights. Substantial benefits accrued to the government in the 1859 treaty, he said, concluding: ". . . surely it was within the competency of the Nation to secure to the Indians such a remnant of the great rights they possessed as 'taking fish at all usual and accustomed places.'"[49] The government had sought to renege on the obligation, but the Court said no.

No discussion of a recent term of Court would be complete without some further word on the status of distant territories. The session's major case was *Rasmussen* v. *United States*, and Justice White interpreted the decision as a personal triumph. Ever since his extensive concurring opinion in *Downes* v. *Bidwell*, where he elaborated on the incorporation theory, White had personally been striving for Court acceptance of his ideological leadership in the area. But in the previous term Harlan had dissented from a majority opinion that had the flavor of White's incorporation doctrine, while Fuller, Peckham, and Brewer had said in their concurring opinion that they placed no reliance on *Downes*. After delivering the Court's opinion in *Rasmussen*, White, having gained the votes of six colleagues, intercepted the reporter and told him to make sure that in his headnotes to the case he indicate that *Downes* was now approved by the Court.[50]

In *Rasmussen* all the Justices agreed that the guarantees of the Bill of Rights were in force in Alaska. The Court held unconstitutional a 1900 statute providing that juries in misdemeanor cases shall consist of only six persons. White said that Alaska was incorporated into the United States by the treaty confirming purchase from Russia in 1868. Incorporation, he continued, made the 1900 act invalid under the Sixth Amendment, since the term *jury* found therein had been consistently interpreted to mean twelve persons. He quoted liberally from his *Downes* opinion on the discretion of Congress to incorporate or not, but Reporter Butler left this reference out of the headnotes. In the wording of the treaty of 1868 White found clear evidence of incorporation. "The inhabitants of the ceded territory . . ," it said, "shall be admitted to the enjoyment of all the rights, advantages and immunities of citizens of the United States; and shall be maintained and protected in the free enjoyment of their liberty, property and religion."[51] When measured against the treaty of annexation, actions of Congress, and repeated decisions of the Court, the contention of the government that Alaska was not incorporated, White ruled, was devoid of merit.

White's need to explain the difference between the Philippines and Alaska was accommodated by all the Justices except Harlan and Brown. Harlan briefly summarized his earlier position and indicated that he could not concur in the incorporation theory. Brown, however, took direct aim on White:

I do not dissent from the conclusion of the court in this case, but I do dissent from the proposition that Congress may not deal with Territories as it pleases, until it has seen fit to extend the provisions of the Constitution to them, which, once done, in my view, is irrevocable. I regret that the disputed doctrine of incorporation should have been made the mainstay of the Court, when the case might so easily have been disposed of upon grounds which would have evoked no utterance of disapproval.

In opposition to Harlan, who maintained that the Constitution was in step with the flag, Brown saw full discretion in Congress to extend or not extend certain constitutional protections. The only exception he made was in favor of "the natural rights of their inhabitants to life, liberty and property."[52]

Perhaps Roosevelt was disturbed by the decision in *Rasmussen*, but the Court's resolution of *Lincoln v. United States* was even more troubling. The case, concerning customs duties, brought the matter of armed Filipino resistance to American rule before the Court. Lincoln and his partners filed a suit in federal district court to recover duties on imports from New York into Manila. Allegedly the duties were justified by a presidential order of July 1898 and ratified by congressional action four years later; Solicitor General Henry M. Hoyt argued that the war power justified the President's order directing that, upon American military occupation of any fort or other place in the Philippines, duties would be levied and collected as "a military contribution." The question was whether this order survived the end of the conflict with Spain. Hoyt argued that the armed insurrection of the Filipinos against the United States continued the duties. Further, he tossed in the suggestion that the 1902 act had ratified the President's earlier action.[53]

In this era before future mammoth accretions to the President's authority as commander-in-chief, Holmes, for a unanimous Court, rejected the government's argument. Noting that the duties involved were collected after ratification of the Treaty of Paris, Holmes said the presidential order was not "a power in blank for any military occasion which might turn up in the future. It was a regulation for and during an existing war, referred to as definitely as it had been named." Concluding that "there is nothing in the Philippine insurrection of sufficient gravity to give to the Islands the character of foreign countries within the meaning of the tariff act," the Justice interpreted the presidential order as dealing with imports from foreign countries, not the United States, and into ports over which the United States did not have "actual military control." Giving the order a more generous interpretation, Holmes said, it still would not apply to American goods imported into Manila, which American forces had occupied since the end of the war with Spain. "The fact that there was an insurrection of natives not recognized as belligerents in another part of the island, or even just outside its walls," he said, "did not give the President power to impose duties on imports from a country no longer foreign."[54] Holmes gave short shrift to the idea of ratification, saying that Congress could only ratify duties legitimately encompassed by the President's order.

With his cavalier treatment of the guerrilla war in the Philippines and his narrowing of presidential authority, Holmes must have further infuriated the President. Apparently Roosevelt pressed Attorney General William H. Moody to petition for a rehearing on the question of congressional ratification of the duties. Since that issue had not been thoroughly argued, the Court granted a rehearing early in the next term. On the rehearing the Court stood by its earlier decision, but the administration's special interest in the case led Chief Justice Fuller to write the Court's opinion. This time Attorney General Moody joined Solicitor General Hoyt in the argument, but the top legal officers of the government succeeded only in prying loose White and McKenna from the former majority.

Fuller confined his opinion to the question of ratification, and cited the passage of the act that specifically "approved, ratified and confirmed" the tariff exaction as specified in the President's order and subsequent amendments. He accepted Holmes's earlier interpretation of the President's order, calling it a "military tax" designed to seize Spanish revenues: "That was what the order meant when it was passed, and a change of circumstances did not change its meaning. Neither was the meaning changed by any amendment." Ratification by Congress, Fuller continued, only reached the order as made, not an order that might have been made by the President. Citing *DeLima*, he imparted knowledge to Congress of Court decisions that, the Chief said, cast grave doubt upon legislative ratification of "a tax under circumstances like the present." Noting "powerful opposition" in Congress on the matter of overseas possessions, Fuller concluded "that the phraseology of the act probably represents all that it was deemed safe to ask."[55] To the argument that such a conclusion made the ratification language meaningless, he responded that the 1902 act legalized both the duties during the war and other duties continued in force after the peace treaty.

White confessed error in his earlier concurrence in Holmes's opinion. Although Fuller commended the argument of the Attorney General, White demonstrated its effect upon him. The Louisiana Justice said his earlier concurrence was based on the doctrine of *stare decisis* and the fact that his attention had not been directed to "public reports and documents throwing light upon the scope of the ratifying act, as was done on the present argument." Now interpreting the ratification act in light of this evidence, he saw "no possible escape from the conclusion that that act was intended to, and did, ratify the collection of the charges complained of."[56] Brown, who believed most strongly in giving Congress a free hand in such matters, did not dissent. Possibly his strong disagreement with White precluded him from changing his mind on the rehearing, or perhaps he simply felt that Holmes and Fuller together had made out the stronger case for limiting the scope of congressional ratification.

This final episode in the *Lincoln* case was yet to come as the term ended, but President Roosevelt had enough evidence to conclude that his first two appointees to the High Bench were too independent. For others, it was *Lochner* that cast a pall over the Court. The hope in this "progressive period" had been that the High Bench was slowly being brought in tune with the changes in society, and although the Justices were far from hostile to change, the public saw only *Lochner*.

When the Justices congregated again in Washington in October 1905, all was normal, including the continued rumors of Fuller's resignation. Justice Brown remarked that the Chief was getting old but that he would never retire. Comments like these did not soothe an anxious William Howard Taft, whose new base in Washington only increased his yearnings for the center seat.[57]

If the *Lochner* decision had seemed to indicate a new willingness to supervise the exercise of state power, the new term revealed no such tendency. Oliver Wendell Holmes, however, found opportunity twice during the term to question the majority's use of the Fourteenth Amendment. Perhaps buoyed by the reception given his dissent in *Lochner*, he quickly overcame his expressed dislike for special opinions and argued with the majority in two cases. In the first decision the majority ruled that a Kentucky tax embracing rolling stock of a company permanently located in another state was a violation of the due process clause of the Fourteenth Amendment. Holmes responded that the Court's determination seemed desirable but then denied that it could be deduced from the Fourteenth Amendment. Desirability alone, according to the man from Massachusetts, did not justify overturning a state court decision. In a second case, involving the validation of a New York regulation of milk sales, Holmes said:

> I do not gather from the statute or from the decision of the Court of Appeals that the action of the board of health was intended to be subject to judicial revision as to its reasonableness. But whether it was or was not, I agree that the statute, which in substance is older than the Fourteenth Amendment, was not repealed or overthrown by the adoption of that Amendment.[58]

Perhaps this was Holmes's way, in absence of cases better framing the issue, of continuing the campaign that he had begun with his *Lochner* dissent.

In the police-power area the Court showed little desire to upset local determinations. A county in Michigan could create a new school district and give it property that was drawn from existing districts. San Francisco could enforce an ordinance requiring all garbage and refuse to be taken to a company for disposition. Iowa could force competition among insurance companies by preventing any combination or agreement to trade information on their operations. In the absence of any federal action, South Carolina could construct a dam to promote the general health of its citizens. Texas could compel a street railway to provide half-fare tickets for school children even though the contract with the municipality did not so specify. California could change its inheritance laws to provide a tax on legacies to brothers and sisters of the decedent while exempting such strangers to the blood as husband, wife, and in-laws. A county in Montana could levy a tax on cattle owned by a Jesuit order whose primary task was to minister to the Indians, and Utah could authorize private mining companies to condemn a right of way. Georgia could exclude a number of occupational groups from jury duty without violating due process of law, and New York could regulate the sale of milk and discriminate between producing and nonproducing vendors.[59]

During the term the Court considered the case of *Security Mutual Life Insurance Company* v. *Prewitt* twice, the first time upholding the right of Kentucky to cancel a permit to do business in the state at the end of its one-year term. The company asked for a rehearing on an issue that was unnecessary to consider in the Court's first opinion—whether a state could revoke a license to do business in the state simply because the insurance company removed a case to the federal court. In the first case the Justices were not aware that the one-year permit had been renewed and subsequently revoked because of such removal. Reviewing precedent, Peckham concluded that the state had a right to put the company on a parity with domestic insurance companies. The company argued that, while a state may prescribe conditions for a company to do domestic business in the state, once so authorized its access to the federal courts could not be barred. Peckham saw no distinction. With Harlan in tow, Day dissented, contending that the right of access to the federal courts cannot be abridged by the state. If all the states followed Kentucky's example, he continued, the right of access to the federal courts would be abrogated. Arguing that such a provision is unconstitutional, he said "no state enactment can lawfully abridge this right or destroy it, directly or indirectly, by affixing heavy penalties to its assertion by those lawfully entitled to its enjoyment."[60]

What the decision shows is the majority's continued willingness to uphold the state police power in its attempt to control corporations. Certainly the dissent is more in harmony with the original purpose of conferring diversity jurisdiction upon the federal courts. But for the moment the idea that the states within their borders had complete control over foreign corporations was too ingrained to be dislodged by the convincing argument of the dissenters.

The Court also approved local actions forcing railroads to undertake considerable expense. A drainage commission in Illinois decided to deepen and widen a creek over which a railroad corporation maintained a bridge. The majority approved the Illinois court's order that required the company to pay for the removal of the present bridge and the full construction costs of a new one. In a broad-ranging defense of the state police power, Harlan drew a distinction "between an incidental injury to rights of private property resulting from the exercise of governmental power, lawfully and reasonably exerted for the public good, and the *taking*, within the meaning of the Constitution of private property for public use." The Justice dismissed any notion that public convenience or prosperity was not a sufficient base for the exercise of such power. Responding to the dissent, Harlan said the claimed exercise of the police power must depend on the individual case and that its exercise must be tested in terms of reasonableness and the sufficiency of its alleged public purpose. Here he found no such taking of private property, for when "the injury complained of is only incidental to the legitimate exercise of governmental powers for the public good, then there is no taking of property for the public use, and a right to compensation, on account of such injury, does not attach under the Constitution."[61]

Such a broad reading of the scope of police power drew the ire of Brewer, who responded in dissent:

It seems to me the police power has become the refuge of every grievous wrong upon private property. Whenever any unjust burden is cast upon the owner of private property which cannot be supported under the power of eminent domain or that of taxation, it is referred to the police power. But no exercise of the police power can disregard the constitutional guarantees in respect to the taking of private property, due process and equal protection, nor should it override the demands of natural justice. The question in the case is not how far the State may go in compelling a railroad company to expend money in increasing its facilities for transportation, but how far it can go in charging upon the company the cost of improving farms along the line of its road.[62]

Although the Justices continued to give a wide berth to local liquor regulation, South Carolina posed special problems. Having monopolized the sale of liquor, the state claimed that because of its sovereign immunity it could not be subjected to the federal tax on the product. Brewer, for the majority, rejected the argument, saying the framers of the Constitution, "in granting full power over license taxes to the National Government, meant that that power should be complete, and never thought that the States by extending their functions could practically destroy it." Starting from this general proposition, he characterized the tax as "not upon the property of the State, but upon the means by which that property is acquired, and before it is acquired."[63] If this smacks of sophistry it was the common coin of the Court in coping both with sovereign immunity and the bar of the Eleventh Amendment.

White dissented, carrying along both Peckham and McKenna. Admitting that the ruling of the Court could be viewed as just, he denied that it comported with the Constitution. By "the ruling and the reasoning sustaining it," the Justice continued, "the ancient landmarks are obliterated and the distinct powers belong to both the National and state Governments are reciprocally placed, the one at the mercy of the other, so as to give to each the potency of destroying the other." Downplaying the significance of this broadening of state functions, White argued the merits of the federal system with the trappings of an outmoded sovereignty concept. Attacking the majority for reasoning from necessity and expediency, he rejected its conception of a malleable Constitution:

> It is not, of course, by me denied that however varying may be the conditions to which the Constitution is applied, that instrument means to-day what it did at the time of its adoption; but I cannot give my assent to the doctrine that a limitation, which it has been decided over and over again arises from the very nature of the Constitution, is not to be enforced in a given condition to which the Constitution applies, because it does not appear that the framers could have contemplated that such conditions might be evolved in the course of the development of our constitutional institutions. To me it seems that no proposition could be more absolutely destructive of constitutional government.[64]

White, the reconstructed Confederate and a man of increasing influence on the Court, seemed to have become the preeminent federalist. Earlier in his career Fuller was sensitive to the authority of the states in the federal union, but White received no support from the Chief.

The 1905 session produced a number of self-incrimination cases dealing with grand jury inquiries into violations of federal antitrust law. Congress in 1903 had passed a general immunity act to insulate executives from prosecution based on their testimony and corporate records. Despite this grant of immunity, a number of witnesses were cited for contempt after refusing to testify and produce documents. Earlier, in considering investigations of the ICC, the Court considered a similar immunity act and upheld it by a divided vote. Now in *Hale* v. *Henkel*, the major case, the matter arose in connection with a grand jury's investigation into violations of the antitrust act by the American Tobacco Company. After disposing of challenges to the grand jury's procedure, Brown, for the Court, reached the Fifth and Fourth Amendment claims. The first major allegation was that the immunity act did not prevent states from prosecuting individuals for a violation of state law disclosed by the compelled testimony. Brown said that because such a danger was "so unsubstantial and remote" it did not justify the witness's refusal to testify.[65] The Justice further responded that the Fifth Amendment protected individuals and was purely a personal privilege, not a corporate one.

Next Brown considered whether the request for documents could be rejected on the basis of the Fourth Amendment's prohibition against unreasonable searches and seizures. Recognizing the practical dimensions of such prosecutions, he said that if an employee as a witness "could refuse to produce the books and documents of such corporation, upon the ground that they would incriminate the corporation itself, it would result in the failure of a large number of cases where the illegal combination was determinable only upon the examination of such papers." But he then added that the Fourth Amendment's prohibition could be invoked by a corporation if the request for the production of documents was so unreasonable as to paralyze the operation of the business. Such a "general subpoena of this description is equally indefensible as a search warrant would be if couched in similar terms." He concluded that the subpoena involved here was "far too sweeping in its terms to be regarded as reasonable." This determination did not help the witness, for his refusal to offer oral testimony, Brown determined, supported the contempt order. Then, worried about the possible implications of finding Fourth Amendment protection for corporations, Brown added the caveat: ". . . in view of the power of Congress over interstate commerce . . . we do not wish to be understood as holding that an examination of the books of a corporation, if duly authorized by act of Congress, would constitute an unreasonable search and seizure within the Fourth Amendment."[66]

Brown spoke for a bare majority of the Court, as Harlan and McKenna concurred in special opinions. Harlan disagreed on the right of a corporation to invoke the personal rights found in the Fourth Amendment. He wondered how six of his colleagues could agree that the Fifth Amendment was not applicable to corporations, yet reach a different result on the applicability of the Fourth. Brewer and Fuller dissented. The Kansan argued that corporations were fully protected by both amendments. He added that since the majority found the subpoena too sweeping and since this issue was the initiator of the problem, the Court should issue the writ of habeas corpus.

During the term the Justices continued to grapple with insular matters. In *Trono v. United States* the Justices again had to contend with the peculiar provisions of Philippine criminal procedure. Trono and two others had been tried for murder and convicted of the lesser charge of assault, but when they appealed the assault conviction the Philippine supreme court found them guilty of murder. Counsel argued that the defendants had been acquitted of murder and a finding of guilty on appeal violated the double jeopardy protection. Writing the plurality opinion, Peckham said the Philippine procedure did not really differ from the widely accepted practice of allowing the trial court on a retrial to find the accused guilty of the higher offense charged. He acknowledged that the states differed on the question, but he said the better view was that on retrial the court was not restricted to the lesser offense. Since here the defendants initiated the appeal, the majority saw this as a waiver that exposed them to jeopardy for the murder offense. Finally, Peckham upheld the action as "a result of the ordinary procedure on the courts of that country."[67] Holmes concurred in the result, but Harlan, White, McKenna, and Fuller dissented.

Relying upon his earlier opinions in the area, Harlan condemned the proceedings for their failure to respect clear constitutional guarantees. "It may be," he concluded, "that the application of these principles to the Philippine Islands and to the people who inhabit them may, particularly in criminal prosecutions, prove sometimes to be inconvenient. But no authority exists anywhere to set aside plain provisions of the supreme law of the land, and substitute the law of convenience for the written fundamental law." White dissented on the basis that the Court had earlier held that a reversal of a verdict of acquittal was double jeopardy, a conclusion he would hold binding here.[68] McKenna agreed, and Fuller registered a dissent without opinion.

Consistently the Court refused to interfere with the enforcement of criminal law, even when a military officer, charged with stopping thefts from a government arsenal, shot and killed a fleeing suspect and was prosecuted for murder in the state court. Various due process claims were rejected from defendants convicted of murder in Vermont, Kentucky, and Illinois. In the latter case the defendant was deaf and unable to hear the evidence; Illinois' failure to take this into account by providing the accused with an opportunity to review the testimony, the Court said, did not violate the defendant's constitutional rights. In a federal prosecution for murder on the high seas the Court saw no error in affording the prosecution considerable latitude in its cross-examination of the defendant, even when it raised other charges of misconduct unconnected with the case. Prejudicial comments by the district attorney, the majority said, were corrected when the prosecutor apologized. Only White dissented in the latter case.[69]

The criminal trial of Senator Joseph R. Burton of Kansas, however, caused the Justices some difficulty. In the lower federal court the Senator was found guilty of a misdemeanor for accepting a fee from a client for rendering services before the Post Office Department. The department was considering the issuance of a fraud order against Burton's client. A first conviction came before the Supreme Court in the preceding term, but the majority found error in the trial. Harlan, in dissenting there, argued that the majority had elevated form over substance. A new trial in Missouri produced another guilty verdict, and John F. Dillon, among other prominent counsel, neglected no plausible issue in urging the Court to reverse. Upholding the federal conflict of interest statute, the majority said its enforcement against a Senator does not infringe the authority of the Senate nor the legitimate work of its members. Harlan, for the majority, after laboriously sifting the claims of counsel, upheld the conviction.[70]

The Court's strongest law and order supporter, David Brewer, with White and Peckham, dissented. Brewer referred to the earlier Court inspection of the case and cited Peckham's opinion, which announced that he, Fuller, Brewer, and White were "of the opinion that the statute does not cover the case as alleged in the indictment." (Obviously the Chief had changed his mind since the first case.) Central to Brewer's dissent was the statutory provision requiring the United States to be "directly or indirectly interested."[71] In Burton's attempt to influence the Post Office Department, the dissenters saw no criminal conduct because of the absence of any pecuniary conflict of interest. General talk of justice and of the need to keep the departments of the government free of possible corruption, the Justice said, was both irrelevant and improper. He noted that Senators can use their influence freely and actually do; they are restrained, he continued, only when they and the government have conflicting financial interests. Concluding, Brewer accused the majority of misreading congressional intent and engaging in judicial legislation.

Hodges v. *United States*, the final case decided during the term, revealed a new vigor in the Justice Department in enforcing legislation protecting blacks. Reuben Hodges and others were convicted of violating the civil rights of eight blacks. Harassment had forced the black workers to leave their employment in a lumber mill, and the lower federal court sentenced all three defendants to jail terms of one year and one day, the maximum provided by the statute. Attesting to the administration's interest in the case was the appearance of Attorney General Moody.

Saying that precedent with its demand for the presence of positive and direct state involvement disposed of the Fourteenth Amendment claim, Brewer, writing for the Court, then turned to the Thirteenth Amendment argument. The Reconstruction amendments, he stated, did not undermine the basic proposition that the federal government is one of delegated powers, a truism from which Brewer then deduced that the Thirteenth Amendment's prohibition against slavery and involuntary servitude "is not an attempt to commit that race to the care of the Nation." In response to the government's contention that interference with the rights of these men was a vestige of slavery and an attempt to reduce them to that condition, Brewer responded that every time an individual wrongs another the same conclusion could be drawn. Attorney General Moody had attempted to compensate for this weakness in his argument by contending that, when such a wrong was inflicted solely because of race, the situation could be clearly distinguished. Unmoved, Brewer invoked the general rule that such private wrongs are to be redressed by the state. Ironically he cited the treatment of the Chinese and the requirement that they carry certificates of residence, saying that, despite division, no Justice ever saw this as a condition of slavery. The decision not to constitute blacks wards of the nation, Brewer maintained, was the result of "believing that thereby in the long run their best interests would be sub-served, they taking their chances with other citizens in the States where they should make their homes."[72] The result was the invalidation of another por-tion of the protective legislation of 1870.

Harlan could be expected to dissent from this perfunctory refusal to con-sider the realities of life in the deep South, and this time he garnered the vote of the man from Ohio, William R. Day. The Thirteenth Amendment, Harlan began, "destroyed slavery and all its incidents and badges, and established freedom." It conferred on all "the right, without discrimination against them on account of their race, to enjoy all the privileges that inhere in freedom." Section two of that amendment, continued the Justice, gave Congress suffi-cient power to pass the type of legislation that is now before the Court. Then addressing himself to the Fourteenth Amendment, Harlan said the liberty there protected from infringement by the state "is neither more nor less than the freedom established by the Thirteenth Amendment." Citing *Allgeyer* with its broad language protecting the individual's right to contract, he asked how the majority can reconcile that result with this one. He con-tinued:

These general principles, it is to be regretted, are now modified, so as to deny to millions of citizen-laborers of African descent, deriving their freedom from the Na-tion, the rights to appeal for National protection against lawless combinations of individuals who seek, by force, and solely because of the race of such laborers, to deprive them of the freedom established by the Constitution of the United States, so far as that freedom involves the right of such citizens, without discrimination against them because of their race, to earn a living in all lawful ways, and to dispose of their labor by contract.

The majority's interpretation, the Kentucky Justice concluded, is "hostile to the freedom established by the supreme law of the land" and tends to neu-tralize the purpose of the Reconstruction amendments.[73]

With the resolution of the *Hodges* case the term came to an end on May 28, 1906, as did Justice Henry B. Brown's fifteen- and one-half-year tenure on the Court. Added to his years on the lower federal bench, his judicial service extended over thirty-one years. Like Shiras, Brown had determined that he would retire at seventy. If his resolution wavered, as was the case with so many who came to the Supreme Court, his failing eyesight and what he called the "inertia" of age overcame any equivocation. On the day following his seventieth birthday he informed both the Chief Justice and the President of his intention to resign at the conclusion of the present term.[74] On the term's last day the customary formal letters were exchanged between the Justice and the remaining members of the Court, and Brown's service was terminated.

Coming to the Court near the beginning of our story as one of President Benjamin Harrison's four appointments, Henry B. Brown's career on the

High Bench spanned a significant period. Unfortunately, the Justice is most often summoned to the modern mind as the author of the Court's opinion in *Plessy* v. *Ferguson*, where in tune with the majority sentiment of the Court and of the nation he placed the imprimatur of constitutionality upon the practice of racial segregation. But to Brown's special credit, before his death in September 1913, he conceded that the Court may have been wrong in *Plessy* and subsequent cases. This opportunity to reflect upon one's work on the High Bench is so often denied Justices. Brown's case was even more unusual because he did not envelop his career in a rosy haze but instead repeatedly subjected it to critical evaluation. He had dissented in *Pollock*, but he was with majority in *Lochner* and was the government's most forceful defender in insular matters. Balance requires some mention of his uncommon understanding of the Indian plight in this country and of his willingness to recognize and promote conservation. His exposure as a Justice to cases where meritorious negligence actions were defeated by the defense of contributory negligence led him in his years of retirement to work to educate both the legal community and the public to the desirability of supplanting the common law by statutes that would enable a jury to apply a standard of comparative negligence.[75]

Brown had strong views, but they defy consistent categorization. At times he sided with Brewer and Peckham, as in *Lochner*, but generally he was a strong supporter of state police power. Although he resisted the broader appeal of due process, he also had some sensitivity to claims asserting the abridgment of individual rights that often was absorbed with an attachment to due process. Quiet and unassuming, Henry B. Brown was one of the many who had served without fanfare and much public notice.

NOTES

1. Roosevelt to Charles S. Mellen, March 12, 1904, in Elting E. Morison, ed., *The Letters of Theodore Roosevelt*, 8 vols. (Cambridge: Harvard University Press, 1951-54), 4:750.

2. Atkin v. Kansas, 191 U.S. 207, 222, 223, 224 (1903).

3. Great Southern Fire Proof Hotel Co. v. Jones, 193 U.S. 532, 549, 550 (1904).

4. For comment that the state courts, not the Supreme Court, stood for a "belated individualism" and "have been over-conservative and . . . largely responsible for the feeling that has been created against the judiciary as the representative of capitalistic and conservative power," see Richard T. Ely, *Property and Contract in Their Relations to the Distribution of Wealth*, 2 vols. (New York: Macmillan Co., 1922), 2:694, and Frederick R. Coudert, *Certainty and Justice: Studies of the Conflict Between Precedent and Progress in the Development of the Law* (New York: D. Appleton & Co., 1914), p. 57.

5. Crossman v. Lurman, 192 U.S. 189 (1904), and Arbuckle v. Blackburn, 191 U.S. 405 (1903); Cronin v. Adams, 192 U.S. 108 (1904); Ohio *ex rel.* Lloyd v. Dollison, 194 U.S. 445 (1904); Rippey v. Texas, 193 U.S. 504 (1904); Fischer v. St. Louis, 194 U.S. 361 (1904); Cable v. United States Life Insurance Co., 191 U.S. 288 (1903); and Missouri, Kansas & Texas Ry. v. May, 194 U.S. 267, 270 (1904).

6. Julian v. Central Trust Co., 193 U.S. 93 (1904); and Fargo v. Hart, 193 U.S. 490 (1904).

7. For a thorough discussion of the inception of this case, its progress through the courts, and its aftermath, see Robert F. Durden, *Reconstruction Bonds & Twentieth-Century Politics: South Dakota v. North Carolina* (Durham, N.C.: Duke University Press, 1962).

8. South Dakota v. North Carolina, 192 U.S. 286 (1904).

9. Citizens' Bank v. Parker, 192 U.S. 73, 93 (1904); and Deposit Bank v. Frankfort, 191 U.S. 499 (1903).

10. Pope v. Williams, 193 U.S. 621 (1904), *overruled by* Dunn v. Blumstein, 495 U.S. 330 (1972); Jones v. Montague, 194 U.S. 147 (1904); and West v. Louisiana, 194 U.S. 258 (1904).

11. Rogers v. Alabama, 192 U.S. 226 (1904).

12. United States v. Lynah, 188 U.S. 445 (1903); Bedford v. United States, 192 U.S. 217 (1904); and Sharp v. United States, 191 U.S. 341 (1903).

13. Buttfield v. Stranahan, 192 U.S. 470, 496 (1904).

14. George E. Mowry, *The Era of Theodore Roosevelt and the Birth of Modern America 1900-1912*, New American Nation Series (New York: Harper & Row, Torchbooks, 1962), pp. 130-33. See also William H. Harbaugh, *The Life and Times of Theodore Roosevelt*, rev. ed. (New York: Crowell-Collier Publishing Co., Collier Books, 1963), pp. 157-60, and R.W. Apple, Jr., "The Case of the Monopolistic Railroadmen," in *Quarrels That Have Shaped the Constitution*, ed. John A. Garraty (New York: Harper & Row, 1964), pp. 159-75.

15. Northern Securities Co. v. United States, 193 U.S. 197, 325 (1904). For a discussion of Knox's strategy in the case, see William Letwin, *Law and Economic Policy in America: The Evolution of the Sherman Antitrust Act* (New York: Random House, 1965), pp. 207-17.

16. Northern Securities Co. v. United States, 193 U.S. 197, 350 (1904).

17. Id. at 364.

18. Id. at 370, 392.

19. Id. at 400-1, 403.

20. Id. at 404, 411.

21. Holmes to Frederick Pollock, April 3, 1910, in *Holmes-Pollock Letters*, ed. Mark D. Howe, 2d ed., 2 vols., (Cambridge: Harvard University Press, Belknap Press, 1961), 1:163.

22. Harbaugh, *Theodore Roosevelt*, p. 161; Roosevelt to Henry Cabot Lodge, September 4, 1906, in Morison, *Letters of Roosevelt* 5:396; and Holmes to Frederick Pollock, February 9, 1921, in Howe, *Holmes-Pollock Letters*, 2:63-64.

23. David J. Brewer, *The Spanish War: A Prophecy or an Exception?* Address before the Liberal Club, Buffalo, New York, February 16, 1899 (New York: Anti-Imperialist League, n. d.); and Brewer, "Two Periods in the History of the Supreme Court," *Report of the Eighteenth Annual Meeting of the Virginia Bar Association* (1906):144-45.

24. Houghton v. Payne, 194 U.S. 88 (1904); Gonzales v. Williams, 192 U.S. 1 (1904); Tom Hong v. United States, 193 U.S. 517 (1904); for instance, see Ah How v. United States, 193 U.S. 65 (1904); and United States v. Sing Tuck, 194 U.S. 161 (1904).

25. United States v. Sing Tuck, 194 U.S. 161, 181-82 (1904).

26. United States v. Ju Toy, 198 U.S. 253, 279-80 (1905).

27. Act of August 2, 1886, ch. 840, 24 Stat. 209, 210, *as amended* Act of May 9, 1902, ch. 784, 32 Stat. 193, 194.

28. *In re* Kollock, 165 U.S. 526, 536 (1897); and McCray v. United States, 195 U.S. 27, 51, 54, 59 (1904).

29. McCray v. United States, 195 U.S. 27, 63 (1904).

30. Crowley v. United States, 194 U.S. 461, 474 (1904).

31. Kepner v. United States, 195 U.S. 100 (1904).

32. Id. at 134, 137.

33. Id. at 137.

34. Dorr v. United States, 195 U.S. 138, 148 (1904).

35. Arthur S. Link, *American Epoch: A History of the United States Since the 1890s*, 2d ed. rev. (New York: Alfred A. Knopf, 1963), pp. 98-99.

36. Clyatt v. United States, 197 U.S. 207, 223 (1905).

37. Fullerton v. Texas, 196 U.S. 192 (1905); Kehrer v. Stewart, 197 U.S. 60 (1905); and Pabst Brewing Co. v. Crenshaw, 198 U.S. 17 (1905).

38. Jacobsen v. Massachusetts, 197 U.S. 11 (1905); National Cotton Oil Co. v. Texas, 197 U.S. 115 (1905); Smiley v. Kansas, 196 U.S. 447 (1905); Aikens v. Wisconsin, 195 U.S. 194 (1904); and Clark v. Nash, 198 U.S. 361, 369 (1905).

39. Charles H. Butler, *A Century at the Bar of the Supreme Court of the United States* (New York: G.P. Putnam's Sons, 1942), pp. 170-71.

40. Briefs, Lochner v. New York, 198 U.S. 45 (1905). For a study of the drive behind the legislation and its aftermath and effects, see Sidney G. Tarrow, "Lochner Versus New York: A Political Analysis," *Labor History* 5 (Fall 1964):277-312.

41. This was the unheeded lament of Charles Warren in "The Progressiveness of the United States Supreme Court," *Columbia Law Review* 13 (April 1913):294-96.

42. Lochner v. New York, 198 U.S. 45, 56, 57, 58, 60, 64 (1905).

43. Id. at 69, 73.

44. Id. at 75, 76.

45. See Holmes to Harold J. Laski, January 8, 1917, in Mark D. Howe, ed., *Holmes-Laski Letters*, abridged by Alger Hiss (New York: Atheneum, 1963), 1:36.

46. See, as examples, "Fussy Legislation," *New York Times*, April 19, 1905; Ernst Freund, "Limitation of Hours of Labor and the Federal Supreme Court," *Green Bag* 17 (July 1905):414-16; and Roscoe Pound, "Liberty of Contract," *Yale Law Journal* 18 (May 1909):454-87. For a summary of the reaction and an anlysis of the decision's reception by state courts, see Barbara C. Steidle, "Conservative Progressives: A Study of the Attitudes of Bar and Bench, 1905-1912" (Ph.D. dissertation, Rutgers University, 1969), pp. 94-111.

47. United States v. United Verde Copper Co., 196 U.S. 207, 216 (1905).

48. Swift & Co. v. United States, 196 U.S. 375, 396, 397, 398-99 (1905).

49. United States v. Winans, 198 U.S. 371, 384 (1905).

50. The case is Dorr v. United States, 195 U.S. 138 (1904); and Butler, *A Century at the Bar*, pp. 92-94.

51. Rasmussen v. United States, 197 U.S. 516, 522 (1905).

52. Id. at 536, 531.

53. Brief for United States, pp. 4, 20, Lincoln v. United States, 197 U.S. 419 (1905).

54. Lincoln v. United States, 197 U.S. 419, 428, 429 (1905).

55. Lincoln v. United States, 202 U.S. 484, 496, 497-98, 498-99 (1906).

56. Id. at 500.

57. Henry F. Pringle, *The Life and Times of William Howard Taft*, 2 vols. (New York: Farrar & Rinehart, 1939), 1:264-65.

58. Union Refrigerator Transit Co. v. Kentucky, 199 U.S. 194 (1905); and New York *ex rel.* Lieberman v. Van De Carr, 199 U.S. 552, 564 (1905).

59. Attorney General *ex rel.* Kies v. Lowrey, 199 U.S. 233 (1905); California Reduction Co. v. Sanitary Reduction Works, 199 U.S. 306 (1905); Carroll v. Greenwich Insurance Co., 199 U.S. 401 (1905); Manigault v. Springs, 199 U.S. 473 (1905); San Antonio Traction Co. v. Altgelt, 200 U.S. 304 (1906); Campbell v. California, 200 U.S. 87 (1906); Montana

Catholic Missions v. Missoula County, 200 U.S. 118 (1906); Strickley v. Highland Boy Gold Mining Co., 200 U.S. 527 (1906); Rawlins v. Georgia, 201 U.S. 638 (1906); and St. John v. New York, 201 U.S. 633 (1906).

60. Security Mutual Life Insurance Co. v. Prewitt, 200 U.S. 446, 202 U.S. 246, 269 (1906). Although the dissenting opinion of Day and Harlan would be paid increasing respect in the near future, the decision here was not formally overruled until 1922 in *Terral* v. *Burke Construction Co.* (257 U.S. 529).

61. Chicago, Burlington & Quincy Ry. v. Illinois *ex rel.* Drainage Commissioners, 200 U.S. 561, 583, 593-94 (1906).

62. Id. at 600.

63. Foppiano v. Speed, 199 U.S. 501 (1905); Cox v. Texas, 202 U.S. 446 (1906); and South Carolina v. United States, 199 U.S. 437, 457, 459 (1905).

64. South Carolina v. United States, 199 U.S. 437, 464, 472 (1905).

65. Act of February 25, 1903, ch. 755, 32 Stat. 854, 904; Brown v. Walker, 161 U.S. 591 (1896); and Hale v. Henkel, 201 U.S. 43, 69 (1906). In *Brown* v. *Walker* the Court had indicated that a federal immunity statute protected individuals against prosecution under state law. That conclusion was questionable then, and now in *Nelson* v. *United States* (201 U.S. 92, 116 [1906]), a companion case to *Hale* v. *Henkel* reaching a similar result on the validity of the new federal immunity act, the unanimous Court said that the act "does not protect, nor has Congress the power to protect" the individual from prosecution under state law.

66. Hale v. Henkel, 201 U.S. 43, 74, 77, 76, 77 (1906).

67. Trono v. United States, 199 U.S. 521, 534 (1905).

68. Id. at 537. White relied on Kepner v. United States, 195 U.S. 100 (1904).

69. United States *ex rel.* Drury v. Lewis, 200 U.S. 1 (1906); Rogers v. Peck, 199 U.S. 425 (1905); Howard v. Kentucky, 200 U.S. 164 (1906); Felts v. Murphy, 201 U.S. 123 (1906); and Sawyer v. United States, 202 U.S. 150 (1906).

70. Burton v. United States, 196 U.S. 283 (1905), 202 U.S. 344 (1906).

71. Burton v. United States, 196 U.S. 283, 296 (1905); and Act of June 11, 1864, ch. 119, 13 Stat. 123.

72. Hodges v. United States, 203 U.S. 1, 16, 20 (1906).

73. Id. at 27, 35, 37. In 1968 in *Jones* v. *Mayer Co.* (392 U.S. 409), the Court overruled the *Hodges* case and expressed its agreement with the dissent of Harlan and Day.

74. Letter responding to Court's formal note of regret dated May 28, 1906, in 202 U.S. vi-vii. Brown scoffed that the notion that retirement from the busy work of the Court brought atrophy and early death, saying "that his health has never been better" and that he never enjoyed life more. He noted that Brewer had also talked of retiring at seventy, but when the moment came the Kansan could not cut himself loose from his judicial duties. Finally, Brown cited the Justices' wives, who enjoyed their social position in Washington, as an additional obstacle to retirement (Brown to Charles A. Kent, February 20, 1908, in Kent, *Memoir of Henry Billings Brown* [New York: Duffield & Co., 1915], pp. 95-96).

75. For Brown's later views on segregation and comparative negligence, see his "Dissenting Opinions of Mr. Justice Harlan," *American Law Review* 46 (May-June 1912):336-38, and "The Status of the Automobile," *Yale Law Journal* 17 (February 1908):229-30.

chapter 7

JUDICIAL RESISTANCE: THE FATEFUL 1907 TERM, 1906-9

Brown's resignation afforded Theodore Roosevelt the opportunity to make his third appointment to the Court. Ironically, the President's desire to remake the High Bench was frustrated by the fact that Brown, like Gray and Shiras before him, had been a consistent supporter of Roosevelt's policies in both insular and antitrust matters. In informing the President of his resignation on March 3, 1906, Brown suggested William Howard Taft as his replacement, or, as a second choice, Philander C. Knox, Roosevelt's former Attorney General and now Senator from Pennsylvania. After consulting Secretary of State Elihu Root, Secretary of War Taft, and Attorney General Moody, the President did offer the seat to Knox. Knox refused, as he had when Roosevelt had tried to appoint him after Taft refused the seat in 1902.[1]

Once again, then, the President offered the seat to Taft. The Secretary of War did not immediately refuse the offer, but he did not accept it either. Taft expressed his anxiety in a diary entry of March 10, saying he hoped he could escape the nomination. Since Roosevelt had declared he would not run again, Taft was the leading candidate for the Republican presidential nomination in 1908. His wife, an ambitious and adamant woman, had her eyes focused on the White House. With it now within reach, she insisted that her husband not throw away the opportunity by ascending the High Bench. Also, Roosevelt had none of the personal need to place Taft on the Court that had induced the pressure he had exerted in 1902. After a discussion with Helen Taft, Roosevelt wrote to the reluctant candidate and outlined the advantages and disadvantages of the choices open to him. The President seemed to agree with Mrs. Taft that the presidency offered her husband the greater challenge.[2]

Not until mid-August did Taft definitely refuse the appointment. Roosevelt had promised that should the chief justiceship become vacant during his tenure Taft would be promoted to the top spot, but both he and Taft realized that this possibility was slim. Stories suggesting that the Chief was considering retirement continued, but Fuller, buttressed by letters from his friends and colleagues, stood fast. If others saw a developing twentieth-century tradition, based upon Shiras, Gray, and Brown, of Justices retiring rather than dying in office, Melville Fuller did not. He and Harlan, whose resignation Roosevelt also sought, were said to have made a pact not to resign "until they have to take us out feet foremost." The newspaper story continued, saying that Fuller's response to Roosevelt's campaign to dislodge the incumbent from the center seat was the following: "My resignation is in the hands of Providence, and I am ready to deliver it anytime that Providence demands it."[3]

With Taft unavailable, Roosevelt moved cautiously in making his third appointment to the Court. Despite Brown's orthodoxy on matters that seemed to mean the most to the President, the retiring Justice had voted with the majority in *Lochner*, and the new appointee could realign the bench on such matters. Both Secretary of War Taft and Justice William Day urged the President to nominate Horace H. Lurton, their former colleague on the Sixth Circuit Court of Appeals. Both men assured Roosevelt of the soundness of this Cleveland Democrat's views, and the President was not adverse to the credit that would accrue from making such a nonpartisan appointment. But Attorney General Moody and Senator Henry Cabot Lodge strongly opposed the choice.[4]

Lodge's personal choice was Moody, a fellow Massachusetts citizen, but Roosevelt had already appointed Holmes from that state and was concerned about the geographical imbalance that would result from Moody's appointment. Lurton's candidacy, Lodge indicated, would be met with partisan opposition, for, after all, Lurton was a former Confederate. Roosevelt, however, did not rule out Lurton until Moody reported that the secretary of the Interstate Commerce Commission had found that the proposed appointee had decided against the government in every case brought before him under the Interstate Commerce Act. With Lurton's candidacy scuttled, Roosevelt focused his attention on Moody.[5]

Moody had earlier informed Roosevelt of his desire to resign the attorney generalship and return to private life. The Rough Rider's relationship with the Attorney General went back to 1895, when Moody was elected to the House of Representatives from Massachusetts. The President chose Congressman Moody to become Secretary of the Navy in May 1902, making him the youngest cabinet member. Moody's work continued to impress the President at a time when the Navy Department was a prime focus for an aggressive foreign policy. When Attorney General Knox resigned to take a seat in the Senate in 1904, Roosevelt turned to Moody, who quickly brought new vigor to the Justice Department. Personally he argued more cases before the Supreme Court than any of his predecessors, and the President's desire to prosecute wrongdoers found an ideal implementer in Moody. The Attorney General's zealous activity led some of the more conservative members of the party to label him a radical, but even a less than orthodox Republican was certainly to be preferred to a Confederate Democrat.[6]

In the end what tipped the scales in favor of Moody, an appointee with no prior judicial experience, was Roosevelt's confidence in the political views of the candidate. The President explained to Lodge that he did not want to place on the Court "any man who from frivolity, or disinclination to think, or ignorance, or indifference to popular moods, goes wrong on great questions." Roosevelt had worked closely with his Attorney General and was convinced that he would have no cause to regret this appointment. Moody's nomination went to the Senate in December, and after some quibbling it was easily confirmed.[7]

On December 17, 1907, Moody took his seat to the far left of the Chief. Nearing age fifty-four, he became the Court's youngest member, four years younger than Day. Standing five feet, ten inches tall, Moody was often mistaken for President Roosevelt, having the same approximate build and a similar mustache. But the new Justice did not wear glasses, and his mustache was thicker and drooped more than Roosevelt's. Moody's full head of hair was parted in the middle, and his arched eyebrows framed intense eyes. His nose and ears were large, though well-proportioned. A broad-shouldered frame gave some hint of his enjoyment of the outdoor life.

With the fall of 1906 came the new term of Court. Brown was gone, and Moody, even after he joined his colleagues, possessed certain disabilities that left the bench at less than full strength. Attorneys general would increasingly be viewed as candidates for the Court, but their appointments posed special problems. Tradition dictated that a Justice not participate in those cases he had handled in one form or another in his earlier employment. Because of the recent activity of the Justice Department, this left a Court of eight to deal with a number of important cases. In fact on the day that Moody took his seat, the Court decided against the United States in a case that the new arrival had presented.[8]

In addition to the appellate review power the Court possesses, the Constitution confers upon the High Bench original jurisdiction when one of the parties to a suit is a state. A number of such cases coalesced in the session. Virginia's suit to compel West Virginia to accept a portion of the pre-Civil War debt, which was to appear on the Court's docket regularly in the next decade, was first instituted in the term. In a unique case Georgia was successful before the Court in gaining an injunction against continued air pollution by a Tennessee copper company, which, the state claimed, had discharged large quantities of sulphur dioxide that were harmful to the air and a threat to forests and vegetation. Although the state could claim ownership of little of the land affected, Holmes, for the Court, held that the state in its sovereign capacity did possess sufficient standing to sue and then granted the injunction.[9]

Kansas was easily rebuffed by the High Court when the state sought to confirm title to land by suing the United States, but the state's second suit, *Kansas* v. *Colorado*, involved the Court in a major inquiry into the nature of the American governmental system.[10] Kansas sought to enjoin Colorado from diverting water from the Arkansas River, used by the latter state for reclamation purposes. The United States intervened in the suit, claiming this controversy between the states was subject to the supervisory authority of the federal government. Counsel for Kansas argued that under the common law its riparian rights should be protected, while opposing counsel argued that the reclamation of arid land was a beneficial use that the common law would permit. In a brief filed by a private Colorado corporation on behalf of the state, the argument was carried further along the lines that the state was sovereign in its use of its waters and no power existed within the federal system to reach the matter. Solicitor General Hoyt under instructions from then Attorney General Moody argued the case for the government. He contended that the federal commerce power embraced conflicting irrigation rights among states in regard to streams crossing state lines. Alternatively, he argued that the power sought here could legitimately be implied from the Constitution and had to be in order to establish federal authority over competing state interests.[11] Moody disqualified himself, and White and McKenna concurred in the Court's resolution without opinion.

Brewer, for the Court, coped with the rival contentions that involved the power of the Supreme Court, Congress, and the states. He first dismissed the argument that the Court has no jurisdiction in the matter. The gap the Solicitor General saw in the federal system Brewer proceeded to fill by asserting the right of the Court to adjudge such controversies. The judicial power, he concluded, embraces "all controversies of a justiciable nature arising within the territorial limits of the Nation, no matter who may be the parties thereto," while the legislative power was bounded by the limits of the delegation found within the Constitution.[12] If the Arkansas River was navigable, Brewer would have conceded national power, but he rejected the claim that Congress possesses authority to exercise a supervisory authority over the matter of reclaiming arid lands.

The argument that federal power must exist where national concerns are apparent the Kansan rejected as incompatible with the nature of the federal union. The Tenth Amendment, with its reservation of undelegated powers to the states or to the people, he said, provides a ready answer to the present contentions of the federal government. He added that this fundamental check upon federal power should be construed liberally "to give effect to its scope and meaning."[13] Although conceding that the United States does have the power to develop reclamation programs for the arid lands in the federal territories, he ruled that it has no power to regulate such matters within the states. Having disposed of the government's contentions, Brewer proceeded to resolve the dispute between Kansas and Colorado largely on the equitable basis that the harm done to the southwestern part of Kansas was small in comparison to the great advantages reaped by reclamation in Colorado.

Approving the present division of the benefits of the Arkansas River, Brewer stated that if the present balance was altered to the detriment of Kansas, the state could reinstitute the suit.

Kansas v. *Colorado* is a reflection of an activist Court willing to use its authority to decide on an *ad hoc* basis disputes that fell into a gap between state and federal authority. The Solicitor General, echoing the views of President Roosevelt, argued that such gaps in legislative authority made no sense and had to be filled by recognizing national interests, but the Court projected its power into the perceived void by broadly defining judicial authority.[14]

Of equal significance was the majority's willingness to read into the Tenth Amendment a check on the power of the federal government. That amendment was the only survivor of a series of proposals made to the first Congress under the Constitution seeking to limit the power of the newly created government beyond provisions protecting individual rights. With the elimination of the adjective *expressly* before the words *powers not delegated* by Congress before the submission of the amendment to the states, the proposal generally was regarded as an obvious declaration of the existing nature of the new government. In 1871 the Court did declare that it had substantial constitutional import in preventing the federal taxation of the salaries of state officials, but no new body of constitutional law was erected upon this foundation. In the *Northern Securities* and *Champion* cases dissenters had relied, in part, upon the Tenth Amendment, but the majority brushed aside the argument.[15] Yet here in 1907 six members of the Court were willing to subscribe to Brewer's words saying the amendment should be construed liberally to accomplish its purpose of checking the range of federal power. Whether this new reliance on the Tenth Amendment would be injected into the mainstream of constitutional law was unclear in 1907, but its appearance was unsettling.

Not only had Colorado been vindicated in its contest with Kansas, but also an unusual action of its highest court passed the scrutiny of the Supreme Court. The members of the Colorado bench took offense at certain newspaper pieces that criticized as partisan the motives and conduct of the judges. In *Patterson* v. *Colorado* a newspaper publisher claimed he was only doing his public duty in exposing the work of the court. Rejecting his offer to prove his allegations, the Colorado tribunal found him in contempt.

Saying that even if the Fourteenth Amendment carries a prohibition similar to the First, a question he left undecided, Holmes, for the Court, ruled that the First Amendment prohibits only prior restraint of speech and does not "prevent the subsequent punishment of such as may be deemed contrary to the public welfare." Holding that the truth of the statements is no defense, the Justice analogized the present criticism of the court to accusing a juror of perjury: even if true, the allegation is a contempt since it "would tend to obstruct the administration of justice, because even a correct conclusion is not to be reached or helped in that way, if our system of trials is to be maintained. The theory of our system is that the conclusions to be reached in a case will be induced only by evidence and argument in open court, and not by any outside influence, whether of private talk or public print." After the litigation is completed, Holmes continued, criticism can follow, "but the propriety and necessity of preventing interference with the course of justice by premature statement, argument, or intimidation hardly can be denied." Just as blithely as he dismissed any violation of free speech, he rejected the argument that in a contempt proceeding judges sit in judgment of their own case. "The grounds upon which contempts are punished are impersonal," said Holmes, adding, "a man cannot expect to secure immunity from punishment by the proper tribunal, by adding to illegal conduct a personal attack."[16] Few of Holmes's opinions are more illustrative of the myopia occasioned by his many years on the bench. His opinion sidesteps the main issues and is grounded in the assumption that judges and their work are sacrosanct in our secular society.

Both Brewer and Harlan dissented. The Kansan challenged the majority's decision that it had no jurisdiction, but beyond finding that Patterson's claim was substantial, Brewer expressed no opinion on the merits of the case. Harlan, however, addressed the substantive matters, as he asserted that the Fourteenth Amendment's protection of the privileges and immunities of the citizens makes the restrictions of the First Amendment applicable to the states. A state, he continued, is prohibited from "impairing or abridging the constitutional rights of such citizens to free speech and a free press."[17] He highlighted the contradiction of the Holmes opinion, which said it left the First Amendment question undecided but then interpreted that amendment as forbidding only prior restraints. Rejecting such a narrow view, Harlan asserted that no concept of public welfare can erode such guarantees. To his mind, the judgment of the majority was a violation of the due process guaranteed by the Constitution against abridgment by either the federal government or the states.

Although Harlan was eloquent in his defense of Patterson's rights, he was untroubled by the alleged violation of rights brought to the Court's attention in *Pettibone* v. *Nichols*. The famous trial attorney Clarence S. Darrow appeared before the Supreme Court and argued that his client deserved his freedom because he was kidnapped from Colorado by local authorities working in conjunction with Idaho officers and carried to the latter state to stand trial for murder. This shortcutting of the legal process, Darrow claimed, was a violation of Pettibone's rights.[18]

Pettibone, Bill Haywood, and Charles Moyer were the prime movers of the Western Federation of Miners and were suspected of complicity in the murder of Frank Steunenberg, the governor of Idaho during the turbulent labor wars of the 1890s. A confession from the assassin procured by James McParland, the manager of Pinkerton's western division, implicated the leaders of the Federation. Since Pettibone and the other men were at the union headquarters in Denver, the governors of Idaho and Colorado reached an understanding that produced warrants for the arrest of the three men. If a normal process of extradition was instituted, the trio would probably have had the opportunity to contest the action in the local courts. To preclude this resort to the judiciary, the wanted men were arrested on a Saturday evening by local officials and then turned over to Pinkertons and Idaho officials who had procured a special train for their transit to Idaho before dawn the next morning. Contesting the legality of the irregular proceedings, Pettibone petitioned for a writ of habeas corpus. It was denied by the lower federal court.[19]

Existing law held that the fact that a defendant was brought into a state by unlawful means was no bar to the exercise of jurisdiction by its courts; the difference here, however, was that this was no private act of kidnapping but a concerted effort of officials of two states involved in a clearly illegal and criminal act. For the majority, Harlan simply brushed aside the apparent distinction, saying the general rule precluded the granting of the petition here. Only McKenna, in dissent, found the whole affair both objectionable and unconstitutional. The California Justice had no argument with the general proposition that the federal courts should not interfere with the operation of the state's criminal process, but he felt that the collusion of government officials here fully justified such interference.[20]

An unwillingness to intervene in *Pettibone* did not prevent the Justices from administering another slap to the Roosevelt administration. Attorney General Moody had argued the case, and the Court reached a unanimous decision before the government advocate had taken his seat on the bench. Congress in 1903 had delegated authority to the Secretary of Agriculture to issue regulations providing for the prevention and spreading of contagious livestock diseases. Citing violation of the Secretary's order, a cattle owner sued a railroad for losses suffered when his stock came into contact with diseased cattle. The transaction concerned a shipment from Tennessee to Kentucky, and apparently this fact led the trial court to grant recovery. Day reversed the verdict on the abstract ground that the sweeping order invaded the reserved powers of the states. He concluded "that this order of the Secretary, undertaking to make a stringent regulation with highly penal consequences, is single in character, and includes commerce wholly within the State, thereby exceeding any authority which Congress intended to confer upon him by the act in question."[21] The Court avoided passing on the 1903 act itself, but it warned Congress to restrict its legislation to matters of interstate commerce. Day also hinted that the Court in the future might scrutinize more carefully allegations of an unlawful delegation of legislative power.

Day's warning was considerably muted when two months later he subscribed to a majority opinion by Harlan that contained clear support for congressional delegation of power to administrative officers. The Secretary of
War ordered alterations to a bridge that was obstructing traffic on an interstate waterway. To the argument that Congress unconstitutionally delegated
both legislative and judicial powers to the Secretary, Harlan responded that
"it is not too much to say that a denial to Congress of the right, under the
Constitution, to delegate the power to determine some fact or the state of
things upon which the enforcement of its enactment depends, would be 'to
stop the wheels of government' and bring about confusion, if not paralysis, in
the conduct of the public business."[22] Only Brewer and Peckham dissented.

Although the Court was sending Congress inconsistent messages upon the
question of its ability to delegate power, in *Ellis* v. *United States* it upheld
legislation passed in 1892 that required all employees engaged in public work
for the United States or the District of Columbia to be employed for no more
than eight hours a day. The Congresses of the 1890s have been criticized for
not using their power to aid workingmen, but actually this was only the first
of a series of prolabor measures passed in that decade that the Court would be
called upon to assess in the early twentieth century. Having upheld in 1903
the right of the state to determine the conditions under which public work
would be performed in *Atkin* v. *Kansas*, the Court, speaking through
Holmes, simply concluded that there was "no reason to deny to the United
States the power thus established for the States."[23] Just this simply, authority
was conceded to the federal government in its position as a contracting party
to insist upon conditions that could not have been imposed through legislation, Congress there being confined within the scope of its delegated powers.
From the Court's rebuff of the claim made in *Ellis* in 1907, the federal government's authority to exert influence through its position as a primary contractor in the economy was clearly established. The elimination of the constitutional objection left for the future only the full exploitation of this source of
federal government power.

All the Justices agreed in *Ellis* that the federal government had the authority
to specify the conditions under which public work was to be done, but they
did differ about the scope of the act. Holmes, for the majority, reversed six
convictions under the 1892 legislation on grounds that men engaged in dredging operations could not properly be labeled either "laborers" or "mechanics." McKenna distinguished the cases and saw half of the convictions sustained by the 1892 act, but it was Moody, joined by Harlan and Day, who
leveled a broad attack on the majority's conclusions. Arguing that all the
convictions should be sustained, he reminded his colleagues "that the object
of this statute, in which is embodied an expression of a great public policy, is
to regulate labor of the kind named."[24] He accused Holmes of frustrating a
clearly expressed congressional policy by a cramped and artificial limitation

of its reach. To the claim that the eight-hour day is difficult to apply to dredging operations, the former Attorney General answered that this was a matter to take before Congress and not the courts. In his maiden effort in dissent, Moody showed his mettle.

His suggestion that the Court's proper role in interpreting congressional legislation was to avoid nice distinctions and effectuate its underlying policy bore fruit in a Court opinion by Holmes that reinterpreted the Safety Appliance Act of 1893 to provide greater protection to an injured employee. In earlier opinions the Justices had recognized that the act eliminated the assumption of risk defense when a safety regulation had been violated, but they had been unwilling to make any inroad on the employer's defense of contributory negligence. In the present case a widow sued a railroad for wrongful death on the ground that the accident had resulted from the failure of the company to provide the automatic couplers required by the federal act. The lower court dismissed the suit on the basis of the deceased's contributory negligence. Holmes, for a five-man majority, reversed. Merging assumption of risk "into negligence as commonly understood," he contended that the statute's purpose would be undermined if the recovery could be defeated by charging the employee "with assumption of risk under another name."[25] The dissenters, Brewer, Peckham, McKenna, and Day, protested against the erosion of the distinction between assumption of risk and contributory negligence. Obviously Roosevelt's appointments had made the difference in the case, for while Fuller had long been sympathetic to modifications of the common law defenses, the reversal here required the votes of at least two of the last three men to join the Court.

The 1906 term seemed to produce a *modus vivendi* between the Court and that first stranger to the American doctrine of the separation of powers, the Interstate Commerce Commission. What was significant in the three cases the Court handled was not the particular subject matter but rather the language in unanimous opinions entrusting to the ICC considerable authority and room to operate. The opinions seemed to concede to the commission, strengthened by statutory amendments pressed by the Roosevelt administration, a primacy in the determination of the reasonableness of interstate rates. Responding to arguments that the ICC erred in giving proper weight to the evidence and that its orders exceeded its authority, the Justices said that determinations of fact would not be disturbed by the Court and that the enabling legislation sufficiently provided for the authority the Commission had exercised. Apparently, finally recognizing the legitimacy of this nonjudicial, fact-finding agency, the Court served notice that appeals from the Commission's authority would be unsuccessful "unless the record establishes that clear and unmistakable error has been committed."[26]

In the matter of overseas possessions the Court maintained its deferential attitude. For instance, the majority, through White, pronounced constitutional a 1906 congressional act ratifying the collection of illegal duties in the Philippines from the time of the President's order of July 12, 1898 to the congressional enactment establishing such duties in 1902. Earlier in *Lincoln* the Court decided that the act of 1902 had not ratified certain duties exacted by the President's order. Now that Congress specifically addressed the matter, the Justices had to face squarely the question of constitutional power. White said that Congress has the right to legalize the actions of its agent, the President, by ratifying them. The duties levied by the President were not illegal because of the absence of power, he continued, but simply because of the absence of proper and specific legislation. Congress could legalize this action, as it had in this case, after commencement of the suit. Brewer and Peckham, obviously attracted to the argument that the plaintiff had been deprived of his property without due process of law, dissented without opinion. Harlan, in a concurring opinion, disassociated himself from the majority, contending in effect that the congressional action taken in response to the *Lincoln* decision had effectively preempted the judicial process.[27]

Despite the fact that the Court decides many cases with political overtones, the self-imposed political question exception to jurisdiction, has been a useful tool for the Justices. Wisely applied, it enables the Court to preserve its integrity and authority by avoiding highly charged questions that should be resolved through the give and take of the ongoing political process. Regarding the overseas possessions, Roosevelt would not be frustrated in his creation and consolidation of an American empire. With the congressional support the President had, the Court in the long run could only defer. Among the Justices there were reluctant holdouts, especially Harlan in Bill of Rights matters, but even when decisions went against the government, room was afforded by the majority for the other branches to accomplish their purposes in ways that would meet the constitutional objection.

In earlier cases Harlan and White had perceived political questions that the Court should not decide, but no member of the High Bench could fail to see the wisdom of avoiding the contentions raised in *Wilson* v. *Shaw*. Warren B. Wilson sought nothing less than the condemnation of the President and the Congress for their actions in acquiring the Panama Canal Zone. He tried to prevent the Secretary of the Treasury, Leslie M. Shaw, from borrowing and disbursing any money for the construction of a canal. Brewer was assigned the opinion for the unanimous Court. After blandly reviewing the history of the acquisition of the Canal Zone, the Justice said: "For the courts to interfere and at the instance of a citizen, who does not disclose the amount of his interest, stay the work of construction by stopping the payment of money from the Treasury of the United States therefore, would be an exercise of judicial power which, to say the least, is novel and extraordinary." Even Brewer gagged at this suit, but the Kansan's activist view of his role led him to deal with some of the plaintiff's major contentions. Any deficiency in presidential authority, Brewer continued, was overcome by Congress's full ratification of the Chief Executive's actions. To Wilson's claim that the government had no authority to construct a canal in an area not part of the United States, Brewer responded that the federal government has broad authority to construct highways. The Court, he concluded, has "no supervising control over the political branch of the Government in its action within the limits of the Constitution."[28]

The suit, with no possibility of success, is illustrative of the way in which individuals have tended to resort to the courts in the mistaken impression that judges are the ultimate rulers, having both the will and the authority to decide all policy matters properly brought to their attention. In our society there is a tendency to recast, either sooner or later, all major policy questions in legal terms. This phenomenon feeds the illusion that disinterested courts are proper forums for deciding issues that deeply divide society.

Wilson's suit was no threat to Theodore Roosevelt, who boasted that while Congress talked he took the Canal Zone, but the President was incensed when newspaper comment suggested that some Americans had financially profited from the canal settlement. The first hint of such a scandal appeared in the *New York World* in the fall of 1908, but Delvan Smith, editor of the *Indianapolis News*, broadened the rumors into an indictment of the administration. Joseph Pulitzer, owner of the *World* and a persistent critic of Roosevelt's leadership, however, bore the brunt of the President's wrath. In a special message to Congress in mid-December 1908 Roosevelt called the accusation not only a libel of individual persons but also "a libel upon the United States Government." With obvious emotion and reference to Pulitzer, the President continued: "It is . . . a high national duty to bring to justice this vilifier of American people, this man who wantonly and wickedly and without one shadow of justification seeks to blacken the character of reputable private citizens and to convict the Government of his own country in the eyes of the civilized world of wrongdoing, of the basest and foulest kind." Apparently seeking to resurrect the crime of seditious libel, the President called upon Attorney General Charles J. Bonaparte to prosecute the wrongdoers. The *World* responded that it would neither be intimidated nor muzzled and would ever "be a fearless champion of free speech, a free press and a free people."[29]

Spurred on by an incensed President, the Justice Department brought suit on the basis that the sale of the offending newspapers in the District of Columbia and on the military reservation at West Point constituted libels in those jurisdictions. The lower federal courts responded to this attempt of a President to silence the press by rejecting the government's theories. Judge A. B. Anderson, the federal judge in Indianapolis, rejected the government's attempt to bring Delvan Smith to Washington for trial. Calling the canal affair "unusual and peculiar," he said that any other disposition of the government's claim would be "a strange result of a revolution where one of the grievances complained for was the assertion of the right to send parties abroad for trial." Roosevelt responded by calling Anderson "a jackass and a crook."[30]

The administration's attempt to punish Pulitzer met a similar fate when the lower federal court in New York determined that a general federal law covering crimes on military reservations did not encompass libel. Pulitzer was not satisfied with his victory until it had been confirmed by the United States Supreme Court, and government counsel played into the publisher's hand by appealing the adverse decision. Without difficulty a unanimous Court sustained the ruling in a bland opinion that gave no hint of the battle that had raged between an intemperate President, intent upon punishing the irresponsible press, and the men of the *World*, who characterized their paper as an institution and Roosevelt as a mere "episode."[31]

Roosevelt's use of Attorney General Bonaparte in his personal vendetta against Pulitzer was still in the future, but Bonaparte's predecessor, spared from this unrewarding service, was making himself felt in the work of the Court. Former Attorney General Moody, despite his late arrival and need to abstain in various cases, wrote fifteen opinions for the Court. Although the term had produced a few decisions of importance, a badly divided Court was unable to reach a decision in a case argued in mid-April that was a highly significant test of congressional power over commerce. How Moody would vote was not in doubt. With his look-alike, the President, Moody was committed to energy in government, and from his perch on the High Court he could be expected to give an eloquent voice to the argument that such legislation was within the authority conferred by the Constitution.

Whether Moody's initiative could persuade his less involved colleagues was the question as the Court convened in full strength for the 1907 term. The Justices knew that the pending case had to be resolved, but they could hardly have known that the coming session would pose the most difficult tests for the Court in over a decade.

For over two months, amid the business pressed upon them, the Justices continued to struggle with the *Employers' Liability Cases*. At issue was a 1906 congressional act regulating the liability of common carriers for employee injuries. It effectively negated the fellow servant defense that railroads had so often used to defeat employee claims by making the carriers responsible for injuries resulting from the negligence of any employee and from any defect in equipment caused by negligence. Also Congress provided that contributory negligence on the part of the employee would not defeat his claim but only reduce the amount of recovery. To prevent judges from using old common law rules to defeat an injured employee's case, the legislation further specified that all such determinations were to be made by juries.[32] With this legislation Congress was trying to redress an imbalance, for courts with their common law doctrines had built up barriers that frustrated employee injury suits. Work on the railroads was still a hazardous enterprise, and, although some of the states had modified the common law defenses by statute to make recovery by injured employees easier, Congress now sought in the wide sector of industrial life that could be reached under its power over commerce to shift the risk of injury to the employing carriers.

That the court had difficulty was attested to not only by the time delay but also by the five opinions filed. White announced the judgment of the Court, in an opinion that only Day joined. White began on a positive note, reminding counsel that the Court is solely concerned with congressional power and not the wisdom of its exercise and that the federal commerce clause contained no limitations as to the permissible subject matter of regulation. Then the Louisianian shifted directions and concluded that the imposition of liability on interstate carriers with no distinction as to whether the injury occurred in interstate commerce "includes subjects wholly outside of the power of Congress to regulate commerce." Despite the duty of the Court to construe an act to save its constitutionality, White said, to read the act to cover only workers employed in interstate commerce would change the effect of the act in the federal territories where Congress was not limited by the commerce clause. Saying that the words of the legislation are free from any ambiguity and that the subjects within and without congressional power "are so interblended in the statute that they are incapable of separation," he pronounced the act "repugnant to the Constitution and nonenforcible [sic]."[33]

White interposed no obstacle to properly circumscribed congressional legislation, but Peckham, Fuller, and Brewer denied that Congress had power to legislate on the subject of master and servant. In dissent, Moody championed the government's case and won support from Harlan and McKenna. Agreeing with all his colleagues that Congress cannot regulate wholly intrastate commerce, Moody discerned in the opening words of the statute a clear limitation of its applicability to interstate commerce. He said the act should be saved by sensibly interpreting it, adding that "the court has never exercised the mighty power of declaring the acts of a co-ordinate branch of the Government void except where there is no possible and sensible construction of the act which is consistent with the fundamental organic law."[34] This is not only a well-established rule of the Court, continued the new appointee, but a rule of conduct resting upon public policy and the separation of powers. Liberally sprinkling words from past decisions in his opinion, he said that reading the term *any employee* to embrace only those employees engaged in interstate commerce is fair, just, and necessary.

To argument of counsel that the absence of such legislation for over a century is evidence of a lack of congressional power, Moody responded that this contention misunderstands "the nature of the Constitution, undervalues its usefulness, and forgets that its unchanging provisions are adaptable to the indefinite variety of the changing conditions of our National life." Demonstrating how this generality had been consistently accepted by the High Bench, he said such precedent leads "to the conclusion that the national power to regulate commerce is broad enough to regulate the employment, duties, obligations, liabilities, and conduct of all persons engaged in commerce with respect to all which is comprehended in that commerce." How else, he asked, could the Court accept the Safety Appliance Act without ever questioning its constitutionality? Moody saw the Constitution entrusting to Congress broad discretion in exercising its lawful powers and warned his colleagues not to trespass "upon a domain which is peculiarly and exclusively the province of the legislative branch."[35] Congress, he argued, has the right to change certain common law doctrines that favored employers, for legislators, not judges, are the determiners of public policy.

Harlan and Holmes also responded in dissent. Condemning White's distorted interpretation of the act of 1906, the Kentuckian, with McKenna again agreeing, said it is well within the orbit of congressional power. Holmes acknowledged that the majority's interpretation of the act was supported by "strong reasons," but he added that the act can be read to save its constitutionality "without violence to the habits of English speech."[36] This he would do.

Although the Employers' Liability Act continued in force in the territories and in the District of Columbia, its primary purpose had been frustrated by the Court's decision. The invalidation of the major portion of this reform legislation on January 6, 1908, was only the beginning, for three weeks later the Court struck again. The second federal act to fall during the month was passed almost a decade earlier. Congress had provided that the dismissal by an interstate carrier of an employee for membership in a labor union was a crime. This particular piece of legislation was inspired by the report of a commission appointed by President Grover Cleveland to investigate the causes of the railway strike of 1894.[37] Passed during the unsettled 1890s, along with legislation like the Safety Appliance Act, the statute revealed that Congress was not as insensitive to the need for reform in the industrial structure as much of the writing of the decade's history suggests. Behind such acts was a sensitivity to labor and a recognition of the inequities brought about by a largely unregulated period of industrial growth. Whatever the reason for this statute of 1898 standing so long upon the books without challenge, the timing of this test was uncanny, coming on the heels of the decision in the *Employers' Liability Cases.*

Adair v. *United States* brought both Attorney General Bonaparte and private attorney William R. Harr, the losers in the *Employers' Liability Cases*, back before the High Bench. A lower federal court had upheld the 1898 act in the conviction of William Adair, an agent of the Louisville and Nashville Railroad Company. Adair had fired O.B. Coppage, a member of the Order of Locomotive Firemen, because of his union membership. Pointing to state decisions holding such acts unconstitutional under the Fourteenth Amendment, Adair's attorneys contended that this alleged regulation of commerce was invalid because the matter regulated was indirect, incidental, and remote. The government spokesmen argued for a broad reading of the commerce power, buttressing the contention with a review of the legislative history of the act.

Harlan wrote the Court's opinion. After reviewing various provisions of the act to demonstrate congressional intent to prevent labor disputes from disrupting the business of the interstate carrier, the Kentuckian addressed section ten, upon which the prosecution was based. First, the Justice condemned the section as repugnant to the Fifth Amendment. Realizing quite well that government has the right to restrict such freedom in the public interest, he maintained that no such interest is involved here. Despite the division in *Lochner*, Harlan said that "there was no disagreement as to the general proposition that there is a liberty of contract which cannot be unreasonably interfered with by legislation." Since the employee is free to quit for any reason, the employer, the Kentuckian continued, is equally free to dismiss the employee, and "any legislation that disturbs that equality is an arbitrary interference with the liberty of contract which no government can legally justify in a free land." Responding next to the argument that Congress had sufficient authority to make such a law in its power over commerce without regard to the Fifth Amendment, he saw no relationship between the statute and a "real or substantial relation to or connection with the commerce regulated." Indulging in the same blindness to reality he condemned in *Lochner*, he pronounced section ten unconstitutional as "an illegal invasion of the personal liberty as well as the right of property of the defendant, Adair."[38]

In his majority opinion, to which five of his colleagues subscribed, Harlan not only whittled away at the reach of congressional control over commerce, but he infused new and vigorous life into the liberty of contract doctrine. During this same term the Justices would begin the process of undermining the *Lochner* precedent, but the assertion of a constitutional right guaranteeing liberty of contract was now strengthened by the adherence of a solid majority of the present Court.

With Moody disqualifying himself, McKenna and Holmes were left to carry the battle in separate dissents. McKenna condemned the majority opinion for being too narrow and too detached from reality. Contending that the Fifth Amendment is not a command to ensure freedom from all restraint and limitation, he said the proper inquiry was, does section ten relate to the act's purpose and is this purpose encompassed by congressional control over interstate commerce? "The provisions of the act are explicit," continued the Justice, "and present a well coordinated plan for the settlement of disputes between carriers and their employes, by bringing the disputes to arbitration and accommodation, and thereby prevent strikes and the public disorder and derangement of business that may be consequent upon them." McKenna commended Congress, as he said, ". . . no worthier purpose can engage legislative attention, or be the object of legislative action."[39] Noting the gratuitous remarks about labor unions tossed off by Harlan, the Justice asked, may not Congress acknowledge their power as factors to be considered in the framing of legislation?

Surveying the history of the bill, he illustrated how Congress modified earlier legislation after the massive railway strike of 1894 to acknowledge the rights of labor unions and integrate them into a plan to solve labor-management disputes without national turmoil and disruption. How, he asked, can this purpose be fulfilled if the carriers are allowed to carry on their war with unions by dismissing their members? "Liberty," he continued, "is an attractive theme, but the liberty which is exercised in sheer antipathy does not plead strongly for recognition." Bolstering his view, he quoted from a Senate committee report on the legislation: "The necessity for the bill arises from the calamitous results in the way of ill-considered strikes arising from the tyranny of capital or the unjust demands of labor organizations, whereby the business of the country is brought to a standstill and thousands of employees, with their helpless wives and children, are confronted with starvation." Congress, McKenna argued, clearly sought to establish a working relationship between unions and management. He denied that the act either required an employer to retain incompetent labor or encouraged disloyalty or dereliction of duty. To the argument that section ten is remote and indirect in its relation to commerce, McKenna said that a

. . . provision of law which will prevent or tend to prevent the stoppage of every wheel in every car of an entire railroad system certainly has as direct influence on interstate commerce as the way in which one car may be coupled to another, or the rule of liability for personal injuries to an employé. It also seems to me to be an oversight of the proportions of things to contend that in order to encourage a policy of arbitration between carriers and their employés which may prevent a disastrous interruption of commerce, the derangement of business, and even greater evils to the public welfare, Congress cannot restrain the discharge of an employé, and yet can, to enforce a policy of unrestrained competition between railroads, prohibit reasonable agreements between them as to the rates at which merchandise shall be carried. . . . May such action be restricted, must it give way to the public welfare, while the other, moved, it may be, by prejudice and antagonism, is entrenched impregnably in the Fifth Amendment of the Constitution against regulation in the public interest.[40]

To McKenna and to many off the Court the answer was obvious.

Despite its length, verbosity, and lack of stylistic grace, McKenna's opinion is impressive, for it clearly exposes the hostility to unionism that lies at the base of the majority's rationale. Despite his long tenure the Californian would never gain great stature on the Court, but he deserves far more recognition than he has been accorded. No man has ever felt personally less qualified to take his seat on the High Bench, and he was often given routine opinions that attracted little public attention. Whether or not the Chief acknowledged it, McKenna had grown into his role with grace and modesty. Not merely a satellite of the more prominent White, he had an inherent sympathy for certain groups and individuals in society. As he grew more confident in his role, he realized there need be no separation between from that often unshared sympathy and his task as a Justice on the Supreme Court. Unlike most of his colleagues, he did not fear a growing labor movement; he strove mightily and successfully to escape his humble background, but in his movement up the American ladder of success he brought with him an understanding and a sensitivity for the underdog, a perspective too little represented in the Court's history. In these two major decisions invalidating congressional acts in January 1908, only McKenna and Holmes consistently supported the attempts to protect the workingman.

Holmes saw little difficulty in the case, believing the law of 1898 was a valid exercise of federal power. Section ten, he said, "simply prohibits the more powerful party to exact certain undertakings, or to threaten dismissal or unjustly discriminate on certain grounds against those already employed." Holmes asserted that "the right to make contracts at will that has been derived from the word liberty in the amendments has been stretched to its extreme by the decision." The Constitution, Holmes argued, should not be read to prevent a legislature from determining that public policy demanded some restraint of this freedom. Section ten he pronounced beneficial in its attempt to encourage arbitration and prevent strikes and then added that no constitutional bar prevented Congress from demanding complete unionization of the railroads. "I could not pronounce it unwarranted," he concluded, "if Congress should decide that to foster a strong union was for the best interest, not only of the men, but of the railroads and the country at large."[41]

In a single month the Court had invalidated two major pieces of congressional legislation, establishing a qualitative if not a quantitative record. In the 1869 term three congressional acts had been struck down, but on balance this new work of the Court was far more threatening, for power was being limited at precisely the time when new demands for federal legislation were being pressed. The adverse decision in the liability cases could be rectified by new legislation, but Harlan's opinion in *Adair* precluded congressional action in the area. From another perspective the decisions seemed to be a manifestation of a new hostility on the part of the Court toward labor. The *Debs* decision in 1895 hinted at this possibility, but the relative absence of cases gave little reading to what *Debs* signified. Now, two congressional statutes aimed at protecting the interests of labor had been annulled. Court watchers did not have to wait long, in fact only one more week, before the Justices were ready to fire another volley against the labor movement.

Loewe v. *Lawlor* provoked no division on the Court, but the decision rumbled ominously through the ranks of organized labor. At issue was whether the Sherman Act embraced the activities of a labor union. In *Debs* the lower federal court had applied the antitrust act, but the Supreme Court expressed no opinion upon its applicability, preferring instead to rely upon the postal and commerce powers of the federal government. *Loewe* v. *Lawlor* posed the question of whether a suit against a union for treble damages suffered by a hat manufacturer could be maintained under the antitrust act. The federal district court had dismissed the suit, and the Court of Appeals certified the question to the Supreme Court.

Dietrich Loewe, a partner in a Connecticut hat manufacturing business, had resisted attempts to unionize his plant. The United Hatters of North America, part of the American Federation of Labor (AF of L), sought to break this resistance by instituting a boycott of Loewe's product by the members of the AF of L. The union had been successful in unionizing seventy out of the eighty-two plants manufacturing fur hats, and this success, plus the nearly 1.5 million membership of the AF of L, gave the case alarming dimensions. Loewe in his complaint outlined the interstate nature of his business and how it was threatened by this combined strength of union men. Fuller, for the unanimous Court, ruled that this activity was a combination "in restraint of trade or commerce among the several states." Attorneys for the union reminded the Court of its decision in *E.C. Knight* and the limitations it had placed upon commerce as regulated by the 1890 act. They contended that the fact that articles are manufactured for export does not subject that manufacturing enterprise to national regulation. Fuller responded, ". . . although some of the means whereby the interstate traffic was to be destroyed were acts within a State, and some of them were beyond the scope of Federal authority, still, as we have seen, the acts must be considered as a whole, and the plan is open to condemnation, notwithstanding a negligible amount of intrastate business might be affected in carrying it out."[42] Apparently, the Court felt no discomfiture in reading the commerce power narrowly in *Adair* and broadly here.

What disturbed observers was the chilling effect the decision would have upon an emerging labor movement and its strategy of coercive action. If organized labor was to succeed, it had to draw upon its members to exert the type of coercion the Court now condemned. Fuller was content to fit the suit into the words of the statute and apparently leave any remedy to the legislative branch, where activity would be centered for the next generation. But fastening upon labor unions liability for threefold damages was a frightening prospect, and the decision was interpreted as part of a new hostility on the part of the Justices toward the interests of unions and the laboring man.[43]

Whether the Sherman Act was ever intended by Congress to cover the activities of labor unions is unclear, but there was no ambiguity when Congress legislated against rebates in the Elkins Act in 1903 or when the legislative body insisted upon compliance with safety regulations by the railroads a decade earlier. In *Armour Packing Company* v. *United States*, the Court gave a generous reading to the Elkins Act, though Brewer, Fuller, and Peckham dissented, claiming the majority had imputed to Congress a desecration of the "sacredness of contracts" that surely could not have been intended. In regard to the Safety Appliance Act, Justice Moody for a unanimous Court rebuffed a railroad's claim that holding the railroads liable for all injuries arising from a failure to conform to the act's requirements could not have been the intent of Congress. He said that harshness and wisdom are not the proper concerns of courts. Then the former Attorney General went on to lend support to the statute, suggesting its clear wording might well have resulted from a congressional determination that the railroads were in the best position to control the causes of such injuries.[44]

Matters affecting Indian tribes again occupied the time of the Justices. In an opinion favoring the rights of Indians on the Fort Belknap Reservation in Montana, McKenna, for the Court, construed an agreement of the United States with the Indians as affording them the use of a tract of arid land. He inferred from this grant of occupancy the right of the Indians to divert water from a river for irrigation purposes. The argument that the admission of Montana to statehood affected a repeal of this arrangement was preemptorily rejected. Only Brewer dissented without opinion. Of all the sitting Justices McKenna was the most favorably disposed to Indian claims, and here seven of his colleagues were willing to deal the rule in *Race Horse*—that Indian claims were abrogated in favor of a newly admitted state—a severe blow.[45]

Just as cases dealing with federal matters made the 1907 term an exceptional one, so did a few cases coming from the states. In *Adair* the Court gave new and forceful approval to the doctrine of liberty of contract, but in *Muller* v. *Oregon* it began to reinspect the states' authority to regulate working hours, the subject matter of *Lochner* in which freedom of contract had been the basis of the Court's decision. *Muller* involved the conviction of a defendant for requiring a woman employed in a laundry to work more than the ten-hour day prescribed by state law. The brief for the defendant emphasized the equality of women and men, saying the rights of women to liberty and property are the same as those of men and that a difference in sex alone cannot justify Oregon's attempt to impair those rights. Louis D. Brandeis, the prominent and wealthy Boston attorney who had begun to devote himself to public service, responded with what has become known as the "Brandeis brief." In an argument stretching over a hundred and thirteen pages, the advocate devoted two pages to legal precedents and the remainder to an exhaustive survey of such laws here and abroad, assessing both their purpose and their wisdom. His brief centered on the physical differences between men and women and the right of the state to pass legislation based upon such differences.[46]

What Brandeis was doing was making a presentation that would normally be made to a legislative body considering the enactment of such protective measures. There the desirability of legislation is the paramount consideration. Repeatedly, each member of the Court during his tenure denied that this was a proper concern of the judicial branch; yet in viewing the majority's confessed inability to see any rational relationship between the state's police power and the regulation of hours in *Lochner*, Brandeis was determined to prove that Oregon had here acted reasonably. What made the brief unusual was not its allusion to considerations of public policy, for this was a part of any good lawyer's argument to the Court, but rather its almost total emphasis upon this factor and its impressive collection of facts and statistics.[47]

Rather than deny that such an argument was proper, the unanimous Court responded with favor. In fact, Brewer, one of the leading proponents of liberty of contract, spoke for the Court. Noting the defendant's reliance on *Lochner*, Brewer responded that such an analogy "assumes that the difference between the sexes does not justify a different rule respecting a restriction of the hours of labor." Defending his resort to the Brandeis collation, the Justice said it "may not be amiss before examining the constitutional question, to notice the course of legislation as well as expressions of opinion from other than judicial sources." He continued:

Constitutional questions, it is true, are not settled by even a consensus of present public opinion, for it is the peculiar value of a written constitution that it places in unchanging form limitations upon legislative action, and thus gives a permanence and stability to popular government which otherwise would be lacking. At the same time, when a question of fact is debated and debatable, and the extent to which a special constitutional limitation goes is affected by the truth in respect to that fact, a widespread and long-continued belief concerning it is worthy of consideration. We take judicial cognizance of all matters of general knowledge.

Then casually Brewer dismissed the freedom to contract argument, saying a state can, "without conflicting with the provisions of the Fourteenth Amendment, restrict in many respects the individual's power of contract."[48]

In two paragraphs that have become a special target for latter-day feminists, the Kansan discoursed on the special and limiting characteristics of the sex. Woman's "physical structure and the performance of maternal functions place her at a disadvantage in the struggle for subsistence." What greater public interest, the Justice insisted, can be imagined than that of preserving "the strength and vigor of the race?" Independent of the maternal dimension, Brewer said that in comparison with men and "looking at it from the viewpoint of the effort to maintain an independent position in life, she is not upon an equality."[49] Woman has been dependent upon man, he continued, and, as with minors, special care must be taken that her rights are preserved. Toward that end, the Justice ruled, she can be placed in a class where legislation specially designed for her protection will be sustained. Upholding the Oregon law, Brewer concluded that the decision should not be read as impugning the validity of *Lochner*.

A final disclaimer could not hold back the march of events, for *Muller* v. *Oregon* was the first wedge hammered into *Lochner*. Despite Brandeis's arguments and Brewer's ready acceptance of sexual differences justifying a departure from the rule of freedom of contract, the distinction that a state could consider the health of women but not of men in regulating the hours of labor could not stand the test of time. We can readily see why those who espouse the complete equality of women are incensed with Brewer's patronizing attitude, but this should neither blind one to the significance of the case as a modification of *Lochner* nor be viewed as an accurate reflection of the Justice's attitude toward the opposite sex.

Brewer took the platform to champion women in their quest for the suffrage long before male support became popular and accepted. In early 1906 in a speech at Vassar College, the Court's finest orator supported the idea of a woman president and suggested that Jane Addams, the prominent Chicago social worker, would make a fine mayor of that city.[50] So his painting of woman as frail, dependent, and maternally hindered should be measured against the Kansan's eloquent espousal of women's rights.

In addition to upholding Oregon's power to regulate the working day for women, the Court showed continued willingness to give the states latitude in regulatory and taxing measures. For instance, though Moody thought a Tennessee oil inspection act violated the commerce clause, the rest of the Justices did not. Kansas could make criminal the transportation into the state of cattle that had not been inspected in conformity with the federal law of 1903; South Carolina could enforce a penalty on carriers for failure to pay a lawful claim; Minnesota could require a railroad to make repairs on a viaduct; and Mississippi could order a railway company to broaden and standardize its narrow-gauge railroad. North Dakota could require manufacturers of paint to affix labels specifying the ingredients used; Vermont could require a corporation to produce its records in court; and New York could levy a tax on cash and notes owned by a foreign corporation doing business as importers without running afoul of the constitutional prohibition against a state tax on imports.[51]

One final case remains from this notable session, that of *Ex Parte Young*, in which the Court made a major exploration into the area of what was and what was not a suit against the state. At issue was the vigorous attempt of Minnesota, through statute and through authority conferred on a railroad and warehouse commission, to set rates and to impose stiff penalties on violators. Nine suits were commenced in the federal circuit court in Minnesota by stockholders against the railroad companies, the state attorney general Edward T. Young, and the state commission. They sought to enjoin the railroads from complying with the orders. Obviously these out-of-state stockholders, in collusion with the companies, were seeking access to the federal courts. Alleging that the rates set were confiscatory, the plaintiffs sought to prohibit the attorney general from instituting proceedings against the railroads. Young appeared and denied the jurisdiction of the federal court, arguing that he was acting in behalf of the state and that the state was immune from suit under the Eleventh Amendment. The circuit court issued a preliminary order enjoining Young from instituting any action in the courts. When Young promptly violated the injunction by bringing suit against the Northern Pacific Railway Company in the state court, the federal circuit judge held the attorney general in contempt of court. Young's petition for habeas corpus brought the matter to the Supreme Court.

Peckham, for the majority, started by acknowledging the significance of the case and its interest to all those concerned with "the practical working of the courts of justice throughout the land, both Federal and state." Somewhat unsure, he further granted that reasonable men could differ concerning the proper result. But then Peckham, equating the Minnesota procedure of setting rates to a situation in which a person was denied an appeal to the courts, ruled that, independent of the question of the sufficiency of the rates, such provisions violated due process. Maintaining that the state has no power through its doctrine of sovereign immunity to insulate an official from the supreme authority of the United States, Peckham said that, when an official seeks to enforce an unconstitutional act, "he is in that case stripped of his official or representative character and is subjected in his person to the consequences of his individual conduct." Referring to the over $1 billion invested in the railway properties and the thousands of people affected, Peckham found a recourse to equitable jurisdiction proper. Also, he ruled that equity can provide the most convenient, comprehensive, and just remedy for all those dependent upon the healthy condition of the railroads. To the final contention that a decision against the authority of the attorney general would excite opposition and injure the federal system, the Justice responded that nothing in the Court's resolution "ought properly to breed hostility to the customary operation of Federal courts of justice in cases of this character."[52] Edward T. Young's petition for habeas corpus was denied.

Alone, Harlan fought against this new inroad upon the Eleventh Amendment. What bothered the Justice was the Court's new ruling that a federal judge could forbid a state access to its own courts by federal order against its chief legal officer. In reading precedent Harlan said the barrier to suits against the state had been surmounted only when officials, acting pursuant to an unconstitutional act, were about "to commit some *specific wrong or trespass,* to the injury of the plaintiff's rights." In fact, during the term the Kentuckian agreed with the Court in such a confined case, but here he saw a clear distinction. Young was no administrative official whose decision was immunized from judicial review; rather, the Justice continued, he was obligated to proceed through the courts. In effect, Harlan added, plaintiffs here sought to test the constitutionality of an act without following proper state procedure. He reminded his colleagues that state courts have obligations to the federal constitution and that some respect should be afforded to their continuous discharge of this responsibility. Minnesota's dignity has been assaulted, lectured Harlan, as he warned the majority about the "pernicious results" the decision might well have. A firm establishment of this new principle, the Justice continued, would work "a radical change in our governmental system" and place the states "in a condition of inferiority never dreamed of when the Constitution was adopted or when the Eleventh Amendment was made part of the Supreme Law of the Land." Even assuming the state acts and regulations were unconstitutional, he argued that a Fourteenth Amendment due process claim could not weaken the force of the Eleventh Amendment. In conclusion he warned his colleagues that the "country should never be allowed to think that the Constitution can, in any case, be evaded or amended by judicial interpretation, or that its behests may be nullified by an ingenious construction of its provisions."[53]

Harlan was not wrong or idiosyncratic in his opinion, a conclusion that might be reached in terms of his failure to garner support, but the majority Justices were willing to break new ground in terms of circumventing the Eleventh Amendment. Behind Peckham's opinion was a disapproval of Minnesota's vigorous railroad regulation program and a desire to protect threatened property rights. In the absence of any possibility of a frontal attack, the Court developed and here extended a fiction, that the official enforcing an unconstitutional act is stripped of the state's immunity and is subject to private suit. Such fictions, born of judicial interpretation, crisscross the law. With the Justices' ability to read the Constitution anew, the resort to fiction is less necessary, but here the precise wording of the Eleventh Amendment makes escape much more difficult.

Ex Parte Young excited the outcry that Harlan had predicted and that Peckham had feared. The Nebraska legislature and the Association of Attorneys General sent memorials to Congress demanding legislation checking the Court in the area. Continued agitation led Congress in 1910 to pass a provision that only partially responded to the critics. The authority of the Supreme Court was untouched, but the new act required that a three-judge trial panel be convened in cases where an injunction was sought against a state official on grounds that the enabling statute was unconstitutional. Some of the criticism engendered by *Ex Parte Young* concerned the power of a lone federal judge to thwart state action; now, although a single federal judge could hand down a temporary restraining order, the formal hearing by three judges was to "be in every way expedited."[54]

With the final decisions of the Court announced on June 1, 1908, the eventful 1907 term came to an end. Rarely had the Court had such a session in which almost all observers could find something to criticize. Congressional power was limited; state immunity from suit was lessened; the laboring man had substantial setbacks both in terms of protective legislation and of labor unionization; interstate carriers found no escape from the rigors of the Elkins Act; and reformers pressing upon state legislatures for measures that would redress the bargaining imbalance in the industrial society were confronted with a stronger-than-ever endorsement by the Court of the sanctity of the freedom to contract. The only ray of hope was *Muller* v. *Oregon.*

During the summer of 1908 Mrs. Taft's dream came true. Her husband, with the sponsorship of Roosevelt, had an easy road to the Republican nomination. The Democrats, so devastated by their defeat in 1904, turned again to William Jennings Bryan, now a third-time candidate for the high office. Indeed, some Democrats did return to the fold in the election in November, but Taft, temporarily at least, was able to soothe concern within his own party and win an easy victory over Bryan. Reformers within the Republican party were cautious in their support of Taft, but generally they were quite willing to give Roosevelt's handpicked successor a chance. In fact, the talent he demonstrated in the Philippines and in the War Department indicated that Taft might well bring to the presidency an administrative competence that Roosevelt had not demonstrated.

As the Chief, now seventy-five, assembled the Court for the 1908 term, he still gave no hint of retirement. He headed an aging Court: Harlan was also seventy-five, Brewer seventy-one, Peckham seventy, and Holmes sixty-seven.[55] But they were all of one mind with Fuller on the subject of retirement. Holmes and White were the workhorses of the Court, but Fuller, Harlan, Brewer, and Peckham were slowing down in terms of opinion output. Buffeted by criticism in the previous session, the Justices seemed especially eager to be accommodating. For instance, in two cases decided early in the term, despite strong dissents by Harlan, the Court was solicitous of state power.

In *Berea College* v. *Kentucky* the Court considered a state law forbidding individuals, corporations, or associations of persons from operating any school that instructed both black and white students together. The Kentucky court had reasoned that, independent of the statute's constitutionality regarding individuals, the state in its power over domestic corporations could amend the college's charter. Brewer's opinion sidestepped the question of whether the state's action violated the Fourteenth Amendment, as it simply accepted the lower court's rationale. Holmes and Moody concurred in the judgment. Day dissented without opinion, but predictably Harlan assailed the decision.[56]

Attacking the majority's evasion of its fundamental responsibility, the Kentucky Justice pronounced the statute "an arbitrary invasion of the rights of liberty and property guaranteed by the Fourteenth Amendment against hostile state action." Although he contended that the right to instruct is a property right that was here abridged, his major argument was that the statute infringed liberty. He speculated on the implications of upholding Kentucky's power, saying the majority opinion afforded sanction to a state prohibiting the meeting of races in any area, including religion. He asked: "Have we become so inoculated with prejudice of race that an American government, professedly based on the principles of freedom, and charged with the protection of all citizens alike, can make distinctions between such citizens in the matter of their voluntary meeting for innocent purposes simply because of their respective races?" Unfortunately, the answer to Harlan's rhetorical question in early twentieth-century America was yes. Avoiding the matter of public schools, "established at the pleasure of the State and maintained at public expense," he denied that Kentucky could make the instruction of black and white students in the same institution a crime.[57]

Harlan had no more success with his colleagues in *Twining* v. *New Jersey*. The case involved the convictions of Albert Twining and David C. Cornell for attempting to deceive a state banking examiner regarding the financial condition of their company. Twining and Cornell were sentenced to jail terms of six and four years respectively. The basis of the defendants' appeal was that their right against self-incrimination was violated by the judge's charge to the jury. Twining and Cornell had neither testified nor produced any witnesses, and in his charge the trial judge alternated between stating that their refusal to testify had no significance and that it did have significance and should be considered by the jury. In the argument before the High Court, counsel noted that New Jersey placed the accused in the position of any party in a civil suit and was alone among all the states and territories in permitting comment upon a defendant's silence. What made the case significant was the Justices' willingness to give extensive consideration to the meaning of due process in the Fourteenth Amendment, especially the question of whether it included the protection against self-incrimination.

Moody, for the Court, reviewed history to show that recourse had to be made to the states in a self-incrimination claim, for the Fifth Amendment only protected an individual from the national government. Did the Fourteenth Amendment, with its obvious restriction upon the authority of the states, result in forcing the state to honor the self-incrimination claim? After noting precedent that saw no protection in the privileges and immunities clause, the former Attorney General addressed the argument that self-incrimination is protected against state abridgment by the due process clause of the Fourteenth Amendment. Moody viewed the contention as plausible, at least to the extent of being willing to consider whether some provisions of the Bill of Rights might be so incorporated, not because they are in the Bill but "because they are of such a nature that they are included in the conception of due process of law." Recognizing that due process is vague, Moody noted that the Court has preferred to move case by case in determining what is and what is not included in the phrase. After citing Anglo-American authority for the proposition that self-incrimation had not been inconsistent with a guarantee of due process, Moody sought to solve the problem independent of these historical antecedents. He cautioned that the Court could not pass on the wisdom and expediency of state law, contending that the power of the citizens to change their laws is really "the greatest security for liberty and justice." Then surveying state constitutional law, he concluded that self-incrimination is not conceived as an integral part of due process of law. With valid law, proper jurisdiction, sufficient notice, and an adequate hearing, Moody continued, "all the requirements of due process, so far as it relates to procedure in courts and methods of trial and character and effect of evidence, are complied with."[58]

Since the Court had built up a considerable body of law saying that due process could be interpreted as a bar to certain state action, counsel was asking the Court to demonstrate a similar willingness to impose the substantive check of the self-incrimination clause upon state criminal procedure. With due process constructed as a vessel into which new meaning could be poured, the doctrinal base for a nationalization of such rights had been established though it would take the Court almost two decades more to begin to build upon this foundation in the cause of individual rights. Revealing present priorities, Moody concluded:

> Even if the historical meaning of due process of law and the decisions of this court did not exclude the privilege from it, it would be going far to rate it as an immutable principle of justice which is the inalienable possession of every citizen of a free government. Salutary as the principle may seem to the great majority, it cannot be ranked with the right to hearing before condemnation, the immunity from arbitrary power not acting by general laws, and the inviolability of private property. The wisdom of the exemption has never been universally assented to .., and it is best defended not as an unchangeable principle of universal justice, but as a law proved by experience to be expedient.[59]

Notice how the majority Justices seemed to require a popular consensus on the importance of the self-incrimination protection. What causes this departure from the Court's practice of determining constitutional questions for itself is the fact that a due process appeal is one made to concepts of fairness, justice, and universality. Of course, if total agreement were required, the

Justices could never find it, even in the matter of the inviolability of private property.

In dissent, Harlan attacked his colleagues for avoiding the threshold question of whether the New Jersey trial judge did, indeed, infringe the defendants' right against self-incrimination. Instead, Harlan said, the majority sought to answer "a question of vast moment, one of such transcendent importance that a court ought not to decide it unless the record before it requires that course to be adopted."[60] What disturbed the Kentuckian, more than the Court's neglect of regular procedure, was the majority's apparent invitation to new intrusions upon the individual's right against self-incrimination.

Coming to grips with the essential issue, Harlan wrote a major dissent. Just as Holmes's dissent in *Lochner*, advising the judiciary to give the legislatures latitude to deal with economic and social matters, charted the future, so here did Harlan anticipate a more distant future. The protection against self-incrimination, he said, is assured state defendants by both the privileges and immunities and due process clauses. Harlan did not really separate the two clauses, contending that a violation of a "privilege," such as that against self-incrimination, is obviously a deprivation of due process. Contrary to the Court's interpretation, he contended that the Fourteenth Amendment was specifically designed to provide some national supervision over deficiencies in the state guarantees. Our history from the break with England through the Bill of Rights, Harlan added, supported the contention that the "privilege" is fundamental. The Fourteenth Amendment shifted the balance in the federal system, he continued, by forbidding the states from violating the rights of citizens. Among the privileges and immunities protected, asserted the Kentuckian, was that against self-incrimination, which even the majority recognized as "universal in American law." The majority entrusted its protection to the states, but the dissenter did not. He asked:

Is it conceivable that a privilege or immunity of such a priceless character, one expressly recognized in the Supreme Law of the Land, one thoroughly interwoven with the history of Anglo-American liberty, was not in the mind of the country when it declared, in the Fourteenth Amendment, that no State shall abridge the privileges or immunities of citizens of the United States? The Fourteenth Amendment would have been disapproved by every State in the Union if it had saved or recognized the right of a State to compel one accused of crime, in its courts, to be a witness against himself. We state the matter in this way because it is common knowledge that the compelling of a person to criminate himself shocks or ought to shock the sense of right and justice to every one who loves liberty.[61]

Even if one was inclined to cripple the amendment with a strained interpretation, the Justice said, its applicability could not be avoided here. Harlan agreed with Moody's characterization of the self-incrimination protection as a shield against unjust and tyrannical prosecutions and as a safeguard to

Americans in their pursuit of political liberty and freedom. While the majority then deduced that its protection was expedient, Harlan deduced that its enforcement against the state was no less than a matter of fundamental law.

Congress ran into trouble with the Court when the federal legislature attempted to extend its control over sexual immorality. In the previous term, the Court upheld an act forbidding the importation of an alien woman for "immoral purposes" in a case where a man had brought a woman into the country to live with him. Now Congress sought to make criminal the harboring, keeping, or controlling of an alien woman for prostitution or other immoral purposes for up to three years after her entry into the country. Recognizing that moral legislation has generally been a concern of the states, Brewer, for the majority, asked whether the federal government's power over the going and coming of aliens supported such legislation. No, he answered. Although Congress has not often attempted such legislation, approval by the Court here, the Justice said, might encourage the legislative body and bring us "face to face with such a change in the internal conditions of this country as was never dreamed of by the framers of the Constitution."[62] The Kansan's rhetoric got the better of him, but the essence of his position was that the federal government should be kept within its prescribed limitations so states could function properly. If the majority Justices expected this setback to discourage Congress in its desire to penalize immorality, they underestimated the ingenuity of the legislative branch.

In the previous term the Court, in connection with the reenactment of the Elkins Act, had flirted with the more significant Hepburn Act of 1906. This new legislation significantly overhauled the Interstate Commerce Act of 1887 by giving rate-making authority to the ICC and broadening its jurisdiction. Congress sought to fill in the gaps that the Court had perceived in earlier legislation and in so doing had finally created in the ICC an effective model for the modern regulatory agency. Now the Justices faced the first substantial challenge to the new legislation based upon a clause seeking to divorce public carrier from private transporter by severing ownership ties between railroads and certain industries. Twelve suits challenging this new authority were consolidated by the Court; all the companies were involved in transporting coal owned by them from the anthracite regions of Pennsylvania. The Attorney General acknowledged that the Hepburn Act was a "radical law" in that it forbade "the carrier who owns the mines and sells the coal, to transport that coal in interstate commerce."[63] The lower federal court had found this commodities clause unconstitutional and had granted an injunction against the enforcement of the ICC orders. During his battle with Congress over the legislation, President Roosevelt was acutely aware that its final provisions would have to surmount the hurdle of the Supreme Court. That constitutional problems lurked within the commodities clause was readily acknowledged by most of the Justices, but White, for the majority, revealed a Court straining to uphold the provision's constitutionality.

White began by shunning questions of inconvenience or harm, saying the Court's only responsibility was to determine whether Congress had power to pass the act. Although raising some important questions affecting the constitutionality of the law, he avoided them by concentrating on an interpretation of the pertinent clause. The Louisianian stated that the Court's responsibility, if a statute is susceptible to more than one construction, is to take the construction that "will save the statute from constitutional infirmity," a precept he ignored in the *Employers' Liability Cases.* The Justice cited precedent supporting the majority's view that congressional action forcing carriers to disassociate themselves from products before transportation would not amount to confiscation. The Court's duty, White maintained, "is to restrain the wider, and as we think, doubtful prohibitions so as to make them accord with the narrow and more reasonable provisions, and thus harmonize the statute." He was especially intent upon repudiating the government's contention that any type of stock relationship was what Congress intended to prohibit, which, for the majority Justices, raised grave constitutional problems. With this creative approach, White narrowed the applicability of the commodities clause and interpreted it as a regulation Congress could make under its commerce power "to which all preexisting rights of the railroad companies were subordinated."[64] So read, he said the due process claim of the railroads was weakened and could now be rejected. His conclusion was that railroads could continue to hold stock in the producing companies but could not at time of shipment have any property interest in the coal. Recognizing that these were test cases designed to gain a reading on the power of Congress and the meaning of the commodities clause, White simply reversed the lower court decisions and directed further proceedings to apply the statute as interpreted.

Harlan dissented from the Court's reading of the commodities clause. Viewing that clause as encompassing stock ownership, the Justice said any other interpretation "will enable the transporting railroad company, by one device or another, to defeat altogether the purpose which Congress had in view, which was to divorce, in a real, substantial sense, production and transportation, and thereby to prevent the transporting company from doing injustice to other owners of coal."[65]

Certainly the majority Justices had limited the range of the commodities clause and rewritten the statute to conform to their ideas of constitutionality. Had they accepted the government's reading, that portion of the act would have been deemed unconstitutional. After the invalidations of the preceding term, the Court here sought some accommodation with Congress, as much in its own self-interest as in any spirit of cooperation. Despite the limitations placed upon the commodities clause by the majority's interpretation, the net result was a victory for Roosevelt and congressional regulatory power. Counsel for the railroads had insisted that the commerce power did not extend to regulation of matters wholly within a state, the effect of which would be to embargo harmless commodities that were useful and necessary to the public. To reject such an argument the Court had to travel a long way from *E.C. Knight*. Congress could regulate matters within a state prior to the time of interstate shipment, said the Court, and with the qualifications here imposed that power could not be limited by due process objections.

Despite the strengthening of its powers the ICC still had to run the gauntlet of the Supreme Court, which insisted that its activities be clearly specified in the enabling legislation. For instance, the commission attempted to coerce testimony from Edward H. Harriman by relying on its authority to keep informed about the conduct of the carrier's business, to enforce the obtaining of reports, and to aid in the recommendation of additional legislation to Congress. Holmes, for the majority, restricted the ICC's right to compel testimony to complaints and investigations directed toward specific violations of the act. The "power to require testimony is limited," he continued, "as it usually is in English-speaking countries, at least, to . . . cases where the sacrifice of privacy is necessary—those where the investigations concern a specific breach of the law."[66] Day, joined by Harlan and McKenna, protested the ruling. Actually, this resort of Holmes to grand principle only masked a hostility that the Justice from Massachusetts bore to the commission. Privately, he said the commission was always trying to expand its authority, and he took pride in being able to write decisions, like the present one, limiting its power through narrow constructions of the enabling legislation. To his English correspondent, Sir Frederick Pollock, he wrote that the Interstate Commerce Commission was unfit for the task of rate making, "even in the qualified way in which it is entrusted."[67]

That the Court, during the session, seemed to be seeking to atone for the decisions of the previous term was evidenced not only by its decision to uphold the commodities clause but also by its curious handling of a South Carolina case raising the issue of sovereign immunity. Since the Court had earlier decided the state could not escape the federal excise tax on liquor by monopolizing its sale, South Carolina had decided to extricate itself from the business. It appointed a commission charged with the task of paying its creditors. A creditor sought to sue the commission, but the Supreme Court upheld the state's claim of sovereign immunity, despite the fact that the appointment of the commission could clearly be read as a consent to suit on the part of the state.[68] Apparently, the reaction caused by the decision in *Ex Parte Young* had some effect on the Justices because a decision the other way was well supported by precedent.

Concerning the police power, the Court continued to allow much latitude. It upheld a penalty of $10,000 imposed upon a company for violating the Arkansas antitrust act, said that Louisiana could impose criminal penalties on a pilot not licensed by the state, and refused to interfere with a Boston building commission's maximum-height regulations. New York could prohibit the possession of game out of season, despite protests that the law violated the due process and the commerce clauses; Chicago could enforce an ordinance destroying food unfit for human consumption without a preliminary hearing; Louisiana could pass and enforce a coal gauging act; and Arkansas could prescribe that miners be paid on the basis of the weight of the coal mined rather than on the basis of its weight after screening. Only Brewer and Peckham saw the latter regulation abridging the freedom of contract. Day, for the majority, responded:

> We are unable to say, in the light of the conditions shown in the public inquiry referred to, and in the necessity for such laws, evinced in the enactments of the legislatures of various States, that this law had no reasonable relation to the protection of a large class of laborers in the receipt of their just dues and the promotion of the harmonious relations of capital and labor engaged in a great industry in the State.[69]

Obviously counsel in such cases, after the Brandeis brief in *Muller*, if not before, sought to convince the Court of the reasonableness of the limitations placed upon the contracting power.

Just one week before the 1908 term ended, the Court handed down its judgment in a unique case that had generated considerable public interest. *United States* v. *Shipp* posed the novel question of whether law officers and mob members who allegedly conspired to lynch a black, whose legal execution had been stayed by order of the Supreme Court, could be found in contempt of the High Bench.

In Hamilton County, Tennessee, a black man, Ed Johnson, was tried and convicted for raping a white woman. He was sentenced to death on February 11, 1906. His petition for habeas corpus on grounds that all blacks had been excluded from the grand and petit juries and that he had been prevented from challenging the jury pool and from moving for a continuance and for a change in venue because of the fear of mob violence was lent a sympathetic ear by Justice Harlan. On March 19 the Supreme Court ordered "that all proceedings against the appellant be stayed, and the custody of said appellant be retained pending this appeal."[70] On the same day Chattanooga newspapers carried the story, and Sheriff John F. Shipp was notified of the Court's action by telegram. That evening the sheriff withdrew the customary guard and left the night jailer, Jeremiah Gibson, in charge. About twelve men broke into the jail, seized Johnson, and lynched him. The allegation was that both Shipp and Gibson, while pretending to fulfill their duties, connived in the illegal action. Both the act of lynching and the conspiracy were viewed as contemptuous, and nine people were so charged, including a second deputy and six members of the mob.

In an unusual preceeding the accused men were brought to Washington and appeared before the Supreme Court in the 1906 term. At that time

Moody, as Attorney General, and Solicitor General Hoyt participated for the government. Holmes, for a unanimous Court, disposed of preliminary challenges and said the question of whether Johnson's appeal was substantial or not did not reach the Court's inherent power to issue orders and punish violators for contempt.[71] Testimony was taken before a commissioner appointed by the Court, and in March 1909 the case was argued before the High Bench. Two months later the Court was ready with its decision.

Delivering the opinion of the Court, Chief Justice Fuller's sense of condemnation was apparent in his rendering of the events. He cited the fact that the dozen men took well over an hour to break through a door that did not respond to the night jailer's key. "It is apparent," the Chief wrote, "that a dangerous portion of the community was seized with the awful thirst for blood which only killing can quench, and that considerations of law and order were swept away in the overwhelming flood." He said that the prior history of Johnson's arrest and conviction should have alerted any law officer to the possibility of violence on the night of the 19th. Fuller made much of an interview that Shipp gave in May 1906 in which the sheriff said that, although he tried to halt the mob, he "*did not attempt to hurt any of them, and would not have made such an attempt.*" In the interview Shipp placed blame for the unlawful action on the Supreme Court "for not allowing the case to remain in our courts" and called this interference "a matter of politics" and "the most unfortunate thing in the history of Tennessee." The Chief condemned the sheriff's view that a hasty trial and a shortcutting of legal procedure were the answer to the problem of mob violence. "Shipp not only made the work of the mob easy," the Chief continued, "but in effect aided and abetted it." Just as the sheriff was guilty for not fulfilling the task assigned to him, so was Gibson. Four members of the mob were also found guilty. The second deputy and two of the alleged lynchers were exonerated because of a lack of evidence.[72]

Peckham, with White and McKenna, dissented. Although joining in condemnation of the crime perpetrated upon Johnson, the New York Justice reminded the majority that the only issue here was the contempt of the defendants to an order of the Court. As far as Shipp was concerned, Peckham said, "there is not one particle of evidence that any conspiracy had ever been entered into or existed on the part of the sheriff." Seeing the sheriff overwhelmed by the mob, Peckham labeled "extraordinary" the finding that a law officer "can be found guilty of a contempt because in fact he did not resist to the death." Contending that the government based its case primarily on Shipp's interview, the Justice pronounced it "wholly insufficient as evidence of the guilt of the sheriff." The fact that Shipp blamed the Supreme Court for the lynching, Peckham concluded, was not "the least evidence of guilt of the sheriff of the contempt with which he is charged, or of any conspiracy to commit it."[73] Although the dissenters thought both Shipp and his deputy

Gibson were free of any contempt, they interposed no objection to the conviction of the other four.

The Supreme Court passed sentence on November 15, 1909. Joseph F. Shipp and the two members of the mob who were identified by an eyewitness were sentenced to ninety days in the jail of the District of Columbia. Jeremiah Gibson, the night jailer, and the two other members of the mob, who had made incriminating statements, were sentenced to sixty days.[74]

As the first instance of a contempt proceeding being initiated by the Supreme Court, the Shipp case is instructive. It had some educational effect in focusing public attention upon lynching as a fact of American life. Within the Southern culture Shipp felt no personal guilt; he was not about to harm himself or his fellow townsmen to save a convicted black rapist. The assembled crowd greatly outnumbered the mob that lynched Ed Johnson, and their support for this vigilante justice was apparent. The United States government had gathered evidence of the guilt of certain individuals, but state authorities in Tennessee were no more inclined to prosecute than officials in other Southern states. What was done by these dozen men was against the written law but in conformity with the overriding unwritten law. Perhaps the Justices pursued this case to assuage the guilt they and the public felt, whether consciously or unconsciously, for such violence condoned by the society. This Court dramatization gave the practice of lynching national publicity on the heels of some notice of its existence in the pages of a national magazine.[75]

The 1908 term had ended with the Justice to the far left of the Chief missing. Looking back, the rather sudden affliction of William Moody, the Court's youngest member, with acute rheumatism was an ominous sign for a bench that had been intact since his accession on December 17, 1906. Previously vigorous, not only because of his age but as a reflection of his personality, the Justice received some treatment at the onset of rheumatoid arthritis both in Washington and New York. After the public session of May 7, 1909, Moody decided to heed his doctor's advice and go to Hot Springs, Virginia, for a rest before the next opinion day. The rheumatism quickly spread through his joints and sapped his energy, and instead of returning to Washington he went to his home in Haverhill, Massachusetts.[76]

William Moody would continue to be counted as a member of the Court but his actual service had come to an end. Despite his nonparticipation in a number of cases he had encountered as Attorney General and despite his freshman standing on the High Bench, he had been a vocal and active Justice. Fulfilling completely Theodore Roosevelt's expectations, Moody was in tune with the view that both Congress and the Chief Executive needed constitutional room to meet the demands of a changing society. These demands, as perceived by Roosevelt and Moody, related to the collective good; so it is not surprising that the former Attorney General in *Twining* demonstrated no more sensitivity to the accused criminal's claim of the abridgment of his constitutional rights than he did to the oft-pressed contention that the government had trespassed upon the property right. In dissent, Moody vigorously challenged the majority's niggardly application of the federal statute commanding the eight-hour day in public work and its refusal to find the Employers' Liability Act constitutional. He was no less an advocate on the bench than off; his forceful presence in his new position brought new ideas and new life to a tired Court. Very possibly on the threshold of his most significant national service, Moody's career was cut painfully short. Both personally and politically, now ex-President Theodore Roosevelt mourned the loss.

Justiceships are conferred for life, and incapacitation is no bar to continued tenure. Since Moody had served less than three years on the Court, he fell far short of meeting the requirements of the general judicial retirement act. His and the Court's friends, however, sponsored special legislation providing for his retirement with full pay. The bill became law in June 1910, but the fallen Justice delayed his resignation for five more months.[77]

The vacancy that Moody's condition presaged was not the first that President Taft would be called upon to fill, for just before the opening of the 1909 term on October 24, Rufus W. Peckham died suddenly. Delaying the opening of the session until November 1, the seven remaining members of the Court journeyed by private train to Albany for the funeral.[78]

A believer in the need for an active Court sensitive to the task of guarding property and contractual rights, his death generated little comment aside from the formal resolutions of the bar and the Court, which were made a part of the record. This was an era of reform in which courts were expected to accommodate the changes society desired, and, though Peckham was not hostile to such change, he insisted upon measuring it carefully against the protections he found in the Constitution. His opinion in *Allgeyer* gave a toehold to the doctrine of freedom of contract that he was able to fortify with the controversial decision in *Lochner*. Along with Brewer, he most often saw impermissible abridgments of this freedom that escaped the majority. Also, the attempt to confine state regulatory power by limiting the concept of property affected with a public interest was attractive to Peckham, though not to the majority. If the Court had been composed of Peckhams, it would have incurred much greater hostility during the period of his service. Yet with his concern for due process in economic matters, he also displayed, under that broad standard, an uncommon sensitivity to certain noneconomic claims. For instance, in cases dealing with Chinese persons he often dissented from the Court's tendency to rubber stamp administrative procedures. Since Peckham's views often coincided with Brewer's, and since the New Yorker was somewhat shy and retiring, he tended to be overshadowed by his more aggressive and colorful colleague from Kansas.

NOTES

1. Paul T. Heffron, "Theodore Roosevelt and the Appointment of Mr. Justice Moody," *Vanderbilt Law Review* 18 (March 1965):545-47.

2. Henry F. Pringle, *The Life and Times of William Howard Taft*, 2 vols. (New York: Farrar & Rinehart, 1939), pp. 313-17. Roosevelt's letter of advice to Taft, dated March 15, 1906, is in Elting E. Morison, ed., *The Letters of Theodore Roosevelt*, 8 vols. (Cambridge: Harvard University Press, 1951-54), 5:183-86.

3. Roosevelt to Elihu Root, August 18, 1906, and Roosevelt to Taft, March 15, 1906, in Morison, *Letters of Roosevelt*, 5:368, 185-86; Willard L. King, *Melville Weston Fuller: Chief Justice of the United States 1888-1910*, Phoenix ed. (Chicago: University of Chicago Press, 1967), pp. 307-8; for the attempt to dislodge Harlan to create an additional vacancy, see Heffron, "Appointment of Moody," pp. 558-59; and *New York Herald*, February 12, 1910.

4. Roosevelt to Lodge, September 4, 1906, in Morison, *Letters of Roosevelt*, 5:396-97; Lodge to Roosevelt, September 10, 1906, in *Selections from the Correspondence of Theodore Roosevelt and Henry Cabot Lodge 1884-1918*, 2 vols. (New York: Charles Scribner's Sons, 1925), 2:229-30; and for Moody's opposition to Lurton, see Heffron, "Appointment of Moody," pp. 559-60.

5. Lodge to Roosevelt, September 10, 1906, in *Correspondence of Roosevelt and Lodge*, 2:230; and Heffron, "Appointment of Moody," pp. 557, 562-65.

6. James F. Watts, Jr., "William Moody," in *The Justices of the Supreme Court of the United States 1789-1969: Their Lives and Major Opinions*, ed. Leon Friedman and Fred L. Israel, 4 vols. (New York: R.R. Bowker Co. and Chelsea House, Publishers, 1969), 3:1805-16.

7. Roosevelt to Lodge, September 12, 1906, in Morison, *Letters of Roosevelt*, 5:407-8; and Heffron, "Appointment of Moody," p. 565, n. 83. Roosevelt's nomination of a man so closely associated with the administration was widely questioned. In an editorial entitled "The Greatest Merger of Them All," a reference to the President's concern over business consolidation, the *New York Times* attacked the appointment. Realizing that a new spate of federal legislation would have to undergo the scrutiny of the Court, the writer said that a nomination to the High Bench should be made on an assessment of the character, ability, independence, and learning of the nominee, not on his political views (*New York Times*, November 9, 1906).

8. Moody had asked the Court to decline jurisdiction in a case where the plaintiff had recovered damages against a railroad for the infection of cattle caused by a violation of the Secretary of Agriculture's quarantine regulations. The unanimous Court not only accepted jurisdiction but found that the rules promulgated by the Secretary were a regulation of internal commerce that could not be authorized by the congressional act involved (Illinois Central R.R. v. McKendree, 203 U.S. 514 [1906]).

9. Virginia v. West Virginia, 206 U.S. 290 (1907); and Georgia v. Tennessee Copper Co., 206 U.S. 203 (1907). Eight years later the Court issued a final order in the case. Three Justices objected to the majority's determination of the cutback in sulphur emissions required. Upon reapplication of the companies in the next session, the order was revised so production could be maintained at roughly the same level as in the past (Georgia v. Tennessee Copper Co., 237 U.S. 474 [1915], 240 U.S. 650 [1916]).

10. Kansas v. United States, 204 U.S. 331 (1907); and Kansas v. Colorado, 206 U.S. 46 (1907).

11. Excerpts from the briefs are in Kansas v. Colorado, 206 U.S. 46, 57-79 (1907).

12. Kansas v. Colorado, 206 U.S. 46, 83 (1907).

13. Id. at 91.

14. In a story speculating upon Hoyt's candidacy for the Supreme Court, the writer said the ideas that Hoyt had urged upon the Justices in *Kansas* v. *Colorado* were those of his superior, President Roosevelt (*New York Sun*, November 5, 1909).

15. Irving Brant, *The Bill of Rights: Its Origin and Meaning* (Indianapolis: Bobbs-Merrill Co., 1965), p. 65; Collector v. Day, 78 U.S. (11 Wall.) 113, 124 (1871); and Northern Securities Co. v. United States, 193 U.S. 197, 364 (1904).

16. Patterson v. Colorado, 205 U.S. 454, 462, 463 (1907).

17. Id. at 464.

18. Brief for Appellant, pp. 15-23, Pettibone v. Nichols, 203 U.S. 192 (1906).

19. Walter Lord, *The Good Years: From 1900 to the First World War* (New York: Harper & Bros., 1960), pp. 150-62.

20. Pettibone v. Nichols, 203 U.S. 192 (1906). Idaho decided to try Haywood first. The trial captured the national spotlight, and Darrow publicized the trial not as a prosecution of a man for a crime but rather as a persecution of unions and men who labored. The jury surmised Haywood's guilt but rendered a verdict of not guilty on the basis of insufficient proof. The acquittal of Haywood led Idaho authorities to release Moyer and Pettibone as well (Lord, *Good Years*, pp. 162-78).

21. Illinois Central R.R. v. McKendree, 203 U.S. 514, 530 (1906).

22. Union Bridge Co. v. United States, 204 U.S. 364, 387 (1907).

23. Ellis v. United States, 206 U.S. 246, 255 (1907).

24. Id. at 266.

25. Schlemmer v. Buffalo, Rochester & Pittsburg Ry., 205 U.S. 1, 12, 13, 14 (1907).

26. Texas & Pacific Ry. v. Abileen Cotton Oil Co., 204 U.S. 426 (1907); Southern Ry. v. Tift, 206 U.S. 428 (1907); and Cincinnati, Hamilton & Dayton Ry. v. ICC, 206 U.S. 142, 154 (1907).

27. United States v. Heinszen, 206 U.S. 370 (1907).

28. Wilson v. Shaw, 204 U.S. 24, 31, 32 (1907).

29. William H. Harbaugh, *The Life and Times of Theodore Roosevelt*, rev. ed. (New York: Crowell-Collier Publishing Co., Collier Books, 1963), p. 204; and W.A. Swanberg, *Pulitzer* (New York: Charles Scribner's Sons, 1967), pp. 363-68.

30. Swanberg, *Pulitzer*, pp. 371-73; United States v. Smith, 173 Fed. 227, 232 (1909); and Roosevelt quoted in Swanberg, *Pulitzer*, p. 380.

31. Swanberg, *Pulitzer*, pp. 382-83; United States v. Press Publishing Co., 219 U.S. 1 (1911); and *New York World*, February 18, 1909.

32. Federal Employers' Liability Act, ch. 3073, 34 Stat. 232 (1906).

33. Employers' Liability Cases, 207 U.S. 463, 498, 504 (1908).

34. Id. at 509.

35. Id. at 521-22, 529, 532.

36. Id. at 541.

37. Erdman Act, ch. 370, 30 Stat, 424, 428 (1898); and U.S., Congress, Senate, United States Strike Commission. *Report on the Chicago Strike of June-July, 1894*, S. Ex. Doc. 7, 53rd Cong., 3d sess., 1895, p. LIII.

38. Adair v. United States, 208 U.S. 161, 174, 175, 178, 180 (1908).

39. Id. at 184. Employés is a variant spelling the Court used inconsistently.

40. Id. at 186, 187, 189-90. In *Lincoln Federal Labor Union* v. *Northwestern Iron & Metal Co.*, 335 U.S. 525 (1949), the Court, in effect, overruled the *Adair* case.

41. Adair v. United States, 208 U.S. 161, 191, 192 (1908). Holmes had arrived at this position in 1873, when he said that "it is no sufficient condemnation of legislation that it favors one class at the expense of another; for much or all legislation does that; and none the less when the *bona fide* object is the greatest good of the greatest number" ("The Gas-

Stokers' Strike," *American Law Review* 7 [April 1873]:584; reprinted and attributed in Felix Frankfurter, "The Early Writings of O. W. Holmes, Jr.," *Harvard Law Review* 44 [March 1931]:795-96).

42. Loewe v. Lawlor (Danbury Hatters' Case), 208 U.S. 274, 292, 301 (1908).

43. See Samuel Gompers, "Labor Organizations Must Not Be Outlawed—The Supreme Court's Decision in the Hatters' Case," *American Federationist* 15 (March 1908):180, and excerpts from letters responding to the decision in ibid., pp. 161-78.

44. Armour Packing Co. v. United States, 209 U.S. 56, 87 (1908); and St. Louis, Iron Mountain & Southern Ry. v. Taylor, 210 U.S. 281 (1908).

45. Winters v. United States, 207 U.S. 564 (1908); and for an indication of McKenna's greater sympathy, see his dissent in *United States* v. *Sisseton & Wahpeton Bands of Sioux Indians* (208 U.S. 561 [1908]).

46. Brief for Appellee, Muller v. Oregon, 208 U.S. 412 (1908).

47. See Alpheus T. Mason, "The Case of the Overworked Laundress," in *Quarrels That Have Shaped the Constitution*, ed. John A. Garraty (New York: Harper & Row, 1964), pp. 176-90, in which the author focuses on the brief and the oral argument and assesses their influence.

48. Muller v. Oregon, 208 U.S. 412, 419, 420-21 (1908).

49. Id. at 421, 422.

50. *New York World*, August 13, 1905. This is a piece written by Brewer based upon his speech at Vassar.

51. General Oil Co. v. Crain, 209 U.S. 211 (1908); Asbell v. Kansas, 209 U.S. 251 (1908); Seaboard Air Line Ry. v. Seegers, 207 U.S. 73 (1907); Northern Pacific R.R. v. Minnesota, 208 U.S. 583 (1908); Mobile, Jackson & Kansas City R.R. v. Mississippi, 210 U.S. 187 (1908); Consolidated Rendering v. Vermont, 207 U.S. 541 (1908); and New York *ex rel.* Burke v. Wells, 208 U.S. 14 (1908).

52. *Ex parte* Young, 209 U.S. 123, 142, 160, 168 (1908).

53. Id. at 192, 204, 175, 183.

54. Charles Warren, *The Supreme Court in United States History*, rev. ed., 2 vols. (Boston: Little, Brown & Co., 1926), 2:717; and Act of June 18, 1910, ch. 309, 36 Stat. 539, 557.

Legislation in 1913 extended the three-judge requirement to cases involving orders by administrative boards and commissions. It further provided that if a suit was pending in the state courts to enforce such an order, the federal courts were mandated to stay proceedings until the state case had been resolved. Only in cases where the suit was not being prosecuted diligently and in good faith was an exception provided (Act of March 4, 1913, ch. 160, 37 Stat. 1013).

55. During the presidential campaign of 1908 the age of the Justices was alluded to in the prediction that the incoming president might well have four vacancies to fill on the Court. (See Eugene P. Lyle, Jr., "The Supreme Court," *Hampton's Broadway Magazine* 21 [October 1908]:437.)

56. Berea College v. Kentucky, 211 U.S. 45 (1908).

57. Id. at 62, 67, 69. Harlan's opinion was praised and the majority's condemned in the *New York Evening Post*, November 11, 1908.

58. Twining v. New Jersey, 211 U.S. 78, 99, 106, 111 (1908).

59. Id. at 113.

60. Id. at 116.

61. Id. at 123. Harlan was vindicated when the Court in *Malloy* v. *Hogan* (378 U.S. 1 [1964]) accepted the conclusion he had urged here.

62. United States v. Bitty, 208 U.S. 393 (1908); and Keller v. United States, 213 U.S. 138, 148-49 (1909).

63. John M. Blum, *The Republican Roosevelt* (Cambridge: Harvard University Press, 1954), pp. 104-5; and oral argument of Attorney General Charles G. Bonaparte quoted in United States v. Delaware & Hudson Co., 213 U.S. 366, 404, 405 (1909).

64. United States v. Delaware & Hudson Co., 213 U.S. 366, 407, 412, 416 (1909).

65. Id. at 419.

66. Harriman v. ICC, 211 U.S. 407, 419-20 (1908).

67. Holmes to Pollock, April 23, 1910, in Mark D. Howe, ed., *Holmes-Pollock Letters*, 2d ed., 2 vols. (Cambridge: Harvard University Press, Belknap Press, 1961), 1:163.

68. Murray v. Wilson Distilling Co., 213 U.S. 151 (1909).

69. Hammond Packing Co. v. Arkansas, 212 U.S. 322 (1909); Leech v. Louisiana, 214 U.S. 175 (1909); Welch v. Swasey, 214 U.S. 91 (1909); New York *ex rel*. Silz v. Hesterberg, 211 U.S. 31 (1908); North American Cold Storage Co. v. Chicago, 211 U.S. 306 (1908); Knop v. Monongahela River Consolidated Coal & Coke Co., 211 U.S. 485 (1909); and McLean v. Arkansas, 211 U.S. 539, 550 (1909).

70. United States v. Shipp, 203 U.S. 563, 571 (1906).

71. Id. at 563.

72. United States v. Shipp, 214 U.S. 386, 414, 417, 418, 423 (1909). Shipp's view that the legal process invited delay and bore some responsibility for the incidence of lynching was shared by some legal commentators. For instance, see Charles J. Bonaparte, "Lynch Law and Its Remedy," *Yale Law Journal* 8 (May 1899):335-43; and Hannis Taylor, "True Remedy for Lynch-Law," *American Law Review* 41 (March 1907):255-66.

73. United States v. Shipp, 214 U.S. 386, 426, 433, 438, 437 (1909).

74. United States v. Shipp, 215 U.S. 580 (1909). Holmes had told Fuller that such a grave offense deserved a one-year sentence (King, *Fuller*, p. 327).

75. See Ray Stannard Baker, "What Is a Lynching?" *McClure's Magazine* 24 (January-February 1905):299-314, 422-30; reprinted in *Following the Color Line* (New York: Doubleday, Page, 1908), pp. 175-215.

76. Charles H. Butler, *A Century at the Bar of the Supreme Court of the United States* (New York: G. P. Putnam's Sons, 1942), pp. 185-86; and Watts, "William Moody," in *Justices of the Supreme Court*, 3:1820.

77. Moody officially retired on November 20, 1910; he died on July 2, 1917.

78. Clerk's Scrapbook No. 7, p. 43, Records of the Supreme Court (Office of the Clerk), Record Group 267, National Archives, Washington, D.C.; and 215 U.S. v-xiii.

chapter 8

IN HIS IMAGE: TAFT REMAKES THE COURT, 1909-12

Still longing for the chief justiceship, Taft brought a unique judicial background to the presidency that made him especially sensitive to the task of making appointments to the High Court. The President had a candidate in mind for the Peckham vacancy, but he had to overcome an obstacle—the appointee's age. Taft worried about senility on the Court and believed that only men under the age of sixty were suitable candidates for the High Bench.[1]

This general rule, however, was not enough to stand in his way of fulfilling a pledge Taft had made to himself—that his former colleague on the Sixth Circuit, Horace H. Lurton, now professor of law at Vanderbilt, should crown his career by service on the Supreme Court. Lurton was a Democrat, but, according to Taft, a right-thinking Southern Democrat. As a young man the appointee had seen considerable action with the Confederate forces. Beginning in 1875 in the judicial system of Tennessee, he worked his way up to the state supreme court, from which he was plucked for service on the Sixth Circuit in 1893. That a nonpartisan appointment might redound to the President's political benefit, an idea that Taft had tried to sell Roosevelt, was far less important to Taft at this juncture than his personal feeling that Lurton deserved a place on the Supreme Court. So the fact that Lurton, at sixty-five, was a risky appointment in terms of tenure did not dissuade the President. Despite some opposition from the AF of L, based primarily upon the nominee's opinion against the constitutionality of a workmen's compensation law, Lurton was speedily confirmed and sworn in on January 3, 1910.[2]

Lurton was short, about the height of his predecessor Peckham, and squarely built. Fairly healthy, he had thinning grey hair, closely cut, and a bushy, full, grey mustache. When he took off his pince-nez, his clear and firmly fixed dark eyes could be seen. Just after Lurton came on the Court, a newspaper picked up a story that Lurton and Harlan were in opposing forces during the Civil War and that Harlan had tried to kill Lurton with a cannonball.[3] But that was long ago, and both men probably appreciated the fact that fortune had spared them to be colleagues on the nation's highest court.

With Peckham dead and Moody disabled, the Court began the term with seven members, and during the session it sought to avoid policy determinations, such as that called for in the antitrust prosecution of the Standard Oil Company. Despite the protests of the business community that the Court's failure to produce a decision was having an unsettling effect on the economy, Fuller preferred to await a full bench. Still there were cases that the Court could not avoid.

The issue of the extent of state power over foreign corporations posed special difficulty for the Justices in a series of decisions that heralded a departure from existing doctrine. The first involved Western Union's protest against Kansas' imposition of a charter fee based upon a certain percentage of the corporation's capital stock as a condition for being allowed to continue a domestic business within the state. Western Union claimed this tax was a burden on interstate commerce. Harlan, joined by Day and Brewer, noted the absent Moody's concurrence and then pronounced the tax "a burden on the company's interstate commerce and its privilege to engage in that commerce."[4] Deeming the levy unconstitutional, Harlan said the state cannot demand its exaction as the price of the company's right to do an intrastate business. White concurred, as he distinguished between a state's power to prescribe the conditions for doing business in the state initially, a situation in which he would acknowledge greater discretion, and the power to impose new conditions upon a foreign corporation that had already met the admission requirements. In the instant case White said the corporation had acquired a property right that was not subject to confiscation.

Holmes wrote the dissenting opinion, joined by Fuller and McKenna. Because Harlan cited Moody's agreement, Holmes noted that Peckham had participated in the case and had sided with the minority. The Massachusetts Justice based his dissent on the long-recognized precedent "that as to foreign corporations seeking to do business wholly within a State, that State is the master, and may prohibit or tax such business at will." Kansas recognized the right of the corporation to do an interstate business in the state, and, to Holmes, it was "more logical and more true to the scheme of the Union to recognize that what comes in only for a special purpose can claim constitutional protection only in its use for that purpose and for nothing else." In a companion case concerning the Kansas imposition, Holmes continued his protest:

I am quite unable to believe that an otherwise lawful exclusion from doing business within a State becomes an unlawful or unconstitutional burden on commerce among States because if it were let in it would help to pay the bills. Such an exclusion is not a burden on the foreign commerce at all, it simply is the denial of a collateral benefit. If foreign commerce does not pay its way by itself I see no right to demand an entrance for domestic business to help it out.[5]

A month later the same majority, now united in a Harlan opinion and still citing Moody's agreement, decided that a company could enjoin the Arkansas secretary of state from proclaiming that it was forbidden, under heavy penalties, from doing any domestic business in the state. At issue again was the right of the state to impose a fee upon a corporation based upon its total capital stock. Holmes, Fuller, and McKenna dissented without further elaboration, but only Fuller and McKenna dissented in the final case in the area. The Court opinion, written by Harlan, now joined by Holmes, held that an out-of-state correspondence school, which had not filed a financial statement, the state prerequisite for gaining access to its courts, was correct in claiming that the Kansas requirement violated the commerce clause. Harlan found the filing of a financial statement a burden on interstate commerce, and, since the prohibition on access to the state courts was intertwined with it, he concluded, the entire statute seeking to regulate foreign correspondence schools was constitutionally invalid.[6]

These decisions imposed new limitations on the hitherto wide discretionary authority enjoyed by states to exclude or regulate foreign corporations in their domestic business. Earlier state regulations and taxes fell because they were clear burdens on interstate commerce. Now the majority took these earlier decisions and widened their application. The directors of interstate corporations had always considered the latitude given to states to regulate foreign corporations an insufferable burden, but until the 1909 term they had repeatedly run into broad Court approval of such state power. The majority now indicated its willingness to give the corporations a wedge to protect themselves from some forms of state regulation. The importance of this change in the law, hammered out in the space of a few months in a single term, cannot be overemphasized. Still this new and sympathetic approach was not reflected in other cases involving corporations and should not be taken as indicative of a broader Court receptivity to corporate claims. For instance, in two cases during the term the Court showed no sympathy for railroads claiming that plaintiffs had collusively joined parties to prevent removal to the federal courts on the basis of diversity jurisdiction.[7]

In most assessments of the constitutionality of state action, the Court came to a conclusion without much internal difficulty, but another case split the bench four to three. The issue raised in *Kuhn* v. *Fairmont Coal Company* was whether a decision of the highest court in West Virginia would be binding on the federal courts. A majority led by Harlan decided the federal courts were not bound. Picking up Justice Field's attack on the idea of a federal common law in the 1890s, Holmes, dissenting with White and McKenna, chided the Court for its refusal to recognize the authority of the state's judge-made law. "The law of a State," he said, "does not become something outside of the state court and independent of it by being called the common law. Whatever it is called, it is the law as declared by the state judges and nothing else."[8] Obviously, the dissenters were recognizing what Field had seen earlier—that rival courts sitting in the same locality administering different laws were an anomaly even within a system of federalism.

In railroad matters the Court ruled that Iowa and Georgia could provide for the attachment of railway cars. Furthermore, in the absence of congressional regulation, Georgia could prescribe requirements for interstate trains in approaching dangerous railway crossings and fasten liability upon the railroads for wrongful death. South Carolina could impose a penalty upon carriers refusing to pay claims for loss of property within a specified time, and Kansas could require a railroad company operating a branch line under a state charter to run a passenger service over that line to the border of the state, despite claims that there were no facilities at the border and no reason to terminate travel there. On the negative side, Arkansas' attempt to enforce a statute requiring railroads to furnish cars to a shipper on demand was viewed as a burden on interstate commerce. Nebraska could not compel a railroad at its own expense and under the compulsion of heavy fines to provide side tracks to reach grain elevators, because such a law violated due process by taking property without compensation. Finally, Missouri's vigorous attempt to force railroads to stop interstate passenger trains at junction points with other lines was deemed a burden on interstate commerce.[9]

Cases coming from the island possessions, especially the Philippines, continued to provide the stimulus for Court excursions into the meaning of the Bill of Rights. Generally the Justices, often with Harlan dissenting, gave Philippine justice a wide berth in approving procedures that seemed to undercut some of the individual guarantees in the Constitution. But this permissive attitude had its limits, as the case of *Weems* v. *United States* illustrates. Paul A. Weems, a disbursing officer of the Bureau of Coast Guard and Transportation, was convicted for falsifying an official document and sentenced to a jail term of fifteen years and fined 4,000 pesetas. Since at the worst Weems had appropriated 612 pesetas, the majority Justices confronted the rigor of the old Spanish law and were appalled.

Speaking of the minimum sentence under the law, McKenna, for a four-man majority, outlined Weems's plight. Confinement is at "hard and painful labor" with chains at the ankle and wrist; even after completing the sentence his liberty is perpetually limited. McKenna continued: "Such penalties for such offenses amaze those who have formed their conception of the relations of a state to even its offending citizens from the practice of the American commonwealths, and believe that it is a precept of justice that punishment for crime should be graduated and proportioned to offense." He quickly got to the contention, not raised in the Philippine courts, that such punishment is cruel and unusual. Although acknowledging that the Court has generally refused to review claims not properly brought to the lower courts' attention,

McKenna cited rules that afforded the High Bench discretion to "notice a plain error not assigned."[10]

The language of the Eighth Amendment barring cruel and unusual punishment was also a part of the Philippine bill of rights, and the two provisions, continued McKenna, must mean the same thing. What is specifically prohibited, the Justice conceded, is unclear, but after detailing the horrors of the Philippine penal law, McKenna concluded that the sentence violates the ban on cruel and unusual punishment. Justifying the liberty he took in his interpretation, he said the provision was clearly intended to check the power of government to define crimes and their punishment. What is proscribed by the constitutional language, the Justice insisted, can and should change over time. He elaborated:

Time works changes, brings into existence new conditions and purposes. Therefore a principle to be vital must be capable of wider application than the mischief which gave it birth. This is peculiarly true of constitutions. . . . In the application of a constitution, therefore, our contemplation cannot be only of what has been but of what may be. Under any other rule a constitution would indeed be as easy of application as it would be deficient in efficacy and power. Its general principles would have little value and be converted by precedent into impotent and lifeless formulas. Rights declared in words might be lost in reality. And this had been recognized. The meaning and vitality of the Constitution have developed against narrow and restrictive construction.[11]

McKenna concluded that since the Philippine law's provision for punishment was in itself a violation of the cruel and unusual bar, neither the conviction nor the law could stand. The lower court was directed to dismiss the prosecution. For the first time the Supreme Court had invoked the words of the Eighth Amendment in behalf of a convicted defendant.

McKenna's manifesto concerning the need to interpret the rights guaranteed the individual by the Constitution liberally and with sensitivity to present conditions is impressive; it could easily have been penned in the 1960s when the Court expanded the protections of the Bill of Rights. McKenna, the Justice from California appointed to fill the shoes of a giant, Stephen J. Field, here not only carried on his predecessor's concern for the protection of certain individual rights but also gave eloquent expression to the very modern rationale that has been primarily responsible for our Constitution's ability to stand the test of time. The initially hesitant and awkward McKenna was now also drafting a blueprint for the future.

White, in a dissent that Holmes joined, pointed to the fact that his four colleagues in interpreting the Eighth Amendment had limited federal legislative power at home as well. Calling the majority's construction of the clause without precedent and an affront to its wording, White said the "interpretation curtails the legislative power of Congress to define and punish crime by asserting a right of judicial supervision over the exertion of that power, in disregard of the distinction between the legislative and judicial department of the Government."[12] As a spokesman for a static view of the Constitution, the Louisianian bristled at the expansive words of McKenna.

The Californian again was the spokesman for a narrow majority in *ICC* v. *Chicago, Rock Island & Pacific Railway Company*, a major ICC opinion delivered on the last day of the term. The Hepburn Act of 1906 had afforded the ICC the power to impose rates subject to judicial review. In this case the lower federal court decided against the commission on the ground that the rates established by the ICC designed to eliminate a competitive rivalry between communities had exceeded its authority. All members of the Court agreed with the lower court that action justified by the commission on that basis would be beyond its statutory mandate, but McKenna ruled that the reduction of freight rates sought by the ICC was based upon a thorough investigation that concluded they were too high. The finding that the pre-existing rate was unreasonable, the Justice concluded, "is peculiarly the province of the commission to make, and that its findings are fortified by presumptions of truth."[13] White, Holmes, and Lurton took issue with the Court's willingness to defer to the administrative agency.

The end of the 1909 term revealed that Lurton, quickly pressed into full service, had responded with a fair share of opinions. But it was the ever ready Holmes who led the Court with thirty-four opinions, over 20 percent of the High Bench's output.

Having begun the session with seven active members, the Court ended the term with the same number. On March 28, 1910, Justice David J. Brewer died in his sleep. In his twenty years of service the Kansan had written 719 opinions, 157 of them in dissent. The words of praise showered upon Brewer in the formal memorial proceedings of the Court seemed more than perfunctory as the members of the bar responded in kind to the late Justice's personal warmth and generosity. Although other observers were not so rash as to label the highly competent Justice unfit, Roosevelt's general impression that Brewer was a benighted judge unswervingly hostile to vigor in government and unduly solicitous of corporate property interests was shared by many.[14] However, the tendency to characterize Justices simply as liberal or conservative, as hostile or friendly to the popular majority, often leads to considerable distortion.

Interpreters of Brewer have been content to follow the outlines sketched by critics who took Brewer's off-the-bench speeches in the 1890s railing against anarchism and the attack of the masses upon property, along with general wording in some of his opinions, as the measure of the man and of the judge. Rarely has any attention been focused on his other speeches, such as those that opposed American colonialism or supported women in their quest for political rights. Interpreters have assumed that Brewer had inherited the mantle of his uncle, Stephen J. Field, and was the ideological leader of the Court, that his platform rhetoric characterized his decision making, and that his concern for property rights exhausted his judicial interest.[15] Brewer was a prime dissenter during his two decades on the High Bench, often fighting a majority that did not budge. To label such a Justice the ideological leader of the Court seems, as best, perverse. Brewer never succeeded in getting the Court to limit the type of property it characterized as affected with a public interest, and though he made some headway with the incorporation of a freedom of contract into constitutional doctrine, the victory was limited. The Kansan did, indeed, fear the power of government and was wary about the increasing governmental activity that seemed to characterize the period, but his role as Justice, if not his general philosophy, led him to approach the task of deciding cases more pragmatically than ideologically. Philosophic certainty was reserved for the platform; it had less serviceability in the conference room. For instance, despite Roosevelt's harsh opinion, it was Brewer who had given the President a victory in the Northern Securities Company prosecution. Also repeatedly the Kansan had shown considerable respect for the exertions of state govenment. He had repeatedly argued that corporations must not be shielded by the Court from the burdens of state taxations.

Aside from considering cases on their facts, he often responded to their moral dimensions. His concept of due process embraced more than the property interest. Brewer's castigation of the Court and the nation for their treatment of the Chinese rings out as clearly as Harlan's castigation of bias against another race. Unwilling to go as far as Harlan, the Kansan, however, saw in the due process clause requirements for fairness and equity that gave to that clause an expansive potential, which, when emptied of its content of property protection, could in the future be refilled with the protection of other individual rights. His good humor and his willingness, despite division, to work as a member of the team were quite apparent. His quality of mind was especially acute in dissent when he dissected the majority's reasoning. Brewer was an activist on the Court, believing the judiciary had a special role to fill within the governmental system and that lack of popular support was no reason to abdicate this role. In this sense he was a doctrinaire on an institutional, not a decision-making, level. Despite Brewer's undeserved reputation as a single-minded servant of outmoded constitutional doctrines, he merits study as a sensitive and responsible Justice seeking to come to grips with himself and his society in a changing age.[16]

Alert to the problems of an undermanned Court, Taft moved quickly to find a replacement for Brewer. In November 1909 the President had expressed unguarded admiration for the governor of New York, Charles Evans Hughes, and indicated a desire to offer him a seat on the Court. Despite Taft's high regard for the Court and its supreme importance in the society, there was more than a hint of political strategy in the President's consideration of Hughes for the Supreme Court. His initial maneuvering with Hughes seemed to suggest a desire to sidetrack a potential rival in 1912. Finding that the New Yorker, who was completing his term as governor, was interested in the appointment, Taft offered it to him. To add inducement the President said that, since the chief justiceship might soon fall vacant, Hughes might consider himself a candidate for succession. Taft added a postscript:

Don't misunderstand me as to the Chief Justiceship. I mean if that office were now open, I should offer it to you and it is probable that if it were to become vacant during my term, I should promote you to it; but, of course, conditions change, so that it would not be right for me to say by way of promise what I would do in the future. Nor, on the other hand, would I have you think that your declination now would prevent my offering you the higher position, should conditions remain as they are.[17]

The President wanted to preserve his freedom of action but not mislead Hughes. Roosevelt, in trying to place his friend on the Court, also promised the reluctant candidate elevation should the center-seat vacancy occur, but Taft always took the promise with a grain of salt. Essentially, the President was seeking to convince Hughes that an acceptance of appointment now would not preclude later elevation. Hughes accepted, and in regard to the center seat he said he wanted Taft "to act freely and without embarrassment in accordance with your best judgment at that time."[18] The President was elated with the acceptance and announced the nomination on April 25, 1910, less than a month after Brewer's death.

Taft's qualified promise of the chief justiceship was a tribute to Hughes's national prominence. Not since Salmon P. Chase in 1864 had an appointee to the Court been as politically visible as Hughes. He had emerged from a successful New York law practice only a little over five years earlier, when he accepted the post of counsel to a state legislative committee investigating gas rates. His success in exposing excessive rates led to his appointment later in the same year as counsel to another committee investigating the insurance industry. This latter work, which brought him not only local but also national attention, paved the way for his successful bid for the New York governorship in 1906. Reelected in 1908, Hughes fought for the passage of workmen's compensation legislation, and sought honest, efficient, and responsible government. The governor shared Taft's respect for the authority and importance of the Supreme Court in the American constitutional system.[19]

Despite the criticism of the oft-defeated Democratic presidential candidate William Jennings Bryan, who labeled the nominee a tool of corporate interests, the appointment was received with enthusiasm, and Hughes was confirmed on May 2, 1910.[20] He continued to serve as governor of New York until the opening of the 1910 term when he resigned and took his seat on the Supreme Court.

At age forty-seven Charles Evans Hughes was the youngest appointee to the Court since John Marshall Harlan's accession in 1877. About five feet, eleven inches tall with a well-proportioned frame, Hughes wore a mustache and closely trimmed beard, both of which were greying. Also his hairline was receding and touches of grey were apparent in his hair. His imposing countenance, with closely set eyes and a generous, straight nose, often led contemporaries to judge him to be a taller man than he was.

An event that had been on the minds of both Taft and Hughes occurred sooner than either man expected. Although the last term had been hard for him, and although his colleagues had begun to see some evidence of the ravages of age, Chief Justice Melville W. Fuller's death of a heart attack at his summer home in Sorrento, Maine, on July 4, 1910, came as a surprise. Fuller, who died at age seventy-seven, had headed the Court for twenty-two years and had carried out his steadfast resolve never to retire.

In his last few years the Chief began to dissent alone and without opinion, apparently disturbed by the drift of the Court. His leadership of the High Bench was primarily administrative, and Holmes, who had the opportunity of serving under four Chief Justices, considered Fuller the most able administrative leader of them all.[21] His role was that of peace maker. Despite decisional division, the harmony of members' relationships was not disturbed due to Fuller's good offices. The Chief had strong ideas about preserving the authority of the states within the federal system, and he repeatedly fought the expansive use of the fellow servant rule to defeat employee injury claims. Often allied with Brewer and Peckham in dissent, he urged more constitutional protection for the rights of property. Dissent bothered Fuller, but he had neither the will nor the skill to curb it during his years on the Court; in fact, his personal readiness to dissent tended to encourage others. To call the Court during his years the Fuller Court is largely a stylistic convention, for though, at times, Fuller led his colleagues, as in *Pollock*, more often he followed. He had outlived the "giants" on the Court into whose circle he had entered with some trepidation. Coming from relative obscurity, Fuller had become Chief Justice of the United States, a position he respected and one for which he demanded respect. He had a few visions of the future, as he focused his efforts upon doing the job imposed upon him in the present. Fuller worried about the growth of government and saw a new era approaching that was different from the one he had known. He was not a great Chief Justice, but he served his country and the Court in a time of difficult transition with competence and humility.

As the President contemplated the vacancy, he was deeply embroiled in a major split within his party over tariff and conservation matters. With considerable longing, he said to William Moody: "It seems strange that the one place in the government which I would have liked to fill myself I am forced to give to another." With feelings in turmoil, he contemplated the task before him: his appointment of a young man like Hughes to the top spot would probably place the chief justiceship permanently beyond his reach. Facing this prospect, he hesitated. Newspapers continually predicted that Hughes would be elevated, but there was no widespread popular demand for Hughes, and Taft was not without advice as to other possibilities. Word reached him revealing John Marshall Harlan's ambition for the post, interpreted as the capping of a long and honorable career on the Court. Taft responded: "I'll do no such damned thing. I won't make the Chief Justiceship a blue ribbon for the final years of any member of the Court. I want someone who will coordinate the activities of the Court and who has a reasonable expectation of serving ten or twenty years on the bench." Harlan was as bitterly disappointed as was Field before him in seeing this honor elude him, and, as with Field, his ambition shifted to establishing a record tenure. Elihu Root, a distinguished constitutional lawyer and former Secretary of War, was also suggested, but Taft said that Root was too old and did not have in him "that length of hard, routine work and constant attention to the business of the Court and to the reform of its methods which a Chief Justice ought to have."[22]

This delay was working against the elevation for Hughes, for when the Court convened in October the former governor was now the most junior member of the bench. Taft asked Attorney General George W. Wickersham to poll the members of the Court as to their preference as to which of the sitting Justices should be elevated to the top spot. Edward D. White, Cleveland's 1894 appointee, garnered the most support. The Louisianian also received support from congressional leaders who called upon the President to indicate their preference for White over Hughes.[23] Although it is difficult to see how conditions had changed between April and July to enable Taft to escape his qualified promise to Hughes, the President simply could not bring himself to seal off his possible access to the position by appointing a young and vigorous Chief Justice. Abstractly he could conceive it; practically he could not go through with it. Instead he appointed a sixty-five year old sitting Justice, certainly not the ideal candidate in terms of age. But age, in fact, was the crucial factor. With good luck, Taft, at fifty-three, might still realize his ambition. Perhaps at the right time White, in responsive gratitude, might retire. Not beyond Taft's ken was the possibility that some future Democratic President might reciprocate by looking for the best possible candidate to replace White and find that eminently qualified Republican, William Howard Taft. At any rate Taft had not, he thought, put the position beyond his ambition. The press was no more surprised than Hughes, who had harbored hopes up to the time of Taft's appointment of White. Not only had the President broken with tradition by elevating a sitting Justice to the center position, but his choice was a Democrat and a Roman Catholic as well.

Actually the President could square his lingering ambition with his obligation to the Court in the appointment of White. Not only did White have the support of most of the sitting Justices, but his sixteen-year record on the Court received Taft's approval. Also, the President hoped this elevation of a member of the Court, thoroughly versed in its procedures, would result in better leadership. What he had in mind was an administrative leader who would use the authority of his position to strive for unanimity and lessen dissent.

The Senate had received White's nomination on December 12; one week later the Louisianian was sworn in as Chief Justice of the United States. On that same December day when Taft sent White's nomination to the Senate, he also sent the names of two other nominees, one to take White's vacated seat and the other to replace Moody, who had officially retired on November 20, 1910. To fill the Moody vacancy the President selected Willis Van Devanter of Wyoming and to fill the Associate's chair that White had vacated, Taft appointed another Southern Democrat, Joseph Rucker Lamar. In the spirit of the White appointment, the Senate acted with uncommon haste and approved both men within a week.

Willis Van Devanter was a Westerner; a proper geographical distribution of the seats and Taft's personal regard had brought a man to the Court who would survive every sitting member. Born in Indiana, Van Devanter moved to Wyoming in his twenty-fifth year and gained the attention of the Republican territorial governor. The new arrival rose quickly in the ranks of power, though he suffered defeat in a Senate race in 1892. His first judicial post was chief justice of the territorial supreme court to which he was appointed at age thirty, but the pay was so poor that Van Devanter quickly returned to private practice. Under McKinley he served in the Interior Department, specializing in public land and Indian matters. His work brought him some attention, for he seemed to have a sensitivity to the problems of the American Indian. Roosevelt placed him on the Court of Appeals for the Eighth Circuit in 1903, and there he remained until Taft picked him for the Supreme Court.[24]

At fifty-one Van Devanter was the Court's second youngest member. About as tall as Hughes, the new appointee's brown hair was thinning and his temples were streaked with grey. His face, with skin that was smooth and flawless, was clean shaven, and his features were well proportioned and regular. He had a vigorous, alert look and manner. His visage was less solemn than that adopted by his colleagues, and he gave the appearance of a ruggedness associated with the West.

Joseph R. Lamar, a relative of L. Q. C. Lamar who had served as Associate Justice of the Supreme Court from 1888 to 1893, was one of Georgia's leading attorneys. He was largely responsible for drafting the state's revised civil code in 1895, and though he had served on the Georgia supreme court from 1903 to 1905, he was in private practice when the call from Taft came.

The President knew Lamar, but his candidacy was primarily the result of the eager advocacy of Archie Butt, the President's military aide, and Attorney General George W. Wickersham.[25] With his party splintering, Taft saw his future with the more conservative wing, and the choice of another Southern Democrat for the High Court could not but help garner support from powerful Southern Congressmen.

An inch shorter than Van Devanter, Lamar reflected his Southern patrician background as completely as his colleague reflected the West. At fifty-three Lamar had a full head of white hair crowning features that were generally well proportioned with a certain softness. His lips were full, and at times they seemed to curl almost of their own will into a smile.

As the Court convened in October 1910, the senior Justice, John Marshall Harlan, according to tradition, was the acting chief. He yearned for appointment to the top spot, but Harlan had probably received some inkling of President Taft's resistance to the idea. Even if he were resigned to simply keeping the center seat warm for the new appointee, Harlan could not have welcomed relinquishing it to the man to his immediate right, Edward Douglas White. First, Harlan was a Republican and White a Democrat, and more significantly, Harlan took vigorous exception to White's views on a number of major issues, including the status of the overseas possessions and the reach of the antitrust law.

The first few months of the 1910 term produced little division; disagreement was registered in only four cases, the most important of which was *Bailey* v. *Alabama*, one of the two major cases decided before Van Devanter and Lamar took their seats. The case involved an exploration into the meaning of peonage or involuntary servitude. Early in the term the Court had unanimously rejected a habeas corpus petition seeking to challenge a conviction for violating the federal statute against peonage, passed under the authority of the Thirteenth Amendment. There the attack was largely procedural and little investigation of the offense itself was necessitated. The case of Alonzo Bailey posed the problem in such a way as to require a major exploration of the meaning of the Thirteenth Amendment's ban. Bailey, a black who had been paid $15 as an advance upon wages, failed to undertake the labor and was convicted in the courts of Alabama for breaching this contract of employment, an offense made criminal by state law. Alabama had provided that, if an employee had obtained money under a written contract of employment and did not perform the work or offer to return the money, a presumption of fraud would be created. Furthermore, the accused could not rebut the presumption with testimony "as to his uncommunicated motives, purpose, or intention."[26] Bailey was found guilty, ordered to pay the employer $15, and then assessed a fine of $30 and costs. In default of payment he was required to serve at hard labor for four and one-half months. The majority of the Supreme Court decided to reverse the conviction. Instead of taking the opinion himself, after years of argument as to the vitality of the Reconstruction amendments, Harlan assigned the task to Hughes. Perhaps the temporary chief thought the new arrival could write an opinion that would win greater support.

Dismissing the plaintiff's color as irrelevant, Hughes focused on the Alabama statute that seemed to mandate a conviction on the basis of the unrebuttable presumption of fraud contained in the law. Reviewing the facts, the new Justice concluded that the law equated the breaking of an employment contract with the intent to defraud. He continued: "Unless he were fortunate enough to be able to command evidence of circumstances affirmatively showing good faith, he was helpless. He stood, stripped by the statute of the presumption of innocence, and exposed to conviction for fraud upon evidence only of a breach of contract and failure to pay."[27] Earlier Alabama legislation, Hughes noted, had tried to limit an employee's contracting rights, but the state supreme court had voided it as an abridgment of the freedom to contract. The same purpose of using the criminal law to enforce personal service contracts, the Justice said, was apparent in the present state statute.

Although acknowledging the state's right to create rules of evidence, Hughes said this authority does not enable the state to avoid constitutional restrictions. The restriction Hughes had in mind was the Thirteenth Amendment, which specifically authorizes Congress to pass legislation to effectuate its guarantees. By statute in 1867, he continued, Congress sought to void state legislation that attempted "to establish, maintain, or enforce, directly or indirectly, the voluntary or involuntary service or labor of any person as peons, in liquidation of any debt or obligation, or otherwise." Hughes ruled that this prohibition against involuntary servitude cannot be evaded by pointing to the voluntary signing of a contract. That contract, he said, subjects the defaulting party to damages but not to enforced labor. Then in a passage that revealed his broad sympathies and realistic approach, Hughes added:

Without imputing any actual motive to oppress, we must consider the natural operation of the statute here in question . . ., and it is apparent that it furnishes a convenient instrument for the coercion which the Constitution and the act of Congress forbid; an instrument of compulsion peculiarly effective as against the poor and the ignorant, its most likely victims. There is no more important concern than to safeguard the freedom of labor upon which alone can enduring prosperity be based. The provisions designed to secure it would soon become a barren form if it were possible to establish a statutory presumption of this sort and to hold over the heads of laborers the threat of punishment for crime, under the name of fraud but merely upon evidence of failure to work out their debts.[28]

Alabama's attempt to make criminal the failure to perform bargained-for service falls, the Justice concluded, under the ban of the Thirteenth Amendment. To reach this end by means of a statutory presumption, he ruled, is no more constitutionally permissible than the use of physical force to accomplish the same objective.

Holmes, here in dissent with Lurton, often searched for the principle, the generality, that would simplify the task of decision making, while cultivating a detachment from the human dimensions of the case. Generally willing to defer to state judgment, the Massachusetts Justice drew no distinction between state action that threatened property interests and that which threatened other human rights. Suggesting, despite Hughes's disclaimer, that in this case both the locale and the defendant's race were highly relevant to the majority's resolution, Holmes argued that a civil action for damages is a powerful impetus to force an employee to continue his service. Labeling the contract breach here "wrong conduct," he saw no impediment to a state intensifying the "legal motive for doing right" by adding criminal sanctions to the preexisting civil ones.[29] Despite his willingness to contend with the majority on these matters, Holmes argued that they were irrelevant to the decision here. The Massachusetts Justice contended that Bailey was not punished because of his breach of an employment contract but rather because of fraud. In the absence of the statutory presumption, Holmes said that as a judge he would have so instructed the jury and would have expected the jurors to arrive quickly at the decision that fraud had been practiced. Holmes found nothing wrong with a state trying to keep its working force in line with the force of the criminal law. The majority's concern and solicitude for the worker seemed to him misplaced, as he implied that a shiftless worker's claim should not be dignified by the mantle of the Constitution.

The second major case decided by the seven-man Court, this time unanimously, was *Muskrat* v. *United States*. Little noticed by historians but known to every student of constitutional law, the litigation posed a fundamental question concerning the source and authority of the Court's power. In 1907 Congress had passed a measure that sought to obtain a reading from the Supreme Court on the constitutionality of certain legislative measures passed since 1902 that endeavored to change aspects of the settlement then reached with the Cherokee Nation. The changes extended restrictions on alienating, encumbering, and leasing allotments and expanded the number of Indians entitled to allotments. The 1907 act attempted to empower certain Indians, whose legal costs were to be borne by the government, to sue the United States in the Court of Claims with an appeal allowed to the Supreme Court.

In a unanimous opinion Day pronounced this special jurisdictional act unconstitutional. Citing Article III, section 2 of the Constitution, he confined the exercise of judicial power to "the right to determine actual controversies arising between adverse litigants, duly instituted in courts of proper jurisdiction."[30] The Justice denied that the suit by Muskrat involved any case or controversy, saying it was simply an attempt to obtain an opinion that would not bind parties legitimately challenging the modifications of the act of 1902. Since such advisory opinions are precluded by the Constitution, Day ruled that Congress had exceeded the reach of its delegated powers in the legislation.

Day's decision, solidly anchored in both precedent and practice, reflects the proposition that the Court has no power of judicial review in the abstract but only as an incident of its need to decide a particular case properly presented by truly adverse parties. In this "progressive era" when the whole concept judicial review was attacked as inconsistent with democracy, the Justices were probably happy to indicate publicly what a circumscribed power it was.

Argued on the same day as *Muskrat* was another case that, without the special help of Congress, squarely presented the question of the constitutionality of one of the federal acts modifying the Cherokee settlement of 1902. Possibly to allow the ruling in *Muskrat* to sink in, the Court withheld a decision in the case of *Tiger* v. *Western Investment Company* and ordered a reargument before a fully manned Court. Late in the term the High Bench reached a unanimous decision that broadly supported the modifying legislation as it affected Indian rights of alienation. Day, again writing for the Court, acknowledged that Congress had full power over Indian matters, including "the right to pass legislation in the interest of the Indians as a dependent people." The legislature alone has the right to determine when its guardianship shall end, he continued, and "it has the right to vary its restrictions upon alienation of Indian lands in the promotion of what it deems the best interest of the Indian."[31] Obviously, Congress did respond to the Interior Department's concern that the landed Indian would not be a match for the shrewdness of land speculators. A vested right was not abridged, the Court ruled, because of the special relationship between the federal government and the Indians. Day's broad language upholding congressional authority tended to give the Secretary of the Interior what he was seeking. The direct route of asking Congress to authorize test cases had failed in *Muskrat*, but the traditional path had brought a case that the Court decided in conformity with the government's wishes.

The undermanned Court also decided *Noble State Bank* v. *Haskell*, in which Holmes, for the unanimous bench, in a characteristically short opinion seemed to narrow the applicability of the due process clause as a check on state authority. Ever since *Lochner* Holmes had raised objections to the use of that clause to check state legislative action. The present case involved an Oklahoma law that had created a state banking board and had authorized it to collect a fund to guarantee deposits by placing an assessment upon each bank's average daily deposits.

Addressing the due process claim, Holmes began by saying the words of the Fourteenth Amendment should not be pressed "to a drily logical extreme." Since many obviously constitutional state laws could, through a "scholastic interpretation," be found to transgress the Constitution, he said that in the absence of scientific criteria to demarcate the line between the police power and constitutional inhibitions, judges should not undermine lawmaking power. Saying that the police power reaches "all the great public needs," Holmes found no unreasonableness in the state's determination that the public welfare requires the security to depositors provided by the legislation. He continued: "The power to compel, beforehand, cooperation, and thus, it is believed, to make a failure unlikely and a general panic almost impossible, must be recognized, if government is to do its proper work, unless we can say that the means have no reasonable relation to the end." To the argument that approval here allows states to create like funds to guarantee the solvency of other business, Holmes responded that lines of decision "are pricked out by the gradual approach and contact of decisions on the opposing sides."[32] He concluded that the states are authorized to regulate banks and even prohibit them on conditions that the state alone can prescribe.

At the same time that he conceded a role to the Court in supervising state action, Holmes seemed to narrow the scope of that role. Apparently his colleagues were not initially disturbed, but when losing counsel petitioned for a rehearing before a full bench some dissatisfaction must have emerged. In his petition counsel argued that the Court had given a new and wider scope to the police power and he pointed specifically to the statement "that an ulterior public advantage may justify a comparatively insignificant taking of private property for what, in its immediate purpose, is a private use." Holmes had said that prior cases had established the proposition, but he cited none. Counsel argued that the Court had eroded a fundamental proposition of law—that private property can only be taken for a public purpose. Holmes's loose phrasing had gotten him into trouble, and although the Court denied the petition for a rehearing, the Justice was forced to modify his earlier words. Contending that counsel was still asking the Court to pass upon the wisdom of the Oklahoma law, Holmes denied that he had intended to provide a new or more expansive reading of the police power. Also, he added that though the taking of property in the case might seem to be for a private use in the most immediate sense, the ultimate purpose was clearly housed under the public use doctrine. Even with such qualifications Holmes's words seemed to promise that new measures of social legislation now working their way through state legislatures would meet an accommodating High Bench.[33]

On January 3, 1911, with the Court whole for the first time since William Moody failed to return late in the spring of 1909, Edward D. White began his tenure as Chief Justice. His enhanced authority would soon be felt as the Court turned its attention to the long delayed matter of reaching decisions in two major antitrust suits. Soon after White's appointment to the Court in

1894, the Louisianian began a campaign to read the adjective *unreasonable* into the Sherman Antitrust Act's prohibition of restraints of trade. To him the blanket prohibition made little sense in a capitalistic economy with its implicit condonation of some restraint of trade. His campaign either to write the word *unreasonable* into the law or stir Congress to action had borne little fruit. Congress seemed unwilling to take the onus of limiting the range of the legislation, both because of the act's symbolic value and because of the vigorous prosecutions under the act in the administrations of Roosevelt and Taft. The advantage White had now was that, as Chief, he could assign himself the important opinions in the *Standard Oil* and *American Tobacco* cases.

Taking advantage of the voluminous record and myriad contentions, Chief Justice White reversed the normal order of consideration and reassessed the meaning of the first two sections of the Sherman Antitrust Act, which dealt respectively with restraints of trade and attempts to monopolize. The new Chief interpreted the environment surrounding the passage of the act and the debates in Congress in 1890 as illustrating the evil at which the act was aimed—the concentration of wealth and corresponding economic power in the hands of a few. After reviewing the common law meaning of restraint of trade and its evolution through changing economic conditions in this country, White concluded that the Sherman Act sought to protect "commerce from being restrained by methods, whether old or new, which would constitute an interference, that is, an undue restraint." Since the language of the law, White continued, is so broad that it could prohibit "every conceivable contract or combination which could be made concerning trade or commerce or the subjects of such commerce," it necessarily calls for the creation of a standard to determine when violations occurred.[34] The Chief said that the standard to be applied is one of reason, which he had found intimately associated with such prohibitions in his historical survey.

Responding to the contention that such an interpretation had been rejected, White, painfully aware of his earlier lack of success, argued his ruling here was not inconsistent with the prior decisions. But recognizing that language in the cases of the 1890s was in conflict with the interpretation now reached, the new Chief overruled the earlier general language. Arguing that the rule of reason had been consistently used to determine whether the factual situation presented was within the terms of the prohibition, he added that without such an implicit recognition, "it is impossible to understand how the statute may in the future be enforced and the public policy which it establishes be made efficacious."[35]

Then taking less space than he did in his defense of the rule of reason, White found that Standard Oil had indeed violated the statute as interpreted. The record clearly showed attempts to exclude others from the market, the absorption of transportation facilities, and the creation of a system of

marketing that excluded rivals; the very success of the enterprise in fashioning its oil empire could, White concluded, be explained only in terms of
unreasonable restraints of trade. In considering the remedy White recognized
that dissolution was appropriate, but he added that such action must be taken
with regard to protecting rights of property that the antitrust act sought to
preserve. White approved the lower court's decision to dissolve the New
Jersey combination but extended the period of compliance from ninety days
to six months. The Chief, however, did object to the broad injunction issued
by the lower court against the stockholders of the subsidiary corporations
attempting to prevent any further action that would restrain trade. By
reading into the trial court's injunction the majority's new interpretation of
the Sherman Act, as allowing subsidiary corporations to enter into lawful
agreements that did not unreasonably restrain trade, White now saw no need
to change the lower court's ruling on this point. Finally, concerned with the
possibility of "an absolute cessation of interstate commerce in petroleum and
its products by such vast agencies," White lifted the ban imposed by the trial
court on all the corporations involved, some thirty-eight all told, from
engaging in any interstate commerce in oil until the dissolution had been
completed.[36]

In partial dissent to the opinion of the Court, Harlan stood alone. He was
especially disturbed by White's language that the subsidiary corporations
could restrain commerce if that restraint was not undue. This, of course, gets
to the heart of Harlan's dispute with White. That the dispute cut deep was
apparent when the Kentuckian accused his colleague and his followers of
usurping legislative functions and causing "alarm for the integrity of our
institutions." Reviewing the environment surrounding the passage of the
antitrust act, Harlan said the unqualified words in the first two sections were
the result of a deliberate attempt to meet popular fear that a new form of
slavery was in the offing—"the slavery that would result from aggregations
of capital in the hands of a few individuals and corporations controlling, for
their own profit and advantage exclusively, the entire business of the country, including the production and sale of the necessaries of life."[37]

What the two sections of the act meant, Harlan continued, was well detailed in the major decisions of the 1890s. Since these decisions fixed the
interpretation of the act, the only question left was the wisdom of the policy
embodied in the language as interpreted by the Court. This question, Harlan
asserted, could properly be considered only by Congress, whose inaction
implicitly had condoned the Court's earlier reading. Harlan had no sympathy
for the view that the new interpretation created more security for business; in
fact, he argued that it substituted chaos for settled law. "I have a strong
conviction," he continued, "that it will throw the business of the country into
confusion and invite widely-extended and harassing litigation, the injurious
effects of which will be felt for many years to come."[38]

For all his willingness to read the Reconstruction amendments broadly and place in the federal government a power to nationalize individual rights and, in so doing, modify substantially the federal system, Harlan expressed in the final paragraphs of his opinion a fervent belief in the separation of powers, and, specifically, in the right of Congress to establish policy independent of judicial interference. With words of warning to his colleagues, he said he sensed "abroad, in our land, a most harmful tendency to bring about the amending of constitutions and legislative enactments by means of judicial construction." Castigating the majority for changing congressional policy, Harlan concluded: "To overreach the action of Congress merely by judicial construction, that is, by indirection, is a blow at the integrity of our governmental system, and in the end will prove most dangerous to all."[39]

More revealing of the attitude of the majority than the *Standard Oil Company* case was its creative handling of the governmental antitrust suit against the American Tobacco Company two weeks later. The government suit had been initiated in 1907. Both the company and the government joined in the appeal of the lower court decision to the Supreme Court, the company because of the dissolution ordered and the government because of the dismissal of the case against certain defendants and the lack of specificity and force in the final order.

White, having interpreted the first two sections of the Sherman Act to his satisfaction in the *Standard Oil* case, proceeded with the rationale of the decision in the normal order. After a more elaborate survey of the factual situation than presented in the previous case, the Chief stated that the undisputed facts demonstrated a coercive pattern of consolidation. Noting that the government's case had presented inconsistent interpretations of the act, on the one hand claiming the letter of the act should be applied, and on the other, trying to reach acts of the subsidiary corporations and their acquisition of property by appealing to the spirit of the Sherman Act, White said that he had resolved this confusion through his interpretation of the antitrust act in *Standard Oil*. What White was arguing was that his new interpretation had made consistent what a literal interpretation of the act could not reconcile. Using his new construction, White said the fact that certain actions of the tobacco corporations are not embraced by the specific language of the statute presents no obstacle to the prosecution. Although reasonable restraints of trade are permissible, the Chief ruled, the first two sections of the act together do embrace "every conceivable act which could possibly come within the spirit or purpose of the prohibitions of the law, without regard to the garb in which such acts were clothed." Matching the facts with the act as interpreted, White saw the history of the combination "replete with the doing of acts which it was the obvious purpose of the statute to forbid," such as monopolizing the tobacco trade and ruthlessly driving out competitors. The company, the Chief continued, manifested "conscious wrongdoing by the form in which the various transactions were embodied from the beginning, ever changing but ever in substance the same."[40]

White concluded that "in order to enable us to award relief coterminous with the ultimate redress of the wrongs which we find to exist, we must approach the subject of relief from an original point of view."[41] This must be done, he added, in a manner that will effectuate the purpose of antitrust policy with as little injury to the general public and to the vast amount of private property interests involved. In setting up these criteria, White revealed what motivated his now successful campaign in the antitrust area— a greater solicitude for the interests of private property. He shared with dominant business leaders the fear that vigorous antitrust action would harm the economy and threaten legitimate property interests.

First, White reversed the lower court's determination of dismissal against certain indicted corporations. Second, he acknowledged the difficulty of the Court in fashioning a decree, saying the mere prohibition of stock ownership was in itself inadequate to meet the complex problems presented. He then rejected two alternatives: the issuance of a permanent injunction against the companies restraining them from participating in interstate commerce, the solution of the court below; and the appointment of a receiver. The first solution, he said, would injure the public by interfering with supply and raising prices. The second, he added, might "cause widespread and perhaps irreparable loss to many innocent people." The Chief's solution was to send the case back to the trial court to hear the parties "for the purpose of ascertaining and determining upon some plan or method of dissolving the combination and of recreating, out of the elements now composing it, a new condition which shall be honestly in harmony with and not repugnant to the law."[42] If such a solution was not found in eight months, the Court would then apply one of the two alternatives it had rejected. Pending this solution, the lower court was directed to enjoin the combination not to increase its power but with care not to injure unnecessarily the public or the stockholders.

Again in partial dissent, Harlan saw nothing wrong with the lower court's order, having little of the sympathy for the wrongdoer that the majority manifested. "I confess my inability to find," the Kentuckian continued, "in the history of this combination, anything to justify the wish that a new condition should be 'recreated' out of the mischievous elements that compose the present combination, which, together with its component parts, have, without ceasing, pursued the vicious methods pointed out by the court." To White's words that only through an erroneous interpretation of the cases of the late 1890s could one fail to see their harmony with the instant rulings, an incensed Harlan replied: "It is obvious from the opinions in the former cases, that the majority did not grope about in darkness, but in discharging the solemn duty put on them they stood out in the full glare of the 'light of reason,' and felt and said time and again that the court could not, consistently with the Constitution, and would not, usurp the functions of Congress by indulging in judicial legislation."[43] Finally, the Justice quite correctly pointed out that change in the settled statutory interpretation was completely unnecessary in these two cases, since all members agreed that the Sherman Act had been violated.

Despite Harlan's logic, backed by unassailable precedent and the firmly established procedure of the Court in interpreting statutes, the "rule of reason" had been fastened upon the Sherman Act.[44] Just as Congress had turned a deaf ear to pleas before 1911 to make a statutory change to limit the Sherman Act to undue or unreasonable restraints, it would after 1911 similarly acquiesce to the Court's new interpretation. If, as Harlan maintained, the Court was stepping beyond its proper bounds and making legislative policy, the majority of Congress, despite the protests of certain of its members, saw no need to reassert its power in the area. Harlan also charged that White's reasoning confused the rational determination of what was a restraint of trade with a determination of what was an unreasonable restraint of trade. This confusion was perhaps purposeful, for clarity worked in favor of Harlan's position.

In rewriting the Sherman Act, White had the obvious satisfaction of winning a battle thought lost. The revival of the question was the result of vigorous enforcement of the Sherman Act under the administrations of Roosevelt and Taft. Fears for the economy, for the security of private property, and for continued growth were real and pressing in the society. Such fears coincided with those White had long entertained; so, while supporting the government's point that Standard Oil and American Tobacco had to be dissolved, he wanted to reassure the economic community that this could be done without widespread dislocation and without endangering the basis of a capitalistic society. What he found in the cases was a vehicle for supporting an antitrust policy while modifying its application and effect. Most of his colleagues obviously shared a similar perception, for they were willing to follow his lead in reshaping congressional policy. The decisions reveal an active Court accepting fully the dimensions of a policy-making role. The decisions were received with some popular satisfaction, for indeed these huge corporations had been pronounced violators of the antitrust act, but White's modification of the act did excite considerable comment in the law journals.[45]

In fairness to White, his opinions did imply a certain sympathy with antitrust policy. In contrast to the literalism of Harlan, White chose flexibility in an effort both to aid the business community and effectuate what he saw as the goal of antitrust policy. The purpose was not revenge but rehabilitation of a competitive system, and though his emphasis on the disadvantages of a literal interpretation might seem specious, there was need for creative remedies in coping with these modern economic problems. In fact White's approach in *American Tobacco*, seeking some type of accommodation between antitrust policy and economic stability, became a model for the future. Taft's Attorney General George W. Wickersham picked up White's idea in *American Tobacco* and sought there and in other cases to obtain consent decrees that would bring about a lawful reorganization that could then be approved by the trial court.[46] This type of largely unofficial settlement could spare the costliness of trial and still accomplish the desired end. Since White's reinterpretation of the Sherman Act, the consent decree arrived at through negotiation between the offending company and the government has become an important tool in antitrust law enforcement.

Apparently willing to allow the Court's decision to rule the antitrust area, Congress paid closer attention when the High Bench interpreted the Pure Food and Drug Act of 1906. The first test of this consumer protection legislation came in *Hipolite Egg Company* v. *United States* in which a unanimous Court repulsed a wide-ranging attack on the act's constitutionality. Upholding the local confiscation of the company's eggs, the Justices said the seizure of such "outlaws of commerce" was clearly within the act's purpose of preventing not only the movement of such adulterated articles but the use of them as well. Such unqualified support for the legislation was eroded when the Court addressed the question of whether bottles of a patent medicine containing the representation that the contents would cure cancer were also "outlaws of commerce." Holmes, for the majority, acknowledged that the representation was misleading, but he refused to consider it the misbranding that was prohibited by the statute. Misbranding, he said, only resulted when the printed contents were not consistent with the results of a chemical analysis. The Massachusetts Justice personally had no interest, and thought the law should have no interest, in saving gullible people from themselves. Saying that honest differences of opinion concerning the curative effects of a medicine were possible, he advised Congress to restrict itself to matters of verifiable fact and not "distort the use of constitutional power to establish criteria in regions where opinions are far apart."[47]

Holmes has so often been heralded as the preeminent practitioner of judicial restraint that observers have missed what he often did in the guise of statutory interpretation. Any close reader of Holmes's opinions cannot miss the obvious hostility that the Justice had for certain legislative measures, despite his oft-repeated conclusion that the judiciary should not pass on the wisdom of such legislation. His displeasure was insinuated through what he considered more acceptable channels of judicial activity, such as statutory interpretation here in *United States* v. *Johnson*.

Hughes's dissent, joined by both Harlan and Day, is more persuasive. Limiting the misbranding section of the act to false statements about ingredients "seems to me," Hughes said, "to be opposed to the intent of Congress, and to deprive the act of a very salutary effect." If the legislature had intended to so limit the act's applicability it could have done so, the Justice continued, but the debates in Congress showed clearly the far-reaching intent behind the statutory language. Recognizing that doctors can differ in assessing the curative power of drugs, Hughes argued that "there still remains a field in which statements as to curative properties are downright falsehoods and in no sense expressions of judgment." The New Yorker saw no justice in allowing purveyors of worthless medicines to escape the prohibitions of the statute. Then reaching Holmes's implications of unconstitutionality in such applications of the statute, Hughes asked: "Why should not worthless stuff, purveyed under false labels as cures, be made contraband of interstate commerce—as well as lottery tickets?"[48]

Congress agreed with Hughes and acted quickly to circumvent the majority's reading by amending the Pure Food and Drug Act in 1912. The amendment extended the prohibition against misbranding to a drug if "its package or label shall bear or contain any statement, design, or devise regarding the curative or therapeutic effect of such article or any of the ingredients or substances contained therein, which is false and fraudulent."[49]

During the term the Court also considered a broad-ranging attack on the constitutionality of the federal corporation tax enacted in 1909, which levied a tax of 1 percent on net income over $5,000. In *Flint* v. *Stone Tracy Company*, Day, for a unanimous Court, upheld the levy. Avoiding the quagmire of *Pollock*, the Justice characterized the tax as "an excise upon the particular privilege of doing business in a corporate capacity." The fact that the corporations were created by the states, Day continued, imposed no bar to federal taxation. If state incorporation in itself would be sufficient to bar federal taxation, the Justice added, "the result would be to exclude the National Government from many objects upon which indirect taxes could be constitutionally imposed."[50] Finally, Day disposed of numerous arguments claiming a violation of due process and equal protection.

With the Court characterizing this corporate income tax as an excise tax, the days of *Pollock* seemed numbered. Before 1909, forty-two amendment proposals to authorize a federal income tax had been introduced in Congress but without success. Then in early 1909 as an addition to the Payne-Aldrich tariff bill the corporate income tax sustained in *Flint* was substituted for a general income tax proposal. To head off a mounting drive to force the Court to reconsider *Pollock* by enacting a new tax bill, conservatives in the Congress, aided by President Taft, threw their force behind the proposal for a constitutional amendment. The hope of those who opposed an income tax but supported the amendment proposal was that the states would be resistant to conferring upon the federal government this new and potentially large source of power and revenue. With such inconsistent support, the amendment proposal easily passed both houses of Congress in mid-July 1909.[51]

As opponents of the tax expected, the state legislatures were in no hurry to ratify the amendment, but the broad support for redistributing the costs of government had been underestimated. Slowly, the states added their concurrences, and on February 25, 1913, the Sixteenth Amendment was formally added to the Constitution. It gave power to Congress "to lay and collect taxes on incomes, from whatever source derived, without apportionment among the several States, and without regard to any census or enumeration." The wording of the amendment accepted the Court's ruling in *Pollock* by assuming that an income tax is a direct tax freed from the restrictions placed on such taxes by the Constitution.[52]

In addition to upholding the federal corporate income tax, the Court in the 1910 term put its full weight behind the authority of Congress to delegate power to the executive branch to make rules and regulations that carried criminal sanctions. Pursuant to general authority granted by Congress to preserve public forest lands, the Secretary of Agriculture mandated that a permit was required before an owner could graze his stock on such land. A lower federal court had dismissed the criminal indictment against Pierre Grimaud for grazing his stock without such a permit, ruling that Congress could not delegate to an administrative officer the legislative power to define crimes. The Supreme Court had heard the case in the preceding term and its eight members divided equally, resulting in the affirmance of the lower court's action. Upon the government's petition a rehearing was granted, and a full bench reconsidered the case.[53]

Justice Lamar, speaking for a surprisingly unanimous Court in *United States* v. *Grimaud*, ruled that "the authority to make administrative rules is not a delegation of legislative power, nor are such rules raised from an administrative to a legislative character because the violation thereof is punished as a public offense."[54] The fact that Congress had specified that a violation of the rules made would be an offense against the United States, Lamar said, was sufficient constitutional authorization to the Secretary. Grimaud, the Justice concluded, would have to stand trial. Once again the Justices had struggled through a knotty constitutional question and had recognized in their decision that the demands placed upon government in an increasingly complex society could not be met by a rigid insistence upon the separation of powers. The authority to promote conservation conferred on the Secretary of Agriculture would be impeded if every rule he promulgated had to be subjected to the legislative process before it would have the force of law.

The reconstituted Court also unanimously approved the Hours of Service Act of 1907 in which Congress had prescribed the number of hours railroad employees engaged in interstate commerce could work. Hughes, for the Court, said that Congress had the authority to provide for the safety of both passengers and employees in this manner. To the contention that intrastate and interstate commerce were so intermingled that the federal law had the effect of regulating local matters, the Justice responded that the legislative branch could not be denied "the effective exercise of its constitutional authority."[55] As easily, Hughes brushed aside the argument that the reports on compliance with the federal law required by the ICC infringed upon any constitutional right.

Of most interest among the term's commerce clause cases was one that challenged Oklahoma's attempt to hoard the state's natural gas supply by prohibiting its shipment out of the state. Earlier the Court had approved state authority to embargo wild game killed in the state and water from important streams, but now the majority drew back. McKenna, for the Court, labeled gas withdrawn from wells personal property that was properly a subject of commerce. Congressional silence he interpreted as a declaration that there should be no state interference with interstate commerce. The California Justice concluded that a contrary decision would threaten the nation's welfare and thwart the purpose of the commerce clause. Holmes, Lurton, and Hughes dissented without opinion.[56]

Oklahoma was unsuccessful in conserving its natural gas supply, but the Court, in *Coyle* v. *Smith*, did side with the state in its controversy with Congress. The question at issue was whether the national legislature could fix the location of the state capital for a period of seven years in the enabling act admitting Oklahoma into the union. Lurton, for a majority, answered no. Under its authority to guarantee each state a republican government, Congress, the Justice continued, cannot impose disabilities that would undermine the new state's equality with others in the union. Although Lurton could have resolved the issue by citing the inconsistency between Congress's words that the state would be admitted upon "an equal footing with the original states" and the restriction, he went further to give long-standing custom secure constitutional standing. Interpreting Article IV, section 3 of the Constitution, he said:

"This Union" was and is a union of States, equal in power, dignity and authority, each competent to exert that residuum of sovereignty not delegated to the United States by the Constitution itself. To maintain otherwise would be to say that the Union, through the power of Congress to admit new States, might come to be a union of States unequal in power, as including States whose powers were restricted by the Constitution, with others whose powers had been further restricted by an act of Congress accepted as a condition of admission.

The Justice concluded that a decision against the action of Congress was necessary to maintain the "harmonious operation of the scheme upon which the Republic was organized."[57]

Despite the Court's less than receptive attitude to labor unions, the Justices, late in the session, refused to be drawn into an attempt to penalize the leaders of the AF of L. The union, through its publication the *American Federationist*, had supported a boycott of Buck's Stove and Range Company. J. W. Van Cleave, the president of Buck's Stove and of the American Manufacturers Association as well, instituted suit against Samuel Gompers and others for the alleged injury the publication did to his business. When this suit came to the Court during the session, the Justices, while listening to oral argument, concluded that the case had become moot and dismissed it. But the main litigation had spawned a subsidiary action against Gompers and two of his associates for failure to obey injunctions issued by the lower court. All three had received prison sentences and the Court now considered their appeals. Although Lamar, for the unanimous Court, rejected the labor leaders' argument that the contempt citations violated their rights of free speech and free press, he ruled that the lower court had incorrectly characterized the contempt as criminal. Pronouncing the actions of the labor leaders a civil contempt, the Justice reversed the decision on grounds that the settlement of the major suit should be reflected in such subsidiary litigation.[58]

Gompers's victory was not yet won, for Lamar added in his closing paragraph that nothing in the opinion would prevent the lower court from exercising power to punish any contempt that might have been committed against it. The decision was handed down on May 15, 1911; the next day the District of Columbia court appointed a committee to determine if Gompers and the others had been guilty of violating the injunction, and, if so, to prosecute charges to that effect. A little over a month later the committee recommended prosecution, and proceedings began on the same day. All three defendants were convicted. Three years later when the new contempt case appeared on the docket the unanimous Court reversed the decision on grounds that the statute of limitations precludes the imposition of punishment.[59] Steadfastly, the High Bench refused to be drawn into what appeared to be a vindictive attempt to penalize the leaders of the preeminent American union.

An eventful term had come to an end, and with no warning at all during the session, so had the career of Justice John Marshall Harlan. Just before the opening of Court in the fall of 1911 and only a term short of besting Field's record for longevity of service, the senior Associate died of a condition diagnosed as acute bronchitis. Harlan did, however, set a record for the most opinions ever written by a member of the Court, 1,161, including 745 for the Court, 100 concurrences, and 316 dissents. Despite his reputation as a dissenter, he agreed with the majority in 92 percent of the over 14,000 decisions reached by the Court during his tenure of almost thirty-four years.[60] He had been appointed by President Hayes in 1877 at the age of forty-four and had been the senior Associate Justice since the retirement of Field late in 1897.

Harlan had a strong and independent mind, and he did not hesitate to tell his colleagues that they were wrong despite their overpowering numerical majority. His stubbornness and independence may have troubled his associates, but, as reflected in his vigorous dissents, those very qualities have endeared him to all recent observers of the Court's history. Despite the praise heaped upon Harlan at his death, most of which neglected his civil rights dissents, students of the Court, until the last few decades, tended to ignore him. During a testimonial banquet honoring Harlan for twenty-five years of service, Brewer did say that his colleague's mistakes were ones in which he could take pride, because they favored human rights, but this bit of contemporary recognition was unusual. Holmes aided the Justice's passage into temporary obscurity with comments like "old Harlan" and "the last of the tobacco-spitting judges." What rehabilitated the Kentuckian was the modern civil rights movement beginning with the reversal of the separate but equal doctrine in *Brown* v. *Board of Education* in 1954. His dissents in the *Civil Rights Cases* and in *Plessy* v. *Ferguson* were rescued from the dusty volumes of reported cases and a new appreciation of the man from Kentucky began to take root.[61]

Protection for the rights of black Americans was only part of Harlan's belief in the Constitution's broad protection of individual rights. He accepted what his fellow Justices would not—that the Reconstruction amendments had revolutionized the federal system. His colleagues did rally to the view that the due process clause of the Fourteenth Amendment imposed substantive checks upon state legislation, but they usually confined the clause's reach to matters affecting property rights. As early as 1884 Harlan had argued that both the privileges and immunities and due process clauses of the Fourteenth Amendment made the protections of the Bill of Rights binding upon the states. This interpretation of the first section of the amendment accorded with that of its primary framer, Representative John Bingham of Ohio, but during Harlan's lifetime, the Court was unwilling to undertake federal responsibility for supervising the operation of state criminal law. Harlan was vindicated by the Warren Court, which completed the process of requiring the states to honor most of the guarantees of the Bill of Rights.

In Harlan, more than in Field, Brewer, or Peckham, we can see how substantive due process as a concept could embrace national protection of rights the society deemed fundamental. Through its economic decisions the Court found meaning in the Fourteenth Amendment, but the Kentuckian's constant dissents showed how that amendment could mean far more than what the consensus at the time was willing to accept. There is no need to apologize for Harlan's acceptance of the Court's role as a supervisor of economic and social legislation; the Justice exercised this responsibility conscientiously, and, after all, the right to be secure in one's own property was considered so precious and special a right that it often blocked out the reality Harlan saw so clearly—that other individual rights were equally precious and equally protected by the same constitutional language.

Despite history's favorable verdict on certain of Harlan's views, the Justice did lose some decisive battles. His attempt to extend full constitutional guarantees to the residents of the new overseas possessions of the United States fell before White's expedient and much more flexible incorporation theory. The

Kentuckian was uncomfortable with a Constitution that did not march abreast of the flag, but the nation and the majority of his colleagues felt differently. His other defeat was in the antitrust area, where again White's judicial embellishment of the Sherman Act won the Court and determined the future. Although he believed in a strong, vigorous, and active judiciary, Harlan argued that the Court's authority to interpret the Constitution was compromised when it responded too eagerly to advocates' invitations to legislate judicially as it had in the antitrust area. Restraint was essential if the Court was to do the job it was empowered to do—uphold the guarantees of the Constitution against challenge.

Harlan had his blind spots, as his decision in *Adair* and his insensitivity to the governmental campaign against the Chinese attest, but the total record cannot be examined without concluding that this was a truly remarkable man who brought to his judicial position rare insight, perception, and a type of moral leadership that demonstrates how this undemocratic institution called the Supreme Court can act as a conscience of the nation. His passionate involvement in his country's welfare often led him to rant and rail and disturb the decorum of the bench. But he lived life to the fullest and left a trail in the annals of the Supreme Court that few can match.

Harlan's death gave President Taft the opportunity to put a fifth man on the Court. The 1910 elections had revealed a deep split in the ranks of the Republican party, resulting in substantial Democratic gains. In addition to a strong Democratic challenge in 1912, Taft also had to face mounting opposition among the "progressives" in his own party, many of whom were drawn to Theodore Roosevelt as the man to unseat Taft. The President was now locked in a political struggle in which election to a second term promised vindication.

Against this political backdrop Taft pondered his choice for the vacancy. In reviewing his years as President, Taft personally took great pride in his nominees to the High Bench. If he were to suffer defeat in the forthcoming election of 1912, he would have the satisfaction of having placed on the Court men who would check what he saw as the radical tendencies abroad in society. With such thoughts in mind the President considered a number of candidates before centering his search in New Jersey. No Justice had come from that state since Joseph P. Bradley, and a nod in that direction could possibly improve Taft's standing at the upcoming Republican convention. Apparently the leading candidate from New Jersey was Francis J. Swayze, a member of the highest court in the state, whose candidacy was pressed upon Taft by state political leaders. Attending a dinner in New Jersey on February 12, 1912, Taft talked over Swayze's qualifications with the state chancellor, Mahlon Pitney, who before attaining the state's highest judicial office had served a term on the New Jersey supreme court. The President must have been impressed with his informant, for one week later Pitney's name was sent to the Senate.[62]

Mahlon Pitney met Taft's standards: he was young enough, and in over eleven years of state judicial service his opinions, which the President had purused, seemed to reveal a kindred judicial philosophy. Also, the nominee had substantial political experience, having served in both the federal and state legislatures. All in all, Taft was proud to crown his list of nominees with Pitney's name. The Senate confirmed the nomination in less than a month, but not without some internal wrangling and a 50-26 vote that reflected the split in Republican ranks. What was responsible for the dispute was the contention that Pitney's earlier judicial record showed more concern for property than for human rights. The opposition pointed to an opinion that Pitney as chancellor had handed down in 1908 as indicating a degree of hostility to organized labor. But the union lobby, even when joined by progressive Republicans like Albert Cummins of Iowa, was still too weak to topple the President's choice.[63]

When Pitney took his seat to the far left of the Chief in the 1911 term, he had just turned fifty-four, and the black robe he donned only crowned his distinguished appearance. His receding hair had almost all turned white, but it still covered his head; he was clean shaven with well proportioned features, clear eyes, and a pleasant visage. He stood tall and erect, drawing attention to his height of about six feet, three inches and his lean frame.

On the first day of the 1911 term Chief Justice White announced the recent death of Justice Harlan and promptly adjourned the Court. McKenna now moved into Harlan's chair as the senior Associate Justice. Although dissents were registered in twenty cases in the last term, the ratio of disagreement would fall in the forthcoming term, with dissents being registered in only fourteen cases. Much of this new consensus could be attributed to Harlan's absence, but White, as Chief, was now reluctant to dissent, and Van Devanter was consistently agreeing with the majority.

Harlan's eloquent voice had been stilled, but during the session Joseph R. Lamar twice wrote lone dissents that carried echoes of Harlan's views. When his colleagues affirmed the constitutionality of a Montana act imposing a license fee of ten dollars upon males engaged in the hand laundry business, Lamar protested. To exclude larger laundries from such taxation, the Justice argued, made no sense, and to discriminate on a basis of sex, an irrelevant personal attribute, was without rational foundation. In *Diaz* v. *United States* the majority saw no constitutional violation when a defendant in the Philippines, for a single act, was tried and convicted of assault and battery and then later of murder. Lamar saw this continuance of the old Spanish procedure in fundamental conflict with the guarantees of the Bill of Rights, specifically made applicable to the Philippines by congressional action in 1902. Without the Harlan fire but with equal conviction, the Georgian asserted that Congress did intend to modify the old Spanish procedure by bringing it abreast of American standards.[64]

Among the matters on the Court's agenda was a decision on the constitutionality of a second Employers' Liability Act passed by Congress in early 1908 after the Court had invalidated the first attempt to provide greater protection for employees injured in interstate commerce. The new legislation contained much the same provisions as the old: the fellow servant doctrine was abolished; contributory negligence could only be considered to diminish and not bar recovery; and assumption of risk was no defense where the carrier had violated any state or federal statutory safety standard. In the *Second Employers' Liability Cases* counsel presented elaborate arguments, but Van Devanter, for a unanimous Court, rejected them all and upheld the act. Broadly supporting the legislation, the Justice said that congressional power reaches every instrument and agent involved in commerce and "may be exerted to its utmost extent over every part of such commerce."[65]

Later in the term the Court passed on a subordinate section of the liability act of 1908 with the same result. That section prevented a carrier from exempting itself from liability created by the act. Contracts making an employee's acceptance of payment from a relief department of the company a bar to further recovery were deemed by the Court to fall within this prohibition. The railroad had argued that legitimate contracts were impaired by the legislation, but Hughes, for the Court, gave short shrift to the contention just as he did in upholding a similar state law in the previous term, saying that accepting such a claim would tend to place "the regulation of interstate commerce in the hands of private individuals and to withdraw from the control of Congress so much of the field as they might choose by prophetic discernment to bring within the range of their agreements."[66]

What continued to pose problems for the Court was determining whether state regulations conflicted with congressional control over interstate commerce. For instance, the Court responded negatively to Colorado and Oklahoma attempts to tax foreign corporations on their interstate business, but, when the legislation was discrete and sensitive to the problem of competing authorities, the Justices did not allow technicalities to inhibit the state's taxing power. This was clear in a Minnesota case where the railroad claimed it was being unconstitutionally taxed on its receipts from a route that traversed a portion of another state in its journey between two points in Minnesota. Chief Justice White responded, showing the type of distinction the Court tried to make in such cases: ". . . we think the statute falls within that class where there has been an exercise in good faith of a legitimate taxing power, the measure of which taxation is in part the proceeds of interstate commerce, which could not, in itself, be taxed, and does not fall within that class of statutes uniformly condemned in this court, which show a manifest attempt to burden the conduct of interstate commerce, such power, of course, being beyond the authority of the State."[67]

Late in the term the High Bench had its first opportunity to inspect the work of the newly created Commerce Court. As early as 1893 the creation of a specialized commerce court was proposed, but not until President Taft, who was always interested in making the judicial machinery more effective, championed the proposal did chances of success improve. Certain Congressmen opposed the new creation on the grounds that such a court would in all likelihood be staffed with individuals who might well prefer the interest of the railroads to that of the public. Supporters of the specialized court included it in what became known as the Mann-Elkins Act, and its merger with many other provisions regulating interstate commerce shielded the court proposal from direct attack. On June 18, 1910, the Commerce Court was approved with hopes that it would be a useful buffer between the Interstate Commerce Commission and the Supreme Court. The idea was to create a body of judges who would develop the expertise required to bring some order out of the chaos caused by many federal courts handling similar matters often in different ways. Essentially the Commerce Court was to have jurisdiction to hear challenges to the orders of the Interstate Commerce Commission. Without great popular or professional support the new court began business in Washington in February 1911 with over thirty pending cases transferred to it. From the Hepburn Act of 1906 until the creation of the Commerce Court, fifty-seven suits had been commenced in the circuit courts, but only twenty-four of them had been resolved.[68]

The Supreme Court's first review of the new tribunal's work was not encouraging. In three of the four cases that came to the High Bench during 1911 term, the Justices reversed the decisions of the Commerce Court.[69] In fact, the Justices would reverse all but two of the first twenty-three decisions of the Commerce Court they reviewed, in part reflecting an environment now more sympathetic to the decision making of the ICC. With Democrats in control of the House after the election of 1910, the Commerce Court became a target. Repeal of the enabling legislation was made part of a major appropriations bill in an effort to head off a veto, but, in August 1912, the President vetoed the bill anyway. To Taft the repeal measure was just another indication of a mounting legislative attack on the judiciary. But the drive to rid the country of the Commerce Court would not be stilled; in fact it was fueled by impeachment proceedings brought against one of its judges, Robert W. Archibald, who was accused of using his influence to secure favors from carriers involved in litigation before him as a district judge and as a member of the Commerce Court.[70]

Although Congress was temporarily stymied in its efforts to do away with the Commerce Court, its worries about legislation affecting Indians and the delegation of power to the Secretary of the Interior, which had led to the abortive attempt to get an early Court reading in *Muskrat*, were largely dissipated by the High Bench's rulings during the term. Without exception the Justices upheld the Secretary's discretion in the area, especially in the matter of determining entitlement to allotments.[71] Seemingly convinced that congressional policy was determined by considering the welfare of the Indian, the Court was willing to defer to the judgment of the legislative branch.

Such judicial deference was never total, however, as the unanimous decision in *Choate* v. *Trapp* illustrates. Indians in Oklahoma had been granted an immunity from state taxation in conjunction with a restriction upon their ability to sell their individual allotments. When Congress removed the restriction on alienation, it also lifted the immunity from taxation. In response to Oklahoma's attempt to tax the land, Justice Lamar, for a unanimous Court, ruled that the federal provision withdrawing the tax exemption was unconstitutional because the immunity was a property right that had vested with the passage of the original act. The Fifth Amendment, he concluded, precluded the congressional action attempted here. Earlier decisions, Lamar continued, did not intimate "that the power of wardship conferred authority on Congress to lessen any of the rights of property which had been vested in the individual Indian by prior laws or contracts."[72]

In addition to suffering this loss of revenue, Oklahoma was rebuffed on another matter relating to its Indian population. In the previous term the Court had said in passing, that, despite the need to respect the equality of the states, certain federal regulations might be justified. *Ex Parte Webb* posed just such a test. Webb was seeking a writ of habeas corpus after his conviction for selling liquor to Indians. He contended that the federal legislation making his conduct criminal did not survive the incorporation of Oklahoma into the union as an equal state. The unanimous opinion was assigned to the new arrival Pitney, who said that, since the enabling act contained a saving clause protecting federal authority over the Indians, the legislation in question clearly survived the incorporation of Oklahoma into the union. Next, he interpreted the restriction, not as a condition of admission nor as a limitation of the state's legislative power, but rather as an assertion of a federal power not affected by state boundaries. In its authority to regulate commerce with the Indians, Pitney concluded, Congress is empowered to continue its enforcement of laws and treaties concerning them.[73]

The unanimity by which the Justices resolved these matters was sundered when they considered *Henry* v. *A. B. Dick*. Patent cases regularly were taken by the Court at its discretion, but rarely did they involve a matter of such far-ranging importance. The question posed was the extent of the patent holder's ability to use his legal monopoly to prevent competition. Henry was sued for infringing a patent by knowingly supplying ink to be used in a patented mimeograph machine purchased under a license that stipulated that supplies had to be obtained from the holder of the machine patent. Lurton, in an extensive majority opinion, cited and accepted "the trend of judicial opinion that such license restrictions annexed to patented articles, when sold, constitute licenses under the patent, and that their violation by persons having notice constitutes an infringement of the patent." White, joined by Hughes and Lamar, overcame his new reluctance to dissent. Considering the patent holder's power, the Chief argued "that its exercise, like every other power, should be subject to the law of the land." By this law of the land White judged the contract here involved contrary to public policy and therefore void. He summoned Congress to amend the patent law to void the implications of the majority decision. In unique language for a member of the judiciary, White told the legislative branch that "if evils arise their continuance will not be caused by the interpretation now given to the statute, but will result from the inaction of the legislative department in failing to amend the statute so as to avoid such evils." The conclusion of the majority, White said, gave the patent holder the "power by contract to extend the patent so as to cause it to embrace things which it does not include; in other words, to exercise legislative power of a far-reaching and dangerous character."[74]

The Chief sought a reversal of *A. B. Dick* with the same type of determination that characterized his efforts in antitrust and insular matters. White would not succeed until 1917, but he did gain some immediate satisfaction in the next term. The question presented in *Bauer & Cie* v. *O'Donnell* was whether a party could control the retail price of his patented product by attaching a notice to it stating that any sale of the drug at less than the stipulated price would constitute an infringement of the patent. Seven members of the Court saw no real distinction between *A. B. Dick* and the instant case, and Pitney, who now considered the issue for the first time, agreed with White and the former dissenters. Pried loose from the former majority was Justice Day, who wrote the opinion and drew a distinction, saying that in the former case the description of the sale as a license to use was supported by the facts while here the concept "is a mere play upon words."[75] By a five to four count the practice was deemed illegal.

Before the 1911 term ended the Justices had to contend with the novel argument that those increasingly popular devices of direct democracy, the initiative and referendum, violated the Constitution. Despite the plea of critics that the people should have faith in the institutions of representative government, the times were ripe for the establishment and use of alternate lawmaking processes. No state electorate was more enthusiastic than that of Oregon, which passed upon thirty-two measures spawned by these devices in 1910 alone.[76] That the state should provide the test case brought to the Supreme Court should occasion no surprise. The Pacific States Telephone & Telegraph Company had levied a massive attack on a 2 percent gross revenue tax proposed through the initiative and enthusiastically approved by Oregon voters by almost a ten to one margin. By the time the case reached the

Supreme Court the challenge was narrowed to an attack on the devices of direct democracy as antagonistic to the guarantee of a republican government found in Article IV, section 4, of the Constitution.

Quoting extensively from *Luther* v. *Borden*, the 1849 case in which the Court found the power to guarantee a republican form of government lodged exclusively in Congress, Chief Justice White responded for the unanimous Court. Concerned with the danger involved in invading the authority of the states, White said the contention pressed, if supported, would have to deny the existence of a lawful government and void all legislation passed since the adoption of the initiative and referendum. Such a ruling, he continued, would involve "the inconceivable expansion of the judicial power and the ruinous destruction of legislative authority in matters purely political." The Chief noted the anomaly of asking the Court to preempt congressional power, thereby guaranteeing "a government republican in form by destroying the very existence of government republican in form in the Nation." White saw certain misconceptions clouding the argument by counsel on both sides, but he maintained that the demarcation between judicial authority and legislative power was clear. Here, he continued, the political nature of the attack was evident, for the government itself "is called to the bar of this court, not for the purpose of testing judicially some exercise of power . . . but to demand of the State that it establish its right to exist as a State, republican in form."[77] Since the question presented was purely political, the Chief concluded, the Court had to dismiss the case.

The initiative and referendum had their day in court, and the outcome was predictable. The Supreme Court was as hesitant to enter into this political thicket as was Congress. Although this grand experiment in direct democracy captured the popular fancy, its accomplishments were minimal. Government at all levels was becoming more complex, and running side by side with this desire to have the people participate more directly in the governmental process was a recognition that the complexity of government required an expertise beyond the capacity of the voters.

Such preemption of the legislative role might not strike all as desirable, but there was growing national support for a reform quite consistent with the traditions of representative government—the direct election of United States Senators. The prevailing system had often led to delay when a candidate could not be agreed upon by the state legislature, and it had come increasingly under attack as the haven of special interest groups. In the era that spawned the initiative, referendum, and recall as indications of distrust of established state government, the direct-election proposal emerged from Congress. In fact, many states had already made changes that directed the legislature to accept as its choice the candidate selected by the voters; by the spring of 1911 thirty-one of the forty-six states in the Union had in one form or another modified the old system. The amendment proposal was sent to the states on

May 12, 1912, and with surprising rapidity was added to the Constitution as the Seventeenth Amendment slightly over a year later.[78]

NOTES

1. Taft's views on the function of the judicial branch are presented in Alpheus T. Mason, *William Howard Taft: Chief Justice* (New York: Simon & Schuster, 1965); pp. 56-65. See also Daniel S. McHargue, "President Taft's Appointments to the Supreme Court," *Journal of Politics* 12 (August 1950): 478-82.

2. Henry F. Pringle, *The Life and Times of William Howard Taft*, 2 vols. (New York: Farrar & Rinehart, 1939), 1:529-30; McHargue, "Taft's Appointments," pp. 483-86; and James F. Watts, Jr., "Horace H. Lurton," in *The Justices of the United States Supreme Court 1789-1969: Their Lives and Opinions*, ed. Leon Friedman and Fred L. Israel, 4 vols. (New York: R. R. Bowker Co. and Chelsea House Publishers, 1969), 3:1849-59.

3. *New York Tribune*, January 8, 1911.

4. Western Union Telegraph Co. v. Kansas *ex rel*. Coleman, 216 U.S. 1, 37 (1910).

5. Id. at 52, 53; and Pullman Co. v. Kansas *ex rel*. Coleman, 216 U.S. 56, 76 (1910).

6. Ludwig v. Western Union Telegraph Co., 216 U.S. 146 (1910); and International Text-Book Co. v. Pigg, 217 U.S. 91 (1910).

7. Illinois Central R.R. v. Sheegog, 215 U.S. 308 (1909); and Southern Ry. v. Miller, 217 U.S. 209 (1910).

8. Kuhn v. Fairmont Coal Co., 215 U.S. 349, 372 (1910).

9. Davis v. Cleveland, Cincinnati, Chicago & St. Louis Ry., 217 U.S. 157 (1910); Cincinnati, New Orleans & Texas Pacific Ry. v. Slade, 216 U.S. 78 (1910); Southern Ry. v. King, 217 U.S. 524 (1910); Atlantic Coast Line R.R. v. Mazursky, 216 U.S. 122 (1910); Missouri Pacific Ry. v. Kansas *ex rel*. Railroad Commissioners, 216 U.S. 262 (1910); St. Louis Southwestern R.R. v. Arkansas, 217 U.S. 136 (1910); Missouri Pacific Ry. v. Nebraska, 217 U.S. 196 (1910); and Herndon v. Chicago, Rock Island & Pacific Ry., 218 U.S. 135 (1910).

10. Weems v. United States, 217 U.S. 349, 364, 366-67, 362 (1910).

11. Id. at 373.

12. Id. at 385.

13. ICC v. Chicago, Rock Island & Pacific Ry., 218 U.S. 88, 110 (1910).

14. The memorial proceeding for Brewer is in 218 U.S. vii-xvi; and for Roosevelt's opinion of the Justice, see his letters to William Allen White, November 26, 1907, November 30, 1908, and to Florence L. La Farge, February 13, 1908, in Elting E. Morison, ed., *The Letters of Theodore Roosevelt*, 8 vols. (Cambridge: Harvard University Press, 1951-54), 5: 855-56, 6: 1392-93, 943.

15. See Arnold Paul, "David J. Brewer," in *Justices of the Supreme Court*, 2:1515-33, and Henry J. Abraham, *Justices and Presidents: A Political History of Appointments to the Supreme Court* (New York: Oxford University Press, 1974), p. 138, for the harsh and prevailing assessment of Brewer's work on the Court.

16. Sympathetic but limited appraisals of Brewer are Robert E. Gamer, "Justice Brewer and Substantive Due Process: A Conservative Court Revisited," *Vanderbilt Law Review* 18 (March 1965):615-41; D. Stanley Eitzen, *David J. Brewer, 1837-1910: A Kansan on the United States Supreme Court*, Emporia State Research Studies, vol. 12, no. 3 (Emporia: Kansas State Teachers College, 1964); and Francis Bergan, "Mr. Justice Brewer: Perspective of a Century," *Albany Law Review* 25 (1961):191-202.

17. Mason, *William Howard Taft*, pp. 35-36.

18. Ibid., p. 36.

19. Samuel Hendel, *Charles Evans Hughes and the Supreme Court* (New York: King's Crown Press, Columbia University, 1951), pp. 5-13.

20. Ibid., pp. 14-15.

21. Willard L. King, *Melville Weston Fuller: Chief Justice of the United States 1888-1910*, Phoenix ed. (Chicago: University of Chicago Press, 1967), p. 290.

22. [Archibald Butt], *Taft and Roosevelt: The Intimate Letters of Archie Butt*, 2 vols. (Garden City, N.Y.: Doubleday, Doran & Co., 1930), 2:439; for an example of newspaper comment, see *Washington Post*, July 6, 1910; and Mason, *William Howard Taft*, pp. 34-35.

23. Pringle, *Life of Taft*, 1:534-35.

24. Van Devanter's campaign for a seat on the Supreme Court is traced in M. Paul Holsinger, "The Appointment of Supreme Court Justice Van Devanter: A Study of Political Preferment," *American Journal of Legal History* 12 (1968):324-35.

25. Leonard Dinnerstein, "Joseph Rucker Lamar," in *Justices of the Supreme Court*, 3:1975-79; Abraham, *Justices and Presidents*, p. 162; and McHargue, "Taft's Appointments," pp. 500-504.

26. Harlan v. McGourin, 218 U.S. 442 (1910); and Bailey v. Alabama, 219 U.S. 219, 228 (1911).

27. Bailey v. Alabama, 219 U.S. 219, 236 (1911).

28. Id. at 241-42, 244-45.

29. Id. at 246. Before coming on the Court Holmes had sought to purge contract law of moral considerations. (See Oliver Wendell Holmes, "The Path of the Law," *Harvard Law Review* 10 [March 25, 1897]:461-62.)

30. Muskrat v. United States, 219 U.S. 346, 361 (1911).

31. Tiger v. Western Investment Co., 221 U.S. 286, 316 (1911).

32. Noble State Bank v. Haskell, 219 U.S. 104, 110, 111, 112 (1911).

33. Id. at 110; Noble Bank v. Haskell, 219 U.S. 575 (1911); and see Charles Warren, "The Progressiveness of the Supreme Court," *Columbia Law Review* 13 (April 1913):310-13.

34. Standard Oil Co. v. United States, 221 U.S. 1, 60 (1911).

35. Id. at 68.

36. Id. at 81.

37. Id. at 83.

38. See United States v. Trans-Missouri Freight Assn., 166 U.S. 290 (1897), and United States v. Joint-Traffic Assn., 171 U.S. 505 (1898); and Standard Oil Co. v. United States, 221 U.S. 1, 102 (1911).

39. Standard Oil Co. v. United States, 221 U.S. 1, 105 (1911).

40. United States v. American Tobacco Co., 221 U.S. 106, 181, 182 (1911).

41. Id. at 184-85.

42. Id. at 187.

43. Id. at 190, 192-93.

44. See the critique in Robert B. Dishman, "Mr. Justice White and the Rule of Reason," *Review of Politics* 13 (April 1951):229-43.

45. See Charles Warren, *The Supreme Court in United States History*, rev. ed., 2 vols. (Boston: Little, Brown & Co., 1926), 2:734, n. 1; and for a discussion of the case and its effect on later legislation, see William Letwin, *Law and Economic Policy in America: The Evolution of the Sherman Antitrust Act* (New York: Random House, 1965), pp. 253-78.

46. Homer Cummings and Carl McFarland, *Federal Justice* (New York: Macmillan Co., 1937), pp. 340-43.

47. Hipolite Egg Co. v. United States, 220 U.S. 45, 58 (1911); and United States v. Johnson, 221 U.S. 488, 498 (1911).

48. United States v. Johnson, 221 U.S. 488, 501, 504, 507 (1911).

49. Act of August 23, 1912, ch. 352, 37 Stat. 416, 417.

50. Flint v. Stone Tracy Co., 220 U.S. 107, 151, 157 (1911).

51. U.S., Congress, House, *Proposed Amendments to the Constitution.* House Doc. 551, 70th Cong., 2d sess., 1928 (Washington: Government Printing Office, 1929), pp. 212-15.

52. Some students of constitutional history see amendments as repudiations of the Court, but such a view is erroneous. The Court never claims more than the right in a properly presented case to interpret the Constitution as it stands. Repassage of legislation found unconstitutional, the other route to change, challenges the High Bench to change its mind or face the censure of Congress. When Congress chooses to submit an amendment to the states, it is an implied tribute to the authority of the Court. President Taft was led by his feeling that the Court's authority was at stake to support the amendment proposal. (See Pringle, *Life of Taft,* 1:233.)

53. Although only Brewer of the previous eight Justices who heard the case the first time had been replaced, the earlier opposition to such an exercise of governmental power withered away. Felix Frankfurter and James M. Landis in *The Business of the Supreme Court: A Study in the Federal Judicial System* (New York: Macmillan Co., 1927), p. 15, n. 43, speculate that Van Devanter with his knowledge of the West and of the public domain might have convinced his hitherto skeptical colleagues of the need to condone such delegation.

54. United States v. Grimaud, 220 U.S. 506, 521 (1911).

55. Baltimore & Ohio R.R. v. ICC, 221 U.S. 612, 618 (1911).

56. Geer v. Connecticut, 161 U.S. 519 (1896); Hudson County Water Co. v. McCarter, 209 U.S. 349 (1908); and West v. Kansas Natural Gas Co., 221 U.S. 229 (1911).

57. Coyle v. Smith, 221 U.S. 559, 566, 567, 580 (1911).

58. Buck's Stove & Range Co. v. American Federation of Labor, 219 U.S. 581 (1911); and Gompers v. Buck's Stove & Range Co., 221 U.S. 418 (1911).

59. Gompers v. United States, 233 U.S. 604 (1914).

60. These statistics come from Louis Filler, "John M. Harlan," in *Justices of the Supreme Court,* 2:1284. See also the extensive memorial proceedings in 222 U.S. v-xxviii.

61. *Washington Post,* December 10, 1902; and Filler, "John M. Harlan," 2:1293-94. See also, Alan F. Westin, "John Marshall Harlan and the Constitutional Rights of Negroes: The Transformation of a Southerner," *Yale Law Journal* 66 (April 1957):637-710, and "Mr. Justice Harlan," in *Mr. Justice,* ed. Allison Dunham and Philip B. Kurland, rev. & enl. ed. (Chicago: University of Chicago Press, Phoenix Books, 1964), pp. 93-128. On Harlan's dissents, see Loren P. Beth, "Justice Harlan and the Uses of Dissent," *American Political Science Review* 49 (December 1955):1085-1104. The first indication of Harlan's modern rehabilitation was Richard F. Watt and Richard M. Orlikoff, "The Coming Vindication of Mr. Justice Harlan," *Illinois Law Review* 44 (March-April 1949):13-40.

62. Abraham, *Justices and Presidents,* p. 163; and Fred L. Israel, "Mahlon Pitney," in *Justices of the Supreme Court,* 3:2001, 2003. See also McHargue, "Taft's Appointments," pp. 504-6.

63. Israel, "Mahlon Pitney," 2:2003-4.

64. Quong Wing v. Kirkendall, 223 U.S. 59 (1912); and Diaz v. United States, 223 U.S. 442 (1912).

65. Second Employers' Liability Cases, 223 U.S. 1, 47 (1912).

66. Philadelphia, Baltimore & Washington R.R. v. Schubert, 224 U.S. 603, 614 (1912).

67. Atchison, Topeka & Santa Fe Ry. v. O'Connor, 223 U.S. 280 (1912); Meyer v. Wells, Fargo & Co., 223 U.S. 298 (1912); and United States Express Co. v. Minnesota, 223 U.S. 335, 348 (1912).

68. Frankfurter and Landis, *Business of the Supreme Court*, pp. 153-64.

69. The Court reversed the lower tribunal's decisions in Proctor & Gamble Co. v. United States, 225 U.S. 282 (1912); Hooker v. Knapp, 225 U.S. 302 (1912); and ICC v. Baltimore & Ohio R.R., 225 U.S. 326 (1912); and affirmed the Commerce Court in United States v. Baltimore & Ohio R.R., 225 U.S. 306 (1912).

70. Frankfurter and Landis, *Business of the Supreme Court*, pp. 162-74. On January 13, 1913, Archibald was found guilty by the Senate and removed from his office (Joseph Borkin, *The Corrupt Judge* [Cleveland: World Publishing Co., Meridian Books, 1962], pp. 199, 221-22).

71. See United States *ex rel.* Turner v. Fisher, 222 U.S. 204 (1911); United States *ex rel.* Lowe v. Fisher, 223 U.S. 95 (1912); Jacobs v. Prichard, 223 U.S. 200 (1912); Fairbanks v. United States, 223 U.S. 215 (1912); Heckman v. United States, 224 U.S. 413 (1912); and Gritts v. Fisher, 224 U.S. 640 (1912).

72. Choate v. Trapp, 224 U.S. 665, 678 (1912). The Tiger case is at 221 U.S. 286 (1911).

73. *Ex parte* Webb, 225 U.S. 663 (1912).

74. Henry v. A. B. Dick Co., 224 U.S. 1, 38, 69, 50, 51-52 (1912). Usually Congress pays little note to such pleas for legislative action, especially when found in dissenting opinions, but the federal legislative branch did attempt to exorcise some of the spectres that the Chief had seen. As part of the Clayton Act of 1914 Congress prohibited the sale of either patented or nonpatented materials by a person engaged in interstate commerce with the stipulation that the purchaser shall not use supplies of a competitor "where the effect of such lease, sale, or contract for sale . . . may be to substantially lessen competition or tend to create a monopoly in any line of commerce" (Clayton Antitrust Act, ch. 323, 38 Stat. 730, 731 [1914]).

75. Bauer & Cie v. O'Donnell, 229 U.S. 1, 16 (1913).

76. Ellis P. Oberholtzer, *The Referendum in America*, rev. ed. (New York: Charles Scribner's Sons, 1912), pp. 410-11.

77. Pacific States Telephone & Telegraph Co. v. Oregon, 223 U.S. 118, 141, 142, 150-51 (1912).

78. *Proposed Amendments to the Constitution*, pp. 215-25.

chapter 9

NEW PATHS FROM CROWDED DOCKETS, 1912-15

Two days after the Court term ended in mid-June 1912 the Republican party, convening in Chicago, raised the curtain on one of the most compelling political dramas of the twentieth century. The split between wings of the party that had been responsible for the Democrats gaining control of the House in 1910 for the first time in eighteen years had only been exacerbated in the interim. Theodore Roosevelt had been drawn into the fray as the challenger to his hand-picked successor, William Howard Taft. Despite Taft's ambivalence about the presidency and his inability to heal the internal wounds of his party, he was not about to relinquish the office to a radicalized Roosevelt. In the spring primaries the former President demonstrated that his popularity had not dimmed. But the party conservatives were not to be steam-rollered, and Taft, showing more political astuteness than had characterized his presidency, gave leadership to the drive for his renomination. When the Taft forces succeeded in early maneuvering to seat their delegates in 235 of 254 contests, renomination of the incumbent was assured. Over 300 Roosevelt delegates left the Convention, vowing that their work was not done. The result was the formation of the Progressive party in August 1912, with Theodore Roosevelt as its standard-bearer.

Progressive party hopes of capturing hitherto disaffected Democrats soon declined because of the candidate that emerged from the Baltimore Convention. Meeting on the heels of the Republicans, the Democrats could sense they were nominating the next President. William Jennings Bryan, the oft-rejected candidate, had little hope, but his call for the party to reject any candidate subservient to large special interests did not go unheeded. The leading contender was the Speaker of the House of Representatives, Champ Clark of Missouri, who from the first ballot on held a commanding lead but not enough to garner the two-thirds vote required. Slowly, a political neophyte, Governor Woodrow Wilson of New Jersey, an active campaigner for the nomination, chipped away at Clark's lead. On the fifty-sixth ballot Wilson emerged victorious. The man who had resigned from the presidency of Princeton University in 1910 to become governor of New Jersey now saw the nation's top office within reach. Despite the convention divisions the Democratic party united behind the candidate.

In the ensuing summer campaign Taft was the forgotten candidate, as Roosevelt and a cautious Wilson squared off. Roosevelt espoused a New Nationalism that departed from the individualistic tradition of American politics. Accepting the inevitability of big business, the program proposed to curb its excesses. At the same time the New Nationalism recognized that workers needed protection that only a federal government willing to take on new responsibilities could provide. Wilson, initially lacking any such comprehensive program, lashed out against the protective tariff, long a target of the Democrats. As Roosevelt developed his ideas Wilson seemed forced to counter, and this he did with the advice of Louis D. Brandeis, a prominent Boston attorney with a devotion to public service work. The Democratic candidate's New Freedom recommended additional antitrust legislation designed to free the nation from monopolistic control and reestablish competitive conditions in the economy. Wilson did not respond to Roosevelt's proposals for specific social legislation, apparently desirous of avoiding commitment and certainly less personally convinced of the necessity of such governmental intervention.[1]

Not long after the Justices convened for the 1912 term, the results were in. Wilson, with only 42 percent of the popular vote, had won a substantial victory in the electoral college. Roosevelt had bested Taft both in popular and electoral votes, while the Socialist candidate, Eugene V. Debs, polled close to 900,000 votes. No matter which way the votes were read, the electorate was voting for change. How much of a change was unclear even to Wilson.

Congress had been quite active during the presidencies of Roosevelt and Taft, and considerable federal legislation was reflected on the Court's docket, and more such cases were in the offing. In the 1890 term the Court had rendered opinions in 293 cases; but with the establishment of the Courts of Appeals, the work load was reduced to slightly over 180 opinions in the 1894 term. In only four terms from the 1897 session through that of 1910 did the Justices produce opinions in over 200 cases. Then in the 1911 term the output skyrocketed to over 240, followed by over 290 in the next two sessions, and over 270 in the 1914 term. What this periodic blooming of cases meant was shorter, more concise opinions, as the Justices coped with as heavy a case load as any faced by their predecessors.

During the 1912 session, in an effort to discourage unnecessary appeals, the Court used authority, long granted but not used in recent years, to penalize a party who prolonged a final judgment through an insubstantial appeal by adding damages for delay to the recovery. In one case where the Justices considered the asserted federal right frivolous, they dismissed the case and levied 5 percent damages plus costs. In another case, where they determined that no question of law had been presented, they affirmed the lower court judgment with an addition of 10 percent damages. In neither opinion did the Court refer to its burdensome case load, but its action in these cases spoke clearly.[2]

As an indication of the impact made by new federal legislation, the Court decided eleven cases under the Federal Employers' Liability Act of 1908. The Justices were willing to effectuate the purposes of the act by shunting aside technical objections in pleading, but they did insist that recovery could only be had by parties in the capacities that the act specified and only for actual pecuniary losses suffered. Although the jury was to be restricted to matters of fact, the need to preserve the jury's authority was clearly recognized by the Court.[3] A majority of the Justices appeared willing to extend the benefits of the legislation to all those who could be reasonably encompassed by it.

Although the Court invalidated some state and municipal regulation because it encroached upon the federal commerce power, the cases where the Justices now pointed to preemptive federal legislation were more numerous. States were told that their rate schedules could not be applied to interstate shipments, and where a particular activity such as ferry transportation was brought under the Interstate Commerce Act, state regulation could not fill in gaps in the federal regulatory scheme. Also, Wisconsin's attempt to require labels, displacing those mandated by the federal food and drug act before sale in the states, was voided by the Court as an attempt to thwart the enforcement of the federal act.[4]

Apparently, the Court had made its peace with the Interstate Commerce Commission, but of all the Justices only the relatively new arrival, Pitney, exhibited a decided preference for shippers in their battles with carriers. The New Jersey Justice seemed to feel that suits by shippers alleging rate discrimination were a useful and perhaps necessary stimulus to force railroads to comply with congressional policy and the directives of the ICC. This attitude is clearly revealed in a series of cases in which Pitney, without support from any of his colleagues, wrote extensive dissents to opinions by Lamar.

In response to a shipper's claim that he should recover the difference between the rates he paid and those paid by others, Lamar ruled that the Interstate Commerce Act limited recovery to the actual pecuniary loss the shipper suffered plus reasonable attorney's fees. Pitney objected to the Court's measure, saying damages should be fixed by the amount of the discrimination. This conclusion, he asserted, was consistent with the language, policy, and legislative history of the basic legislation, and the practice of the ICC. Pitney called the majority's decision "a virtual denial of private remedy for the most common and harmful of those discriminations that the Interstate Commerce Act was designed to prevent and to redress."[5] Why the requirement that actual damages be proved would deny a remedy lies in the fact that, since the shipper passed the increased charge on to its customer, no pecuniary loss resulted. So Pitney's dissent was as much anchored in the effective enforcement of the regulatory legislation as in protecting shippers' interests. Of all the Justices who sat on the Court since the enactment of the Interstate Commerce Act, none before Pitney demonstrated a similar empathy for the essential purposes of this type of regulation.

The next two cases involved matters of discrimination that the majority said could not be the subject of a suit until a ruling on the practices had been made by the Interstate Commerce Commission. Pitney dissented, arguing that the Court's resolution of such cases so restricted the right of shippers "that it is difficult to conceive of a case where the injured shipper can, by the simple and direct mode of an action at law, recover any substantial compensation for the discrimination practiced upon him by the carrier."[6]

Battling against a certain residue of hostility on the Court to this whole regulatory scheme, Pitney shared none of the majority's qualms. His extensive dissents did not flow easily, nor were they filled with epigrams, but their inherent logic could only be resisted by the majority's refusal to accept the underlying purpose of such commercial regulation. Since Congress had sought to make the courts partners in this system of regulation, the majority attitude frustrated the successful application of the legislative policy. The New Jersey Justice was the term's leading dissenter, and though his image is often interpreted through the lens of other cases, his plea here for the implementation of congressional policy is impressive.[7]

Holmes had little of Pitney's empathy with congressional policy as revealed in the actions of the ICC or in prosecutions under the antitrust act, but the Massachusetts Justice did write an opinion for the Court upholding the criminal provisions of the Sherman Act. A defendant claimed the charge of conspiring to restrain trade was too vague to alert an individual to what actually was illegal conduct. Holmes, for the majority, brushed aside these claims as insubstantial. The Justice's dislike for the substantive provisions of the antitrust law was subordinated to his interest in seeing criminals brought to bar of justice. In another case he offered his opinion that the safeguards surrounding the accused criminal were excessive.[8]

This same impression is clearly generated in an opinion by Holmes, for a unanimous Court, in one of the self-incrimination cases of the session. Charles R. Heike was summoned before a grand jury investigating possible antitrust violations by the American Sugar Refining Company. Among the documents he produced was a corporate memorandum that later was used against him in a federal prosecution for defrauding the government of lawful revenue. In appealing his conviction Heike argued that the use of the memorandum violated the statutory immunity he had been granted in testifying before the grand jury. Holmes said the immunity was restricted to a violation of the antitrust law and did not extend to a prosecution entirely unrelated to the original investigation. "We see no reason," he concluded, "for supposing that the act afforded a gratuity to crime."[9]

No more sympathetic did William A. Ensign find the Court to his claim that he had been forced to incriminate himself. Ensign had been forced into involuntary bankruptcy and, pursuant to the federal law, he filed schedules of his property. The 1898 federal bankruptcy act provided that "no testimony given by him shall be offered in evidence against him in any criminal proceeding." Pennsylvania authorities, however, used the schedules and convicted Ensign of receiving deposits as an insolvent banker. Pitney, for a unanimous Court, upheld the conviction. First, the Fifth Amendment's protection against self-incrimination, said the Justice, was not applicable to the states. Next, the Justice read the protection in the bankruptcy law to pertain only to oral testimony. Since no oral testimony had been used in the state prosecution, he concluded, the claim could not be sustained.[10] This evasion enabled the Court to sidestep the question of whether the provision in the federal bankruptcy law, even restricted as it was to oral testimony, was binding on state courts. The result of an affirmative decision would have been to immunize certain individuals from the operation of the state's criminal law. In other areas the Court did not hesitate to find federal preemption, but here in a matter of criminal law it drew back.

Additionally, the Court found that no personal privilege against self-incrimination attached to records of a dissolved corporation in the hands of individuals. Contempt citations were upheld by the Court. Corporate records, no matter in whose possession, were, the Justices said, "subject to inspection and examination when required by competent authority."[11] Consistently the Court brushed aside claims of personal privilege in such cases. Much of the problem in this area resulted from the need for a choice between competing values. Obviously, the producer of the books and records was being forced to incriminate himself, but the Court seemed to say the individual had brought this plight upon himself and should not be able to hide behind the privilege against self-incrimination to frustrate legitimate investigation into either corporate activities or those of an insolvent individual.

Free press and due process challenges to new requirements established by Congress in 1912 for admission to second-class mailing privileges were also considered by the Court. Newspaper and periodical publishers were required to publish their average circulations, the names of the editors, publishers, owners, stockholders, and principal creditors, and to mark all paid-for reading material "advertisement." Chief Justice White painstakingly met the various contentions, but his response was well summarized in the following segment:

... we are concerned not with any general regulation of what should be published in newspapers, not with any condition excluding from the right to resort to the mails, but we are concerned solely and exclusively with the right on behalf of the publishers to continue to enjoy great privileges and advantages at the public expense, a right given them by Congress upon condition of compliance with regulations deemed by that body incidental and necessary to the complete fruition of the public policy lying at the foundation of the privileges accorded.[12]

White did, however, suggest some limitation might exist upon the power of the government to classify the mails. The prominent attorneys involved in the case, including James M. Beck, who now was appearing frequently before the High Bench, did succeed in getting the Court to entertain the idea that a case might some day arise in which the judiciary would have to act to check arbitrary action by the Postal Department.

Under both the postal and immigration statutes, Congress sought to regulate sexual morality, a subject that advocates before the High Bench repeatedly argued was exclusively a matter of state concern. Consistently the Court rebuffed such arguments, even when Congress moved further into the area with the notorious Mann Act. Heeding rumors of thriving national prostitution rings, Congress passed the Mann Act to curtail this form of commercialized vice. Popularly called the White Slave Act, it found support among those who concluded that the states had been too lax in stamping out sexual immorality. Passed under the federal commerce power, the legislation made criminal the transportation of a woman across state lines "for the purpose of prostitution or debauchery, or for any other immoral purpose."[13]

In rather cursory fashion the Court upheld four convictions under the new legislation. In the major case of *Hoke* v. *United States* the Justices found no constitutional impediment in the act. Effie Hoke and Basile Economides were both charged with enticing two young women to go from New Orleans to Beaumont, Texas, for purposes of prostitution. Both defendants received a sentence of two years on each of the three counts in the indictment, an indication of the fervor with which trial judges greeted the new legislation. McKenna handled this case, along with the remaining three, for a unanimous Court.

After dealing with particular objections to the trial in *Hoke*, the Californian concentrated his opinion on the legitimacy of the act as an exercise of congressional power over commerce. McKenna rejected the idea that prostitution regulation is an exclusive matter for state control, saying "we are one people; and the powers reserved to the States and those conferred on the Nation are adapted to be exercised, whether independently or concurrently, to promote the general welfare, material and moral." He continued:

This is the effect of the decisions; and surely if the facility of interstate transportation can be taken away from the demoralization of lotteries, the debasement of obscene literature, the contagion of diseased cattle or persons, the impurity of food and drugs, the like facility can be taken away from the systematic enticement to and the enslavement in prostitution and debachery of women, and, more insistently, of girls.

The apparent fact that the two girls were well established prostitutes in New Orleans did not sidetrack McKenna. He concluded that congressional power over commerce embraced means "convenient to its exercise," even though the legislation "may have the quality of police regulations."[14]

In *Anthanasaw* v. *United States* the Court explicated the meaning of debauchery. Involved was a seventeen-year-old Georgia girl, who, when she answered an advertisement for chorus girls, received a ticket for transportation to Tampa, Florida. Apparently one of her duties was to mingle intimately with the guests in the theater, but her protests found a sympathetic ear, and the police were called. Since no sexual intercourse had taken place the defendants argued that she had not been debauched. Taking his cue from the trial court, McKenna read the term as indicating a prohibition against leading a women to corrupt her sexual morality whether the actual corruption had taken place or not.[15]

The remaining two cases relied upon technical objections that McKenna quickly disposed of.[16] Strangely enough, three defendants involved in these two cases were women, as was Effie Hoke. This first High Court brush with the Mann Act revealed little of that high-powered commercialized vice that apparently was the target of the act. Here all the defendants were involved in trying to profit on a small-time basis from sexual immorality, but hardly were they the vice entrepreneurs whose assumed activities had stirred congressional action.

Whether in the Mann Act cases the Court was implementing or extending congressional policy is a moot question, but clear evidence of cooperation with another branch of the government can be seen in *Charlton* v. *Kelly*. Italy had requested the extradition of an American citizen for the crime of murder, relying upon treaties with the United States for the reciprocal return of fugitives. In the past the United States had repeatedly been rebuffed in its requests for the extradition of Italian citizens under the treaties, the Italian government contending that the term *persons* in the treaty did not embrace citizens. Now Italy sought, for the first time, to test the sincerity of the American government's interpretation. The Justices were not without advice, for the Secretary of State filed a memorandum in which he said the United States recognized its obligation to surrender an American citizen to Italian justice. Interpreting this as a waiver of the breach, the Court, quite willing to support State Department policy in the case, allowed Charlton to be returned.[17] Without such State Department intervention, the Court would probably have looked at the foreign country's practice under the treaty and reciprocated in kind.

The Court did not hesitate to reject a claim that a jury trial had been denied on grounds that the party requesting the trial had not followed the prescribed procedure, but by a narrow majority the Justices resisted pressure to make any direct inroad on this basic right. In *Slocum* v. *New York Life Insurance*

Company, Van Devanter, for the majority, ruled that a lower federal court could only order a new trial and not reverse a jury verdict. Although federal courts were required to follow state practice, and although New York practice permitted a judgment notwithstanding the verdict, the Justice stated that federal courts were limited by the Seventh Amendment's provision for jury trials in civil suits. With considerable scholarship Van Devanter demonstrated that in 1791, when the Seventh Amendment was adopted, the common law, as incorporated in the amendment, required the result reached here. Hughes dissented with Holmes, Lurton, and Pitney. The dissenting opinion was couched in terms that somewhat disguised the innovation it proposed, but its basic thrust was in the direction of judicial economy. Hughes called the lower court's action no more than a simplification of procedure designed to avoid unnecessary litigation. He argued, in contending with the Seventh Amendment, that it protects the defendant's right not to have fact determinations made by a jury reexamined and that, since there was no factual dispute involved in the case, the constitutional provision could not have been violated.[18]

Some constitutional provisions carry general language that can be interpreted differently over time; others tend to be fixed by the meaning the terms had at the time they became a part of the Constitution. Despite professional criticism of the *Slocum* decision, it did recognize, in a manner the dissenters sought to avoid, that certain constitutional language should retain its historical meaning.[19] At times the attempt to search for the original meaning of constitutional language is both illusory and counterproductive; at other times, as in this instance, it reaches the essence of what a constitution is.

Advocates continued to press due process claims upon the Court, though the vast majority were consistently rejected. For instance, South Dakota could prohibit unfair competition; Indiana could regulate mines; Chicago could fix the weight of bread; and a city in Georgia could mandate water closets.[20] But the argument retained its appeal because the general language that a person could not be deprived of his property without due process of law seemed to confer an air of legitimacy on claims alleging a wide variety of injuries. Combined with the inherent indefiniteness of the standard was the fact that the Justices often responded inconsistently to similar claims because of their reaction to the particular facts in the case. Cases coming from the neighboring states of Nebraska and Kansas provide a good illustration.

For violation of the maximum time allowed for the shipment of livestock, Nebraska specified the damages that could be recovered by the injured shipper. The railroad's argument that its property was being taken without due process of law was rejected by the lower court, which justified the fixed amount as necessary because of the difficulty of determining actual damages. The shipper recovered $1,640 plus attorney's fees for the twenty-five violations alleged. McKenna, for a unanimous Court, simply accepted the argument that the statute in question "was enacted to meet conditions which had arisen from the conduct of carriers, and which, in the judgment of the legislature, demanded a remedy." A little over two months later the Court, again unanimously, decided that similar Kansas legislation violated the due process clause. The state had sought to strengthen its enforcement of interstate rates for common carriers by affording aggrieved shippers a set amount of damages plus attorney's fees for every charge in excess of the established rates. Now substituting its judgment for that of the Kansas legislature, the Court, through Van Devanter, said "the imposition of $500 as liquidated damages is not only grossly out of proportion to the possible actual damages but is so arbitrary and oppressive that its enforcement would be nothing short of the taking of property without due process of law."[21] What in one case had been a reasonable exercise of police power was now condemned as a violation of due process. No wonder the Court's docket was bulging!

As the last business in the term that extended to mid-June 1913, the Court announced its decision in a host of cases challenging rate regulation in Minnesota, Missouri, West Virginia, Oregon, and Arkansas. With the recent activity of the federal government in the area of rate regulation, corporations now leveled a massive challenge upon similar state action. Justice Hughes was assigned the task of coping with this complex problem, not only to settle the present litigation but to provide guidelines for the future. The decisive opinion was issued in the *Minnesota Rate Cases*. All cases were decided without dissent, and all decisions upheld the basic authority of the states to regulate. The three Minnesota cases were stockholder suits brought to enjoin the enforcement of state rates upon interstate carriers. In all three plaintiffs had won in the lower court. The state rates were assailed on three grounds: first, that they interfered with interstate commerce; second, that they were confiscatory; and third, that the penalties for violation were so severe they amounted to a deprivation of due process and equal protection.

Hughes took these contentions in order. Accepting as "given" a federal system that has institutionalized competing authority and that has hindered a truly national system of rate regulation, Hughes recognized that much that is done locally has effect beyond the state's borders. But, he said, this is no bar to state action so long as it does not directly burden interstate commerce. Throughout his opinion the New York Justice extensively quoted precedent to support his generalities. He then ruled that state authority to regulate railroad rates was clearly established. When in the federal legislature's judgment, Hughes continued, the blending of intrastate and interstate commerce makes such separation unworkable, Congress has the power to act. But any failure to act, he added, cannot be interpreted as a bar to state action.

Next, the Justice considered the allegation that the rates were confiscatory. Whether the rates allow a fair return upon the investment requires, first of all, a consideration of how the property is to be valued. This cannot be done,

Hughes said, by preordained rules, but rather must be done after considering all the facts. Unable to come up with any better detailing of facts to consider, Hughes resorted to the Court's first such summary in the landmark case of *Smyth* v. *Ames*, decided in 1897. If the cases were designed to elicit greater precision from the Court on the matter of valuation, this aim was frustrated by Hughes's reliance upon the early case. Valuation in each instance was a complex economic matter that the Court apparently felt could best be judged on the basis of the individual case. However, Hughes added that the Court will insist that the carriers come in with hard evidence of confiscation, for the "general estimates of the sort here submitted, with respect to a subject so intricate and important, should not be accepted as adequate proof to sustain a finding of confiscation."[22] Only in one of the three Minnesota cases was the allegation of confiscation established to the Court's satisfaction, and there Hughes modified an injunction to permit the trial court to proceed further on an initiative from the state in changed circumstances.

With the general principles stated in the *Minnesota Rate Cases*, Hughes responded similarly to the other challenges to state regulation.[23] Although the Court gave notice that it would still inspect such state action and pass judgment on its constitutionality under the due process clause, the opinions gave new life and support to state rate-making power. In an era of growing federal regulation of the railroads, operators hoped to free themselves from the patchwork quilt of state regulation. Their arguments testified to the need for a consistent pattern of national regulation, but they were battling an entrenched federal system and a Congress that had neither the temerity nor the desire to make further inroads on state power.

While the Court was in recess President Woodrow Wilson and his administration kept Washington buzzing. Long a student of government and the presidential office, Wilson was now ready to turn his plurality victory into a mandate for reform along the lines of his New Freedom platform. Theodore Roosevelt had given initial shape to the modern presidency, but Wilson extended and strengthened the powers of the office and wedded them to party leadership. He realized the key to his success was the ability to work with his party in Congress.[24] By early October 1913 Wilson's theories of leadership had been tested, and he emerged with the first substantial downward revision of the tariff since the Civil War. Before the end of the year the President would also sign legislation establishing the Federal Reserve, which provided the banking and currency reform long demanded. The passage of the Clayton Antitrust Act and the establishment of the Federal Trade Commission in 1914 brought to fruition the three major goals of the President. Organized labor had been able to lobby successfully for changes in antitrust legislation that seemed to promise unions some relief from the injunctive processes of the courts. The New Freedom had been predicated upon the assumption that government had to redress certain functional imbalances in the industrial society and free the competitive spirit. With the completion of the New Freedom program the question became one of whether the President could be moved to champion other types of legislation, more clearly embraced under Roosevelt's New Nationalism, that recognized a qualitatively different role for the federal government. Whatever the future held it was clear that the presidency had passed from a passive Taft to an active Wilson.

Returning in October 1913 the Justices found another clogged docket. The prospect of another long session characterized by short opinions loomed ahead. To handle as many cases as possible the Court cut its Christmas recess to less than two weeks. Dissents would be registered in less than 10 percent of the cases, and less than a quarter of them resulted in written opinions. In addition, the Justices readily avoided substantive questions when cases could be dismissed on procedural grounds.

Hughes, for the unanimous Court, served notice in the first opinion of the new term that the words he uttered in the *Minnesota Rate Cases* clearly expressed the Court's policy in regard to claims of confiscation. He told a carrier that the simple ratio between total operating expenses and revenues over the entire line was insufficient to make out a case of confiscation under Indiana's intrastate rate making.[25] The presumption of good faith would be accorded state action. As long as the states confined their regulatory and taxing enactments to what was essentially intrastate commerce, the Court tended to uphold such measures and regularly rejected due process and equal protection claims.

Ever since *Munn* v. *Illinois* in 1877 confined the state's ability to set rates to those businesses affected with a public interest, litigants argued that the decision implied the existence of private business beyond the regulatory power of the state. Generally, the targets of state regulations were railroads and other public service corporations. *German Alliance Insurance Company* v. *Lewis*, however, squarely brought to the Justices the issue of whether an insurance company could be forced to respect the schedule of rates and charges for fire insurance established by Kansas. Although the insurance industry had been the subject of state regulation for many decades, German Alliance argued that the state's power did not embrace the setting of rates for what were essentially private contracts.

Rejecting the contention that state regulatory power is confined to areas where the use of property is public or where a public trust is imposed upon the property, McKenna, for the majority, ruled that "a business, by circumstances and its nature, may rise from private to be of public concern and be subject, in consequence, to governmental regulation." Addressing the subject of fire insurance, he said its fundamental object is to spread individual loss over as wide an area as possible. Because a large portion of the public wealth is protected by insurance, such private contracts, he continued, have greater public consequence than ordinary commercial transactions. Counsel had argued that the Court had shown special concern for protecting freedom of contract, especially in matters of price regulation, but the Justice responded that once the state's power to regulate is established it can set prices. With Lurton temporarily absent from the bench, McKenna's opinion commanded only a majority of five. Lamar, in a dissent joined by White and Van Devanter, picked up the refrain of losing counsel and contended that the majority had now determined that "the citizen holds his property and his individual right of contract and of labor under legislative favor rather than under constitutional guaranty."[26]

The words in *Munn*, suggesting that certain businesses were beyond state regulatory power, could have become the basis for a new doctrine of constitutional law, but the growing recognition of the wide ambit of state power militated against success in the period. White had sided with Brewer in his unsuccessful attempt to reverse *Munn* in 1894, and the Chief, as indicated here, continued to see limits on the state police power as it related to the setting of rates. Many observers criticized *Munn* for its suggestion of constitutional limitations upon the subject matter of regulation, but the wisdom of the Court had prevailed since 1877 in not building upon the distinction suggested.

In *German Alliance* the dissenters also saw an interference with the freedom to contract, and despite the majority's rejection of it there, that doctrine was far from dead. But the Court tended to restrict its use to certain regulations of labor, perhaps wary that its broader use would impede substantially the exercise of state power. During the term the majority did invoke the doctrine, over Holmes's silent dissent, to invalidate a Texas law that sought to impose a requirement that a conductor of a freight train have at least two years prior experience as a brakeman or freight conductor. Lamar had the satisfaction of writing the opinion. He concluded that the statute under the guise of the police power created a privileged class and deprived others of "the liberty to work in a calling they were qualified to fill with safety to the public and benefit to themselves."[27]

Chief Justice White, during the term, sought to reinforce the Court's new policy on whether a state could revoke a company's license to do business in the state when that company sought to remove a case to the federal court. Weakly distinguishing the earlier inconsistent decisions of the Court, he wrote forceful words that charted clearly the new direction of the Court:

. . . the judicial power of the United States as created by the Constitution and provided for by the Congress pursuant to its constitutional authority, is a power wholly independent of state action, and which therefore the several States may not by any exertion of authority in any form, directly or indirectly, destroy, abridge, limit, or render inefficacious. The doctrine is so elementary as to require no citation of authority to sustain it.[28]

Despite his refusal to acknowledge the conflict with past decisions, White clearly indicated that the Court would not allow the states in the exercise of their substantial power over domestic business to deny interstate corporations access to the federal courts.

Perhaps not too much should be made of the Court's decision in *Patsone* v. *Pennsylvania*, but the case seems to demonstrate just how willing the Justices were to give wide berth to the police power. In 1909 Pennsylvania passed a law making the killing of any wild bird or animal or the ownership or possession of a shotgun by an alien illegal. Patsone contended that the statute discriminated against aliens as a class and deprived him of his property without due process of law. Assuming the question of discrimination could be resolved, Hughes said, there was no problem in upholding the means of enforcement Pennsylvania chose. A state may classify with reference to a particular evil, he continued, and regulate only those within a designated class. At the heart of the matter, the Justice continued, was the question of whether the Court can pronounce Pennsylvania's assumption that aliens posed a particular threat to wildlife unwarranted. Since a determination cannot be made in ignorance of local conditions, he concluded, the Court cannot call the judgment of the state legislature wrong.[29] Admittedly, the Court's decision here did not threaten any substantial vested interest in the society. Only the Chief dissented in this strange case; the rest of the Justices were willing to suspend logic in deference to the authority of the state.

During the term the Court gave continued support to the federal government's campaign against sexual immorality, both of the domestic and foreign variety. Just how far the Court was willing to trod this path with the federal government is revealed in the case of Samuel Lewis. Current law provided that an alien bringing a prostitute into the country was guilty of a felony and was also deportable. Lewis was found not guilty of the criminal offense, and he pleaded his acquittal as a bar to deportation proceedings. Pitney resolved the conflict and upheld the deportation order, saying that "the acquittal under the indictment was not equivalent to an affirmative finding of innocence, but merely to an adjudication that the proof was not sufficient to overcome all reasonable doubt of the guilt of the accused."[30] Indeed, a person found not guilty by a jury may actually be guilty of the offense, but to argue this speculative possibility as a justification for inconsistent action seems to allow the other branches of the government to proceed unimpeded by the guarantees afforded by the Constitution.

A Court so deferential to administrative action could hardly be expected to tangle with the Congress directly over a related matter. When a statute created a legislative presumption that any naturalized citizen who took up permanent residence in a foreign country within five years after becoming an American citizen did not have the requisite intention of becoming a citizen and therefore could have his naturalization certificate canceled for fraud, the

Court saw no deficiency of power in Congress. Van Devanter, for the unanimous bench, seemed slightly uncomfortable with the statute, suggesting that a five-year period might be too long and that the presumption would weaken as the period lengthened between naturalization and the taking up of residence abroad. In this case where a doctor, immediately after finishing his medical training, left for South Africa and then fought in the Boer War, the Justice seemed sure of the result.[31]

By far the most significant case of the 1913 term was *Weeks* v. *United States*, dealing with the Fourth Amendment's protection against unreasonable searches and seizures. In 1886 the Court had said the Fourth Amendment applied "to all invasions on the part of the government and its employees of the sanctity of a man's home and the privacies of life," but no ruling was then required on the question of the admissibility of evidence that had been illegally seized.[32] Now in 1914 the Justices were confronted with the conviction of Fremont Weeks for using the mails to transport lottery tickets. He was arrested at his place of employment. About the same time a Kansas City police officer went to Weeks's home, where he found a helpful neighbor who told him where Weeks kept a key to the house. The officer entered the house, searched it, and found certain papers and articles that he turned over to a United States marshal. On the same day the marshal returned with local police officers for a further search; they were admitted by a boarder. The second search turned up some letters and envelopes in a chest of drawers. Weeks was convicted on the basis of the lottery tickets and written material regarding the lottery found in the two searches. His Fourth Amendment objections were overruled at the trial, presumably upon the ground that as long as the material was competent the court would not inquire into the manner by which it was obtained, a rule with some lineage in the law.

Reaffirming the Court's earlier words, Day, for the unanimous Court, ruled that even accused criminals have rights that must be respected by the courts, whose duty must involve the supervision of unlawful official activity destructive of fundamental rights. Dismissing the relevance of searches incident to a lawful arrest, Day said this case involved the right of the court to use evidence seized in the defendant's house without his permission by a United States marshal holding neither a warrant for arrest nor a warrant for a search of the premises. The Justice argued that if such material could be seized and used against the defendant, the Fourth Amendment is meaningless. Although the attempt to catch criminals may be praiseworthy, he continued, it cannot be "aided by the sacrifice of those great principles established by years of endeavor and suffering which have resulted in their embodiment in the fundamental law of the land."[33] Under the color of his office, the marshal, Day continued, had violated the Constitution, and the conviction must be reversed. Such strong language in defense of an accused criminal's rights was unusual during this period.

A victory had been achieved for the rights of the individual under the Fourth Amendment, but that victory was limited. Evidence seized without a proper warrant or not pursuant to a lawful arrest by federal officials would be excluded from the trial, the established "exclusionary rule." But since the amendment was not binding upon the states, their police officers could seize evidence and then turn it over to federal prosecutors. For obvious reasons this practice was labeled the "silver platter doctrine." With the states having the primary responsibility for the enforcement of criminal law, the loophole left by *Weeks* was great.[34]

By the time the Justices reached a batch of cases coming up from the Commerce Court, that specialized tribunal had been legislated out of existence. With its demise on October 22, 1913, the Commerce Court had experienced a short life of a little less than two years and eight months. Almost from the very beginning it was a political target, but its seeming hostility to the Interstate Commerce Commission and the impeachment and removal of Judge Robert W. Archibald sealed its doom, which came with the Wilson administration.[35]

Despite the Supreme Court's early wariness in dealing with the Interstate Commerce Commission, at this time it was much more in tune with the commission than was the specialized court allegedly set up to bring a needed expertise to this area.[36] Still, in the most significant of these ICC cases to come to the Court in the 1913 term, the Shreveport Rate Case, the ICC, the Commerce Court, and a majority of Justices agreed. At issue was the question of whether the ICC could override intrastate railroad rates set by Texas for the purpose of eliminating a discrimination in interstate commerce. The case came to the commission in a proceeding initiated by the Railroad Commission of Louisiana, which claimed that the roads were discriminating against traffic from Shreveport into Texas. Finding such discrimination, the ICC ordered the lowering of the interstate rate. In its investigation it also found that shippers from Dallas and Houston to points east had to pay intrastate rates substantially less than shippers from Shreveport for approximately the same distance, and the commission ordered an equalization of these rates. Since the interstate rate was now deemed reasonable by the ICC, the Commerce Court ordered an increase in the intrastate rates. The obvious argument on appeal was that the commission was not authorized to set intrastate rates because Congress either could not or did not empower it to set such rates. Only Lurton and Pitney were impressed by this argument.

Noting that Congress was given control over commerce to overcome local rivalry, Hughes, for the Court, ruled that whenever "the interstate and intrastate transactions of carriers are so related that the government of the one involves the control of the other, it is Congress, and not the State, that is entitled to prescribe the final and dominant rule." Although Congress has no power to regulate intrastate commerce as such, Hughes continued, "it does possess the power to foster and protect interstate commerce, and to take all measures necessary or appropriate to that end, although intrastate transactions of interstate carriers may thereby be controlled."[37] He then had no trouble finding that the commission was authorized to remedy the type of discrimination it found.

In relatively clear language a majority of the Court was willing to recognize that regulation of some intrastate commerce was needed to accomplish the goal of regulating commerce for a nation. In the commerce clause the Court found power for the federal government to pass legislation that affected subject matter earlier assumed to be exclusively within the jurisdiction of the states. Now in the Shreveport case it recognized that effective control over interstate commerce could necessitate the regulation of matters within a state's borders. Attuned to the realities of a national economy, the decision clearly illustrates the way in which the Court was developing the commerce clause as a vehicle for national action.

Pitney was silent in his dissent in the Shreveport case, but not in *Boston & Maine Railroad Company* v. *Hooker* in which he criticized his colleagues for their favoritism to public carriers and their frustration of clear congressional policy. Earlier a unanimous Court had interpreted the Carmack amendment, a part of the Hepburn Act of 1906, to allow railroads to limit their liability for loss to goods by filing a schedule for increased costs for liability beyond the minimum contained in the established tariff. If a shipper wanted to cover his goods for their full value, he could pay the additional cost. What the present case asked was whether a passenger who had no knowledge of the practice could be limited to a minimal recovery for the loss of her luggage through the railroad's negligence. The lower court in Massachusetts followed its common law rules of liability and awarded the passenger full recovery for her loss. Day, speaking for the Court majority, reversed on grounds that the Carmack amendment was applicable and that it limited the passenger's recovery to the minimum amount. Placing the burden upon the passenger to procure the added coverage, Day said, was altogether proper, despite the fact that additional coverage had not been offered her and that no schedules of cost were posted. The Ohio Justice brushed aside any differences between a bill of lading and a baggage ticket or between a loss caused by the carrier's negligence and by an act of God.[38] The majority had turned a legislative provision designed to meet the relative equities of shippers and carriers into a trap for the unwary passenger. Furthermore, the Court's new reading provided a limitation of a carrier's liability in cases of its own negligence, hitherto a major target of state and federal regulatory legislation.

Pitney passionately responded that the majority's resolution was inconsistent with its earlier holdings on the responsibility of common carriers. The federal legislation, which the majority interpreted as necessitating the result, Pitney read as clearly expressing an intent to hold the carrier responsible for its own negligence. The New Jersey Justice accused the majority of ignoring consistent precedent and sabotaging clear congressional intent. His long dissent here is incisive and persuasive, but Pitney convinced none of his colleagues to stem the tide of what he saw so clearly as a reactionary development—the insulation of common carriers from liability for their own negligence.[39]

Pitney, as many Justices on the Court, has often been characterized as a conservative, if not a reactionary, Justice on the basis of a small portion of his opinions. We must recognize the worth of the conservative approach. What bothered Pitney was the fact that the Court was departing from precedent and the tradition of the common law in the present case, and his look backward brought a far more equitable result, as did Horace Gray's in *Wong Kim Ark*. One decision does not a career make, but Pitney's forceful stand here reveals a thoughtful and sensitive decision maker.

All Justices were present on the last opinion day, June 22, 1914, when the Court closed the term, but Lurton's absence in midterm had spawned rumors of resignation. The Justice, who had turned seventy in late February, scotched rumors by returning to the Court in April after a vacation in Florida with his family. Perhaps he had returned to duty too soon, for four weeks after the Court adjourned, Horace H. Lurton died of a heart attack in Atlantic City. Joining the Court in the 1909 term, his total service in the state and federal judiciary exceeded thirty-two years.[40] His steady and reliable work on the Sixth Circuit Court of Appeals had commended him to Taft, who appointed Lurton to the High Bench as he was nearing the age of sixty-six. Perhaps Taft hoped Lurton would be another Holmes, who though over sixty at the time of his appointment, was still on the Court after a dozen years. But such was not to be, as Lurton became the first of Taft's appointees to fall.

In the eulogies showered upon Lurton at the formal Court ceremony, the refrain was that the man had been a solid, reliable, and conscientious judge. The Attorney General added that he "rendered no startling or sensational decisions."[41] Lurton did not hesitate to dissent, generally in the company of others, but his contribution to the work of the Court is largely submerged in the institutional work product. Although he wrote some opinions that recognized the scope of federal power, he was more reluctant than most of his colleagues to override states' rights arguments. He was less inclined to read the silence of Congress as a bar to state regulatory action, and he was more niggardly in determining the scope of the commerce power of Congress as an inroad on the state's police power. His dissent in the Shreveport Rate Case is a good illustration of where Lurton and the majority parted company. During his short term on the Court he probably met Taft's expectations.

Lurton's death on July 12, 1914, gave President Woodrow Wilson his first opportunity to name a man to the Court. The new President was more of a prior student of his office than either of his two predecessors, but he, unlike them, seemed to treat the task now confronting him rather casually. Roosevelt and Taft spent considerable time and personal effort in selecting nominees to the High Bench, convinced that the function of appointment was one of the most significant and far-reaching responsibilities of the office. Wilson initially neglected the importance of the Supreme Court or, at the very least, subordinated its importance in his thinking. Roosevelt wanted to put party men on the Court to assure decisions in step with his administration, and Taft wanted to staff the Court with solid and reliable judicial minds that would exercise a conservative check on social innovation, but Wilson considered his first appointment with no real appreciation of the significance of the matter, either to his administration or to his governmental philosophy. In fact, the President apparently used the vacancy to rid himself of a cabinet member. If this was his prime motivation, the fact that the nominee would not be a "progressive" in the Wilsonian sense should occasion no surprise.

James C. McReynolds had served as Assistant Attorney General from 1903 to 1907 and as special governmental counsel in certain antitrust prosecutions in the Taft administration. His vehement objection to George W. Wikersham's compromise on the final settlement of the *American Tobacco Company* case led him to resign his governmental post to return to private law practice in New York. His image as a trustbuster had been securely lodged in the popular mind, and because of the relatively few acceptable candidates for the job, Wilson appointed the Tennessee Democrat to be Attorney General. Although a foe of monopoly, McReynolds held a rigidly limited view of the role that government should play in the economy, and before long he was advising Wilson to assuage the alarms of business as to the antitrust program of the administration. But it was not this advice to slow down reform that made McReynolds more and more of a liability in the cabinet but rather his abrasive personality. He mixed little with his colleagues and saw himself as a man of great rectitude, quite different from the politicians who filled the other cabinet posts.[42]

As Attorney General, McReynolds repulsed his cabinet colleagues' requests that certain individuals be considered for appointments in the Justice Department. McReynolds also alienated some powerful Senators, who charged that the Justice Department was softening in its attitude toward trusts. Furthermore, the Attorney General's attempt to supervise the performance of federal judges, which included a proposal that if lower federal judges did not retire at age seventy new judges were to be appointed to sit with them on the bench, led to charges of spying and interference with the judiciary.[43] This appointment was causing headaches for Wilson. McReynolds was never easy to work with, but matters seemed to be worsening when the vacancy developed on the Supreme Court. Apparently Wilson made the decision without much thought, for a month after Lurton's death McReynolds's name was sent to the Senate. With strong party backing the nomination was approved in ten days. The cabinet had been purged, but the Court had been burdened.

Historians looking backward from Wilson's other appointments, made within a different framework at a different time, have assumed the President put McReynolds on the Court because of his "progressivism." This was simply not so; Wilson got exactly what he deserved in the nomination. What he got was a Justice who became increasingly truculent on the Court and increasingly restrictive in his view of the permissible range of governmental activity. McReynolds' conservatism was not hidden from view at the time of his appointment, for in commenting upon the appointment the *New York World* said: "... while Mr. McReynolds may not be classed as an extreme reactionary, he has repeatedly exhibited mental traits and inclinations that have given much comfort to reactionaries."[44] Wilson had not been misled; he simply underestimated the importance of the task he faced.

Rarely is a man replaced on the Court so smoothly, for James C. McReynolds was ready to be sworn in on the first day of the 1914 term. The appointment of another man from the Justice Department again meant that an eight-man Court would have to decide a significant number of cases because of the new appointee's participation in them while in his former office. This would be a factor throughout the decade.

The fifty-two-year-old Justice who took his seat to the far left of the Chief was a bachelor. The Court's last bachelor was Moody and before him Gray, but McReynolds felt so strongly about bachelorhood that he excluded all married or engaged individuals from consideration for his clerkships, but then he excluded smokers and Jews as well.[45] About six feet in height, McReynolds was of medium build. He had a roughhewn, squarish face with a hawklike nose and large ears. His hair was receding, and his clear eyes were capped with light eyebrows. His lips were thin and his jaw prominent.

Early in the term the Court first considered the constitutionality of state workmen's compensation legislation. The new variety of law was designed to compensate employees injured in the course of their employment by creating an employers' insurance system. The old common law defenses—contributory negligence, fellow servant, and assumption of risk—were abolished, and in return the employer was immunized from a personal injury suit. Ohio drafted legislation to eliminate any constitutional barrier that might arise from making the system compulsory, as it gave the employer of five or more persons an option: he could join the system and gain the immunity it offered, or he could refuse and be subject to suit but without recourse to the common law defenses. The Jeffrey Manufacturing Company had opted not to join the plan, and in the state court the injured employee gained a recovery. The company claimed it had been denied equal protection because companies employing less than five workers were exempt from the law and had access to the full panoply of common law defenses in such suits. In a unanimous opinion by Day the Court saw no arbitrariness or unreasonableness in such a classification. The Justice simply said the state legislature has the right to make such distinctions, and its judgment, not the Court's, makes the law.[46]

This bland opinion reflects none of the drama surrounding the subject of workmen's compensation laws, an episode of which had just culminated in congressional action enlarging the Supreme Court's review authority over state court decisions. Behind this change effected in late 1914 lies an interesting story that revealed a problem inherent in the federal system. In 1911 in *Ives* v. *South Buffalo Railway Company* the New York Court of Appeals provoked national dismay by invalidating the state's workmen's compensation act as a violation of the due process clause found in both the state and the federal constitutions. The New York court accurately summarized the social and economic purposes behind the law and recognized the argument that this system of compensation would better spread the loss and eliminate antagonism between employer and employee, but then it added that if such arguments "can be allowed to subvert the fundamental idea of property, then there is no private right entirely safe, because there is no limitation upon the absolute discretion of legislatures, and the guarantees of the Constitution are a mere waste of words."[47]

Theodore Roosevelt expressed well the feelings of many, when he wrote:

Such decisions are profoundly anti-social, are against the interests of humanity, and tell for the degradation of a very large proportion of our community; and, above all, they seek to establish as an immutable principle the doctrine that the rights of property are supreme over the rights of humanity, and that this free people, this American people, is not only forbidden to better the conditions of mankind, but cannot even strive to do the elementary justice that, among even monarchies of the Old World, has already been done by other great industrial nations.[48]

For once in his mounting campaign against the backwardness and unresponsiveness of courts, the former President was supported by a host of legal scholars and constitutional lawyers. The Supreme Court had moved away from *Lochner* and in *Muller* v. *Oregon* had directly alluded to the relevance of the economic and social factors highlighted in the Brandeis brief. The consensus was that the New York Court of Appeals had interpreted the due process clause in a manner that would not have commanded the agreement of the Supreme Court. Although state courts had been interpreting their own constitutions and the federal constitution more conservatively than the Supreme Court for years, the *Ives* decision with its cursory refusal to consider the social and economic situation as legally relevant focused attention on the fact that no appeal to the Supreme Court was possible from the New York decision. The High Bench could only review cases in which the state court had decided against the validity of a federal constitutional claim; here that claim had been upheld.

Responding to the situation the American Bar Association drafted a bill to give the Supreme Court the right to review cases in which state laws were invalidated on federal grounds. So as to not further burden an already over-burdened Court the original version was changed in the Senate to give the Justices the discretion to hear an appeal under a writ of certiorari, rather than make review obligatory under a writ of error. In this form the bill became law in December 1914.[49]

Throughout the whole campaign to rid the nation of decisions such as *Ives*, there seemed to be a consensus that the new legislation would eliminate the finality of decisions like that made by the New York Court of Appeals. The Supreme Court could now insist upon consistent interpretations of the Con-stitution throughout the United States, but this modification in no way inter-fered with the rights of the high court of each state to utter the final word on the meaning of its constitution. Where the state court based its decision on state and federal constitutional grounds, the Court, in the past, had been quite ready to dismiss such appeals because the decision could be supported on an independent state ground. Even a due process clause in the state consti-tution could be interpreted to mean something different from the federal due process clause. Still, the furor caused by *Ives* might also have served the purpose of alerting state judiciaries to the temper of the times. For the first time since the basic judiciary act of 1789, the Court's jurisdiction was ex-panded. The legislation, supported by many as a curb on reactionary tenden-cies of state judiciaries, also seemed to express a vote of confidence in the United States Supreme Court.

The decision approving Ohio's workmen's compensation law seemed to indicate that such confidence in the Court was justified, but when protection for the workingman concerned unions the majority of Justices were much more suspicious. Seven terms ago the Court had ruled that a suit for triple damages against the United Hatters and the American Federation of Labor for engaging in a secondary boycott against Dietrich Loewe was permitted under the antitrust act. Now the Justices considered a substantial verdict in Loewe's favor. Despite the change in six seats since the initial determination, the Court unanimously upheld the recovery.[50]

A second case, *Coppage* v. *Kansas*, provided more of a challenge to the Court, as it also brought back memories of the fateful 1907 term. In *Adair* v. *United States* the Court had ruled by a vote of six to two that a federal statute outlawing the yellow-dog contract was not a legitimate exercise of congres-sional power to regulate interstate commerce. Harlan had written the opin-ion, but both McKenna and Holmes had dissented vigorously. Now, in the 1914 term, both dissenters were still on the Court, but only two of the Justices in the majority remained, White and Day. At issue was the constitutionality of a Kansas law attempting the same type of regulation under the state police power. If Taft in his remaking of the Court had such an issue in mind, he had done his job well, for the majority, in a six to three decision, ruled that the state law was equally invalid. Pitney's majority opinion garnered the votes of two of the three other Taft appointees still on the bench, Van Devanter and Lamar, White, McReynolds, and, surprisingly, McKenna. Day, who switched places with McKenna, wrote a dissent, as did Holmes.

Noting the similarity between the instant case and *Adair*, Pitney addressed the argument that the state has a legitimate interest in redressing the bargaining imbalance between employer and employee. Such police power action, the New Jersey Justice continued, must be consistent with the guarantees of the federal constitution. He read those guarantees to include both a liberty to contract and a protection for private property, which, he maintained, must inevitably result in "inequalities of fortune that are the necessary result of the exercise of those rights."[51] To argue that the public good requires the removal of such inequalities, he concluded, is tantamount to denying the rights upon which they are based. Just as the federal statute seeking to protect workers from employer reprisals fell before the requirements of the Fifth Amendment's due process clause, so, too, Pitney ruled, must this state statute fall before the clause in the Fourteenth Amendment. *Coppage* v. *Kansas* is often cited as characteristic of Pitney's attitudes while on the Court. Although such an attribution considerably distorts and simplifies Pitney as a Justice, the opinion does reveal his and the majority's unwillingness to accept the legitimacy of labor unions as a counterforce to organized capital.

Holmes, in dissent, insisted that *Adair* was wrongly decided. Liberty of contract, he contended, can only be meaningful when the parties are relatively equal. The Massachusetts Justice saw no barrier to state action seeking to ensure this equality. Day, joined by Hughes, was willing to distinguish *Adair* on grounds that the state police power extended beyond the federal commerce power. He expressed concern that the decision of the majority limited not only Kansas but also fourteen other states with similar statutes. Responding to the barrier Pitney raised by summoning up freedom of contract, the Ohio Justice concluded quite correctly "that the right of contract is not absolute and unyielding, but is subject to limitation and restraint in the interests of the public health, safety and welfare." Day indicated his general sympathy with such state action, saying it does no more than seek to create for the employee the same freedom of action enjoyed by the employer: "the right to make such lawful affiliations as he may desire with organizations of his choice." The Justice contended that a ruling that destroys the liberty of one citizen to protect that of another is certainly unnecessary. Kansas did not, he concluded, "go beyond a legitimate exercise of the police power, when it sought, not to require one man to employ another against his will, but to put limitations upon the sacrifice of rights which one may exact from another as a condition of employment."[52] Day's dissent clearly illuminates the bias inherent in a majority taking refuge in abstractions, neither well supported by other Court activity in the area, nor in the greater world beyond. Day, Hughes, and Holmes were free of the antiunion bias that characterized the majority, and they were keenly aware of the need to afford states sufficient latitude to legislate on such matters.

When union activity was not involved the Justices generally gave wide berth to state labor regulations. Ohio's law establishing the manner in which workers were to be paid for coal mined, even though it imposed substantial penalties for violation, was upheld unanimously. Indiana could by statute require coal mine operators to provide washrooms; and California could prosecute hotel and hospital owners for employing female workers in excess of the eight hours a day mandated by statute.[53] No member of Court in any of these cases saw any unconstitutional infringement of the freedom to contract.

Coppage also did not indicate that the Court was generally imposing any new limitations on the state police power. In fact, in a matter of first impression the Court ruled that motion pictures could be censored. In *Mutual Film Corporation* v. *Industrial Commission of Ohio* McKenna, for a unanimous Court, disposed of the argument that such censorship infringes upon interstate commerce by saying the law does not take effect until the film is mingled with other property in the state. But the main contention in the case was that the regulation violated the right of free speech protected by the Ohio constitution. The board of censors was directed to approve only those films with "a moral, educational, or amusing and harmless character." The company had argued it should not be restrained from distributing its wares, for it remained liable under state law for any injury or harm it caused. Speech in all its manifestations, counsel contended, is protected by the free speech clause. Noting that other states had also instituted programs of censorship to protect the public morality, McKenna responded that the "judicial sense supporting the common sense of the country is against the contention." With a myopia not uncommon as the judicial mind confronts new technology, the Justice concluded "that the exhibition of moving pictures is a business pure and simple, originated and conducted for profit, like other spectacles, not to be regarded, by the Ohio Constitution, we think, as part of the press of the country or as organs of public opinion."[54] Viewing the pictures as vivid and entertaining representations of ideas already published and known, the Justice said they possess a power for evil that can be regulated by government.

In many ways this unanimous opinion illustrates well the wisdom of the Court's general rule of not considering matters not properly brought before it for decision. Only because of the commerce clause contention was the case heard, but the Justices decided to go beyond that issue and meet the free-speech argument. What the Supreme Court did here was decide prematurely an issue to which time would have afforded more dimension. Well over a generation would have to pass before this limiting conception of motion pictures would be overturned by the Court.[55]

Equally supportive was the Court of federal attempts to protect the public morality. What had led to the Mann Act's passage were lurid details of how innocent young women were trapped into a life of prostitution, but in *United States* v. *Holte* the Court clearly undercut the rationale of the legislation by holding that a woman could be charged with conspiring to violate the act through her own transportation for purposes of prostitution. In a biting dissent Lamar, joined by Day, reminded his colleagues that Congress has no power to punish immorality. Inspecting the purpose of the Mann Act, he viewed the government's prosecution for conspiracy as "a sword with which to punish those whom the Traffic Act was intended to protect."[56] Lamar and Day had less sympathy for the woman trapped in the governmental net than they did for what they considered the boundaries of the federal system. Not only was Congress using its power under the commerce clause to enter new areas of activity, but its ready ally, the Supreme Court, now seemed eager to push the government's reach even further than the legislators had intended.

Just as the Court was willing to give latitude to federal prosecutors, it also refused to interfere with the operation of state criminal law processes. Two cases of peculiar human interest illustrate well the unwillingness of the Court to undertake a supervisory role. The first, *Drew* v. *Thaw*, revived the drama surrounding the shooting of the prominent socialite and architect Stanford White by Harry K. Thaw. Convinced that he was losing the affections of his wife, Evelyn Nesbit, reputedly the model for the Gibson girl, to White, Thaw killed the architect. Thaw was adjudged insane and committed to an asylum. He escaped and found his way to New Hampshire, where he was finally located. New York authorities sought to use its obstruction of justice statute to hold Thaw guilty of a misdemeanor and thereby pave the way for his extradition. A federal district judge ordered Thaw's release on the ground that he had committed no crime that would justify extradition. In the Supreme Court the escapee's counsel ingeniously argued that his client if insane could not be found guilty of any crime and if sane was entitled to his discharge from the mental hospital. Holmes, for a unanimous Court, ignored the argument and reversed the lower court's decision, saying that a habeas corpus proceeding was not intended to speculate on what would be the result of a trial and thereby impede the demands of state justice.[57] Although Holmes saw no grounds for interference with New York justice he bristled when the majority came to a similar conclusion in *Frank* v. *Mangum*.

Before the case came to the High Bench it had become a national cause célèbre, summoning up thoughts of the Dreyfus affair in France and anticipating the Sacco and Vanzetti case of the 1920s. Leo Frank, a Jewish superintendent and part owner of the National Pencil Factory in Atlanta, Georgia, had been convicted of murdering a thirteen-year-old employee, Mary Phagan. The community's thirst for vengeance was met by the county solicitor who constructed a case using highly suspect testimony, much of which was later repudiated, to obtain a guilty verdict. The appeal for a new trial was rejected by the trial judge, apparently because he feared the highly visible and vocal throng outside the courtroom would not suffer it, for in his denial he indicated his personal doubts as to Frank's guilt. The Georgia Supreme Court passed over the judge's doubts, affirmed his decision, and later rejected additional pleas for a new trial.[58]

After considerable legal manuevering by Louis Marshall, the president of the American Jewish Committee and a seasoned constitutional lawyer, the Supreme Court finally agreed to hear the case under its habeas corpus jurisdiction.[59] Marshall argued that the absence of Frank and his counsel when the verdict was rendered was a fatal defect in the conviction. The absence was suggested by the trial judge, who feared that a not-guilty verdict might leave Frank and his defender subject to mob action. Marshall also argued that the threat of mob action that hung over the court's proceeding vitiated the verdict.

Inspecting whether Frank had been deprived of his liberty without due process of law, Pitney, for the majority, said the entire process of Georgia justice must be considered. Agreeing that if a mob had actually intimidated the jury and the trial court, the decision should be reversed, the New Jersey Justice concluded this was not the case here. He was willing to defer to the mature judgment of the highest state court in its inspection of the trial proceedings. To accept counsel's claim that outside pressure undermines the jurisdiction of the court, Pitney added, "would in a very practical sense, impair the power of the states to repress and punish crime; for it would render their courts powerless to act in opposition to lawless public sentiment."[60] Addressing Frank's absence when the jury returned its verdict, Pitney said that nothing within the due process clause prevents a defendant from waiving his right to be present. Even if the waiver was not voluntary, the Justice concluded that the failure to cite the matter as error in Frank's first appeal to the highest state court precluded its consideration here.

Holmes could accept unwise measures from a legislature and he could accept good-faith errors in the administration of justice, but when the sanctity of the courtroom was violated no condemnation could be too strong. Often respectful of the argument that the High Court should not limit the state's ability to punish the guilty, Holmes, joined by Hughes, now argued that the supremacy of the federal constitution should be asserted to insist that trials be conducted free of outside interference. Although unwilling to pronounce Frank's absence from the courtroom a denial of due process, the Massachusetts Justice said that the judge's decision to ask counsel and the defendant to leave was an overwhelming presumption "that the jury responded to the passions of the mob."⁶¹ Lynch law, he concluded, was equally reprehensible whether practiced by a regularly drawn jury or a mob.

The Supreme Court was willing to allow Georgia justice to claim its victim, but Governor John M. Slayton, saying he would not be a modern Pontius Pilate by turning another Jew over to the mob, commuted Frank's sentence. In the prison farm to which he was transferred Frank survived a fellow inmate's attack, but he did not survive the lynching party that extracted him from the farm and did its grizzly work.⁶²

Such deference to state judgment, which characterized the Court's work in the criminal area, did not extend to other claims of a violation of due process. Although the High Bench continued to uphold state and local railroad regulation, it carefully inspected the contentions pressed. So a Minnesota commission could not compel a railroad to install a scale at a certain station for the convenience of stockmen and farmers; and Wisconsin could not order railroads to maintain unoccupied upper berths in their fixed position in sleeping cars to enable the person in the lower berth to enjoy greater freedom. The Court seemed inclined to allow rates set by local government to go into operation despite claims of confiscation, but it did not hesitate to reinspect the situation and uphold a resubmitted claim. In cases coming from North Dakota and West Virginia, with only Pitney dissenting, the Court found that the prescribed rates for certain traffic did not allow much, if any, profit. Rejecting the states' claim that the entire system of state regulation should be considered, the Court ruled that the due process clause required that each part of the road's operation should be allowed to return a profit and that one part should not be made to subsidize another.⁶³

Regularly and often routinely the Court passed upon legislation enacted by Congress and action taken under it by officials in the executive department, but the Court docket was usually free of cases in which the authority of the President himself was the crucial issue. Not one but three such cases appeared for decision in the 1914 term. The first and most significant of the trio was *United States* v. *Midwest Oil Company*, in which the Justices considered the inherent power of the President to withdraw land for conservation purposes. The case was instituted by the government to recover certain tracts of oil lands from private companies. At the heart of the suit was a presidential order of September 27, 1909, temporarily withdrawing certain oil lands "from all forms of location, settlement, selection, filing, entry, or disposal under the mineral or nonmineral public-lands laws."⁶⁴ President Taft worried about his authority to take such action in view of legislation in 1897 opening such land to settlement, a concern that had not plagued Roosevelt in his enthusiastic protection of the public lands. Taft had hoped to get retroactive authorization from Congress, but when the legislative body acted in 1910 it authorized withdrawal prospectively.

Lamar, for the majority, ruled that the basic question of the President's authority to modify congressional policy need not be confronted, for the "case can be determined on other grounds and in the light of the legal consequences flowing from a long continued practice to make orders like the one involved here." No law empowers the President to remove lands for military or Indian reservations or bird reserves, but Congress, Lamar continued, has consistently acquiesced in such action. Citing the President's capacity to determine when the public interest necessitates such action, he concluded that such tacit congressional approval "operated as an implied grant of power in view of the fact that its exercise was not only useful to the public but did not interfere with any vested right of the citizen."[65] Lamar saw no distinction between creating a reservation and effecting a temporary withdrawal in anticipation of new legislation. He also placed weight on the episode that took place in Roosevelt's administration when the Secretary of the Interior was requested by the Senate to state the authority of the President to make such withdrawals. The Secretary listed various withdrawals of land and said this long-accepted practice confirmed the right of the executive to take such action. Congress received the report and took no action, a response Lamar interpreted as implied approval. Congressional failure to respond to Taft's plea to ratify the proclamation the Justice saw as a decision to leave the matter to the courts. Lamar accepted this challenge and determined that consistent presidential action in the area had foreclosed any independent consideration of the matter. In other words, the practice had hardened into constitutional custom.

In dissent, Day, joined by McKenna and Van Devanter, challenged the majority's assessment. Undeterred by custom, he asserted that there "is nothing in the Constitution suggesting or authorizing such augmentation of Executive authority or justifying him in thus acting in aid of a power which the framers of the Constitution saw fit to vest exclusively in the legislative branch of the Government."[66] The majority's accommodation of history, the Justice argued, cannot be squared with a proper respect for the separation of powers. Day conceded that earlier withdrawals of land had been approved by the Court, but he said they all involved action taken by the President either in pursuance of a declared congressional policy, such as the establishment of military or Indian reservations, or in the absence of such a clearly expressed policy. Here, on the other hand, Day continued, a clear legislative policy was violated by the presidential action.

The second case, *Burdick* v. *United States*, was one in which the incumbent President figured. George Burdick, the city editor of the *New York Tribune*, was summoned to appear before a grand jury investigating fraud in the collection of customs duties. Two articles had been run in the *Tribune* on the matter, and the grand jury sought to uncover the writer's sources. Burdick refused to answer on Fifth Amendment grounds, but he was instructed to reappear. When he returned he found a pardon from President Wilson tendered; Burdick would not accept the pardon and again refused to answer the questions. He was found guilty of contempt. Burdick denied that his privilege against self-incrimination was affected by the unaccepted pardon, that the pardon fully immunized him, or that the President had the power to pardon for an offense neither defined nor confessed. Since the law did not recognize a privilege behind which newsmen could shield their sources, the only way informants could be protected was for newsmen to claim that answers to such requests would tend to incriminate them.[67] Unless the claim was clearly without foundation, it would be honored.

McKenna, for the Court, first addressed the question of whether the acceptance of a pardon is necessary before a person can be compelled to testify. The Justice answered yes, saying that otherwise executive power can be thrust upon such a person to the detriment of his rights. Even assuming the pardon's effectiveness, McKenna continued, Burdick could refuse it and still have access to his Fifth Amendment right. The Californian had one last hurdle to surmount, the 1896 case of *Brown* v. *Walker*, where after a grant of legislative immunity the witness was compelled to testify. Although an immunity carries no imputation of guild, McKenna continued, a pardon does. Then equating the immunity granted in *Brown* with amnesty, he distinguished amnesty and pardon, not denying the similarity of their ultimate effect but highlighting their difference in character and purpose:

The one overlooks offense; the other remits punishment. The first is usually addressed to crimes against the sovereignty of the State, to political offenses, forgiveness being deemed more expedient for the public welfare than prosecution and punishment. The second condones infractions of the peace of the State. Amnesty is usually general, addressed to classes or even communities, a legislative act, or under legislation, constitutional or statutory, the act of the supreme magistrate. There may or may not be distinct acts of acceptance. If other rights are dependent upon it and are asserted, there is affirmative evidence of acceptance. . . . If there be no other rights, its only purpose is to stay the movement of the law. Its function is exercised when it overlooks the offense and the offender, leaving both in oblivion.[68]

Burdick remains as the Court's most thorough consideration of the matters of pardon and amnesty.

Late in the session the Justices considered the final case concerning presidential power. A citizen in the District of Columbia brought suit to oust a local commissioner appointed by the President because the appointee did not meet the residency requirement. The trial court agreed with the plaintiff and ordered the ouster. Reversing, the majority of the Supreme Court said that a citizen of the District, because of the absence of any distinct personal interest, did not have the requisite standing to challenge the appointment. Lamar's majority opinion read into this minor issue major implications. To find standing in this case, the Georgian asserted, would expose all federal officials appointed by the President to similar attacks. Van Devanter saw the matter as discretely confined to the peculiar situation of the District of Columbia and would have denied the appeal, while McKenna and Pitney probably agreed that the majority had blown a minor case out of all proportion. But Lamar and his colleagues in the majority wanted to protect the authority of the President by leaving the removal of all such appointed officials to him.[69]

In addition to this excursion into presidential authority, the Justices also decided a number of cases during the session that involved the rights of blacks in American society. In *United States* v. *Reynolds* the Court was again confronted with the complex provisions of Alabama law seeking to assure a continuing labor force. State law provided that a person convicted of an offense could have his fine and costs paid by another person, who then entered into a contract with the convicted man for labor over a certain period to discharge the debt. In the event of default the laborer could be convicted of violating the contract of service, have another surety appear, and be forced to enter into a contract for a longer period of service. The federal government prosecuted two such sureties as violaters of the law against peonage; the federal court in Alabama found no offense, but the Supreme Court found the indictments good.

Looking at the substance of the matter, Day saw such labor being performed under the constant threat of rearrest and conviction, a coercion "as potent as it would have been had the law provided for the seizure and compulsory service of the convict." In this manner the man can be rearrested and forced into a longer period of service, "chained to an ever-turning wheel of servitude."[70] In one instance the maximum penalty that could have been assessed was hard labor for four months, but the contract with the surety provided for over nine months of such labor. To the contention that the Court must respect state law Day responded that the system established must be judged by its operation on the rights secured by the Constitution and on the offenses punishable under federal law. Although the state had authority to exact compulsory service as punishment for a crime, concluded the Justice, it could not authorize such compulsory service for the benefit of private parties. Because the invalid Alabama statute afforded no protection, the defendants could properly be indicted for violating the federal antipeonage law. Holmes, who dissented in *Bailey*, arguing that a state can make the breach of a contract a crime, now concurred, saying the logical outcome of the Alabama system, human nature being what it is, is a series of such employment contracts, each for a longer term than the one displaced.

On the same day that *Reynolds* was decided the Justices considered a suit by a group of blacks attempting to enjoin railroads in Oklahoma from complying with a state statute commanding segregation. All members of the Court agreed the injunction could not issue because the allegations were too vague and none of the plaintiffs had shown they had requested service and had been denied it. But five members of the Court, in an opinion by Hughes, were willing to rule on certain issues. The New York Justice invalidated a section of the law that made the furnishing of equal accommodations dependent on the volume of traffic. Rejecting counsel's argument that blacks must demonstrate they will actually use the accommodations to afford the road a reasonable profit, Hughes responded that respect for a personal constitutional right cannot be contingent upon "the number of persons who may be discriminated against."[71] Implying that the high cost of segregation is constitutionally irrelevant, the New Yorker said that equal protection requires a carrier, acting under state law, to furnish similar facilities and conveniences to all passengers. For the first time a bare majority of the Court seemed to place real emphasis upon the equality rather than the separateness of accommodations. Unwilling to trod this road with the majority, White, Holmes, Lamar, and McReynolds simply concurred in finding no grounds for issuing the injunction requested.

Near the end of the session the Justices confronted the grandfather clause, a device installed by some Southern states and municipalities to control, if not eliminate, black suffrage. The major case was *Guinn* v. *United States*, which presented the question of the constitutionality of a 1910 amendment to the Oklahoma constitution. Generally prescribing a literacy test that required a would-be voter to read and write any section of the state constitution, the amendment exempted from this requirement all those entitled to vote under any form of government or those living in a foreign country as of January 1, 1866, and their lineal descendants. Since race was not a specified criterion for the distinction, state authorities claimed that to deny use of these standards would infringe the right of the state to set qualifications for voting, in itself a constitutional guarantee.

Although he proceeded ponderously, White had little difficulty in concluding that the provision's purpose was to create "a standard of voting which on its face was in substance but a revitalization of conditions which when they prevailed in the past had been destroyed by the self-operative force of the [Fifteenth] Amendment."[72] Since the obvious purpose of the law was to exclude whites from the literacy test while applying it to blacks, the Chief implied that the absence of language of racial exclusion does not save it from condemnation under the Fifteenth Amendment. White then went on to invalidate the entire Oklahoma amendment, for to uphold it without the intended exemption would leave a measure far different from the one designed by the state. Ruling that the abortive state amendment afforded no justification for barring blacks from voting for a qualified candidate for Congress, the Chief cleared the way for the Court of Appeals to assess the liability of election officials for discriminating against the blacks involved. White obviously wrote this opinion because of the importance he attached to the issue involved. Despite the fact that the Court in the past had avoided digging beneath the surface in charges of discrimination, the grandfather clause was really a very unsubtle disenfranchisement device. How its advocates could have expected the Court to have taken the absence of language of racial exclusion as conclusive of the constitutional issue taxes the imagination. Despite White's labored reasoning the matter presented to the Court was without real difficulty.

The Court concluded its work in this area with its decision in *United States v. Mosley*. The Justices held good an indictment against the defendants for conspiring to omit certain precinct returns from their count in a congressional election. The general section of the federal statutes outlining the crime of conspiracy to hinder the exercise of a person's civil rights was originally part of the Ku Klux Klan Enforcement Act of 1870 and still contained some language indicating its origin. Specific sections dealing with the franchise had been deleted over the years, and the question was whether this broader section, obviously not originally designed to cover the instant matter, could now be read as embracing it. Holmes, for the majority, experienced no difficulty with this problem, contending that the general wording of section 19 in its present form reached the conspiracy here prosecuted. Even assuming, said the Justice, that the present interpretation would not have been held correct under the original section of the Enforcement Act, "we cannot allow the past so far to affect the present as to deprive citizens of the United States of the general protection which, on its face, 19 most reasonably affords."[73] In dissent, Lamar argued that the repeal of the earlier sections relating to elections left no law to support the indictment.

With this decision the term came to an end on June 21, 1915. The session had produced more than its share of interesting cases, but of greatest significance were the decisions reinvigorating federal law in the guarantee of certain basic rights. Looking backward, the invalidation of peonage laws and grandfather clauses was significant, but much more revealing of the future was the Supreme Court's sympathetic reading of federal law, constitutional and statutory, in behalf of black citizens seeking to gain their basic rights, whether to equal accommodations or to the ballot box. Although a Southern President in the White House was segregating government employees, the Court, through its decisions during the session, had begun to respond to claims of racial discrimination. The march toward the goal of providing full equality for all black citizens was still to be long and troubled, and the Justices could not see what lay ahead. But in this and other areas, such as its approval of a wide-ranging exercise of the commerce power and of presidential initiative, the Court was charting the future.

NOTES

1. This material on the political situation is drawn from Arthur S. Link, *Woodrow Wilson and the Progressive Era, 1910-1917*, New American Nation Series (New York: Harper & Row, Torchbooks, 1963), pp. 14-22.

2. Deming v. Carlisle Packing Co., 226 U.S. 102 (1912); and Texas & Pacific Ry. v. Prater, 229 U.S. 177 (1913).

3. On the points mentioned, see Missouri, Kansas & Texas Ry. v. Wulf, 226 U.S. 570 (1913); St. Louis, San Francisco & Texas Ry. v. Seale, 229 U.S. 156 (1913); Michigan Central R.R. v. Vreeland, 227 U.S. 59 (1913); and Pedersen v. Delaware, Lackawanna & Western R.R., 209 U.S. 146 (1913).

4. Texas & New Orleans R.R. v. Sabine Tram Co., 227 U.S. 111 (1913); New York Central & Hudson River R.R. v. Board of Chosen Freeholders, 227 U.S. 248 (1913); and McDermott v. Wisconsin, 228 U.S. 115 (1913).

5. Pennsylvania R.R. v. International Coal Mining Co., 230 U.S. 184, 247 (1913).

6. Morrisdale Coal Co. v. Pennsylvania R.R., 230 U.S. 304 (1913); and Mitchell Coal & Coke Co. v. Pennsylvania R.R., 230 U.S. 247, 303 (1913).

7. That the image of Pitney conveyed by so much of the literature on the Supreme Court is in need of revision is further supported by the results of a recent sociometric analysis of the Court in which the author concludes that of all the sitting Justices Pitney was the most consistent supporter of national reform legislation. (See Donald C. Leavitt, "Attitude Change of the Supreme Court, 1910-1920," *Michigan Academician* 4 [Summer 1971]: 61-62.)

8. Nash v. United States, 229 U.S. 373 (1913); and Donnelly v. United States, 228 U.S. 243, 278 (1913).

9. Heike v. United States, 227 U.S. 131, 142 (1913).

10. Federal Bankruptcy Act, ch. 541, 30 Stat. 544, 548 (1898); and Ensign v. Pennsylvania, 227 U.S. 592 (1913).

11. Grant v. United States, 227 U.S. 74, 80 (1913); and Johnson v. United States, 228 U.S. 457 (1913).

12. Lewis Publishing Co. v. Morgan, 229 U.S. 288, 316 (1913).

13. For instance, see Bartell v. United States, 227 U.S. 427 (1913); Zakonaite v. Wolf, 226 U.S. 272 (1912); and Bugajewitz v. Adams, 228 U.S. 585, 591 (1913); Mann Act, ch. 395, 36 Stat. 825 (1910). For a discussion of the cases brought to the Supreme Court under this legislation, see Edward H. Levi, *An Introduction to Legal Reasoning* (Chicago: University of Chicago Press, Phoenix Books, 1961), pp. 33-54.

14. Hoke v. United States, 227 U.S. 308, 322, 323 (1913).

15. Athanasaw v. United States, 227 U.S. 326 (1913).

16. Bennett v. United States, 227 U.S. 333 (1913); and Harris v. United States, 227 U.S. 340 (1913).

17. Charlton v. Kelly, 229 U.S. 447 (1913).

18. Dill v. Ebey, 229 U.S. 199 (1913); and Slocum v. New York Life Insurance Co., 228 U.S. 364 (1913).

19. Continued acceptance of the historical meaning of a particular constitutional term militates against a change of meaning, but this is not to say that the Court is foreclosed from redefining the language. For instance, in 1970 a majority of the Justices, despite spirited internal opposition, in the case of *Williams* v. *Florida* (399 U.S. 78), decided that the hitherto consistent reading of the term *jury* in the Sixth Amendment as meaning a twelve-person panel did not prevent the Court from casting the historical meaning aside and determining that a six-man jury essentially met the functional purpose of the constitutional protection.

20. Central Lumber Co. v. South Dakota, 226 U.S. 157 (1912); Barrett v. Indiana, 229 U.S. 26 (1913); Schmidinger v. Chicago, 226 U.S. 578 (1913); and Hutchinson v. Valdosta, 227 U.S. 303 (1913).

21. Chicago, Burlington & Quincy R.R. v. Cram, 228 U.S. 70, 84 (1913); and Missouri Pacific Ry. v. Tucker, 230 U.S. 340, 351 (1913).

22. Minnesota Rate Cases, 230 U.S. 352, 465-66 (1913).

23. See Missouri Rate Cases, 230 U.S. 474 (1913); Chesapeake & Ohio Ry. v. Conley, 230 U.S. 513 (1913); Oregon R.R. & Navigation Co. v. Campbell, 230 U.S. 525 (1913); and Allen v. St. Louis, Iron Mountain & Southern Ry., 230 U.S. 553 (1913).

24. Link, *Woodrow Wilson and the Progressive Era*, pp. 34-35.

25. Wood v. Vandalia R. R., 231 U.S. 1 (1913).

26. German Alliance Insurance Co. v. Lewis, 233 U.S. 389, 411, 419 (1914).

27. Smith v. Texas, 233 U.S. 630, 638 (1914).

28. Harrison v. St. Louis & San Francisco R.R., 232 U.S. 318, 328 (1914).

29. Patsone v. Pennsylvania, 232 U.S. 138 (1914).

30. Lewis v. Frick, 233 U.S. 291, 302 (1914). Pitney, however, was correct in saying that the distinction between sanctions that were criminal and those that were not was well established in the law, despite the obvious fact that deportation could be more personally punitive than a jail sentence.

31. Luria v. United States, 231 U.S. 9 (1913).

32. Boyd v. United States, 116 U.S. 616, 630 (1886).

33. Weeks v. United States, 232 U.S. 383, 393 (1914).

34. This loophole was not closed until 1960 in *Elkins* v. *United States* (364 U.S. 206).

35. Felix Frankfurter and James M. Landis, *The Business of the Supreme Court: A Study in the Federal Judicial System* (New York: Macmillan Co., 1927), pp. 170-73.

36. For instance, the High Bench overruled the Commerce Court and made rate rulings by the ICC immune from inspection if they were based upon the evidence (The Los Angeles Switching Case, 234 U.S. 294 [1914]).

Albro Martin, *Enterprise Denied: Origins of the Decline of American Railroads, 1897-1917* (New York: Columbia University Press, 1971), pp. 352-67, argues that legislation, such as the Mann-Elkins Act of 1910, and an Interstate Commerce Commission that was unwilling to authorize railroads to raise rates to the point of attracting needed capital were the prime factors in the decline of American railroads. For a contrary view on the effect of railroad regulation—one that maintains the ICC aided the railroads in protecting profits—see Gabriel Kolko, *Railroads and Regulation, 1877-1916* (Princeton: Princteon University Press, 1965), p. 212.

37. Houston, East & West Texas R.R. v. United States (Shreveport Rate Case), 234 U.S. 342, 351-52, 353 (1914).

38. Boston & Maine R.R. v. Hooker, 233 U.S. 97, 119 (1914).

39. In two other cases decided on the same day involving race horses, Pitney again dissented from the majority's reading of the Carmack Amendment that had limited the injured shipper's recovery to the unrealistic schedule (Atchison, Topeka & Santa Fe Ry. v. Robinsin, 233 U.S. 173 [1914]; and Atchison, Topeka & Santa Fe Ry. v. Moore, 233 U.S. 182 [1914]).

40. James F. Watts, Jr., "Horace H. Lurton," in *The Justices of the United States Supreme Court 1789-1969: Their Lives and Major Opinions*, 4 vols. (New York: R. R. Bowker Co. and Chelsea House, Publishers, 1969), 3:1847.

41. Memorial service for Lurton, 237 U.S. xviii.

42. David Burner, "James C. McReynolds," in *Justices of the Supreme Court*, 3:2025-26; and Arthur S. Link, *Wilson: The New Freedom* (Princeton: Princeton University Press, 1956), p. 117.

43. Charles H. Butler, *A Century at the Bar of the Supreme Court of the United States* (New York: G. P. Putnam's Sons, 1942), pp. 201-5; and Burner, "James C. McReynolds," in *Justices of the Supreme Court*, 3:2026.

44. See Henry J. Abraham, *Justices and Presidents: A Political History of Appointments to the Supreme Court* (New York: Oxford University Press, 1974), p. 166; and *New York World* quoted in *Literary Digest* 49 (September 5, 1914):406.

45. Abraham, *Justices and Presidents*, p. 167.

46. Jeffrey Mfg. Co. v. Blagg, 235 U.S. 571 (1915). For an analysis of the development of workmen's compensation legislation, see Lawrence M. Friedman and Jack Ladinsky, "Social Change and the Law of Industrial Accidents," *Columbia Law Review* 67 (January 1967):50-82. For a discussion of big business support of such legislation, see James Weinstein, *The Corporate Ideal in the Liberal State:1900-1918* (Boston: Beacon Press, 1968), pp. 40-61; and for a discussion of bar support, see Barbara C. Steidle, "Conservative Progressives: A Study of the Attitudes of Bar and Bench, 1905-1912" (Ph.D. dissertation, Rutgers University, 1969), pp. 180-226.

47. Ives v. South Buffalo Ry., 201 N.Y. 271, 295 (1911).

48. Roosevelt and others quoted in Frankfurter and Landis, *Business of the Supreme Court*, pp. 193-95, n. 37, 42.

49. Ibid., pp. 196-98; and Act of December 23, 1914, ch. 2, 38 Stat. 790.

50. Lawlor v. Loewe, 235 U.S. 522 (1915).

51. Coppage v. Kansas, 236 U.S. 1, 17 (1915).

52. Id. at 28, 40, 42.

53. Rail & River Coal Co. v. Yaple, 236 U.S. 338 (1915); Booth v. Indiana, 237 U.S. 391 (1915); Miller v. Wilson, 236 U.S. 373 (1915); and Bosley v. McLaughlin, 236 U.S. 385 (1915).

54. Mutual Film Corp. v. Industrial Commission, 236 U.S. 230, 240, 244 (1915).

55. See Joseph Burstyn, Inc., v. Wilson, 343 U.S. 495 (1952).

56. See United States v. Portale, 235 U.S. 27 (1914); and United States v. Holte, 236 U.S. 140, 148 (1915).

57. Drew v. Thaw, 235 U.S. 432 (1914). In 1915 Thaw was acquitted of the conspiracy charge and later released after a New York court found him sane (*New York Times*, March 14, July 17, 1915).

58. Leonard Dinnerstein, *The Leo Frank Case* (New York: Columbia University Press, 1968), pp. 1-109.

59. Ibid., pp. 90-91, 105-9. The Court rejected an appeal in *Ex parte* Frank, 235 U.S. 694. (1914).

60. Frank v. Mangum, 237 U.S. 309, 337 (1915).

61. Id. at 349. Eight years later in a similar case Holmes would win the Court to his position and return a petition to the trial court for a rehearing. (See Moore v. Dempsey, 261 U.S. 86 [1923].)

62. Dinnerstein, *Leo Frank Case*, pp. 114-29, 136-47.

63. Great Northern Ry. v. Minnesota, 238 U.S. 340 (1915); Chicago, Milwaukee & St. Paul R.R. v. Wisconsin, 238 U.S. 491 (1915); for instance, see Des Moines Gas Co. v. Des Moines, 238 U.S. 153 (1915); Northern Pacific Ry. v. North Dakota *ex rel.* McCue, 236 U.S. 585 (1915); and Norfolk & Western Ry. v. Conley, 236 U.S. 605 (1915).

64. United States v. Midwest Oil Co., 236 U.S. 459, 467.

65. Id. at 469, 475.

66. Id. at 491-92.

67. For a fuller discussion of the case's background and the newsman's privilege issue, see Margaret A. Blanchard, "The Fifth Amendment Privilege of Newsman George Burdick," *Journalism Quarterly* 55 (Spring 1978):29-36, 67.

68. Burdick v. United States, 236 U.S. 79, 95 (1915).

69. Newman v. United States *ex rel.* Frizzel, 238 U.S. 537 (1915).

70. United States v. Reynolds, 235 U.S. 133, 146-47 (1914).

71. McCabe v. Atchison, Topeka & Santa Fe Ry., 235 U.S. 151, 161-62 (1914).

72. Guinn v. United States, 238 U.S. 347, 363-64 (1915); and Meyers v. Anderson, 238 U.S. 368 (1915).

73. United States v. Mosley, 238 U.S. 383, 388 (1915).

chapter 10

"RADICALIZING" THE COURT: THE NEW WILSON APPOINTEES, 1915-17

As the Court completed the term in late June 1915, there was no indication of impending vacancies. Holmes, at seventy-four, was the Court's oldest member, but he gave no intimation of approaching senility; neither did McKenna at seventy-one. The Chief at sixty-nine, despite rumors, offered no hint of retirement. Day was sixty-six, and the remaining Taft appointees, Hughes, Van Devanter, Lamar, and Pitney, and Wilson's lone appointee, McReynolds, were in their fifties.

During the summer of 1915, as news of the war in Europe occupied the front pages, the Justices were more immediately concerned by the news that Joseph Rucker Lamar had suffered a paralytic stroke. Recovery was slow, and when the Court convened for the new term in October, Lamar was absent. In December the stricken Justice caught a severe cold that resulted in the inflammation of his lungs. The end came on January 2, 1916, after Lamar had experienced a heart attack. Like his earlier relation, Joseph R. Lamar's tenure on the Court was too short, less than five terms, to etch his name firmly in the annals of Supreme Court history. His early dissents indicated sensitivity on his part to the rights of individuals, but this early intimation that the Georgian might follow in the footsteps of Harlan perhaps was not fairly tested by his short career. He seemed, though, to have little of his predecessor's sensitivity to the plight of blacks. Lamar was eulogized for his integrity, modesty, and judicial skill, but later interpreters criticized him for looking backward rather than forward.[1] Yet in his willingness to recognize and condone the exercise of presidential and administrative authority and in his unsuccessful attempt to get his colleagues to recognize that sexual discrimination was unconstitutional, his ideas have a modern ring to them.

The vacancy on the Supreme Court came at a politically opportune time for a troubled President, worried about his and his party's fortunes in facing a reunited Republican party in the upcoming election. What had brought Wilson his victory in 1912 was the split within the dominant party; now, with Theodore Roosevelt back in the fold and with the demise of the Progressive party, the opposition was formidable. In his first term the President had admirable success in fulfilling the pledges of his New Freedom platform. With its enactment, despite pleas for social legislation at the national level, he called a halt to further reform. Although this stand had considerable support within the Democratic party, Wilson was an astute politician who saw the need to bend with the political winds if his leadership was to survive the coming battle. To win in 1916 he had to capture a substantial segment of the vote received by the Progressives in 1912 by convincing such voters that the Democrats were capable of fulfilling their dreams. With the President's new conviction, leadership, and political skill, the Democratic Congress would, by the fall of the year, enact into law most of the Progressive platform of 1912. Included in that activity of 1916 was legislation providing for rural credits, a workmen's compensation law for federal employees, and an act regulating child labor.

On January 28, 1916, the first public indication of this shift in strategy came with Wilson's choice for the Court—Louis D. Brandeis. Rarely had such an announcement from the White House created the shock waves this one did. Wilson had indirectly consulted only one member of the Senate, Progressive Republican Senator Robert M. La Follette. Large segments of the business and legal communities considered the nomination a personal affront; attiring this "radical" in a black robe and placing him on the nation's highest court seemed a cruel joke. But Wilson knew exactly what he was doing; he had come a long way since his casual appointment of James McReynolds to the Supreme Court. That the choice of Brandeis was a symbolic act none could doubt, and the President knew he had a fight on his hands.[2] Wilson's appointment of a close and trusted advisor to the Supreme Court hardly seems surprising, but Brandeis was a highly visible lawyer with a unique public image.

Brandeis's early practice in Boston was in the field of corporate law, and through his skill and service he soon amassed a small fortune. Increasingly, with the coming of the twentieth century, Brandeis involved himself in the live and controversial issues of the day. The famous brief he submitted for the state of Oregon in the *Muller* case, relying upon sociological and economic data collected to convince the Court of the state's reasonableness in regulating the workday for women, was simply one of his many achievements. He was enlisted into service by *Collier's* after that magazine had published material critical of Taft's Secretary of the Interior, Richard A. Ballinger. In the ensuing congressional investigation Brandeis, through acute questioning, discredited Ballinger. President Taft, who viewed the conservation issue as central to his credibility and the success of his administration, saw Brandeis as the principal villain.[3] The Massachusetts lawyer brought not only his legal skills but also his pen to bear. His writings, coupled with his espousal of the public interest, unsettled segments of the business community, which readily pronounced him a radical. The label was primarily an epithet without much substantive content, for though Brandeis was a consumer advocate and a critic of business methods and big business irresponsibility, he believed in the capitalistic system. He wanted to endow it with a conscience and make it more truly competitive. Lawyers generally seek low visibility, but here was Brandeis in the thick of public affairs with a passion and dedication for making the society a better one. There were no models for Brandeis's view of the interventionist lawyer serving the public; that such activity appeared unseemly to the staid corporate bar is understandable.

Wilson had made the nomination, but it would have to run the gauntlet of the Senate, upon which the forces coalescing on both sides would try to work. The battle would not be easy nor short, but Wilson resolved to stand behind his choice and, with able leadership, he could use his position to keep defections from Democratic ranks to a minimum.

The nation's press responded first, revealing the ideological lineups. The *Boston Post* and the *New York World* applauded the appointment, but the reactions of the *Wall Street Journal* and the *Detroit Free Press* were more typical. The *Journal* singled Brandeis out as the most conspicuous anticorporation agitator: "Where others were radical he was rabid; where others were extreme he was super-extreme; where others would trim he would lay the ax to the root of the tree." The *Free Press*, branding the appointee "in temperament and in training perhaps the least fit for the calm, cold, dispassionate work of the Supreme Court of the United States," asked the Senate to do its duty and reject the nomination.[4]

Ex-President Taft, who many considered the ideal candidate for the vacancy, first reacted privately and then publicly to the nomination. He confided that the nomination was "one of the deepest wounds I have had as an American and a lover of the Constitution and a believer in progressive conservatism." Then he expounded upon the deficiencies of Brandeis, calling him "a muckraker, an emotionalist for his own purposes, a socialist, prompted by jealousy, a hypocrite, a man who has certain high ideals in his imagination, but who is utterly unscrupulous in method in reaching them, a man of infinite cunning, of great tenacity of purpose, and, in my judgment, much power for evil."[5] Taft signed a statement submitted by Elihu Root and six past presidents of the American Bar Association pronouncing Brandeis unfit for the post of Supreme Court Justice. The former President heartily approved the move, indicating the widespread private grumbling, to which he eagerly contributed, should be made public. Taft's public expression led some to question his impartiality as they remembered the role Brandeis had played in the Ballinger affair. Other lawyers joined in the attack, and a good representation of the Boston bar, which had once accepted Brandeis as one of its own, joined in the chorus claiming his unfitness.[6]

Even if it were inclined to do so, the Senate Judiciary Committee could not escape the task of giving the nomination close scrutiny. A subcommittee was appointed, consisting of three Democrats and two Republicans, and charged with examining the candidate's fitness. This group sifted the accusations.

Lurking behind some of the protest was a lingering anti-Semitism and a concern about the candidate's Zionist views, but coming to the fore were two main charges: first, that Brandeis had not acted ethically as a lawyer; and second, that his wholehearted and passionate advocacy of certain causes meant that he lacked the requisite judicial temperament of impartiality. Among the indictments under the first count was the charge that he acted improperly in his dealings with the United Shoe Machinery Company. In the 1890s as the company's legal counsel and as a stockholder and director, Brandeis had defended certain monopolistic practices of the company. Later he resigned and aided both the government in an antitrust prosecution and a group of shoe manufacturers seeking to break the company's stranglehold on the industry.[7]

This episode was representative of the evidence submitted to the subcommittee. Brandeis appeared as a turncoat, a private counselor who took advantage of his privileged position to later aid the enemy. To this crusader the barren ethical standards of the profession were less significant than the rightness of the cause; he switched sides because of a conviction that United Shoe's practices were wrong. Convinced he was not using any information gained in his earlier capacity as counselor to the company, Brandeis saw no obstacle to doing what he thought was right. Other episodes were revealed in the hearings, but the charge of unethical conduct was difficult to sustain when the accusers were confronted by the fact that the bar had never received any such complaints and that no investigation of Brandeis had ever been instituted. The nominee was an untraditional lawyer, the type that makes others of his profession nervous, but such complaints about the man's professional ethics seemed dwarfed by his own well-projected personal moral code. Specific allegations of unethical conduct could be countered, but this was not so on the other area of concern—judicial temperament.

How can judicial temperament be judged? Brandeis had never been a judge, but neither had many of the appointees to the High Bench. What his critics were saying was not that the advocate was disabled from being a judge, for judges indeed are drawn from the practicing bar, but rather that Brandeis was too involved an advocate, too much interested in the cause he represented, too certain he knew what was right. The traditional advocate provided representation for his client: the rightness or wrongness or even the nature of the matter contested was not a subject of personal importance. He was a person employed as a professional to exact the best bargain he could with the law. Indeed, he could enjoy the fruits of victory; and winning was important, not because the advocate considered the cause just, but because his skill had been exercised to secure victory within the parameters of the game. Brandeis saw himself as a representative of the public interest, a "people's lawyer." Winning for him was more than enjoying the satisfaction of a game well played; it was a successful struggle against entrenched forces to secure fairness for the public, an interest even in the "progressive era" that was too little represented.[8] If the cries that Brandeis did not have a judicial temperament meant that the new appointee could not be impartial on the pressing issues of the day, the critics were right. While critics bemoaned such advocacy, supporters emphasized that the Court needed a Justice with a different point of view and a different set of priorities.

From early February to early April the subcommittee, headed by Senator William E. Chilton of West Virginia, received materials and held hearings on the nomination. On April 3, 1916, the subcommittee approved the nomination by a straight party vote of three to two. Chilton responded to the criticism of the nominee's dealings with United Shoe by suggesting that prior employment could lay no claim on a man's conscience. Brandeis had returned half of the fee he charged the Western Alliance of Shoe Manufacturers in the suit against United Shoe while turning over the other half to his law partners. He did this not because of any feeling that his acceptance would violate any standard of professional ethics but because he considered his service in this matter public. Chilton acknowledged that the nominee's advocacy had led to some bitterness, which he saw mirrored in evidence of a systematic campaign to discredit the candidate and which he credited with influencing the nominee's opponents. The Republican minority members professed sympathy with the social and economic views of the candidate, but both men found his methods and his professional ethics suspect.[9]

The eighteen-man Senate Judiciary Committee, composed of ten Democrats and eight Republicans under the chairmanship of Charles A. Culberson of Texas, now had to act. With the chairman still not sure of the Democratic votes and the Republicans in no hurry to vote, time passed. At the request of Culberson, President Wilson addressed a letter to the commitee, indicating his complete commitment to Brandeis, calling him "singularly enlightening, singularly clear-sighted and judicial, and, above all, full of moral stimulation." During the delay the anti-Brandeis campaign pressed on, while the nominee's supporters took their campaign to the people. Finally, on May 24, 1916, almost four months after hearings had begun, the Senate Judiciary Committee favorably reported out the nomination with a straight party-line vote of ten to eight. The Republican Senators, eager to adjourn in time for the presidential nominating convention in Chicago, conceded defeat and agreed to a vote of the full Senate. On June 1, 1916, the Senate voted on the Brandeis appointment and approved it by a vote of forty-seven to twenty-two. After the months of inquiry, charges and countercharges, party loyalty proved to be the decisive factor in the voting, with only one Democrat and three progressive Republicans defecting.[10] The unsettled political picture during the spring of 1916 had resulted, even more than usual, in ensuring the type of party loyalty that Wilson needed to carry his fight.

As the eight-man Court convened for the 1915 term the Justices perhaps surmised that a replacement for Lamar would be in the offing, but they could have had no inkling that the Supreme Court and the qualifications for appointment to it would consume so much public debate. Neither could they anticipate that the Republican party's search for a standard-bearer to challenge Wilson in 1916 would again draw the High Bench into the political arena.

Early in the session the Court responded to a number of cases dealing with ramifications of the great wave of immigrants coming to this country in the early years of the twentieth century—about 8,000,000 from Europe in the first decade alone. Organized labor was alarmed and began lobbying for restrictive legislation, a drive that would eventually bring success in the 1920s. What the Court considered was one federal and two state attempts to limit competition from immigrants. Encouraged by the Justices' willingness to defer to administrative handling of aliens, the New York commissioner of immigration ordered the deportation of two aliens bound for Portland, Oregon, because that city's labor supply was already overabundant. The officer relied on wording in an immigration act allowing the deportation of "persons likely to become a public charge."[11]

Holmes, for a unanimous Court, granted a writ of habeas corpus to the two Russians involved, saying the cited wording is restricted to paupers, prostitutes, and others whose personal characteristics make them objectionable. To consider local conditions, as the commissioner did in this instance, would be improper, Holmes added, because the statute deals with admission to the United States, not to any specific locality. Noting that the act provides the President with power to act if he finds an oversupply of labor in the entire country, the Justice pointed out the anomaly of a commissioner taking unto himself even greater authority than that conferred on the Chief Executive himself.[12]

Hughes responded for the Court in *Truax* v. *Raich*, which involved a state attempt to limit the employment of aliens. Arizona had passed a law requiring that all employers of more than five workers ensure that 80 percent of their work force be composed of citizens or qualified electors. Mike Raich, an alien of Austrian descent employed as a cook, sought to enjoin the enforcement of the law as inconsistent with the Fourteenth Amendment. Arizona claimed the suit was against the state and therefore prohibited by the Eleventh Amendment, that the federal courts had no authority to enjoin the enforcement of a state criminal statute, and that such a statute was adequately supported by the state's police power.

Hughes quickly disposed of the first claim on the basis of precedent, saying that if a statute is unconstitutional the officers of the state cannot invoke the state's immunity. As easily, he dismissed the second objection, maintaining that the federal courts have often enjoined the enforcement of state criminal laws when necessary to safeguard the rights of property. "The right to earn a livelihood and to continue in employment unmolested by efforts to enforce void enactments," he added, "should similarly be entitled to protection." Although recognizing the breadth of the police power, Hughes asserted that a state cannot justify the denial "to lawful inhabitants, because of their race or nationality, the ordinary means of earning a livelihood." The right to work, he continued, "is of the very essence of the personal freedom and opportunity that it was the purpose of the Amendment to secure." Then in language that implied the state act also violated the equal protection clause, the Justice concluded: "The discrimination is against aliens as such in competition with citizens in the described range of enterprises, and in our opinion it clearly falls under the condemnation of the fundamental law."[13]

In the *Truax* opinion Hughes clearly demonstrated the ease by which analogies protecting other individual rights could be drawn from the Court's use of substantive due process in the property area. In fact, the first litigation inviting an interpretation of the Fourteenth Amendment by the Supreme Court concerned not the protection of investment capital but rather the right to work at one's chosen profession free from state interference. The protesting butchers in the *Slaughter-House Cases* had to obtain their redress from a reformed Louisiana legislature, but the Court now read the amendment to protect the rights of aliens to earn a living. The constitutional foundation for a protection of a wider range of individual rights was clearly established.

If Arizona could not blanket all employment in the state with a regulation of alien labor, could New York confine employment on its public works projects to its citizens? In two unanimous opinions McKenna answered yes. The first case dealt with the successful attempt of a state public service commission to declare certain contracts void because of a breach of the state alien labor law. McKenna disposed of the contention that this discrimination against aliens is unconstitutional by citing *Atkin* v. *Kansas*, in which the Court had said the state can determine the conditions under which public work is to be done. The Justice interpreted these general words to encompass a prohibition of alien labor. The second New York case involved a criminal prosecution for violation of the act, but McKenna added nothing new, except the bare statement that a distinction between aliens and citizens is not an unreasonable classification that would violate the equal protection clause.[14] As a result of these decisions a state could restrict employment on its public works to citizens and, showing some rational basis, could exclude aliens from other specific types of employment, but a wholesale restriction was prohibited.

Congress could provide a naturalization process making aliens citizens, but could that body by fiat turn a native-born American into an alien? In

Mackenzie v. *Hare* the Court passed upon a 1907 act divesting American women of their citizenship when they married foreigners. Ethel Mackenzie sought to vote but was barred on the basis that she was no longer a citizen. She had married a British subject residing in California and had lived there since her marriage. Mrs. Mackenzie claimed the intent of the 1907 act, as demonstrated by its history, was only to regulate the status of such women living abroad.

Ruling that the clear wording of the act does embrace the claimant, McKenna for the unanimous Court, assessed the legislation's validity. Mrs. Mackenzie argued that her right to citizenship is accrued at birth and as such was a right conferred by the Constitution that could only be divested by punishment for crime or by voluntary expatriation. McKenna avoided a direct confrontation with the argument presented by noting that the federal law is based upon the ancient conception of the identity of husband and wife with dominance in the husband, a proposition that the Californian still saw as valid in terms of both domestic and international policy. Although acknowledging that the government cannot arbitrarily withdraw citizenship, McKenna ruled that Mrs. Mackenzie's decision to marry an alien was a voluntary acceptance of the consequences. His only justification was that international considerations necessitated this result. So Mrs. Mackenzie was told her act of marriage to a foreigner "is as voluntary and distinctive as expatriation and its consequence must be considered as elected."[15]

Ethel Mackenzie's problem, the Court had said, was that the broad congressional pronouncement had left no room for exceptions, but when the notorious Ida May Innes found gaps in the federal extradition policy the High Bench proceeded to fill them. She was found in Oregon and·extradited to Texas where she was acquitted of murder charges. Her hopes for returning to the Northwest were dashed when Georgia reached out its long arm and requested her extradition. She sought a writ of habeas corpus, claiming she had not fled into Texas, having been brought there involuntarily from Oregon. The federal statute, she said, only provided for extradition from a state to which the fugitive had fled. White, for the unanimous Court, acknowledged that the statute fell short of the extent of congressional power in the area, but he said the gap could be filled by state authority until the federal legislature chose to act. Revealing the policy basis upon which his decision rested, the Chief added that a contrary holding would protect an individual acquitted in one state after extradition from ever being removed to answer criminal charges, no matter how heinous, in another state.[16]

During the session the Court contended with the amendment to the Pure Food and Drug Act that Congress had passed in response to the limiting decision that Holmes had written in *Johnson*. The new case involved the seizure by the federal government of another patent medicine, this time one promising a cure for tuberculosis. With obvious pleasure and for a unanimous Court, Hughes sustained the amendment's constitutionality. Quickly disposing of the claim that the law invaded the reserved powers of the states, the New Yorker answered counsel's contention that the preparation was not illicit, immoral, or harmful, the distinguishing words the Court had used earlier to place subjects of commerce within the prohibitory power of Congress. Hughes found "no ground for saying that Congress may not condemn the interstate transportation of swindling preparations designed to cheat credulous sufferers and make such preparations, accompanied by false and fradulent statements, illicit with respect to interstate commerce, as well as, for example, lottery tickets." Then exorcising Holmes's spectre in *Johnson*, he added: "The fact that the amendment is not limited, as was the original statute, to statements regarding identity or composition . . . does not mark a constitutional distinction." Honest differences of opinion and "absolute falsehoods" can be distinguished, said Hughes, as the 1912 amendment validly does. The government, concluded the Justice, had made its case, and, he added, "we are not at liberty to indulge in hypercriticism to escape the plain import of the words used."[17]

Later in the term, again in a unanimous opinion, Hughes decided that the government's case against Coca-Cola, on grounds that the formula contained an ingredient that might be dangerous to health and that the product was misbranded because it contained no coca and no cola, could proceed to trial. The Justice sought to correct what he called a misinterpretation of the basic act. The legislation, he said, not only seeks to eliminate deception by requiring disclosure of ingredients but also protects "the public from lurking dangers caused by the introduction of harmful ingredients."[18] Hughes had won the Court to a broad, supportive reading of the Pure Food and Drug Act, though he had to be helped by additional congressional action.

Also, the Court had no trouble upholding a congressional act banning the entry of prize-fight films into the country. Again the law was attacked on the ground that Congress sought, under the commerce clause, to exercise a police power that the states alone possessed. Chief Justice White responded that, within its ambit, congressional power over commerce was supreme and that any consideration of legislative motive as a restriction upon the power was improper.[19] This sweeping statement seemed to give a blank check to Congress, but in Supreme Court adjudication there is much leeway between the general proposition and the deduction reached in a specific situation.

Presumably the Sixteenth Amendment had settled the question of the federal government's authority to levy an income tax, but this fundamental bar did not stop litigants from challenging the particular act that Congress had passed implementing its new authority. In a series of cases, of which *Bushaber* v. *Union Pacific Railroad Company* was the primary one, the Chief Justice painstakingly sifted through the contentions. On the basis of an historical reading of the taxing power of Congress and the text of the constitutional change, White ruled that "the whole purpose of the Amendment was to relieve all income taxes when imposed from apportionment [and] from a consideration of the source whence the income was derived." Claims of implied limitations on the nature and character of an income tax, the Chief continued, "find no support in the text and are in irreconcilable conflict with the very purpose which the Amendment was adopted to accomplish." This addition to the Constitution, he said, "was drawn with the object of maintaining the limitations of the Constitution and harmonizing their operation."[20]

White then considered the specific objections to the law. Its retroactive application the Chief sustained on the grounds that it extended back no further than the effective date of the amendment. He listed the other specific provisions attacked, all of which dealt with detailed aspects of the law involving deductions and exemptions, and then responded that they were all based on an erroneous reading of the requirement of uniformity. When the tax is levied throughout the United States, he said, it meets the geographical test that uniformity demands. To the challenge to the progressive feature of the tax, White answered that the Fifth Amendment's due process clause places no limitation on the taxing power. Summarizing the Court's response, the Chief declared that claims of injustice stemming from the exercise of lawful legislative power cannot be entertained by a Court that accepts the limits of its authority.[21]

With a similar attitude of accommodation, the Court viewed some new exertions of state police power. When Florida and Washington sought to use their taxing power to prohibit the use of trading stamps and redeemable coupons, McKenna, for the unanimous bench, rejected the argument that the states were regulating interstate commerce, though both the insertion and redemption of such stamps or coupons involved transactions beyond the state's borders. These schemes, the Justice said, "are not designed for or executed through a sale of the original package of importation, but in the packages of retail and sale to the individual purchaser and consumer." Then citing "the duty and function of the legislature to discern and correct evils," McKenna rejected the challenge to the tax based on infringement of the right to contract, equal protection, and due process grounds. In the second case, the Californian covered much the same ground and concluded that such taxes were within the police power, which, quoting the words of Justice Brown earlier, "is coextensive with the necessities of the case and the safeguard of the public interests."[22]

With this attitude of deference to the legislative branch, the session drew to a close amid some interesting developments. On June 5, 1916, Louis D. Brandeis, after the historically long Senate deliberation over his appointment, filled the vacant seat on the Court. His ideological leanings and seniority put him to the far left of the Chief, but his age of fifty-nine put him in the center of the High Bench. A little over six feet tall, Brandeis had a sensitive, deeply lined face with sunken and piercing eyes, crowned by bushy eyebrows. His nose and ears were large, and his generous mouth, even when solemnly posed, gave a hint of a smile. His bushy, brown hair, tinged with grey, seemed to resist taming; its disorder coupled with his intent eyes provided an image for the radicalism that some saw in the man.

Five days after Brandeis was seated, Charles Evans Hughes resigned his seat to accept the Republican party's presidential nomination. Reaction to Hughes's departure from the bench was mixed; few denied that he was presidential timber, but some viewed his sudden departure as unseemly. The *New York Times* forecasted the Republican's defeat as a rebuke to politicians seeking to raid the Court.[23] The newspaper seemed to feel the High Bench would become easy prey for politicians seeking a leader, but the Justices, although publicly visible, were out of the political mainstream. What made Hughes different was that he was a prominently mentioned presidential candidate before he donned his robe.

As early as 1908 Hughes was recognized as a contender, but when his name came up in the crowded race for the nomination in 1912, he indicated clearly that he did not wish to be considered. Overtures in 1916 found Hughes noncommittal, but failure to remove himself made him available to a party desperately in search of a candidate unsullied by the fiasco of 1912.[24] Hughes was attractive; his position on the Supreme Court had removed him from intraparty battles, and his record during his six-year tenure on the Court, despite the grumbling of certain party conservatives, had only increased his stature. In a year in which the Republicans would need a strong candidate to contend with Woodrow Wilson, whose political moves in 1916 had strengthened his bid for reelection, the New Yorker seemed an ideal choice.

While on the Court Hughes had carved a record that has impressed critics of the Court. He wrote 115 opinions, more than any other Justice during his tenure, and in only 9 of those cases were dissents registered. In addition, he wrote 32 dissenting opinions, also a record during the period.[25] Despite his belief in the integrity of the federal structure, he was willing to interpret generously federal regulation under the commerce and taxing clauses. His opinion in the Shreveport Rate Case recognized the meshing of interstate and intrastate commerce and the need to project federal control over some aspects of local commerce. His dissent in *Johnson* and his vindication when Congress overruled the decision with new legislation illustrated the sympathetic view he took of federal legislation, such as the Pure Food and Drug Act. His forceful opinions outlawing Alabama's laws permitting peonage and Arizona's attempt to discriminate against aliens in employment speak to his sensibilities. In the areas where he contended with Holmes, the New Yorker tended to have the advantage. Where Holmes was often concerned with technicalities and tended to write opinions that lacked clarity, Hughes was interested in reaching the substantive issues in opinions that were generally clear and precise. Also, he had an interest in and an understanding of economic matters that Holmes would not or could not share.

His departure from the Court left a void, but after the Brandeis appointment Wilson experienced little indecision as to the type of man he wanted to place on the Court. There was only one Brandeis, but there were others whose approach might run parallel to the man who had recently survived the scrutiny of the Senate. Newton D. Baker, Wilson's Secretary of War, had convinced the President in 1914 to make John H. Clarke, a close associate from Ohio, a federal district judge, and now Baker urged Wilson to elevate Clarke. Baker pointed to the judge's "progressive" record, which had occasioned some opposition in the Senate upon his initial judical appointment. Brandeis also supported Clarke's candidacy, and in certain ways the two men had parallel careers. As corporation lawyers, both men came to question such service. Brandeis found no appeal in political office, but Clarke was deeply involved in reform politics in Ohio and twice was an unsuccessful candidate for the Senate. Clarke advocated increased national power and supported reforms such as the direct election of Senators, home rule for cities, publicity of campaign expenditures, municipal ownership of street railways, and woman suffrage. Clarke's two years on the federal bench had not endeared him to practicing attorneys; he seemed cold and matter-of-fact and did not hesitate to instruct the bar on questions of general morality. Yet no one questioned his legal competence.[26]

After reading over Clarke's opinions, the President seemed quite impressed, but before making the appointment he sent his Secretary of War to visit the candidate. Baker returned with a report that pleased Wilson, who now concluded that Clarke "could be depended upon for a liberal and enlightened interpretation of the law."[27] In July he sent the nomination to the Senate.

Headlines read, "Wilson Names Another Radical To The Court." Especially noted were Clarke's politics and his unusual sympathy as a judge toward the underprivileged. Fellow Ohioan William Howard Taft opposed the choice, but neither the nation nor the Senate, in the midst of a presidential campaign, had the desire to contest the nomination. Clarke was confirmed unanimously within ten days.[28]

John H. Clarke had just turned fifty-nine as he displaced Brandeis to the far left of the Chief at the opening of Court for the 1916 term. He stood about five feet, five inches tall, was squarely built, and had a courtly air. His silvery hair was receding, but it still was wavy and full as it ran down into long sideburns. His face was fleshy and smooth, and his nose was broad. Distinguished in appearance, he conveyed a determined and even pugnacious air, as small men sometimes do. Standing in the back of the seated Justices for the official Court photograph, Clarke was dwarfed by the trio of Brandeis, Pitney, and

McReynolds, but the man from Ohio would prove that he could hold his own.

The 1916 race for the presidency was somewhat disappointing to those who thought the two candidates would set a record for high level campaigning. As the incumbent, Wilson had the advantage over Hughes, but, as one of his biographers has said, Hughes's campaign "was mostly negative in character, critical rather than constructive, rarely elevated in tone, and rarely convincing as to future courses of action."[29] The New Yorker had been a politically astute governor, but now, after six years of service on the High Court, he seemed to have lost his feel for politics—that understanding of how a successful campaign must be waged.

Still, despite the disappointing campaign of Hughes the election was close, very close. Wilson's strategy of pushing for measures of social justice, coupled with the slogan of "He kept us out of war," as a reminder of the worsening world situation, brought support Wilson's way, but the election would hinge on the vote of a single state. By the closest of margins Wilson captured California and the election. The President's campaign of "progressivism and peace" had paid off, as he won nearly 3 million more votes than he had in 1912. The final tally gave Wilson one-half million more votes than Hughes and a majority of twenty-three in the electoral college, but the Democrats suffered losses in both the House and Senate.[30] For the first time in his career Charles Evans Hughes had suffered political defeat; he retired to private practice and would return often to the Supreme Court to argue before his former colleagues.

How Wilson's last two appointments to the Court would affect its decision making was a question posed as the Justices assembled for the 1916 Term. White had decided to order reargument of the cases left undecided in the previous term. This enabled both Brandeis and Clarke to become full time members of the Court at the outset of their service.

Repeatedly, litigation under the Federal Employers' Liability Act of 1908 brought considerable work to the Court. In the previous term 13 percent of the Court's opinions dealt with this matter, and in the 1916 term such litigation accounted for 10 percent of the opinion workload. Such litigation added unnecessarily to the Court's work. Most often the High Bench was called upon to determine whether the injured employee was engaged in interstate commerce or to evaluate instructions to the jury as to the liability of the railroads. In either instance the Justices were not spending their time in the most profitable manner.

Relief was on the way, however, for this burden placed on the Supreme Court had not gone unnoticed by Congress. Without much debate or consideration, unlike earlier efforts at legislation affecting the federal judiciary, the lawmakers responded quickly to the cry for remedial action. James McReynolds had recognized the growing problem as Attorney General and now was

the principal drafter of the new legislation.[31] The bill focusing on relieving the
Court of its duty to review the liability act and like cases easily became law on
September 6, 1916. What the act did was to make the judgments of the Courts
of Appeals final in cases arising under the federal liability, hours of service,
and safety appliance acts, as well as the bankruptcy act, while preserving for
the Court the authority to review such cases at its discretion on a writ of
certiorari.

Although this section of the legislation was the center of attention, the new
law also further cut down the Court's obligation to hear other appeals,
affording the Justices greater discretion in accepting cases for review. Obligatory jurisdiction was now confined to decisions of state courts in which a
treaty, federal statute or any other exercise of federal authority was held
invalid, or a state statute or exercise of state authority was upheld against
the claim of its repugnancy "to the Constitution, treaties, or laws of the
United States." All other state cases were subject to the Court's discretionary review power. One final provision of the 1916 measure shifted the beginning of the Supreme Court's term from the second to the first Monday in
October. The Chairman of the House Judiciary Committee, Edwin Y. Webb
of North Carolina, explained the change by saying the men on the Court
wanted "a shorter vacation and more time to do work when the weather is
better."[32]

Early in the session the Court was forced to contend with an escalated attack on various state workmen's compensation laws. Two terms ago the
Justices unanimously sustained an Ohio law that was drawn to eliminate the
compulsory feature many states had adopted. Apparently, a number of employers and their counsel thought the earlier decision had not foreclosed
attack upon this new type of state act, for broad-ranging challenges were
mounted against the New York, Iowa, and Washington statutes. In *New
York Central Railroad* v. *White*, the Court considered the New York act
passed after a state constitutional amendment had overturned *Ives*.

Pitney, for a unanimous Court, after noting that the High Bench had
consistently held that states can abolish the common law defenses in em-
ployee-injury cases without running afoul of federal constitutional guarantees, added that no one "has a vested interest in any rule of law entitling him
to insist that it shall remain unchanged for his benefit." Although the New
Jersey Justice did agree that the law limits the liberty to contract, he said such
a limitation is justified when it arises from a reasonable exercise of the state's
police power. Recognizing a clear public interest in the area of hazardous
employment, he ruled that "laws regulating the responsibility of employers
for the injury or death of employees arising out of the employment bear so
close a relation to the protection of the lives and safety of those concerned
that they properly may be regarded as coming within the category of police
regulations."[33] Pitney then concluded that the system of compulsory com-

pensation, established by the New York law, does not violate the Fourteenth Amendment.

With similar ease the Court upheld the Iowa statute, but the Washington scheme split the bench.[34] The new wrinkle in the Washington legislation was the requirement that all employers involved in hazardous work were required to pay premiums into a state fund on the basis of a percentage of their payrolls. Injured employees were to be compensated from this fund. In *Mountain Timber Company* v. *Washington*, Pitney wrote for a five-man majority that was willing to accommodate the Washington plan.

From the standpoint of the employee, he began, the act is not appreciably different from New York's, though the burden placed upon the employer is. What makes the difference is the enforced contribution that the Washington law demands. Quickly disposing of other arguments, Pitney came to the most serious portion of the attack—"that since the act unconditionally requires employers in the enumerated occupations to make payments to a fund for the benefit of employees, without regard to any wrongful act of the employer, he is deprived of his property, and of his liberty to acquire property, without compensation and without due process of law." The Justice said the question for the Court to determine was whether the scheme was a reasonable exercise of the police power, noting that presumptions are in favor of the state and the burden is placed upon the defendant to prove otherwise. This consideration he broke into three parts: whether the legislation is for the public rather than a private interest; whether the burden imposed upon employers is reasonable; and whether it is fairly distributed. On the first point Pitney equated the power of the state to provide pensions for soldiers to the power to compensate those who are wounded not by a bullet but by a machine. Then determining that the scale of compensation was reasonable, he considered the burden imposed upon employers and concluded that "it cannot be deemed arbitrary or unreasonable for the State, instead of imposing upon the particular employer entire responsibility for losses occurring in his own plant or work; to impose the burden upon the industry through a system of occupation taxes limited to the actual losses occurring in the respective classes of occupations."[35] He accepted the state's argument that industrial accidents are inevitable and that an apportionment of responsibility on the basis of payrolls is not unreasonable.

Upholding the act against challenge, Pitney expressed concern about a single feature, the requirement that employers not deduct from the worker's wages any part of the cost of the premiums paid to the state. The Justice indicated that the wording might be construed so broadly that it would interfere with the freedom of contract. But, he added, it has not been so construed, and the Court would not assume a construction that would bring the law into conflict with the Constitution. Pitney probably added this concluding paragraph to work through his own doubts; certainly the other members of the majority—Holmes, Day, Brandeis, and Clarke—did not seem to share such reservations.

Noting disagreement with the decision, White, McKenna, Van Devanter, and McReynolds said nothing. What was significant in this dissenting alignment was the presence of McKenna, who had repeatedly penned opinions that expressed in broad terms the range of the state police power. In 1908 when the Court decided *Adair* and overturned the federal law seeking to outlaw the yellow-dog contract, McKenna had dissented, but in *Coppage* in 1915 he seemed to find new appeal in the freedom to contract doctrine. Now here in the 1916 term he joined a trio of colleagues who had been generally more suspicious of exercises of state power. If his votes in these two cases indicated a shift in McKenna's position, the President's plan to remake the Court with his recent nominees was in trouble.

Wilson's two appointees, Brandeis and Clarke, had made the difference in this battle for affording states considerable latitude in drafting workmen's compensation laws, but they were unable to hold this shaky coalition together in *New York Central Railroad Company* v. *Winfield*. What the case asked was, if the injury did occur in interstate commerce, did the existence of the federal act preclude recovery under the state compensation law? Winfield had been injured in the course of his employment but without negligence on the part of the railroad. His recovery under the New York compensation act was reversed by the majority of the Court in an opinion by Van Devanter. The Justice ruled that the federal act preempted the field and barred the application of state law; any other decision, he said, would undermine the uniformity commanded by the federal statute, since each state would be free to add to the interstate carrier's liability by holding it responsible, irrespective of negligence, for injuries suffered in the course of employment. No state, Van Devanter asserted, "is at liberty thus to interfere with the operation of a law of Congress."[36]

Brandeis, with Clarke joining, disagreed in a dissent that resembles the brief Brandeis penned in *Muller* v. *Oregon*. Maintaining that Congress could preempt the whole field of injuries suffered by employees in interstate commerce, he labeled the 1908 act an emergency measure that is devoid of any preemptive intent and designed to cope with a rising incidence of employee injuries. The scope of the federal law, Brandeis added, is narrow and based upon common law principles; it assures "a more efficient means of making the wrongdoer indemnify him whom he has wronged." In no way, he asserted, does it deny to the states the right to grant relief to workers injured through no fault of the railroad, an area the Justice claimed was left open by the federal act. Examining the nature of the state compensation acts, Brandeis argued that they reflected the conclusion that individual justice must be supplanted by social justice. He noted that when Congress passed the liability act in 1908 not one of the thirty-seven states or territories now having compensation legislation then had such laws. In an eloquent passage the Justice said the states within our federal system are held primarily responsible for preventing social unrest, destitution, and the denial of opportunity. "Surely," Brandeis continued, "we may not impute to Congress the will to deny to the States the power to perform either this duty to humanity or their fundamental duty of self-preservation."[37] Whatever means a state uses to provide a compensation system, he added, is a matter left solely to its discretion. This first written dissent of Brandeis fully justifies both his critics and his supporters, who claimed his elevation to the High Bench would not still his advocacy.

The Court also divided five to four on the question of whether a workman's compensation act could be applied to an injury occurring on board a ship docked in New York harbor. A longshoreman had been killed in an accident on the gangplank of an ocean-going ship, and his widow sought recovery under the state compensation act. All the Justices agreed that the federal liability act did not cover the injury, but they disagreed on the authority of New York law.

McReynolds, for the majority in *Southern Pacific Company* v. *Jensen*, read the Constitution and precedent to say that "Congress has paramount power to fix and determine the maritime law which shall prevail throughout the country. And further, that in the absence of some controlling statute the general maritime law as accepted by the federal courts constitutes part of our national law applicable to matters within the admiralty and maritime jurisdiction." The Justice recognized that the Court had approved state legislation that had affected the general maritime law, but he ruled that such legislation is invalid "if it contravenes the essential purpose expressed by an act of Congress or works material prejudice to the characteristic features of the general maritime law or interferes with the proper harmony and uniformity of that law in its international and interstate relations." If New York can subject such vessels to its compensation act, McReynolds continued, so can other states. The result would be "destruction of the very uniformity in respect to maritime matters which the Constitution was designed to establish; and freedom of navigation between the States and with foreign countries would be seriously hampered and impeded." The former Attorney General acknowledged that the maritime law specifically preserves common law remedies, but a compensation act, unknown to the common law, he said, is not permitted by the grant of exclusive jurisdiction to the federal government. Then in an unusual passage that revealed the reason for the contortions present in the opinion, McReynolds concluded: "And finally this remedy is not consistent with the policy of Congress to encourage investments in ships" as manifested in acts that provide for the limited liability of shipowners.[38]

What had given McReynolds a majority was the defection of Day from the ranks of those Justices who had voted to uphold the Washington workmen's compensation law. Holmes and Pitney wrote dissents in *Jensen*, and Brandeis and Clarke joined in both expressions of opinion. Actually the strained opinion of the majority provided an easy target.

Holmes saw no valid distinction between reserving actions under the common law and reserving actions under statutory law. He cited precedent to indicate that congressional silence does not exclude "the statute or common law of a State from supplementing the wholly inadequate maritime law of the time of the Constitution, in the regulation of personal rights." Attempting to dismiss the spectre of uniformity, Holmes pointed to the fact that the Court had consistently held interstate carriers responsible to the varying laws of the state. In a much more extensive dissent Pitney continued the attack on the majority. He contended that its views that "non-action by Congress amounts to an imperative limitation upon the power of the States to interpose where maritime matters are involved" was novel, far-reaching, and unsupported by precedent.[39] In a scholarly treatment of both history and past decisions, Pitney showed that the reservation of a common law remedy in maritime actions included statutory changes and that neither the Constitution nor federal legislation had sought to provide a uniform substantive law, let alone one concerning procedure.

Rarely in the Supreme Court's history have dissents so completely exposed the fallacies of a majority opinion, but logic was not enough to dislodge a protective feeling toward owners of merchant ships. Perhaps the movement of war closer to home had some effect. The majority refused to heed the *Jensen* dissenters, but Congress, moved both by the logic and humaneness of their position, responded with curative legislation. On October 6, 1917, less than five months after the Court's opinion, the lawmakers passed a bill allowing such claimants "the right and remedies under the Workmen's Compensation Law of any state."[40]

Of even greater importance than interpreting the relationship between federal and state law in the matter of employee injuries was the Justices' reaction to both federal and state statutes regulating conditions of employment. Over a dozen years earlier a bare majority of the Court in *Lochner* had held that state police power was checked by the due process clause's requirement to safeguard the freedom of contract. In the interim the Justices upheld an Oregon law regulating the hours of female employment and a federal statute prescribing maximum hours for employees involved in public work. Now the Court confronted the Adamson Act, which established an eight-hour day for railway employees involved in interstate commerce and two Oregon statutes, one prescribing the ten-hour day in mills, factories, and manufacturing establishments and the other setting a minimum wage for women. As the cases were argued in January 1917, the public eagerly awaited the outcome of the Court's deliberations.

After President Wilson's personal intervention in the dispute between the railroads and the railroad brotherhoods had failed, and with a general strike of the workers in the offing, Congress passed the Adamson Act. The eight-hour day that the unions had fought for was now realized by congressional action. The business community was stirred to anger.[41] Fair-minded men could accept the wisdom of the policy that the administration now chose to follow, but the Supreme Court had to square it with the Constitution. The case of *Wilson* v. *New* was expedited by the trial court acting in concert with the parties; it enjoined the enforcement of the act on grounds of its unconstitutionality, and a direct appeal came to the High Bench.

Acknowledging the importance of the issue, the Chief Justice took the opinion himself. Citing precedent, he concluded that the power to establish the eight-hour day was "so clearly sustained as to render the subject not disputable." White then noted that the legislation by setting hours and preventing any reduction in pay resulted in setting wages as well. White posed the question the Court faced: Did Congress under the commerce power have the authority to exert its will on a wage scale and make it binding for a limited time? This was the heart of the matter, for, although the Justices could accept a maximum-hours law, some of them had severe reservations about governmental interference with employment contracts to the point of determining wages. White identified with the latter group, but he found an exception to the general rule. Facing the interruption of interstate commerce and considering the resultant damage to the public interest, the Chief continued, Congress had the right to devise a remedy and provide "for a standard of wages to fill the want of one caused by the failure to exert private right on the subject." White refused to believe "that the existence of the public right and the public power to preserve it was wholly under the control of the private right to establish a standard by agreement."[42]

Agreeing that an emergency situation cannot in itself create power where there was none before, he then said:

... nevertheless emergency may afford a reason for the exertion of a living power already enjoyed. If acts which, if done, would interrupt, if not destroy, interstate commerce may be by anticipation legislatively prevented, by the same token the power to regulate may be exercised to guard against the cessation of interstate commerce threatened by a failure of employers and employees to agree as to the standard of wages, such standard being an essential prerequisite to the uninterrupted flow of interstate commerce.[43]

Viewing the Adamson Act within the inherent authority of Congress, White suggested that it, in fact, compelled arbitration, which he deemed a legitimate goal of Congress in seeking to protect interstate commerce. But the Chief did not flinch from the other interpretation—that the congressional act was a direct fixing of wages—saying that from either perspective the legislative branch has power to act and that no claim of the invasion of private rights can inhibit such action.

Three dissenting opinions were written by Day, Pitney, and McReynolds, with Van Devanter joining Pitney's dissent. Day acknowledged congressional power in the area, but he added that it could not be exercised to the detriment of fundamental rights secured to individuals under the Constitution. Day called the act a clear illustration of taking the property of one and giving it to another in violation of the Fifth Amendment's due process clause. To the majority's emphasis upon the emergency situation, Day said: "Constitutional rights, if they are to be available in time of greatest need, cannot give way to an emergency, however immediate, or justify the sacrifice of private rights secured by the Constitution." Pitney asserted that the act is not within Congress's commercial power, for its subject matter is not directly connected to interstate transportation. To the contention that it was passed to remove the threat of a strike, Pitney responded that such an argument is immaterial to the law. Calling the act unprecedented, he found it a clear deprivation of property without due process of law. Investments in railroads, the New Jersey Justice added, had been made "without any anticipation or reason for anticipating that a law of this character would be adjudged to be permissible, either as a regulation of commerce or on any other ground."[44] McReynolds argued that the majority had confirmed congressional authority to fix wages and hours, to compel arbitration, and to protect the flow of commerce without limit. This does not strike the modern mind as a parade of horribles. In fact, had the majority Justices not been enamored with the archaic notion of freedom of contract, the case would have posed little difficulty.

In the Court's consideration of the two Oregon cases Brandeis had to withdraw from participation because, before coming to the High Bench, he had advised Felix Frankfurter, counsel for the state, in the preparation of the briefs. This left an eight-man court to wrestle with the problems presented. *Bunting* v. *Oregon* involved the conviction of an employer for his refusal to pay overtime wages for hours worked beyond the ten a day mandated by state law. The statute permitted an employee to work an additional three hours a day, but it required the employer to compensate the worker at one and one-half times his normal hourly rate. Counsel for Bunting contended that a law drawn in this form was neither a health regulation nor a law establishing the maximum workday; instead it was an attempt to set wages.

Recognizing a certain appeal in the argument that the law permitted an employee to work thirteen hours but commanded that he be paid for fifteen and one-half, McKenna, for a five-man majority, said its plausibility disappears when one realizes that the provision for overtime is permissive. He added that the purpose of the provision is "to deter by its burden and its adequacy for this was a matter of legislative judgment under the particular circumstances."[45] Pronouncing reasonable the legislature's recognition of differing employment situations, the Justice suggested that the lawmakers might have determined that such a conditional restraint would prove more

effective than an absolute prohibition. Thus viewing the law as one regulating hours, McKenna saw such legislation amply supported as a health
measure in conformity with national and world standards.

In his opinion McKenna did not deal with the freedom of contract issue
that was central to the decision in *Lochner*, though it had been raised by
counsel. The result of *Bunting* was to overrule implicitly the application of
that doctrine to such regulations by the state. From the Court that decided
Lochner only three Justices remained in 1917, and they all had been dissenters
in the 1905 case: Holmes and Day were with the majority now, but the Chief
apparently had changed his mind. Free from the obligation he must have felt
toward the federal government in *Wilson* v. *New*, he could follow his new
conviction. But neither White nor the other dissenters, Van Devanter and
McReynolds, chose to write an opinion.

Brandeis's vote had not been needed in *Bunting*, but his absention in the
second Oregon case, *Stettler* v. *O'Hara*, left the Court evenly divided. The
result of the equal division was to uphold the state court's decision that the
law establishing a minimum wage for women was constitutional, but this
decision by default carried no precedential weight. The even division of the
Justices revealed just how tenuous was the constitutional standing of such
legislation delving into the details of the employee-employer relationship.[46]

The Oregon law discussed in *Bunting* was typical of state legislation
responding to desires of workers, who were campaigning not for more leisure
time but rather for better wages. A law that made the ten-hour day compulsory would have fallen short of the desired goal. Because of the continuing
constitutional objections to governmental power to prescribe wages, states
had to proceed indirectly. Such indirection was accepted in *Bunting*, enabling
the worker to improve his salary by offering his services at a higher rate
beyond the workday now deemed standard. The episode well illustrates that
obstacles to a direct approach to a perceived problem do not imply that the
goal cannot be reached. We can condemn the Court's myopia in failing to
accept definitively governmental power to regulate wages in an industrial
society characterized by unequal bargaining power between employer and
employee, but, as is illustrative of the entire period under study, the Justices
rarely interposed the Constitution as a barrier that could not be overcome by
the imagination and dedication of those serving the public interest.

In addition to passing upon congressional power in *Wilson* v. *New*, the
Justices sustained the Webb-Kenyon Act of 1913, which sought to give states
greater control over liquor traffic. Passed over the constitutional objections
of President Taft in the waning days of his administration, the legislation
forbad the interstate shipment of liquor to be used in violation of state law.
Despite the attempt of Congress to afford the states greater control over
liquor traffic in the Wilson Act of 1890, the Court had consistently limited the
range of permissible state regulation in the interest of protecting interstate

commerce. Prohibitionist forces had now succeeded with Congress in affording the states greater latitude in enforcing their laws. The test of the new legislation came in *James Clark Distilling Company* v. *Western Maryland Railway Company*, when the distiller sought to force the railroad company to accept shipments destined for the dry state of West Virginia.

For a six-man majority White wrote the opinion. Brushing aside the question of whether personal use can be prohibited by saying the state can restrict the means by which persons obtain the product, he contended with the question of whether Congress can authorize such a state burden upon interstate commerce. Congress clearly has the authority, the Chief began, to ban all interstate shipments of liquor, as it had banned the shipment of lottery tickets and the transportation of women for immoral purposes. It is not then a want of power, White continued, but the fact that Congress had departed from uniform regulation and subjected the traffic to the various laws of the states that posed the problem. But, he added, Congress had not delegated its control over interstate commerce to the states, for the states can act in accordance with their own policies only because Congress willed this result. As to uniformity, White said the Constitution does not impose such a requirement upon Congress under the commerce clause. Not fully content to rely on precedent, White ruled that, since Congress could prohibit the liquor traffic in interstate commerce, it certainly could recognize the federal system and cooperate with the states, thereby "making it impossible for one State to violate the prohibitions of another through the channels of interstate commerce."[47] Probably because McReynolds was troubled by the expansive wording of White's opinion, he concurred in the result, but Holmes and Van Devanter dissented without opinion.

Perhaps the dissenters worried about the Court's eager accommodation of the prevailing morality, but in *Caminetti* v. *United States* they did join their colleagues in extending federal power over sexual immorality. Caminetti and his friend, Diggs, both of whom were married, found willing girls of about nineteen and took off for Reno, Nevada, where they set up housekeeping. When their cozy arrangement was exposed, newspapers in California highlighted the story. Caminetti's father was prominent in state politics and was shortly to be appointed Commissioner of Immigration by President Wilson. Apparently the younger Caminetti thought his political connections insulated him from prosecution, but the United States attorney, John L. McNab, responded to the popular outcry and charged both men with violations of the Mann Act. When the elder Caminetti accepted the federal post, he indicated that he wanted to return to California for his son's trial. But in the early months of the Wilson administration, the Secretary of Labor decided he could not spare the new Commissioner of Immigration. Then Attorney General McReynolds was approached to obtain a delay of the trial; he agreed and sent word to McNab. Convinced that justice was to be sacrificed on the altar of politics, McNab responded in a public letter to the President in which the United States attorney, accusing the administration of favoritism, resigned his federal post. As the national press picked up the story, Wilson acted to nip the budding scandal by appointing a special prosecutor to see that justice would be done in the *Caminetti* case.[48] The administration had not acted improperly in the matter, despite the suspicions of McNab, but the President himself must have breathed a sigh of relief when the special prosecutor obtained the conviction.

Earlier litigation under the Mann Act had embraced far more than white slavery, but the *Caminetti* case now asked the Court to interpret the meaning of the prohibition of transportation "for any immoral purposes."[49] The companions of Caminetti and Diggs were not the naive creatures pictured by the local press; indeed, they may have been misled, but they were objects of pleasure, not profit.

Had Caminetti and Diggs violated legislation that ostensibly was aimed at those who sought financial profit from sexual immorality? Justice Day, for the majority, answered yes. To the argument that the statute was concerned only with commercialized vice, the Justice responded that such a limitation, despite the popular title of the act, cannot be found in its wording. Relying upon the interpretation by the Court of the same phrase in an immigration act in 1908, Day said the concubinage involved in the *Caminetti* case is properly embraced by the catchall wording. "To say the contrary," the Justice continued, "would shock the common understanding of what constitutes an immoral purpose when those terms are applied, as here, to sexual relations." The fact that the interpretation now given to the act would make it a useful vehicle for blackmail, Day added, was a matter properly addressed to Congress and not to the Court. To the argument that this act is not, as interpreted, a regulation of commerce, he responded that "the authority of Congress to keep the channels of interstate commerce free from immoral and injurious use has been frequently sustained, and is no longer open to question."[50] After finding no error committed in the trial, Day upheld the conviction, which carried a sentence of eighteen months for Caminetti.

McReynolds, with his earlier embarrassing connection with the case did not participate, and the Chief and Clarke joined in a dissenting opinion written by McKenna. The California Justice assaulted the simplistic approach of the majority, which, he said, failed to put the phrase *for any other immoral purpose* into the context of the statute. The words of a statute can properly be extended or restricted to effectuate its purpose, McKenna argued, both to rescue legislation from absurdity and to recognize the inherent limitations of language. To the charge he was recommending that the Court legislate, McKenna said that, on the contrary, his was "seeking and enforcing the true sense of a law notwithstanding its imperfection or generality of expression." Acknowledging that the facts of the case excited emotion, he argued that judicial consideration must be guided solely by reason. Everyone knows, McKenna continued, that differences exist "between the occasional immoralities of men and women and that systematized and mercenary immorality epitomized in the statute's graphic phrase 'White-slave traffic.' "[51] Sensing danger in extending the statute beyond its clear purpose, he saw in the blackmail possibility the substitution of one evil for another.

After the Supreme Court decision in *Caminetti*, President Wilson was no more sympathetic to the pleas for a pardon coming from the defendant's mother and California Democrats.[52] The whole affair had burned him earlier, and even if the conviction, absent its political setting, had moved him to respond mercifully, Wilson had little political choice but to reject the pardon requests.

The result of the Court's reading of the commerce power of Congress both in *Wilson* v. *New* and in *Caminetti* was that it encompassed wide-ranging regulatory possibilities. The majority had read the power as broadly as it ever would be read.

Two cases of the term considered substantive matters relating to the Sherman Antitrust Act. A unanimous Court upheld a district court's decision allowing an aggrieved party to recover treble damages. The Court of Appeals had reversed on the ground that the major antitrust decision of 1911 provided immunity for restraints that were reasonable. Finding no basis for such a conclusion, McKenna said White's opinions in the 1911 cases were misread. Allegations that a restraint of trade was beneficial to commerce, the Justice claimed, were insufficient to overcome a clear showing in the trial court of a restraint prohibited by the antitrust act. Good motives, McKenna continued, do not preclude a violation. Here the plaintiff had been able to show an injury from a combination of ocean carriers between New York and South African ports that restricted his ability to ship goods.[53]

In *Paine Lumber Company* v. *Neal* a number of companies sought to enjoin a union of carpenters from interfering with the use of nonunion-made materials. Both lower courts found no special damage to the plaintiffs that would merit an injunction. Holmes, for the majority, said that, even assuming the Sherman Act was violated, the legislation did not give a private party the right to sue for an injunction, that right being reserved for the government. Acknowledging that the Clayton Antitrust Act of 1914 did recognize the right of private parties to sue for an injunction, Holmes found that provision limited by others that, he said, sought to preclude the issuance of injunctions in labor disputes of the kind involved here. Finally, responding to the claim that New York law allowed the issuance of an injunction, the Justice refused to believe "that the ordinary action of a labor union can be made the ground of an injunction under those laws until we are so instructed by the New York Court of Appeals."[54]

With McKenna and Van Devanter in tow, Pitney detailed his disagreement, and McReynolds dissented alone. The New Jersey Justice said the Sherman Act does not forbid the issuance of an injunction when a boycott in restraint of interstate commerce is clearly shown. Pitney went on to deal with the prolabor sections in the Clayton Act. Neither in the act nor in its legislative history, he claimed, "is there any indication of a purpose to render lawful or legitimate anything that before the act was unlawful, whether in the objects of such an organization or its members or in the measures adopted for accomplishing them." To assert that the boycott involved here is unlawful, he continues, is "a libel upon the labor organization and a serious impeachment of Congress."[55] The anti-injunction provision, Pitney argued, applies only to strikes and does not preclude injunctions in such situations. Holmes's opinion in the case was murky, but Pitney's dissent was not. The dissent is significant because it suggested that organized labor had misread the protection offered by the recent legislation.

As the Justices put the divisive matter of union activity behind them they all agreed the House of Representatives had exceeded its power in the case of *Marshall* v. *Gordon*. At issue was the power of the House of Representatives to arrest a person for contempt. The controversy arose out of the charges and countercharges of a member of the House and a federal attorney in New York. The exasperated lawyer sent a letter to the chairman of a subcommittee, charged with taking testimony on the question of whether the government attorney was guilty of impeachable conduct, that was itself considered defamatory and insulting by the House. The attorney was arrested, and he sued for a writ of habeas corpus. A unanimous Court granted the writ, as White ruled that the inherent power of contempt in the legislative branch could only be used "to prevent acts which in and of themselves inherently obstruct or prevent the discharge of legislative duty or the refusal to do that which there is an inherent legislative power to compel in order that legislative functions may be performed."[56]

Although White believed it to be the Chief Justice's duty to remind a coordinate branch of the federal government of the limits of its power, he delegated the task of writing the Court's opinion to Clarke in another case in which the Chief had considerable personal interest. In his spirited dissent in *A. B. Dick* White had been alarmed by the majority's ruling that a patent holder could condition a sale with a license that restricted the buyer to the exclusive use of nonpatented materials sold by the patent holder.[57] From the four-man majority in *A. B. Dick*, Holmes, McKenna, and Van Devanter remained, but only the Chief survived from the dissenting trio. Day did not participate in the earlier case, and Pitney had not yet become a member of the Court. Both of them and all three subsequent appointees joined with White to reverse the earlier case.

Perhaps because of his own strong views and his desire to secure as large a majority as possible, the Chief assigned the opinion to Clarke. The case involved the sale of a motion picture projector with the notice that it was to be used only to show certain films provided by the patent holder. The lower federal court's decision was based on the statutory change made by Congress in response to *A. B. Dick*, but Clarke confronted the earlier case and overruled it. Such a restriction, he said, which "would give to the plaintiff such a potential power for evil over an industry which must be recognized as an important element in the amusement life of the nation . . . is plainly void, because wholly without the scope and purpose of our patent laws and because, if sustained, it would be gravely injurious to that public interest, which we have seen is more a favorite of the law than is the promotion of private fortunes."[58] With Clarke's words White had won his victory. McReynolds simply concurred in the result, but Holmes wrote in dissent, carrying along the surviving members of the *A. B. Dick* majority. The Massachusetts Justice, who generally did not share his generation's concern with monopoly, saw the patent and copyright laws conferring a broad monopolistic power. He said there is no public interest in a patented product, for the patent holder has the right to withhold the product from the public. If he has this right, the Justice continued, he may conditionally withhold it. Holmes criticized the majority for disturbing a rule of property that many had relied upon for the last decade and a half.

Claims of contract. impairment were frequently presented during the session, and in contending with them the Justices demonstrated that, although some avenues of successful argument had been closed, others, surprisingly, were not. Two of the term's cases are illustrative. *Long Sault Development Company* v. *Call* involved New York's conferral of substantial rights upon a company to improve navigation, develop power, construct a bridge, and establish factories using the waters and bed of the St. Lawrence River. In 1913 the legislature repealed this act, a clear violation of the constitutional protection against the impairment of contracts, McKenna and Pitney argued in dissent. But not so, said the majority in an opinion by Clarke, which accepted the New York court's sidestepping of the constitutional provision. The state court had pronounced the 1907 act void on the grounds that navigable waters "are held by the State on such a trust for the public use that the legislature has no power to authorize the conveyance of them to a private corporation to maintain navigation."[59] Since the lower court did not consider the repeal act of 1913, but instead ruled that the original granting act was void, Clarke concluded, the constitutional prohibition has not been violated.

In the second case the Court was forced to contend with Owensboro, Kentucky's battle against the local waterworks company. In 1913 the Court had decided that the municipality had granted a telephone company a per-

petual franchise; now the majority reached a similar conclusion in litigation involving a water company. Clarke dissented, saying the finding of what
amounted to a perpetual franchise was a most serious burden upon the city
and a ruling that violated two well-established rules of construction regularly
used by the Court: first, that any such grant must be made in clear and
unequivocal terms; and second, that any ambiguity should be interpreted as
the parties themselves interpret it. Brandeis agreed with Clarke, and Day
joined Clarke on the basis that grants of this character should be construed in
favor of the public interest.[60] The dissenters seemed concerned that a new
majority was coalescing that would be willing to twist previously established
court doctrine.

In other matters relating to the police power, the Court was supportive
with an important exception. Iowa could regulate the butterfat content of ice
cream, Atlanta could regulate private detectives, and New Jersey could require street railways to provide free transportation for all police officers.
McKenna dissented when the rest of the Justices found no objection to a
Chicago ordinance regulating the construction of billboards, but he was the
writer for the Court in a number of important police power cases.[61]

California, McKenna ruled, could require faith healers or "drugless practitioners" to complete a course of study and take an examination before being
licensed, even though those who sought to heal by prayer were exempted
from the statutory requirements. Then in three opinions he upheld laws
regulating the sale of securities in Ohio, South Dakota, and Michigan.
Designed to protect the investing public, the laws essentially presented the
same constitutional questions. Perceiving an evil that justified the exercise of
the state police power, McKenna disposed of due process and equal protection claims. In the absence of congressional action, he concluded, the states
had the authority to place this indirect burden on interstate commerce.[62] The
only dissenter in the cases was McReynolds, the author of the one opinion in
the term imposing a substantial limit upon the police power.

Adams v. *Tanner*, decided on the last day of the term, ended the session on
a sour note. To protect workers from extortion voters in the state of Washington had used the initiative and referendum to pass a law prohibiting the
collecting of fees for furnishing individuals with information leading to
employment. Although private agencies were not precluded from obtaining
fees from employers, there was general agreement that the legislation had the
practical effect of prohibiting such agencies. In the previous term McReynolds wrote for a unanimous Court in upholding the regulation of such
agencies by Michigan, but now he and a majority of his colleagues concluded
that Washington had gone too far.[63]

Abuses justify regulation, McReynolds said, but "this is not enough to
justify destruction of one's right to follow a distinctly useful calling in an
upright way." Differing with the initiators of the Washington act and those

who voted it into law, the Justice ruled that the Constitution protects such businesses from destruction by skillfully "directed agitation." Quoting earlier decisions of the Court, including *Allgeyer*, concerning the check that the Fourteenth Amendment imposes upon the state police power, he concluded that the present measure "is arbitrary and oppressive, and that it unduly restricts the liberty of appellants, guaranteed by the Fourteenth Amendment, to engage in a useful business."[64]

McKenna dissented, saying the Court's reading of the police power, in cases so recent as not to merit citation, clearly upholds the Washington measure. The Californian's brief response to the majority was followed by an extensive dissent by Brandeis, who was joined by Holmes and Clarke. Brandeis cited precedent to deny that a legal distinction can be drawn between regulation and prohibition. The action of the legislature, he said, is final unless arbitrary or unreasonable, and this determination, the Justice continued, must be made not upon assumptions but rather upon the relevant facts. This is necessary, he asserted, "in order that we may have a system of living law." Then with the same justification that produced his brief in *Muller*, Brandeis plunged into facts, not to establish the wisdom of the approach taken here but rather to demonstrate that it can hardly be labeled unreasonable. Quoting extensively from two federal government reports that clearly delineated both the abuses and the inadequacy of such private agencies, the Justice noted that widespread regulation had not cured the abuses. He also suggested that the electorate could have "considered the elimination of the practice a necessary preliminary to the establishment of a constructive policy for dealing with the subject of unemployment." Quoting from *Holden* v. *Hardy*, in which the Court gave its support to the adjustment of law "to new conditions of society, and particularly to the new relations between employers and employes as they arise," Brandeis seemed to be asking his colleagues if their predecessors almost two decades earlier did not have a better understanding of their role.[65]

Day and Pitney held the balance of power in the Oregon and Washington cases; as they voted, the Court decided. White, Van Devanter, and McReynolds voted to invalidate both state acts, while McKenna, Holmes, Brandeis, and Clarke voted to sustain them.

With *Adams* v. *Tanner* the term ended on June 11, 1917. The careful observer could not have failed to note indications of a hardening of positions and a willingness to reinspect doctrines favoring the exercise of both state and federal power in the public interest. Some things were clear. The two new Wilson appointees had lived up to their reputations, not as "radicals" but as men sensitive to the claims of social justice. Their realism and judicial honesty were apparent, and not since the accession of Moody in 1906 had recent appointees brought a clearly new perspective to the Court. In the term's thirty-seven divided cases, Brandeis and Clarke agreed in thirty-two, the highest incidence of agreement between any two Justices. Their votes were decisive in nine of the divided cases. The Brandeis dissent proved as distinctive as the Brandeis brief, and although Clarke did not use the same approach, his attacks on the majority's resolution were precise and hard hitting.

During the past term dissent had increased 50 percent over the level of the two previous sessions. White disagreed with the majority only seven times in the previous two sessions but ten times during the 1916 session. His early reluctance to dissent as Chief had been overcome. McKenna was the Court's leading dissenter with fifteen, the mean for the Justices being ten. McReynolds was the Justice most hesitant to approve governmental action. He usually wrote short opinions relying heavily on quotations, and at this time he rarely explained his dissents. Van Devanter wrote fewer opinions than any of his colleagues; he has been called "opinion shy," a characterization denoting the difficulty he had in handling writing assignments. This reflected no lack of legal ability but simply a substantial personal difficulty in writing. Holmes continued to pull a heavy work load at his own urging, but his opinions, which always were short, were now at times murky and cryptic, unable to stand on their own without reference to the briefs or dissenting opinions to fill in the facts and establish the precise grounds of law involved. Although the Massachusetts Justice was seventy-six, this opinion problem was not an indication of approaching senility but rather simply an accentuation of a characteristic that Holmes brought with him to the Court fifteen years earlier. Pitney wrote the longest opinions, whether for the Court or in dissent, and he tended to chart his own way through the cases, at times agreeing with the new Wilson appointees and at other times taking a position in opposition to them.

When the Court adjourned, its members scattered into a society on a war footing. The war that Wilson had been given credit for avoiding in the campaign of 1916 had come, when, on April 6, 1917, Congress followed the President's lead and declared war on Germany. Mobilizing a society ill prepared for war was a herculean task. New legislation providing for the waging of war was quickly enacted. The draft was authorized in May 1917, and less than a month later obstruction of the war effort was made a crime by the Espionage Act. Then in August Congress gave what appeared to be dictatorial authority to the President to control the production, distribution, and pricing of food and fuel essential to the war effort. The Lever Food and Drug Control Act subjected the economic life of the nation to the war effort under the President's direction. Those forces fighting so successfully for prohibition of alcoholic beverages were rewarded with a provision in the Lever Act enacting wartime prohibition. Some of the measures would find their way to the Supreme Court where the Justices would be pressed to harmonize them with the Constitution, just as they had to square the Adamson Act in the recently completed term.

During the recess of the Court Brandeis remained in Washington to assist the administration in mobilizing the country for war. Wilson continued to solicit the Justice's advice on a wide range of matters, much more so than Cleveland did with Fuller or Roosevelt with Moody. Brandeis was reputed to have great influence with the President, an impression that Wilson himself fostered when he confided to a visitor that he had need for Brandeis "everywhere." Such a relationship between a Justice and a President has, in more recent times, become a subject of concern, but neither Brandeis nor Wilson thought it involved any impropriety. However, Chief Justice White, who had believed that Hughes's resignation to run for the presidency demeaned the Court, did veto Brandeis's participation on a three-man commission designed to soothe troubled Mexican-American relations.[66] The Chief had approved similar service for Lamar in 1913 and had himself participated as an arbitrator in a boundary dispute between Costa Rica and Panama in 1910, but now White was less hospitable to such raids upon the Court's personnel.

NOTES

1. Leonard Dinnerstein, "Joseph Rucker Lamar," in *The Justices of the United States Supreme Court 1789-1969: Their Lives and Major Opinions*, ed. Leon Friedman and Fred L. Israel, 4 vols. (New York: R.R. Bowker Co. and Chelsea House Publishers, 1969), 3:1987-88; and memorial proceeding for Lamar in 241 U.S. v-xx.

2. A. L. Todd, *Justice on Trial: The Case of Louis D. Brandeis* (New York: McGraw-Hill Book Co., 1964), pp. 37-39, 69-72, 65-67.

3. Ibid., pp. 75-77.

4. Ibid., p. 73.

5. Alpheus T. Mason, *William Howard Taft: Chief Justice* (New York: Simon & Schuster, 1965), pp. 66-72; and Todd, *Justice on Trial*, p. 78.

6. Mason, *William Howard Taft*, pp. 73-74; and petition from the fifty-five members of the Boston bar is in Alpheus T. Mason, *Brandeis: A Free Man's Life* (New York: Viking Press, 1946), pp. 472-73.

7. On the United Shoe matter, see Mason, *Brandeis*, pp. 214-29, and Todd, *Justice on Trial*, pp. 49-51, 111-14. The Todd volume concentrates on the fight over Brandeis's nomination to the Court.

8. For a summary of Brandeis's legal career and attitudes, see Todd, *Justice on Trial*, pp. 40-68, and Melvin I. Urofsky, *A Mind of One Piece: Brandeis and American Reform* (New York: Charles Scribner's Sons, 1971), pp. 17-42.

9. Todd, *Justice on Trial*, pp. 185-87, 512, 190-192.

10. Ibid., pp. 192-94, 199-200, 212-15, 240-44. For Brandeis's assessment of the nomination fight, see his letter to Charles F. Amidon, June 27, 1916, in Mason, Brandeis, 505-6.

11. Act of February 20, 1907, ch. 1134, 34 Stat. 898, 899, *as amended*, Act of March 26, 1910, ch. 128, 36 Stat. 263.

12. Gegiow v. Uhl, 239 U.S. 3 (1915).

13. Truax v. Raich, 239 U.S. 33, 38, 41, 43 (1915).

14. Heim v. McCall, 239 U.S. 175 (1915); and Crane v. New York, 239 U.S. 195 (1915).

15. Mackenzie v. Hare, 239 U.S. 299, 312 (1915). Congress repealed that portion of the Act of March 2, 1907, ch. 2534, 34 Stat. 1228, that had deprived Mrs. MacKenzie and

others similarly situated of their citizenship by the Act of September 22, 1922, ch. 411, 42 Stat. 1021. Women trapped by the earlier provisions, such as Mrs. Mackenzie, did not automatically resume their American citizenship; rather they were required to pass through a naturalization proceeding. Under the 1922 act American women marrying aliens declared ineligible for naturalization were still stripped of their American citizenship and certain presumptions were raised about the effect of living outside the country. Over the next eighteen years these disabilities were removed, the final removal coming with the Nationality Act of 1940, ch. 876, 54 Stat. 1137, 1172.

16. Innes v. Tobin, 240 U.S. 127 (1916).

17. United States v. Johnson, 221 U.S. 488 (1911); and Seven Cases v. United States, 239 U.S. 510, 516-17, 518 (1916).

18. United States v. Coca Cola Co., 241 U.S. 265, 276 (1916).

19. Weber v. Freed, 239 U.S. 325 (1915).

20. Brushaber v. Union Pacific R.R., 240 U.S. 1, 18, 19 (1916). The Union Pacific was precluded by the tax law from challenging the exaction before its payment, but the device used in *Pollock*—a shareholders' suit against the company seeking to enjoin the payment of the tax—was again permitted by the Court. Also, the government was allowed to intervene and participate in the argument.

21. The Court dealt similarly with challenges to the income tax in the following: Stanton v. Baltic Mining Co., 240 U.S. 103 (1916); Tyee Realty Co. v. Anderson, 240 U.S. 115 (1916); Dodge v. Osborn, 240 U.S. 118 (1916); and Dodge v. Brady, 240 U.S. 122 (1916).

22. Rast v. Van Deman & Lewis Co., 240 U.S. 342, 360, 357 (1916); and Tanner v. Little, 240 U.S. 369, 386 (1916).

23. *New York Times* and other newspaper reaction quoted in Samuel Hendel, *Charles Evans Hughes and the Supreme Court* (New York: King's Crown Press, Columbia University, 1951), p. 69.

24. Merlo J. Pusey, *Charles Evans Hughes*, 2 vols. (New York: Macmillan Co., 1951), 1:233-39, 300-301, 315-27. William Howard Taft offered his support but lamented that Wilson could "almost destroy the Court" by filling the coming vacancies with men like Brandeis (pp. 319-20).

25. See Arthur M. Allen, "The Opinions of Mr. Justice Hughes," *Columbia Law Review* 16 (November 1916):565-66, and Fred Rodell, *Nine Men: A Political History of the Supreme Court of the United States from 1790 to 1955* (New York: Random House, Vintage Books, 1955), p. 223; and Hendel, *Hughes and the Supreme Court*, p. 18.

26. Henry J. Abraham, *Justices and Presidents: A Political History of Appointments to the Supreme Court* (New York: Oxford University Press, 1974), p. 171; and David Burner, "John H. Clarke," in *Justices of the Supreme Court*, 3:2079-81.

27. Hoyt L. Warner, *The Life of Mr. Justice Clarke* (Cleveland: Western Reserve University Press, 1959), p. 116.

28. See *Literary Digest* 53 (July 29, 1916):240-41, and Burton J. Hendrick, "Another Radical for the Supreme Court," *World's Work* 33 (November 1916):95-98.

29. Dexter Perkins, *Charles Evans Hughes and American Democratic Statesmanship* (Boston: Little, Brown & Co., 1965), p. 55.

30. Arthur S. Link, *Woodrow Wilson and the Progressive Era, 1910-1917*, New American Nation Series (New York: Harper & Row, Torchbooks, 1963), pp. 247-50.

31. Felix Frankfurter and James M. Landis, *The Business of the Supreme Court* (New York: Macmillan Co., 1927), pp. 210-14; and Abraham, *Justices and Presidents*, p. 172.

32. Act of September 6, 1916, ch. 448, 39 Stat. 726, 727; and Webb quoted in Frankfurter and Landis, *Business of the Supreme Court*, p. 211, n. 114.

33. New York Central R.R. v. White, 243 U.S. 188, 198, 207 (1917).

34. Hawkins v. Bleakly, 243 U.S. 210 (1917); and Mountain Timber Co. v. Washington, 243 U.S. 219 (1917).

35. Mountain Timber Co. v. Washington, 243 U.S. 219, 235, 244 (1917).

36. New York Central R.R. v. Winfield, 244 U.S. 147, 153 (1917).

37. Id. at 164, 166.

38. Southern Pacific Co. v. Jensen, 244 U.S. 205, 215, 216, 217, 218, (1917). The Court's hostility to granting seamen access to common or statutory law for redress of their injuries was further demonstrated in the subsequent term, when the same majority, with Holmes concurring in the result, speaking again through McReynolds, concluded that an injured seaman was limited to an action for wages, maintenance and care under admiralty law. The basic legislation of 1789 seemed to preserve a common law remedy, but the majority limited its reach. Pitney, Brandeis, and Clarke did not add to their words in *Jensen* (Chelentis v. Luckenbach Steamship Co., 247 U.S. 372 [1918]).

39. Southern Pacific Co. v. Jensen, 244 U.S. 205, 223, 224-25 (1917).

40. Act of October 6, 1917, ch. 97, 40 Stat. 395.

41. See Link, *Woodrow Wilson and the Progressive Era*, pp. 235-38.

42. Wilson v. New, 243 U.S. 332, 346, 348 (1917).

43. Id. at 348.

44. Id. at 372, 388.

45. Bunting v. Oregon, 243 U.S. 426, 436 (1917).

46. Stettler v. O'Hara, 243 U.S. 629 (1917). Although the Court issues no opinion in such a case and does not reveal the lineup of the Justices, here the division seems easy to call. The majority in *Bunting* included McKenna, Holmes, Day, Pitney, and Clarke; in *Stettler* one of its members defected to the former minority of White, Van Devanter, and McReynolds. McKenna in the *Adamson* case had indicated his willingness to uphold the setting of wages as a legitimate governmental power, and the new arrival Clarke was known to be in sympathy with such legislation. Holmes might privately question the wisdom of a wage-setting law, but he had long accepted the view that his private judgment should not be elevated into a constitutional objection. Day, for all his worry in *Adamson* and other cases about the reach of federal power, had long interpreted the state police power broadly. This leaves Pitney as the Justice who distinguished *Bunting*. The New Jersey Justice had a teachable intellect in many matters, but in the matter of wage setting his mind seemed closed.

47. James Clark Distilling Co. v. Western Maryland Ry., 242 U.S. 311, 331 (1917).

48. *Current Opinion* 55 (August 1913):76-79.

49. Mann Act, ch. 395, 36 Stat. 825 (1910).

50. Caminetti v. United States, 242 U.S. 470, 486, 491 (1917). The 1908 case is United States v. Bitty, 208 U.S. 393.

51. Caminetti v. United States, 242 U.S. 470, 501, 502 (1917).

52. *New York Times*, March 31, 1917.

53. Thomsen v. Cayser, 243 U.S. 66 (1917).

54. Paine Lumber Co. v. Neal, 244 U.S. 459, 471 (1917).

55. Id. at 484.

56. Marshall v. Gordon, 243 U.S. 521, 542 (1917).

57. Henry v. A. B. Dick Co., 224 U.S. 1, 49 (1912).

58. Motion Picture Patents Co. v. Universal Film Mfg. Co., 243 U.S. 502, 519 (1917). On the same day the Court decided that the holder of a patent could not control the retail price of his product. Holmes, McKenna, and Van Devanter again dissented (Straus v. Victor Talking Machine Co., 243 U.S. 490 [1917]).

59. Long Sault Development Co. v. Call, 242 U.S. 272, 278 (1916).

60. Owensboro v. Cumberland Telephone & Telegraph Co., 230 U.S. 58 (1913); and Owensboro v. Owensboro Water Works Co., 243 U.S. 166 (1917).

61. Hutchinson Ice Cream Co. v. Iowa, 242 U.S. 153 (1916); Lehon v. Atlanta, 242 U.S. 53 (1916); Sutton v. New Jersey, 244 U.S. 258 (1917); and Thomas Cusack Co. v. Chicago, 242 U.S. 526 (1917).

62. Crane v. Johnson, 242 U.S. 339, 343 (1917); Hall v. Geiger-Jones Co., 242 U.S. 539 (1917); Caldwell v. Sioux Falls Stock Yards Co., 242 U.S. 559 (1917); and Merrick v. N. W. Halsey & Co., 242 U.S. 568 (1917).

63. Brazee v. Michigan, 241 U.S. 340 (1916); and Adams v. Tanner, 244 U.S. 590 (1917).

64. Adams v. Tanner, 244 U.S. 590, 594, 597 (1917). In 1949 the Court said in *Lincoln Federal Labor Union* v. *Northwestern Iron & Metal Co.* (335 U.S. 525, 535) that the Adams decision had been "clearly undermined" by *Olson* v. *Nebraska* (313 U.S. 296 [1941]).

65. Adams v. Tanner, 244 U.S. 590, 600, 614-15, 616. Both of Brandeis's dissents during the term were written to promote a recognition of the relationship between law and social and economic facts. They were designed to educate not only his colleagues on the bench but the public as well. (See Mason, *Brandeis*, p. 518.)

66. Mason, *Brandeis*, pp. 520-25; and *Washington Evening Star*, August 13, 1916.

chapter 11

OMINOUS RUMBLINGS, 1917-19

     In the previous session a narrow majority of the High Court had refused to grant an injunction against a labor union under the antitrust law, but early in the 1917 term the Justices contended with a similar request. The dissent last term in *Paine Lumber Company*, written by Pitney and joined by McKenna and Van Devanter, had indicated hostility to the methods and goals of organized labor, but for various reasons, some of which were technical, enough Justices resisted the blandishments of what became the minority opinion.[1] The question to be resolved in *Hitchman Coal & Coke Company* v. *Mitchell* was whether the former dissenters could gain the additional support needed to become the voice of the Court.

     Hitchman had been pressured into unionizing its coal mines in 1903, but after a strike in 1906 the company made the signing of a yellow-dog contract a prerequisite for reemployment. Shortly thereafter the United Mine Workers renewed its activity with the miners, hoping to force management to recognize the workers' right to organize. Seeking to prevent interference with its employee relationships, the company sought an injunction against the union. Although Hitchman alleged that the union had violated the antitrust law, it also pressed for an injunction against the union organizers on grounds of an irreparable loss to property. Generally accepting Hitchman's contentions, the trial court granted the injunction, but its decision was reversed by the federal appellate court. The Supreme Court reached for the case by invoking its discretionary jurisdiction. First argued before Brandeis and Clarke took their seats, the case was one of the matters upon which the Chief had ordered reargument before a full bench. Now the three-man minority in *Paine Lumber Company* augmented by the Chief, Day, and McReynolds, became a majority.

     Pitney, as the Court's spokesman, said the employer is free to require his employees to sign yellow-dog contracts and that such contracts are deserving of legal protection. "The fact that the employment is at the will of the parties, respectively," he continued, "does not make it one at the will of others." Contending that the majority does not dispute the right of workmen to join unions, the Justice insisted that union objectives must be proper and legitimate. Counsel for the union organizers had contended they were not attempting to break any contract by inducing the workers to join the union, for all the contract required was that the worker sever his employment with Hitchman after becoming a union member. Pitney responded that, in equity, a court "looks to the substance and essence of things and disregards matters of form and technical nicety." To the argument that the recruitment drive was peaceful, the New Jersey Justice answered the intentions of the union organizers cannot be ignored and the absence of violence is irrelevant. "In our opinion," he continued, "any violation of plaintiff's legal rights contrived by defendants for the purpose of inflicting damage, or having that as its necessary effect, is as plainly inhibited by law as if it involved a breach of peace. A combination to procure concerted breaches of contract by plaintiff's employees constitutes such a violation."[2] Defendants' attempt to cause a strike with resulting financial loss to the plaintiff, Pitney concluded, is an unlawful purpose pursued by unlawful and malicious means. He reversed the appellate court and upheld the trial court's injunction.

Brandeis wrote for the dissenters, who included Holmes and Clarke. First noting agreement with the decision of the court of appeals, which had reversed the district court on the grounds that no unlawful action was shown and that no contracts of employment were breached, Brandeis then systematically undermined the majority's opinion. First, he emphasized that the union is not an unlawful organization nor an unlawful conspiracy. Contending that the mines cannot be unionized without the employer's consent, the Justice found the methods used here to extract this consent were not unlawful. This is not coercion in a legal sense, he contended, for the employer is free to accept it or not. "Indeed," he continued, "the plaintiff's whole case is rested upon agreements secured under similar pressure of economic necessity or disadvantage." Next, Brandeis denied that any employment contract was broken, since the contract created an employment terminable by either party at will and did not preclude union membership. He noted that no evidence of any employee joining the union was introduced, saying all the organizers sought to get were promises to join. As to defendants conspiring to induce employees to quit their jobs, Brandeis said: "It should not, at this day, be doubted that to induce workingmen to leave or not to enter an employment in order to advance such a purpose is justifiable when the workmen are not bound by contract to remain in such employment."[3] Step by step, he exposed the antiunion sentiment of a majority still not ready to accept the reality of labor organizations in a capitalistic society. Holmes had come to this position quite early, and now Brandeis gave it forceful expression.

Hitchman Coal & Coke Company revealed a polarized bench and support for the contention that the Court was hostile to organized labor. What made the injunction such a formidable weapon against organized labor was its ability to crush unionization drives under the guise of protecting the employer's property. This equitable proceeding, allowing no room for a trial of the facts by a jury, gave judges considerable room to vent their feelings about unions. In later comments Brandeis criticized this tendency, arguing the courts were not protecting legitimate property rights but rather endowing property with an "active, militant power, which would make it dominant over men."[4] But the Justice's advice not to apply concepts drawn from property law to conflicts between labor and capital seemed to many of his colleagues no less than a request that they abdicate their fundamental judicial responsibility.

Still a Court that divided clearly on some issues could heal wounds and arrive at unanimous decisions: although the tactics of organized labor seemed per se unlawful to a majority of the High Bench, all members agreed in a case involving the rights of black Americans. *Buchanan* v. *Warley* was a suit for specific performance of a contract by a white seller against a black buyer. The fact that the contract of sale contained a stipulation that the buyer not be denied occupancy of the residence under any city or state law indicates that the two parties were trying to get the courts to declare unconstitutional a Louisville ordinance restricting such residency. The city justified its law as a measure designed to prevent conflict between the races and to promote the local welfare; it prevented both whites and blacks from moving into any block where the majority of residences were occupied by members of the other race.

Day quickly disposed of the contention that the plaintiff could not claim standing to invoke the rights of blacks, saying the right of the white plaintiff to have the sale executed was directly involved. Noting that the police power has always been subject to checks interposed by the Fourteenth Amendment, the Justice concluded that segregation statutes cannot be sustained "where the exercise of authority exceeds the restraints of the Constitution," as the ordinance did here. To the argument that property values would be eroded, Day simply responded that "undesirable white neighbors" can pose a similar threat, as he pronounced the Louisville ordinance "in direct violation of the fundamental law enacted in the Fourteenth Amendment of the Constitution preventing state interference with property rights except by due process of law."[5]

Although the decision in *Buchanan* v. *Warley* fits well into the Court's tendency to view more critically exercises of police power when rights of property are involved, its significance should not be lost by such a categorization. Here the Justices were reinspecting the rights of blacks with sympathy; perhaps the greater distance from the period of Civil War and Reconstruction was a factor. In other areas the Court seemed willing, at times, to revive old doctrines as checks upon the popular will, but in this area its movement toward a greater recognition and consequent protection of blacks was consistent. Along with the outlawing of peonage statutes and grandfather clauses and a finding of federal governmental power in old civil rights acts, the Justices, for the first time, invalidated a segregation statute, and a residential one at that. Unfortunately, it did not appreciably diminish segregated neighborhoods; the private restrictive covenant that was made part of the deed would fill in the gap left by the decision and survive for another generation.[6] Still, a start had been made by a unanimous Court.

So, too, the Justices agreed on the constitutionality of the Selective Service Act of 1917. Six cases were ushered expeditiously through the lower federal courts and combined under the title *Selective Draft Law Cases*. They all involved convictions under the statute. Two years earlier the unanimous Court had held that a Florida law commanding service on the state's roads was an obligation of citizenship and not inconsistent with the Thirteenth Amendment's injunction against involuntary servitude.[7] Was the noble task of defending one's country in time of war any less an obligation of citizenship?

Of course not, said Chief Justice White, who insisted that the argument that the citizen's "performance of his supreme and noble duty of contributing to the defense of the rights and honor of the nation as the result of a war" is involuntary servitude "is refuted by its mere statement." Actually White spent most of his opinion on other aspects of the challenge to the Selective Service Act. In the constitutional provision giving Congress the power to raise armies the Chief found sufficient authority to enact a conscription measure. To the argument that the provision envisioned a volunteer army, he responded that a power which can only be exercised with the citizen's consent is no power at all. Next, he addressed the objection that the act deprived individuals of their freedom without due process of law. White had no difficulty dealing with this argument, for it seemed to him it was answered by self-evident propositions. The "very conception of a just government and its duty to the citizen," he continued, "includes the reciprocal obligation of the citizen to render military service in case of need and the right to compel it." To the argument that the power given to Congress to call up the state militia limited the means it could use to raise an army, White answered that the two powers are separate and should not be confounded "to the end of confusing both the powers and thus weakening or destroying both." After reviewing history to 1868, he asked if the Fourteenth Amendment limited congressional power. On the contrary, he asserted, that amendment "broadened the national scope of the Government under the Constitution by causing citizenship of the United States to be paramount and dominant instead of being subordinate and derivative, and therefore . . . leaves no possible support for the contentions made."[8]

After disposing of claims of the unlawful delegation of authority to administrative and judicial officials, White addressed the argument that the statute's exemption from service of those whose religious affiliations forbade participation in war was repugnant to the First Amendment's guarantee of the free exercise of religion. Again, as in his response to the Thirteenth Amendment contention, White said that the claim's unsoundness was revealed by its statement.

One week later the Court upheld the prosecutions of four individuals for conspiring to induce resistance to the draft law and three others for procuring a violation of the act. Emma Goldman and Alexander Berkmen, prominent anarchists, were convicted of conspiring to induce persons not to register for the draft. Again for the unanimous Court, White upheld the Selective Service Act. To the contention that the conspiracy had not accomplished its purpose, the Chief responded that success was not necessary to the conviction. The same result was reached in the prosecution of two others decided on the same day. In a third case three Socialist defendants were charged with procuring a violation of the act, which meant their attempt to dissuade an individual from registering had succeeded. The defendants argued that the jury, composed of capitalists, was not one of their own peers and that the trial judge erred in failing to instruct the jury on the difference between socialists and anarchists. White dismissed both contentions, and, as briefly, disposed of some technical objections to the indictment and trial.[9]

Then late in the term, despite the forceful argument of counsel, the Chief in ruling upon a petition for habeas corpus, disposed of the last remaining argument of those who fought the draft. A popular conception was that, though it had the right to conscript, Congress could not deploy the force raised outside the continental United States. The asserted legal basis for this distinction was that in the militia clause Congress was limited to "calling forth the Militia to execute the Laws of the Union, suppress Insurrections, and repel Invasions." White again said the militia clause of the Constitution does not limit Congress in its ability to raise an army and that the power to conscript implies the authority to deploy troops overseas.[10]

One final point the Chief dealt with in the opinion was Solicitor General John W. Davis's request that a portion of opposing counsel's brief be expunged from the files. Hannis F. Taylor, primary counsel for the defendant, was greatly concerned over the aggrandizement of executive power, and he berated Congress for abetting a constitutional revolution that had created a political dictatorship under Wilson's control. The President's decision to commit American troops abroad, Taylor argued, now converted a political dictatorship into a military one. To this sixty-seven-year-old lawyer, who had written extensively on historical and legal subjects and had served as government counsel in a number of international matters, the drift of the nation away from its constitutional moorings necessitated strong and direct language. Actually Solicitor General Davis treated the brief and its contentions rather lightly on the basis of the Court's recent decisions upholding the draft. Taylor's sixty-plus page effort was answered by the government in four short pages, which included the request for the removal of three and one-half pages of the petitioner's brief from the public record and snide comments directed to the "burning valor" of both the defendant and his counsel. Taylor's oral argument on the constitutionality of committing drafted troops to overseas action was so emotionally tinged that Justice Holmes referred to the presentation as a "pompous row." White agreed with the Solicitor General's description of particular passages in the brief, but he refused to strike them, saying "they would best serve to indicate to what intemperance of statement and absence of self-restraint or forgetfulness of decorum will lead."[11]

Those challenging the draft had no chance of success, but they were allowed their day in court. The opinions are not very satisfactory, simply because White and the others could not even entertain the thought of substance behind the challenge. Self-evident truths were uttered to meet the arguments of the defendants; and no weaponry exists, even in the legal arsenal, with which to respond.

Early in the session the Court majority afforded evidence that its decision in the *Owensboro* case the previous term was no aberration. The Court again ruled that an unqualified grant to a street railway containing no time limitation was a perpetual franchise barring the state from ousting the railway. The state court had interpreted the grant as terminable at will by either party, but McReynolds, for the majority, said it would affront "common experience to conclude that rational men wittingly invested large sums of money in building a railroad subject to destruction at any moment by mere resolution of county commissioners." Clarke, joined by Brandeis, concluded that "it is impossible for me to agree that any grant is perpetual unless the language used in it is so express and clear that reasonable men cannot differ in giving to it that effect."[12]

Concerning the related area of freedom to contract, the majority reiterated the *Allgeyer* ruling of 1897 and seemed to push it even further. Giving birth to the doctrine of freedom of contract as a part of the due process clause of the Fourteenth Amendment, that decision freed a contracting party to an out-of-state insurance contract from the requirements of state law. What was new in a Missouri case, *New York Life Insurance Company* v. *Dodge*, was that the foreign insurance company had been admitted into the state under a condition that it abide by local law. McReynolds, for the majority, ruled that the state could not in this indirect way control the terms of the insurance company's contracts with Missouri citizens. The state law was intended to protect the policyholder from forfeiture, but the majority held that it could not reach a contract made in New York. Brandeis dissented, joined by Day, Pitney, and Clarke, saying the recitation in the contract that it was made in New York could not stand in face of the facts. Even if the contract was made in New

York, he continued, that fact could not preclude the attachment to it of provisions of Missouri law. Noting that the 1897 decision confirmed that the liberty protected was that of natural persons, the junior Massachusetts Justice added that the protection does not extend to corporations seeking to use their ties to other states to shield themselves from the state's police power.[13]

Other decisions of the term limited the price that states could extract from foreign corporations for the privilege of doing a local business. As the cases holding that a state cannot deny such a corporation access to the federal courts demonstrate, the Court had been moving away from its early position that the cost assessed was exclusively a matter for individual states to determine. Now the Justices seemed ready to limit state authority in the area even further. A state could still impose a fine upon a corporation for not getting a certificate to do business in the state, but when states sought to lay a heavy tax burden upon business as the price of admission, the unanimous Court balked. Texas and Massachusetts sought to fix this price by levying taxes on the companies' capital stock, but they were told their exactions directly burdened interstate commerce and violated due process by subjecting property beyond the state's confines to its taxing power.[14]

The novelty of these decisions was hidden behind citations to precedent establishing limits to the state's taxing power, but here, although a tax was involved, the corporation had the option of not doing a local business in the state if it determined that the price of admission was too high. By equating the issue to the general reach of the state taxing power, the Court was able to avoid the confrontation with its own precedents broadly supporting state authority in the area. The best the Court could do was rely on *Western Union Telegraph Company* v. *Kansas*, a 1910 decision, but there the company had already been licensed by the state.[15] The myriad of state admissions standards had long kept counsel for corporations busy and had been a great annoyance to large interstate businesses; now the Court was freeing such businesses from what the majority considered exorbitant admission prices.

Cases during the term in which counsel argued that state action had violated the Fourteenth Amendment were few in number in comparison to past terms. The Court experienced no difficulty in concluding that states could proscribe the personal possession of liquor, as it said such a proscription was neither arbitrary nor unreasonable in light of the inherent difficulties in stopping the liquor traffic. Except for a rate-setting case all state action challenged under the due process clause was upheld. The exception involved Denver's attempt to fix rates charged by the local water company. Pitney, for a majority, agreed with company's counsel that the base upon which to assess the return the rates would yield was the value of the company as a going concern, despite the expiration of its franchise. Taking this evaluation as the base, Pitney calculated a present profit of a little over 4 percent. In assessing its reasonableness the Justice looked at local conditions and circumstances, from which he determined that a 6 percent return would be reasonable. Since the 4 percent rate was inadequate, he pronounced the action of Denver in violation of the due process clause. Holmes responded in dissent, joined by Brandeis and Clarke. The Justice saw the expiration of the franchise as central to the case, for the city had the right to require the company to remove its pipes, thereby rendering its investment practically valueless. Holmes saw no obstacle to Denver insisting upon its rates as a condition for the company's continued operation beyond the life of its franchise.[16]

In the area of shipper-carrier conflicts over the liability for loss in shipment, the term did produce a case that placed limits on a carrier's ability to limit its liability in a bill of lading. In *Boston & Maine Railroad* v. *Piper* the shipper had consigned his cattle to a carrier under a uniform livestock contract stipulating that liability for unusual delay or confinement of the livestock caused by the carrier's negligence was limited to the furnishing of food and water during the period of delay. The shipper could have opted for greater liability at an increase of 10 percent in the rates. Responsible for the undoing of the carrier and the drafters of the uniform livestock contract was the specific exemption of the carrier from responsibility for negligence, for it was this wording that the Court seized upon to distinguish this case from the dozens of others that had accepted as conclusive the agreement of the shipper and carrier. Here, in a unanimous opinion by Day, the Court ignored the stipulation in the bill of lading and allowed full recovery to the shipper. Alluding to cases, though not citing any, the Justice said the exemption from negligence "is not within the principle of limiting to an agreed valuation which had been made the basis of a reduced freight rate." The limitation here is illegal, Day continued, and the fact that it was filed with the ICC does nothing to save it from condemnation. In many of the other cases railroads had been able to limit their liability in instances where their own negligence was involved.[17] The shift of opinion here was less the result of a change of attitude by the Court or the result of guidance provided by Congress in new legislation that was not applicable here, than it was the inartful drafting of the uniform livestock contract.

Generally, the Justices supported rulings of the ICC that came before the bench. In one case the unanimous Court, through McKenna, broadly sustained the commission's inquisitorial powers. A railroad president had refused to answer questions, contending that they inquired into matters beyond the powers of the ICC. The commission wanted to know if money had been spent to keep other railroads from the territory, to maintain lobbyists, to contribute to political campaigns, and to mold public opinion, and whether such expenditures had been charged to operating or legal expenses. Finding in the enabling legislation wide discretionary authority, McKenna said that

... the investigating and supervising powers of the Commission extend to all of the activities of carriers and to all sums expended by them which could effect in any way their benefit or burden as agents of the public. If it be grasped thoroughly and kept in attention that they are public agents, we have at least the principle which should determine judgement in particular instances of regulation or investigation.[18]

Although the Court looked with favor upon the actions of the Interstate Commerce Commission, it stymied two government prosecutions under the Sherman Antitrust Act. The first involved the government's attempt to enjoin the enforcement of a rule of the Chicago Board of Trade that stopped its members from purchasing grain arriving after the exchange's close at other than the closing price. The Board had insisted its purpose was not to prevent competition or control prices but rather to establish a business day and break a monopoly of the grain trade maintained by some warehouse operators. Striking this response as irrelevant and immaterial, the district court agreed with the government that the rule constituted an illegal restraint of trade.

Brandeis, for a unanimous Court, began by condemning this simplistic approach, saying every agreement is designed to restrain trade to some extent and that the true test is whether the agreement "merely regulates and perhaps thereby promotes competition or whether it is such as may suppress or even destroy competition." To avoid misinterpretation the Justice added that although a good intention does not save an objectionable restraint, "knowledge of intent may help the court to interpret the facts and to predict the consequences."[19] Concluding that the Board's action had no appreciable effect on general market prices and that it actually helped to improve market conditions, Brandeis pronounced the rule a reasonable regulation of trade consistent with the antitrust act.

All Justices agreed that the government had erred in its prosecution of the Chicago Board of Trade, but *United States* v. *United Shoe Machinery Company* divided the Court and posed special problems. Both McReynolds and Brandeis had to withdraw from participation because of their earlier connection with the government's prosecution. Had the two Justices not been so disabled, the decision would probably have gone the other way. As it was, the Court split four to three against the government. McKenna wrote the majority opinion, and Day, Pitney, and Clarke dissented in opinions by both Day and Clarke.

United Shoe Machinery Company was organized in 1899 by combining seven shoe machinery companies. A report to the stockholders of one of the combined companies asserted the great advantages of consolidation and the intention to acquire other shoe machinery companies. Over the years United Shoe had acquired a great many patents covering machinery used in the making of shoes. Fortified by such protection the company entered into leases that were the focal point of Brandeis's earlier attack on the combination. Running for a term of seventeen years, the leases substantially restricted the freedom of shoe manufacturers with provisions that mandated the exclusive use of United Shoe machines, that provided for the cancellation of all leases for default on any one, and that required the purchase of certain material used in fastening shoes from the company. United Shoe Machinery Corporation clearly dominated the field; for instance, of the more than 7,000 machines producing shoe forms in the country only seven escaped the company's control. Even the House Judiciary Committee in considering the Clayton Antitrust Act cited United Shoe as a prime example of a monopoly. The entire shoe-making industry, apart from individual cobblers, was under the control of United Shoe. In 1913 a unanimous Court, speaking through Holmes, had ruled that no violations of the antitrust act had been committed in the formation of the company.[20]

Acknowledging some bewilderment at the complexity of the machines and processes used in the making of shoes, McKenna in *United Shoe* placed considerable weight on the district judge's findings. The lower court had repulsed the government's attempt to dissolve the combination and the alleged conspiracy and to have the leases and agreements declared void. McKenna agreed that the companies combined and later acquired were not competitive and that the various acquisitions of patents and companies over the years were independent of each other and "not coordinated acts in a scheme of oppression." The Justice accepted the leases as legitimate offspring of the patent law. Distinguishing the cases limiting the range of a patent holder over the sale of his product under certain licenses, he found the crucial difference to be that the arrangement here was, in fact, one of lessor-lessee with the implicit restriction on use which that relationship recognizes. Using words that must have elicited scorn from shoe manufacturers throughout the country, he concluded that "it is impossible to believe, . . . that the great business of the United Shoe Machinery Company has been built up by the coercion of its customers and that its machinery has been installed in most of the large factories of the country by the exercise of power, even that of patents."[21]

The dissenters responded in two stages. In retracing the consolidation of the company, Clarke perceived a clear monopolistic intent. The actions of United Shoe he said were clearly embraced by Holmes's words in *Swift Company* v. *United States*: "Even if separate elements of such a scheme are lawful, when they are bound together by a common interest as parts of an unlawful scheme to monopolize interstate commerce the plan may make the parts unlawful." Reading the words of the management of United Shoe after one of its acquisitions, Clarke saw as clearly established the company's desire to stifle competition in violation of the antitrust act. The Justice could not agree "that this now securely entrenched monopoly is an innocent result of normal business development."[22] In the second part of the dissent for the trio, Day contended with the company's leasing contracts. A mere statement of their terms, he argued, shows an attempt to monopolize trade. Then the Justice dealt with the majority's justification of such contracts as an incident of the rights granted under the patent law. Noting that the case was decided by the trial court when *A. B. Dick* was the law of the land, Day said the over-ruling of that case had considerably narrowed the rights of a patent holder. The Justice concluded that there is nothing in the patent law that gives the holder of a patent a license to violate the antitrust law, which these leases, he insisted, surely do.

Day's words harkened back to White's dissent in the *A. B. Dick* case, where the Chief bitterly complained about the extension of patent protection to encompass immunity from the general law.[23] Now White was silent. In the recent cases overruling *A. B. Dick* in which White had concurred, McKenna, Holmes, and Van Devanter, the remainder of the former majority, had dissented. Now with White, their forceful adversary in that case, joining them the trio was able to salvage substantial protection for the holder of patents. Holmes, who never had much sympathy for the antitrust law, had great feelings of paternalism for the rights of the patent holder. This major setback for the government and shoe manufacturers everywhere was in reality the result of internal squabbling over the patent issue on the Court for the past six years. With Brandeis and McReynolds forced to sit out the *United Shoe Machinery* case, the irony is that White, who protested against the decision in *A. B. Dick* so vehemently, should now join his rivals on the issue and become the decisive vote against the position he earlier espoused.

On its next to last opinion day the Court was ready to announce its decision in a case that had excited great public attention when it was argued in mid-April. *Hammer* v. *Dagenhart* challenged the constitutionality of the federal Child Labor Act enacted in the late summer of 1916. Congress had based the law upon the commerce power, in which the Court had found a very substantial reservoir of federal authority that legitimated federal regulation of lottery tickets, impure and misbranded food and drugs, sexual immorality, and wages. The Justices had delivered only two setbacks to the use of such congressional power, both in the 1907 term. New legislation was passed eliminating the Court's objection to the first federal liability act, so the only permanent barrier the Court had interposed in reading the commerce clause was *Adair*, in which Congress was found powerless to ban the yellow-dog contract. Against this background *Hammer* v. *Dagenhart* was decided.

Despite the fact that more and more states throughout the first decade and a half of the twentieth century had enacted and strengthened their legislation limiting child labor, demand for a federal law was widespread. States had varying limitations on a minimum age, for the pull of conscience was met by a concern for profits and worries about competitive disadvantages. The first such proposals for a national law were introduced in Congress in 1906, but it took a decade and President Wilson's revived leadership in 1916 to get the bill through Congress. The act provided for the prohibition of goods in interstate commerce coming from establishments where children between the ages of fourteen and sixteen had worked for more than eight hours a day or more than six days a week.[24] Just before the law took effect on September 1, 1917, an injunction had been granted against its enforcement by a district court in North Carolina at the behest of Roland H. Dagenhart, the father of two young millworkers.

Even a nation at war was not invulnerable to the shock the decision caused when it was announded on June 3, 1918. By a five to four count the Court pronounced the Child Labor Act of 1916 unconstitutional.

Day, for the majority, began his opinion with quotes from the key cases in which congressional regulation under the commerce clause had been upheld, concluding that in "each of these instances the use of interstate transportation was necessary to the accomplishment of harmful results. In other words, although the power over interstate transportation was to regulate, that could only be accomplished by prohibiting the use of the facilities of interstate commerce to effect the evil intended." Here, Day continued, the statute really seeks to standardize the age of children employed, for the goods to be shipped are in themselves harmless. The fact that the goods were produced for interstate commerce, the Justice asserted, did not subject their production to federal control. Citing *Kidd* v. *Pearson*, the 1888 case that introduced the distinction between commerce and manufacturing into constitutional law, Day said the matter of production is subject only to state control. To the contention that Congress sought to close the channels of interstate commerce to prevent unfair competition with states having more protective legislation, the Justice responded that the commerce clause gives Congress no power "to control the States in their exercise of the police power over local trade and manufacture." In fact, he added, the grant of the commerce power "was not intended to destroy the local power always existing and carefully reserved to the States in the Tenth Amendment of the Constitution."[25] To uphold such an act and with it the authority of Congress to use its power over commerce to reach local matters, Day maintained, would result in the destruction of the freedom of commerce and the elimination of the exclusive power of the states to deal with local matters. The majority had taken the Tenth Amendment, which states the obvious—the reservation of power not delegated to the federal government to the people and to the states—and turned it into a substantive limitation on the exercise by Congress of one of its delegated powers.

Holmes responded for the dissenters, who included McKenna, Brandeis, and Clarke. The senior Massachusetts Justice agreed that the federal government cannot directly interfere with methods of production, but he could not see how, if an act is based upon a conceded power, its indirect effects are in any way relevant to a constitutional determination. The only possible argument that the statute is unconstitutional, he continued, must proceed on a collateral ground—that it interfered with the states that have direct control over the subject matter. But precedent, Holmes asserted, had clearly established "that the power to regulate commerce and other constitutional powers could not be cut down or qualified by the fact that it might interfere with the carrying out of the domestic policy of any State." With uncharacteristically heavy citations to the Court decisions in the area, he undergirded his generality. Alluding to the distinction that the channels of interstate commerce could be closed only to things considered evil, he said all civilized countries agree that "premature and excessive child labor" is an evil. Holmes called attention to the majority's inconsistency in saying that prohibition is "permissible as against strong drink but not as against the product of ruined lives." The Justice denied that the act interfered with the rights of the states within the federal system, for those rights are subordinated to Congress when products cross state boundaries. "The national welfare as understood by Congress," Holmes concluded, "may require a different attitude within its sphere from that of some self-seeking State. It seems to me entirely constitutional for Congress to enforce its understanding by all the means at its command."[26]

Reaction to the Court's obstruction of the national will was strong and clear, so strong and clear that Congress set in motion another child labor bill that became law on February 24, 1919, less than nine months after the decision in *Hammer* v. *Dagenhart*. Stymied under the commerce clause, Congress based the new legislation on its taxing power. The act provided for heavy taxes on goods introduced into interstate commerce that were produced by an establishment employing child labor.[27] What Congress was relying upon was the Court's consistent ruling that the broad authority of the federal government precludes the courts from looking behind the tax to assess motive and purpose. The drive to save the nation's children from the evils of early labor had succeeded again in Congress, but the new measure also would have to run the judicial gauntlet.

On the last day of the term the Justices decided a case of much lower public profile but one that again revealed the majority's protective attitude toward the courts and its insensitivity to First Amendment claims. *Toledo News-paper Company* v. *United States* involved the power of a federal trial judge summarily to find a newspaper guilty of contempt for publishing material critical of the court's consideration and handling of a pending case.

Eleven years earlier the Court, in an opinion by Holmes, dismissed a case that involved a state court punishing a publisher for contempt in a similar situation. But now in this federal proceeding the Justices could not avoid confronting the free speech issue. The case concerned a controversy between Toledo and a street railway. After the railway's franchise had expired, the city government imposed a three-cent fare. Creditors of the company attacked the ordinance and sought an injunction. After the city had been made a party to the suit in March 1914, the *Toledo News-Bee*, a newspaper long associated with local reform sentiment, began publishing news and comment relating to the conflict between Toledo and the street railway. Early in the legal action the *News-Bee* had published a cartoon showing the railway as a sick man with one of his bedside friends suggesting that "Doc Killits" be called in. John M. Killits was the federal district judge considering the injunction, which he finally granted on September 12. When a local Socialist was cited for contempt for a speech attacking the ruling, the newspaper renewed its criticism of the court. Then on September 15 the managing editor of the newspaper was cited for contempt, and after continuing critical publication, so was the newspaper company. Killits sat in judgment in the contempt matter and found the editor and the newspaper company guilty.[28] Well settled was the authority of the trial judge to punish for contempt, but just how far did this summary power extend beyond the courtroom? For the majority White answered at least as far as the offices of the newspaper.

The Chief accepted the dividing line between a summary procedure and one affording the benefits of trial, but here he ruled that the newspaper campaign had tended to obstruct the discharge of judicial duty. Judge Killits had made his contempt ruling on the basis that the newspaper stories had impugned his integrity, subjected him to popular hatred, and advocated disobedience to the order he issued. Giving short shrift to the contention that the order interfered with the freedom of the press, White said that "however complete is the right of the press to state public things and discuss them, that right, as every other right enjoyed in human society, is subject to the restraints which separate right from wrong-doing." Finally to the argument that there was no evidence from which an obstruction of justice could be deduced, the Chief answered that the failure to sway the judge is not the critical factor; rather it is "the reasonable tendency of the acts done to influence or bring about the baleful result is the test."[29]

The two Ohioans on the Court, Day and Clarke, because of their acquaintance with Judge Killits did not participate in the case, but Holmes dissented in an opinion joined by Brandeis. The senior Massachusetts Justice, who had been the Court's writer in the earlier case, said that endowing the same person with the functions of accusing and judging is generally contrary to our system of justice. Possible obstruction of justice he saw as insufficient to support a summary contempt procedure, and misbehavior, he added, "means something more than adverse comment or disrespect." Reviewing the facts, Holmes found nothing in the newspaper's campaign "that would have affected a mind of reasonable fortitude, and still less ... anything that obstructed the administration of justice in any sense that I possibly can give to those words."[30] Although assuring his colleagues that he took a back seat to no man in his strong support for order in the courtroom and the need to command obedience to court decrees, Holmes objected to the use of the judge's summary procedure here, where there was no pressing matter requiring an immediate response.

With this decision the Court ended the session, a less divisive one in that only 28 of the 248 cases produced division, but one during which the nation had been stunned by the decision against the federal Child Labor Act. Unpopular decisions had been made before, but rarely had they been so obstructive of the public will and so devastating to the range of congressional power. The check imposed by the Court on the police power in the previous term when it declared unconstitutional Washington's prohibition of private employment agencies paled before the decision in *Hammer* v. *Dagenhart*. Whether such rulings were aberrations or were indications of a more restrictive view of the range of governmental power was, as yet, unclear.

In the summer of 1918 American forces were making a decisive difference in Europe. Earlier in the year President Wilson had outlined his plan for a just and lasting peace, and now with a conviction that the world could be made safe for democracy he began the initiative for an armistice. By early fall he was succeeding, and the actual date of the termination of hostilities was obviously only a matter of time. On November 11, 1918, the war ended, leaving in its wake a host of problems.

The Supreme Court was left with the task of squaring the many extraordinary war measures taken by the Wilson administration with the Constitution. For the next few terms a good portion of the Justices' time would be spent dealing with such measures and their ramifications. The coming of peace gave their deliberations less urgency but no less significance. For as the Court decided present controversies it sketched the contours of the future as well. Unlike a presidential administration that would concentrate its full resources on a particular matter, the Court had to consider cases challenging wartime measures as part of a total work load that saw customary challenges to state and federal action. Facing this weighty burden, the Court, as it approached the 1918 term, had one advantage—stable membership. The previous two sessions had given the Justices the opportunity to take each other's measure. What had become apparent in the past two terms was the fact that differences would be aired and that cases would have a full and complete hearing.

In one of the early decisions the Justices contended with the novel question of whether there was a property right in news. The Associated Press (AP) sought an injunction to stop its competitor, the International News Service (INS), from pirating news stories. Since the news was uncopyrighted, the only ground of possible relief was that equity could enjoin what amounted to an unfair trade practice, and this was the basis of Pitney's majority opinion. The New Jersey Justice sought to slide by the novelties the case presented, content to point to the substantial effort the AP expended to obtain its news as reason for concluding that "the right to acquire property by honest labor or the conduct of a lawful business is as much entitled to protection as the right to guard property already acquired."[31] To the contention that first publication abandoned any property right to the public, Pitney responded that such abandonment was not supported by the clear intent of the AP, which, he continued, has the right to be protected in the limited purpose of its publication. Clarke did not participate in the case; Holmes, joined by Mc-Kenna, wrote a special opinion that amounted to a dissent; and Brandeis, in a long and thorough opinion, dissented alone.

Holmes, led to question the majority's decision by Brandeis's opinion, limited his consideration to the appropriation of the AP stories. The senior Massachusetts Justice seemed to acknowledge the difficulty of finding a protected property right in news, but he saw nothing wrong in providing relief to cure the misrepresentations of INS. Holmes would solve the problem by sending the case back to the trial court with instructions to specify a period of hours in which the AP would be protected from INS encroachment in the absence of some clear acknowledgment of the story's source. With proper credit afforded, Holmes made no objection to allowing INS to pick up stories as soon as they were published in one form or another.

Lurking behind the Holmes opinion is Brandeis's dissent, which masterfully delineated why the Court should defer to action by the legislative branch in this matter. "The rule for which the plaintiff contends," Brandeis began, "would effect an important extension of property rights and a corresponding curtailment of the free use of knowledge and of ideas; and the facts of this case admonish us of the danger involved in recognizing such a property right in news, without imposing upon news-gatherers corresponding obligations." Grasping the future, the Justice placed primary emphasis on the public's right to know, cautioning legislators not to provide a remedy to the alleged injury by opening "the door to other evils, greater than that sought to be remedied." Although not insensitive to the substance of the AP's claim, the Justice concluded:

Courts are ill-equipped to make the investigations which should precede a determination of the limitations which should be set upon any property right in news or of the circumstances under which news gathered by a private agency should be deemed affected with a public interest. Courts would be powerless to prescribe the detailed regulations essential to the full enjoyment for enforcement of such regulations. Considerations such as these should lead us to decline to establish a new rule of law in the effort to redress a newly disclosed wrong, although the propriety of some remedy appears to be clear.[32]

Here Brandeis was the practitioner of judicial restraint, not Holmes, who was willing to trust the courts to fashion appropriate remedies on a case-by-case basis. Pitney and the five-man majority espoused judicial activism, believing that a wrong was shown and that the judiciary, through the process of analogy to other equitable proceedings, could find a way both to establish a property interest and then protect it.

The absence of law in the *Associated Press* case give the majority the opportunity to free-lance, but when Congress speaks the rules of the game are changed, or at least they should be. In three cases argued in early November the Court had its first opportunity to inspect the provisions of the La Follette Seamen's Act of 1915. This legislation was the result of the continuing campaign of Andrew Furuseth, the president of the International Seamen's Union of America, who, since his early residence in this country in the 1880s, had been lobbying for legislation that would adequately protect the rights of seamen. The 1915 legislation was a far-ranging attempt to provide a seamen's bill of rights.[33]

That the Justices would move warily in the area was clearly indicated in the previous term when the majority read a statute freeing seamen from furnishing bonds for court costs to apply only to the trial court and not to any appellate tribunal. In the 1918 term the Court confined its attention to the applicability of a section of the Seamen's Act prohibiting the advance payment of wages and giving seamen the right to demand full pay without deduction if the shipowner had violated this provision. The petitioners in the first case were British seamen who had been recruited for a British ship with the inducement of an advance of wages. When the seamen reached the United States they found their claim for wages met with a payment that included a deduction for the advance made. They then sued on the basis of the 1915 act. Furuseth's interest in his cause had resulted in a bill drafted broadly to cover not only American citizens and American ships but any sailor in any ship requesting clearance from an American port. The act further abrogated any conflicting treaty provisions.[34]

For a bare majority of the Court, Day refused to read the law that broadly. He did not deny congressional power to so act, but he ruled that the language of the statute did not clearly express such an intent. Since the application of the statute to the matter here would undermine legal foreign contracts, Day refused to accept the result. Impliedly, he accepted the argument that such an interpretation would lead to an imposition of the American "conception of the rights of seamen upon the whole world in violation of the comity of nations." McKenna, joined by Holmes, Brandeis, and Clarke, dissented. Replying to Day's worry about international ramifications, the Californian said Congress, by including the provision overriding inconsistent treaty obligations, forcefully demonstrated the breadth of its policy in the area. To limit the scope of the act, McKenna continued, is to "take us from the certainty of language to the uncertainties of construction dependent upon the conjecture of consequences."[35] Seeing that the language was clearly broad enough to embrace the present fact situation, the Justice would rule in favor of the seamen and reverse the lower court.

The Court lineup was the same in the second case, in which American seamen entered service in Argentina on an American merchantman sailing for New York. Citing the prior opinion, Day saw no essential difference in the two cases. Revealing the majority's lack of sympathy with the congressional provision, he concluded that "we are unable to discover that in passing this statute Congress intended to place American shipping at the great disadvantage of this inability to obtain seamen when compared with the vessels of other nations which are manned by complying with local usage." That the majority was substituting its determination for that of Congress was made clear by McKenna's dissent. The Justice reminded the majority that talk of faraway countries did nothing to dislodge the control that Congress can and has exercised over ships found in the ports of the United States. To change the policy clearly outlined in the statute, McKenna argued, resort must be made to Congress and not the Court. Reiterating his conclusion that the language of the law is clear, he pronounced it "a barrier against alarms and fault-finding."[36]

Since the majority denied the act's application in the cases of the term, it did not have to address constitutional objections. But a case the Court sent back to the lower court appeared for review in the next term. Exercising its own judgment in *Strathearn Steamship Company* v. *Dillon*, the Fifth Circuit court had upheld the act. The case concerned a British seaman employed in Great Britain on a British merchantman. His contract of employment provided for no advance and no payment before the completion of the voyage, which could extend up to three years. Dillon sued in conformity with the 1915 act for one-half of his accrued wages while the ship was in Pensacola, Florida.

While the Court was considering the case Justice Brandeis wrote a draft opinion on the matter. His close connections with both Senator La Follette and Andrew Furuseth made him especially knowledgeable about the act of 1915. Why his opinion did not succeed in winning the Court was apparent, for Brandeis's broad exploration of the legislative history of the act, though well done, had the effect of casting doubt on the correctness of the recent decisions.[37] Since the Justices in conference had voted to sustain the act and its application, Brandeis chose not to weaken the Court's opinion by entering into the record one of his own. The Chief assigned the opinion to Day, who had the task of squaring the present decision with those reached in the previous session.

Day began by seeking to distinguish the section involved here with the earlier one, saying that in the instant case Congress in clear terms provided that relevant stipulations in contracts to the contrary shall be void. Although such words were omitted from the previously construed section, this was a matter of hasty drafting rather than an attempt to preserve the exception that the majority had found. No matter how contrary to his conception of the proper policy Day found this provision, he could not escape its applicability to the present case. Having found the half-pay provision applicable, Day addressed the challenge to the act's constitutionality. The result was anti-climatic, for he cited a 1903 case upholding an earlier federal statute prohibiting the advance payment of wages to seamen controlling the decision here. The Justice said, ". . . we have no doubt as to the authority of Congress to pass a statute of this sort, applicable to foreign vessels in our ports and controlling the employment and payment of seamen as a condition of the right of such foreign vessels to enter and use the ports of the United States."[38]

In addition to construing the Seaman's Act in the 1918 term, the Court also had to come to grips with the Harrison Narcotic Drug Act of 1914. This was a much more delicate matter, for presumably Congress could override a niggardly interpretation of the Seamen's Act, but the question the drug legislation posed cut much deeper. In 1916 the Court had considered whether mere possession of a drug was made a crime under the statute. There, Holmes read the act to embrace only those compelled by the terms of the statute to register as dealers in drugs. Such a construction, he said over the dissent of Hughes and Pitney, was necessary to avoid grave doubts about the constitutionality of this revenue measure.[39]

That this federal drug act of 1914 was ostensibly passed as a taxing measure tells us much about our federal system. In recent years the commerce clause had been much more frequently used as a basis for enacting legislation with quasi-police power dimensions, though the early federal tax on margarine illustrated the taxing power's potential in this area. Congress generally preferred the commerce power as a basis for this type of regulation, but in the area of drug control the taxing power seemed productive of greater reach. Repeatedly the Court had ruled that, when a tax was imposed within the authority of Congress, the bench could not question the purpose or the intent of the tax. This drug control act was passed well before the Court's limiting decision on the commerce power in *Hammer* v. *Dagenhart*, but the redrafting of a federal child labor act based on the taxing power illustrated the faith Congress had in prior decisions of the Court.

The Harrison Act imposed a tax of $1 a year and registration requirements upon those who dealt in drugs. With certain exceptions provided for physicians, dentists, and veterinarians, the statute made it unlawful for any person to engage in the proscribed activity without registering and paying the excise tax. All such transactions were to be made only on forms issued by the Commissioner of Internal Revenue and records were to be kept for two years.[40]

In *United States* v. *Doremus* the government prosecuted a physician registered under the statute, who supplied an addict with heroin. Under the terms of the statute a physician was exempted from the requirements of the act if he dispensed drugs as part of his professional treatment, but here the government alleged that supplying an addict with heroin was not a matter of proper professional treatment of any disease and that the requisite form required for the dispensing of drugs in all other situations had not been filled out. Day, for a bare majority of the Court, wrote an opinion upholding the federal law. The Justice ruled that the nonrevenue provisions of the act were clearly related to the tax involved, for "they tend to keep the traffic above-board and subject to inspection by those authorized to collect the revenue. They tend to diminish the opportunity of unauthorized persons to obtain the drugs and sell them clandestinely without paying the tax imposed by the federal law."[41] McKenna, Van Devanter, and McReynolds joined in the Chief's dissent, which was confined to a single sentence supporting the lower court's decision that the matters embraced by the federal act went beyond the delegated powers of Congress and invaded the reserved police power of the states. This ominous rumbling from four members of the Court willing to challenge precedent on the scope of inquiry into a taxing statute came only one week after the new child labor bill had become law.

When the Justices approached matters stemming from the American war effort, the divisions so apparent in the above cases faded away. To maintain the wholesomeness of military life, Congress had banned the sale of liquor to men in uniform and delegated authority to the executive department to pro-scribe brothels near military installations. The Secretary of War set up a range of five miles, and the unanimous Court upheld the conviction of a madam in Georgia for violating this perimeter. Day disposed of the conten-tion that Congress had no power to pass such legislation, saying that in raising an army the legislative branch could establish regulations looking toward the men's health and welfare. To the argument of unlawful delega-tion, the Justice responded that the details of the regulations could properly be left to the Secretary of War.[42]

The legitimacy of the federal government's takeover of the railroads and the nation's telephone and telegraph systems during the war was a question presented indirectly to the Court in a pair of cases from the Dakotas. North Dakota had succeeded in getting its supreme court to issue a writ of manda-mus against the Director General of the Railroads to prevent him from collecting intrastate rates that differed from the state schedule. Supporting the emergency measures, which did indeed seek to safeguard the interests of private property, White, for the unanimous bench, delineated the scope of the war power:

The complete and undivided character of the war power of the United States is not disputable. . . . On the face of the statutes it is manifest that they were in terms based upon the war power, since the authority they gave arose only because of the existence of war, and the right to exert such authority was to cease upon the war's termination.

To interpret, therefore, the exercise of the power by a presumption of the continuance of a state power limiting and controlling the national authority was but to deny its existence.

Since the enabling legislation allowed the President's delegate to file rates with the Interstate Commerce Commission, the Chief concluded that those rates so filed displaced those set under prior state authority. In the second case White responded similarly, adding only a caution that the wisdom of the governmental actions cannot be questioned by courts.[43]

Only Brandeis had some doubts about the Court's resolution of these matters. He concurred in the North Dakota case and dissented in the one from South Dakota, though without opinion. In all likelihood he did not contest governmental authority to take control of these businesses, but he wondered if the public interest was being well served by displacing carefully established state rate schedules, especially with the government's very special interest in the matter.

Of most significance among the war-related cases was *Schenck* v. *United States*, in which the Court, for the first time in its history, consciously sought to square the First Amendment's prohibition against the abridgment of free speech with restrictive federal legislation. Charles T. Schenck, the general secretary of the Socialist party, was in charge of the party headquarters from which was circulated a leaflet to men who had been called for military service under the Selective Service Act. The leaflet equated the draftee to a convict and maintained that conscription was a violation of the Thirteenth Amendment's ban on involuntary servitude. Calling upon its recipient not to bow down to Wall Street, it advocated only peaceful measures of resistance. "If you do not assert and support your rights," the leaflet continued, "you are helping to deny or disparage rights which it is the solemn duty of all citizens and residents of the United States to retain." Arguments in support of the draft, it added, came from greedy capitalists and conniving politicians. Schenck and an associate, Elizabeth Baer, were convicted of conspiring to cause insubordination in the military and to obstruct the recruiting service in violation of the Espionage Act of June 15, 1917.[44]

Earlier Holmes had interpreted the free-speech clause solely as a prohibition against prior restraint, but now, for a unanimous Court, he suggested that the First Amendment may mean more. He conceded that the words Schenck circulated would ordinarily be housed within the constitutional protection, but then he added, "the character of every act depends upon the circumstances in which it is done. . . . The most stringent protection of free speech would not protect a man falsely shouting fire in a theater and causing a panic." Seeking to generalize, Holmes put forward the following standard:

The question in every case is whether the words used are used in such circumstances and are of such a nature as to create a clear and present danger that they will bring about the substantive evils that Congress has a right to prevent. It is a question of proximity and degree. When a nation is at war many things that might be said in time of peace are such a hindrance to its effort that their utterance will not be endured so long as men fight and that no Court could regard them as protected by any constitutional right.[45]

The Justice said the intent and tendency of the writing was to obstruct recruitment, and since the enabling act punishes conspiracies, he saw no grounds for overruling the conviction.

The government, as in all the war-related cases, had been sustained, but the Chief's assignment of the case to Holmes gave the Massachusetts Justice an opportunity to discourse in a limited fashion upon the Constitution's guarantee of free speech. Holmes himself referred to his words as dealing with the subject "somewhat summarily," but he had enunciated what became known as "the clear and present danger test." Holmes privately indicated he was willing to afford speech greater protection than most of the majority, but the test he enunciated was quite compatible with his relativistic view.[46] Viewing free speech as a right conditioned by factual circumstances, he believed that the courts could be trusted to determine when an individual could be prosecuted for his words.

One week after this decision Holmes again delivered unanimous opinions in two other such cases, *Frohwerk* v. *United States* and *Debs* v. *United States*, upholding convictions under the Espionage Act. The first was a conspiracy prosecution charging Frohwerk with acting with another to cause disloyalty in the armed forces. He had published twelve articles in a German-language newspaper critical of the American war effort. Taking the opportunity to extend an analogy he made in *Schenck*, the senior Massachusetts Justice said the paper may have circulated "in quarters where a little breath would be enough to kindle a flame and that the fact was known and relied upon by those who sent the paper out." On such suppositions were convictions sustained; if Holmes was temperamentally ready to provide greater protection for speech, only an inkling can be found in the opinion, such as in his statement, that we "do not lose our right to condemn either measures or men because the Country is at war."[47]

The difference in the second case was not the charge but rather the public visibility of the defendant, Eugene V. Debs, the former leader of the American Railway Union and now the country's leading Socialist. The charge against Debs stemmed from a public speech in which he expressed hatred of war and militarism and castigated the government for prosecuting those who sought to defend the rights of workingmen in resisting the war effort. Many critics saw the government's prosecution of Debs as an attempt to use the issue of war to silence a prominent agitator. Holmes privately questioned the wisdom of such prosecutions. He deplored the prevalent jingoism of the federal trial judges and expressed hope that pardons for the convicted men would be forthcoming. Separating his personal convictions from his professional duty, the Justice upheld the conviction, holding that the generalities in the speech did not preclude a finding that it was designed to obstruct the government's recruiting effort. In affirming the sentence to ten years imprisonment, the Justice added no further words on the First Amendment.[48]

Although the Justices chose to defer to congressional action limiting free speech, they actually had little discretion left in the area of liquor regulation. In March 1917 Congress, in the Reed Amendment to a Postal Appropriations Act, had seemed to close the last gap in state control over interstate commerce in liquor. The provision made the shipment of liquor into any state that prohibited the manufacture of liquor illegal, whether the intended use violated state law or not. The Court's first consideration of this legislation led to a broad reading of its provisions, holding it applicable to a person who purchased liquor in Kentucky and carried it into West Virginia, where its manufacture was prohibited. That the state permitted the introduction of liquor for personal use, Day, for the majority, said, did not preclude Congress from making the shipment criminal. McReynolds, dissenting in an opinion that Clarke joined, accused the majority of inviting the destruction of the control of the states over local matters. Whether the dissent gave the majority pause or not, three months later a unanimous Court ruled that a passenger carrying liquor in his baggage in transit through a dry state could not be prosecuted.[49]

Only in the matter of adjusting the interests of shippers and carriers did the Court seem to deviate from congressional policy. Earlier Pitney had lectured his colleagues with regard to the proper interpretation of the Carmack Amendment as it applied to shipper-carrier conflicts, but during the 1918 term Clarke and McKenna emerged as the two members of the Court most concerned with the majority's inclination to favor the interest of the carrier over that of the shipper. New federal legislation had provided more protection for shippers, but in three cases instituted before its passage the two men dissented, complaining about the majority's strained interpretation of the basic act.[50] Adjusting shipper-carrier interests was a complex matter, but most Justices approached the issue on an abstract level detached from the realities involved. They seemed to see their function more as arbitrators between the parties rather than as partners with Congress in upholding the policy behind the statutory rules.

Repeatedly the Justices were asked to square the commerce clause with the state's police power. Where there was some intrastate business the Justices continued to rule that states or municipalities could levy taxes.[51] But when Georgia tried to levy a tax on a foreign tank car company based upon the miles traveled in the state compared to the total miles traversed in the United States, the majority said the result of the valuation scheme was so unreasonable that it violated both the due process and the commerce clauses. Pitney, dissenting with Brandeis and Clarke, found nothing wrong with Georgia's system of valuation; if it resulted in an inequitable burden, he said, the company had the obligation to seek relief from the state.[52] The New Jersey Justice was inclined here, as Holmes was in other cases, to force the company to deal with the state by cutting off easy access to the federal judiciary through a claim of confiscation of property.

Actually the Court seemed especially willing to harmonize state regulation with existing federal law. When Missouri sought to enforce a grain-weighing act, the contention that the federal government had preempted the area with the United States Grain Standards Act of 1916 was rejected, as was the claim that South Dakota could not prevent the shipment of game birds out of the state because of the Federal Migratory Bird Act of 1913. More significantly, the Justices took a sympathetic view toward state pure food and drug laws. In judging the constitutionality of a Wisconsin statute making the sale of any product containing benzoic acid or benzoates unlawful, Holmes, for the unanimous Court, said the state power to regulate after completion of the shipment in interstate commerce is unimpaired by federal food and drug legislation. Since the state law dealt with retail sales, Holmes read the statute not as an attempt to supplement congressional action but rather as an "exercise of an authority outside of that commerce that always had remained in the States."[53]

Pitney, in a unanimous opinion in *Corn Products Refining Company* v. *Eddy*, went one step further in undermining the original package doctrine in this area. Under authority conferred by Kansas law the state board of health required all table syrups to contain a listing of ingredients with their proportions. The state court had not addressed the question of the law's application to original packages, but Pitney saw such applicability assumed in the lower court decision. In upholding this inroad on the original package doctrine Pitney relied heavily upon a 1912 decision in which Hughes, for a unanimous Court, upheld an Indiana inspection statute requiring the placement of labels upon commercial feeding stuffs imported into the state. Since the Court had consistently upheld inspection laws as only incidental burdens upon commerce, it had had no occasion to consider the original package rule. In *Corn Products Refining Company* counsel had contended that the Pure Food and Drug Act specifically protected the very trade formulas that Kansas said had to be disclosed. Even with such a direct conflict in the statutes, Pitney said the protective language of the federal law "merely relates to the interpretation of the requirements of the federal act, and does not enlarge its purview or establish a rule as to matters which lie outside its prohibitions."[54] The result was that states could now act with substantial discretion in supplementing federal law by state regulation. At times the Court seemed quick on the preemption trigger, but here it worked out a sensible accommodation that provided room for both federal and state action.

Once again the Justices confronted the issue of determining the rights of a public service corporation after the expiration of its franchise. A street railway's franchise had expired and the city of Detroit had the right to oust the corporation, but the majority, reiterating its earlier conclusion, said that, if it chose to keep the railway in operation, Detroit had the obligation of assuring the company a fair return on its investment. Clarke, in dissent with Holmes and Brandeis, could not fathom how, if the city had complete power to dislodge the railway, it was prevented from dictating terms upon which the railway could continue to operate.[55]

With this exception the Court rejected all other due process and equal protection claims, but this bland conclusion submerges the drama behind the Court's consideration of the Arizona Employers' Liability Act. In 1917 the Justices had upheld workmen's compensation acts establishing liability without negligence, and only in a Washington case where employers were forced to pay into a state fund an amount based upon their payrolls had the Court divided. There White, McKenna, Van Devanter, and McReynolds dissented without opinion. Now the Justices were faced with an even more novel solution to the problem of industrial accidents. The Arizona constitution directed the legislature to enact both an "Employers' Liability Law" and a "Workmen's Compulsory Compensation Law." The first act was to be confined to "all hazardous occupations" and the second to "workmen engaged in manual or mechanical labor in such employments as the legislature may determine to be especially dangerous." An employee injured in hazardous employment had three options: first, he could sue his employer at common law, and although the fellow servant rule had been abolished, the employer could rely upon the assumption of risk and contributory negligence defenses; or second, he could sue under the Employers' Liability Law and be defeated only when the injury was caused by his own negligence; or third, he could accept the recovery provided by the compulsory compensation law.[56] Obviously, the most favored route for recovery, where the injury could not be attributed to the employee's own negligence, was under the Employers' Liability Law, since the size of the award was not limited by the schedules of the compensation act. This was the crux of the problem posed for the Justices, for the law made the non-negligent employer liable but did not provide the compensating advantage of limiting the injured employee's recovery to an established schedule. By this scheme Arizona was entering into an age of collectivism while at the same time giving the individual worker more choice than had been afforded by any other state in the Union.

Three cases coming from the federal district court in Arizona, in which injured employees obtained verdicts under the state liability act, first came to the Supreme Court for oral argument in January 1918. No opinion in the cases was issued before the end of the term, but Brandeis returned to the Court in October with a draft dissent. Assuming that the four dissenters in the case involving Washington's workmen's compensation act were even more disturbed with the Arizona scheme, the old majority had cracked. Holmes, Brandeis, and Clarke, we can assume, were ready to sustain the Arizona law, leaving Day and Pitney as the potential defectors. Despite his qualms about the exercise of a quasi-police power on the part of the federal government, Day seemed ready to acquiesce in a wide variety of state regulations. If he remained firm in his conviction that state regulation of industrial accidents was constitutional—and his tendency to hold firm convictions was noted by his colleagues—Pitney was the wavering Justice. Indeed, Pitney's doubts may have precluded an opinion from being issued in the 1917 term. That the Justice could be reached and could change his mind was quite possible, for both Holmes and Brandeis commented upon his personal integrity and his willingness to learn.[57] At any rate, Brandeis's draft dissenting opinion seemed well pitched to Pitney's concerns.

Apparently Brandeis succeeded in fending off a decision to invalidate the Arizona law, for the Chief scheduled oral argument in April 1919 for one of two other cases, coming up through the Arizona state courts, that had also granted recovery under the state liability act. This second argument produced a decision in favor of the law with the former majority in the Washington workmen's compensation case again coalescing. Holmes sought to write the opinion for the majority. When Holmes returned his draft to the other Justices in the majority, only Brandeis and Clarke concurred. The senior Justice from Massachusetts justified his conclusions broadly, and after the agony that the cases had caused, neither Day nor Pitney would accept the opinion. Since Holmes was not about to rewrite the opinion to conform especially with Pitney's requirement that it be harmonized with words that the New Jersey Justice had written earlier, Holmes left the task to Pitney, who turned out the opinion of the Court.[58] Holmes added his words in a supplemental concurrence, joined by Brandeis and Clarke.

Addressing the innovations in the Arizona legislation favoring workers' interests, Pitney said novelty is not a constitutional objection and that the Fourteenth Amendment leaves to the states a wide range of discretion not subject to censure by the courts. Prior decisions, he continued, have established the fact that states, without encountering any legitimate claim of vested rights, may legislate in the public interest on the employer's responsibility for injury to his employees. So long as such state action "does not interfere arbitrarily and unreasonably, and in defiance of natural justice, with the right of employers and employees to agree between themselves respecting the terms and conditions of employment," the Justice asserted, common law rules in the area are not placed beyond the reach of state power.[59] Requiring the employer to compensate employees for injuries, which he can do by lowering wages or increasing the selling price, Pitney added, provides as rational a basis for such legislation as can be found. Then, contending with counsel's claim that the Arizona statute held the employer to an unlimited liability, the Justice responded that liability is limited solely to compensation for the injury suffered. That a jury might award an extravagant recovery, he said, can hardly support a claim of a denial of due process. Confronting his own wording in the Washington workmen's compensation case, Pitney noted that the opinion there left the precise question this case presented open for future consideration. Any reading of the earlier opinion, he contended, that suggested a state must meet a removal of the requirement of negligence with a fixed schedule of compensation is erroneous. If the prior method is constitutional, he argued, the approach used here, where the amount of compensation was to be determined by the facts of each case, is equally free from constitutional objection.

Holmes's original opinion is labeled a concurrence. It is easy to see why Pitney and Day were dissatisfied with the opinion, which was short, imprecise, and not well developed or fully responsive. Although Holmes regularly complained about Pitney's long and labored prose, Pitney quite likely found his colleague's style equally unsatisfactory. Probably as disturbing here was Holmes's wholesale approach, broadly supporting state regulation of the employer-employee relationship:

It is reasonable that the public should pay the whole cost of producing what it wants and a part of that cost is the pain and mutilation incident to production. By throwing that loss upon the employer in the first instance we throw it upon the public in the long run and that is just. If a legislature should reason in this way and act accordingly it seems to me that it is within constitutional bounds.[60]

McKenna dissented in an opinion joined by White, Van Devanter, and McReynolds. What bothered the Californian was the extension given here to the workmen's compensation cases of 1917, which, he said, were "difficult to decide against the contentions and conservatism which opposed them. . . . I hope that it is something more than timidity, dread of the new, that makes me fear that it is a step from the deck to the sea—the metaphor suggests a peril in consequences." From this bit of introspection McKenna moved to the level of abstraction. No camouflage of public policy, he argued, can cloak the invidious discrimination found in the Arizona system. "It seems to me to be of the very foundation of right—of the essence of liberty as it is of morals—to be free from liability if one is free from fault." The Justice accused the majority of erecting the denial of this principle "into a principle of law and governmental policy." Revealing some of the emotion the matter generated, McKenna contended that "the difference between the position of employer and employee, simply considering the latter as economically weaker, is not a justification for the violation of the rights of the former, and that individual rights cannot be made to yield to philanthropy."[61]

In speculating upon the consequences of the majority's decision, he said that constitutional rights are being sacrificed by succumbing to a popular opinion that seeks to give labor "immunity from the pitilessness of life." The California Justice was further concerned with the "attractive speciousness" of the argument that the employer can pass along any additional costs to the public. As a principle, he pronounced it dangerous, for it could be used to justify any burden placed upon industry. McKenna, of course, was quite right; while others embraced the principle, he recoiled from it. Here, he simply called attention to the fact that additional costs of production would put the employer at a competitive disadvantage in other states.[62] McKenna was a strange and peppery figure, who at times cut through abstractions with abandon to reach the facts of the situation, but here, unwilling to reinspect the modern employment situation, he retreated to the mountain top and drew his thunderbolts from an arsenal of abstractions.

McReynolds added a longer opinion in which the other dissenters concurred. Its length, structure, and reproduction of the state statutory and constitutional provisions suggest it may have, at the time Brandeis wrote his draft dissent, been constructed as the majority opinion. The Fourteenth Amendment, McReynolds began, stripped "the States of all power to deprive any person of life, liberty, or property by arbitrary or oppressive action." The former Attorney General said that the Constitution must be imposed as a bulwark against the "whims or caprices or fanciful ideas" of the popular majority and that the Court's function is to support the old order until it is superseded through proper methods. Ridiculing the view that employers who have furnished their employees with a chance to earn a living should be forced to bear the responsibility for injury, he argued that the Arizona law operated "to stifle enterprise, produce discontent, strife, idleness and pauperism."[63] With no fair attempt to balance the interests involved, he concluded that the Arizona scheme lacked the necessary rationality to bring it within the legitimate scope of the police power.

Members of the Court had wrangled over cases before and would again, but this struggle was truly titanic. The case is a useful lens through which to view fundamental attitudes of the Justices. The battle lines drawn here would long remain. Yet, despite all the criticism of the Court for its insensitivity to the laboring man, a majority had recognized the human dimensions of the problem involved and suppressed any constitutional qualms in affording state legislatures the right to use their judgment in regulating industrial accidents. Accepting this wholesale change to common law liability and tipping the scale from old rules that favored the employer to new ones that distinctly favored the employee required the Justices to take a broad view of the realities involved. Holmes, Brandeis, and Clarke were willing to proceed boldly, rejecting the old and accepting the new, but to Day and Pitney this course appeared hazardous, and they had to find their own ways to combat their prejudices and predispositions to reach a result that could be squared with the Constitution and the needs of society. Although Pitney turned a deaf ear to pleas of labor unions, his crucial vote here shows an understanding of the problems inherent in an industrial society. Fears that the Arizona scheme would spread were unfounded, for other state legislatures, not immune from various lobbies, continued to accept the balance between liability without fault and limited compensation as an equitable solution to the problem.

The two previous terms of Court had ended on sour notes—the invalidation of Washington's law prohibiting private employment agencies and of the federal Child Labor Law—but here the decision in the *Arizona Employers' Liability Cases*, despite the close division, brought the 1918 term to a close on a note affirming the right of the legislative branch to represent the popular will. Any optimism, however, would have to be tempered by a recognition of the strong internal attack on the majority's permissive view.

One of the striking developments of the term was the erosion of the Brandeis-Clarke bloc in divided cases. In the previous term they had agreed in twenty-four of twenty-six divided cases; now in twenty-four divided cases in which both participated, they agreed in only fourteen. Clarke and McKenna were the term's leading dissenters with ten each, and Brandeis followed closely with nine. Van Devanter, who disagreed four times, still did not write any dissenting opinions. But McReynolds, who previously also had been silent in dissent or had subscribed to the views of others, wrote opinions in three of six cases in which he disagreed with the majority.

During the past term Brandeis and Holmes moved closer together. They agreed in fifteen of twenty-five divided cases. What made this developing relationship intriguing was the fact that the two Justices were so unalike. Brandeis was committed, but Holmes prided himself on his detachment. Brandeis saw the need to research cases thoroughly, digging into the facts and placing them in the context of the larger social and economic environment, but Holmes was content to respond to a case in terms of general principles. Brandeis tailored his work and effort to the task of winning the votes of others, but Holmes, though not unwilling to compromise, was both less able and less willing to court his fellow Justices. Finally, Brandeis wrote highly organized and precise opinions, but Holmes often dashed off a few paragraphs that seemed to him sufficient to meet the main arguments raised. Yet from these very different starting points the two men often reached similar results.[64]

With their increasingly close relationship, Brandeis felt confident enough to try to educate his older colleague, especially with regard to conditions in the real world. After a trying session of Court Holmes would seek escape from the law and the controversies that surround it. In Beverly Farms, Massachusetts, he would spend a leisurely summer reading books on history and government, biographies, and some contemporary nonfiction. Just before the end of the 1918 term Brandeis made some suggestions concerning how his senior colleague might profitably spend the coming summer. Holmes detailed his reaction in a letter to his English correspondent, Sir Frederick Pollock:

Brandeis the other day drove a harpoon into my midriff with reference to my summer occupations. He said you talk about improving your mind, you only exercise it on the subjects with which you are familiar. Why don't you try something new, study some domain of fact. Take up the textile industries in Massachusetts and after reading the reports sufficiently you can go to Lawrence and get a human notion of how it really is. I hate facts. I always say the chief end of man is to form general propositions—adding that no general proposition is worth a damn. Of course a general proposition is simply a string for the facts and I have little doubt that it would be good for my immortal soul to plunge into them, good also for the performance of my duties, but I shrink from the bore—or rather I hate to give up the chance to read this and that, that a gentleman should have read before he dies.[65]

As the Justices scattered during the summer recess it was apparent that the end of war the previous autumn had not brought peace to a troubled society. The emotions played upon and the fears elicited by the mobilization of a people for war had not dissipated with the signing of an armistice. Demobilization was expected to bring a deep recession, as former soldiers flooded the labor market, but, although industrial production took an immediate drop, it quickly resumed its upward trend and easily absorbed the returning veterans. Consumer demand moved faster than supply, and the result was a period of growing inflation. Caught in this pinch and desirous of preserving wartime gains and extending unionization, workers used the weapon of the strike. In 1919 alone there were 2,665 strikes involving over 4,000,000 workers. This clear evidence of labor unrest, coupled with the founding of the Third International in Moscow in 1919 with its drive to free the workers of the world from the yoke of capitalism, created fear. While Woodrow Wilson was promoting another brand of internationalism in his quest for American participation in the League of Nations, anxiety caused by the Moscow variety gave birth to the Red Scare.[66]

When on the eve of a May Day celebration in 1919 the New York City Post Office found bombs in sixteen packages addressed to officials in state and federal governments, including Justice Holmes, the fear seemed well grounded. One month later the residence of the new Attorney General, A. Mitchell Palmer, was partially destroyed by a bomb that claimed the life of its wielder. Such explosions in eight cities in the spring of 1919 were viewed as further evidence of anarchistic and communistic activity designed to overthrow the American way of life. Attorney General Palmer, whether motivated by the invasion of his residence or political ambitions, launched a crusade to rid the country of the reds. The famous Palmer raids brought the man notoriety and led to the deportation of hundreds of aliens, few of whom could be considered a threat to anyone. Well into 1920 this fear of a disillusioned American people was exploited in a persecution of largely harmless aliens.[67]

The summer of 1919 also saw an American people adjusting, more or less, to prohibition. National prohibition had come as a wartime measure, and the forces behind this movement to save man from the evils of alcohol were able to capitalize upon the war atmosphere to push through an amendment to the Constitution. Congress had been especially accommodating to the antiliquor forces with legislation giving the states greater and greater control over the trade. The problem with a federal constitutional amendment on the subject of prohibition was that it would delegate primary control to the federal government. This objection was raised, as was the charge that such an amendment regulating matters of personal conduct rather than governmental relationships would be a unique and dangerous addition to the Constitution. But the time was right for the prohibitionists to accomplish their goal, and such worries were shunted aside. By the end of 1913 only ten states were dry, but four years later that number had swelled to twenty-six and would be augmented by six more over the next two years. This growing state support was reflected in the halls of Congress, where resolutions for a prohibition amendment in each session began to mount. The resolution introduced on April 14, 1917, an especially auspicious time considering the American war declaration, slowly moved through Congress and was submitted to the states eight months later. The world was to be made safe for democracy and the United States was to be freed from the evils of drink, twin expectations that would founder on the rocks of reality in the coming years. In less than thirteen months, ratifications were obtained from the requisite number of states, and the Eighteenth Amendment, prohibiting "the manufacture, sale, or transportation of intoxicating liquors," was scheduled to take effect in January 1920.[68]

Well before the Eighteenth Amendment became law, Congressman Reuben L. Haskell of New York proposed a resolution for an amendment calling for a popular referendum on the question of whether alcoholic beverages should be permitted in the United States. To show where his sympathies really rested, Haskell also presented a resolution seeking repeal of the recently ratified amendment. His proposals were not then taken seriously, but they would be later when the nation acknowledged its error.[69] Rarely in the history of mankind has a people's mistake been so clearly etched into their fundamental law.

NOTES

1. Paine Lumber Co. v. Neal, 244 U.S. 459 (1917).

2. Hitchman Coal & Coke Co. v. Mitchell, 245 U.S. 229, 251, 255, 257 (1917). The decision stimulated employer use of yellow-dog contracts. (See Felix Frankfurter and Nathan Greene, *The Labor Injunction* [New York: Macmillan Co., 1930], pp. 148-49.)

    3. Hitchman Coal & Coke Co. v. Mitchell, 245 U.S. 229, 271, 273 (1917).
    4. Truax v. Corrigan, 257 U.S. 312, 368 (1921).
    5. Buchanan v. Warley, 245 U.S. 60, 81, 82 (1917).
    6. In 1948 in *Shelly* v. *Kraemer* (334 U.S. 1) the Supreme Court ruled that the enforcement of such restrictive covenants by a resort to the courts was unconstitutional.
    7. Butler v. Perry, 240 U.S. 328 (1916).
    8. Selective Draft Law Cases, 245 U.S. 366, 390, 378, 384, 389 (1918).
    9. Goldman v. United States, 245 U.S. 474 (1918); Kramer v. United States, 245 U.S. 478 (1918); and Ruthenberg v. United States, 245 U.S. 480 (1918).
    10. U.S. Const., art. 1, sec. 8; and Cox v. Wood, 247 U.S. 3 (1918).
    11. Brief for Appellant, pp. 53-57, and Brief for United States, p. 4, Cox v. Wood, 247 U.S. 3 (1918); Holmes to Pollock, June 14, 1918, in Mark D. Howe, ed., *Holmes-Pollock Letters*, 2d ed., 2 vols. (Cambridge: Harvard University Press, Belknap Press, 1961), 1:267; and Cox v. Wood, 247 U.S. 3, 7 (1918).
    12. Owensboro v. Owensboro Water Works Co., 243 U.S. 166 (1917); Northern Ohio Traction & Light Co. v. Ohio *ex rel.* Pontius, 245 U.S. 574, 585, 594 (1918). The same result was reached in *Covington* v. *South Covington & Cincinnati Street Ry.* (246 U.S. 413 [1918]).
    13. Allgeyer v. Louisiana, 165 U.S. 578 (1897); and New York Life Insurance Co. v. Dodge, 246 U.S. 357 (1918). Holmes cast the deciding vote in this latter case, possibly on the technical basis that the contract was made in New York.
    14. Dalton Adding Machine Co. v. Virginia, 246 U.S. 498 (1918); Looney v. Crane Co., 245 U.S. 178 (1917); and International Paper Co. v. Massachusetts, 246 U.S. 135 (1918).
    15. Western Union Telegraph Co. v. Kansas, 216 U.S. 1 (1910).
    16. Crane v. Campbell, 245 U.S. 304 (1917); and Denver v. Denver Union Water Co., 246 U.S. 178 (1918).
    17. Boston & Maine R.R. v. Piper, 246 U.S. 439, 445 (1918). Day does mention *Kansas City Southern R.R.* v. *Carl* (227 U.S. 639 [1913]), but that case is illustrative of the Court's prior approval of limited carrier liability.
    18. Smith v. ICC, 245 U.S. 33, 42-43 (1917).
    19. Board of Trade v. United States, 246 U.S. 231, 238 (1918).
    20. United States v. United Shoe Machinery Co., 247 U.S. 32, 89-90 (1918); and United States v. Winslow, 227 U.S. 202 (1913). The present case concerned practices of the company after its formation.
    21. United States v. United Shoe Machinery Co., 247 U.S. 32, 55, 66 (1918).
    22. Id. at 86, 90.
    23. Henry v. A. B. Dick Co., 224 U.S. 1, 49 (1912).
    24. For a comprehensive discussion of the movement for child labor reform, see Stephen B. Wood, *Constitutional Politics in the Progressive Era: Child Labor and the Law* (Chicago: University of Chicago Press, 1968); and Child Labor Act, ch. 432, 39 Stat. 675 (1916).
    25. Hammer v. Dagenhart, 247 U.S. 251, 271, 273-74 (1918). What Day and the majority were doing was calling a halt to the Court's expansive reading of the federal commerce power and establishing a rival precedent that could be summoned when needed to escape what, except for *Adair*, had been a consistent line of Court decisions. (See John P. Roche, "Entrepreneurial Liberty and the Commerce Power: Expansion, Contraction and Causistry in the Age of Enterprise," *University of Chicago Law Review* 30 [Summer 1963]:702-3.)
    26. Hammer v. Dagenhart, 247 U.S. 251, 278, 280, 281. Holmes expressed pride in his dissent in *Hammer* and in the subsequent case (Holmes to Pollock, June 14, 1918, in Howe, *Holmes-Pollock Letters*, 1:267). In *United States* v. *Darby* (312 U.S. 100 [1941]) the Court agreed with Holmes's opinion and overruled the *Hammer* decision.

27. Child Labor Tax Act, ch. 18, 40 Stat. 1138 (1918).

28. Patterson v. Colorado, 205 U.S. 454 (1907); and Toledo Newspaper Co. v. United States, 247 U.S. 402 (1918).

29. Toledo Newspaper Co. v. United States, 247 U.S. 402, 419-20, 421 (1918). The Court in *Nye* v. *United States* (313 U.S. 33 [1941]) overruled the Toledo Newspaper decision, citing the Holmes's dissent approvingly and saying the majority had misconstrued the federal statute involved.

30. Holmes to Pollock, June 14, 1918, in Howe, *Holmes-Pollock Letters*, 1:267; and Toledo Newspaper Co. v. United States, 247 U.S. 402, 423, 425 (1918).

31. International News Service v. Associated Press, 248 U.S. 215, 236 (1918).

32. Id. at 263, 264, 267

33. Arthur S. Link, *Woodrow Wilson and the Progressive Era, 1910-1917*, New American Nation Series (New York: Harper & Row, Torchbooks, 1963), pp. 61-63; and Seaman's Act, ch. 153, 38 Stat. 1164 (1915).

34. *Ex parte* Abdu, 247 U.S. 27 (1918); Sandberg v. McDonald, 248 U.S. 185 (1918); Neilson v. Rhine Shipping Co., 248 U.S. 205 (1918); and Seaman's Act, ch. 153, 38 Stat. 1164, 1165 (1915).

35. Sandberg v. McDonald, 248 U.S. 185, 202. (1918).

36. Neilson v. Rhine Shipping Co., 248 U.S. 205, 213, 215 (1918).

37. For Brandeis's draft opinion and an assessment of the Court's response to the Seaman's Act, see Alexander Bickel, *The Unpublished Opinions of Mr. Justice Brandeis* (Chicago: University of Chicago Press, Phoenix Books, 1967), pp. 34-60.

38. Strathearn Steamship Co. v. Dillon, 252 U.S. 348, 356 (1920). The 1903 case is Patterson v. Bark Eudora, 190 U.S. 169.

39. United States v. Jin Fuey Moy, 241 U.S. 394 (1916).

40. Harrison Narcotic Drug Act, ch. 1, 38 Stat. 785, 789 (1914).

41. United States v. Doremus, 249 U.S. 86, 94 (1919).

42. McKinley v. United States, 249 U.S. 397 (1919).

43. Northern Pacific Ry. v. North Dakota *ex rel.* Langer, 250 U.S. 135, 149-50 (1919); and Dakota Central Telephone Co. v. South Dakota *ex rel.* Payne, 250 U.S. 163 (1919).

44. Quoted in Schenck v. United States, 249 U.S. 47, 51 (1919); and Espionage Act, ch. 30, 40 Stat. 217, 219. (1917).

45. Patterson v. Colorado, 205 U.S. 454 (1907); and Schenck v. United States, 249 U.S. 47, 52 (1919).

46. Holmes to Pollock, April 5, 1919, in Howe, *Holmes-Pollock Letters*, 2:7. On the same opinion day, Brandeis spoke for the unanimous Court in *Sugarman* v. *United States* (249 U.S. 182 [1919]) and upheld a similar conviction.

47. Frohwerk v. United States, 249 U.S. 204, 209, 208 (1919).

48. Holmes to Pollock, April 5, 1919, in Howe, *Holmes-Pollock Letters*, 2:7; Holmes to Harold J. Laski, March 16, 1919, in Mark D. Howe, ed. *Holmes-Laski Letters*, abrig. ed., 2 vols. (New York: Atheneum, 1963), 1:142; and Debs v. United States, 249 U.S. 211 (1919).

49. Act of March 3, 1917, ch. 162, 39 Stat. 1058, 1069; United States v. Hill, 248 U.S. 420, 428 (1919); and United States v. Gudger, 249 U.S. 373 (1919).

50. See Southern Pacific Co. v. Stewart, 248 U.S. 446 (1919), Baltimore & Ohio R.R. v. Leach, 249 U.S. 217 (1919), and Erie R.R. v. Shuart, 250 U.S. 465 (1919).

51. See Postal Telegraph-Cable Co. v. Richmond, 249 U.S. 252 (1919); MacKay Telegraph & Cable Co. v. Little Rock, 250 U.S. 94 (1919); Pure Oil Co. v. Minnesota, 248 U.S. 158 (1918); and Standard Oil Co. v. Graves, 249 U.S. 389 (1919).

52. Union Tank Line Co. v. Wright, 249 U.S. 275, 295 (1919).

53. Merchants Exchange v. Missouri *ex rel.* Barker, 248 U.S. 365 (1919); Carey v. South Dakota, 250 U.S. 118 (1919); and Weigle v. Curtice Brothers Co., 248 U.S. 285, 288 (1919).

54. Savage v. Jones, 225 U.S. 501 (1912); Corn Products Refining Co. v. Eddy, 249 U.S. 427, 439 (1919).

55. Detroit United Ry. v. Detroit, 248 U.S. 429 (1919). In the previous term the same Court majority had reached a similar conclusion in Denver v. Denver Union Water Co., 246 U.S. 178 (1918).

56. Mountain Timber Co. v. Washington, 243 U.S. 219 (1917); and Ariz. Const. art. 18, secs. 7-8, and Ariz. Rev. Stats., sec. 23, chs. 5-6.

57. For the draft dissent and commentary on the Court's consideration of the cases, see Bickel, *Unpublished Opinions of Brandeis*, pp. 61-76. The comments on Day and Pitney are found on pp. 65-68.

58. Bickel, *Unpublished Opinions of Brandeis*, p. 65. Bickel assumes the Holmes's opinion was written after the first hearing of the case (p. 68), but this cannot be so since it bore the title of one of the additional cases not submitted to the Court until April 1919.

59. Arizona Employers' Liability Cases, 250 U.S. 400, 421-22. (1919).

60. Id. at 433.

61. Id. at 434, 436, 437.

62. Id. at 438, 439.

63. Id. at 450, 451, 452.

64. For a comprehensive study of the two men during their years of mutual service on the Court, see Samuel J. Konefsky, *The Legacy of Holmes and Brandeis: A Study in the Influence of Ideas* (New York: Crowell-Collier Publishing Co., Collier Books, 1961). On the specific matter mentioned, see pp. 260-79. See also, G. Edward White, *The American Judicial Tradition* (New York: Oxford University Press, 1976), pp. 150-77.

65. Holmes to Pollock, May 26, 1919, in Howe, *Holmes-Pollock Letters*, 2:13-14.

66. Arthur S. Link, *American Epoch: A History of the United States Since the 1890s*, 2d ed. rev. (New York: Alfred A. Knopf, 1963), pp. 234-37.

67. Ibid., pp. 238-40. See also William Preston, Jr., *Aliens and Dissenters: Federal Suppression of Radicals, 1903-1933* (New York: Harper & Row, Torchbooks, 1966), pp. 192-237, and John Higham, *Strangers in the Land: Patterns of American Nativism* (New York: Atheneum, 1963), pp. 222-33.

68. U.S., Congress, House, *Proposed Amendments to the Constitution*. H. Doc. 551, 70th Cong., 2d sess., 1928 (Washington: Government Printing Office, 1929), pp. 227-28, 233-37. Section two of the amendment read: "The Congress and the several States shall have concurrent power to enforce this article by appropriate legislation," and the amendment was to become effective one year after its ratification.

69. *Proposed Amendments to the Constitution*, p. 237. The Eighteenth Amendment was repealed by the Twenty-first Amendment late in 1933.

chapter 12

ENDING AN ERA: PRAGMATISM IN ECLIPSE, 1919-21

Although the *Arizona Employers' Liability Cases* had revealed a divided Court on the issue of the flexibility of the Constitution, the Justices could not have anticipated what lay ahead in the 1919 term—the most divisive session in the Court's history to that point. In one hundred and eighty cases, the lightest opinion load since the 1910 session, dissents were registered in fifty-eight cases, almost a third of the total. In the four terms before the arrival of Brandeis and Clarke divided decisions comprised 10 percent or less of the total opinion load. Then in the 1916 term dissents were registered in 20 percent of the cases, and disagreement in the next two sessions ran between 12 and 14 percent. The drastic escalation that came with the present term reflected fundamental differences among the Court's members.[1]

As the Justices confronted further prosecutions of individuals for criticizing the American war effort, the unanimity that had characterized their work in the area collapsed. If the clear and present danger test that the entire Court had accepted in *Schenck* now meant condoning these dissenters to the war effort, the majority was willing to look elsewhere for its guidelines. This evasion became apparent in *Abrams* v. *United States,* which brought before the High Bench the Sedition Act of May 16, 1918 that had amended the earlier Espionage Act. This new law proscribed the making of false statements that would interfere with the American war effort, obstructing the sale of government bonds, inciting disloyalty or hindering recruitment, abusing the government, Constitution, flag, or uniform of the armed services, urging the curtailment of production of anything necessary to the national interest, or supporting by word or deed the cause of the enemy.[2] As if compliant juries had not made the government's task easy enough under the provisions of the original act, Congress now gave the administration a license to prosecute all dissent to the war effort.

That the administration quickly took advantage of the broad wording of the act is well illustrated in the *Abrams* case. Five Russians Jews had published two leaflets bitterly criticizing President Wilson's decision to send American troops into Russia in an attempt to aid the overthrow of the Bolsheviks, who had gained control of the revolution. The disheartened protestors assailed the hypocrisy of a President seeking to save the world for democracy by embarking upon a venture designed to suppress the cause of workers everywhere. Justice Clarke, for the majority, disposed of the First Amendment claim, saying it had been answered by the decisions in *Schenck* and the successor cases and then found the evidence sufficient to support the maximum sentence provided by the law.[3]

Holmes, who had been the Court's spokesman in the earlier cases, now gave vent to the reservations he had suppressed in accepting the Chief's earlier assignments.[4] Joined by Brandeis, Holmes looked at the four counts of the indictment and immediately concluded that two, which alleged an attack on the form of government of the United States, were wholly unsupported. Another count, he continued, required proof of an intent to hinder the prosecution of the war. Abrams had told workers they were producing bullets to kill fellow workers and urged a general strike, but the Justice argued the statute must be read literally to avoid imputing criminality to a whole range of actions that might well trap unwary individuals. Although abiding by his earlier opinions for the Court and recognizing that governmental power over speech is greater in wartime "because war opens dangers that do not exist at other times," Holmes said that "only the present danger of immediate evil or an intent to bring it about . . . warrants Congress in setting a limit to the expression of opinion. . . . Congress certainly cannot forbid all effort to change the mind of the country." The Justice ridiculed the notion "that the surreptitious publishing of a silly leaflet by an unknown man, without more, would present any immediate danger." On the final count involving a conspiracy to provoke resistance to the war, Holmes interpreted the statute to require "some forcible act of opposition to some proceeding of the United States in pursuance of the war." Finding no intent on the part of the defendants to accomplish such a purpose, he shook his head at a sentence of twenty years for the publishing of leaflets that the defendants "had as much right to publish as the government has to publish the Constitution of the United States now vainly invoked by them."[5] These men, he concluded, were punished for their creed rather than for any crime against the government.

Holmes's dissents in the past were often admirable and now and then sprinkled with epigrammatical phrases, but they lacked the passion that comes from true personal concern. In recent years Holmes's generalities had been less satisfactory and his opinions less sparkling, but here he found an issue of substance, and not procedure, that seemed to stir him as a concerned individual. He wound up his dissent in *Abrams* with a paragraph that still echoes in the cause of freedom:

Persecution for the expression of opinions seems to me perfectly logical. If you have no doubt of your premises or your power and want a certain result with all your heart you naturally express your wishes in law and sweep away all opposition. . . . But when men have realized that time has come to upset many fighting faiths, they may come to believe even more than they believe the very foundations of their own conduct that the ultimate good desired is better reached by free trade in ideas—that the best test of truth is the power of the thought to get itself accepted in the competition of the market and that truth is the only ground upon which their wishes safely can be carried out. That at any rate is the theory of our Constitution. It is an experiment, as all life is an experiment. Every year if not every day we have to wager our salvation upon some prophecy based upon imperfect knowledge. While that experiment is part of our system I think that we should be eternally vigilant against attempts to check the expression of opinions that we loathe and believe to be fraught with death, unless they so imminently threaten immediate interference with the lawful and pressing purposes of the law that an immediate check is required to save the country. . . . Of course I am speaking only of expressions of opinions and exhortations, which were all that were uttered here, but I regret that I cannot put into more impressive words my belief that in their conviction upon this indictment the defendants were deprived of their rights under the Constitution of the United States.

Holmes had found a cause, and he felt good about it and about the opinion he penned. The relativism he expressed in this passage is quite characteristic, but his sympathy for a convicted criminal and his broad espousal of at least a part of the Bill of Rights as a substantial check upon governmental power is not. His words, aimed at a society convulsed by the Red Scare, appealed to saner minds and brought the Justice an entirely new following. He basked in this new admiration, and it seemed to bring new life to the seventy-eight-year-old man.[6]

Four months after the decision in *Abrams* the Court was ready to announce its judgment in *Schaefer* v. *United States*, a collection of five cases argued on the same day as *Abrams*. All five defendants were connected with a German-language newspaper in Philadelphia and were convicted in the same proceeding on an indictment containing nine counts of violating the Espionage Act of 1917.

McKenna, for the majority, used the same approach White had earlier to dismiss the challenge that the draft constituted involuntary servitude. The California Justice scoffed at the argument that a right of free speech allowed individuals to disregard clearly drawn statutes designed to assure the success of the war effort. The previous convictions and their affirmance by the Supreme Court, he continued, conclusively respond to a claim "invoked to justify the activities of anarchy or of the enemies of the United States." Not mentioning Holmes's test of a clear and present danger, McKenna seemed to use a much more permissive criterion, the bad tendency test:

The tendency of the articles and their efficacy were enough for offense—their "intent" and "attempt," for those are the words of the law, and to have required more would have made the law useless. It was passed in precaution. The incidence of its violation might not be immediately seen, evil appearing only in disaster, the result of the disloyalty engendered and the spirit of mutiny.[7]

Although McKenna's opinion was not well written, the result he reached was clear. Two of the defendants, including Schaefer, were entitled to directed verdicts in their favor because of the absence of evidence connecting them with the publications, but the convictions of the other three were upheld.

Brandeis, joined by Holmes, dissented from the decision upholding the convictions. Citing the clear and present danger test enunciated by Holmes in *Schenck*, Brandeis said it preserves "the right of free speech both from suppression by tyrannous, well-meaning majorities and from abuse by irresponsible, fanatical minorities." Its proper application, he argued, requires good judgment to which "calmness is, in times of deep feeling and on subjects which excite passion, as essential as fearlessness and honesty." That calmness, the Justice continued, was characteristic of neither judge nor jury in these convictions, for the jury convicted these men for a "disloyal heart" under unsupportable instructions from the judge. Claiming that such convictions threaten an already endangered press, Brandeis found no solace in the era of the Red Scare:

In peace, too, men may differ widely as to what loyalty to our country demands; and an intolerant majority, swayed by passion or by fear, may be prone in the future, as it has often been in the past, to stamp as disloyal opinions with which it disagrees. Convictions such as these, besides abridging freedom of speech, threaten freedom of thought and of belief.[8]

Finally, Clarke, the Court's writer in *Abrams*, dissented in an opinion that rejected both the majority's view and that of the other dissenters. Looking at the record, he saw the case as a "flagrant mistrial" and criticized the majority for not exercising the "power, which it undoubtedly possesses, to correct, in this calmer time, errors of law which would not have been committed but for the stress and strain of feeling prevailing in the early months of the late deplorable war."[9]

One week after *Schaefer* the Court decided *Pierce* v. *United States* with the predictable result of upholding further convictions under the Espionage Act. Again the defendants were tried jointly for speaking against the war effort and for distributing a pamphlet. Pitney, the fourth writer for the Court on these matters, disposed of the constitutional questions by citing the unbroken chain of recent precedent. Brandeis, in a long and thorough opinion joined by Holmes, dissented, contending that the failure of the government to prove intent and to produce evidence that there was a clear and present danger should have forced the judge to direct a verdict for the defendants. To urge fellow men to better their lot by seeking new legislation and new institutions, Brandeis argued, cannot be labeled a criminal act "merely because the argument presented seems to those exercising judicial power to be unfair in its portrayal of existing evils, mistaken in its assumptions, unsound in reasoning, or intemperate in language."[10] No more nor less than that was at issue here, the Justice concluded.

Despite the majority's casual handling of the free speech claim, a substantial dialogue had begun that would bear fruit in the future. None of the Justices interposed the Constitution as a barrier to congressional acts limiting the right of free speech in times of assumed emergency, but the cases did sensitize the Court and the nation to a problem that too few had hitherto perceived. The war had changed society, and in the aggrandizement of federal power new threats were posed to the exercise of individual rights. One reason the majority of the Justices reacted to the free-speech claim with such insensitivity was its relative novelty. Judges and Justices must be educated, and what is novel today can, through continual argument, become acceptable tomorrow. Just as substantive due process in the property area gained constitutional legitimacy through its continual argument to the Court, so, too, would the idea that a government can afford individuals in practical terms the theoretical rights the system provides and still function effectively. Looking backward, the ferment of the Court's handling of the free-speech claim in these war-related cases was a new and significant beginning.

Although the majority Justices demonstrated little sensitivity to the First Amendment questions presented in the war-related cases, most of them followed Holmes as he traveled the more well-trodden path of Fourth Amendment litigation. In *Silverthorne Lumber Company* v. *United States*, Holmes, with only White and Pitney dissenting, ruled that a corporation was as fully protected from illegal search and seizure as was an individual. Holmes said that to permit knowledge gained by the government's wrongdoing to be used against the corporation's officers would violate the Bill of Rights.[11]

The term also produced two cases in which the unanimous Court, perhaps reflecting American society's switch from worrying about the Chinese to worrying about the Japanese, rescued Chinese persons from administrative determinations. In the first case Chin Fong claimed he was a merchant and, as such, was entitled to reentry upon return from a temporary visit to China. The commissioner of immigration concluded that his first entry into the country had been unlawful and ordered his deportation. McKenna said the commissioner, in effect, ignored the question presented and instead attempted to reopen another question settled at a different time by a different tribunal. The government had argued that its fundamental policy in the area should override such technicalities, but McKenna insisted on the need for judicial supervision. In the second case Justice Clarke spread upon the record the strange machinations of a commissioner of immigration in the case of Kwock Jan Fat. Before the young man left for a visit to China he filed a request for a determination of his claim of American citizenship; three white witnesses appeared and supported Kwock Jan Fat's testimony, and he was given a copy of the approved petition. On his return he was denied entry and held for deportation. Relying upon the testimony of a witness whose name he would not reveal and the statement of an unidentified Chinese person, the commissioner sent his new decision to the Secretary of Labor, who concurred in the recommendation. Reliance upon such anonymous testimony over that of three white men with fine reputations in the San Francisco community, Clarke said, was manifestly unfair and grounds for reversal of the determination. In words reminiscent of Brewer, Clarke condemned such arbitrary administrative treatment of the Chinese:

The acts of Congress give great power to the Secretary of Labor over Chinese immigrants and persons of Chinese descent. It is a power to be administered, not arbitrarily and secretly, but fairly and openly, under the restraints of the tradition and principles of free government applicable where the fundamental rights of men are involved, regardless of their origin or race.

"It is better," the Justice concluded, "that many Chinese immigrants should be improperly admitted than that one natural born citizen of the United States should be permanently excluded from his country."[12] Perhaps the Court's rubber stamping of such administrative determinations had finally come to an end.

Since the adoption of the Sixteenth Amendment and the laws enacted thereunder, the Court rejected wholesale challenges to the new taxing law, but in 1918 the Justices unanimously opened the door to a claim that might be pressed to the Sixteenth Amendment itself. Holmes, in *Towne* v. *Eisner*, had ruled that the government erred in its attempt to tax a stock dividend as income, concluding that the transaction was simply a change in the form of capital ownership. Perhaps because of the government's limited argument, the Court avoided the constitutional question. Holmes said "it is not necessarily true that income means the same thing in the Constitution and the act."[13]

This evasion could only be temporary, for the Court would be pressed to determine if a tax on stock dividends was permitted by the Sixteenth Amendment. How Charles Evans Hughes would have viewed this question from the other side of the bench we cannot know, but in the 1919 term he returned before his former colleagues to press the constitutional issue in *Eisner* v. *Macomber*. This time the government was prepared for the larger confrontation. The struggle inside the conference room must have matched that of the advocates, because Holmes now saw the tax on a stock dividend embraced by the amendment, while the majority Justices followed what they felt were the clear implications of their colleague's words in *Towne*.

Pitney, writing for the majority in *Macomber*, said that a bona fide stock dividend does increase the shareholder's capital investment, but it adds nothing to his income. Since the Sixteenth Amendment only frees income from the direct tax requirement of apportionment, the Justice continued, neither Congress nor the courts can disregard through loose construction the limitation the amendment imposes. Limiting the range of the power conferred upon Congress, Pitney ruled that the provision in the 1916 act taxing a stock dividend in the amount of its cash value was unconstitutional. It is a direct tax on property, the Justice continued, which the Sixteenth Amendment does not save from the requirement of apportionment.[14] Apportionment was, of course, impossible, and the result was to deny Congress power to reach stock dividends.

In a single paragraph opinion joined by Day, Holmes dissented, saying of the amendment that he had no "doubt that most people not lawyers would suppose when they voted for it that they put a question like the present to rest."[15] Brandeis, with Clarke, disagreed with the majority in an opinion that grappled with the economic realities of a stock dividend. Contending that whether cash or stock is distributed is a matter of private financial management that cannot affect congressional power, the Justice accused the majority of backing away from its previous broad construction of the amendment to a narrow and cramped interpretation. He claimed the Court had strained to find an act of Congress unconstitutional in the face of an amendment that obviously sought to give the legislative branch the power to include everything that by a reasonable understanding could be classed as income. Such a conclusion, he contended, affronted the view not only of the common people but also of the financiers, investors, and most of the courts in the country.

Three days before the Court announced its result in *Macomber*, it heard argument in another case that questioned the reach of the Sixteenth Amendment: could the salary of federal judges be subjected to the income tax in view of the constitutional provision prohibiting any diminution of their salaries? *Evans* v. *Gore* is unique, for every judge involved in deciding the case had an obvious personal interest in its outcome. Such personal interest generally called for nonparticipation, but if every member of the federal judiciary withdrew, there could have been no disposition. Rather than accept this anomaly, the judges involved, including those on the Supreme Court, simply ignored the question of their self-interest.

Van Devanter, for the Court, extolled the virtues of the judiciary and the need to preserve its independence. Unless clear conflict between the amendment and the guarantee of judge's salaries cannot be avoided, the Justice said, both should be given effect, for "a purpose to depart from or imperil a constitutional principle so widely esteemed and so vital to our system of government as the independence of the judiciary is not lightly to be assumed."[16] He decided that even such a nondiscriminatory tax would diminish the salary of a federal judge and found no evidence that the Sixteenth Amendment was designed to reach new or exempted subjects. Without a note of the self-interest involved—in fact masking it behind a facade of judicial independence—Van Devanter pronounced the pertinent section of the taxing act of 1919 unconstitutional.

Holmes, joined by Brandeis, dissented. Responding to the majority, the senior Massachusetts Justice said the independence of the judiciary does not exonerate the federal judge "from the ordinary duties of a citizen, which he shares with all others. . . . I see nothing in the purpose of this clause of the Constitution to indicate that the judges were to be a privileged class, free from bearing their share of the cost of the institutions upon which their well-being, if not their life, depends."[17] Holmes concluded with an attack on Van Devanter's reading of the Sixteenth Amendment, which, he said, was designed to tax income no matter what its source.

Although the majority had thus limited the taxing authority of the federal government, it was willing to give the states considerable latitude in the same area. With McReynolds dissenting, the Court upheld state income taxes against Fourteenth Amendment challenges in Oklahoma, New York, and Massachusetts.[18] Of all the state taxing cases, the one that posed by far the greatest challenge to the capitalistic system was *Green* v. *Frazier*. The state was North Dakota, where strange things had been happening. Dissatisfaction with the agricultural policy of the dominant Republican party led the farmers of that state to support the Nonpartisan League. By 1918 the league had elected both a governor and a majority of both houses in the state legislature. Laws providing for the establishment of a state bank, warehouse, grain elevator, flour mill system, and a home-building project were enacted. Governor Lynn L. Frazier and William Langer, the attorney general, were the defending parties in a suit challenging as unconstitutional the taxes contemplated to finance these new state endeavors.

Day, for a unanimous Court, noted that taxes must be imposed only for a public, not a private, purpose, but then he added: "When the constituted authority of the State undertakes to exert the taxing power, and the question of the validity of its action is brought before this court, every presumption in its favor is indulged, and only clear and demonstrated usurpation of power will authorize judicial interference with legislative action." Saying that neither wisdom nor the legislation's potential for good or evil is a proper judicial consideration, the Justice ruled that government can go beyond expenditures absolutely necessitated and embrace others that will promote the general welfare of its people. Recognizing the novelty of the North Dakota action, Day could find precedent only in a relatively recent case in which the Court sustained the authority of Portland, Oregon, to establish a municipal fuel supply from which residents would be supplied at cost. The Justice translated the holding of that case into the proposition "that the judgment of the highest court of the State, declaring a given use to be public in its nature, would be accepted by this court unless clearly unfounded." Applying this principle to the facts in the instant case, Day concluded that "if the state sees fit to enter upon such enterprises as are here involved, with the sanction of its constitution, its legislature and its people, we are not prepared to say that it is within the authority of this court, in enforcing the observance of the Fourteenth Amendment, to set aside such action by judicial decision."[19] In no other case had the capitalistic system been so broadly challenged; yet all the Justices were willing to defer to the state's judgment. Despite the Court's support the Nonpartisan League's hold on North Dakota's government did not survive the 1920 election.

Since the Court increasingly had found that federal action and authority had preempted inconsistent state action, the ruling in *South Covington & Cincinnati Street Ry. Company* v. *Kentucky* came as a surprise. Decisions late in the 1917 term had afforded some hope that the Court was demonstrating a greater sensitivity toward and a greater respect for the rights of black men and women, but now the Justices seemed ready to bend commerce clause doctrine to accommodate segregationists in Kentucky. The street railway involved was principally engaged in transporting passengers from Covington, Kentucky, across the Ohio River to Cincinnati, a distance of some six miles. Earlier when the defendant railway had been subjected to regulation by the city of Covington, a unanimous Court in 1915 said that the terms of an ordinance affecting the load the cars could carry and the temperature that had to be maintained were unconstitutional burdens on interstate commerce. But the Court did uphold city regulations affecting passengers on platforms, cleanliness, ventilation, and fumigation as only incidental burdens supportable in the absence of congressional action.[20]

McKenna, for the majority, equated the Kentucky law requiring separate cars or separate compartments with the type of regulation upheld in 1915, saying it "affects interstate business incidentally and does not subject it to unreasonable demands." The state acknowledged that it could not directly regulate interstate commerce, contending that the burdens placed on a Kentucky corporation simply prescribed a rule governing travel within the state. Agreeing with the state legislature, McKenna ruled that the corporation could not "escape its obligations to the state, under the circumstances presented by this record, by running its coaches beyond the state lines." This is a strange statement, but the Justice cited the "equal necessity, under our system of government, to preserve the power of the States within their sovereignties as to prevent the power from intrusive exercise within the National sovereignty."[21] Day, the author of the 1915 opinion, dissented and was joined by Van Devanter and Pitney. Looking at the practical operation of such a statute, he said it would force the railway to provide separate cars or redesign its cars to create separate compartments for blacks in intrastate travel; if the railway continued the trip across the river in conformity with the Kentucky law, it would be met by an Ohio statute that forbade such segregation. To hold that the railway, for a small portion of the trip, would have to comply with the state segregation statute, Day declared, is an unreasonable burden upon interstate commerce.

Whether a burden on interstate commerce was direct or indirect was normally a conclusion the Court stated as a reason for striking down or upholding state action, but here the restraint on the interstate carrier appeared more substantial than in many other cases where the Court decided the burden was oppressive and direct. The adherence of Holmes, Brandeis, and Clarke to the majority in this Kentucky case is quite instructive. Generally more tolerant of state action than their colleagues, they were no more inclined to strike down this segregation statute than they were to invalidate any other state measure that the local legislature deemed to be in the public's interest. Critics often assailed the Court for placing obstacles in the path of responsive state govenment and called upon the Justices to narrow the scope of judicial review. Holmes, Brandeis, and Clarke seemed to heed that call. That a later generation would support the maintenance of national standards, often at the expense of state discretion, such as in the matter of desegregation, should remind us that any judicial technique or approach can be evaluated meaningfully only within the context of the society its practitioners serve.

Although the segregation decision seemed especially accommodating of state power, the majority of the Court balked when Congress acted to increase the ambit of that power by providing that states could apply their workmen's compensation acts to maritime injuries. Surprisingly, the congressional enactment designed to overrule the Court's interpretation in *Southern Pacific Company* v. *Jensen* changed not a single Justice's mind. *Knickerbocker Ice Co.* v. *Stewart* was decided by the same five to four lineup that had disposed of the earlier litigation.[22]

McReynolds, for the majority, began by saying the Constitution "took from the States all power, by legislation or judicial decision, to contravene the essential purposes of, or to work material injury to, characteristic features of such law or to interfere with its proper harmony and uniformity in its international and interstate relations." Then, in rereading the constitutional provisions, he found a new limitation on congressional power. Instead of acting in the area, he said, Congress had delegated its power in a manner that destroyed the uniformity upon which the grant of power is conditioned. Noting precedents in the area of prohibition that cut across the grain of the unlawful delegation argument, McReynolds argued that here "we are concerned with a wholly different constitutional provision—one which, for the purpose of securing harmony and uniformity, prescribes a set of rules,

empowers Congress to legislate to that end, and prohibits material interference by the States."[23] The former Attorney General's opinion holding the
statute unconstitutional on the assumption that a granted power was limited
is clearly anticipatory of the Court's later response to federal legislation in the
mid-1930s. Obviously unsympathetic to the problem that Congress sought to
remedy by this statute, McReynolds read his lack of sympathy into the
Constitution itself.

The *Jensen* dissenters—Holmes, Pitney, Brandeis, and Clarke—were back
in full force. Holmes spoke for the quartet, saying their earlier views had now
been validated by the deliberate action of Congress. The Justice chided the
majority for its failure to concede that much of maritime law had been
continually supplemented by the states, whose power had been conceded
under the basic legislation of 1789. Holmes saw no constitutional bar to a
federal act allowing for the imposition of differing rules in different places,
finding both adequate reason and precedent to support liability that varied
with location and with differing conditions. Citing the Court's consistent
approval of congressional action in the matter of liquor regulation, he said
this answers the unlawful delegation argument of the majority. Pointing to
the fact that the common law liability of master-servant does not provide for
uniformity now, Holmes exposed fully the weakness of the majority's
reasoning.

The decision in *Stewart* when coupled with the two opinions restricting the
reach of federal power under the income tax amendment resulted in the
invalidation of three congressional acts during the session. The cramped and
artificial rationales that the majority put forward in these cases hardly
justified the assertion of judicial power. Instead, the Court gave indications
of following an ideological bent that threatened the healthful pragmatism
that had generally characterized its work over the past generation.

McReynolds in *Stewart* relied, in part, upon a static view of the Constitution, but Holmes, speaking for the majority in another case, viewed the
fundamental law quite differently. He said:

... when we are dealing with words that also are a constituent act, like the Constitution of the United States, we must realize that they have called into life a being the
development of which could not have been foreseen completely by the most gifted of
begetters. It was enough for them to realize or to hope that they had created an
organism; it has taken a century and has cost their successors much sweat and blood
to prove that they created a nation. The case before us must be considered in the light
of our whole experience, and not merely in that of what was said a hundred years
ago.[24]

Holmes was speaking here in the case of *Missouri* v. *Holland* in which Van
Devanter and Pitney, but not McReynolds, dissented.

Missouri sought to enjoin federal authorities from enforcing the Migratory Bird Treaty Act under regulations promulgated by the Secretary of Agriculture. Alleging a proprietary interest in game birds, Missouri claimed the federal act invaded the reserved powers of the state under the Tenth Amendment. What gave substance to the state claim were lower federal court decisions holding unconstitutional an earlier federal statute seeking to regulate game birds under the commerce power. The government did not seek review of those adverse decisions; instead, pursuant to a treaty with Great Britain involving the migration of birds between the United States and Canada ratified in 1916, Congress passed new legislation.[25] The question now posed was: could a properly ratified treaty confer power on the federal government that it otherwise did not possess?

Noting that a treaty becomes the supreme law of the land, Holmes rejected the argument that the federal government is limited in its treaty-making power to subjects clearly delegated to it by the Constitution. The Justice broadly asserted "that there may be matters of the sharpest exigency for the national well-being that an act of Congress could not deal with but that a treaty followed by such an act could, and it is not lightly to be assumed that, in matter requiring national action, 'a power which must belong to and somewhere reside in every civilized government' is not to be found." Contending that the treaty did not contravene any prohibition found in the Constitution, Holmes brushed aside the Tenth Amendment argument, saying Missouri's authority to regulate the birds did not survive this new accretion of power to Congress. Stressing the need for finding the requisite power, Holmes concluded that the national interest "can be protected only by national action in concert with that of another power. We see nothing in the Constitution that compels the Government to sit by while a food supply is cut off and the protectors of our forests and of our crops are destroyed."[26]

Probably the Court would not have agreed with the lower courts' earlier holding that the federal government lacked power to regulate migratory birds, but the absence of an appeal there forced this case into a strange framework. A Court that had lectured Congress on the limitations of its power under the Sixteenth Amendment and of the necessity of legislating on maritime matters to promote uniformity was here seemingly saying that, through the treaty process, the federal government could expand its power beyond the dimensions of the authority delegated. What precedential value the decision would have was left for the future to determine; for the present, the approval of federal control over migratory birds made good sense.

In contrast to the decision in *Missouri* v. *Holland*, which was sure to engender new criticism of the Court, Chief Justice White's opinion in a case involving the Philippines sought to lay to rest charges of the Justices' inability to agree on the constitutional status of the nation's overseas territories. With nary a voice raised in opposition the Chief ruled that the Philippines were not incorporated into the United States. A due process challenge had been levied against a congressional statute requiring ships engaged in the coastal trade in the Philippines to carry the mail without charge. The claim here, the Chief said, "arises from the erroneous assumption that the constitutional limitations of power which operate upon the authority of Congress when legislating for the United States are applicable and are controlling upon Congress when it comes to exert . . . legislative power over territory . . . not incorporated therein."[27] Longevity had aided the Chief in gaining total victory for his incorporation theory with its built-in deference to the will of Congress.

During the session the Justices expressed continued willingness to defer to the expertise and good faith of the ICC, but this attitude did not extend to another administrative agency, the Federal Trade Commission (FTC) created in 1914. Hope existed that the Court's slow but relatively consistent accommodation to the ICC would aid in its acceptance of the new agency's work. The decision in *Federal Trade Commission* v. *Gratz* dashed that hope.[28] The FTC had issued a cease and desist order against a partnership preventing it from using an "unfair method of competition"—selling steel ties for bailing cotton only in conjunction with a like number of jute bags for wrapping the fiber.

McReynolds, for the majority, ruled that what is an "unfair method of competition" is ultimately a matter for the courts to decide. Seeing the words inapplicable to practices not previously condemned "as opposed to good morals because characterized by deception, bad faith, fraud or oppression, or as against public policy because of their dangerous tendency unduly to hinder competition or create monopoly," he said the Federal Trade Commission Act was not designed to hamstring fair and free competition. The Justice found no grounds for condemning this practice of the partnership, saying that a private merchant may tie together the sale of closely related articles. If real competition is to continue, McReynolds concluded, "the right of the individual to exercise reasonable discretion in respect of his own business methods must be preserved."[29]

Pitney concurred in the decision without opinion, but Brandeis, joined by Clarke, dissented. Noting that the majority disposed of the case on the basis that the complaint was deficient, he said such an approach had not been taken by the Court toward the ICC. Feeling that both agencies should be equally respected, Brandeis advocated giving the FTC the opportunity to establish its case. Inquiring into the purpose behind the creation of the new agency, he called attention to the commission's novel task of discouraging unfair practices. Its work, Brandeis argued, is advisory, for either it or the company affected must take the initiative in gaining a judicial reading of the legitimacy of the commission's order. After tracing the history of antitrust regulation, the Justice asserted that the Federal Trade Commission was a departure from the past regulation in two ways: first, it was designed to preserve competition through supervisory rather than punitive action; and second, it was left the task of defining what was an "unfair practice." Since unfair competition was already covered by preexisting law, Brandeis concluded, the FTC was created to deal with unfair practices before they spread and suppressed competition.

Brandeis's recommendations to President Wilson had led to the creation of the Federal Trade Commission, and his opinion conveyed a keen knowledge of its intended function. The majority, however, still mired in the old ways and the old considerations, simply could not adjust to this new creation with its new functions. Brandeis tried to inform his colleagues that the purpose of the FTC was to anticipate problems rather than remedy them after the fact, but as with the ICC, the Court's adjustment to the FTC would be slow.[30]

This most eventful session also saw the Court finally issue an opinion in the long-pending antitrust suit seeking the dissolution of the United States Steel Corporation. The case had been instituted by the Taft administration in 1911 and was first argued to the Court in 1917. Both Brandeis and McReynolds had to withdraw from participation because of earlier involvement, leaving a seven-man bench to handle the case. No decision had been reached by the beginning of the 1919 term when, as the first matter of business, the case was reargued. United States Steel Corporation was a holding company with stock in the operating manufacturers. All the Justices agreed that the company attained its commanding position in the industry in the decade from 1901 to 1911 in part by methods condemned by the Sherman Act. But now confronting the government's suit for dissolution, the Justices split four to three against the government.

McKenna, for the majority, was willing to overlook the past and concentrate on what the corporation was doing now. Having seen reformation in company practices since 1911, he believed its important position in the economy of the nation and of the world was a matter that deserved special consideration. Although it controlled almost half the total market, McKenna ruled that United States Steel was not a monopoly. He explained:

The Corporation is undoubtedly of impressive size and it takes an effort of resolution not to be affected by it or to exaggerate its influence. But we must adhere to the law and the law does not make mere size an offense or the existence of unexerted power an offense. It, we repeat, required overt acts and trusts to its prohibition of them and its power to repress or punish them.[31]

McKenna rebuffed the government's request for dissolution, as he cited the public interest in encouraging the foreign trade in which the corporation was substantially engaged. Relating the continued existence of the corporation to the national welfare, the Justice said prominent consideration must be given to such public interest in the enforcement of the Sherman Act.

Writing for Pitney and Clarke, Day dissented, as he demonstrated what a novel opinion in antitrust law the majority had written. Viewing the record as establishing that the corporation violated the Sherman Act in its formation and in its practices, thereby enabling it to build up the power to fix prices and restrain commerce "upon a scale heretofore unapproached in the history of corporate organization in this country," Day saw a clear case calling for dissolution. Only this remedy, he concluded, would reestablish competitive conditions in the trade and "carry into effect the policy of the law."[32] Day was quite correct in both his assessment of precedent and the policy inherent in the Sherman Act. But the times had changed, and as the nation headed into the 1920s the Court seemed to anticipate a much more favorable attitude toward big business.

If *United States Steel* suggested a departure in the Court's view of the proper application of antitrust policy, the last major series of cases during the term demonstrated the Court's eager willingness to support the new policy of national prohibition. A brief summary of federal action in the area serves as a useful prelude. The Webb-Kenyon Act of 1913 sought to afford the states sufficient power to enforce their prohibitionist policies with regard to interstate shipments; it attempted to fill in the gaps created by the Court's interpretation of the Wilson Act of 1890. When the Justices read the Webb-Kenyon legislation as allowing interstate shipment into the state for purposes not specifically forbidden by state law, Congress responded with the Reed Amendment in early 1917 banning interstate shipments of liquor into dry states. With the coming of war prohibitionists were successful in getting Congress to write into the Lever Food Control Act of August 10, 1917, authority for the President to regulate the use of food products in the production of liquor. In four proclamations President Wilson effectuated this policy, but the last two restricted prohibition to beverages that were intoxicating. Then, on November 21, 1918, Congress enacted the Wartime Prohibition Act, which provided for a period within which liquors could be disposed of free from any regulation of the federal government. Then, from its effective date until the termination of the war emergency, the act made unlawful the sale of liquor for beverage purposes. After the Wartime Prohibition Act was passed brewery operators contended that the law did not preclude the production and sale of beer and other malt liquors that were not intoxicating. Congress eventually responded with the Volstead Act of October 28, 1919, passed over President Wilson's veto, which brought within the prohibition all beverages containing at least 0.5 percent alcohol. Finally, the Eighteenth Amendment became effective in January 1920.

The first case the Court considered involved an attack upon the Wartime Prohibition Act by two companies owning a large supply of distilled beverages. Counsel for the owners contended that the act violated the Fifth Amendment because it took property without due process of law, that it had expired because of the termination of the war emergency, and that it was repealed by the Eighteenth Amendment. The unanimous bench rejected these arguments. Then in early January 1920 the Court announced its only decision saving a defendant from government enforcement of the prohibition act. Interpreting the wartime act as not embracing nonintoxicating beer or malt liquor, a unanimous Court held that a brewery manufacturing such beer could not be prosecuted under that act. Of course, the conclusion the Justices reached had already been accepted by Congress, which had filled the gap with the Volstead Act of 1919. On the same day the Court considered the change made by that statute in *Ruppert* v. *Caffey*. This time the Justices split five to four in upholding the new congressional enactment. Brandeis wrote for the majority, while McReynolds dissented, joined by Day and Van Devanter, and Clarke dissented alone and without opinion.[33]

Brandeis detailed how various states and courts had coped with regulations similar to the Volstead Act and concluded that such facts demonstrated that if liability is predicated on showing that the particular beverage is intoxicating, "it is deemed impossible to effectively enforce either prohibitory laws or other laws merely regulating the manufacture and sale of intoxicating liquors." The war power, the Justice said, is as complete as the state's police power, and all means necessary to administer the law effectively are encompassed by it. McReynolds based his dissent on the view that "active hostilities have ended, and demobilization has been completed." The Justice said the rights of a citizen might be less in a period of war, but he contended that the rights asserted here must be viewed in a peacetime setting. Finding no power in Congress to pass the Volstead Act, he argued that if the war power can proscribe plaintiff's beer there is no checking the federal government in implying powers from those delegated. Citing both the Fifth and Tenth Amendments, he was ready to pronounce the Volstead Act unconstitutional, saying the Constitution should not "suffer emasculation by any strained or unnatural construction."[34] Even McReynolds, whose personality and general decision making hardly excited admiration, could pen an opinion that appeals to a later generation.

The federal government had been captured by the prohibitionists, and the majority of the Court would not interfere with this inexorable march to save Americans from the evils of liquor. In *Ruppert* the minority came close to restricting the excesses of this drive, but both White and McKenna, perhaps the most vulnerable of the majority Justices to the minority's reasoning, were unwilling to interfere with the federal legislative program. Even Clarke, who would not subscribe to McReynolds's words, found the Brandeis opinion more than he could accept. Clarke did speak as the lone dissenter in a case in which the Court held that an individual bringing liquor for his own use into a dry state in his automobile could be prosecuted by the federal government. The Justice argued that the Reed Amendment as applied was unconstitutional, for, the "grant of power to Congress is over commerce—not over isolated movements of small amounts of private property, by private persons for their personal use."[35]

The Court's conversion to prohibition is perhaps best illustrated by its decision in an Ohio case. The state legislature had ratified the Eighteenth Amendment, but antiprohibitionists sought to invoke the state's referendum procedure to undo that ratification. State courts had refused to enjoin the referendum, but the Justices unanimously reversed the decision. Day, for the Court, evaded precedent by saying that in prior decisions the use of the devices of popular government had been restricted to legislative functions. The ratification task, he ruled, is not legislative and therefore not subject to modifications by state law; it can only be exercised by the body specified in the Constitution. The appeal of such an artificial distinction perhaps can best be understood in terms of the Court's conversion to prohibition.[36]

On the last decision day of the term the Justices faced the Eighteenth Amendment in a series of cases known as the *National Prohibition Cases*. After its acquiescence in the national prohibition drive, the Justices were not about to find a fundamental deficiency in the new amendment to the Constitution. The Court responded predictably, but with McKenna and Clarke in dissent. Chief Justice White assigned the opinion to Van Devanter, who found the contentions in the case overwhelming. Unable to write a traditional opinion, he stated eleven conclusions. Technical arguments relating to the question of Congress's belief in the necessity of the amendment and to the question of whether two-thirds of a quorum in each house was sufficient to pass the resolution were summarily disposed of. So was a major argument of the antagonists, the contention that the subject matter of the amendment was improper. The first section of the amendment, Van Devanter said, "invalidates every legislative act—whether by Congress, by a state legislature, or by a territorial assembly—which authorizes what the section prohibits."[37] Considering the subject of concurrent state and federal enforcement power, Van Devanter responded that it does not enable the states to thwart federal policy, that the states are not required to concur in federal law enacted under it, and that the federal power it created is coextensive with the territorial limits of the country. Congressional authority, he concluded, is sufficient to validate the Volstead Act as well, and though limits to the exercise of such power may exist, this legislation of 1919 did not transgress them.

In concurring in the resolution White implied that he appreciated Van Devanter's difficulty, although he regretted that in a case of such great importance the Court had responded only in terms of ultimate conclusions. The Chief was most dissatisfied with his colleague's discussion of the meaning of "concurrent power." He concentrated on counsel's argument, which urged that concurrent action by the state was necessary before enforcement could take place. Rejecting such a suggestion the Chief said "no reason exists for saying that a grant of concurrent power to Congress and the States to give effect to, that is, to carry out or enforce, the Amendment as defined and sanctioned by Congress, should be interpreted to deprive Congress of the power to create, by definition and sanction, an enforceable amendment."[38] White had neither the stamina nor the resolve to do the job Van Devanter had been assigned.

McKenna, dissenting, also criticized Van Devanter's work, saying it "will undoubtedly decrease the literature of the court if it does not increase lucidity."[39] Clearly contending with White, McKenna denied that the concurrent power of the states and the federal government can mean the subordination of one to another; such a reading, he said, affronts both precedent and the common definition of words. If the supremacy of Congress in the matter was intended by the amendment, as the government had argued, the Justice found this interpretation inconsistent with the wording. Its text, he continued, requires concurrent action of the part of the states and the federal government. Problems arising from this joint enterprise, he concluded, are not matters the Court can consider.

Clarke's dissent was focused on Van Devanter's treatment of the Volstead Act. Like McKenna, he could not square the majority's decision with the Eighteenth Amendment's conferral of power upon the states as well as the federal government. Looking at the legislative history, Clarke saw abundant reason not to read words out of the amendment. The Volstead Act seemed to be just the type of intrusion on state legislation that the amendment forbad. The Justice would read "concurrent power" as limiting the reach of federal legislation to matters within a state's boundaries "only when concurred in by action of Congress and of such State." This type of state-federal cooperation, he continued, "would, to a great extent, relieve Congress of the burden and the general government of the odium to be derived from the antagonism which would certainly spring from enforcing, within States, federal laws which must touch the daily life of the people very intimately and often very irritatingly."[40] Should the state refuse such cooperation, Clarke added, the first section prohibiting the manufacture, sale, and transportation of alcoholic beverages would still be the law of the land. This would leave the states, he said, free to act in the limited field that the first section does not preempt.

Clarke realized such an interpretation would not satisfy the prohibitionists, but he said it accorded with well-established rules of constitutional construction, which are "intended to prevent courts from rewriting the Constitution in a form which judges think it should have been written instead of giving effect to the language actually used in it." To the majority's upholding of the Volstead Act's proscription of nonintoxicating beverages, Clarke replied that no constitutional base for such action can be found in the first section of the Eighteenth Amendment. He conceded that it may be found in the state police power or the federal war power, but he was at a loss to see how the scope of the first section could be enlarged by the limiting language of the second section. Finally, he cited the *Slaughter-House Cases* as an illustration of how the Court resisted the pressure to reduce the ambit of state police power and indicated his regret that the "present questions of like character to, and of not less importance than, those which were presented in those great cases" have not evoked a similar response from the Court.[41]

Despite the array of counsel in these cases and the welter of arguments that were poorly served by the opinions, the only real dispute among the Justices was over the meaning of concurrent state and federal jurisdiction. As White, McKenna, and Clarke all indicated, the basic question was how much power remained in the states to stem this successful national tide in favor of prohibition. Prohibitionists had succeeded in forging a new nationalism with the help of a Court that interpreted concurrent jurisdiction of the states as a subordinate jurisdiction limited to effectuating what the Court accepted as national policy. The provision for concurrent jurisdiction was a potential troublemaker in the amendment, but the majority here obligingly eliminated the problem. In a few short years the tables had turned. Before 1917 the federal government had put its force behind the liquor policy of the states, but after that date, aided by the war effort, the trend was reversed and culminated in the federal government setting a policy from which no state could deviate.

With the decision in the *National Prohibition Cases* the tumultuous 1919 term came to an end. Registering dissents in almost every third case decided, the Justices had set a new record. Clarke led the pack with twenty-two dissents, followed by Pitney with sixteen, McReynolds and Brandeis with fifteen, and Holmes with thirteen. Clarke and Brandeis agreed in 62 percent of the divided cases, and Holmes and Brandeis agreed in excess of 85 percent.

At the other end of the spectrum McReynolds and Clarke agreed in only 32 percent of such cases. In fact, these two men together were responsible for dividing the Court six times; each of them dissented three times alone and without opinion when the other rendered the decision of the Court. This was just one indication of the antagonism between the two men. Clarke had received his first appointment to the federal bench at the urging of Attorney General McReynolds; so, when the Ohioan came to the Court, apparently the more senior Justice expected his new colleague to be a disciple. Clarke's siding with Brandeis so consistently in their early tenure on the Court became a continuing annoyance to McReynolds. More than any other member of the Court, Clarke became the butt of his sponsor's sarcasm and ill humor. Regularly McReynolds impugned his colleague's competence and "liberal" tendencies. It was a most unpleasant experience for Clarke, who only became more depressed as Brandeis drifted away from him and closer to Holmes. As Attorney General, McReynolds had worked with Brandeis, apparently with some mutual respect, but now he refused to accept invitations that would bring him into social contact with his Jewish colleague. McReynolds was a vocal anti-Semite, but Brandeis's confidence provided him with an invulnerability that Clarke lacked.[42]

The Court that ended the 1919 term had been intact for four full sessions; it would be only a matter of time before vacancies would develop. In fact, a still anxious William Howard Taft estimated that the President elected in 1920 would make four appointments to the Court. Realizing that a Republican President would look with favor upon the focus of his great ambition, Taft plunged into the campaign.[43] In calculating four seats the pretender had in mind Holmes, who was seventy-nine, McKenna, who would turn seventy-seven over the summer, White, who was seventy-four, and Day, who was seventy-one. Taft was especially interested in the Chief Justice. Age had taken its toll on Edward White, who was suffering from a loss of hearing and impaired eyesight. However, the other senior members gave little indication of either retirement or incapacitation. They were carrying their share of the work, more so than the youthful Van Devanter with his writing block.

President Wilson's vigorous campaign for American membership in the League of Nations, upon which he staked his party's leadership and his personal health, was a failure. He suffered a stroke on October 2, 1919, that disabled him. His desire to run again to give the people a chance to express their opinion of the League was never seriously entertained by Democratic party chieftains. No matter who emerged as the Democratic candidate, the party was the target of disillusionment in the aftermath of war.

Republicans, sensing victory, met first. As the strong contenders fought to a standstill on the early balloting, a group of Senators and other influential party members decided to break the deadlock by selecting the nondescript, loyal party follower, Senator Warren G. Harding of Ohio, whose choice the convention ratified. No less confusing was the Democratic party's convention. William G. McAdoo, Wilson's son-in-law and former Secretary of the Treasury, battled in the early going with the Attorney General, A. Mitchell Palmer, who had sought to turn his activities in hounding radicals into a presidential bid. On the forty-fourth ballot one of the favorite sons, James M. Cox, also from Ohio, emerged victorious. The election in November bore out the predictions, with Cox gaining the electoral votes of only eleven Southern states and losing by a majority of 7,000,000 votes out a total of a little over 25,000,000 cast. With over 60 percent of the popular vote, Harding won the most lopsided victory in the presidential sweepstakes since the vote was first counted.

To Taft the victory was indeed sweet, for had not the present Chief Justice promised to resign when he could be assured that his successor would be the former President? Taft would have to wait at least until March, when Harding would be sworn in, and he did not hide his impatience. Yet at sixty-three, after years of frustration, the ex-President now saw his goal within reach. White would have to be persuaded to vacate the top spot on the Court, and Harding would have to be persuaded to appoint Taft, but both were well within the realm of the possible.[44]

In addition to the presidential contest the summer of 1920 also brought a new addition to the Constitution, the Nineteenth Amendment, providing for women's suffrage. The first congressional proposal for a women's suffrage amendment came in 1866 during the Reconstruction period when there was some agitation seeking to gain the right seemingly conferred upon blacks. From this time on each succeeding Congress entertained proposals for an amendment enfranchising women. Such resolutions began to mount in number in 1911, coinciding with renewed activity at the state level. With the campaign picking up, the Senate presented an obstacle to the proposed amendment by rejecting such a measure once in 1918 and twice in early 1919. Some of the opposition came from those who believed the power of the states over the suffrage should not be displaced, but this concern for protecting the interests of the states, which appeared to the women activists as a specious type of reasoning, was finally overridden. The attempt in the final resolution to afford states concurrent jurisdiction over the matter failed to win the necessary support; Congress could not yet know that the Court would shortly find a similar provision in the Eighteenth Amendment all but meaningless. With the President's backing the resolution sailed through the House and got by the Senate in a little over two weeks.[45]

That the time was indeed right was proved by the relatively quick ratification of the Nineteenth Amendment. Tennessee became the necessary thirty-sixth state to ratify, and the amendment went into effect on August 18, 1920. Some have suggested the fruition of this movement for women's suffrage was less an acknowledgment by men that a democratic theory mandated the move or the result of an irresistible drive by a united sisterhood than it was a recognition of the advantage of offsetting the votes of the wave of Eastern and Southern European immigrants entering the country in the decade and a half before the war.[46] The presence of women at the ballot box neither brought the disaster to family life some feared, nor did it result in making the society appreciably better, but it was one product of the war in which the society could take pride.[47] The contrast with the Eighteenth Amendment is indeed stark.

The 1919 term had taken its toll upon the Justices, and the nine men who returned to Washington early in October for the 1920 session still reflected some of the tension and weariness produced by the preceding term. Although they would decide forty-three more cases during the 1920 term than in the preceding one, dissent was halved, as only one in six cases provoked disagreement.

Early in the session the Justices heard arguments in a series of cases that challenged criminal indictments under section four of the Lever Act. Conspiring to charge or charging excessive prices for necessities was punishable by a jail term up to two years and/or a fine up to $5,000. In all cases the defendants filed demurrers to the indictments, and lower federal courts in Missouri, Colorado, and Michigan found the indictments bad, while federal courts in Mississippi, New York, Ohio, and Georgia upheld them. *United States* v. *Cohen Grocery Company*, in which the company was indicted for charging an excessive price for sugar, provided the focal point for the Court. The main thrust of the attack was levied at the vagueness of the statutory language. Defendants' lawyers claimed their clients' Fifth and Sixth Amendment rights were violated by the legislation.

In reviewing the lower court's decision against the government, White, for the majority, approved the trial judge's conclusion "that the mere existence of a state of war could not suspend or change the operation upon the power of Congress of the guaranties and limitations of the Fifth and Sixth Amendments as to questions such as we are here passing upon." The Chief ruled that the criminal provision in the Lever Act was repugnant to the amendments cited because it negated the prohibitions "imposed upon Congress against delegating legislative power to courts and juries, against penalizing indefinite acts, and against depriving the citizen of the right to be informed of the nature and cause of the accusation against him." Pitney, concurring in the result, saw no need for reaching the constitutional issue in the case, and Brandeis agreed. Interpreting the statute, Pitney concluded that it "was not intended to control the individual dealer with respect to prices that he might exact." The conspiracy portion of the provision he saw as clearly subject to the criminal penalties, a conclusion he and Brandeis stated in one of the other cases.[48] The two Justices followed the old adage that constitutional issues should not be resolved if they could be avoided in deciding the case before the Court. Here both men would not have placed a precedent on the books talking in terms of the unlawful delegation of power by Congress. The result of the litigation was the voiding of section four of the Lever Act well after the war emergency and without any questioning of the power of the federal government to regulate prices under the war power.

The Court also split on a matter related to the Sixth Amendment's provision for a fair trial. In a prosecution for violating the Espionage Act by speaking against the war effort, Victor L. Berger, the prominent American Socialist and former congressman, claimed that presiding judge Kenesaw Mountain Landis had a personal bias against German-born defendants and supported the claim with the evidence of the judge's views. Landis, who had just left the bench to assume a firm hand over professional baseball as its commissioner in the wake of the Black Sox Scandal of 1919, had said that one "must have a very judicial mind, indeed, not to be prejudiced against the German Americans in this country." At another time he added: "If anybody has said anything worse about the Germans than I have I would like to know it so I can use it."[49] Landis rejected the challenge and proceeded with the trial in which Berger was sentenced to twenty years. The court of appeals divided and certified certain questions to the High Bench.

McKenna responded for the majority and found applicable the section in the Judicial Code requiring the challenged judge to excuse himself from the case. Less worried about perjury or impugning the integrity of federal judges than about the defendant's right to a fair trial, the California Justice ruled that "an affidavit upon information and belief satisfies the section and that upon its filing, if it show the objectionable inclination or disposition of the judge, which we have said is an essential condition, it is his duty to 'proceed no further' in the case." Joined by Pitney, Day dissented, bothered by the majority's decision to make Berger's affidavit a final adjudication of the claim it contained. The Justice argued that this procedure threatened the independence of the judge and opened a door to the abuse of the statutory provision. The Court's holding that a judge's condemnation of a class subjects him to disqualification in dealing with members of that class took direct aim on the personal prejudices of McReynolds. In dissent, the Justice responded:

Intense dislike of a class does not render the judge incapable of administering complete justice to one of its members. A public officer who entertained no aversion toward disloyal German immigrants during the late war was simply unfit for his place. And while "An overspeaking judge is no well tuned cymbal" neither is an amorphous dummy unspotted by human emotions a becoming receptacle for judicial power. It was not the purpose of Congress to empower an unscrupulous defendant seeking escape from merited punishment to remove a judge solely because he had emphatically condemned domestic enemies in time of national danger. The personal concern of the judge in matters of this kind is indeed small, but the concern of the public is very great.[50]

Of course, the dissenters were quite right in implying that in cases brought under the Espionage Act, there was not much impartiality on the part of judges and juries, but the Berger decision did help introduce some sanity into a society that had released its pent-up frustrations in the Red Scare.

Having found merit in Berger's claim, the Justices unanimously decided in *Gouled* v. *United States* that the Fourth Amendment had been violated. Gouled was suspected of conspiring with others to defraud the government, and pursuant to the investigation a military intelligence officer visited the suspect and carried away some papers. Later, under a search warrant, other material was taken. For the Court, Clarke said the fact that the first documents were seized without force or illegal coercion was irrelevant, for the amendment should be construed liberally to protect individuals from having their rights eroded "by imperceptible practice of courts or by well-intentioned but mistakenly over-zealous executive officers." The Justice said a warrant could not justify "gaining access to a man's house or office and papers solely for the purpose of making search to secure evidence to be used against him in a criminal or penal proceeding."[51]

Brandeis and Holmes were willing to go further than their colleagues in making the Fourth Amendment protection fully effective, as their dissent in *Burdeau* v. *McDowell* illustrated. In a prosecution for using the mails to defraud, the government had been presented with documents stolen from McDowell. The majority, in an opinion by Day, simply held that since the record showed no participation by the government in the procurement of the papers, no bar existed to their use by the prosecution. Brandeis asked, should the government be able to use materials gained by theft? No, he responded, saying that a proper respect "for law will not be advanced by resort, in its enforcement, to means which shock the common man's sense of decency and fair play."[52]

In a term that brought a number of Bill of Rights cases to the Court, Holmes and Brandeis also dissented from the Court's resolution of a free speech and free press claim asserted against action taken by the Postmaster General. A section of the Espionage Act said that any newspaper violating the law shall not be "conveyed in the mails or delivered from any post office or by any letter carrier." Acting under this authority and that conferred upon him by the general postal statutes, the Postmaster General revoked the second-class mailing privileges of the Milwaukee Social Democratic Publishing Company, publisher of the *Milwaukee Leader*. The *Leader's* primary voice was that of Victor Berger. Charges included publishing false reports with intent to hinder the country's military operations, aiding the cause of the enemy, and obstructing the recruitment and enlistment service. The company responded with a denial of the requisite authority in the Postmaster General and a claim that the alleged statutory authorization violated the due process of law, the right to trial, and the free speech and free press clauses of the Constitution. Clarke, for the majority, found ample support for the denial of second-class mailing privileges. Briefly touching upon the type of articles published, Clarke said rather than seek changes in the law they were designed to create hostility to, and encourage violations of, the law. The First Amendment, he concluded, is certainly not intended "to serve as a protecting screen for those who while claiming its privileges seek to destroy it."[53]

Brandeis responded in dissent. Although the issue involved here arose in wartime, he began, it "presents no legal question peculiar to war." What the Justice saw involved was no less than a determination of whether "our press shall be free." Reviewing precedent, Brandeis found that even where Congress had declared certain material nonmailable, only those issues containing such material could be proscribed. If the Postmaster could ban all issues of a paper, the Justice added "he would, in view of the practical finality of his decisions, become the universal censor of publications."

Allowing, as the majority did, the Postmaster to deny such rates to all future issues of the paper, especially when each issue had to be submitted for inspection under the law, raised grave constitutional problems for Brandeis. To the question of whether the postal power is subject to limitation, the Justice answered, yes, of course. Congress may not limit the freedom of press indirectly any more than it can directly. Upholding the censorship imposed here, continued Brandeis, seriously abridges the freedom of expression, for it denies to a publication effective access to the mails by saying that such access is only a privilege terminable upon an administrative determination that the views expressed do not accord with dominant public policy. The Justice solved the problem by saying that Congress had afforded a right to those who met the specified criteria for second-class mailings. Brandeis concluded that the power to classify the mails could not justify the order issued here. Questioning whether the majority's decision left much substance in the Bill of Rights, he warned that "in every extension of governmental functions lurks a new danger to civil liberty."[54]

After seeing Brandeis's dissent, Holmes said he changed his mind in the case, having come to a realization that a denial of second-class rates would make the circulation of the paper impossible and that the Postmaster had no authority in the classification statute to act as a censor of the mails. The senior Massachusetts Justice asserted that it would take exceedingly clear language to convince him that Congress had conferred such power upon the official considering "the ease with which the power claimed by the Postmaster could be used to interfere with very sacred rights."[55]

That Brandeis was emerging from the 1920 term as the High Bench's most fervent advocate of an effective right of free speech was confirmed by his eloquent dissent in *Gilbert* v. *Minnesota*. This time the senior Massachusetts Justice refused to follow his younger colleague's lead. Even in the cause of free speech Holmes did not seem ready to deviate from what he considered the Court's proper role of not using the Fourteenth Amendment's due process clause to invalidate decisions made by state legislatures. Gilbert was convicted for violating a notorious state sedition statute that prohibited the teaching or advocacy of certain proscribed ideas. He had made a speech questioning the nature of the American democracy and the real choice it afforded the people in the selection of federal and state officials. He suggested that "if they conscripted wealth like they have conscripted men, this war would not last over forty-eight hours."[56] For this he was fined $500 and sentenced to a year in jail. Gilbert contended that federal legislation had preempted the field and that his conviction under the state law had violated his right of free speech.

McKenna, writing for the majority, said the Constitution does not insist upon a technical separation of state and federal power, for "the constituted and constituting sovereignties must have power of cooperation against the enemies of all." Minnesota had not usurped a national power, he proclaimed, but rather it had rendered a service to its people. Although the Justice reserved the question of whether the federal guarantee of free speech limited the states, he conceded the possibility. This concession, however, did not aid Gilbert. Citing recent precedent on the meaning of free speech, McKenna concluded that it "would be a travesty" to allow the defendant to find protection within the constitutional clause.[57]

Both White and Brandeis dissented. The Chief argued quite simply that congressional legislation on the subject had preempted the field, a conclusion so obvious that only the red flag of disloyalty could blind the majority to its soundness. Brandeis saw the Minnesota statute far more compromising of the right of free speech than its federal counterpart, for, he said, the state measure was not war related, and it, in effect, censored belief and banned the teaching of pacifism for all time. Again citing the need to find a clear and present danger before speech can be proscribed, the Justice had no difficulty in holding the free speech guarantee binding upon the states. He contended that the federal government alone had the power to determine when the right of free discussion should be curtailed in the national interest. When enacted, Brandeis added, the Minnesota law was inconsistent with federal law permiting free discussion, and when the Espionage Act was passed, the state law was still out of phase, for the federal act never prohibited the teaching of any doctrine but only tangible obstructions to the war effort. Chiding his colleagues, he concluded: "I cannot believe that the liberty guaranteed by the Fourteenth Amendment includes only liberty to acquire and to enjoy property."[58]

Gilbert v. *Minnesota* is an important case because of the majority's willingness to acknowledge the possibility that a personal guarantee in the Bill of Rights, heretofore held applicable only to the federal government, could also be interposed as a bar to inconsistent state action. John Marshall Harlan had long contended that the Fourteenth Amendment had made the Bill of Rights binding upon the states, but his position had garnered no support. Now, Brandeis again suggested the way in which the guarantee of free speech could be read into the protection of liberty in the Fourteenth Amendment. Five years after *Gilbert*, the Court would accept this position, in much the same way that an earlier Court had accepted the argument that a corporation was a person for purposes of the protection afforded by the Fourteenth Amendment.[59] Although there were certain indications that the Court might be moving toward a more miserly view of the extent of governmental power, *Gilbert* suggested that this greater willingness to view official action with suspicion could bring forth a new era in extending the protection of individual rights substantially beyond the right to hold and enjoy property. Despite the dramatic appeal of changes that come suddenly, significant shifts in direction often come slowly, almost imperceptibly.

The Court demonstrated no willingness to get involved in a suit to enjoin a strike when the matter could be avoided on jurisdictional grounds, but the Justices did not flinch when a case seeking an injunction against labor activity was properly presented. In 1917 in *Paine Lumber Company* a narrow majority of the Court had avoided considering the extent of protection afforded by the Clayton Act to organized labor. Now, *Duplex Printing Press Company* v. *Deering* squarely brought before the High Bench the prolabor provisions of the legislation.[60]

The Duplex Printing Company manufactured printing presses in Battle Creek, Michigan, and employed its workers under an open-shop policy. To force the company to unionize the International Association of Machinists instituted a boycott. Duplex sought an injunction against the boycott, which it claimed, was "in furtherance of a conspiracy to injure and destroy its good will, trade and business—especially to obstruct and destroy its interstate trade."[61] The lower court had dismissed the bill on grounds that the Clayton Act precluded such an injunction, but the Supreme Court, with both the Chief and Day defecting from the *Paine* majority, reversed by a vote of six to three. White assigned the opinion to Pitney, who had written the earlier opinions checking labor union activity. It was Pitney's authorship of these relatively few opinions that has led interpreters of the Court to see this Justice primarily through the lens of the work he did in this area.

Finding the company threatened with irreparable loss, Pitney said injunctive relief is appropriate when a threat is posed by the union's violation of antitrust law. What is involved here, he continued, is a secondary boycott, a combination designed "to exercise coercive pressure upon such customers, actual or prospective, in order to cause them to withhold or withdraw patronage from complainant through fear of loss or damage to themselves should they deal with it." The fact that such coercion was peaceful rather than violent, Pitney ruled, is of no legal consequence. After reading section six of the Clayton Act to condone only lawful methods not specifically condemned by the antitrust law, the Justice confined section twenty's prohibition against injunctions "to parties standing in proximate relation to a controversy." He rejected the lower court's reading of "employers" and "employees" as generic terms and restricted the statutory protection to disputes between particular employers and their employees. How and why Pitney reached such a conclusion is well revealed in the following passage:

Section 20 must be given full effect according to its terms as an expression of the purpose of Congress; but it must be borne in mind that the section imposes an exceptional and extraordinary restriction upon the equity powers of the courts of the

United States, and upon the general operation of the anti-trust laws, a restriction in the nature of a special privilege or immunity to a particular class, with corresponding detriment to the general public; and it would violate rules of statutory construction having general application and far-reaching importance to enlarge that special privilege by resorting to a loose construction of the section, not to speak of ignoring or slighting the qualifying words that are found in it.[62]

Brandeis dissented in an opinion joined by Holmes and Clarke. On the basis of common knowledge of industrial disputes and the evidence here adduced, he concluded that "the defendants and those from whom they sought cooperation have a common interest which the plaintiff threatened." In a brief survey of the industrial struggle and the hostile attitude of the courts, Brandeis said the prolabor sections in the Clayton Act were "designed to equalize before the law the position of working men and employer as industrial combatants." The Justice criticized the majority's reading of section twenty, saying that to conclude that this case did not arise out of a dispute concerning the conditions of work simply misperceived the facts. Avoiding any moral pronouncement, Brandeis found a clearly communicated decision of Congress to allow the organized forces on both sides of the industrial struggle to push their cause to the limits of self-interest. Although he recognized that a danger to the community might be posed, the Justice argued:

It is not for judges to determine whether such conditions exist, nor is it their function to set the limits of permissible contest and to declare the duties which the new situation demands. This is the function of the legislature which, while limiting individual and group rights of aggression and defense, may substitute processes of justice for the more primitive method of trial by combat.[63]

Brandeis's eloquent plea for the Court to stay its hand in the area of union-management conflict and trust Congress to resolve problems within a larger and more meaningful context made little impression upon the majority.

The *Duplex Printing Company* decision confirmed the interpretation of most of the lower federal courts to the effect that the Clayton Act had not imposed much of a bar to the granting of injunctions in labor disputes. Historians have generally concluded that Samuel Gompers had misread the prolabor provisions as "the industrial magna charta" and that judicial interpretations were consistent with both the words of the act and its legislative history.[64] Clearly, the Clayton Act did not condone a secondary boycott, but did the facts present a secondary boycott? Brandeis challenged Pitney's characterization by demonstrating that the workers involved ran the direct risk of losing the benefits they had gained through union negotiation if Duplex was able to persist in its antiunion stance. Brandeis was supported in his view that the union activity could not validly be characterized as a secondary boycott not only by Holmes and Clarke but also by the prestigious Second Circuit Court of Appeals, whose decision was reversed in *Duplex Printing Company*.

Certainly the Clayton Act had not exempted unions from the operation of antitrust law, but the conclusion that the Supreme Court simply rejected the exaggerated claims of union leaders and faithfully interpreted the law rests on a superficial reading of opinions such as *Duplex Printing Company*. That the Court majority had little sympathy with the tactics of organized labor and therefore tailored its rendering of the facts to fit the pattern of a secondary boycott seems clear.[65] This judicial approach ruled the area for over a decade until 1932 when Congress passed specific legislation severely limiting the issuance of injunctions in labor disputes.

During the recent war most labor unions demonstrated their loyalty to the American effort and moderated their conflicts with management for the duration of hostilities, but the Industrial Workers of the World (IWW), a revolutionary labor organization that had capitalized upon the failure of other unions to embrace unskilled labor, opposed the American war effort and did not hesitate to strike. Hostility to the union was fanned by a super-patriotism that led to vigilante activity. Most vigilante action, because of its nature, never became the subject of litigation, but *United States* v. *Wheeler* did bring to the Supreme Court a sordid instance of such activity.

Strikes by the IWW in the copper mines of Arizona in the summer of 1917 brought retaliatory action. The success of a vigilante group in the town of Jerome in deporting sixty-seven striking Wobblies to California may have sparked the imagination of leaders of the Citizens Protective League and officials of the copper companies in Bisbee, where a strike had been in progress for over two weeks. In the early morning of July 12, 1917, under the leadership of Sheriff Harry E. Wheeler of Cochise County, five armed bands of men swept through the workers' district, captured the workers, and confined them in the local baseball park. A special train was procured and the men were herded into boxcars for a trip to New Mexico. They were dropped at a little desolate station in Hermanas, New Mexico, and told never to return to Arizona.[66]

The rabidly antiunion *Los Angeles Times* commended the action as "a lesson that the whole of America would do well to copy," but Samuel Gompers and other labor leaders protested to the President. Wilson condemned the action taken and appointed a mediation commission to investigate the labor situation in Arizona. Although the commission eventually concluded that the deportation was illegal under both state and federal law, the leader of the vigilante group was acquitted in a state prosecution.[67] A federal indictment of twenty-five men for conspiracy to violate the rights of citizens, here the right to reside freely in Arizona, was prosecuted in the federal district court. The trial judge quashed the indictment, and Charles

Evans Hughes appeared before the High Bench asking for an affirmance of that decision. Essentially the government argued that the indictment was based upon the power of the federal government under the privileges and immunities clause.

Chief Justice White, speaking for eight members of the Court, said the constitutional clause only prevented states from discriminating in favor of their citizens to the detriment of those of other states. It did not, he continued, empower the federal government to prosecute individual wrong done by one citizen to another. If a crime has been committed, White concluded, it is an offense under state and not federal law. Even with the celebrated nature of this episode and with the failure of the state to protect the rights of its citizens, the Court pointed to the federal system as a barrier to any redress. Without opinion Clarke dissented.[68]

To gain a conviction in the *Wheeler* case, the federal government needed to overcome the Court's consistent and limited view of the privileges and immunities clause, but the task of government prosecutors seemed much easier in *United States* v. *Newberry*. The Federal Corrupt Practices Act provided that "no candidate for Senator of the United States shall give, contribute, expend, use, or promise any sum, in the aggregate, exceeding ten thousand dollars in any campaign for his nomination and election." Contesting Henry Ford for the party nomination, Truman H. Newberry was convicted for conspiring to violate the federal act by spending over $100,000 in his primary campaign. The entire Court agreed the conviction should be reversed, but only five agreed on the grounds that the law, when applied to a primary, was unconstitutional. McReynolds, for the Court, said the power given by the Constitution to regulate the manner of holding elections could not justify legislation whose "exercise would interfere with purely domestic affairs of the State and infringe upon liberties reserved to the people."[69] White and Pitney wrote concurring opinions, and the latter was joined by Brandeis and Clarke. Because Pitney and White found deficiencies in the instructions of the trial judge that had prejudiced the accused, they agreed with the reversal, but they insisted that the congressional act was constitutional. All four Justices were much disturbed by the majority's miserly interpretation of federal power in an area crucial to the functioning of the democratic process.

McReynolds's opinion in the *Newberry* case was becoming increasingly typical of his tendency to read limitations into the governing power, whether at the state or federal level. Holmes's vote gave McReynolds the majority in *Newberry*, and the senior Massachusetts Justice revealed again how inadequately his decision making is encompassed by the theory of judicial restraint. All the Justices agreed the conviction of Newberry should be reversed, and one would think that Holmes would have preferred the narrow ground for reversal that would have avoided the constitutional question, but this was not the way he voted.

Temporary government ownership of the railroads and telegraph companies occasioned a number of cases that came before the Court in the 1920 term. With McKenna, Van Devanter, Pitney, and McReynolds dissenting, the Court said a complaint against the freight tariff schedules established by the Director General of Railroads would first have to be filed with the ICC. Because of the delay this procedure involved, the decision effectively ruled against the challenge. The Court was not inclined to put a precedent on the books that would afford parties the opportunity to challenge such emergency measures by the government. This conclusion is further supported by the Court's action in refusing to hold either the government or railroad companies liable for violations of state law during the period of wartime control.[70]

With equal unanimity the Court broadly upheld the right of the government to confiscate enemy property during the war. In the Trading with the Enemy Act of October 1917, Congress delegated authority to the President to deal with enemy property. An alien property custodian was appointed with full authority of the President. In the major case of *Stoehr* v. *Wallace* the Court found sufficient power in Congress to take such action under the constitutional provision giving the legislative body the right to "make Rules concerning Captures on Land and Water." The custodian could seize such property on his belief that it was enemy owned, for provision was made for the return of the property in case of mistake.[71]

An ever-present advocate before the High Bench during the term was ex-Justice Hughes. When he argued against the assessment of an excess profits tax against his corporate client, he met defeat, as his former colleagues broadly supported the war revenue measure. Hughes, however, was successful when he urged the Court to uphold the constitutionality of the Federal Farm Loan Act of 1916. He represented a corporation defending an action by a shareholder seeking to enjoin an investment by the company in farm loan bonds. That the primary purpose of the legislation was to make loans to farmers available at low rates of interest, the Court said, does not rise to the level of a constitutional objection to clearly ordained congressional power. Even the beleaguered Detroit United Railway sought salvation in the advocacy of the vigorous former Supreme Court Justice. An earlier decision had protected the railway from confiscatory rates established after the expiration of its franchise, although the Court had recognized the city's right to dispossess the railway. The Justices simply said that if the railway was allowed to continue its service, its rates would have to yield a reasonable profit. Detroit city officials got the clear message and moved to acquire the railway. Valiantly, Hughes argued that the earlier municipal ordinances had committed the city to a course of action that precluded the contemplated drastic action and that the suggested purchase price was a deprivation of due process. Showing no sympathy for their former colleague's arguments, the Justices unanimously rejected his claims.[72] Despite the hopes of his clients, Hughes was able to work no miracles with the High Bench.

Since municipalities in the nineteenth century had often bound themselves in contracts with public service corporations that could not be broken because of the constitutional provision against the impairment of contracts, many states passed legislation limiting the contracting power of cities. This protective action backfired in two cases the Court considered. Both Iowa and Texas so limited the contracting powers of municipalities, and in each state a city had entered into a franchise agreement with a public service corporation setting certain rates for the duration of the franchise. The corporations challenged the rates as confiscatory, and the unanimous Court upheld the claim. The Justices recognized that a fully binding contract would preclude such a claim, but in both cases they found limitations upon the contracting power of the city that gave substance to the corporation's argument.[73] As in many instances where a remedy for one problem is obtained, new problems arise from the solution.

A final pair of cases near the end of the term raised the question of whether the local police power could justify action in times of emergency that the Court had found housed within the war power at the national level. The Justices considered legislation in both the District of Columbia and the state of New York allowing tenants to maintain their occupancy at the same rent after their leases ran out. In both cases the Court divided five to four in upholding the regulation.[74] With customary realism Holmes wrote for the majority in both cases. In *Block* v. *Hirsh*, the District of Columbia case that produced the major opinions, the tenant asserted that he had a right to maintain occupancy under a congressional act relating to the District passed in October 1919 to run for maximum of two years. Congress justified the legislation on the basis that the emergency produced by the war had created rental conditions in the District that endangered the public health, burdened public officials, and resulted in embarrassment to the federal government.

That emergency conditions existed, Holmes began, was "a publicly notorious and almost world-wide fact." He asserted that matters of purely private concern can become matters of public concern and clothe government with a regulatory power it would not otherwise possess. That power, the Justice continued, extends to real property and to the subject of rent as well. Noting that the legislation provides for a reasonable rent, Holmes ruled that it does no more than deprive the landlord of profiteering from crowded conditions. Stating that such governmental action is common to all civilized countries, the Justice saw no validity in the constitutional objections.[75]

McKenna wrote the dissenting opinion, joined by White, Van Devanter, and McReynolds. It was another one of those McKenna opinions, of rather recent vintage, that dealt with matters abstractly, or as he put it: "The grounds of the dissent are the explicit provisions of the Constitution of the

United States; the specifications of the grounds are the irresistible deductions from those provisions and, we think, would require no expression but for the opposition of those whose judgements challenge attention." The Justice ridiculed the justification of such a rent control law on grounds that housing is a necessity, asking whether all necessities were now to be disposed of by the government. What this law did, he claimed, was deprive the owner of his property by subjecting the contracts he had made in good faith "to the fiat of a subsequent law." In another rhetorical flight, he concluded:

Have conditions come . . . that are not amenable to passing palliatives, so that socialism, or some form of socialism, is the only permanent corrective or accommodation? It is indeed strange that this court, in effect, is called upon to make way for it and, through the instrument of a constitution based on personal rights and the purposeful encouragement of individual incentive and energy, to declare legal a power exerted for their destruction.[76]

Holmes disposed of the contentions in the New York case with as little difficulty, though here the arguments focused much more upon the contract clause. The Justice simply responded that all contracts are subject to justifiable exercises of the police power. The four dissenters protested once more, saying the Constitution's clear authority should not be weakened by "refined dialectics" or bent out of shape by claims of emergency or by impulse. Obviously agitated over the whole matter, McKenna took a direct swipe at Holmes by quoting from his dissent in *Northern Securities Company*, which cautioned against "some accident of immediate overwhelming interest which appeals to the feeling, and distorts the judgment."[77]

That the statutes involved in these cases infringed upon the preexisting obligations of contract is really quite clear, and it is this fact, coupled with Holmes's tendency to emphasize the practical and not expend time or effort in attempting to square clearly the present decisions with constitutional doctrine, that provoked the bitter dissent. The acrimony here was as great as can be found in any dissent in the annals of the Supreme Court, for the minority accused the majority not only of bad judgment but also of subverting the Constitution. Yet both Pitney and Day, who were generally sensitive to impairment of contract claims, cast the decisive votes in favor of upholding such governmental regulation.

Only the future could determine the precedential weight such decisions would have.[78] What was clear, however, was a hardening of ideological positions in the last two terms that was clearly reflected in the Justices' decision making. More and more in matters of wider social import, a number of the Justices found a lodging for their general social and economic views in abstract interpretations of the Constitution. Court opinions in the past had contained such generalized statements, but the decisions reached were not simple deductions from such principles but rather were solidly anchored in the particular fact situations presented. Rhetoric sometimes clouded this fact, but the operative principle was pragmatism, a concentration on the desirable result in the prevailing social and economic context. Although intimations of a shift to ideological decision making could be seen in earlier terms, the indications were now more pronounced. The positions of Clarke and McReynolds were illustrative of the ideological cleft on the Court. They were the leading dissenters, with sixteen and fifteen respectively, but only in one prohibition case did they agree, but even there they went their separate ways. Increasingly McReynolds, Van Devanter, White, and, more recently, McKenna voted as a block insisting upon their static view of the Constitution. In opposition were Clarke, Holmes, and Brandeis. The swing votes were those of Day and Pitney, and more often than not they were able to accommodate the exercises of governmental power under the Constitution. If Taft had been correct in predicting that the president elected in 1920 would, in effect, remake the Court, the balance that had been maintained over the last few years was precarious indeed. A Court remade in the image of McReynolds was far more likely than one remade in Clarke's.

Chief Justice White appeared to be surviving the 1920 term quite well, writing his share of opinions and being only partially hampered by a cataract condition. Rumors of retirement he met with the same rebuff that his predecessor had, but on May 13, 1921, he was rushed to a Washington hospital. The prognosis was grave, and six days later the Chief Justice died. He had served the Court for a little over twenty-seven years, the last ten and one-half as Chief. During that tenure the Court had handed down over 7,000 opinions, 10 percent of which were written by White.[79]

As Chief, White did not bring the administrative skill to the post that President Taft had expected. He did his job competently but with little of that high degree of organization and efficiency that some see as the most desired quality of a chief justice. White opposed a new building for the Court and rejected the suggestion that Justices should lobby for bills affecting the judiciary. He also tended to hold onto cases of substantial interest and delay decisions by ordering rearguments; his desire to have the case heard by a full bench or to make certain that the matters were fully aired and deliberately considered struck others as procrastination. Certainly this practice did not enhance the Court's reputation for efficiency. Despite remedial legislation designed to aid the Court in its processing of cases, the pace of decision making was relatively slow.[80]

The Chief's administrative shortcomings should not suggest that he had little influence during his tenure. In both the antitrust area and in the matter of the overseas possessions White eventually led the Court to embrace his personal point of view. In the late 1890s, as the Court began to find some meaning in the Sherman Antitrust Act, White argued in favor of reading into the law the proscription of only unreasonable restraints of trade, a position the Court accepted in 1911. In the matter of the overseas territories, White evolved the doctrine of incorporation, which afforded Congress the discretion to determine when the full range of constitutional guarantees should be extended to distant and diverse possessions, and eventually won the Court to his view.

For the first half of his tenure on the High Bench, White was quite willing to accept considerable discretion on the part of both state and federal governments. He dissented in both *Pollock* and *Lochner* and fully supported the federal quasi-police power activity of Congress under both the commerce and taxing powers. Indications of a change in White's position appeared in the 1907 term when he refused to save the first Federal Employers' Liability Act and when he decided that Congress could not ban yellow-dog contracts. Although he read the war power broadly and sustained emergency measures of the federal government, including the Adamson Act, White, after the arrival of Brandeis and Clarke, clearly aligned himself with the Justices who saw greater constitutional restriction on the range of governmental power. The arrival of Wilson's last two appointees seems to have led the Chief into a position of more direct opposition, which he was willing to support with the weight of his office. When the Court decided in *Bunting* that states could establish the workday, White dissented, as he did when the majority in *Doremus* refused to look at the effects of a federal taxing statute. Also, he was with the majority when it invalidated the federal child labor law. In his final term he dissented in the rent-control cases. White's progression then from a much more expansive view of the scope of both state and federal governmental power to one in which the Court had the duty to interpose its will on the exercise of discretion is really quite pronounced.[81]

Edward Douglas White could hardly be considered a great Chief Justice in the tradition of Marshall and Taney, but he was a man who left his imprint upon constitutional law. His death set in motion a series of events that would enable President Harding to remake the aging and ailing Court.

NOTES

1. In a study of the Court from 1910 to 1920, using social science methodology to chart attitude change, Donald C. Leavitt concluded that Brandeis and Clarke were key reference figures. Contending that Brandeis led both Holmes and Day to more "liberal" positions, Leavitt attributed White's shift to a more restrictive position to Clarke, and McKenna's to Brandeis. Both Brandeis and Clarke, the author said, were factors contributing to the staunch "conservatism" of McReynolds. (See Leavitt, "Attitude Change on the Supreme Court, 1910-1920," *Michigan Academician* 4 [Summer 1971]:55-59.)

2. Sedition Act, ch. 75, 40 Stat. 553 (1918). Only once before had the federal government imposed such a ban upon political criticism—the ill-fated Sedition Act of 1798—which had only succeeded in strengthening the Republican attack on the Federalist administration of John Adams.

3. Abrams v. United States, 250 U.S. 616 (1919).

4. Holmes wrote to Harold J. Laski saying he "greatly regretted having to write" the earlier opinions, adding that he felt that the government should never have pressed the cases (Holmes to Laski, March 16, 1919, in Mark D. Howe, ed., *Holmes-Laski Letters*, abridg. ed., 2 vols. [New York: Atheneum, 1963], 1:142). The Justice also wrote to Herbert Croly, editor of the *New Republic*, expressing similar convictions but drawing a line between constitutionality and wisdom of federal legislation limiting free speech. Personally, Holmes said, "I am for aeration of all effervescing convictions—there is no way so quick for letting them get flat" (Holmes to Croly, May 12, 1919, in ibid., 1:153).

5. Abrams v. United States, 250 U.S. 616, 628, 629 (1919).

6. Id. at 630-31. For examples of some of the praise the dissent received, see Laski to Holmes, November 12, 27, 1919, April 2, 1920, in Howe, *Holmes-Laski Letters*, 1:168, 169, 202, and the piece by Herbert Croly in *New Republic*, November 26, 1919, pp. 360-62.

7. Schaefer v. United States, 251 U.S. 466, 477, 479 (1920).

8. Id. at 482, 483, 493, 495.

9. Id. at 501.

10. Pierce v. United States, 252 U.S. 239, 273 (1920). Holmes privately said that if Justice Clarke could be persuaded to read the dissents in these free-speech cases he would join his two colleagues from Massachusetts (Holmes to Laski, March 21, 1920, in Howe, *Holmes-Laski Letters*, 1:197).

11. Silverthorne Lumber Co. v. United States, 251 U.S. 385 (1920).

12. White v. Chin Fong, 253 U.S. 90 (1920); and Kwock Jan Fat v. White, 253 U.S. 454, 464 (1920).

13. Towne v. Eisner, 245 U.S. 418, 425 (1918). The opinion also contained one of Holmes's most quoted sentences: "A word is not a crystal, transparent and unchanged; it is the skin of a living thought and may vary greatly in color and content according to the circumstances and the time in which it is used" (Id. at 425).

14. Eisner v. Macomber, 252 U.S. 189 (1920).

15. Id. at 220.

16. Evans v. Gore, 253 U.S. 245, 259 (1920).

17. Id. at 265. In *O'Malley v. Woodrough* (307 U.S. 277 [1939]) the Supreme Court overruled the *Evans* opinion and vindicated the two dissenters.

18. Shaffer v. Carter, 252 U.S. 37 (1920); Travis v. Yale & Towne Mfg. Co., 252 U.S. 60 (1920); and Maguire v. Trefry, 253 U.S. 12 (1920).

19. Green v. Frazier, 253 U.S. 233, 239, 242, 243 (1920). The Portland case is Jones v. Portland, 245 U.S. 217 (1917).

20. See South Covington & Cincinnati Street Ry. v. Covington, 235 U.S. 537 (1915).

21. South Covington & Cincinnati Street Ry. v. Kentucky, 252 U.S. 399, 404 (1920).

22. Southern Pacific Co. v. Jensen, 244 U.S. 205, 215 (1917). Congress had attempted to override the Jensen decision with the Act of October 6, 1917, ch. 97, 40 Stat. 395.

23. Knickerbocker Ice Co. v. Stewart, 253 U.S. 149, 160, 166 (1920).

24. Missouri v. Holland, 252 U.S. 416, 433 (1920).

25. United States v. Shauver, 214 Fed. 154 (1914), and United States v. McCullagh, 221 Fed. 288 (1915); and Migratory Bird Treaty Act, ch. 128, 40 Stat. 755 (1918).

26. Missouri v. Holland, 252 U.S. 416, 433, 435 (1920).

27. Board of Public Utility Commissioners v. Ynchausti & Co., 251 U.S. 401, 406-7 (1920).

28. See, for instance, Spiller v. Atchison, Topeka & Santa Fe Ry., 253 U.S. 117 (1920); and FTC v. Gratz, 253 U.S. 421 (1920).

29. FTC v. Gratz, 253 U.S. 421, 427, 428-29 (1920).

30. Alpheus T. Mason, *Brandeis: A Free Man's Life* (New York: Viking Press, 1946), pp. 402-4, 405-6. Actually, the Federal Trade Commission was not very active; its members were closely identified with the businesses regulated (Paul M. Murphy, *The Constitution in Crisis Times 1918-1969*, New American Nation Series [New York: Harper & Row, Torchbooks, 1972], p. 35).

31. United States v. United States Steel Corp., 251 U.S. 417, 451 (1920).

32. Id. at 460, 466.

33. Hamilton v. Kentucky Distilleries & Warehouse Co., 251 U.S. 146 (1919); United States v. Standard Brewery, 251 U.S. 210 (1920); and Ruppert v. Caffey, 251 U.S. 264 (1920).

34. Ruppert v. Caffey, 251 U.S. 264, 282, 304-5, 310 (1920).

35. United States v. Simpson, 252 U.S. 465, 468 (1920).

36. Hawke v. Smith, 253 U.S. 221, 231, 227 (1920). Although there is a difference between legislating and ratifying a federal constitution amendment, those functions are placed in the same body and surely are subject to the same direction from the people. The circumvention before 1913 of the constitutional requirement that Senators be elected by state legislatures casts further doubt on the Court's resolution here. Before the Seventeenth Amendment became part of the Constitution, most of the states had made a popular vote binding upon the state legislature in its choice of Senators. According to Day's definition this function could not be considered a legislative one either, but it was an accepted practice that was not challenged as unconstitutional.

37. National Prohibition Cases, 253 U.S. 350, 386-87 (1920).

38. Id. at 392.

39. Id. at 393.

40. Id. at 408.

41. Id. at 410, 411.

42. Hoyt L. Warner, *The Life of Mr. Justice Clarke* (Cleveland: Western Reserve University Press, 1959), pp. 59-60, 65-66, 75; Mason, *Brandeis*, pp. 402, 405, 455-56, 537; and Henry J. Abraham, *Justices and Presidents: A Political History of Appointments to the Supreme Court* (New York: Oxford University Press, 1974), pp. 166-67.

43. Alpheus T. Mason, *William Howard Taft: Chief Justice* (New York: Simon & Schuster, 1965), p. 160. Taft had been horrified in 1896 when the Democratic presidential contender, William Jennings Bryan, had brought the Supreme Court into the political fray by suggesting that the voters could alter the High Bench's composition by electing the right man president, but here in 1920 Taft was making the same argument (p. 158).

44. Mason, *William Howard Taft*, pp. 76-77.

45. U.S., Congress, House, *Proposed Amendments to the Constitution*. House Doc. 551, 70th Cong., 2d sess., 1928 (Washington: Government Printing Office, 1929), pp. 246-53.

46. See Alan P. Grimes, *The Puritan Ethic and Woman Suffrage* (New York: Oxford University Press, 1967).

47. Women later would claim their sisters had placed too much emphasis on the suffrage to the detriment of other goals seeking the equal rights of the sexes. Yet as early as 1923 the first proposal for an equal rights amendment was introduced in Congress. As with other ultimately successful amendment proposals, such resolutions would have to multiply before Congress gave the matter serious consideration. The Equal Rights Amendment was finally passed by Congress and sent to the states for ratification in 1972.

48. United States v. Cohen Grocery Co., 255 U.S. 81, 88, 87, 96 (1921); and Weeds, Inc. v. United States, 255 U.S. 109 (1921). The related cases follow *Cohen Grocery* in the official reports and are all decided upon the authority of the major case.

49. Berger v. United States, 255 U.S. 22, 28 (1921).

50. Sec. 21 of Judicial Code, ch. 231, 36 Stat. 1087, 1090 (1911); and Berger v. United States, 255 U.S. 22, 35, 43 (1921).

51. Gould v. United States, 255 U.S. 298, 304, 309 (1921). In 1967 the Court in *Warden v. Hayden* (387 U.S. 294) narrowed the protection afforded by the *Gould* case, saying that evidence proving a crime had been committed was subject to legitimate seizure.

52. Burdeau v. McDowell, 256 U.S. 465, 477 (1921).

53. Espionage Act, ch. 30, 40 Stat. 217, 230 (1917); and United States *ex rel.* Milwaukee Social Democratic Publishing Co. v. Burleson, 255 U.S. 407, 414 (1921).

54. United States *ex rel.* Milwaukee Social Democratic Publishing Co. v. Burleson, 255 U.S. 407, 417, 423, 436 (1921).

55. Id. at 438.

56. Gilbert v. Minnesota, 254 U.S. 325, 327 (1920). Eleven states and territories had supplemented the federal legislation with harsh sedition statutes of their own. (See Zechariah Chafee, Jr., *Free Speech in the United States* [New York: Atheneum, 1969], pp. 100-2, 285-90).

57. Gilbert v. Minnesota, 254 U.S. 325, 329, 333 (1920).

58. Id. at 343.

59. See Gitlow v. New York, 268 U.S. 652 (1925).

60. Niles-Bement-Pond Co. v. Iron Moulders Union, 254 U.S. 77 (1920) (Pitney and McReynolds dissenting); Paine Lumber Co. v. Neal, 244 U.S. 459 (1917); and Duplex Printing Press Co. v. Deering, 254 U.S. 443 (1921).

61. Duplex Printing Press Co. v. Deering, 254 U.S. 443, 460 (1921).

62. Id. at 466, 471-72. For the pertinent portions of the statute, see *Clayton Antitrust Act* (ch. 323, 38 Stat. 730, 731, 738 [1914]).

63. Duplex Printing Press Co. v. Deering, 254 U.S. 443, 482-83, 484, 488 (1921).

64. Samuel Gompers, "The Charter of Industrial Freedom," *American Federationist* 21 (November 1914):971; and see Arthur S. Link, *Wilson: The New Freedom* (Princeton: Princeton University Press, 1956), pp. 427-33.

65. For analysis of the prolabor sections of the Clayton Act and their judicial interpretation, see Felix Frankfurter and Nathan Greene, *The Labor Injunction* (New York: Macmillan Co., 1930), pp. 157-76.

66. United States v. Wheeler, 254 U.S. 281 (1921); and H.C. Peterson and Gilbert C. Fite, *Opponents of War 1917-1918* (Madison: University of Wisconsin Press, 1957), pp. 52-54.

67. Peterson and Fite, *Opponents of War*, pp. 54-55.

68. United States v. Wheeler, 254 U.S. 281 (1920).

69. Federal Corrupt Practices Act, ch. 392, 36 Stat. 822 (1910), *as amended*, ch. 33, 37 Stat. 25, 28 (1911); and Newberry v. United States, 256 U.S. 232, 258 (1921). *United States v. Classic* (313 U.S. 299 [1941]) in effect overrruled the *Newberry* precedent.

70. Director General of Railroads v. Viscose Co., 254 U.S. 498 (1921); and Missouri Pacific R.R. v. Ault, 256 U.S. 554 (1921), and Western Union Telegraph Co. v. Poston, 256 U.S. 662 (1921).

71. U.S. Const. art. I, sec. 8; and Stoehr v. Wallace, 255 U.S. 239 (1921).

72. La Belle Iron Works v. United States, 256 U.S. 377 (1921); Smith v. Kansas City Title & Trust Co., 255 U.S. 180 (1921); and Detroit United Ry. v. Detroit, 255 U.S. 171 (1921). The earlier case is Detroit United Ry. v. Detroit, 248 U.S. 429 (1919).

73. Southern Iowa Electric Co. v. Chariton, 255 U.S. 539 (1921); and San Antonio v. San Antonio Public Service Co. 255 U.S. 547 (1921).

74. Block v. Hirsch, 256 U.S. 135 (1921); and Brown Holding Co. v. Feldman, 256 U.S. 170 (1921).

75. Block v. Hirsh, 256 U.S. 135, 154 (1921).

76. Id. at 159, 161, 162-63.

77. Brown Holding Co. v. Feldman, 256 U.S. 170, 201 (1921).

78. An attempt to extend the period of rent control in the District of Columbia into 1924 was held invalid by the Court in an opinion by Holmes on the basis that the emergency that had earlier sustained the legislation no longer existed. Brandeis concurred in the disposition of the case, but he preferred to withhold judgment on the basic legislation until the facts were more clearly developed. (See Chasleton Corp. v. Sinclair, 264 U.S. 543 [1924]).

79. Mason, *William Howard Taft*, pp. 79-80; and memorial proceeding in 257 U.S. xv.

80. Mason, *William Howard Taft*, pp. 136-37, 194, 196.

81. White's biographer, Sister Marie Carolyn Klinkhamer, has argued that the Chief Justice's legal philosophy was really quite unified and consistent. (See Klinkhamer, *Edward Douglas White: Chief Justice of the United States* [Washington: Catholic University Press, 1943], pp. 28-31, and "The Legal Philosophy of Edward Douglas White," *University of Detroit Law Journal* 35 [December 1957]:197-99.)

EPILOGUE

With Warren G. Harding's smashing victory in 1920, the ever-present suitor for the center seat on the Court, William Howard Taft, now sixty-three, was elated. To head off any possibility that the President-elect was considering him for an Associate Justice's position, Taft informed Harding that he was available only for the top spot. Hopeful that Chief Justice White would anticipate Harding's inauguration with a retirement announcement, Taft began to worry when mid-March arrived with no such word. When White died two months later Taft's hopes for a quick announcement of his succession were scuttled by Harding's vacillation.[1]

The President had promised a seat on the Court to the former Senator from Utah, George Sutherland, and although Harding seemed willing to give the center seat to Taft, only a single vacancy existed. The former President joined in a campaign to provide a second seat by suggesting that Holmes might find retirement more attractive with an appointment to the Disarmament Commission in London, but this approach met with no success. Feelers sent out to Day and McKenna produced the same response. Attorney General Harry M. Daugherty used his significant leverage with Harding and pressed for a decision on the Taft appointment before July. With the hope of prying a sitting Justice loose fading, the President faced the inevitable. Placing Sutherland on the Shipping Board for an interim period, Harding sent Taft's nomination to the Senate on June 30, 1921. Confirmation came immediately, as only four renegade Republicans voted against the appointee. On July 11, 1921, William Howard Taft became the ninth man to be confirmed as Chief Justice.[2]

For years Taft had been contemplating the chief justiceship. He conceived of the role more in terms of administrative than of ideological leadership. What was needed was a judicial tribunal that spoke authoritatively with as little dissent as possible. Since the Court took far too much time to get to the cases on its docket, some streamlining was essential to promote the efficiency that the "solid people" of the country had a right to expect from their highest court. Also the Justices should be afforded greater discretion in determining what cases they would hear so their time could be spent on matters truly worthy of their stature within the judicial system. Finally, the Court should be housed in a building of its own—a physical representation of the grandeur and significance of this third branch of the federal government. William Howard Taft would serve in his cherished post for less than a decade; yet in that relatively short time he achieved the administrative goals he had set, owing chiefly to his dedication to them and his willingness to become a prime lobbyist for the judiciary.[3]

Despite Taft's deliberate attempt to win the favor of the sitting Justices, he was unable to reduce the level of dissent during his first term. Earlier the new Chief had established contact with Brandeis, who was man enough to put Taft's vehement opposition to his appointment behind them both. As Chief Justice, Taft quickly developed respect for his former adversary, both because of the quality of Brandeis's mind and his dedication to the work of the Court. The two men, though often in disagreement, were able to establish a good working relationship. The Chief's strong desire to hold down dissent had some effect on Brandeis, who earlier had recognized the tactical advantages of suppressing some of his disagreement with the majority. Although courteous and friendly to the Court's elder statesmen, Holmes and McKenna, Taft thought they should retire. He said Holmes's presence on the Court effectively gave Brandeis two votes. The senior Massachusetts Justice was plagued by asthma and prostate gland trouble in 1922, but the old man snapped back with considerable vigor. McKenna's case was different. At age seventy-eight during Taft's first term, the Californian showed a tendency to wander and lose his train of thought, a problem that worsened as the terms went by. Taft sought McKenna's resignation, but the Justice held on in the belief that Holmes should be the first to go. When invited to join a delegation of Justices calling upon McKenna to urge retirement, Holmes refused to be pressed into such compromising service.[4]

Day, always frail and prone to some ailment, had the grippe in the spring of 1922, and Taft refused to assign him any cases. Initially expecting more of Pitney, Taft also struck him from the list of opinion writers when the New Jersey Justice late in the 1921 term suffered from a nervous disorder. Van Devanter was still opinion shy, and the new Chief had no more success than his predecessor in extracting from the Westerner his fair share of opinions. McReynolds was quite healthy but just as irritating to Taft as he was to the other Justices. The Chief called his colleague lazy and "too stiff-necked and too rambunctious" and said "we ought not to have too many men on the Court who are as reactionary on the subject of the Constitution as McReynolds." Clarke, the most junior Associate, was restless. Disturbed by the fact he and Brandeis, so close in their first two terms, now saw important matters differently and plagued by a feeling that his work was unrewarding, as well as by the continued badgering of McReynolds, he considered resigning. Taft was critical of Clarke's decision making, which the Chief believed was more reflective of a legislative, rather than of a judicial, frame of mind.[5]

With the close of Taft's first term on the Court the judicial careers of Clarke, Day, and Pitney came to an end. During the summer Clarke, after six terms on the High Bench, opted for retirement. He had decided to leave the burden of judicial service and devote his remaining years working to realize the Wilsonian dream of American membership in the League of Nations. Clarke believed a peaceful future hinged on American acceptance of international responsibility. Hearing news of the resignation, Woodrow Wilson sent the Justice a note lamenting his departure from the High Bench. The former President said he had been counting upon Clarke and Brandeis "to restrain the Court in some measure from the extreme reactionary course which it seems inclined to follow." Wilson was troubled by his vision of a near future in which "the courts will more and more outrage the common people's sense of justice and cause a revulsion against judicial authority which may seriously disturb the equilibrium of our institutions." Denying that his presence could modify the growing conservatism of the Court, Clarke detailed the concerns that had led him to leave "a deplorable and harassing" situation. McReynolds responded to the resignation with a final gesture of contempt when he refused to sign the Court's formal letter of regret.[6]

Clarke's resignation was shortly followed by the resignations of Day and Pitney. William R. Day, whose frail constitution had endured almost twenty years of service on the High Court, was the next to leave. His illness in the previous term, from which he had not fully recovered, left him temperamentally, if not physically, unable to face another heavy load of cases. He decided to retire with the coming of the 1922 term, and within a year he was dead. Mahlon Pitney suffered a stroke in August 1922 that left him physically and mentally incapacitated after ten years on the Court. His formal departure from the High Bench came on the last day of the year, though he survived almost two years longer.

When Clarke resigned in September 1922 President Harding acted immediately to fulfill his promise to George Sutherland. The Senate honored its former colleague by approving the nomination on the day of its receipt. Harding and Sutherland had been close since their days in the Senate, and the man from Utah had been an advisor to his former colleague in the recent campaign. The new appointee had no prior judicial experience, but he had a great deal of governmental experience at both the state and federal level and was regarded as an expert on constitutional law. Sutherland's appointment delighted Taft, who shared with the ex-Senator a similar judicial philosophy.[7] Because of his intellect and energy, Sutherland would emerge as the ideological leader of the remade Court. He took his seat at the outset of the 1922 term.

Harding had needed no help with the Sutherland nomination, but shortly after his own confirmation Taft had offered his services to the administration as an advisor on judicial appointments and related matters. With a shrewd understanding of the politics involved, the Chief, with the eager support of Attorney General Daugherty, undertook a unique advisory role to the administration. Taft's influence was clearly revealed in the choice of Day's successor. With what he hoped was the imminent retirement of the only Roman Catholic on the Court, McKenna, the Chief suggested that an appointee of the same religious persuasion made good sense. Also, he believed, in conformance with his actions as President, that candidates of the opposing political party should be considered for the Court, in part to avoid the criticism of packing the High Bench. For these reasons, buttressed by a personal respect for the man and his "sound" philosophy, Taft selected Pierce Butler, a little-known Minnesota attorney whose practice in the corporate field had earlier brought him before the Court. At times personally directing Butler's candidacy, Taft fed information to the White House that undermined other candidates and accentuated the availability of Butler. Mobilizing support from the Catholic hierarchy and from the Middle West, Taft made Butler an all but irresistible choice. The nomination caused some controversy, sparked by claims of Butler's unfitness and by protests that the Court was being staffed with men hostile to change, but the Senate approved the choice by a vote of sixty-one to eight. Butler was sworn in on January 2, 1923.[8]

On the matter of Pitney's replacement, Taft seemed to have exercised little direct influence, though he heartily approved of a nominee with prior judicial experience, which neither Sutherland nor Butler had had. Furthermore, the Chief liked the idea of recognizing merit through the elevation of lower federal court judges. The Court had no Southern representative since the death of White, and Tennessee, which had delivered its electoral vote to Harding, appeared to be good hunting ground. Daugherty suggested Edward Terry Sanford, who had been a federal district judge in the state since 1908. Since Sanford had considerable support among Republicans, Tennessee Democrats, and the very labor leaders who had found Pitney so objectionable, the nomination encountered no difficulty in the Senate. The new Justice took his seat late in January 1923.[9]

The replacement of White by Taft probably made little difference in the makeup of the Court, but the loss of Clarke, Day, and Pitney was most significant. From today's perspective Clarke, with the exception of his insensitivity to the free speech issue, was the Court's most consistent "liberal." The fact that he dissented fifteen times during his last term of service tends to support his estimate of the drift of the Court. In that final term Clarke protested the Court's invalidation of the second federal child labor law, and Pitney agreed with him in dissent when Clarke would have found sufficient power for Arizona to prohibit the issuance of injunctions to stop picketing or boycotts in labor disputes.[10] Pitney had been the most consistent supporter of congressional policy as detailed in the Interstate Commerce Act, with its various amendments, and in the antitrust law. But all three Justices—Clarke, Day, and Pitney—were more sympathetic than their colleagues to government prosecutions under the antitrust law and were willing to allow states greater latitude in dealing with corporations, whether such regulation was attacked on federal preemption or due process grounds. They also consistently supported workmen's compensation laws and were less inclined to accept common law defenses in suits by injured employees. Finally, their votes were essential to sustaining the authority of local government to establish rent and occupancy controls during periods of emergency. The replacement of Clarke, Day, and Pitney would increase opposition to many of the rulings that they helped write into the law and lessen or eliminate the disagreement they had expressed.

During the 1922 term, when the vacated seats were filled by Harding's appointees, the rate of dissent was halved from that of the previous term. Sutherland, who had filled Clarke's seat, also succeeded to the role of leading dissenter, though from the opposite position—that the Court was too permissive, not too restrictive. In the last few terms of the Court under Chief Justice White, we have noted the sporadic presence of a majority less receptive to new exercises of state and federal power; the Harding appointments now consolidated that majority.

Although the record of the Court of the 1920s, with Harlan Fiske Stone replacing McKenna in 1925 and providing some support for Brandeis and Holmes, should not be treated simplistically, evidence of a new hostility to government exertion is abundant. When recent precedents could be exploited they were eagerly grasped by the new majority to write some new constitutional law. *Hammer* was ideal for this purpose, for in that decision the Court had interposed the Tenth Amendment as a limitation on the federal commerce power. In 1919 the Court had refused to read that amendment as a check upon the federal taxing power, but the reconstituted High Bench felt differently. In 1922 the Court invalidated the Child Labor Tax Act, widening the reach of the Tenth Amendment by ignoring consistent precedent that had held the purposes and effects of an otherwise legitimate federal tax were constitutionally irrelevant.[11]

Much recent precedent, however, not only failed to provide a wedge for the new majority's views but also was hostile to the results sought. Still, the majority did not have to construct its new restrictive readings from whole cloth, for the Justices could piece together remnants, no matter how threadbare and unfashionable they had become, drawn from older cases. This judicial tendency to conceal innovation by citing earlier decisions should not lead to the conclusion that equally creditable lines of precedent were available or that the sins of the Court of the 1920s should be visited upon its predecessors. Such conclusions ignore the qualitative change that took place in Supreme Court decision making in the 1920s. For instance, even Chief Justice Taft balked when the majority resuscitated *Lochner* as the basis for its invalidation of a minimum-wage law for women in the District of Columbia.[12]

Admittedly the Court of the previous generation had developed the due process clause as a potential check upon the arbitrariness of state and local action, but it increasingly presumed the reasonableness of governmental action and consistently refused to place any business beyond the pale of regulation. That the remade Court was willing to change the ground rules became clear in 1923.[13] In the following year the new majority found a state law regulating the weight of bread an interference with private business and therefore a violation of due process. Although the majority noted a unanimous decision in 1913 to the contrary, it expended no effort in trying to distinguish the two cases. Then in 1927 the Court invalidated a New York law regulating the resale of theatre tickets, ruling that such a business was not one affected with a public interest.[14] Advocates before the Court had long argued that *Munn* v. *Illinois* had implied the existence of a category of business that was immune from governmental regulation, but only in the mid-twenties, almost fifty years after that decision, did the argument succeed with the High Bench.

Perhaps more than anything else this tendency of the Court of the 1920s to exploit distinctions and language found in earlier opinions, which the High Bench of the preceding generation had chosen wisely to ignore, and to use as precedents decisions that were bitterly attacked at the time of their issuance gave credence to the contention that the period from the depression of the 1890s to that of the 1930s could be interpreted meaningfully as a whole. The two dozen or so decisions beginning with *E. C. Knight* and extending through *Hammer* excited contemporary opposition and gained a notoriety that attracted historical attention. When the Court of the 1920s built upon such precedents to extend the reach of their questionable doctrines, this tendency seemed to confirm the importance of the earlier opinions and justify a focus upon them as characteristic of the Court's decision making in the preceding generation. By providing such a lens through which the 1890 to 1920 period could be viewed, the Court of the 1920s gave a dwarfed and misleading reading of its predecessor's work.

This qualitative shift in the Court's decision making had substantial quantitative implications that belied the predictions of informed observers who had been sounding the death knell for the due process clause as a judicially imposed restriction on state action.[15] From the 1870s, when the Fourteenth Amendment's due process clause first became a subject of litigation to 1921, the Court had invalidated only thirteen state and local acts in the 195 due process cases presented, less than 7 percent. Votes by Justices against the constitutionality of such legislation had not exceeded 10 percent, but from 1921 through 1926 such votes climbed to over 30 percent. In considering 53 cases over these five years in which a due process challenge was mounted, the Court found 15 valid claims or 28 percent of the total—a fourfold increase in the ratio of the preceding half-century. That this new activity heralded a new era in the Court's history was confirmed by Felix Frankfurter, a noted constitutional scholar and future Justice, who, writing in 1930, concluded that in the last decade the High Bench had resurrected antiquated views to overturn more legislation that the Court had invalidated in the previous half century.[16]

Initially, the Court's new activity engendered congressional protest. In the period from 1898 through 1921 six bills had been introduced in Congress seeking to curb the power of the Court, either through limiting its review authority or in requiring more than a simple majority to invalidate legislation, but in the two years from 1922 to 1924, eleven such bills were introduced. Apparently the Court had reflected the changes in the society better than Congress, for the Justices continued to hand down similar decisions after 1924 but with little congressional protest. In the period from 1925 to 1934 only two bills seeking to check the power of the Court were introduced in Congress.[17]

With the election of Harding and the change in personnel, the Court, often building upon the views of Van Devanter, McReynolds, Sutherland, and Butler,[18] tended to view its primary function in inhibitory terms. With this tendency, however, came a new willingness to see the due process clause as protective of more than property rights. An anticipation of this development can be seen in certain opinions of Field, Harlan, Brewer, Hughes, and Brandeis. Throughout these pages the writer has suggested that the interpretation of due process as a substantive limitation on state action concerning property interests may be seen as an evolutionary step in the direction of the Court's reading that clause to embrace other rights. Not long after his arrival and with unabating vigor over his tenure, Harlan argued that the first section of the Fourteenth Amendment made the entire Bill of Rights binding upon the states. He made no headway with his colleagues, but when they accepted the due process clause as a protection of property, they opened the door to a broader interpretation of the check the amendment imposed upon state action. Property is only one of a trio of attributes protected from deprivation by the states; the other two are life and liberty, both potential heirs to an expansive reading of the amendment. In 1920 a majority of the Court had suggested that one of the protections afforded by the Bill of Rights might be deemed so fundamental it might be interposed against state action.

Picking up this suggestion, the Court of the 1920s and 1930s, using the due process clause of the Fourteenth Amendment, determined that certain provisions in the Bill of Rights now also limited state governments. The first step on this long road leading into the 1960s was taken in 1925 when the Court ruled that the free speech guarantee limited state action; two years later the Justices invalidated the application of a state law on this ground. Over the next decade the Court found binding upon the states the guarantee of a free press, the right to counsel, and the right to assemble and the protection of religious freedom. In addition, the Court invalidated a black man's conviction for rape on grounds that members of his race were not tapped for jury service, despite the absence of any bar to such service in the controlling statute. In 1937 the Court sought to sum up its recent work, indicating that protection would be afforded against state action when the individual right invaded constituted part of the "essence of a scheme of ordered liberty" and was rooted in basic principles of justice.[19] This language became the springboard for further extensions of the Bill of Rights in the years ahead.

So the Court remade in the early 1920s was embarking upon twin paths. The first path, characterized by finding new limitations on governmental attempts to deal with real and pressing economic problems, came to an abrupt end with the showdown between Franklin D. Roosevelt and the Court in 1937. This dead end forced the Court more clearly onto the second path, characterized by the Justices discovering rights that must be afforded the individual by all government within a democratic society. Slowly, and at first hesitantly, the Court emerged over the next generation as a protector of the claims of the dispossessed.

No matter what its course over the immediate future, the Supreme Court in the 1890 to 1920 period found its primary task in responding to the invitation to sanctify under the Constitution new exertions of government at all levels. Whether completely consciously or not, the Justices forged constitutional doctrine that modernized the fundamental law and made it workable in the complex world of the twentieth century. The precedents created might be limited or distinguished, as they were in the 1920s and early 1930s, but they made up a body of constitutional law that could not long be ignored.

When the Justices erred in their decisions, as they did, a critique of their work often was initiated internally by one or more dissenting colleagues. Spread on the public record, then, was a dialogue that escaped the confines of the conference room to lend itself to reevaluation over time. When the majority during this generation did not solidly lay the foundation of modern constitutional law, certain Justices suggested the ways in which such foundations could be constructed.

If the approach of courts to the task of applying the law can be characterized as formalistic or mechanistic during the 1890 to 1920 period, as both contemporary legal critics and historians have suggested, the Supreme Court is a decided exception.[20] Repeatedly, the author has called the Court's decision making pragmatic, that is, attuned to law's use as an instrument for the effectuation of certain ends. A formalistic approach, on the other hand, draws deductions from fixed principles or from precedent, heedless of the result dictated by the process. Confusion in characterizing the work of courts can stem from concentrating on the rhetoric of the reasoning to the neglect of the result actually reached, for some formalism is an integral part of our cultural conception of law. In fact, constitutional adjudication necessitates some formalistic reasoning, for the Justices are called upon to justify their decisions in terms of the Constitution. Within the broad phrases of the fundamental law there is much room for differing interpretations, not only of the phrases themselves but also of their applicability to different fact situations. But the crucial question must always be whether formalistic rhetoric substantially hinders the adaptation of that law to the needs of society. Less concerned with belaboring the Court's reasoning, this study has focused on results. From this perspective the overwhelming body of the Court's work was responsive to the practical realities facing the society it served.

In responding to the litigation in the period from 1890 to 1920, the Justices accommodated the new exertions of the power of a federal government seeking national solutions to national problems. In the commerce clause primarily, but also within the taxing provision, the Court found a reservoir of power that enabled Congress to reach matters long considered to be the exclusive preserve of the states and to legislate on the basis of a recognition of the interconnectedness of the national economy. The setbacks the Court delivered to Congress in *Adair* and *Hammer*, on the subjects of yellow-dog contracts and child labor respectively, were exceptions to the commerce clause doctrine developed by the Court during the period. Such inconsistencies could not really weather the test of time. The argument, first accepted in 1918 in *Hammer* v. *Dagenhart*, that the Tenth Amendment's reservation of undelegated power to the states or the people imposed a substantive limitation on the exercise of authority by Congress had, up to that time, been consistently rejected by the Court.[21] Repeatedly the High Bench had said that, if power resides in Congress under the Constitution, there can be no objection to its exercise on grounds it had internal effects on state policy. As with a number of the latter cases in the period, *Hammer* is anticipatory of the Court of the 1920s and 1930s rather than reflective of its work in the earlier generation. The only roughly analogous case that can be found within the period, though the Tenth Amendment was not mentioned, was *E.C. Knight* in 1895. But the Court's decision there that manufacture was not commerce and hence could not be reached by Congress was weakened by later decisions in the antitrust area. Under the commerce power the Justices approved a host of regulatory measures, including the prohibition of interstate transportation of lottery tickets and of women for immoral purposes. The power, the majority concluded, even encompassed the temporary setting of wages in the Adamson Act.

Also the taxing power of the federal government was construed broadly. Its quasi-police power potential was approved by the Court in instances of margarine and drug regulation. The 1895 decision against the validity of an income tax was overcome by the Sixteenth Amendment in 1913, though the Court, independent of the change in fundamental law, seemed to be approaching a similar conclusion.

Finally, American participation in World War I forced the Court to consider the dimensions of the war power, and its exploration resulted in a broad reading that found little limitation on the type of action that could be taken in support of the war effort. The Justices even deferred to the administration on the question of when the exercise of the war power was no longer needed.

That Court decisions do not always please Congress is to be expected within our governmental system, but most often during this generation the Justices, by anchoring their decisions in statutory interpretation, gave the legislative branch the opportunity to change prospectively the Court's readings. In numerous instances Congress so acted. The self-created Court rule that congressional silence after a judicial determination indicates acquiescence in the interpretation often has a hollow ring, but the many occasions on which the legislative branch did respond with corrective measures indicates that the general rule is not without some validity. Such legislative changes necessitated by a too restrictive judicial reading were numerous, but the process is perhaps best illustrated by amendments to the Interstate Commerce Act of 1887. This new administrative agency was a strange creature in terms of the country's long devotion to the separation of powers concept, and the Court greeted it with suspicion, finding no authority in the commission unless it was clearly specified in the legislation. When this was done through precise amendments to the basic act, the High Bench interposed no obstacles.

As long as the Justices interpret statutes and not the Constitution, Congress has this revisory power, but this does not mean that its exercise is always politically possible. For instance, the Court's interpretation of the Mann Act clearly diverged from the legislation's white slave focus, but despite some protest both on the Court and in Congress, the majority of the legislators preferred to avoid the issue of sexual immorality for fear of offending their constituents. Also, in the antitrust area the Court first concluded that all restraints of trade were unlawful under the Sherman Act and then changed its mind in favor of the prohibition only of undue or unreasonable restraints. After both interpretations pleas were made in Congress to alter the judicial reading, and although the subject matter appeared less incendiary than sexual immorality, the people's representatives were content to let the Court rule the area. When the Justices etched their own path in the law, they often did so in default of congressional action and not because of any limitation imposed upon the legislative power.

Within the dimensions of the federal system the Court during the period tended to accommodate the exertions of state and local authority as it had federal power. In the formation of the Constitution limitations were imposed upon the states in favor of the new federal government, the law of which was declared to be supreme. From the beginning of the Court's existence one of its primary tasks was to demarcate the boundaries of state and federal authority. During the 1890 to 1920 period the Justices continued to perform this function, and with increasing federal legislation moving into new areas, further limitations were imposed upon state power. In these areas of conflict between state and federal authority opinions could differ on whether a conflict truly existed, but no dispute was possible over the supremacy of federal law. Especially in the area of interstate commerce, where Congress was quite active, the Court saw more and more matters preempted by new legislation, and, at times, the silence of Congress was interpreted to mean that the channels of commerce should go unregulated. But narrowly drawn statutes seeking to protect the state's interest were most often approved.

Before 1868, when the Fourteenth Amendment was added to the Constitution, no generalized check, except for the supremacy clause, was imposed upon the exertion of state power. The amendment's broad wording prohibiting states from abridging the privileges and immunities of citizens and from denying any person the equal protection of the law, or life, liberty, or property without due process of law granted substantial new supervisory authority to the federal government. The extent of this centralization of power and what it encompassed spawned litigation that continues to the present. Initially in the 1870s the Court, by reading the privileges and immunities section so narrowly as to deprive it of any substantial meaning, seemed to drain the amendment of its revolutionary potential. But the due process clause remained vital, and litigation challenged the Court to supervise state action under this mandate.

Much has been said in constitutional commentary about how the Court came to view due process in substantive rather than procedural terms and how the Court invalidated procedurally regular actions on the ground that the state had impermissibly deprived a person, either natural or artificial, of his property. The Fourteenth Amendment had limited state action; the Court in the 1890s assumed authority under the amendment to review state action in terms of whether that action was a reasonable exercise of state or local police power. In the decade they found a deprivation of due process when a state denied a fair return on property and when it unjustifiably abridged the individual's freedom to contract. Critics generalized from the cases decided on these grounds and pictured a Court, hostile to the need for new and vigorous governmental action, which substituted its own judgment for that of popularly elected legislatures. Holmes's dissent in *Lochner*, accusing the majority of reading the Constitution with an economic philosophy out of touch with the times, struck a responsive chord in the generation. But how typical was *Lochner* of the Court's reaction to exertions of state power?

Even when substantive due process was read into the Fourteenth Amendment, the new doctrine had to run the gauntlet of the well-established police power. That the Justices would have to exercise their judgment when these doctrines conflicted is clear, but equally so is the fact that due process, though repeatedly argued, won relatively few victories. Throughout the period 1890-1920 the Court did indeed pass judgment on whether state action resulted in the confiscation of property, but few practical inhibitions were placed on the range of the police power. In no instance during this generation did the Court rule that any business was beyond the regulatory power of the states, and only late in the era did a majority decide that the power to regulate did not encompass the authority to prohibit a lawful business. Even North Dakota's venture into competing state-owned businesses was unanimously approved. The ruling in *Lochner* that the state could not regulate the workday was, in effect, overruled a dozen years later. Like the federal government, the state could not outlaw yellow-dog contracts under its police power, but one is hard pressed to find other such unqualified prohibitions imposed by the Court during the period.

In conformity with its restrained use of the Fourteenth Amendment to check state action, the Court rejected Harlan's attempt to extend the amendment's range to make the Bill of Rights binding upon the states. Why Harlan's interpretation, the result of which has now been almost completely accepted, was resisted during the generation stretching from 1890 to 1920 can only be understood within the context of the times. During this period government at all levels sought to cope with the problems of an industrialized society, and since vigorous government then posed the primary threat to property interests, courts were drawn by the insistent stream of litigation into the task of adjudicating disputes between government and the property right. A balance would have to be struck, and the fear of those who advocated a greater role for government was that courts would enshrine the property interest and block the enactment of legislation designed to serve the public. In suggesting that state and local government be further limited, Harlan seemed to be fighting a battle ahead of its time, before the threat expanded government posed to other individual rights could be fully recognized and appreciated and before such cases could be generated in sufficient numbers to engage the Court's attention.

While Harlan wanted to lead the Court on a crusade to free the black man from his inferior status and to guarantee to the individual certain rights against the power of government at all levels, his colleagues were content to work within the boundaries of the prevailing consensus. Time has worked in favor of Harlan's views, but this fact should not hinder our understanding of how the Court from 1890 to 1920, for the most part, reflected well the society it served.

The one area of traditional criticism that is justified in the period is the allegation of the Court's hostility to union activity. Sometimes this charge has been broadened to include a hostility to the workingman, but except for *Lochner* and *Hammer* the Court consistently upheld legislation aiding the laborer. Even the Arizona scheme of compensating industrial accident victims, which so revolutionized the common law, gained the sanction of a majority of the High Bench. So it was not this type of remedial legislation that incurred the Court's censure, but only laws that encouraged unionism. Except for its approval of the sweeping injunction against Debs in the Pullman strike, the Justices considered few cases in the early period dealing with union activity. Beginning in 1908 with *Adair* and *Loewe* v. *Lawlor*, the Court's attitude more clearly emerged: the federal government could not protect unionization by making yellow-dog contracts illegal; and unions would be held to the strict accountability of the antitrust law. Similar state attempts to insulate union men from hostile employers likewise fell before the scrutiny of the High Bench. Even though historians now agree that the Clayton Act did not free unions from the injunction process, the antiunion bias of the majority in *Duplex Printing Press Company* is clear. The country's adjustment to organized labor as a countervailing force to organized capital came slowly, and in this area, more than in any other, the Justices lagged behind the people's representatives in adjusting the law to the realities of an industrialized society. Organized labor could only succeed in overcoming the self-interest of employers by using coercive tactics, which seemed, to the majority of the Court, to be clearly illegal. Brandeis tried to persuade his colleagues to defer to legislative handling of the industrial conflict, but they believed the judiciary was the proper agency for affording relief to the threatened property interests.[22]

In evaluating the work of the Supreme Court we must grasp what a strange and unique agency of government it truly is. Much of this character stems from the Court's power of judicial review, which has invited litigation framed in terms of competing policy choices. In interpreting the language of the Constitution, the Court makes and remakes law, for it can ignore precedent as erroneous in light of a new reading of the fundamental law. Authority to judge state legislation by the standard of the fundamental law was provided in the first judiciary act in 1789, and like authority to review federal legislation was assumed by the Court. That such a tremendous power should be the target for attack in a democratic society is readily understandable, for here are nine men, appointed for life, passing judgment on expressions of the popular will. Why proposals to limit the Court's power have consistently failed deserves some explanation. First, the sanctity of the Constitution has, in part, cloaked the Court. Second, its critics have not coalesced, and some have realized that limits imposed now may lead to unforeseen and undesirable results later. Finally, the Justices have not been divorced from the society they serve. Their ability to accommodate change within the generalities of the Constitution has been both the key to the survival of the Constitution and to the power of the Court.

Changes in membership obviously contribute to the Court's sensitivity to society, but equally important has been the willingness of some Justices to bend with the times. No two cases are ever the same, and the talent of distinguishing the instant case from a prior one enables the Court to change its mind without directly overruling precedent. What we must realize is that significant provisions of the Constitution are far from tightly drawn; rather they are general statements that invite interpretation and permit changes in that interpretation over time. History has favored a flexible interpretation of the Constitution—not so flexible that the fundamental law loses its contours but resilient enough to enable its eighteenth-century wording to cope with the much changed world of the twentieth century. Accommodating the new without visible distortion of the old has been both the hallmark and genius of our constitutional system.

Yet the Court's role does encompass the task of nay-saying to some desires of the moment. One indication of a stable society is its ability to endure frustration, for some frustration is inevitable. In interpreting the Constitution, which has a dual purpose of conferring legitimacy and empowering the government to act effectively and of checking its operation so it does not become oppressive, the Court has wide latitude. Judicial review stems from a distrust of unrestrained majority rule, for without that suspicion this check would make no sense. Such distrust is reinforced periodically and has become too engrained to be dislodged, and for better or worse we resort to the Court as a final arbitration panel. We may not always like the result, and we may expect more from the Justices, drawn as they are from the society at large, than they can deliver, but the alternative of legislative supremacy has held little appeal. Perhaps we have been willing to endure frustrating judgments of the Court for the same reason we endure a democratic system of government, not because it is ideal, but rather because the alternatives to it are undesirable. Often the advantage of a definitive interpretation of the Constitution lies in the fact that a final decision has been reached, independent of what that decision is.

In the period from 1890 to 1920 the surprising fact is not that the Court placed some obstacles in the path of the popular will but rather that these inhibitions were so relatively few. This characterization holds true for the entire period, and those observers who have suggested that the Court became more "progressive" in the second decade of the twentieth century have over-emphasized the subject matter of the litigation to the detriment of the relative consistency of the judicial doctrine applied. Except for the substantial reading of the war power, these latter decisions often only extended doctrines forged in the preceding years.

Although the Court is an institution and speaks with a collective voice, it is also an assemblage of individuals whose ideas, attitudes, approaches, sympathies, and antagonisms are an essential part of the Court's story. Parading through these pages have been some twenty-six Justices, more than a quarter of all those who have sat on the Supreme Court. Most of them have slipped away into the obscurity of the past, and some were so reticent that they excited little notice even at the time. But they comprised the Supreme Court at a time of substantial activism, and whether leaders or followers, their votes helped chart the future. The writer has not suggested that these men did not have or espouse legal or social and economic philosophies, but he has argued that the Justices most of the time responded to cases with a sensitivity to the effect of their resolution on society, rather than on the basis of deductions from shared or individual preconceptions. None of the men escaped his past or his prejudices, and though some decisions could be selected to reveal an a priori approach, the total record belies such an overall appraisal.

Most of the Justices left behind a substantial work product that must be inspected before their decision making can be usefully characterized. Supreme Court historians have long lamented the fact that most of the members of the High Bench died without leaving a legacy of private papers, and although our potential knowledge is thereby limited, much can be gleaned about these men and the role they played from the Court's official record. The failure to examine this record closely has resulted in stereotypes rather than characterizations. Picturing Holmes as the model of judicial restraint neglects the fact that often he insinuated his dislike of certain legislative measures into his decisions through narrow and cramped readings of the law. Portrayers of Brewer have apparently paid more attention to his rhetoric than they have to his decision making, for his off-the-bench railing against the inroads of government upon the property right must be balanced by his substantial support for both state and federal regulation of property. Viewing Pitney through the lens of his antiunion opinions excludes completely his fervent support of the antitrust law and his openness on the subject of the permissible range of state regulatory power. The list could be lengthened, but the point is clear.

Throughout these years, certain Justices heard the cries of the dispossessed and responded. Most often their protests went unheeded, but their words enriched the record of the Court and helped sensitize the society. Field and Fuller criticized the majority's technical application of the fellow servant rule to defeat the recovery of injured workmen. Gray battled successfully to secure American citizenship for those children of Chinese parents born in the United States, and Brewer vehemently protested his colleagues' unwillingness to override administrative determinations hostile to the Chinese. Brown, who had second thoughts about his opinion sanctioning segregation, took up the cause of the American Indian with an understanding of native culture that his fellow Justices could not or would not share. Holmes and Brandeis eloquently called attention to government persecution of dissenters to the war effort. Yet when this roll is called one name stands out above all others—John Marshall Harlan. His fervent attachment to the constitutional guarantees designed to protect individuals and minority groups made him the defender of blacks against the tide of segregation and the accused criminal, whether prosecuted stateside or in the island possessions, whose plea of a violation of his rights under the Constitution was little heeded by the other Justices. Harlan was grasping a future beyond the vision of his brethren, and only recently has that vision been incorporated into constitutional law.

In reviewing the men of the Supreme Court we are impressed with McKenna, who grew into his role with a certain grace, skill, and even sophistication, and by Moody, Hughes, Brandeis, and Clarke, who brought with them to the Court a practical knowledge of the world beyond and who saw the imperative need to view the Constitution flexibly enough to accommodate the exertions of government in the public interest.

If the Court's history from 1890 to 1920 had not been obscured through a stereotyping of Justices and through studies emphasizing only the negative aspect of the Court's work or those concentrating on narrow subject areas that purportedly illuminate the Court's fundamental attitude, the crucial role of the High Bench during this generation would long have been recognized. To stress *Pollock* in the 1890s, *Lochner* in the 1900s, and *Hammer* in the 1910s presents a distorted image of the Court, which during these three decades was struggling, most often successfully, with the task of accommodating the law to the demands of a changing society.

NOTES

1. Alpheus T. Mason, *William Howard Taft: Chief Justice* (New York: Simon & Schuster, 1965), pp. 76-80.

2. Ibid., pp. 80-85

3. For Taft's efforts as a lobbyist for the federal judiciary and its highest court, see Mason, *William Howard Taft*, pp. 121-37.

4. Alpheus T. Mason, *Brandeis: A Free Man's Life* (New York: Viking Press, 1946), pp. 537-38; Henry F. Pringle, *The Life and Times of William Howard Taft* (New York: Farrar & Rinehart, 1939), 2:968-70; and Mason, *William Howard Taft*, pp. 199-205, 161, 213-15.

5. Mason, *William Howard Taft*, pp. 213, 195, 164, 215-17.

6. Hoyt L. Warner, *The Life of Mr. Justice Clarke* (Cleveland: Western Reserve University Press, 1959), pp. 112-16; and Wilson to Clarke, September 5, 1922, and Clarke to Wilson, September 9, 1922, in Mason, *William Howard Taft*, pp. 165-67. Clarke lived until 1945, dying just after the creation of the United Nations. The Warner volume details Clarke's career after leaving the Court (pp. 119-205).

7. Walter F. Murphy, "In His Own Image: Mr. Chief Justice Taft and Supreme Court Appointments," *1961 Supreme Court Review*, ed. Philip B. Kurland (Chicago: University of Chicago Press, 1961), pp. 167-68.

8. Mason, *William Howard Taft*, pp. 160-63; and David J. Danelski, *A Supreme Court Justice Is Appointed* (New York: Random House, 1964). A shorter treatment of the Butler appointment and confirmation can be found in Murphy, "In His Own Image," pp. 168-76.

9. Mason, *William Howard Taft*, pp. 171-72; and Murphy, "In His Own Image," pp. 176-83. Taft was more influential in nipping the candidacies of others than in the appointment of Sanford.

10. Bailey v. Drexel Furniture Co., 259 U.S. 20 (1922); and Truax v. Corrigan, 257 U.S. 312 (1921).

11. Bailey v. Drexel Furniture Co., 259 U.S. 20 (1922). *Atherton Mills* v. *Johnson* (259 U.S. 13 [1922]), a companion case, was first argued in December 1919, but the Court that Chief Justice White headed was unable to resolve the matter. For a discussion of this earlier episode, including a draft opinion by Brandeis seeking to dismiss the case on jurisdictional grounds, see Alexander M. Bickel, *The Unpublished Opinions of Mr. Justice Brandeis* (Chicago: University of Chicago Press, Phoenix Books, 1967), pp. 1-20.

12. Adkins v. Children's Hospital, 261 U.S. 525 (1923).

13. Wolff Packing Co. v. Court of Industrial Relations, 262 U.S. 522 (1923).

14. Burns Baking Co. v. Bryan, 264 U.S. 504 (1924); Schmidinger v. Chicago, 226 U.S. 578 (1913); and Tyson & Brothers v. Banton, 273 U.S. 418 (1927).

15. See Charles M. Hough, "Due Process of Law—To-day," *Harvard Law Review* 32 (January 1919):218-33; and Robert E. Cushman, "The Social and Economic Interpretation of the Fourteenth Amendment," *Michigan Law Review* 20 (May 1922):737-64.

16. Ray A. Brown, "Due Process of Law, Police Power, and the Supreme Court," *Harvard Law Review* 40 (May 1927):943-45; and Felix Frankfurter, "The United States Supreme Court Molding the Constitution," *Current History* 32 (May 1930):239.

17. Stuart S. Nagel, "Court-Curbing Periods in American History," *Vanderbilt Law Review* 18 (June 1965):925-27. For a discussion of the bills introduced from 1922 to 1924, and in earlier periods as well, see Maurice S. Culp, "A Survey of the Proposals to Limit or Deny the Power of Judicial Review by the Supreme Court of the United States," *Indiana Law Journal* 4 (March-April 1929):386-98, 474-90.

18. G. Edward White, *The American Judicial Tradition* (New York: Oxford University Press, 1976), p. 198, calls the four Justices "the last representatives of the oracular theory of judging."

19. Gitlow v. New York, 268 U.S. 652 (1925); Fiske v. Kansas, 274 U.S. 380 (1927); Near v. Minnesota, 283 U.S. 697 (1931); Powell v. Alabama, 287 U.S. 45 (1932); De Jonge v. Oregon, 299 U.S. 353 (1937); Hamilton v. Regents of the University of California, 293 U.S. 245 (1934); Norris v. Alabama, 294 U.S. 587 (1935); and Palko v. Connecticut, 302 U.S. 319, 325 (1937).

20. For such a characterization, see William E. Nelson, "The Impact of the Antislavery Movement Upon Styles of Judicial Reasoning in Nineteenth Century America," *Harvard Law Review* 87 (January 1974):513-15. Nelson does, however, recognize that formalistic reasoning does not inevitably lead to a formalistic result (p. 515, n. 12).

21. In only one case before *Hammer* in the 1890 to 1920 period did the Court invoke the Tenth Amendment as an answer to a federal governmental claim. The government had intervened in *Kansas* v. *Colorado* (206 U.S. 46 [1907]), which involved a dispute over the use of the waters of the Colorado River, and had argued that such disputes had to be resolved in the context of the national interest and therefore the Court should imply such power in the federal government. The Court rebuffed the government and cited the Tenth Amendment as a bar to the claim. The Court censuring of such a naked assertion of authority lent little support to the use of the Tenth Amendment in *Hammer*.

22. The traditional interpretation of the Court as a protector of business interests or of entrepreneurial liberty finds its greatest support in the series of cases in which the Justices decided against the legitimacy of union activity or the legitimacy of governmental intervention to protect union organization. (See John P. Roche, "Entrepreneurial Liberty and the Fourteenth Amendment," *Labor History* 4 [Winter 1963]:8-15.)

SELECTED BIBLIOGRAPHY

BASIC SOURCE MATERIAL, INDICES, AND BIBLIOGRAPHICAL AIDS

A. SUPREME COURT CASES

1. Opinions

Decisions of the Supreme Court have been published by the U.S. Government Printing Office since 1882 under the title *United States Reports*, cited as U.S. In addition, two commercial editions are published: The *Supreme Court Reporter* by West Publishing Company, cited as S. Ct.; and the *Lawyers' Edition* by the Lawyers Co-operative Publishing Company, cited as L. Ed. Both commercial editions contain periodic annotations on areas of constitutional law, and the *Lawyers' Edition* has regularly contained more material excerpted from briefs filed in the cases.

Both of the commercial firms also provide multivolumed digests of Supreme Court opinions that annotate the decisions under certain key words and phrases. The digests are designed to provide doctrinal and subject references to the cases for the purpose of serving the legal profession, but they can also be of use to the historian.

The single most convenient guide to significant cases interpreting the Constitution is *The Constitution of the United States of America: Analysis and Interpretation* (Washington: Government Printing Office, 1972; supplements, 1974, 1976). It annotates the cases under the various provisions of the Constitution and contains useful appendixes detailing cases in which federal acts, state laws, and local ordinances were held unconstitutional by the Supreme Court. A final appendix lists decisions later overruled by the Court along with the overruling cases.

A final research tool of considerable value to historians is *Shepard's United States Citations: Cases*. Under the official citation of the Supreme Court case are citations to all state and federal court opinions that refer to the decision. Also notations are provided to indicate whether the case has been distinguished or overruled by subsequent decisions.

2. Briefs and Records

All briefs and records that have weathered the years relating to Supreme Court cases from the inception of the Court to the early 1950s are housed in the National Archives in Washington, D.C. as part of Record Group 267. The National Archives began a microfilm publication program of some of these records, making available, for instance, the appellate case files through 1831. Commercial companies have since assumed the task of making this material more generally available and have now published in either microfilm or microfiche the complete set of the records and briefs of all cases, both appellate and original, since 1831. They are available in a number of research libraries, including the law library at the University of North Carolina at Chapel Hill.

The briefs and arguments in some of the Supreme Court's most significant decisions have been published in Philip B. Kurland and Gerhard Casper, eds., *Landmark Briefs and Arguments of the Supreme Court of the United States: Constitutional Law*, 80 vols. (Arlington, Va.: University Publications of America, 1975.) Term supplements, with the volumes numbered sequentially, keep the series relatively current.

B. FEDERAL STATUTES

United States Statutes at Large, cited as Stat., is a compilation of federal laws by the Congress in which they were enacted; the *United States Code* contains statutes currently in force. The annotated version of the *Code* is useful to the historian, for it includes citations to cases in which the statute was interpreted along with other historical notes.

Shepard's United States Citations: Statutes, which covers the Constitution, Code, and Statutes at Large, is especially useful for tracing the history of legislation no longer in effect.

C. THE SUPREME COURT

All of the official records of the United States Supreme Court from its beginning to the early 1950s are deposited in the National Archives in Washington, D.C. under the title Records of the Supreme Court (Record Group 267). Although the case files constitue most of the records, small collections from the Offices of the Clerk and of the Marshal contain useful information.

Scrapbooks kept by the Clerk of Court, most consistently from the late 1880s to 1912, contain a variety of information, mostly in the form of clippings from newspapers and magazines commenting on the work of the Court or on the Justices. Also a series of folders in the records from the Office of the Marshal contain additional material on the Justices and their working environment.

As with the briefs and records of the cases, the engrossed minutes of the Supreme Court from 1790 to 1950 and the engrossed dockets from 1791 to 1950, contained in the collection in the National Archives, have been made available as microfilm publications. For a close tracing of the Court's work, this material is very helpful.

A voluminous secondary literature on the Court exists, and its retrieval is aided by a number of bibliographical tools. Law journals publish not only relatively contemporaneous comment on the Court but historical articles as well, and access to this material is provided by the *Index to Legal Periodicals* under author, subject, and case-name entries. Two general bibliographies that seek to draw from all sources are Stephen M. Millet, *A Selected Bibliography of American Constitutional History* (Santa Barbara, Calif.: American Bibliographical Center Clio Press, 1975), and Dorothy C. Thompkins, comp., *The Supreme Court of the United States: A Bibliography* (Berkeley: Bureau of Public Administration, University of California, 1959). In addition, most historical studies on the Court or the Constitution contain useful and often informative bibliographies, the most comprehensive of which is that found in Alfred H. Kelly and Winfred A. Harbison, *The American Constitution: Its Origins and Development*, 5th ed. (New York: W. W. Norton & Co., 1976).

GENERAL BIBLIOGRAPHY

A. NEWSPAPERS AND PERIODICALS

American Federationist
Current Opinion

Harper's Weekly
Literary Digest
New Republic
New York Evening Post
New York Herald
New York Recorder
New York Sun
New York Times
New York Tribune
New York World
St. Louis Republic
Washington Evening Star
Washington Post

B. PRIMARY AND DOCUMENTARY SOURCES

Bickel, Alexander. *The Unpublished Opinions of Mr. Justice Brandeis.* Chicago: University of Chicago Press, Phoenix Books, 1967.

Brewer, David J. *The Spanish War: A Prophecy or an Exception?* Address before the Liberal Club, Buffalo, New York, February 16, 1899. New York: Anti-Imperialist League, n.d.

———. "Two Periods in the History of the Supreme Court." *Report of the Eighteenth Annual Meeting of the Virginia Bar Association* 19 (1906): 133-54.

Brown, Glenn. *History of the United States Capitol,* 56th Cong., 1st sess., 1900, *Senate Document No. 60.* 2 vols. Washington: Government Printing Office, 1900-1903.

Brown, Henry B. "Dissenting Opinions of Mr. Justice Harlan." *American Law Review* 46 (May-June 1912):321-52.

———. "The Status of the Automobile." *Yale Law Journal* 17 (February 1908):223-31.

[Butt, Archibald]. *Taft and Roosevelt: The Intimate Letters of Archie Butt.* 2 vols. Garden City, N.Y.: Doubleday, Doran & Co., 1930.

Danelski, David J., and Tulchin, Joseph S. *The Autobiographical Notes of Charles Evans Hughes.* Cambridge: Harvard University Press, 1973.

Farrand, Max, ed. *The Records of the Federal Convention of 1787.* Rev. ed. 4 vols. New Haven: Yale University Press, 1937; also in paperback edition by the same publisher, 1966.

Holmes, Oliver Wendell. *Collected Legal Papers.* New York: Harcourt, Brace & Co., 1921.

———. "The Gas Stokers' Strike." *American Law Review* 7 (April 1873):582-84; reprinted and attributed in *Harvard Law Review* 44 (March 1931):795-96.

———. "The Path of the Law." *Harvard Law Review* 10 (March 25, 1897): 457-78.

Howe, Mark D., ed. *Holmes-Laski Letters.* Abridged ed. 2 vols. New York: Atheneum, 1963.

———. *Holmes-Pollock Letters.* 2d ed. 2 vols. Cambridge: Harvard University Press, Belknap Press, 1961.

Hughes, Charles Evans. *The Supreme Court of the United States.* New York: Columbia University Press, 1928.

Kent, Charles A. *Memoir of Henry Billings Brown.* New York: Duffield & Co., 1915.

Morison, Elting, ed. *The Letters of Theodore Roosevelt.* 8 vols. Cambridge: Harvard University Press, 1951-54.

Porter, Kirk H., and Johnson, Donald B., comps. *National Party Platforms 1840-1960.* 2d ed. Urbana: University of Illinois Press, 1961.

Richardson, James D., ed. *Compilation of the Messages and Papers of the Presidents, 1789-1897.* 53d Cong., 2d sess., 1894, *House Miscellaneous Document No. 210.* 10 vols. Washington: Government Printing Office, 1896-99.

Selections from the Correspondence of Theodore Roosevelt and Henry Cabot Lodge 1884-1918. 2 vols. New York: Charles Scribner's Sons, 1925.

U.S. Congress. House. *Proposed Amendments to the Constitution.* House Doc. No. 551, 70th Cong., 2d sess., 1928. Washington: Government Printing Office, 1929.

U.S. Congress. House. Committee on the Judiciary. *Associate Justice William O. Douglas: Final Report by the Special Subcommittee on H. Res. 920.* 91st Cong., 2d sess., 1970.

U.S. Congress. Senate. *Report on the Chicago Strike of June-July, 1894.* Senate Executive Doc. No. 7, 53rd Cong., 3d sess., 1895.

U.S. Department of Justice. *Annual Report of the Attorney-General.* 1894.

Westin, Alan F. *An Autobiography of The Supreme Court: Off-the-Bench Commentary by the Justices.* New York: Macmillan Co., 1963.

C. SECONDARY SOURCES

Abraham, Henry J. *Freedom and the Court: Civil Rights and Liberties in the United States.* 3rd ed. New York: Oxford University Press, 1977.

_____. "John Marshall Harlan: A Justice Neglected." *Virginia Law Review* 41 (November 1955):871-91.

_____. *Justices and Presidents: A Political History of Appointments to the Supreme Court.* New York: Oxford University Press, 1974.

Allen, Arthur M. "The Opinions of Mr. Justice Hughes." *Columbia Law Review* 16 (November 1916):565-84.

Baker, Ray Stannard. "What is a Lynching?" *McClure's Magazine* 24 (January-February 1905):299-314, 422-30. Reprinted in *Following the Color Line.* New York: Doubleday, Page, 1908.

Bearss, Ed, and Gibson, Arrell M. *Fort Smith: Little Gibralter on the Arkansas.* Norman: University of Oklahoma Press, 1969.

Bergan, Francis. "Mr. Justice Brewer: Perspective of a Century." *Albany Law Review* 25 (1961):191-202.

Beth, Loren P. *The Development of the American Constitution 1877-1917.* New American Nation Series. New York: Harper & Row, Torchbooks, 1971.

_____. "Justice Harlan and the Uses of Dissent." *American Political Science Review* 49 (December 1955):1085-1104.

Blanchard, Margaret A. "The Fifth Amendment Privilege of Newsman George Burdick." *Journalism Quarterly* 55 (Spring 1978):29-36, 67.

Blum, John M. *The Republican Roosevelt.* Cambridge: Harvard University Press, 1954.

Bonaparte, Charles J. "Lynch Law and Its Remedy." *Yale Law Journal* 8 (May 1899): 335-43.

Borkin, Joseph. *The Corrupt Judge.* Cleveland: World Publishing Company, Meridian Books, 1962.

Boudin, Louis B. *Government by Judiciary,* 2 vols. New York: William Godwin, 1932.

Bowen, Catherine Drinker. *Yankee from Olympus: Justice Holmes and His Family.* Boston: Little, Brown & Co., 1944.

Brant, Irving. *The Bill of Rights: Its Origin and Meaning.* Indianapolis: Bobbs-Merrill Co., 1965.

Brown, Ray A. "Due Process of Law, Police Power, and the Supreme Court." *Harvard Law Review* 40 (May 1927):943-68.

_____. "Police Power—Legislation for Health and Personal Safety." *Harvard Law Review* 42 (May 1929):866-98.

Butler, Charles H. *A Century at the Bar of the Supreme Court of the United States.* New York: G. P. Putnam's Sons, 1942.

Carson, Hampton L. *The Supreme Court of the United States: Its History.* 2d ed. 2 vols. Philadelphia: A. R. Keller Co., 1892.

Chafee, Zechariah, Jr. *Free Speech in the United States*. New York: Atheneum, 1969.
———. *Thirty-Five Years with Freedom of Speech*. New York: Roger N. Baldwin Civil Liberties Foundation, 1952.
Clark, Floyd B. *The Constitutional Doctrines of Justice Harlan*. Johns Hopkins University Studies in Historical and Political Science. Series XXXIII, No. 4. Baltimore: Johns Hopkins Press, 1951.
Collins, Charles W. *The Fourteenth Amendment and the States*. Boston: Little, Brown & Co, 1912.
Corwin, Edward. *The Commerce Power versus States Rights*. Princeton: Princeton University Press, 1936.
———. *Court over Constitution: A Study of Judicial Review as an Instrument of Popular Government*. Princeton: Princeton University Press, 1938.
———. *Liberty Against Government: The Rise, Flowering and Decline of a Famous Juridical Concept*. Baton Rouge: Louisiana State University Press, 1948.
———. *The Twilight of the Supreme Court*. New Haven: Yale University Press, 1934.
Coudert, Frederic R. *Certainty and Justice: Studies of the Conflict Between Precedent and Progress in the Development of the Law*. New York: D. Appleton & Co., 1914.
Croy, Homer. *He Hanged Them High*. New York: Duell, Sloan & Pearce, 1952.
Culp, Maurice S. "A Survey of the Proposals to Limit or Deny the Power of Judicial Review by the Supreme Court of the United States." *Indiana Law Journal* 4 (March-April 1929):386-98.
Cummings, Homer, and McFarland, Carl. *Federal Justice: Chapters in the History of Justice and the Federal Executive*. New York: Macmillan Co., 1937.
Cushman, Robert E. *The Independent Regulatory Commissions*. New York: Oxford University Press, 1941.
———. "The Social and Economic Interpretation of the Fourteenth Amendment." *Michigan Law Review* 20 (May 1922):737-64.
Danelski, David J. *A Supreme Court Justice Is Appointed*. New York: Random House, 1964.
Dinnerstein, Leonard. *The Leo Frank Case*. New York: Columbia University Press, 1968.
Dishman, Robert R. "Mr. Justice White and the Rule of Reason." *Review of Politics* 13 (April 1951):229-43.
Dunham, Allison, and Kurland, Philip B., eds. *Mr. Justice*. Revised and enlarged ed. Chicago: University of Chicago, Phoenix Books, 1964.
Durden, Robert F. *Reconstruction Bonds and Twentieth-Century Politics: South Dakota v. North Carolina (1904)*. Durham, N.C.: Duke Univeristy Press, 1962.
Eitzen, D. Stanley. *David J. Brewer, 1837-1910: A Kansan on the United States Supreme Court*. Emporia State Research Studies. Vol. 12, no. 3. Emporia: Kansas State Teachers College, 1964.
Ellis, Elmer. "Public Opinion and the Income Tax." *Mississippi Valley Historical Review* 27 (September 1940):225-42.
Ely, Richard T. *Property and Contract in Their Relations to the Distribution of Wealth*. 2 vols. New York: Macmillan Co., 1922.
Fairman, Charles O. *Mr. Justice Miller and the Supreme Court*. Cambridge: Harvard University Press, 1939.
———. "What Makes A Great Justice: Mr. Justice Bradley and the Supreme Court." *Boston University Law Review* 30 (January 1950):49-102.
Farrelly, David G. "Harlan's Dissent in the Pollock Case." *Southern California Law Review* 24 (February 1951):175-82.
Frankfurter, Felix. *Mr. Justice Holmes and the Supreme Court*. Cambridge: Harvard University Press, 1938.
———. "The United States Supreme Court Molding the Constitution." *Current History* 32 (May 1930):235-40.

_____, and Greene, Nathan. *The Labor Injunction*. New York: Macmillan Co., 1930.

_____, and Landis, James M. *The Business of the Supreme Court: A Study in the Federal Judicial System*. New York: Macmillan Co., 1927.

Freund, Ernst. "Limitation of Hours of Labor and the Federal Supreme Court," *Green Bag* 17 (July 1905):414-16.

Friedman, Lawrence M., and Ladinsky, Jack. "Social Change and the Law of Industrial Accidents." *Columbia Law Review* 67 (January 1967):50-82.

Friedman, Leon, and Israel, Fred L., eds. *The Justices of the United States Supreme Court 1789-1969: Their Lives and Major Opinions*. 4 vols. New York: R. R. Bowker Co. and Chelsea House, Publishers, 1969.

Fuller, Paul. "Is there a Federal Police Power?" *Columbia Law Review* 4 (December 1904): 563-88.

Gamer, Robert E. "Justice Brewer and Substantive Due Process: A Conservative Court Revisited." *Vanderbilt Law Review* 18 (March 1965): 615-41.

Garraty, John A., ed. *Quarrels That Have Shaped the Constitution*. New York: Harper & Row, 1964.

Ginger, Ray. *Age of Excess: The United States from 1877-1914*. New York: Macmillan Co., 1965.

Gompers, Samuel. "Labor Organizations Must Not be Outlawed—The Supreme Court's Decision in the Hatters' Case." *American Federationist* 15 (March 1908):180.

Grantham, Dewey W. "The Progressive Movement and the Negro." *South Atlantic Quarterly* 54 (October 1955):461-77.

Gregory, Charles N. "Government by Injunction." *Harvard Law Review* 11 (March 25, 1898):487-511.

Grimes, Alan P. *The Puritan Ethic and Woman Suffrage*. New York: Oxford University Press, 1967.

Hale, Robert L. *Freedom through Law: Public Control of Private Governing Power*. New York: Columbia University Press, 1952.

Halsell, W. D., "L. Q. C. Lamar, Associate Justice of the Supreme Court." *Journal of Mississippi History* 5 (April 1943):59-78.

Hamilton, Walton H. "The Path of Due Process of Law." *Ethics* 48 (April 1938):269-96.

Harbaugh, William H. *The Life and Times of Theodore Roosevelt*. Rev. ed. New York: Crowell-Collier Publishing Co., Collier Books, 1963.

Harmon, Samuel W. *Hell on the Border: He Hanged Eighty-Eight Men*. Indian Heritage ed. Edited by Jack Gregory and Rennard Strickland. Muskogee, Okla.: Indian Heritage Association, 1971.

Harrington, Fred H. *Hanging Judge*. Caldwell, Idaho: Caxton Printers, 1951.

Hays, Samuel P. *The Response to Industrialism, 1885-1914*. Chicago: University of Chicago Press, 1957.

Heffron, Paul T. "Theodore Roosevelt and the Appointment of Mr. Justice Moody." *Vanderbilt Law Review* 18 (March 1965): 545-68.

Hendel, Samuel. *Charles Evans Hughes and the Supreme Court*. New York: King's Crown Press, Columbia University, 1951.

Henrick, Burton J. "Another Radical for the Supreme Court." *World's Work* 33 (November 1916):95-98.

Higham, John. *Strangers in the Land: Patterns of American Nativism*. New York: Atheneum, 1963.

Holsinger, M. Paul. "The Appointment of Supreme Court Justice Van Devanter: A Study in Political Preferment." *American Journal of Legal History* 12 (1968):324-35.

Hurst, J. Willard. *Law and the Conditions of Freedom in the Nineteenth-Century United States*. Madison: University of Wisconsin Press, 1956.

Ingersoll, Henry H. "The Revolution of 20th May, 1895." *Proceedings of the Fourteenth Annual Meeting of the Bar of the Association of Tennessee* (1895):161-80.

Jacobs, Clyde D. *Law Writers and the Courts: The Influence of Thomas M. Cooley, Christopher G. Tiedeman, and John F. Dillon upon American Constitutional Law*. Berkeley: University of California Press, 1954.

King, Willard L. *Melville Weston Fuller: Chief Justice of the United States 1888-1910*. Phoenix ed. Chicago: University of Chicago Press, 1967.

Klinkhamer, Sister Marie Carolyn. *Edward Douglas White: Chief Justice of the United States*. Washington: Catholic University Press, 1943.

———. "The Legal Philosophy of Edward Douglas White." *University of Detroit Law Journal* 35 (December 1957):174-99.

Kolko, Gabriel. *Railroads and Regulations, 1877-1916*. Princeton: Princeton University Press, 1965.

———. *The Triumph of Conservatism: A Reinterpretation of American History, 1900-1916*. Glencoe, Ill.: Free Press, 1965.

Konefsky, Samuel J. *The Legacy of Holmes and Brandeis: A Study in the Influence of Ideas*. New York: Crowell-Collier Publishing Co., Collier Books, 1961.

Leavitt, Donald C. "Attitude Change on the Supreme Court, 1910-1920." *Michigan Academician* 4 (Summer 1971):53-65.

Leech, Margaret. *In the Days of McKinley*. New York: Harper & Bros., 1959.

Letwin, William. *Law and Economic Policy in America: The Evolution of the Sherman Antitrust Act*. New York: Random House, 1965.

Levi, Edward H. *An Introduction to Legal Reasoning*. Chicago: University of Chicago Press, Phoenix Books, 1961.

Levitan, David M. "The Jurisprudence of Mr. Justice Clarke." *Miami Law Quarterly* 7 (December 1952):44-72.

———. "Mahlon Pitney—Labor Judge." *Virginia Law Review* 40 (October 1954):733-70.

Lewis, William D. "Protest Against Administering Criminal Law by Injunction—the Debs Case." *American Law Register & Review* 42 (December 1894):879-83.

Link, Arthur S. *American Epoch: A History of the United States Since the 1890s*. 2d ed. rev. New York: Alfred A. Knopf, 1963.

———. *Wilson: Campaigns for Progressivism and Peace 1916-1917.* Princeton: Princeton University Press, 1965.

———. *Wilson: The New Freedom*. Princeton: Princeton University Press, 1956.

———. *Woodrow Wilson and the Progressive Era, 1910-1917*. New American Nation Series. New York: Harper & Row, Torchbooks, 1963.

Lord, Walter. *The Good Years: From 1900 to the First World War*. New York: Harper & Bros., 1960.

Lowell, Abbott L. "The Status of Our New Possessions—A Third View." *Harvard Law Review* 13 (November 1899):155-76.

Lowry, Edward G. "Justice at Zero: The Frigid Austerities Which Enrobe the Members of the United States Supreme Court." *Harper's Weekly*, May 21, 1910, pp. 8+.

Lyle, Eugene P., Jr., "The Supreme Court." *Hampton's Broadway Magazine* 21 (October 1908):435-46.

Martin, Albro. *Enterprise Denied: Origins of the Decline of American Railroads, 1897-1917*. New York: Columbia University Press, 1971.

Mason, Alpheus T. *Brandeis: A Free Man's Life*. New York: Viking Press, 1946.

———. *Organized Labor and the Law*. Durham, N.C.: Duke University Press, 1925.

———. *William Howard Taft: Chief Justice*. New York: Simon & Schuster, 1965.

McCloskey, Robert G. *American Conservatism in the Age of Enterprise 1865-1910*. New York: Harper & Row, Torchbooks, 1964.

McCurdy, Charles W. "Justice Field and the Jurisprudence of Government-Business Relations: Some Parameters of Laissez-Faire Constitutionalism, 1863-1897." *Journal of American History* 61 (March 1975):970-1005.

McDevitt, Brother Matthew. *Joseph McKenna: Associate Justice of the United States.* Washington: Catholic University Press, 1946; reprint ed., New York: Da Capo Press, 1974.

McHargue, Daniel S. "President Taft's Appointments to the Supreme Court." *Journal of Politics* 12 (August 1950):478-510.

McLean, Joseph E. *William Rufus Day: Supreme Court Justice From Ohio.* Johns Hopkins University Studies in Historical and Political Science. Vol. 44. Baltimore: Johns Hopkins University Press, 1946.

McMurry, Donald L. *Coxey's Army: A Study of the Industrial Army Movement of 1894.* Boston: Little, Brown & Co., 1929.

Mott, Rodney L. *Due Process of Law: A Historical and Analytical Treatise of the Principles and Methods Followed by the Courts in the Application of the Concept of the 'Law of the Land'.* Indianapolis: Bobbs-Merrill Co., 1926.

Mowry, George E. *The Era of Theodore Roosevelt and the Birth of Modern America 1900-1912.* New American Nation Series. New York: Harper & Row, Torchbooks, 1962.
———. *The Progressive Era, 1900-20: The Reform Persuasion.* AHA Pamphlet no. 212. Washington: American Historical Association, 1972.

Murphy, Paul M. *The Constitution in Crisis Times 1918-1969.* New American Nation Series. New York: Harper & Row, Torchbooks, 1972.

Murphy, Walter F. "In His Own Image: Mr. Chief Justice Taft and Supreme Court Appointments." *1961 Supreme Court Review.* Edited by Philip B. Kurland. Chicago: University of Chicago Press, 1961.

Myers, Gustavus. *History of the Supreme Court of the United States.* Chicago: Charles H. Kerr & Co., 1912.

Nagel, Stuart S. "Court-Curbing Periods in American History." *Vanderbilt Law Review* 18 (June 1965):925-44.

National American Woman Suffrage Association. *Victory: How Women Won It, A Centennial Symposium 1840-1940.* New York: H. W. Wilson Co., 1940.

Nelson, William E. "The Impact of the Antislavery Movement Upon Styles of Reasoning in Nineteenth Century America." *Harvard Law Review* 87 (January 1974):513-66.

Nevins, Allan. *Grover Cleveland: A Study in Courage.* New York: Dodd, Mead & Co., 1933.

Noblitt, Harding C. "The Supreme Court and the Progressive Era." Ph.D. dissertation, University of Chicago, 1955.

Oberholtzer, Ellis P. *The Referendum in America.* Rev. ed. New York: Charles Scribner's Sons, 1912.

Paul, Arnold M. *Conservative Crisis and the Rule of Law: Attitudes of Bar and Bench, 1887-1895.* Torchbook Ed. New York: Harper & Row, 1969.

Paul, Randolph E. *Taxation in the United States.* Boston: Little, Brown & Co., 1954.

Perkins, Dexter. *Charles Evans Hughes and American Democratic Statesmanship.* Boston: Little, Brown & Co., 1965.

Peterkin, W. G. "Government by Injunction." *Virginia Law Register* 3 (December 1898): 549-63.

Peterson, H. C. and Fite, Gilbert C. *Opponents of War 1917-1918.* Madison: University of Wisconsin Press, 1957.

Pound, Roscoe. "Liberty of Contract." *Yale Law Journal* 18 (May 1909):454-87.

Preston, William, Jr. *Aliens and Dissenters: Federal Suppression of Radicals, 1903-1933.* New York: Harper & Row, Torchbooks, 1966.

Pringle, Henry F. *The Life and Times of Wlliam Howard Taft.* 2 vols. New York: Farrar & Rinehart, 1939.

Pusey, Merlo J. *Charles Evans Hughes.* 2 vols. New York: Macmillan Co., 1951.

Ratner, Sidney. *American Taxation: Its History as a Social Force in Democracy.* New York: W. W. Norton & Co., 1942.

Roche, John P. "Civil Liberty in the Age of Enterprise." *University of Chicago Law Review* 31 (Autumn 1963):103-35.

———. "Entrepreneurial Liberty and the Commerce Power: Expansion, Contraction and Causistry in the Age of Enterprise." *University of Chicago Law Review* 30 (Summer 1963):680-703.

———. "Entrepreneurial Liberty and the Fourteenth Amendment." *Labor History* 4 (Winter 1963):3-31.

———. *The Quest for the Dream: The Development of Civil Rights and Human Relations in Modern America.* New York: Macmillan Co., 1963.

———. *Sentenced to Life.* New York: Macmillan Co., 1974 (contains above three articles, pp. 205-308).

Rodell, Fred. *Nine Men: A Political History of the Supreme Court of the United States from 1790 to 1955.* New York: Random House, Vintage Books, 1955.

Roe, Gilbert E. *Our Judicial Oligarchy.* New York: B. W. Heubsch, 1912.

Roelofs, Vernon W. "Justice William Day and Federal Regulation." *Mississippi Valley Historical Review* 37 (June 1950):39-60.

Schmidhauser, John R. *The Supreme Court as Final Arbiter in Federal-State Relations 1789-1957.* Chapel Hill: University of North Carolina Press, 1958.

———. *The Supreme Court: Its Politics, Personalities, and Procedures.* New York: Holt, Rinehart & Winston, 1960.

Semonche, John E. "Conflicting Views on Crime and Punishment in the 1890s: 'Hanging Judge' Parker Confronts the United States Supreme Court," publication forthcoming.

Shiras, George, III. *Justice George Shiras, Jr. of Pittsburgh.* Edited and completed by Winfield Shiras. Pittsburgh: University of Pittsburgh Press, 1953.

Shirley, Glenn. *Law West of Fort Smith: A History of Frontier Justice in the Indian Territory 1834-1896.* New York: Henry Holt & Co., 1957.

Smith, John M. "Mr. Horace Gray of the United States Supreme Court." *South Dakota Law Review* 6 (Fall 1961):221-47.

Spector, Robert M. "Legal Historian on the United States Supreme Court: Justice Horace Gray, Jr., and the Historical Method." *American Journal of Legal History* 12 (1968): 181-210.

Steidle, Barbara C. "Conservative Progressives: A Study of the Attitudes and Role of Bar and Bench, 1905-1912." Ph.D. dissertation, Rutgers University, 1969.

Sutherland, William A. "Is Congress a Conservator of the Public Morals?" *American Law Review* 38 (January-February 1904):194-208.

Swaine, Robert T. *The Cravath Firm and Its Predecessors, 1819-1947.* 3 vols. New York: privately printed by Ad Press for Cravath, Swaine & Moore, 1946-48.

Swanberg, W. A. *Pulitzer.* New York: Charles Scribner's Sons, 1967.

Swindler, William F. *Court and Constitution in the Twentieth Century: The Old Legality 1889-1932.* Indianapolis: Bobbs-Merrill Co., 1969.

Swisher, Carl B. *Stephen J. Field: Craftsman of the Law.* Washington: Brookings Institution, 1930.

Tarrow, Sidney G. "Lochner Versus New York: A Political Analysis." *Labor History* 5 (Fall 1964):277-312.

Taylor, Hannis. "True Remedy for Lynch-Law." *North American Law Review* 41 (March 1907):255-66.

Todd, A. L. *Justice on Trial: The Case of Louis D. Brandeis.* New York: McGraw-Hill Book Co., 1964.

Twiss, Benjamin R. *Lawyers and the Constitution: How Laissez Faire Came to the Supreme Court.* Princeton: Princeton University Press, 1942.

Urofsky, Melvin I. *A Mind of One Piece: Brandeis and American Reform.* New York: Charles Scribner's Sons, 1971.

Waite, Edward F. "How 'Eccentric' Was Mr. Justice Harlan?" *Minnesota Law Review* 37 (February 1953):173-87.

Warner, Hoyt L. *The Life of Mr. Justice Clarke.* Cleveland: Western Reserve University Press, 1959.

Warren, Charles. "A Bulwark to the State Police Power—the United States Supreme Court." *Columbia Law Review* 13 (December 1913):667-95.

_____. *Congress, the Constitution, and the Supreme Court.* Boston: Little, Brown & Co., 1925.

_____. "The Progressiveness of the United States Supreme Court." *Columbia Law Review* 13 (April 1913):294-313.

_____. *The Supreme Court in the United States History.* Rev. ed. 2 vols. Boston: Little, Brown & Co., 1926.

Watt, Richard F., and Orlikoff, Richard M. "The Coming Vindication of Mr. Justice Harlan." *Illinois Law Review* 44 (March-April 1949):13-40.

Weinstein, James. *The Corporate Ideal in the Liberal State: 1900-1918.* Boston: Beacon Press, 1968.

Westin, Alan F. "John Marshall Harlan and the Constitutional Rights of Negroes: The Transformation of a Southerner." *Yale Law Journal* 66 (April 1957):637-710.

_____. "Stephen J. Field and the Headnote to O'Neil v. Vermont: A Snapshot of the Fuller Court at Work." *Yale Law Journal* 67 (January 1958):363-83.

_____. "The Supreme Court, the Populist Movement and the Campaign of 1896." *Journal of Politics* 15 (February 1953):3-41.

White, G. Edward. *The American Judicial Tradition.* New York: Oxford University Press, 1976.

_____. "The Rise and Fall of Justice Holmes." *University of Chicago Law Review* 39 (Fall 1971):51-77.

Wiebe, Robert H. *Businessmen and Reform: A Study of the Progressive Movement.* Cambridge: Harvard University Press, 1962.

_____. *The Search for Order, 1877-1920.* New York: Hill and Wang, 1967.

Wood, Stephen B. *Constitutional Politics in the Progressive Era: Child Labor and the Law.* Chicago: University of Chicago Press, 1968.

Wright, Benjamin F. *The Contract Clause of the Constitution.* Cambridge: Harvard University Press, 1938.

INDEX

About the Author

John E. Semonche is a professor of history at the University of North Carolina at Chapel Hill. His last book is *Ray Stannard Baker: A Quest for Democracy in Modern America, 1870-1918.* He has published in *The American Journal of Legal History, UCLA Law Review,* and the *North Carolina Law Review.*